THE IVORY PORTER.

THE LAKE REGIONS
OF
CENTRAL AFRICA

RICHARD F. BURTON

DOVER PUBLICATIONS, INC.
NEW YORK

" Some to discover islands far away."—Shakspeare.

Published in Canada by General Publishing Company, Ltd., 30 Lesmill Road, Don Mills, Toronto, Ontario.

Bibliographical Note

This Dover edition, first published in 1995, is an unabridged, slightly altered, republication of the work originally published by Harper & Brothers, New York, in 1860 under the title *The Lake Regions of Central Africa, A Picture of Exploration*. The map of Burton's routes, which originally followed the Preface, has been moved to the inside back cover and noted in the list of illustrations.

Library of Congress Cataloging-in-Publication Data

Burton, Richard Francis, Sir, 1821–1890.
   The lake regions of Central Africa / Richard F. Burton.
        p.   cm.
   Originally published: New York : Harper, 1860.
   Includes index.
   ISBN 0-486-28618-5 (pbk.)
   1. Africa, Central—Description and travel.   I. Title.
DT361.B96   1995
916.704'23—dc20   94-46004
                                                                         CIP

Manufactured in the United States of America
Dover Publications, Inc., 31 East 2nd Street, Mineola, N.Y. 11501

TO

MY SISTER,

MARIA STISTED,

THESE PAGES

Are Affectionately Inscribed.

PREFACE.

I HAD intended this record of personal adventure to appear immediately after my return to Europe, in May, 1859. The impaired health, the depression of spirits, and, worse still, the annoyance of official correspondence, which to me have been the sole results of African exploration, may be admitted as valid reasons for the delay.

In April, 1860, the Royal Geographical Society of Great Britain honored me by publishing a detailed paper, forming the XXIXth volume of their journal, from which the topographical descriptions contained in the following pages have, with their kind permission, been extracted. I have now attempted to combine with geography and ethnology a narrative of occurrences and an exposition of the more popular and picturesque points of view which the subject offers.

When I communicated to my friends the publishers certain intentions of writing exclusively a "light work," they protested against the project, stating that the public appetite required the addition of stronger meat. In compliance, therefore, with their suggestion, I have drawn two portraits of the same object, and mingled the gay with the graver details of travel, so as to produce an antipathetic cento.

Modern "hinters to travelers" direct the explorer and the missionary to eschew theory and opinion. We are told somewhat peremptorily that it is our duty to gather actualities, not inferences—to see and not to think; in fact, to confine ourselves to transmitting the rough material collected by us, that it may be worked into shape by the professionally learned at home. But why may not the observer be allowed a voice concerning his own observations, if at least his mind be sane and his stock of collateral knowledge be respectable?

I have not attempted to avoid intruding matters of a private and personal nature upon the reader; it would have been impossible to avoid egotism in a purely egotistical narrative. The official matter, however, has been banished into Appendix II. In publishing it, my desire is to avoid the possibility of a charge being concealed in the pigeon-holes of the India House, to be produced, according to custom, with all the effect of a surprise, whenever its presence is convenient. I know the conditions of appealing from those in office to a higher tribunal—the Public. I well know them and I accept them. *Avant tout, gentilhomme!*

I have spoken out my feelings concerning Captain Speke, my companion in the expedition which forms the subject of these pages. The history of our companionship is simply this:—As he had suffered with me in purse and person at Berberah, in 1855, I thought it but just to offer him the opportunity of renewing an attempt to penetrate into Africa. I had no other reasons. I could not expect much from his assistance; he was not a linguist —French and Arabic being equally unknown to him—nor a man of science, nor an accurate astronomical observer. The Court of Directors officially refused him leave of absence; I obtained it for him by an application to the local authorities at Bombay. During the exploration he acted in a subordinate capacity; and, as may be imagined, among a party of Arabs, Baloch, and Africans, whose languages he ignored, he was unfit for any other but a subordinate capacity. Can I then feel otherwise than indignant, when I find that, after preceding me from Aden to England, with the spontaneous offer, on his part, of not appearing before the society that originated the expedition until my return, he had lost no time in taking measures to secure for himself the right of working the field which I had opened, and that from that day he has placed himself *en evidence* as the *primum mobile* of an expedition in which he signed himself " surveyor"—*cujus pars minima fuit?*

With deference to the reader's judgment, I venture to express a hope that whatever of unrefinement appears in these pages may be charged to the subject. It has been my duty to draw a Dutch picture, a cabaret-piece which could not be stripped of its ordonnance, its boors, its pipes, and its pots. I have shirked nothing of the unpleasant task—of recording processes and not only results; I have entered into the recital of the maladies, the weary squabbles, and the vast variety of petty troubles, without which the *coup d'œil* of African adventure would be more like a Greek saint in effigy—all lights and no shade—than the chapter of accidents which it now is.

The map and the lists of stations, dates, etc., have been drawn upon the plan adopted by Mr. Francis Galton, F.R.G.S. The outline of Africa, the work of Mr. Weller, F.R.G.S., contains the latest and the best information concerning the half-explored interior of the continent. The route-map has been borrowed by permission from the laborious and conscientious compilation of Mr. Findlay, F.R.G.S., accompanying the paper forwarded by me to the Royal Geographical Society. The latter gentleman has also kindly supplied a profile of the country traversed, showing the eastern limits of the Great Depression, and the "elevated-trough formation" of Central Africa.

In conclusion, I would solicit forbearance in all that concerns certain errors of omission and commission scattered through these pages. The migratory instinct is now hurrying me toward the New World; I have, therefore, been obliged to content myself with a single revise.

10th April, E.I.U.S. Club, 14 St. James's Square.

DATES OF JOURNEYING.

1856	September	Left England.
	2d December	Sailed from Bombay.
	19th December	Arrived at Zanzibar Island.
1857	6th January	Left Zanzibar the first time
	14th June	Left Zanzibar the second time.
	27th June	Set out from Kaole on the coast.
	7th November	Arrived at Unyanyembe of Unyamwezi.
1858	14th February	Reached Ujiji on the Tanganyika Lake.
	26th April	Arrived at Uvira on the north of the Tanyanyika Lake.
	26th May	Left Ujiji.
	19th June	Returned to Unyanyembe.
	26th September	Left Unyanyembe.
1859	3d February	Reached Konduchi on the coast.
	4th March	Landed at Zanzibar Island.
	4th May	Left Aden.
	20th May	Landed at Southampton.

LIST STASIMETRIC AND HYPSOMETRIC.

NAMES OF KHAMBI OR STAGES MADE BY THE EAST AFRICAN EXPEDITION, AND
HEIGHTS OF THE SEVERAL CRUCIAL STATIONS.

FIRST REGION.

	FROM KAOLE ON THE COAST TO ZUNGOMERO, CHIEF DISTRICT OF K'HUTU.	H.	M.
1	Kaoli to Mgude or Kuingani	1	30
2	Kuingani to Bomani	1	30
3	Bomani to Mkwaju la Mvuani.	0	30
4	Mkwaju to Nzasa (of Uzaramo)	3	20
5	Nzasa to Kiranga-Ranga	6	0
6	Kiranga-Ranga to Tumba Ihere	3	30
7	Tumba Ihere to Muhonyera	4	40
8	Muhonyera to Sagesera	2	45
9	Sagesera to Tunda	7	0
10	Tunda to Dege la Mhora	2	30
11	Dege la Mhora to Madege Madogo.	3	0
12	Madege Madogo to Kidunda.	3	0
13	Kidunda to Mgeta Ford.	7	0
14	Mgeta Ford to Kiruru in K'hutu	6	0
15	Kiruru to Dut'humi	6	40
16	Dut'humi to Bakera.	2	0
17	Bakera to Zungomero.	7	0
⊙17		67	55

Kaole, Latitude, South, 6° 25′. Longitude, East, 38° 51′.
Zungomero, " 7° 27′. " 37° 22′.
Altitude of Zungomero, 330 feet above sea level. Average altitude of First Region,
by B. P. Therm., 230 feet.

SECOND REGION.

	FROM ZUNGOMERO, OVER THE MOUNTAINS OF USAGARA TO UGOGI.	H.	M.
1	Zungomero to Mzizi Mdogo (in Usagara)	5	0
2	Mzizi Mdogo to Chya K'henge	4	30
3	Chya K'henge to Rufuta River	4	30
4	Rufuta River (up the Goma Pass) to Mfu'uni	1	50
5	Mfu'uni to " Overshot Nullah"	6	10
6	" Overshot Nullah" to Zonhwe	2	0
7	Zonhwe to Muhama	4	45
8	Muhama to Makata	6	30
9	Makata to Myombo River	4	30
10	Myombo River to Mbumi	4	30
11	Mbumi to Kadetamare	5	55
12	Kadetamare to Muinyi	8	10
13	Muinyi to Nidabi	4	50
14	Nidabi to Rumuma	5	30
15	Rumuma to Marenga Mk'hali	3	30
16	Marenga Mk'hali to ⊙ in Jungle	5	0
17	Jungle to Inenge	4	0
18	Inenge to first gradient of Rubeho Pass	6	30
19	First gradient to second gradient ditto	2	0
20	Second gradient to summit of Rubeho	1	45
21	Summit to ⊙ one quarter of the way down the counterslope	3	0
22	From ⊙ on slope to ⊙ below half-way	5	0
23	From ⊙ below half-way to Ugogi at the base	4	0
⊙23+27 (carried forward)=33 ⊙'s		103	25
	Carried forward	67	55
	Total hours from the coast to Ugogi	171	20

Rubeho Pass, (about) Latitude, South, 6° 38′.   Longitude, East, 36° 19′.
Ugogi,   "   6° 40′.   "   36° 6′.
Altitude of Rubeho summit, 5700. Altitude of Ugogi at western Counterslope, by
B. P. Therm., 2770.

THIRD REGION.

		FROM UGOGI, THROUGH MARENGA MK'HALI, UGOGO, AND MGUNDA MK'HALI, TO TURA OF UNYAMWEZI.	H.	M.
Marenga Mk'hali.	⊙1	Ugogi to ⊙ in Jungle	4	0
	2	Jungle to Marenga Mk'hali (second of that name)	4	40
	3	Marenga Mk'hali to ⊙ in Jungle	4	10
	4	⊙ in Jungle to ⊙ in Jungle	5	0
	5	⊙ in Jungle to Ziwa or tank (on frontier of Ugogo)	2	0
Ugogo.	6	Ziwa to Kifukuru	3	0
	7	Kifukuru to ⊙ in Jungle	5	40
	8	⊙ in Jungle to Kanyenye	1	25
	9	Kanyenye to Kanyenye of Magomba	2	45
	10	Kanyenye of Magomba to ⊙ in Jungle	5	0
	11	⊙ in Jungle to K'hok'ho	7	40
	12	K'hok'ho to Mdaburu	6	20
	13	Mdaburu to ⊙ in Jungle of Mgunda Mk'hali	6	30

THIRD REGION—*continued.*

				H.	M.
Mganda Mk'hali.	14	Mgunda Mk'hali to Mabunguru		6	0
	15	Mabunguru to Jiwe la Mkoa		7	0
	16	Jiwe la Mkoa to Kirurumo		3	10
	17	Kirurumo to Jiweni of Uyanzi		4	30
	18	Jiweni to Mgongo Thembo		2	20
	19	Mgongo Thembo to ☉ Tura Nullah		7	0
	20	☉ Tura Nullah to Tura in Unyamwezi		5	30

☉ 20+33 (carried forward)=53 .... 93 40

Carried forward... 171 20

Total hours from the coast to Tura... 265 0

Eastern limit of Tura, Latitude, South, 5° 27′. Longitude, East, 34°.
Altitude, by Bath Thermometer, 4125 feet.

FOURTH REGION.

THROUGH UNYAMWEZI, UGARA, UWENDE, AND UVINZA, TO FORD OF MALAGARAZI RIVER.

		H.	M.
1	Eastern limit of Tura to Western Tura	1	30
2	Western Tura to Kwale Nullah	6	30
3	Kwale Nullah to Eastern Rubuga	5	45
4	Eastern Rubuga to Western Rubuga	2	40
5	Western Rubuga to Ukona	2	15
6	Ukona to Kigwa	5	5
7	Kigwa to Hanga village	6	30
8	Hanga to Kazeh (Arab ☉)	5	0
9	Kazeh to Zimbili Hill	1	40
10	Zimbili to Yombo	2	0
11	Yombo to Pano (clearing in Jungle)	4	0
12	Pano to Eastern Mfuto	1	40
13	Eastern Mfuto to Western Mfuto	2	0
14	Western Mfuto to Eastern Wilyankuru	6	30
15	Eastern Wilyankuru to Central Wilyankuru	2	50
16	Central Wilyankuru to Western Wilyankuru	2	0
17	Western Wilyankuru to Masenge	2	30
18	Masenge to Eastern Kirira	2	0
19	Eastern Kirira to Western Kirira	3	0
20	Western Kirira to Eastern Msene	4	0
21	Eastern Msene to Western Msene (Arab ☉)	2	0
22	Western Msene to Mbhali	1	30
23	Mbhali to Sengati	2	0
24	Sengati to Sorora or Solola	0	45
25	Sorora to Ukungwe	2	15
26	Ukungwe to Panda	1	50
27	Panda to Kajjanjeri	1	30
28	Kajjanjeri to Eastern Usagozi	3	45
29	Eastern Usagozi to Western Usagozi	1	0
30	Western Usagozi to Masenga of Wagara	2	0
31	Masenga to Mukozimo of Wawende	2	45
32	Mukozimo to Uganza of Wanyamwezi	3	15
33	Uganza to Usenye of Wavinza	4	0
34	Usenye to Rukunda	2	20
35	Rukunda to Wanyika	3	0
36	Wanyika to Unyanguruwwe	4	50
37	Unyanguruwwe to Ugaga on the Malagarazi River	3	0

(Items 17–21 marked "Expedition separated." Items 33–37 bracketed "Uvinza.")

☉ 37+53 (carried over)=90 .... 110 30

Carried forward...... 265 0

Total hours from coast to Malagarazi River...... 375 30

Kazeh, Latitude, South, 5° 1′. Longitude, East, 33° 3′.
Malagarazi Ferry, " 5° 7′. " 31° 13′.
Altitude of Kazeh, by Bath Therm., 3490 feet.
" Usenye " 3190 "

FIFTH REGION.

	FROM THE MALAGARAZI FERRY TO UKARANGA ON THE TANGANYIKA LAKE.	H. M.
1	Ugaga on left to Mpete on right hand............................	0 25
2	Mpete to Kinawani..	5 20
3	Kinawani to ⊙ in Jungle...	5 25
4	⊙ in Jungle to Jambeho..	1 40
5	Jambeho to Salt-pans of Rusugi River	5 15
6	Salt-pans to ⊙ in Jungle	4 20
7	⊙ in Jungle to Ruguvu River	3 30
8	Ruguvu River to Unguwwe River	4 40
9	Unguwwe River to ⊙ in Jungle	7 35
10	⊙ in Jungle to Ukaranga on Lake	6 35
⊙10+90 (carried forward)=100		44 45
	Carried forward......	375 30
	Total hours from the coast to the Tanganyika Lake......	420 25
	Ukaranga, Latitude, South, 4° 58'. Longitude, East, 30° 3' 30''. Altitude by Bath Therm., 1850.	

The distance from Kaole to Ujiji is of 540 rectilinear geographical miles; or, in statute miles, allowing one for windings of the road, thus:

> From Kaole to Kazeh, statute miles......................... 520
> From Kazeh to Ujiji   "   276
>   ———
>   796
> Add one fifth for detour—159 miles.............. 159
> Total of statute miles................................. 955

Assuming the absolute time of traveling to be 420 hours, this will give a marching rate of 2.27 miles per hour.

CONTENTS.

APPENDICES.

LIST OF ILLUSTRATIONS.

ZANZIBAR TOWN FROM THE SEA.

THE

LAKE REGIONS OF CENTRAL AFRICA.

CHAPTER I.

WE QUIT ZANZIBAR ISLAND IN DIGNIFIED STYLE.

At noon, on the 16th of June, 1857, the corvette Artémise, after the usual expenditure of gunpowder which must in Eastern lands announce every momentous event, from the birth of a prince to the departure of a bishop, slowly gliding out of Zanzibar harbor, afforded us a farewell glance at the whitewashed mosques and houses of the Arabs, the cadjan-huts, the cocoa-grown coasts, and the ruddy hills striped with long lines of clove. Onward she stole before a freshening breeze, the balmy breath of the Indian Ocean, under a sun that poured a flood of sparkling light over the azure depths and the bright-green shallows around, between the "elfin isles" of Kumbeni, with its tall trees, and Chumbi, tufted with dense thickets, till the white sand-strip mingled with the blue ocean, the gleaming line of dwarf red cliff and scaur dropped into the water's edge, the land faded from emerald to brown, and from brown to hazy purple, the tufts of the trees seemed first to stand out of, then to swim upon the wave, and as evening, the serenest of tropical evenings, closed in over sky, earth, and sea, a cloud-like ridge, dimly discernible from our quarter, was all that remained of Zanzibar.

I will not here stay the course of my narrative to inform the reader that Zanzibar is not, as the cyclopedias declare, "an island of Africa, governed by a king who is subject to the Portuguese;" that it is not, as the Indian post-offices appear to believe, a part of the Persian Gulf; nor, as home-keeping folk, whose notions of African geography are somewhat dim and ill-defined, have mentally determined, a rock in the Red Sea, nor a dependency of the Niger, nor even an offshoot of the Cape of Storms.

The Artémise is a kind of "jackass-frigate," an 18-gun corvette, teak-built in Bombay, with a goodly breadth of beam, a slow sailer, but a sure. In the days of our deceased ally, Sayyid Said, the misnamed "Imaum of Muscat," she had so frequently been placed by his highness at the disposal of his old friend Lieutenant Colonel Hamerton, that she had acquired the sobriquet of "the Balyuz, or consul's yacht." On this occasion she had been fitted up for a cruise to the main land; her yards, usually struck, had been swayed up and thrown across; her top spars had been transferred from the hold to their proper place; her ropes and rigging, generally hanging in tatters about her sticks, had been carefully overhauled; her old sails had been bent, and her usual crew, a few slaves that held their own with difficulty against a legion of rats and an army of cockroaches, had been increased to its full complement of twenty men. His highness the Sayyid Majid, who after the demise of his father had assumed the title of "Sultan of Zanzibar and the Sawahil," came on board, accompanied by his four brothers, of whom two—Sayyids Jamshid and Hamdan—died of small-pox before our return, and one—Sayyid Barghash—has lately become a state prisoner at Bombay, to bid what proved a last adieu to his father's friend. At the same time his highness honored me through his secretary, Ahmed bin Nuuman, more generally known as Wajhayn, or "Two-faces," with three letters of introduction, to Musa Mzuri, the Indian doyen of the merchants settled at Unyamwezi, to the Arabs there resident, and to all his subjects who were traveling into the interior.

The Artémise conveyed the *personnel* and the *matériel* of the East African Expedition, namely, the two European members— my companion and myself—two Portuguese, or rather half-caste Goanese "boys," two negro gun-carriers, the Seedy Mubarak Mombai (Bombay), and Muinyi Mabruki, his "brother," and finally, eight so-called "Baloch" mercenaries, a guard appointed by the sultan to accompany me. Lieutenant Colonel Hamerton, at that time her majesty's consul and Hon. East India Company's agent at Zanzibar, though almost lethargic from the effects of protracted illness—he lived only in the evening—had deemed it his duty to land us upon the coast, and to superintend our departure from the dangerous sea-board. He was attended by Mr. Frost, the apothecary attached to the consulate, whose treatment for a fatal liver-complaint appeared to consist of minute doses of morphia and a liberal diet of sugar.

By Lieut. Colonel Hamerton's advice, I ventured to modify the scheme of the East African Expedition, as originally proposed by the Expeditionary Committee of the Royal Geographical Society of London. In 1855, Mr. Erhardt, an energetic member of the hapless "Mombas Mission," had on his return to London offered to explore a vast mass of water, about the size of the Caspian, which, from the information of divers "natives," he had deposited in slug or leech shape in the heart of intertropical Africa, thus prolonging the old "Maravi" or "Moravim Lake" of Portuguese travelers and school atlases to the north of the equator, and thus bringing a second deluge upon sundry provinces and kingdoms thoroughly well known for the last half century. He had proposed to land, with an outfit of three hundred dollars,* at Kilwa, one of the southern ports of the Zanzibar main land, to hire a score of Wasawahili porters, to march with a caravan upon the nearest point of his own water, and to launch an adventurous canoe upon a lake which, according to his map, could not be traversed under twenty-five days. Messrs. Erhardt and Krapf, of the "Mombas Mission," spent, it is true, a few hours at Kilwa, where they were civilly entreated by the governor and the citizens; but they egregriously deceived themselves and others when they concluded that they could make that place their ingress-point. Lieutenant Christopher, I.N., who visited the East African coast in 1843, wisely advised explorers to avoid the neighborhood of Kilwa. Wisely, I repeat: the burghers of that proud old settlement had, only a year before my arrival, murdered, by means of the Wangindo savages, an Arab merchant who ventured to lay open the interior.

At the same time I had laid before the council of the Royal Geographical Society my desire to form an expedition primarily for the purpose of ascertaining the limits of the "Sea of Ujiji, or Unyamwezi Lake," and secondarily, to determine the exportable produce of the interior and the ethnography of its tribes. I have quoted exactly the words of the application. In these days every explorer of Central Africa is supposed to have set out in quest of the coy sources of the White Nile, and when he returns without them, his exploration, whatever may have been its value, is determined to be a failure. The council honored my plans with their approval. At their solicitation, the Foreign Office granted the sum of £1000 for the outlay of the exploration, and the defunct Court of Directors of the late East India Company, who could not be persuaded to contribute toward the expenses, generously allowed me two years' leave of absence from regimental duty, for the purpose of commanding the expedition. I also received instructions to report myself to his Excellency the Lord Elphinstone, then Governor of Bombay, and to Lieut. Colonel Hamerton, from whose influence and long experience much was expected.

---

* The sum was wholly inadequate. M. Erhardt has, I have been told, expended as much on a week's march from Pangani Town to Fuga. The smallest of Wasawahili peddlers would hardly deem an outfit of three hundred dollars sufficient. M. Erhardt was, even according to his own reduced ideas of distance, to march with twenty followers 400 miles, and to explore a lake 300 miles in breadth and of unknown length. In 1802, when cloth and beads were twice their present value in Africa, the black Pombeiros sent by M. Da Costa, superintendent of the "Cassangi Factory," carried with them, for the necessary expenses and presents, goods to the value of nearly £500. M. Erhardt's estimate was highly injurious to future travelers: either he knew the truth, and he should have named at once a reasonable estimate, or he was ignorant of the subject, and he should have avoided it. The consequence of his proposal was simply this: With £5000 instead of £1000, the limited sum of the government grant, the East African Expedition could have explored the whole central area; nothing but the want of supplies caused their return at the time when, after surmounting sickness, hardship, and want of discipline among the party, they were ready to push to the extreme end.

When the starting-point came to be debated, the consul strongly objected to an expedition into the interior *viâ* Kilwa, on account of the opposition to be expected at a port so distant from the seat of government, where the people, half-caste Arabs and Wasawahili, who are under only a nominal control, still retained a strong predilection for protection, and a violent hostility to strangers. These reasons led him to propose my landing upon the coast opposite Zanzibar, and to my thence marching with a strong escort, dispatched by the Arab prince, through the maritime tribes, whose cruel murder of M. Maizan, the first European known to have penetrated beyond the sea-board, was yet fresh in the memories of men. This notion was accepted the more readily, as, during my short preliminary sojourn at Zanzibar, I had satisfactorily ascertained from Arab travelers that the Maravi or Kilwa Lake, is distinct from the " Sea of Ujiji;" that the former is of comparatively diminutive dimensions; that there is no caravan route between the two; and therefore that, by exploring the smaller, I should lose the chance of discovering the larger water. Moreover, the general feeling of the Zanzibarites—of the Christian merchants, whom I had offended by collecting statistics about copal-digging, ivory, and sesamum—of the Bhattias, or Hindoos of Cutch, who systematically abuse the protection of the British flag to support the interest of the slave-trade—of the Arabs, who remembered nothing but political intrigue in the explorations of the " Mombas Mission" and the lamentable result of Dr. Krapf's political intrigues—and of the Africans generally, who are disposed to see in every innovation some new form of evil—had been conveyed to my ears explicitly enough to warrant my apprehensions for the success of the expedition, had I insisted upon carrying out the project proposed by M. Erhardt.

I must here explain that, before my departure from England, the Church Missionary Society had supplied me, after a personal interview in Salisbury Square, with a letter to their *employé*, M. Rebmann, the last remnant of that establishment at Mombasah, which had, it is said, expended about £12,000 with the minimest of results. The missionaries had commenced operations with vigor, and to the work of conversion they had added certain discoveries in the unknown lands of the interior, which attracted the attention of European geographers. Unhappily Dr. Krapf, the principal, happened to commit himself by the following assertion: " The Imaum of Muscat has not an inch of ground on the coast between the Island of Wassin and the Pangani River; this tract, in fact, belonging to King Kmeri, of Usumbara, down from 4° 30′ to 5° 30′ S. The tract, which is very low, is inhabited by the Wasegua tribes, and is the chief slave-market for supplying Zanzibar."

This " information," put forth in the Journal of the Royal Geographical Society (vol. i., p. 203), was copied into the proceedings (vol. xxiii., p. 106), with the remark that the territory alluded to was a "supposed possession" of the Imaum. Orientals are thin-skinned upon questions of land; the assertion was directly opposed to fact, and the jealousy of the rival representatives at Zanzibar, each on his own side, exaggerated its tendency. Lieut. Colonel Hamerton, who felt his influence sapped by this error on the part of his protégé, had reported the facts to his government. Dr. Krapf had quitted the scene of his labors and discoveries, but his highness the Sultan and the sadat, or court, retained a lively remembrance of the regretable incident. Before the arrival of the expedition, "Muhiyy-el-Din," the shafei kazi of the island, had called upon Lieut. Colonel Hamerton, probably by direction of his superiors, and had received an answer, fortified by an oath, that the expedition was wholly independent of "Dutchmen," as the missionaries were called by the Zanzibarites. I was compelled, somewhat unwillingly, to dispense with urging M. Rebmann's presence. By acting in any other way I should have lost the assistance of the consul; and the Arabs, with a ready display of zeal, would have secured for me an inevitable failure.

At six P.M. on Wednesday, the 17th of June, 1857, the Artémise cast anchor off Wale Point, a long, low, bush-grown sandspit, about eighty-four miles distant from the little town of Bagamoyo. Our sailing-master, Mohammed bin Khamis, anchored in deep water, throwing out double the length of chain required. For this prudence, however, there was some reason. The roadsteads are open; the muddy bottom shelves gradually, almost imperceptibly; the tides retire ten or eleven feet, and a strong gale, accompanied by the dangerous raz de marée, or rollers from seaward, especially at the seasons of the syzygies, with such a shore to leeward, is justly dreaded by the crews of square-rigged vessels.

There is a something peculiarly interesting in the first aspect of the "Mrima," the hill-land, as this part of the African coast is called by the islanders of Zanzibar. On one side lies the Indian Ocean, illimitable toward the east, dimpled with its "anerithmon gelasma," and broken westward by a thin line of foam, creaming upon the whitest and finest of sand, the detritus of coralline and madrepore. It dents the coast deeply, forming bays, bayous, lagoons, and back-waters, where, after breaking their force upon bars and black ledges of sand and rock, upon diabolitos, or sun-stained masses of a coarse conglomerate, and upon strong weirs planted in crescent shape, the waters lie at rest in the arms of the land like sheets of oil. The points and islets formed by these sea-streams are almost flush with the briny surface, yet they are overgrown with a profuse vegetation, the result of tropical suns and copious showers, which supply the want of rich soil. The banks of the back-waters are lined with forests of white and red mangrove. When the tide is out, the cone-shaped root-work supporting each tree rises naked from the deep sea-ooze; parasitical oysters cluster over the trunks at water-level, and between the adults rise slender young shoots, tipped with bunches of brilliant green. The pure white sand is bound together by a kind of convolvulus, whose large fleshy leaves and lilac-colored flowers creep along the loose soil. Where raised higher above the ocean-level, the coast is a wall of verdure. Plots of bald old trees, bent by the regular breezes, betray the positions of settlements which, generally sheltered from sight, besprinkle the coast in a long straggling line, like the suburbs of a populous city. Of these thirteen were counted in a space of three miles. The monotony of green that clothes the soil is relieved in places by dwarf earth-cliffs and scaurs of rufous hue—East Africa is mostly a red land—and behind the foreground of littoral or alluvial plain, at a distance varying from three to five miles, rises a blue line of higher level, conspicuous even from Zanzibar Island, the sandy raised beach now the frontier of the wild men. To this sketch add its accompaniment; by day, the plashing of the wave and the scream of the gull, with the perpetual hum and buzz of insect life; and, after sunset, the deep, dead silence of a tropical night, broken only by the roar of the old bull-crocodile at his resting-time, the qua-qua of the night-heron, and the shouts and shots of the watchmen, who know from the grunts of the hippopotamus, struggling up the bank, that he is quitting his watery home to pay a visit to their fields.

We were delayed ten days off Wale Point by various preliminaries to departure. Said bin Salim, a half-caste Arab of Zanzibar, who, sorely against his will, was ordered by the prince to act as ras kafilah, or caravan-guide, had, after ceaseless and fruitless prayers for delay, preceded us about a fortnight, for the purpose of collecting porters. The timid little man, whose nerves were shaken to weeping-point by the terrors of the way, and by the fancy that, thus co-operating with the exploration, he was incurring the hatred of his fellows, had "taken the shilling," in the shape of 500 dollars, advanced from public funds by the consul, with a promise of an ample reward in hard coin, and a gold watch, "si se bene gesserit:" at the same time Lieut. Colonel Hamerton had warned me against trusting to a half-caste. Accompanied by a Cutch banyan of the Bhattia caste, by name Ramji—of whom more anon—he had crossed over, on the 1st of June, to the main land, and had hired a gang of porters, who, however, hearing that their employer was a muzungu, a "white man," at once dispersed, forgetting to return their hire. About one hundred and seventy men were required; only thirty-six were procurable. The large amount of carriage was necessitated by the bulky and ponderous nature of African specie, cotton cloth, brass wire, and beads, of which a total of seventy loads was expended in one year and nine months. Moreover, under the impression that "vert and venison" abounded in the interior, I had provided ammunition for two years—ten thousand copper caps of sizes, forty boxes, each restricted, for convenience of porterage, to forty pounds, and containing ball, grape, and shot, six fire-proof magazines, and two small barrels of fine powder, weighing in total fifty pounds, together with four ten-pound kegs of a coarser kind for the escort—in all, two hundred rounds for each individual of the party. This supply was deemed necessary on account of the immense loss to which ammunition is subjected by theft and weather in these lands.

On the second day after anchoring off Wale Point a native boat brought on board the Artémise Ladha Damha, the collector of customs at Zanzibar, who, in compliment to Lieut. Colonel Hamerton, of old his friend and patron, had torn himself from his beloved occupations to push the departure of the expedition. Ladha, hearing that the Arab merchants had hastened to secure their gangs before corrupted by the more liberal offers of the "white men"—"pagazi," or porters, being at that time scarce, because the caravans from the interior had not yet reached the coast—proposed to send forward the thirty-six fellows hired by Said bin Salim, with orders to await the arrival of their employer at Zungomero, in the land of K'hutu, a point situated beyond the plundering maritime tribes. These men carried goods to the value of 654 dollars German crowns (each 4s. 2d.), and they received for hire 124 dollars; rations, that is to say, 1.50 lbs. of grain per diem, not included: they preferred to travel with the escort of two slave-musketeers rather than to incur the fancied danger of accompanying a "muzungu," though followed by a well-armed party. For the personal baggage and the outfit necessary for crossing the maritime region, which reached by waste the figure of 295 dollars, asses were proposed by Ladha Damha: Zanzibar and the main-land harbors were ransacked, and in a short time thirty animals, good, bad, and indifferent, were fitted for the roads with large canvass bags and vile Arab pack-saddles, composed of damaged gunny-bags stuffed with straw. It was necessary to leave behind, till a full gang of porters could be engaged, the greater part of the ammunition, the iron boat which had proved so useful on the coasting voyage to Mombasah, and the reserve supply of cloth, wire, and beads, valued at 359 dollars. The Hindoos promised faithfully to forward these articles, and received 150 dollars for the hire of twenty-two men, who were to start in ten days. Nearly eleven months, however, elapsed before they appeared; caravan after caravan came up from the coast, yet the apathetic Bhattias pretended want of porters as the cause of their delay. Evidently my preparations were hurriedly made; strong reasons, however, urged me on—delay, even for a few days, might have been fatal.

During the brief detention off Wale Point, the latitudes and longitudes of the estuary of the Kingani, the main artery of these regions, and of the little settlements Bagamoyo and Kaole—strongly against the advice of Lieut. Colonel Hamerton, who declared that by such proceedings the expedition was going to the bad—were laid down by my companion: a novice lunarian, he was assisted by Mohammed bin Khamis, who had read his "Norie" in England. Various visits to the hippopotamus haunts produced little beyond the damaging of the corvette's gig, which, suddenly uplifted from the water upon the points of two tusks, showed two corresponding holes in her bottom. Nor did I neglect to land as often as possible at Kaole, the point of departure upon the main land, for the purpose of making sketches with the pen and pencil, of urging on preparations, and of gathering those items of "bazar-gup," *i. e.*, tittle-tattle, that represents the labors of the "fourth estate" in Eastern lands.

The little settlement of "Kaole"—an abbreviation of Kaole Urembo, meaning literally, in the ancient dialect of the coast, "to show beauty"—is the normal village-port in these regions, which, from Mombasah southward to Kilwa, still ignore a town of masonry. You land, when the tide is out, upon half a mile of muddy sand, and if a "swell," you are carried by four men upon the kitanda—cot or cartel—which is slung along the side of your craft. Arrived at the strip of dry ground that marks the limit of the tide, you are let down, and amid the shouts of the men, the shrieks of the women, and the naïve remarks of the juvenile population, you ascend by a narrow foot-path, worn through the thick jungle and through the millet-fields which press upon the tattered palisade, a dwarf steep bank, on whose summit the settlement lies. Inside the fence are a dozen pent-roofed houses, claret-chests of wattle and dab, divided into three or more compartments by dwarf party-walls of the same material: each messuage is jealously separated from its neighbor by large inclosed "compounds," or courtyards appropriated to the women and children. The largest timber is that of the mangrove; the flying thatch-roof, so raised that, though windows are unknown, the interior enjoys tolerable ventilation, is of jauli, or rude cocoa-plaits, and under the long and projecting eaves, which rest upon strong perpendiculars, are broad earth-benches, divided by the entrance, and garnished with mats: these form the shops and sitting-rooms of the settlement. Some houses have a partial second story, like a ship's bunk, a planking supported by rafters, and used as a store-closet or a dormitory. Around the larger habitations cluster masses of hovels, and the characteristic African haycock huts. With closed doors in still weather, these dens are unendurable to a European; the people, however, fearing thieves and wild beasts, never fail to barricade themselves within at night. The only attempt at masonry in the settlement is the "gurayza," or fort, a square of lime and coralline, with store-rooms for the banyan's goods below, and provided with a creneled terrace for watchmen.

In the "garrison-towns" the soldiers and their families form the principal part of the population. These men, who call themselves Baloch, are, with few exceptions, originally from Mekran and from the lowlands about Guadel. Many of them had been born and bred in Arabia. In former days their fathers migrated from their starving homes to Maskat, in the Arab dows which visited their ports to buy horses and to collect little cargoes of wheat and salt. In Arabia they were fakirs, sailors, porters, and day-laborers, barbers, date-gleaners, asinegos, beggars, and thieves. Sultan Bin Hamid, the father of the late Sayyid Said, first conceived the bright idea of putting matchlocks into their hands, and of dubbing them askar, or soldiers, as a slight upon his less docile compatriots. The son of Sultan followed his sire's plan, and succeeded in dividing and ruling by means of the antipathy prevailing between the more disciplinable mercenary and the unruly Arab subject. The Baloch are, however, rather hated than feared. They hang, say the Semites, their benefits behind their backs, while they wear their grievances in full view, woman-like, upon their breasts. Loud in debate, and turbulent in demeanor, they are called by the Arabs a "light folk," and are compared to birds fluttering and chirruping round a snake. Abject slaves to the Great Gaster, they collect in swarms round a slaughtered goat, and they will feast their eyes for hours on the sight of a rice-bag. When in cantonment on the island or the coast, they receive as pay from 2.50 to 5 dollars per mensem; when in the field or on outpost duty, a "batta" of 10 dollars—a sensible system, which never allows them to become, like the Indian sepoy, independent. They are not averse to active service, as, when so employed, they have full permission to "pill and poll." In camp they are commanded by a jemadar, who, assisted by a "moollah"—some wretch who has retained, as sole traces of his better days, a smattering of reading, writing, and arithmetic—robs them and his government with the recklessness of impunity. Thus the jemadar, or C. O., who also dispenses promotion, is a man having authority. Similarly our colonels in India, by superior position and allowances, commanded the respect of their men before centralization, falling upon the land like a pestilence, systematically monopolized all power, and then rained blame upon those who had lost it. These Baloch are a tame copy of the Turkish bashi buzuk, or "madcap," far inferior as desperadoes to the Kurd and Arnaut. They live the life of the Anglo-Indian soldier of the past generation, drinking beer when they can "come by it," smoking, chatting, and arguing; the younger wrestle, shoot, and exchange kit; and the silly babbling patriarchs, with white beards and venerable brows, tell wondrous tales of scenes long gone by, and describe to unbelieving ears the ice and snow, the luscious fruits and the sweet waters of the mountains and valleys of far Balochistan.

The other items of the population are the Wamrima*—Western negroids of a mixed Arab and African descent, who fringe the shore in a thin line. These "coast-clans" support themselves in idleness and comparative luxury, by amicably plundering the down-caravans, and by large plantations of cereals and vegetables, with which they, or rather their slaves, supply the Island of Zanzibar, and even the shores of Arabia. The Wamrima are an ill-conditioned race; they spend life in eating, drinking, and smoking, drinking and dancing, visits, intrigue, and low debauchery. They might grow cotton and coffee, and dig copal to almost any extent; but while a pound of grain remains in bin, no man will handle a hoe. The feminine part of the community is greatly superior in number to the masculine, and this leads to the usual result: on a "siku ku," or fête-day, the ladies of the village, with yellow pigment over their faces and their woolly heads, perform in their cups impromptu dances upon the open, enter a stranger's house as if it were their own, and call for something to drink, as if they had been educated at Cremorne or the Rue Cadet. The Wamrima are ruled by diwans, or headmen, locally called "chomwi;" these officials are subject to Zanzibar, and their numbers are every where in inverse ratio to the importance of the places. The chomwi enjoys the privileges of "dash," fines and extortions; he has also certain marks of distinction. For instance, he is authorized to wear turbands and the wooden pattens called by the Arabs "kabkab;" he may also sit upon cots, chairs, and the mkeka, a fine dyed mat; whereas a commoner venturing upon such display would infallibly be mulcted in goats or cattle. At the ngoma ku, or great dance, which celebrates every event in this land of revelry, only the chomwi may perform the morris with drawn sword before the admiring multitude. A subject detected in intrigue with the wife of a headman must, under penalty of being sold, pay five slaves; the fine is reduced to one head in the case of a plebeian. With this amount of dignity the diwan naturally

---

* It must be borne in mind that, in the Kisawahili and its cognates, the vowel *u* prefixed to a root, which, however, is never used without some prefix, denotes, through a primary idea of causality, a country or region, as Uzaramo, the region of Zaramo. Many names, however, exceptionally omit this letter, as the Mrima, K'hutu, Fuga, and Karagwah. The liquid *m*, or, before a vowel and an aspirated h, *mu*, to prevent hiatus, being probably a synæresis of *mtu*, a man, denotes the individual, as Mzaramo, a man or woman of Zaramo. When prefixed to the names of trees, as has been instanced, it is evidently an abbreviation of mti, a tree. The plural form of *m* and *mu* is Wá, a contraction of Wátu, men, people; it is used to signify the population, as Wamrima, the "coast-clans," Wazaramo, the people or tribe of Zaramo, and Wasawahíli (with a long accent upon the penultimate, consonant with the spirit of the African language, and contrary to that of the Arabic), the population of the Sawahil. Finally, the syllable *ki*—prefixed to the theoretical root—denotes any thing appertaining to a country, as the terminating *ish* in the word English. It especially refers in popular usage to language, as Kizaramo, the language of Zaramo; Kisawahíli, the language of the Sawahil, originally called Ki-ngozi, from the district of Ngozi, on the Ozi River. It has been deemed advisable to retain these terse and concise distinctions, which, if abandoned, would necessitate a weary redundance of words.

expects to live, and to support his family with the fat of the land, and without sweat of brow. When times are hard, he organizes a kidnapping expedition against a weaker neighbor, and fills his purse by selling the proceeds. But his income is derived chiefly from the down-caravans bringing ivory and slaves from Unyamwezi and the far interior. Though rigidly forbidden by the Prince of Zanzibar to force caravans to his particular port, he sends large armed parties of his kinsmen and friends, his clients and serfs, as far as 150 and 200 miles inland, where they act less like touters than highwaymen. By every petty art of mercantile diplomacy —now by force, then by fraud, by promises, or by bribes of cloth and sweetmeats—they induce the caravan to enter the village, when the work of plunder begins. Out of each frasilah (thirty-five lbs. avoirdupois) of ivory, from eight to fourteen dollars are claimed as duties to the government of Zanzibar; the headmen then demand six dollars as their fee, under various technical names, plus one dollar for "ugali," or porridge—the "manche" —and one dollar for the use of water—the "pour boire." The owner of the tusk is then handed over to the tender mercies of the Banyan, from whom the diwan has received a bribe, called his "rice;" and the crafty Hindoo buys for eighteen to twenty dollars an article worth, at Zanzibar, fifty. If the barbarian be so unwise as to prefer cash, being intellectually unfit to discriminate between a cent and a dollar, he loses even more than if he had taken in barter the coarse and trashy articles provided for him by the trade. An adept at distinguishing good from bad cloth and a cunning connoisseur in beads of sorts, he has yet no choice: if he reject what is worthless, he must return home with his ivory and without an investment. Such is an outline of the present system. It is nowhere the same in its details; but every where the principle is one—the loss is to the barbarian, and the profits are to the coast-clans, the Wamrima and their headmen. Hence the dislike to strangers and the infinite division into little settlements, where people might be expected to prefer the comfort and safety of large communities. The 10th article of the commercial treaty, concluded on the 31st May, 1839, between her majesty's government and his highness Sayyid Said of Muscat and Zanzibar, secured to the possessors of the Mrima a monopoly in the articles of ivory and gum-copal on that part of the east coast of Africa from the port of Tangata (Mtangata), situated in about 5½° S. lat., to the port of Quiloa (Kilwa) lying in about 7° S. of the equator. It is not improbable that the jealousy of European nations, each fearing the ambitious designs of its neighbor, brought about this invidious prohibitionist measure.

Besides the Baloch and the Wamrima, the settlements usually contain a few of the " Washenzi," or barbarians from the interior, who visit them to act as day-laborers, and who sometimes, by evincing a little disrespect for the difference between the "mine" and the "thine," leave their heads to decorate tall poles at the entrance. The Wazaramo tribe send, when there is no blood-feud, numbers to Kaole, where they are known by their peculiar head-dress, a single or a double line of pips or dilberries of ochre and grease surrounding the head. They regard the stranger with a wild and childish stare, and whenever I landed they slunk away from me, for reasons which will appear in the course of this narrative. The list of floating population concludes with a few Banyans—there are about fifty in Kaole and its vicinity—a race national as the English, who do their best to import into Eastern Africa the cows and curries, the customs and the costumes, of Western India.

The first visit to Kaole opened up a vista of unexpected difficulties. My escort had been allowed to leave the Artémise, and their comrades in arms had talked them half crazy with fear. Zahri, a Baloch, who had visited Unyamwezi, declared that nothing less than 100 guards, 150 guns, and several cannon could enable them to fight a way through the perils of the interior. Tulsi, the Banyan, warned them that for three days they must pass among savages, who sit on trees and discharge poisoned arrows into the air with such dexterity that they never fail to fall upon the traveler's pate; he strongly advised them, therefore, under pain of death, to avoid trees—no easy matter in a land all forest. Then the principal chomwi assured them that the chiefs of the Wazaramo tribe had sent six several letters to the officials of the coast, forbidding the white man to enter their country. Ladha Damha also obscurely hinted that the Wazaramo might make caches of their provisions in the jungle, and that the human stomach can not march without feeding. Divers dangers of the way were incidentally thrown in: I learned for the first time that the kargadan, or rhinoceros, kills 200 men, that armies of elephants attack camps by night, and that the craven hyena does more damage than the Bengal tiger. In vain I objected that guns with men behind them are better than cannon backed by curs, that mortals can die but once, that the Wazaramo are unable to write, that rations might be carried where not purchasable, and that powder and ball have been known to conquer rhinoceroses, elephants, and hyenas. A major force was against me.

Presently the cause of intimidation crept into sight. The jemadar and the eight Baloch detached by his highness the Sayyid Majid of Zanzibar could not march without a re-enforcement of four others, afterward increased by a fifth in the person of an "Ustad," a tailor-boy. The garrison of Kaole, having no employment, was ready, with the prospect of the almighty dollar, to march any where on this side of Jehannum. The perils of the path rendered it absolutely necessary that we should be escorted by a temporary guard of thirty-four men and their jemadar Yaruk: and they did not propose to do the good deed gratis. Ramji, the Banyan clerk of the customs at Zanzibar, had a number of slaves whom he called his "sons;" they were "eating off their heads" in idleness at Zanzibar. He favored me by letting out ten of these youths at the rate of thirty dollars a head for a period of six months: for the same sum every man might have been purchased in the market. When asses were proposed ass-men were necessary; in the shortest space of time five were procured, and their pay for the whole journey was fixed at thirty dollars, about twice the sale-value of the article. I can not plead guilty to not having understood the manœuvre—a commercial speculation on the part of the rascal Ramji. Yet at times—need I say it?—it is good to appear a dupe. It is wise, when your enemies determine you to be that manner of sable or ermine contrivance into which ladies insert their fair hands, to favor the hypothesis. I engaged the men, I paid the men, and mentally I chronicled a vow that Ramji should in the long run change places with me.

Presently Mr. Frost, with brow severe and official manner, informed me that the state of Lieut. Colonel Hamerton's health forbade a longer stay near the coast. To this there was no reply: I contented myself with remarking once more that morphia appeared a curious cure for a confirmed liver complaint, and I made preparations for landing at once. Mr. Frost replied that the doses of morphia were very "little ones"—an excuse which, according to Captain Marryat, has been urged under somewhat dissimilar circumstances by the frail ancilla. I confided to Mr. Frost's care two MSS. addressed through the Foreign Office, one to Mr. John Blackwood, the other to Dr. Norton Shaw, of the Royal Geographical Society. As the former arrived in safety, while the latter—a detailed report concerning the commerce and capabilities of Zanzibar—was lost, I can not help suspecting that it came somehow to an untimely end. Lieut. Colonel Hamerton had repeatedly warned me that, by making inquiries into the details of profit, I was exciting the jealousy of the natives and the foreigners of Zanzibar. According to him, the mercantile community was adopting the plan which had secured the foul murder of M. Maizan: the Christians had time and opportunity to alarm the Banyans, and the latter were able to work upon the Wasawahíli population. These short-sighted men dreaded that from throwing open the country competition might result: Oriental-like, thinking only of the moment, of themselves, they could not perceive that the development of resources would benefit all concerned in their exploitation. There were, however, honorable exceptions, among whom I am bound to mention M. Bérard, agent to Messrs. Rabaud, frères, of Marseilles, who, by direction of his employers, offered me every manner of assistance; and the late M. Sam. Masury, a Salem merchant, to whose gratuitous kindness I was indebted for several necessaries when separated from civilization by one half of Africa. They contrasted sharply with the rest of the community. In the case of a certain young gentleman, Lieut. Colonel Hamerton was, he informed me, compelled to threaten a personal chastisement unless he ceased to fill native ears with his malignant suspicions.

The weary labor of verifying accounts and of writing receipts duly concluded, I took a melancholy leave of my warm-hearted friend, Lieut. Colonel Hamerton, upon whose form and features death was written in legible characters. He gave me his last advice, to march straight ahead, despising " walnut and velvet-slipper men," who afford opinions, and conciliating the Arabs as much as possible. Then he spoke of himself: he looked forward to death with a feeling of delight, the result of his religious convictions; he expressed a hope that if I remained at Kaole he might be buried at sea; and he declared himself, in spite of my entreaties, determined to remain near the coast until he heard of our safe transit through the lands of the dreaded Wazaramo. This courage was indeed sublime. Such examples are not often met with among men.

After this affecting farewell, I took leave of the Artémise and landed definitively at Kaole. The Baloch driving the asses were sent off to the first station on the road westward, headed by my companion, on the same evening, lest a longer sojourn in the lands of semi-civilization should thoroughly demoralize them. The Wanyamwezi porters, whose open faces and laughing countenances strongly prepossessed me in their favor, had already passed beyond their centre of attraction, the coast. I spent that evening with Ladha Damha, inside the gloomy gurayza. He lectured me for the last time upon my development of what the French cartomantiste calls " la bosse de la témérité." Might not the sahib be a great sahib in his own land, Cutch or Guzerat? Are there not other great sahibs there, A—— Sahib and B—— Sahib, for instance, who only kill pigs, and ignore the debtor and creditor side of an account in Guzeratee?

I must mention that, on the morning of the same day, I was present at a conversation held by the Ladha, the respectable collector of the customs, with the worthy Ramji, his clerk. I had insisted upon their inserting in the estimate of necessaries the sum required to purchase a boat upon the " Sea of Ujiji."

" Will he ever reach it?" asked the respectable Ladha, conveying his question through the medium of Cutchee, a dialect of which, with the inconsequence of a Hindoo, he assumed me to be profoundly ignorant.

" Of course not," replied the worthy Ramji; " what is he that he should pass through Ugogi?" (a province about half way.)

At the moment I respected their " sharm," or shame, a leading organ in the Oriental brain, which apparently has dwindled to inconsequential dimensions among the nations of the West. But when Ladha was alone, I took the opportunity to inform him that

I still intended to cross Ugogo, and to explore the "Sea of Ujiji."
I ended by showing him that I was not unacquainted with Cutchee,
and even able to distinguish between the debits and the credits of
his voluminous sheets.

During the conversation, the loud wail of death rang wildly
through the grave-like stillness of night. "O son, hope of my
life! O brother, dearest of brothers! O husband! O husband!"
these were the cries which reached our ears. We ran to the door
of the gurayza. The only son of the venerable diwan Ukwere,
who had been ascending the Kingani River on a mercantile expedition with five slaves, had been upset by a vengeful hippopotamus, and, with two of his attendants, had lost his life.
"Insaf karo! be honest!" said the Banyan, with whom I had
had many discussions as to whether it be lawful or unlawful to
shoot the hippopotamus, "and own that this is the first calamity
which you have brought upon the country by your presence."

I could only reply with the commonplaces of polemics. Why
should Ladha, who by purchasing their spoils encouraged the destruction of herds of elephants, object to the death of a "creek-
bull?" and why should the man who would not kill the "creek-
bull" be ready to ruin a brother man for making a better bargain
about its tusks? Ladha received these futile objections contemptuously, as you would, right reverend father, were I to suggest that
you, primate and spiritual peer, are not exactly following in the
footsteps of certain paupers whom you fondly deem to have been
your prototypes—your exemplars.

When Ladha left, my spirits went with him. In the solitude
and the silence of the dark gurayza, I felt myself the plaything
of misfortune. At Cairo I had received from the East India
House an order to return to London, to appear as a witness on a
trial by court-martial then pending. The missive was, as usual,
so ineptly worded, that I did not think proper to throw overboard
the Royal Geographical Society—to whom my services had been
made over—by obeying it: at the same time I well knew what
the consequences would be. Before leaving Egypt, an interview
with the Count d'Escayrac de Lauture had afforded me an opportunity of inspecting an expedition thoroughly well organized by
his highness Said Pasha, of military predilections, and the contrast between an Egyptian and an English exploration impressed
me unpleasantly. Arrived at Aden, I had enlisted the services
of an old and valued friend, Dr. Steinhaeuser, civil surgeon at that
station: a sound scholar, a good naturalist, a skillful practitioner;
endowed, moreover, with even more inestimable personal qualities, his presence would have been valuable in a land of sickness,
skirmishes, and sporting adventures, where the people are ever
impressed with the name of "medicine-man," and in a virgin field
promising subjects of scientific interest. Yet though recommended for the work by his Excellency the Governor of Bombay, Dr.

Steinhaeuser had been incapacitated by sickness from accompanying me: I had thus with me a companion and not a friend, with whom I was "strangers yet." The Persian war had prevented the fitting out of a surveying vessel, ordered by the Court of Directors to act as a base of operations upon the African coast; no disposable officer of the Indian navy was to be found at the Presidency; and though I heard in Leadenhall Street of an "observatory sergeant" competent to conduct the necessary astronomical and meteorological observations, in the desert halls of the great bungalow at Colaba only a few lank Hindoos met my sight. Nor was this all. His highness the late Sayyid Said, that estimable ally of the English nation, had for many years repeatedly made the most public-spirited offers to his friend Lieut. Colonel Hamerton. He was more than once upon the point of applying for officers selected to map the caravan routes of Eastern Africa, and he professed himself willing to assist them with men, money, and the weight of his widely-extended influence. This excellent prince had died forty days before the expedition arrived at Zanzibar. Lieut. Colonel Hamerton, also, whose extraordinary personal qualities enabled him to perform any thing but impossibilities among the Arabs, was compelled by rapidly-failing health, during my stay at Zanzibar, to lead a recluse life, which favored the plans of my opponents. Finally, as Indian experience taught me, I was entering the unknown land at the fatal season, when the shrinking of the waters after the wet monsoon would render it a hot-bed of malaria.

The hurry of departure, also, had caused a necessary neglect of certain small precautions, which, taken in time, save much after trouble. I should have shunned to have laid down limits of space and time for the expedition, whereas my friend and adviser had specified the "Sea of Ujiji." I intended to have drawn out every agreement in an official form, registered at the consulate, and specifying all particulars concerning rations and presents for the escort, their ammunition, and their right of sporting—that is to say, of scaring the game before it could be shot—their reward for services, and their punishments for ill conduct. Lieut. Colonel Hamerton's state of health, however, rendered him totally unfit for the excitement of business; and, without his assistance, a good result was not to be expected from measures so unfamiliar, and therefore so unpalatable, to the people whom they most concerned.

Excuse, amiable reader, this lengthy and egotistical preface to a volume of adventure. Do not think that I would invert the moral of the frog fable, by showing that what is death to you may become fun to me. As we are to be companions—not to say friends—for an hour or two, I must put you in possession of certain facts, trivial in themselves, and all unworthy of record, yet so far valuable, that they may enable us to understand each other.

Au reste, to quote the ballad so much admired by the authoress of " Our Village:"

> " The Pindar of Wakefield is my style,
>   And what I list I write ;
> Whilom a clerk of Oxenford,
>   But now—a banished wight."

CHAPTER II.

ZANZIBAR AND THE MRIMA EXPLAINED.

THE history of the word Zanzibar is curious. Its Persian origin proves that the Iranians were in early days a more maritime people than Vincent and other writers imagine. Zanzibar, signifying Nigritia, or Blackland, is clearly derived from the "Zang," in Arabic Zanj, a negro, and "bar," a region. This Zangbar was changed by the Arabs, who ignore in writing the hard *g*, into Zanjíbár; they still, however, pronounce Zangbar, and consider it synonymous with another popular expression, "Mulk el Zunuj," or "the Land of the Blacks." Thus the poet sings,

نسميت ملك الز نوج جميعها

"And it hath been called Land of the Blacks, all of it."

Traces of the word may be found in the earliest geographers. Ptolemy records a Zingis, or Zingisa, which, however, with his customary incorrectness, he places north of the equator. According to Cosmas Indicopleustes, the Indian Ocean beyond Barbaria is called Zingium. "Sinus Barbaricus" seems to have been among the Romans the name of the belt of low land afterward known as "Zanzibar," and it was inhabited by a race of Anthropophagi, possibly the fathers of the present "Wadoe" tribe. In more modern times, the land of the Zunuj has been mentioned by a host of authors, El Novayri and others.

The limits of Zanzibar—a word indiscriminately applied in former times to the coast, the island, and even to the principal town—are variously laid down by geographers. Usually it is made to extend from Cape Delgado, in S. lat. 10° 41′ to the equator, or, more strictly, to S. lat. 0° 15′, at the mouth of the Vumbo, or the Webbe Ganana, which appears in our maps under the deceptive corruptions "Juba" and "Govind," from the Somali "Gob," a junction, and "Gob-wen," a large junction. Mr. Cooley (Inner Africa Laid Open, p. 111) corrects the great error of the Portuguese historian, de Barros, who has made the embouchure of the Obi—in Somali Webbe, meaning any river—the demarkation line between "Ajan" on the north, and "Zanguebar" in the south, and has placed the mouth of that stream in 9° N. lat., which would extend Zanzibar almost to Cape Guardafui. Asiatic authors, according to M. Guillain (Documents sur l'Histoire, etc., de l'Afrique Orientale. Première partie, p. 213), vary

A TOWN ON THE MRIMA.

in opinion concerning the extent of the "land of the Zunuj" and its limits; some, as El Masudi, make it contain the whole country, including Sofala, between the embouchure of the Juba River (S. lat. 0° 15') and Cape Corrientes (S. lat. 23° 48'): others, like El Idrisi and Ibn Said, separate from it Sofala. In local and modern usage, the word Zanjibar is generally confined to the chief town upon the island, the latter being called by Arabs, as well as by the negroids, Kisiwa, "insula," in opposition to the Barr el Moli, a barbarized Semitic term for the continent.

As usual throughout these lands, where comprehensive geographical names are no longer required, there is no modern general word for East Africa south of the equator. The term "Sawahil," or "the shores," in present parlance is confined to the strip of coast beyond the half-Somali country, called from its various ports—Lamu, Brava, and Patta—Barr el Banadir, or Harbor-land. The "Sawahil" extend southward to Mombasah, below which the coast suddenly falling flat, is known as Mrima, or the Hill, and its people as Wamrima, the "hill-men." It is limited on the south by the delta of the Rufiji River, whose races are termed Watu wa Rufiji, Rufiji clans, or, more shortly, Warufiji.

The country, properly called the Mrima, has no history beyond its name, while the towns immediately to the north and south of it—Mombasah and Kilwa—have filled many a long and stirring page. The Arab geographers preceding the Portuguese conquest mention only five settlements on the coast between Makdishu (Magadoxo) and Kilwa, namely, Lamu, Brava, Marka, Malindi (Melinda), and Mombasah. In Captain Owen's charts, between Pangani and the parallel of Mafiyah (Monfia Island), not a name appears.

The fringe of Moslem negroids inhabiting this part of the East African coast is called by the Arabs Ahl Maraim, and by themselves Wamrima, in opposition to the heathen of the interior. These are designated in mass the Washenzi—conquered or servile—properly the name of a Helot race in the hills of Usumbara, but extended by strangers to all the inner races. The Wasawahili, or people of the Sawahil, mulattoes originally African, but semiticized, like the Moplahs of Malabar, by Arab blood, are in these days confined to the lands lying northward of Mombasah, to the Island of Zanzibar, and to the regions about Kilwa.

The Mrima is peopled by two distantly connected families, the half-caste Arabs and the coast-clans. The former are generally of Bayazi or Khariji persuasion; the latter follow the school of El Shafei; both, though the most imperfect of Moslems, are fanatical enough to be dangerous. They own a nominal allegiance to the suzerain of Zanzibar, yet they are autonomous and free-spoken as Bedouins, when removed a few miles from the coast, and they have a rooted aversion to the officials of the local government, whom they consider their personal enemies. Between them and the pure Arabs of Oman, who often traverse, but who now never settle upon the Mrima, there is a repugnance increased by commercial jealousy; they resent the presence of these strangers as an intrusion, and they lose no opportunity of thwarting and discouraging them from traveling into the interior. Like their ancestors, they dislike Europeans personally, and especially fear the Beni Nar, or Sons of Fire—the English—"hot as the Ingrez," is in these lands a proverb. In their many riwayat, hadisi, and ngoma—tales, traditions, and songs—they predict the eventual conquest of the country that has once felt the white man's foot.

The half-caste Arab is degenerate in body and mind; the third generation becomes as truly negroid as the inner heathen. Even creoles of pure blood, born upon the island and the coast of Zanzibar, lose the high nervous temperament that characterizes their ancestors, and become, like Banyans, pulpy and lymphatic. These mestiços, appearing in the land of their grandsires, have incurred the risk of being sold as slaves. The peculiarity of their physiognomy is the fine Semitic development of the upper face, including the nose and nostrils, while the jaw is prognathous, the lips are tumid and everted, and the chin is weak and retreating. The cranium is somewhat rounded, and it wants the length of the negroid's skull. Idle and dissolute, though intelligent and cunning, the coast Arab has little education. He is sent at the age of seven to school, where in two or three years he accomplishes the Khitmah, or perfection of the Koran, and he learns to write a note in an antiquated character, somewhat more imperfect than the Cufic. This he applies to the Kisawahili, and, as nothing can be less fitted for the Semitic tongues than the Arabic syllabarium, so admirably adapted to its proper sphere, his compositions require the deciphering of an expert. A few prayers and hymns conclude the list of his acquirements. His mother-tongue knows no books except short treatises on bao, or geomancy, and specimens of African proverbial wisdom. He then begins life by aiding his father in the shop or plantation, and by giving himself up to intoxication and intrigue. After suffering severely from his excesses —in this climate no constitution can bear up against over-indulgence long continued—at the age of seventeen or eighteen he takes unto himself a wife. Estranged from the land of his forefathers, he rarely visits Zanzibar, where the restraints of semi-civilization, the decencies of Oriental society, and the low estimation in which the black skin is held, weary and irritate him. His point of honor seems to consist chiefly in wearing publicly, in token of his Arab descent, a turban and a long yellow shirt, called el dishdasheh.

The Wamrima, or coast-clans, resemble even more than the half-caste Arabs their congeners the Washenzi. The pure Omani will not acknowledge them as kinsmen, declaring the breed to be aajam, or gentiles. They are less educated than the higher race, and they are more debauched, apathetic, dilatory, and inert; their favorite life is one of sensual indolence. Like the Somal, they appear to be unfitted by nature for intellectual labor; of the former people there is but one learned man, the Shaykh Jami of Harar, and the Kazi Muhiyy-el-Din of Zanzibar is the only literato among the Wasawahili. Study, or indeed any tension of the mind, seems to make these weak-brained races semi-idiotic. They can not answer yes or no to the simplest question. If, for example, a man be asked the place of his tribe, he will point to a distance, though actually living among them; or if questioned concerning some particular of an event, he will detail every thing but what is wanted. In the earlier days of exploration, I have repeatedly collected the diwans, and, after a careful investigation and comparison of statements, have registered the names and distances of the stages ahead. These men, though dwelling upon the threshold of the regions which they described, and being in the habit of traversing them every year, yet could hardly state a single fact correctly; sometimes they doubled, at other times they halved the distance; they seldom gave the same names, and they almost always made a hysteron-proteron of the stations. The reader may gather from this sample some idea of the difficulties besetting those who would collect information concerning Africa from the Africans. It would not have happened had an Arab been consulted. I soon resolved to doubt for the future all Wasawahili, Wamrima, Washenzi, and slaves, and I found no reason for regretting the resolution.

The Wamrima are of darker complexion, and are more African in appearance than the coast Arabs. The popular color is a dull yellowish bronze. The dress is a fez, or a Surat cap; a loin-cloth, which, among the wealthy, is generally an Arab check or an Indian print, with a similar sheet thrown over the shoulders. Men seldom appear in public without a spear, a sword, or a staff; and priding themselves upon the possession of umbrellas, they may be seen rolling barrels, or otherwise working upon the sands, under the luxurious shade. The women wear a tobe, or long cloth, wrapped tightly round the body, and extending from beneath the arms to the ankles. It is a garb ungraceful as was the European "sacque" of by-gone days. It spoils the figure by depressing instead of supporting the bosom, and it conceals none of its deficiencies, especially the narrowness of the hips. The murungwana, or free-woman, is distinguished from the slave-girl, when outside the house, by a cloth thrown over the head. Like the women of the Bedouins and of the Persian Iliyat, even the matrons of the Mrima go abroad unmasked. Their favorite necklace is a string of sharks' teeth. They distend the lobes of the ears to a prodigious size, and decorate them with a rolled-up strip of variously-dyed cocoa-leaf, a disk of wood, a plate of chakazi or raw gum-copal, or, those failing, with a betel-nut, or with a few straws. The left wing of the nose is also pierced to admit a pin of silver, brass, lead, or even a bit of manioc-root. The hair, like the body, is copiously anointed with cocoanut or sesamum oil. Some shave the head wholly or partially across the brow and behind the ears; others grow their locks to half or full length, which rarely exceeds a few inches. It is elaborately dressed, either in double rolls rising like bears' ears on both sides of the head, or divided into a number of frizzly curls which expose lines of scalp, and give to the head the appearance of a melon. They have also a propensity for savage "accroche-cœurs," which stand out from the cheek-bones, stiffly twisted like young porkers' tails. In early youth, when the short, soft, and crisp hair resembles Astrachan wool, when the muscles of the face are smoothly rounded, and when the skin has that life and texture, and the countenance has that vivacity and amiability which belong only to the young, many of the girls have a pretty piquancy, a little minois chiffonné, a coquettishness, a natural grace, and a caressing look, which might become by habit exceedingly prepossessing. In later life their charms assume that peculiar solidity which is said to characterize the beauties of Mullingar, and, as a rule, they are shockingly ugly. The Castilian proverb says that the English woman should be seen at the window, the French woman on the promenade, and the Spanish woman every where—the African woman should be seen nowhere, or in the dark. The children mostly appear in the graceful costume of the Belvidere Apollo; not a few of them have, to the European eye, that amusing prettiness which we admire in pug-pups.

The mode of life in the Mrima is simple. Men rise early, and repair to either the shop, the boat, or the plantation; more commonly they waste the morning in passing from house to house "ku amkía"—to salute neighbors. They ignore "manners;" they enter abruptly with or without the warning cry of "Hodi! hodi!" place their spears in the corner, and without invitation squat and extend themselves upon the floor, till, wearied with conversation, they take "French leave." Life, to the European so real and earnest, is with them a continued scene of drumming, dancing, and drinking, of gossip, squabble, and intrigue. The favorite inebriants are tembu or cocoa toddy, and mvinyo, its distillation, pombe or millet-beer, opium, bhang, and sometimes foreign stimulants purchased at Zanzibar. Their food is mostly ugali, the thick porridge of boiled millet or maize flour, which represents the "staff of life" in East Africa. They usually feed twice a day, in the morning and at nightfall. They employ the cocoanut extensively. Like the Arabs of Zanzibar, they boil their rice in the thick juice of the rasped albumen kneaded with water, and they make cakes of the pulp mixed with the flour of various grains. This immoderate use of the fruit, which, according to the people, is highly refrigerant, causes, it is said, rheumatic and other diseases. A respectable man seen eating a bit of raw or undressed cocoanut would be derided by his fellows. They chew tobacco with lime, like the Arabs, who, under the influence of Wahhabi tenets, look upon the pipe as impure, and they rarely smoke it like the Washenzi.

The Wamrima as well as the Wasawahili are distinguished by two national peculiarities of character. The first is a cautiousness bordering upon cowardice, derived from their wild African blood; the second is an unusual development of cunning and deceitfulness, which partially results from the grafting of the semi-civilized Semite upon the Hamite. The Arabs, who are fond of fanciful etymology, facetiously derive the race-name "Msawahili" from "Sawwá hílah,"* *he played a trick*, and the people boast of it, saying, "Are we not Wasawahili?" that is, "artful dodgers." Supersubtle and systematic liars, they deceive when duller men would tell the truth; the lie direct is no insult, and the offensive word "muongo!" (liar) enters largely into every dialogue. They lie like Africans, objectlessly, needlessly, when sure of speedy detection, when fact would be more profitable than falsehood; they have not discovered with the civilized knave that "honesty is the best policy;" they lie till their fiction becomes subjectively fact. With them the lie is no mental exertion, no exercise of ingenuity, no concealment, nor mere perversion of the truth; it is apparently a local instinctive peculiarity in the complicated madness of poor human nature. The most solemn and religious oaths are with them empty words; they breathe an atmosphere of falsehood, manœuvre, and contrivance, wasting about the mere nothings of life—upon a pound of grain or a yard of cloth—ingenuity of iniquity enough to win and keep a crown. And they are treacherous as false; with them the salt has no signification, and gratitude is unknown even by name.

Though partially Arabized, the Wamrima, as well as the Wasawahili, retain many habits and customs derived from the most degraded of the Washenzi savagery. Like the Wazegura heathen of Eastern Africa, and the Bangala of the Kasanji (Cassange) Valley, in the west, the uncle sells his nephews and nieces by an indefeasible vested right, with which even the parents can not in-

---

* Dr. Krapf, in the Preface to his "Outlines of the Kisuahelí Language," deduces the national name from Síwá 'a hílah, which would mean exactly the reverse of astute—"without guile." He has made other curious linguistic errors: he translates, for instance, the "Quilimancy" River—the ancient name for the Ozi or Dana—"water from the mountain," after a Germanic or Indo-European fashion, whereas, in the Zangian languages, the compound word would, if admissible, signify "a mountain of water." It is curious that the learned and accurate Mr. Cooley, who has charged Dr. Krapf with "puerile etymologies," should have fallen into precisely the same error. In the "Geography of N'yassi," p. 19, "Mazingia" is rendered the "road or land along the water;" but Mají Njíá, if the elision of the possessive affix ya be allowed in prose as in poetry—Mají Njíá for Mají yá Njíá—would mean only the "water of the road." As a specimen of Dr. Krapf's discoveries in philology the following may suffice. In his vocabulary of the Engutuk Eloikob or Kikuafi dialect, he derives olbitir, a *pig*, from the Arabic el batrah, a *young ass*, or from el basir, a *sharpseeing dog!*

terfere. The voice of society even justifies this abomination. "What!" exclaim the people, "is a man to want when his brothers and sisters have children?" He is thus encouraged in doing, on the slightest pretext, that of which the heathen rarely approve, except to save themselves from starvation. At the same time the Wamrima, holding the unchastity of woman as a tenet of belief, consider the sister's son—the "surer side"—the heir, in preference to the son. They have many superstitions, and before all undertakings they consult a pagan mganga, or medicine-man. If the k'hunguru or crow caws from the house-top, a guest is coming; if a certain blackbird cries "chee! chee!" in front of a caravan, the porters will turn back, saying that there is blood on the road, and they will remain four or five days till the "chika! chika!" of the partridge beats the "general." An even number of wayfarers met in early morning is a good omen, but an odd number, or the bark of the mbweha—the fox—before the march, portends misfortune. Strong minds of course take advantage of these and a thousand other follies of belief, and when there is not, as in civilized countries, a counteracting influence of skepticism, the mental organization of the people becomes a mass of superstitious absurdities.

The chief industry of the Mrima, namely, the plundering of caravans, has already been alluded to; it will be here described with somewhat more of detail. The industrious and commercial nations near Kilwa and the southern regions delay but a few days on the coast; the Wanyamwezi, on the line now to be described, will linger there from three to six months, enjoying the dear delights of comparative civilization. Many old campaigners have so far overcome their barbarous horror of water-traveling, which has been increased by tales of shipwreck and drowning, as to take boat and carry their ivory to the more profitable market in this land of Zanzibar, where the Wanyamwezi occupy their own quarter. Arrived within two marches of the coast town, the head of the caravan calls a halt till the presents promised by an escort of touters have arrived and have been approved of. He then delays as long as possible, to live gratis upon those with whom he proposes to deal. After a time, the caravan enters in stately procession, a preliminary to the usual routine of commercial operations. Having settled the exorbitant claims of the village headmen and the charges of the Zanzibar government, which are usually levied in duplicate by the local authorities, the barbarian has recourse to the Indian Banyan. Bargains are usually concluded at night: to a civilized man the work would be an impossible trial of patience. A lot of two hundred tusks is rarely sold under four months. Each article is laid upon the ground, and the purchaser begins by placing handsome cloths, technically called "pillows," under the point and bamboo of the tusk, and by covering its whole length with a third; these form the first perquisites of the seller.   After a few days, during which rice and ghee, sugar and sweetmeats must be freely supplied, commences the chaffering for the price.   The Banyan becomes excited at the ridiculous demand of his client, screams like a woman, pushes him out of doors, and receives a return of similar treatment with interest.   He takes advantage of his knowledge that the African in making a bargain is never satisfied with the first offer, however liberal; he begins with a quarter of the worth, then he raises it to one half, and, when the barbarian still hesitates, he throws in some flashy article which turns the scale.   Any attempt at a tariff would be contemptuously rejected by both parties.   The African delights in bargaining, and the Indian having brighter wits relies upon them for a profit, which the establishment of fair prices would curtail.   It were in vain to attempt any alteration in this style of doing " business;" however despicable it may appear in the London market, it is a time-honored institution in East Africa.

The Wazaramo Tribe.

CHAPTER III.

TRANSIT OF THE VALLEY OF THE KINGANI AND THE MGETA
RIVERS.

It was a gallant sight to see the Baloch, as with trailed matcn-
locks, and in bravery of shield, sword, and dagger, they hurried
in Indian file out of the Kaole cantonments, following their blood-
red flag, and their high-featured, snowy-bearded chief, the "Sahib
Mohammed"—old Mohammed. The band, "like worms," as they
expressed its numbers, which amounted to nearly a hundred,
about one third of the venerable jemadar's command, was marching forth to bid us farewell, in token of respect, at Mgude or
Kuingani, "the cocoa-plantation near the sea." It is a little settlement, distant an hour and a half's walk from Kaole: hither
my companion had preceded me, and hence we were to make our
second departure. Accompanied by Said bin Salim, Valentine,
my Goanese servant, three Baloch, and two slaves, I followed in
the wake of the main body, bringing up the rear of the baggage

on three Unyamwezi asses bought that morning at the custom-house. The animals had been laden with difficulty; their kick-ing and plunging, rearing and pawing, had prevented the nice adjustment of their packs, and the wretched pads, which want of time had compelled me to take instead of panels or pack-saddles, loosely girthed with rotten coir rope, could not support a heap of luggage weighing at least 200 pounds per load. On the road they rushed against one another, they bolted, they shied, and they threw their impediments with such persistence, that my servant could not help exclaiming, " Unká nám gadha"—" Their name *is* jack-ass." At last, as the sun neared the salt sea, one of these half-wild brutes suddenly sank, girth-deep, in a patch of boggy mire; and the three Baloch, my companions, at once ran away, leaving us to extricate it as best we could. This little event had a pecul-iar significancy to one about to command a party composed prin-cipally of asses and Baloch.

The excitement of finding myself on new ground, and the pe-culiarities of the scenery, somewhat diverted melancholy forebod-ings. Issuing from the little palisade of Kaole, the path winds in a southwesterly direction over a sandy soil, thick with thorns and bush, which in places project across the way. Thence as-cending a wave of ground where cocoas and the wild arrow-root flourish, it looks down upon park land like that described by travelers in Caffraria, a fair expanse of sand veiled with humus, here and there growing rice, with mangoes and other tall trees regularly disposed as if by the hand of man. Finally, after cross-ing a muddy grass-grown swamp, and a sandy bottom full of wa-ter when rain has been heavy, the path, passing through luxuriant cultivation, enters Kuingani. Such is the "nakl," or preparatory stage of Arab travelers—an invariable first departure, where por-ters who find their load too heavy, or travelers who suspect that they are too light, can return to Kaole and re-form.

The little settlement of Kuingani is composed of a few bee-hive huts, and a bandani, or wall-less thatched roof—the village pala-ver-house—clustering orderless round a cleared central space. Outside, cocoas, old and dwarfed, mangoes almost wild, the papaw, the cotton shrub, the perfumed rayhan or basil, and a sage-like herb, the sugar-cane, and the Hibiscus, called by the Goanese "ro-sel," vary the fields of rice, holcus, and "turiyan," or the Cajanus Indicus. The vegetation is, in fact, that of the Malabar coast; the habitations are peculiarly African.

The 28th of June was a halt at Kuingani, where I was visited by Ramji and two brother Bhattias, Govindji and Kesulji. The former was equipped, as least becomes the Banyan man, with sword, dudgeon, and assegai. But Ramji was a heaven-made soldier; he had taken an active part in the military operations directed by his highness the late Sayyid Said against the people of the main land, and about thirteen years ago he defended Kaole against a host of Wazaramo, numbering, it is said, 3000 men, when, lacking balls, he had loaded his honeycombed cannon and his rusty matchlocks with pointed sticks. The Europeans of Zanzibar called him "Rush"—the murderer. His fellow-countrymen declared him to be a "sharp practicer," who had made a reputation by spending other people's money, and I personally had proofs which did not allow me to doubt his "savoir faire."

The nights at Kuingani were not pleasant. The air was stifling, the musquitoes buzzed without intermission, and I had neglected to lay in "essence of pennyroyal" against certain other plagues. On the second evening, seeing by the hang-dog look of my jemadar that he was travailing in mind, I sent for a mganga or medicine-man, and having previously promised him a Surat skull-cap for a good haul of prophecy, I collected the Baloch to listen. The mganga, a dark old man, of superior rank, as the cloth round his head and his many bead necklaces showed, presently reappeared with a mat bag containing the implements of his craft. After taking his seat opposite to me, he demanded his fee—here, as elsewhere, to use the words with which Cleon excited the bile of Tiresias,

"Τὸ μαντικὸν γὰρ πάν φιλάργυρον γένος;"

—without which prediction would have been impossible. When gratified, he produced a little gourd snuff-box, and indulged himself with a solemn and dignified pinch. He then drew forth a larger gourd which contained the great medicine, upon which no eye profane might gaze: the vessel, repeatedly shaken, gave out a vulgar sound, as if filled with pebbles and bits of metal. Presently, placing the implement upon the ground, Thaumaturges extracted from the mat bag two thick goat's horns connected by a snake-skin, which was decorated with bunches of curiously-shaped iron bells; he held one in the left hand, and with the right he caused the point of the other to perform sundry gyrations, now directing it toward me, then toward himself, then at the awe-struck bystanders, waving his head, muttering, whispering, swaying his body to and fro, and at times violently rattling the bells. When fully primed by the spirit of prophecy, and connected by ekstasis with the ghosts of the dead, he spake out pretty much in the style of his brotherhood all the world over. The journey was to be prosperous. There would be much talking, but little killing. —Said bin Salim, in chuckling state, confessed that he had heard the same from a mganga consulted at Zanzibar.—Before navigating the Sea of Ujiji, a sheep or a parti-colored hen should be killed and thrown into the lake.—Successful voyage.—Plenty of ivory and slaves.—Happy return to wife and family.

This good example of giving valuable advice was not lost upon Mr. Rush Ramji. He insisted upon the necessary precautions of making a strong kraal and of posting sentinels every night; of wearing a kerchief round the head after dark, and of avoiding the dangerous air of dawn; of not eating strange food, and of digging fresh wells, as the Wazaramo bewitch water for travelers; of tethering the asses, of mending their ropes, and of giving them three lbs. of grain per diem. Like the medical directions given to the French troops proceeding to China, the counsel was excellent, but impracticable.

The evening concluded with a nautch. Yusuf, a Baloch, produced a saringi—the Asiatic viol—and collected all the scamps of the camp with a loud scraping. Hulluk, the buffoon, acted dancing-girl to perfection. After the normal pantomime, somewhat broadly expressed, he did a little work in his own character; standing on his head, with a peculiar tremulousness from the hips upward, dislocating his person in a sitting position, imitating the cry of a dog, cat, ape, camel, and slave-girl, and finally reproducing me with peculiar impudence before my face. I gave him a dollar, when, true to his strain, he at once begged another.

All accounts and receipts being finally duly settled with the Hindoos, the last batch of three donkeys having arrived, and the baggage having been laden with great difficulty, I shook hands with old Mohammed and the other dignitaries, and mounting my ass, gave orders for immediate departure from Kuingani. This was not effected without difficulty: every one and every thing, guide and escort, asses and slaves, seemed to join in raising up fresh obstacles. Four P.M. sped before we turned out of the little settlement. Among other unpleasant occurrences, Rahmat, a Baloch knave, who had formed one of my escort to Fuga, leveled his long barrel, with loud "Mimí ná pigá" (I am shooting him), when his company was objected to. His jemadar, Yaruk, seized the old shooting-iron, which was probably unloaded, and Rahmat, with sotto-voce snarls and growls, slunk back to his kennel. A turbaned negroid, who appeared on the path, was asked to point out the way, and, on his refusal, my bull-headed slave Mabruki struck him on the face, when, to the consternation of all parties, he declared himself a diwan. The blow, according to the jemadar, would infallibly lead to bloodshed.

After a second short march of one hour and a half, we pitched tents and obtained lodgings in Bomani, "the Stockade," a frontier village, but within the jurisdiction of Bagamoyo. On this road, which ascended the old sea-beach, patches of open forest and of high rank grass divided cultivated clearings, where huts and hamlets appeared, and where modest young maidens beckoned us as we passed. The vegetation is here partly African, partly Indian. The mbuyu—the baobab, Adansonia digitata, monkey-bread, or calabash, the mowana of the southern and the kuka of the northern regions—is of more markedly bulbous form than on the coast, where the trunk is columnar; its heavy extremities, depressed by the wind, give it the shape of a lumpy umbrella shading the other wild growths. There appear to be two varieties of this tree, similar in bole but differing in foliage and in general appearance. The normal mbuyu has a long leaf, and the drooping outline of the mass is convex; the rarer, observed only upon the Usagara Mountains, has a small leaf, in color like the wild indigo, and the arms striking upward assume the appearance of a bowl. The lower bottoms, where the soil is rich, grow the mgude, also called mparamusi (Taxus elongatus, the geel hout or yellow-wood of the Cape?), a perfect specimen of arboreal beauty. A tall tapering shaft, without knot or break, straight and clean as a main-mast forty or forty-five feet in height, and painted with a tender greenish-yellow, is crowned with parachute-shaped masses of vivid emerald foliage, while sometimes two and even three pillars spring from the same root. The mvumo—a distorted toddy tree, or hyphæna, allied to the Daum palm of Egypt and Arabia —has a trunk rough with the drooping remnants o withered fronds, above which it divides itself into branches resembling a system of Y's. Its oval fruit is of a yellowish red, and when full-sized it is as large as a child's head; it is eaten even unripe by the people, and is said to be the favorite food of the elephant. Pulpless, hard, and stringy, it has, when thoroughly mature, a slight taste of gingerbread; hence it is also called the gingerbread-tree. The ukhindu, or brab, of whose fronds mats and the grass kilts worn by many of the tribes are made, flourishes throughout the country, proving that the date-tree might be naturalized. The nyara, or Chamærops humilis, the dwarf fan-palm or palmetto of Southern Europe, abounds in this maritime region. The other growths are the mtogwe and the mbungo-bungo, varieties of the nux vomica; the finest are those growing in the vicinity of water. The fruit contains within its hard rind, which, when ripe, is orange-colored, large pips, covered with a yellow pulp of a grateful agro-dolce flavor, with a suspicion of the mango. The people eat them with impunity; the nuts, which contain the poisonous principle, being too hard to be digested. The mtunguja (the Punneeria coagulans of Dr. Stocks,) a solanaceous plant, called by the Indians jangli bengan, or the wild egg-plant, by the South Africans toluane, and by the Baloch panír, or cheese, from the effect of the juice in curdling milk, is here, as in Somaliland, a spontaneous growth throughout the country. The same may be said of the castor-plant, which, in these regions, is of two kinds. The mbono (Jatropha curcas?) is the gumpal of Western India, a coarse variety, with a large seed; its fetid oil, when burnt, fouls the lamp; yet, in Africa, it is used by all classes as an unguent. The mbarika, or Palma Christi, the irindi of India, is employed in medicine. The natives extract the oil by toasting and pounding the bean, adding a little hot water, and skimming off what appears upon the surface. The Arabs, more sensibly, prefer it "cold-drawn." These plants, allowed to grow unpruned, often attain the height of eighteen to twenty feet.

The 30th June was another forced halt, when I tasted all the bitterness that can fall to the lot of those who explore regions unvisited by their own color. The air of Bomani is stagnant, the sun fiery, and clouds of musquitoes make the nights miserable. Despite these disadvantages, it is a favorite halting-place for up-caravans, who defer to the last the evil days of long travel and short rations. Though impressed with the belief that the true principle of exploration in these lands is to push on as rapidly and to return as leisurely as possible, I could not persuade the Baloch to move. In Asia, two departures usually suffice; in Africa there must be three—the little start, the great start, and the start κατ᾽ ἐξοχήν. Some clamored for tobacco—I gave up my cavendish; others for guitar-strings — they were silenced with beads; and all, born donkey-drivers, complained loudly of the hardship and the indignity of having to load and lead an ass. The guide, an influential Mzaramo, promised by the Banyans Ladha and Ramji, declined, after receiving twenty dollars, to accompany the expedition, and from his conduct the Baloch drew the worst of presages. Much ill-will was shown by them toward the European members of the expedition. "Kafir end, márá bandirá na khenen" (they are infidels, and must not carry our flag)—it was inscribed with the usual Moslem formula—was spoken audibly enough in their debased Mekrani to reach my ears: a faithful promise to make a target of the first man who might care to repeat the words stopped that manner of nuisance. Again the most childish reports flew about the camp, making these jet-bearded and fierce-eyed hen-hearts faint with fears. Boxes had been prepared by the barbarians for myself, and gates had been built across the paths to arrest my party. P'hazi Mazungera, M. Maizan's murderer, had collected a host that numbered thousands, and the Wazaramo were preparing a levée *en masse*. To no purpose I quoted the Arab's proverb—"The son of fifty dieth not at thirty;" all *would* be heroic victims marching to gory graves. Such reports did real damage: the principal danger was the tremulous alacrity with which the escort prepared upon each trivial occasion for battle and murder, and sudden death. At one place a squabble among the villagers kept the Baloch squatting on their hams with lighted matches from dusk till dawn. At another, a stray fisi or cyn-hyena entering the camp by night, caused a confusion which only the deadliest onslaught could have justified. A slave hired on the road, hearing these horrors, fled in dismay; this, the first of desertions, was by no means the last. The reader may realize the prevalence and the extent of this African traveler's bane by the fact that during my journey to Ujiji there was not a soul in the caravan, from Said bin Salim the Arab, to the veriest pauper, that did not desert or attempt to desert.

Here, at the first mention of slaves, I must explain to the reader why we were accompanied by them, and how the guide and escort contrived to purchase them. All the serving-men in Zanzibar Island and on the coast of East Africa are serviles; the Kisawahili does not contain even a word to express a hired domestic. For the evil of slave-service there was no remedy: I therefore paid them their wages and treated them as if they were freemen. I had no power to prevent Said bin Salim, the Baloch escort, and the "sons of Ramji," purchasing whomever they pleased; all objections on my part were overruled by, "We are allowed by our law to do so," and by declaring that they had the permission of the consul. I was fain to content myself with seeing that their slaves were well fed and not injured, and indeed I had little trouble in so doing, as no man was foolish enough to spoil his own property. I never neglected to inform the wild people that Englishmen were pledged to the suppression of slavery, and I invariably refused all slaves offered as return presents.

The departure from Bomani was effected on the 1st of July with some trouble; it was like driving a herd of wild cattle. At length, by ejecting skulkers from their huts, by dint of promises and threats, of gentleness and violence, of soft words and hard words, occasionally backed by a smart application of the "bakur" —the local "cat"—by sitting in the sun, in fact by incessant worry and fidget from 6 A.M. to 3 P.M., the sluggish and unwieldy body acquired some momentum. I had issued a few marching orders for the better protection of the baggage: two Baloch were told off for each donkey, one to lead, the other to drive; in case of attack, those near the head of the file, hearing the signal, three shots, were to leave their animals and hurry to the front, where my companion marched, while the remainder rallied round my flag in the rear: thus there would have been an attacking party and a reserve, between which the asses would have been safe. The only result of these fine manœuvres was, that after a two-mile tramp through an umbrageous forest in which caravans often lose the way, and then down an easy descent across fertile fields, into a broken valley, whose farther side was thick with luxuriant grass, tall shrubs, and majestic trees, a confused straggling line—a mere mob of soldiers, slaves, and asses, arrived at the little village of Mkwaju la Mvuani—the "tamarind in the rains."

The settlement is composed as usual of a few hovels and a palaver-house, with a fine lime-tree, the place of lounging and gossip, grain-husking, and mat-weaving, in the open centre. Provisions and rough muddy water being here plentiful, travelers often make a final halt to polish their weapons, and to prepare their minds for the Wazaramo. It is the last station under the jurisdiction of Bagamoyo; from Changahera, the crafty old diwan, I obtained the services of his nephew Muinyi Wazíra, who received seventeen dollars as an inducement to travel in the interior, and was at once constituted linguist and general assistant to Said bin

Salim. The day passed as usual; a snake was killed, and a gun-shot heard in the distance supplied conversation for some hours. The " sons of Ramji" carefully lost half a dozen of the axes, bill-hooks, and dibbles with which they had been supplied, fearing lest they might be called upon to build the síwá or bomá, the loose thorn fence with which the halting-place ought to be sur-rounded before the night, and 7 P.M. had passed before I could persuade the Baloch to catch, tether, and count the asses. One of the escort, Ismail, was attacked with dysentery and required to be mounted, although we were obliged by the want of carriage to wend our way on foot. During the last night, Said bin Salim had taken charge of three Wanguru porters, who, freshly trapped by Said el Hazrami, had been chained *pro tempore* to prevent deser-tion. The Arab boasted that he was a bad sleeper, but bad sleep-ers are worse watchers, because when they do sleep they sleep in earnest. The men were placed for the night in Said's tent, sur-rounded by his five slaves, yet they stole his gun, and, carry-ing off an axe and sundry bill-hooks, disappeared in the jungle. The watchful Said, after receiving many congratulations on his good fortune—fugitive slaves sometimes draw their knives across the master's throat, or insert the points into his eyes—sent off his own attendants to recover the fugitives. In the jungle, however, search was of scant avail: the Wanguru feared that, if caught by the Baloch, they would lose their ears; three days would enable them to reach their own country; and their only risk was that if trapped by the Washenzi before their irons—a valuable capture to the captors—could be removed, they might again be sold to some traveling trader. As the day wore on, Said's face assumed a deplorable expression: his slaves had not appeared, and though several of them were muwallid, or born in his father's house, and one was after a fashion his brother-in-law, he sorely dreaded that they also had deserted. He was proportionably delighted when, in the dead of the night, entering Mkwaju la Mvuani, they re-ported ill success; and though I could little afford the loss, I was glad to get rid of this chained and surly gang.

On the next day we began loading for the third and final de-parture, before dawn, and at 7 30 A.M. were on the dew-dripping way. Beyond the settlement a patch of jungle led to cultivated grounds belonging to the villagers, whose scattered and unfenced abodes were partially concealed by dense clumps of trees. The road then sweeping parallel with the river plain, which runs from N.W. to S.E., crossed several swamps, black muddy bottoms cov-ered with tall thick rushes and pea-green paddy, and the heavily laden asses sunk knee-deep into the soft soil. Red copaliferous sand clothed the higher levels. On the wayside appeared for the first time the khambi or substantial kraals which evidence un-safe traveling and the unwillingness of caravans to bivouac in the villages. In this region they assumed the form of round huts and

long sheds or boothies of straw or grass, supported by a frame-
work of rough sticks firmly planted in the ground and lashed together with bark strips.   The whole was surrounded with a deep
circle of thorns which—the entrance or entrances being carefully
closed at nightfall, not to reopen until dawn—formed a complete
defense against bare feet and naked legs.   About half-way a junction of the Mbuamaji road was reached, and the path became
somewhat broader and less rough.   Passing on the right a hilly
district, called Dunda or " the Hill," the road fell from the ancient
sea-beach into the alluvial valley of the Kinganí River; presently
rising again, it entered the settlement of Nzasa, a name interpreted
" level ground."

Nzasa is the first district of independent Uzaramo.   My men
proceeded to occupy the Bandani, in the centre of the hamlet,
when Said bin Salim, discovering with the sharp eye of fear a
large drum, planted in readiness for the war-signal or the dance-
signal, hurried about till he had turned all hands out of the village into a clump of trees hard by, a propitious place for surprise
and ambuscade.   Here I was visited by three p'hazi, or headmen,
Kizaya, Tumba Ihere or the "poison gourd," and Kombe la Simba
or the "lion's hide."   They came to ascertain whether I was bound
on peaceful errand or—as the number of our guns suggested—I
was marching to revenge the murder of my "brother" muzungu.
Assured of our unwarlike intentions, they told me that I must
halt on the morrow and send forward a message to the next chief.
As this plan invariably loses three days—the first being a *dies non*,
the second being expended in dispensing exoteric information to
all the lieges squatting in solemn conclave, while on the third the
real message is privily whispered into the chieftain's ear—I replied through Said that I could not be bound by their rules, but
was ready to pay for their infraction.   During the debate upon
this fascinating proposal for breaking the law, Yusuf, one of the
most turbulent of the Baloch, drew his sword upon an old woman
because she refused to give up a basket of grain.   She rushed,
with the face of a black Medusa, into the assembly, and provoked
not very peaceable remarks concerning the peaceful nature of
our intentions.   When the excitement was allayed, the principal
p'hazi began to ask what had brought the white man into their
country, and in a breath to predict the loss of their gains and commerce, their land and liberty: "I am old," pathetically quoth the
p'hazi, " and my beard is gray, yet I have never beheld such a
calamity as this!"   "These men," replied Said, "neither buy nor
sell; they do not inquire into price, nor do they covet profit.
Moreover," he pursued, " what have ye to lose?   The Arabs take
your best, the Wasawahili your second best, and your trifling tribute is reduced to a yoke of bullocks, a few clothes, or half a dozen
hoes."   An extravagant present—at that time ignorance of the
country compelled me to intrust such matters to the honesty of

Said bin Salim—opened the headmen's hearts: they privily termed me Murungwana Sana, a real freeman, the African equivalent for the English "gentleman," and they detached Kizaya to accompany me as far as the western half of the Kingani Valley. At 4 P.M. a loud drumming collected the women, who began to perform a dance of ceremony with peculiar vigor. A line of small, plump, chestnut-colored beings, with wild beady eyes, and a thatch of clay-plastered hair, dressed in their loin-cloths, with a profusion of white disks, bead necklaces, a little square bib of beads called a t'hando, partially concealing the upper bosom, with short coils of thick brass wire wound so tightly round the wrists, the arms above the elbows, and the fat ankles, that they seemed to have grown into the flesh, and—hideous perversion of taste!—with ample bosoms tightly corded down, advanced and retired in a convulsion of wriggle and contortion, whose fit expression was a long discordant howl, which seemed to

"Embowel with outrageous noise the air."

I threw them a few strings of green beads, which for a moment interrupted the dance. One of these falling to the ground, I was stooping to pick it up when Said whispered hurriedly in my ear, "Bend not; they will say 'He will not bend even to take up beads!' "

In the evening I walked down to the bed of the Kingani River, which bisects a plain all green with cultivation—rice and holcus, sweet potato and tobacco—and pleasantly studded with huts and hamlets. The width of the stream, which here runs over a broad bed of sand, is about fifty yards; it is nowhere fordable, as the ferry-boat belonging to each village proves, and thus far it is navigable, though rendered dangerous by the crocodiles and the hippopotami that house in its waters. The color is tawny, verging upon red, and the taste is soft and sweet, as if fed by rain. The Kingani, like all streams in this part of the continent, is full of fish, especially a dark green and scaleless variety (a Silurus?) called kambari, and other local names. This great "miller's thumb" has fleshy cirri, appears to be omnivorous, and tastes like animal mud. The night was rendered uncomfortable to the Baloch by the sound of distant drums, which suggested fighting as well as feasting, and by the uproar of the wild men, who, when reconnoitred by the scouts, were found to be shouting away the hippopotami.

In the hurry and the confusion of loading on the next morning one ass was left behind, and the packs were so badly placed that the fatigue of marching was almost doubled by their repeated falls. While descending the well-wooded river terrace, my portion of the escort descried an imaginary white flag crossing the grassy valley below. This is the sign of a diwan's expedition or commando: it is unwisely allowed by the Arabs, whose proper colors are a plain blood-red. After marching a few miles over undulating ground, open and park-like, and crossing rough and miry beds, the path disclosed a view verging upon the pretty. By the wayside was planted the peculiarly African mzimu, or fetiss hut, a penthouse about a foot high, containing, as votive offerings, ears of holcus or pombe-beer in a broken gourd. There, too, the graves of the heathen met the eye. In all other parts of East Africa a mouldering skull, a scattered skeleton, or a few calcined bones, the remains of wizards and witches dragged to the stake, are the only visible signs of man's mortality. The Wazaramo tombs, especially in the cases of chiefs, imitate those of the Wamrima. They are parallelograms, seven feet by four, formed by a regular dwarf paling that incloses a space cleared of grass, and planted with two uprights to denote the position of head and feet. In one of the long walls there is an apology for a door. The corpse of the heathen is not made to front any especial direction; moreover, the centre of the oblong has the hideous addition of a log carved by the unartistic African into a face and a bust singularly resembling those of a legless baboon, while a white rag, tied turbanwise round the head, serves for the inscription "this is a man." The Baloch took notice of such idolatrous tendency by spitting and by pronouncing certain national anathemas, which literally translated might sound unpleasant in Europeans' ears. The abomination of iconism is avoided in the graves of Moslem travelers: they are usually cleared ovals, with outlines of rough stone and a strew of smooth pebbles, according to the custom of the Wasawahili. Several stumps of wood planted in the earth show that the corpse faces Mecca, and, as among the Jinga of Western Africa, the fragments of a china bowl or cup lying upon the ground are sacred to the memory of the departed. In Zanzibar Island, also, saucers, plates, and similar articles are mortared into the tombstones.

The number of these graves made the blackness of my companions pale. They were hurrying forward with sundry "la haul!" and with boding shakes of the head, when suddenly an uproar in the van made them all prepare for action. They did it characteristically by beginning with begging for ranjak—priming-powder. Said bin Salim, much excited, sent forward his messmate Muinyi Wazira to ascertain the cause of the excitement. One Mviraru, the petty lord of a neighboring village, had barred the road with about a dozen men, demanding "dash," and insisting that Kizaya had no right to lead on the party without halting to give him the news. My companion, who was attended only by "Bombay," his gun-carrier, and a few Baloch, remarked to the interferers that he had been franked through the country by paying at Nzasa. To this they obstinately objected. The Baloch began to light their matches and to use hard words. A fight appeared imminent. Presently, however, when the Wazaramo saw my flag rounding the hill-shoulder with a fresh party, whose numbers were exaggerated by distance, they gave way; and finally, when Muinyi Wazira opened upon them the invincible artillery of his tongue, they fell back and stood off the road to gaze. The linguist returned to the rear in great glee, blowing his finger-tips, as if they had been attached to a matchlock, and otherwise deriding the overboiling valor of the Baloch, who, not suspecting his purport, indulged in the wildest outbreak of boasting, offering at once to take the whole country and to convert me into its sultan. Toward the end of the march we crossed a shallow, salt, bitter rivulet, flowing cold and clear toward the Kingani River. On the grassy plain below noble game—zebra and koodoo—began to appear; while guinea-fowl and partridge, quail, green-pigeon, and the cuculine bird, called in India the Malabar pheasant, became numerous. A track of rich red copaliferous soil, wholly without stone, and supporting black mould, miry during the rains, and caked and cracked by the potent suns of the hot season, led us to Kiranga-Ranga, the first dangerous station in Uzaramo. It is the name of a hilly district, with many little villages embosomed in trees, overlooking the low cultivated bottoms where caravans encamp in the vicinity of the wells.

Before establishing themselves in the kraal at Kiranga-Ranga, the two rival parties of Baloch—the prince's permanent escort and the temporary guard sent by Ladha Damha from Kaole—being in a chronic state of irritability, naturally quarreled. With the noise of choughs gathering to roost they vented their bile, till thirteen men belonging to a certain Jemadar Mohammed suddenly started up, and without a word of explanation set out on their way home. According to Said bin Salim, the temporary guard had determined not to proceed beyond Kiranga-Ranga, and this desertion was intended as a preliminary to others by which the party would have lost two thirds of its strength. I at once summoned the jemadars, and wrote in their presence a letter reporting the conduct of their men to the dreaded Balyuz, the consul, who was supposed to be still anchored off Kaole. Seeing the bastinado in prospect, the Jemadar Yaruk shouldered his sabre, slung his shield over his arm, set out in pursuit of the fugitives, and soon succeeded in bringing them back. He was a good specimen of the true Baloch mountaineer—a tall, gaunt, and large-boned figure, with dark complexion deeply pitted by small-pox, hard, high, and sun-burnt features of exceeding harshness; an armory in epitome was stuck in his belt, and his hand seemed never to rest but upon a weapon.

The 4th of July was a halt at Kiranga-Ranga. Two asses had been lost, the back-sinews of a third had been strained, and all the others had been so wearied by their inordinate burdens, to which on the last march the meat of a koodoo, equal in weight to a young bullock, had been superadded, that a rest was deemed indispensable. I took the opportunity of wandering over and of prospecting the country. The scene was one of admirable fertility; rice, maize, and manioc grew in the rankest and richest crops, and the uncultivated lands bore the corindah bush (Carissa carandas), the salsaparilla vine, the small whitish-green mulberry (the Morus alba of India), and the crimson flowers of the rosel. In the lower levels near the river rose the giants of the forest. The mparamusi shot up its tall head, whose bunchy tresses rustled in the breeze when all below was still. The stately msufi, a bombax or silk-cotton tree, showed as many as four or five trunks, each two to three feet in diameter, rising from the same roots; the long tapering branches stood out stiffly at right angles from the bole; and the leaves, instead of forming masses of foliage, were sparsely scattered in small dense growth. The msukulio, unknown to the people of Zanzibar, was a pile of dark verdure, which dwarfed the finest oaks and elms of an English park. No traces of game appeared in the likeliest of places; perhaps it preferred lurking in the tall gross grass, which was not yet in a fit state to burn.

At Kiranga-Ranga the weather began to be unpropitious. The mcho'o, the heavy showers which fall between the masika or vernal, and the vuli or autumnal rains, set in with regularity, and accompanied us during the transit of the maritime plain. I therefore refused to halt more than one day, although the p'hazi or chiefs of the Wazaramo showed, by sending presents of goats and grain, great civility—a civility purchased, however, by Said bin Salim at the price of giving to each man whatever he demanded; even women were never allowed to leave the camp unpropitiated. I was not permitted in this part to enter the villages, although the Wazaramo do not usually exclude strangers who venture upon their dangerous hospitality. Girls are appointed to attend upon them, and in case of sickness or accident happening to any one in the settlement, they are severely interrogated concerning the morality of the guest, and an unfavorable account of it leads to extortion and violence. The Wazaramo, like the Wagogo, and unlike the other East African tribes, are jealous of their women; still, "damages" will act, as they have acted in other lands, as salve to wounded honor and broken heart.

On the 5th of July we set out betimes, and traversing the fields around Kiranga-Ranga, struck through a dense jungle, here rising above, there bending into the river valley, to some stagnant pools which supply the district with water. The station, reached in 3hrs. 30m., was called Tumba Ihere, after the headman who accompanied us. Here we saw cocos emerging from a fetid vegetation, and, for the last time, the mwembe or mango, a richly-foliaged but stunted tree, which never attains the magnificent dimensions observed at Zanzibar. Several down-caravans were halted at Tumba Ihere. The slaves brought from the interior were tied together by their necks, and one obstinate deserter was so lashed to a forked pole with the bifurcation under his chin, that when once on the ground he could not rise without assistance. These wretches scarcely appeared to like the treatment; they were not, however, in bad condition. The Wanyamwezi porters bathed in the pools, and looked at us without fear or shame. Our daily squabble did not fail to occur. Riza, a Baloch, drew his dagger on one of Said bin Salim's "children," and the child pointed his Tower-musket at the Baloch; a furious hubbub arose; the master, with his face livid and drawn like a cholera patient's, screamed shrilly as a woman, and the weapons returned to their proper places bloodless as those wielded by Bardolph, Nym, and ancient Pistol. My companion began to suffer from the damp heat and the reeking miasma; he felt that a fever was coming on; and the fatigue of marching under these circumstances prevented our mustering the party. The consequence was, that an ass laden with rice disappeared—it had probably been led out of the road and unburdened by the Baloch — while axes, cords, and tethers could nowhere be found when wanted.

On the next morning we left Tumba Ihere, and tramped over a red land through alternate strips of rich cultivation and tangled jungle, which presently opened out into a forest where the light-barked msandarusi, or copal-tree, attains its fullest dimensions. This is one of the richest "diggins," and the roadsides are every where pitted with pockets two or three feet deep by one in diameter. Rain fell in huge drops, and the heaviness of the ground caused frequent accidents to the asses' loads. About noon we entered the fine grain-fields that gird the settlements of Muhogwe, one of the most dreaded in dreaded Uzaramo. In our case, however, the only peril was the levée en masse of the fair sex in the villages, to stare, laugh, and wonder at the white men. "What should you think of these whites as husbands?" asked Muinyi Wazira of the crowd. "With such things on their legs? Sivyo! not by any means!" was the unanimous reply, accompanied with peals of merriment.

Beyond Muhogwe all was jungle and forest, tall trees rising from red copaliferous sand, and shading bright flowers and blossoming shrubs. After crossing a low mud overgrown with rush and tiger-grass, and a water-course dotted with black stagnant pools, we ascended rising, well-forested ground, and lastly debouched upon the kraals of Muhonyera.

The district of Muhonyera occupies the edge of the plateau forming the southern terrace of the Kingani River, and the elevated sea-beach is marked out by lines of quartzose pebbles running along the northern slope of the hill upon which we encamped. Water is found in seven or eight reedy holes in the valley below. It acquires from decomposed vegetation an unnaturally sweet and slimy taste. This part of the country, being little inhabited by reason of its malarious climate, abounds in wild animals. The guides speak of lions, and the cry of the fisi or cyn-hyena was frequently heard at night, threatening destruction to the asses. The fisi, the wuraba of the Somal, and the wilde honde of the Cape, is the wolf of Africa, common throughout the country, where it acts as scavenger. Though a large and powerful variety, it seldom assaults man, except when sleeping, and then it snatches a mouthful from the face, causing a ghastlier disfigurement even than the scalping of the bear. Three asses belonging to the expedition were destroyed by this beast. In all cases they were attacked by night with a loud wrangling shriek, and the piece of flesh was raggedly torn from the hind quarter. After affording a live rump-steak, they could not be driven like Bruce's far-famed bullock. These, however, were the animals brought from Zanzibar; that of Unyamwezi, if not tied up, defends itself successfully against its cowardly assailant with teeth and heels, even as the zebra, worthy of Homeric simile, has, it is said, kept the lion at bay. The woods about Muhonyera contain large and small gray monkeys with black faces. Clinging to the trees, they gaze for a time at the passing caravan imperturbably, till, curiosity being satisfied, they slip down and bound away with long, plunging leaps, like a greyhound at play. The view from the hill-side was suggestive. The dark green plain of sombre monotony, with its overhanging strata of mist-bank and dew-cloud, appeared in all the worst colors of the Oude Tirhai and the Guzerat jungles. At that season, when the moisture of the rainy monsoon was like poison distilled by the frequent bursts of fiery sunshine, it was a valley of death for unacclimatized travelers. Far to the west, however, rose Kidunda, "the hillock," a dwarf cone breaking the blurred blue line of jungle, and somewhat northward of it towered a cloud-capped azure wall, the mountain crags of Duthumi, upon which the eye, long weary of low levels, rested with a sensation of satisfaction.

It was found necessary to halt a day at Muhonyera: according to some authorities no provisions were procurable for a week; others declared that there were villages on the road, but were uncertain whether rations could be purchased. Said bin Salim sent Ambari, a favorite slave, back to buy grain at Muhogwe, whence he had hurried us on in fear of the Wazaramo; and the youth, after wasting a day, returned on the evening of the 2d July with about sixty lbs.—a poor supply for eighty-eight hungry bodies. This proceeding naturally affronted the Baloch, who desired for themselves the perquisites proceeding from the purchases. Two of their number, Yusuf and Salih Mohammed, came to swear officially on the part of their men that there was not an ounce of grain in camp. Appearing credulous, I paid them a visit about half an hour afterward; all their shuffling and sitting upon the bags could not conceal a store of about 100 lbs. of fine white rice, whose quality—the Baloch had been rationed at Kaole with an inferior kind—showed whence it came.

After repairing the "boma," or fenced kraal—it had been burned down, as often happens, by the last caravan of Wanyamwezi —I left my companion, who was prostrate with fever, and went out, gun in hand, to inspect the country, and to procure meat, that necessary having fallen short. The good p'hazi Tumba Ihere accompanied me, and after return he received an ample present for his services, and departed. The Baloch employed themselves in cleaning their rusty matchlock-barrels with a bit of kopra—dried cocoanut-meat—in weaving for themselves sandals, like the spartelle of the Pyrenees, with green palmetto leaves, in preparing calabash fibre for fatilah or gun-matches, and in twisting cords for the asses. The best material is supplied by an aloetic plant, the hig or haskul of Somaliland, here called by the Arabs bag, and by the natives mukonge. The mananazi, or pineapple, grows wild as far as three marches from the coast, but its fibrous qualities are unknown to the people. Ismail, the invalid Baloch, was the worse for remedies, and two other men gave signs of breaking down.

During the first week, creeping along at a slug's pace, we heard the booming of the Artémise's evening gun, an assurance that refuge was at hand. Presently these reports ceased. Lieutenant Colonel Hamerton, seized with mortal sickness, had left Kaole suddenly, and he died on board the Artémise on the 5th July, shortly after his return to Zanzibar. The first letters announcing the sad event were lost: with characteristic African futility the porter dispatched with the parcel from the island, finding that the expedition had passed on to the mountains of Usagara, left his charge with a village headman, and returned to whence he came. Easterns still hold that

"Though it be honest, it is never good,
    To bring bad news."

The report, spread by a traveling trader, was discussed throughout the camp, but I was kept in ignorance of it till Khudabakhsh, a Baloch, who had probably been deputed by his brethren to ascertain what effect the decease of the consul would have upon me, "hardened his heart," and took upon himself the task of communicating the evil intelligence. I was uncertain what to believe. Said bin Salim declared, when consulted, that he fully trusted in the truth of the report, but his reasons were somewhat too Arabo-African to convince me. He had found three pieces of scarlet broadcloth damaged by rats—an omen of death; and the color pointed out the nationality of the departed.

The consul's death might have proved fatal to the expedition, had its departure been delayed for a week. The court of Zanzibar had required the stimulus of a strong official letter from Lieutenant Colonel Hamerton, before it would consent, as requested by the Foreign Office, " to procure a favorable reception on the coast, and to insure the protection of the chiefs of the country" for the travelers. The Hindoos, headed by Ladha Damha, showed from first to last extreme unwillingness to open up the rich regions of copal and ivory to European eyes: they had been deceived by my silence during the rainy season at Zanzibar into a belief that the coast fever had cooled my ardor for further adventure; and their surprise at finding the contrary to be the case was not of a pleasant nature. The homesick Baloch would have given their ears to return, they would have turned back even when arrived within a few marches from the lake. Said bin Salim took the first opportunity of suggesting the advisability of his returning to Zanzibar for the purpose of completing carriage. I positively refused him leave; it was a mere pretext to ascertain whether his highness the Sayyid Majid had or had not, in consequence of our changed position, altered his views.

Lieutenant Colonel Hamerton's death, however, was mourned for other than merely selfish considerations. His hospitality and kindness had indeed formed a well-omened contrast with my unauspicious reception at Aden in 1855, before my departure to explore the Eastern Horn of Africa, when the coldness of some, and the active jealousy of other political authorities, thwarted all my projects, and led to the tragic disaster at Berberah.* Lieutenant Colonel Hamerton had received two strangers like sons, rather than like passing visitors. During the intervals between the painful attacks of a deadly disease, he had exerted himself to the utmost in forwarding my views; in fact, he made my cause

---

* Captain R. L. Playfair, Madras Artillery and First Assistant Pol. Resident, Aden, in a selection from the records of the Bombay government (No. 49, new series, Bombay, printed for government, at the Education Society Press, Byculla, 1859), curiously misnamed "A History of Arabia Felix, or Yemen," transports himself, in a "supplementary chapter," to East Africa, and thus records his impressions of what happened in the "Somali Country:"

1855.—"During the afternoon of the same day (the 18th of April), three men visited the camp, *palpably as spies*, and as such *the officers of the expedition were warned against them by their native attendants.* Heedless of this warning, they retired to rest at night in the fullest confidence of security, and without having taken any extra, *or even ordinary means*, to guard against surprise."

The italics are my own: they designate mis-statements unpardonable in an individual whose official position enabled him to ascertain and to record the truth. The three men were represented to me as spies, who came to ascertain whether I was preparing to take the country for the Chief Shermarkay, then hostile to their tribe, not as spies to spy out the weakness of my party. I received no warning of personal danger. The "ordinary measures," that is to say, the posting of two sentinels in front and rear of the camp during the night, were taken, and I can not blame myself because they ran away.

I will not stop to inquire what must be the value of Captain Playfair's 193 pages touching the history of Yemen, when in five lines there are three distinct and willful deviations from fact.

I am well aware that after my departure from Aden, in 1855, an inquiry was instituted during my absence, and without my knowledge, into the facts of the disaster which occurred at Berberah. The "privileged communication" was, I believe, in due course, privily forwarded to the Bombay government, and the only rebuke which this shuffling proceeding received was from a gentleman holding a high and honorable position, who could not reconcile himself to seeing a man's character stabbed in the back.

his own. Though aware of his danger, he had refused to quit, until compelled by approaching dissolution, the post which he considered his duty to hold. He was a loss to his country, an excellent linguist, a ripe Oriental scholar, and a valuable public servant of the old Anglo-Indian school; he was a man whose influence over Easterns, based upon their respect for his honor and honesty, his gallantry and determination, knew no bounds; and at heart a "sad good Christian"—the heavens be his bed!

On the 8th of July we fell into what our Arab called Wady el Maut and Dar el Jua—the Valley of Death and the Home of Hunger—the malarious river-plain of the Kingani River. My companion was compelled by sickness to ride, and thus the asses, now back-sore and weak with fatigue, suffered an addition of weight, and a "son of Ramji," who was upon the point of deserting openly, required to be brought back at the muzzle of the barrel. The path descending into a dense thicket of spear-grass, bush, and thorny trees based on sand, with a few open and scattered plantations of holcus, presently passed on the left Dunda Nguru, or "Seer-fish hill," so called because a man laden with such provision had there been murdered by the Wazaramo. After 2$^{\text{hrs.}}$ 45$^{\text{m.}}$ a ragged camping-kraal was found on the tree-lined bank of a half-dry fiumara, a tributary of the neighboring Kingani: the water was bad, and a mortal smell of decay was emitted by the dark dank ground. It was a wild day. From the black brumal clouds driven before furious blasts battered rain-drops like musket bullets, splashing the already saturated ground. The tall stiff trees groaned and bent before the gusts; the birds screamed as they were driven from their perching-places; the asses stood with heads depressed, ears hung down, and shrinking tails turned toward the weather, and even the beasts of the wild seemed to have taken refuge in their dens. Provisions being unprocurable at "Sagesera," the party did what men on such occasions usually do—they ate double quantities. I had ordered a fair distribution of the rice that remained, consequently they cooked all day. Yusuf, a jemadar of inferior rank, whose friends characterized him as "sweet of tongue but bitter at heart," vainly came to beg, on plea of hunger, dismissal for himself and his party; and another Baloch, Wali, reported as uselessly that a sore foot would prevent him advancing.

Despite our increasing weakness, we marched seven hours on the 9th of July over a plain wild but prodigiously fertile, and varied by patches of field, jungle, and swamp, along the right bank of the Kingani River, to another ragged old kraal, situated near a bend in the bed. This day showed the ghost of an adventure. At the "Makutaniro," or junction of the Mbuamaji trunk-road with the other lines branching from various minor sea-ports, my companion, who was leisurely proceeding with the advance-guard, found his passage barred by about fifty Wazaramo standing across the path in a single line that extended to the travelers' right, while a reserve party squatted on the left of the road. Their chief stepping to the front and quietly removing the load from the foremost porter's head, signaled the strangers to halt. Prodigious excitement of the Baloch, whose loud "Hai, hui!" and nervous anxiety contrasted badly with the perfect *sang froid* of the barbarians. Presently Muinyi Wazira, coming up, addressed to the headman a few words, promising cloth and beads, when this African modification of the "pike" was opened, and the guard moved forward as before. As I passed, the Wazaramo stood under a tree to gaze. I could not but admire the athletic and statuesque figures of the young warriors and their martial attitude, grasping in one hand their full-sized bows, and in the other sheaths of grinded arrows, whose black barbs and necks showed a fresh layer of poison.

At Tunda, "the fruit," so called from its principal want, after a night passed amid the rank vegetation, and within the malarious influence of the river, I arose weak and depressed, with aching head, burning eyes, and throbbing extremities. The new life, the alternations of damp heat and wet cold, the useless fatigue of walking, the sorry labor of waiting and reloading the asses, the exposure to sun and dew, and last, but not least, of morbific influences, the wear and tear of mind at the prospect of imminent failure, all were beginning to tell heavily upon me. My companion had shaken off his preliminary symptoms, but Said bin Salim, attacked during the rainy gusty night by a severe mkunguru or seasoning-fever, begged hard for a halt at Tunda—only for a day —only for half a day—only for an hour. Even this was refused. I feared that Tunda might prove fatal to us. Said bin Salim was mounted upon an ass, which compelled us to a weary trudge of two hours. The animals were laden with difficulty; they had begun to show a predilection for lying down. The footpath, crossing a deep nullah, spanned a pestilential expanse of spear-grass, and a cane, called from its appearance gugu-mbua, or the wild sugar-plant, with huge calabashes and natural clearings in the jungle, where large game appeared. After a short march, I saw the red flag of the vanguard stationary, and turning a sharp corner found the caravan halted in a little village, called, from its headman, Báná Dirungá. This was premature. I had ordered Muinyi Wazira to advance on that morning to Dege la Mhora, the "large jungle-bird," the hamlet where M. Maizan's blood was shed. Said and Wazira had proposed that we should pass it ere the dawn of the next day broke; the advice was rejected: it was too dangerous a place to show fear. The two diplomatists then bethought themselves of another manœuvre, and led me to Báná Dirungá, calling it Dege la Mhora.

We halted for a day at the little hamlet, embosomed in dense grass and thicket. On our appearance the villagers fled into the bush, their country's strength; but before nightfall they took heart of grace and returned. The headman appeared to regard us with fear: he could not comprehend why we carried so much powder and ball. When reassured, he offered to precede us, and to inform the chief of the "large jungle-bird" that our intentions had been misrepresented—a proposal which seemed to do much moral good to Said, the jemadar, and Wazira.

On the eleventh day after leaving Kaole, I was obliged to mount by a weakness which scarcely allowed me to stand. After about half an hour, through a comparatively open country, we passed on the left a well-palisaded village, belonging formerly to P'hazi Mazungera, and now occupied by his son Hembe, or the "wild buffalo's horn." Reports of our warlike intentions had caused Hembe to "clear decks for action;" the women had been sent from the village, and some score of tall youths, archers and spearmen, admirably appointed, lined the hedges, prepared, at the leveling of the first matchlock, to let loose a flight of poisoned arrows, which would certainly have dispersed the whole party. A halt was called by the trembling Said, who at such conjunctures would cling like a woman to my companion or to me. During the few minutes' delay, the "sons of Ramji," who were as pale as blacks could be, allowed their asses to bump off half a dozen loads. Presently Hembe, accompanied by a small guard, came forward, and after a few words with Wazira and Said, the donkey from which I had not dismounted was hurried forward by the Baloch. Hembe followed us with a stronger escort to Madege Madogo, the next station. Illness served me as an excuse for not receiving him: he obtained, however, from Said a letter to the headmen of the coast, bespeaking their good offices for certain of his slaves sent down to buy gunpowder.

An account of the melancholy event which cut short at Dege la Mhora the career of the first European that ever penetrated beyond this portion of the coast may here be inserted.

M. Maizan, an *enseigne de vaisseau*, and a pupil of the Polytechnic School, after a cruise in the seas off Eastern Africa, conceived, about the end of 1843, the project of exploring the lakes of the interior, and in 1844 his plans were approved of by his government. Arrived at Bourbon, he was provided with a passage to Zanzibar, in company with M. Broquant, the Consul de France, newly appointed after the French commercial treaty of the 21st Nov., 1844, on board the corvette Le Berceau, Capitaine, afterward Vice-admiral, Romain Desfossés commanding. At the age of twenty-six M. Maizan had amply qualified himself by study for travel, and he was well provided with outfit and instruments. His "kit," however, was of a nature calculated to excite savage cupidity, as was proved by the fact that his murderer converted the gilt knob of a tent-pole into a neck ornament, and tearing out the works of a gold chronometer, made of it a tobacco-pouch. He has been charged with imprudence in carrying too much luggage

—a *batterie de déjeuner*, a *batterie de dîner*, and similar superfluities. But he had acted rightly, when bound upon a journey through countries where outfit can not be renewed, in providing himself with all the materials for comfort. On such explorations a veteran traveler would always attempt to carry with him as much, not as little as possible—of course prepared to abandon all things, and to reduce himself, whenever the necessity might occur, to the "*simple besace du pélerin.*" It is easy to throw away a superfluity, and the best preparation for severe "roughing it" is to enjoy ease and comfort while attainable.

But M. Maizan fell upon evil times at Zanzibar. Dark innuendoes concerning French ambition—that nation being even suspected of a desire to establish itself in force at Lamu, Pangani, and other places on the coast of East Africa—filled Hindoo and Hindi with fear for their profits. These men influenced the inhabitants of the island and the sea-coast, who probably procured the co-operation of their wild brethren in the interior. For the purpose of learning the Kisawahili, M. Maizan delayed nearly eight months at Zanzibar, and, seeing a French vessel entering the harbor, he left the place precipitately, fearing a recall. Vainly also M. Broquant had warned him against his principal confidant, a noted swindler, and Lieut. Colonel Hamerton had cautioned him to no purpose that his glittering instruments and his numerous boxes, all of which would be supposed to contain dollars, were dangerous. He visited the coast thrice before finally landing, thus giving the Wasawahili time and opportunity to mature their plans. He lowered himself in the eyes of the Arabs by "making brotherhood" with a native of Unyamwezi. Finally, fearing Arab apathy and dilatoriness, he hastened into the country without waiting for the strong-armed escort promised to him by his highness the late Sayyid Said.

These were grave errors; but they were nothing in comparison with that of trusting himself unarmed, after the fatal habit of Europeans, and without followers, into the hands of an African chief. How often has British India had to deplore deaths "that would have dimmed a victory," caused by recklessness of danger or by the false shame which prevents men in high position from wearing weapons where they may be at any moment required, lest the safe mediocrities around them should deride such excess of cautiousness!

After the rains of 1845 M. Maizan landed at Bagamoyo, a little settlement opposite the Island of Zanzibar. There leaving the forty musketeers, his private guard, he pressed on, contrary to the advice of his Mnyamwezi brother, escorted only by Frédérique, a Madagascar or Comoro man, and by a few followers, to visit P'hazi Mazungera, the chief of the Wákámbá, a sub-tribe of the Wazaramo, at his village of Dega la Mhora. He was received with a treacherous cordiality, of which he appears to have been completely the dupe. After some days of the most friendly intercourse, during which the villain's plans were being matured, Mazungera, suddenly sending for his guest, reproached him as he entered the hut with giving away goods to other chiefs. Presently working himself into a rage, the African exclaimed, "Thou shalt die at this moment!" At the signal a crowd of savages rushed in, bearing two long poles. Frédérique was saved by the p'hazi's wife: he cried to his master to run and touch her, in which case he would have been under her protection; but the traveler had probably lost presence of mind, and the woman was removed. The unfortunate man's arms were then tightly bound to a pole lashed crosswise upon another, to which his legs and head were secured by a rope tied across the brow. In this state he was carried out of the village to a calabash-tree, pointed out to me, about fifty yards on the opposite side of the road. The inhuman Mazungera first severed all his articulations, while the war-song and the drum sounded notes of triumph. Finding the sime, or double-edged knife, somewhat blunt, he stopped, when in the act of cutting his victim's throat, to whet the edge, and, having finished the bloody deed, he concluded with wrenching the head from the body.

Thus perished an amiable, talented, and highly-educated man, whose only fault was rashness—too often the word for enterprise when fortune withholds her smile. The savage Mazungera was disappointed in his guest's death. The object of the torture was to discover, as the mganga had advised, the place of his treasures, whereas the wretched man only groaned and implored forgiveness of his sins, and called upon the names of those friends whose advice he had neglected. The p'hazi then attempted to decoy from Bagamoyo the forty musketeers left with the outfit, but in this he failed. He then proceeded to make capital of his foul deed. When Snay bin Amir, a Maskat merchant — of whom I shall have much to say—appeared with a large caravan at Dege la Mhora, Mazungera demanded a new tribute for free passage; and, as a threat, he displayed the knife with which he had committed the murder. But Snay proved himself a man not to be trifled with.

Frédérique returned to Zanzibar shortly after the murder, and was examined by M. Broquant. An infamous plot would probably have come to light had he not fled from the fort where he was confined. Frédérique disappeared mysteriously. He is said now to be living at Marungu, on the Tanganyika Lake, under the Moslem name of Muhammádí. His flight served for a pretext to mischievous men that the prince was implicated in the murder: they also spread a notoriously false report that Mazungera, an independent chief, was a vassal of the suzerain of Zanzibar.

In 1846 the brig-of-war Le Ducoüedic, of the naval division of Bourbon, M. Guillain, Capitaine de Vaisseau, commanding, was charged, among other commercial and political interests, with insisting upon severe measures to punish the murderers. In vain his highness Sayyid Said protested that Mazungera was beyond his reach; the fact of the robber-chief having been seen at Mbuamaji on the coast after the murder was deemed conclusive evidence to the contrary. At length the Sayyid dispatched upcountry three or four hundred musketeers, mercenaries, and slaves, under command of Juma Mfumbi, the late, and Bori, the present, Diwan of Saadani. The little troop marched some distance into the country, when they were suddenly confronted by the Wazaramo, commanded by Hembe, the son of the Mazungera, who, after skirmishing for a couple of days, fled wounded by a matchlock ball. The chief result of the expedition was the capture of a luckless clansman who had beaten the war-drum during the murder. He was at once transferred to Zanzibar, and passed off by these transparent African diplomatists as P'hazi Mazungera. For nearly two years he was chained in front of the French Consulate; after that time he was placed in the fort, heavily ironed to a gun under a cadjan shed, where he could hardly stand or lie down. The unhappy wretch died about a year ago, and Zanzibar lost one of its lions.

After the slaughter of M. Maizan the direct route through Dege la Mhora was long closed, it is said, and is still believed, by a "ghul," a dragon, or huge serpent, who, of course, was supposed to be the demon-ghost of the murdered man. The reader will rejoice to hear that the miscreant Mazungera, who has evaded human, has not escaped divine punishment. The miserable old man is haunted by the p'hepo or spirit of the guest so foully slain: the torments which he has brought upon himself have driven him into a kind of exile; and his tribe, as has been mentioned, has steadily declined from its former position, with even a greater decline in prospect. The jealous national honor displayed by the French government on the occasion of M. Maizan's murder has begun to bear fruit.

Its sensitiveness contrasts well with our proceedings on similar occasions. Rahmat, the murderer of Captain Milne, still wanders free over the hills in sight of Aden. By punishing the treacherous slaughter of a servant of government, the price of provisions at the coal-hole of the East would have been raised. Au Ali, the murderer of Lieut. Stroyan, is still at large in the neighborhood of Berberah, when a few dollars would have brought in his head. The burlesque of a blockade—Capt. Playfair, in a work previously characterized, has officially mistermed it, to the astonishment of Aden, "a rigid blockade," a "severe punishment," and so forth—was considered sufficient to chastise the Somal of Berberah for their cowardly onslaught on strangers and guests; and though the people offered an equivalent for the public and private property destroyed by them, the spirit of centralization, by an exercise of its peculiar attributes, omniscience and omnipresence, decided that the indemnity, which in such cases is customary throughout the East, must not be accepted, because—forsooth!—it was not deserved by the officers. This is a new plan, a system lately adopted by the nation once called "la plus orgueilleuse et la plus perilleuse"—to win and preserve respect in lands where prestige is its principal power. The Arabs of Yemen have already learned from it to characterize their invaders as Sahib Hilah—a tricky, peddling manner of folk. They—wiser men than we—will not take upon themselves the pains and penalties of subject-hood, without its sole counter-weight, the protection of their rulers, in cases where protection is required.

At Madege Madogo, the "little birds," so called in contradistinction to its western and neighboring district, Madege Makuba, the "great birds," we pitched tent under a large sycamore; and the Baloch passed a night of alarms, fancying in every sound the approach of a leopard, a hippopotamus, or a crocodile. On the 13th July, we set out after dawn, and traversing forest, jungle, and bush, checkered with mud and morass, hard by the bending and densely-wooded line of the Kingani River, reached in three hours' march an unwholesome camping-ground, called from a conspicuous land-mark Kidunda, the "little hill." Here the scenery is effective. The swift, yellow stream, about fifty yards broad, sweeps under tall, stiff earth-works, ever green with tangled vegetation and noble trees. The conical huts of the cultivators are disposed in scattered patches to guard their luxuriant crops, while on the northern bank the woody hillock, and on the southern rising ground, apparently the ancient river-terrace, affect the sight agreeably after the evergreen monotony of the river-plain. A petty chief, Mvirama, accompanied by a small party of armed men, posted himself near the cantonment, demanding rice, which was refused with asperity. At this frontier station the Wazaramo, mixed up with the tribes of Udoe, K'hutu, and Usagara, are no longer dreaded.

From Kidunda, the route led over sandy ground, with lines and scatters of water-worn pebbles, descended the precipitous inclines of sandstone, broken into steps of slabs and flags, and crossed the Manyora, a rough and rocky fiumara, abounding in blocks of snowy quartz, gray and pink syenites, erratic boulders of the hornblende used as whetstones, and strata of a rude sandstone conglomerate. Thence it spanned grass, bush, and forest, close to the Kingani, and finally leaving the stream on the right hand, it traversed sandy soil, and, ascending a wave of ground, abutted upon the Mgeta or rivulet, a large perennial influent, which, rising in the mountains of Duthumi, drains the head of the river-valley.

This lower portion of the Mgeta's bed was unfordable after the heavy rains: other caravans, however, had made a rude bridge of trees, felled on each side, lashed with creepers, and jammed together by the force of the current. The men, perched upon the trunks and boughs, tossed or handed to one another the loads and packages, while the asses, pushed by force of arm down the banks, were driven with sticks and stones across the stream. Suddenly a louder cry than usual arose from the mob; my double-barreled elephant-gun found a grave below the cold and swirling waters. The Goanese Gaetano had the courage to plunge in; the depth was about twelve feet; the sole was of roots and loose sand, and the stream ran with considerable force. I bade farewell to that gun—by-the-by, it was the second accident of the kind that had occurred to it; the country people can not dive, and no one ventures to affront the *genius loci*, the mamba or crocodile. I found consolation in the thought that the expedition had passed without accident through the most dangerous part of the journey. In 18 days, from the 27th of June to the 14th of July, I had accomplished, despite sickness and all manner of difficulties, a march of 118 indirect statute miles, and had entered K'hutu, the safe rendezvous of foreign merchants.

Resuming our march on the 15th July, we entered the "Doab," * on the western bank of the Mgeta, where a thick and tangled jungle, with luxuriant and putrescent vegetation, is backed by low, grassy grounds, frequently inundated. Presently, however, the dense thicket opened out into a fine park country, peculiarly rich in game, where the calabash and the giant trees of the sea-board gave way to mimosas, gums, and stunted thorns. Large gnus, whom the porters regard with a wholesome awe, declaring that they are capable of charging a caravan, pranced about, pawing the ground, and shaking their formidable manes; hartebeest and other antelopes clustered together on the plain, or traveled in herds to slake their thirst at the river. The homely cry of the partridge resounded from the brake, and the guinea-fowls looked like large blue-bells upon the trees. Small land-crabs took refuge in the pits and holes, which made the path a cause of frequent accidents; while ants of various kinds, crossing the road in close columns, attacked man and beast ferociously, causing the caravan to break into a halting, trotting hobble, ludicrous to behold. While crossing a sandy fiumara, Abdullah, a Baloch, lodged by accident four ounces of lead, the contents of my second elephant-gun, in the head of an ass. After a march of six hours we entered Kiruru, a small, ragged, and muddy village of Wak'-hutu, deep in a plantation of holcus, whose tall, stiff canes nearly swept me from the saddle. The weather was a succession of raw mist, rain in torrents, and fiery sunbursts; the land appeared rotten, and the jungle smelt of death. At Kiruru I found a cottage, and enjoyed for the first time an atmosphere of sweet warm smoke.

* This useful word, which means the land embraced by the bifurcation of two streams, has no English equivalent. "Doab," "dhun" (dhoon), "nullah," and "ghaut," might be naturalized with advantage in our mother tongue.

My companion remained in the reeking, miry tent, where he partially laid the foundation of the fever which threatened his life in the mountains of Usagara.

Despite the danger of hyenas, leopards, and crocodiles to an ass-caravan, we were delayed by the torrents of rain and the depth of the mud for two days at Kiruru. According to the people, the district derives its name, "palm leaves," from a thirsty traveler, who, not knowing that water was near, chewed the leaves of the hyphæna-palm till he died. One of the Baloch proposed a "hammam"—a primitive form of the "lamp-bath," practiced in most parts of Central Asia—as a cure for fever: he placed me upon one of the dwarf stools used by the people, and under the many abas or hair cloaks with which I was invested he introduced a bit of pottery containing live coal and a little frankincense. At Kiruru I engaged six porters to assist our jaded animals as far as the next station. The headman was civil, but the people sold their grain with difficulty.

On the 18th July we resumed our march over a tract which caused sinking of the heart in men who expected a long journey under similar circumstances. Near Kiruru the thick grass and the humid vegetation, dripping till mid-day with dew, rendered the black earth greasy and slippery. The road became worse as we advanced over deep thick mire interlaced with tree-roots through a dense jungle and forest, chiefly of the distorted hyphæna-palm, in places varied by the mparamusi and the gigantic msukulío, over barrens of low mimosa, and dreary savannas cut by steep nullahs. In three places we crossed bogs from 100 yards to a mile in length, and admitting a man up to the knee; the porters plunged through them like laden animals, and I was obliged to be held upon the ass. This "yegea mud," caused by want of water-shed after rain, is sometimes neck-deep; it never dries except when the moisture has been evaporated by sun and wind during the middle of the kaskazi or N.E. monsoon. The only redeeming feature in the view was a foreground of lovely hill, the highlands of Dut'humi, plum-colored in the distance, and at times gilt by a sudden outburst of sunshine. Toward the end of the march I forged ahead of the caravan, and, passing through numerous villages surrounded by holcus-fields, arrived at a settlement tenanted by Sayf bin Salim, an Arab merchant, who afterward proved to be a notorious "mauvais sujet." A Harisi from Birkah, in Oman, he was a tall thin-featured venerable-looking man, whose old age had been hurried on by his constancy to pombe-beer. A long residence in Unyamwezi had enabled him to incur the hostility of his fellow-merchants, especially one Salim bin Said el Sawwafi, who, with other Arabs, persuaded Mpagamo, an African chief, to seize upon Sayf, and after tying him up in full view of the plundering and burning of his store-house, to drive him out of the country. Retreating to Dut'humi, he had again collected a small stock in trade, especially of slaves, whom he chained and treated so severely that all men predicted for him an evil end. "Msopora," as he was waggishly nicknamed by the Wanyamwezi, instantly began to backbite Said bin Salim, whom he pronounced utterly unfit to manage our affairs; I silenced him by falling asleep upon a cartel placed under the cool eaves of a hut. Presently staggered in my companion almost too ill to speak; over-fatigue had prostrated his strength. By slow degrees, and hardly able to walk, appeared the Arab, the Baloch, the slaves and the asses, each and every having been bogged in turn. On this occasion Wazira had acted guide, and used to "bog-trotting," he had preferred the short cut to the cleaner road that rounds the swamps.

At Dut'humi we were detained nearly a week; the malaria had brought on attacks of marsh fever, which in my case lasted about 20 days; the paroxysms were mild compared with the Indian or the Sindhian type, yet, favored by the atonic state of the constitution, they thoroughly prostrated me. I had during the fever-fit, and often for hours afterward, a queer conviction of divided identity, never ceasing to be two persons that generally thwarted and opposed each other; the sleepless nights brought with them horrid visions, animals of grisliest form, hag-like women and men with heads protruding from their breasts. My companion suffered even more severely; he had a fainting-fit which strongly resembled a sun-stroke, and which seemed permanently to affect his brain. Said bin Salim was the convalescent of the party; the two Goanese yielded themselves wholly to maladies brought on mainly by hard eating, and had they not been forced to rise, they would probably never have risen again. Our sufferings were increased by other causes than climate. The riding-asses having been given up for loads, we were compelled, when premonitory symptoms suggested rest, to walk, sometimes for many miles in a single heat, through sun and rain, through mud and miasmatic putridities. Even ass-riding caused over-fatigue. It by no means deserves in these lands the reputation of an anile exercise, as it does in Europe. Maître Aliboron in Africa is stubborn, vicious and guilty of the four mortal sins of the equine race, he shies and stumbles, he rears and runs away: my companion has been thrown as often as twice in two hours. The animals are addicted to fidgeting, plunging, and pirouetting when mounted; they hog and buck till they burst their frail girths, they seem to prefer holes and hollows, they rush about pig-like when high winds blow, and they bolt under tree-shade when the sun shines hot. They must be led, or, ever preferring the worst ground, they disdain to follow the path, and when difficulties arise the slave will surely drop the halter and get out of harm's way. If a pace exceeding two miles an hour be required, a second man must follow and flog each of these perfect slugs during the whole march. The roundness of their flanks, the shortness of their backs, and their want of shoulder, combine to make the meagre Arab pack-saddle unsafe for any thing but a baboon or a boy, while the straightness and the rigidity of their goat-like pasterns render the pace a wearisome, tripping hobble. We had, it is true, Zanzibari riding-asses, but the delicate animals soon chafed and presently died; we were then reduced to the koroma or half-reclaimed beast of Wanyamwezi. The laden asses gave us even more trouble. The slaves would not attend to the girthing and the balancing of parcels—the great secret of donkey-loading—consequently the burdens were thrown at every mud or broken ground: the unwilling Baloch only grumbled, sat down and stared, leaving their jemadars with Said bin Salim and ourselves to reload. My companion and I brought up the rear by alternate days, and sometimes we did not arrive before the afternoon at the camping-ground. The ropes and cords intended to secure the herd were regularly stolen, that I might be forced to buy others: the animals were never pounded for the night, and during our illness none of the party took the trouble to number them. Thus several beasts were lost, and the grounding of the expedition appeared imminent and permanent. The result was a sensation of wretchedness hard to describe; every morning dawned upon me with a fresh load of cares and troubles, and every evening reminded me, as it closed in, that another and a miserable morrow was to dawn. But "in despair," as the Arabs say, "are many hopes; though sorrow endured for the night—and many were "white" with anxiety—we never relinquished the determination to risk every thing, ourselves included, rather than to return unsuccessful.

Dut'humi, one of the most fertile districts in K'hutu, is a plain of black earth and sand, choked with vegetation where not corrected by the axe. It is watered by the perennial stream of the same name, which, rising in the islands, adds its quotum to the waters of the Mgazi, and eventually to the Mgeta and the Kingani Rivers. In such places artificial irrigation is common, the element being distributed over the fields by hollow ridges. The mountains of Dut'humi form the northern boundary of the plain. They appear to rise abruptly, but they throw off southerly lower eminences, which diminish in elevation till confounded with the almost horizontal surface of the champaign; the jagged broken crests and peaks argue a primitive formation. Their lay is to the N.N.W.; after four days' journey, according to the guides, they inosculate with the main chain of the Usagara Mountains, and they are probably the southern buttress of Ngu, or Nguru, the hill region westward of Saadani. This chain is said to send forth the Kingani River, which, gushing from a cave or fissure in the eastern, is swollen to a large perennial stream by feeders from the southern slopes, while the Mgeta flows from the western face of the water-parting, and circles the southern base. The cold tem-

perature of these cloud-capped and rainy crags, which never expose their outlines except in the clearest weather, affects the
plains; by day bleak northeast and northwest gusts pour down
upon the sun-parched Dut'humi, and at night the thermometer
will sink to 70°, and even to 65° F. Water is supposed to freeze
upon the highlands, yet they are not unhealthy; sheep, goats, and
poultry abound; betel-pepper grows there, according to the Arabs,
and, as in the lowlands, holcus and sesamum, manioc and sweet
potatoes (Convolvulus batata), cucumbers, the turai (Luffa acutan-
gula), and beans, plaintains, and sugar-cane, are plentiful. The
thick jungle at the base of the hills shelters the elephant, the rhinoceros in considerable numbers, the gnu, and the koodoo, which,
however, can rarely be found when the grass is high; a variety
of the ngole—a small dendraspis—haunts the patriarchs of the
forest, and the chirrup of the mongoose, which the people enjoy,
as Europeans do the monotonous note of the cricket, is heard in
the brakes at eventide. This part of the country, about six hours'
march northward from Dut'humi, is called the Inland Mgogoni;
and it is traversed by the "Mdimu" nullah, which falls into the
Mgeta River. The fertile valleys in the lower and southern folds
are inhabited by the Wákumbáku (?),* and by the Wásuop'hángá tribes; the higher elevations, which apparently range from
3000 to 4000 feet, by the Waruguru. They are compelled to fortify themselves against the cold and the villainous races around
them. The plague of the land is now one Kisabengo, a Mzegura of low origin, who, after conquering Ukami, a district extending from the eastern flank of the Dut'humi hills seaward, from its
Moslem diwan, Ngozi, alias Kingaru, has raised himself to the
rank of a shene khambi, or principal headman. Aided by the
kidnapping Moslem coast-clans of Whinde, a small coast-town
opposite the Island of Zanzibar, and his fellow tribemen of Uze-
gura, he has transferred by his frequent commandos almost all
the people of Ukámí, chiefly Wásuop'hángá and Wárúgúrú, to
the slave-market of Zanzibar, and, thus compelled to push his
depredations farther west, he has laid waste the lands even beyond the Mukondokwa river-valley. The hill tribes, however,
still receive strangers hospitably into their villages. They have
a place visited even by distant Wazaramo pilgrims. It is described as a cave where a p'hepo or the disembodied spirit of a
man, in fact a ghost, produces a terrible subterraneous sound, called by the people kurero or bokero; it arises probably from the
flow of water underground. In a pool in the cave women bathe
for the blessing of issue, and men sacrifice sheep and goats to obtain fruitful seasons and success in war. These hill-races speak

---

* This unsatisfactory figure of print will often occur in these pages. Ignorance,
error, and causeless falsehood, together with the grossest exaggeration, deter the
traveler from committing himself to any assertion which he has not proved to his own
satisfaction.

peculiar dialects, which, according to the guides, are closely connected with Kik'hutu.

Despite the bad name of Dut'humi as regards climate, Arabs sometimes reside there for some months for the purpose of purchasing slaves cheaply and to repair their broken fortunes for a fresh trip to the interior. This keeps up a perpetual feud among the chiefs of the country, and scarcely a month passes without fields being laid waste, villages burnt down, and the unhappy cultivators being carried off to be sold.

At Dut'humi a little expedition was sent against Manda, a petty chief, who, despite the presence of the Sayyid's troops, had plundered a village and had kidnapped five of the subjects of Mgota, his weaker neighbor. I had the satisfaction of restoring the stolen wretches to their hearths and homes, and two decrepit old women that had been rescued from slavery thanked me with tears of joy.

This easy good deed done, I was able, though with swimming head and trembling hands, to prepare accounts and a brief report of proceedings for the Royal Geographical Society. These, together with other papers, especially an urgent request for medical comforts and drugs, especially quinine and narcotics, addressed to Lieut. Colonel Hamerton, or, in case of accidents, to M. Cochet, Consul de France, were intrusted to Jemadar Yaruk, whom, moreover, I took the liberty of recommending to the prince for the then vacant command of the Bagamoyo garrison. The escort from Kaole, reduced in number by three desertions, was dismissed. All the volunteers had been clamoring to return, and I could no longer afford to keep them. Besides the two supplies of cloth, wire, and beads, which preceded, and which were left to follow us, I had been provided by Ladha Damha with a stock of white and blue cottons, some handsome articles of dress, 20,000 strings of white and black, pink, blue, and green, red and brown porcelain beads, needles, and other articles of hardware, to defray transit charges through Uzarama. This provision, valued at 295 dollars, should have carried us to the end of the third month; it lasted about three weeks. Said bin Salim, to whom it had been intrusted, had been generous, through fear, to every half-naked barbarian that chose to stretch forth the hand of beggary; moreover, while too ill to superintend disbursements, he had allowed his "children," aided by the Baloch and the "sons of Ramji," to "loot" whatever they could seize and secrete. Ladha Damha, unable to complete our carriage, had hit upon the notable device of converting eighteen pieces of American domestics into saddlecloths for the asses: the stuff was used at halts as bedding by the Baloch and others; and—a proof that much had fallen into wrong hands—the thirteen men composing our permanent guard increased the number of their laden asses from two to five; moreover, for many weeks afterward, the "sons of Ramji" could

afford to expend four to five cloths upon a goat.   On the 21st of
July the escort from Kaole departed with a general discharge of
matchlocks.   Their disappearance was hailed as a blessing; they
had pestered me for rations, and had begged for asses till midnight.   They were the refuse of their service; they thought of,
they dreamed of nothing but food; they would do no work;
they were continually attempting violence upon the timid Wa-
k'hutu, and they seemed resolved to make the name of Baloch
equally hateful and contemptible.

I had been careful to bring from Zanzibar four hammocks,
which, slung to poles, formed the conveyance called by the Indians "manchil;" by the Portuguese "manchila;" and in West Africa " tipoia."   Sayf bin Salim agreed for the sum of ten dollars
to hire his slaves as porters for ourselves and our outfit.   On the
24th of July, feeling strong enough to advance, we passed out of
the cultivation of Dut'humi.   Crossing a steep and muddy bed,
knee-deep even in the dry season, we entered fields under the outlying hillocks of the highlands.   These low cones, like similar
formations in India, are not inhabited; they are even more malarious than the plains, the surface is rocky, and the woodage, not
ceasing as in higher elevations, extends from base to summit.
Beyond the cultivation the route plunges into a jungle, where the
European traveler realizes every preconceived idea of Africa's aspect, at once hideous and grotesque.   The general appearance is
a mingling of bush and forest, which, contracting the horizon to a
few yards, is equally monotonous to the eye and palling to the
imagination.   The black greasy ground, veiled with thick shrubbery, supports in the more open spaces screens of tiger and spear
grass, twelve and thirteen feet high, with every blade a finger's
breadth; and the towering trees are often clothed from root to
twig with huge epiphytes, forming heavy columns of densest verdure, and clustering upon the tops in the semblance of enormous
birds'-nests.   The foot-paths, in places " dead"—as the natives
say—with encroaching bush, are crossed by llianas, creepers and
climbers, thick as coir-cables, some connecting the trees in a
curved line, others stretched straight down the trunks, others
winding in all directions around their supports, frequently crossing one another like net-work and stunting the growth of even
the vivacious calabash, by coils like rope tightly encircling its
neck.   The earth, ever rain-drenched, emits the odor of sulphu-
reted hydrogen, and in some parts the traveler might fancy a
corpse to be hidden behind every bush.   To this sad picture of
miasma the firmament is a fitting frame: a wild sky, whose heavy
purple nimbi, chased by raffales and chilling gusts, dissolve in
large-dropped showers; or a dull, dark gray expanse, which lies
like a pall over the world.   In the finer weather the atmosphere
is pale and sickly; its mists and vapors seem to concentrate the
rays of the oppressive " rain-sun."   The sensation experienced at

once explains the apathy and indolence, the physical debility, and the mental prostration that are the gifts of climates which moist heat and damp cold render equally unsalubrious and uncomfortable. That no feature of miasma might be wanting to complete the picture, filthy heaps of the rudest hovels, built in holes in the jungle, sheltered their few miserable inhabitants, whose frames are lean with constant intoxication, and whose limbs, distorted by ulcerous sores, attest the hostility of Nature to mankind. Such a revolting scene is East Africa from central K'hutu to the base of the Usagara Mountains.

Running through this fetid flat, the path passed on the left sundry shallow salt-pits, which, according to the Arabs, are wet during the dry, and dry during the wet season. Presently, after breaking through another fence of holcus, whose cane was stiffer than the ratans of an Indian jungle, we entered and found lodgings in Bakera, a pretty little hamlet ringed with papaws and plantains, upon which the doves disported themselves. Here, on our return in 1859, a thick growth of grass waved over the ground-marks of hearth and roof-tree. The African has a superstitious horror of stone walls; he is still a semi-nomade, from the effects of the Wandertrieb, or man's vagabond instinct, uncurbed by the habits of civilization. Though vestiges of large and stable habitations have been discovered in the barbarous Eastern Horn, in these days, between the parallels of Harar and the ruined Portuguese towns near the Zambezi Rivers, Inner Africa ignores a town of masonry. In our theoretical maps, the circlets used by cartographers to denote cities serve only to mislead; their names prove them to be saltanats—lordships, districts, or provinces.

Resuming our course on the next day through hollows and rice-swamps, where almost every ass fell or cast its load, we came, after a long tramp, to the nearest outposts of the Zungomero district; here were several caravans with pitched tents, piles of ivory and crowds of porters. The gang of thirty-six Wanyamwezi, who had preceded us, having located themselves at a distant hamlet, we resumed our march, and presently were met by a number of our men headed by their guard, the two "sons of Ramji." Ensued a general sword and spear play, each man with howls and cheers brandished his blade or vibrated his missile, rushing about in all directions, and dealing death among ideal foes with such action as may often be observed in poultry-yards when the hens indulge in a little merry pugnacity. The march had occupied us four weeks—about double the usual time—and the porters had naturally begun to suspect accidents from the Wazaramo.

Zungomero, the head of the great river-valley, is a plain of black earth and sand, prodigiously fertile. It is inclosed on all sides except the eastern, or the line of drainage; northward rise the peaks of Dut'humi; westward lie the little Wigo hills and the other spurs of Usagara, uncultivated and uninhabited, though the coun-

try is populous up to their feet; and southward are detached
cones of similar formation, steep, rocky, and densely wooded.
The sea-breeze is here strong, but beyond its influence the atmosphere is sultry and oppressive; owing to maritime influences, the
kosi, or southwest wind, sometimes continues till the end of July.
The normal day, which varies little throughout the year, begins
with the light milky mist which forms the cloud-ring; by degrees
nimbi and cumuli come up from the east, investing the heights
of Dut'humi, and, when showers are imminent, a heavy line of
stratus bisects the highlands and overlies the surface of the plain.
At the epochs of the lunar change rain falls once or twice during
the day and night, and, when the clouds burst, a fiery sun sucks
up poison from the earth's putridity. The early nights are oppressive, and toward the dawn condensation causes a copious deposit of heavy dew, which even the people of the country dread.
A prolonged halt causes general sickness among the porters and
slaves of a caravan. The humidity of the atmosphere corrodes
every thing with which it comes in contact; the springs of pow-
der-flasks exposed to the damp snap like toasted quills; clothes
feel limp and damp; paper, becoming soft and soppy by the loss
of glazing, acts as a blotter; boots, books, and botanical collections
are blackened; metals are ever rusty; the best percussion caps,
though labeled water-proof, will not detonate unless carefully stow-
ed away in waxed cloth and tin boxes; gunpowder, if not kept
from the air, refuses to ignite, and wood becomes covered with
mildew. We had an abundance of common German phosphor
matches, and the best English wax lucifers; both, however, became equally unserviceable; the heads shrank and sprang off at
the least touch, and the boxes frequently became a mere mass of
paste. To future travelers I should recommend the "good old
plan;" a bit of phosphorus in a little phial half full of olive oil,
which serves for light as well as ignition. When accompanied
by matchlock-men, however, there is no difficulty about fire; their
pouches always contain a steel and flint, and a store of cotton, or
of the wild bombex, dipped in saltpetre or gunpowder solution.

Yet Zungomero is the great bandári or centre of traffic in the
eastern, as are Unyanyembe and Ujiji in the middle and the western regions. Lying upon the main trunk-road, it must be traversed by the up and down caravans, and, during the traveling
season, between June and April, large bodies of some thousand
men pass through it every week. Kilwa formerly sent caravans
to it, and the Wanyamwezi porters have frequently made that
port by the "Mwera road." The Arab merchants usually pitch
tents, preferring them to the leaky native huts, full of hens and
pigeons, rats and mice, snakes and lizards, crickets and cockroaches, gnats and flies, and spiders of hideous appearance, where
the inmates are often routed by swarms of bees, and are ever in
imminent danger of fires. The armed slaves accompanying the

caravan seize the best huts, which they either monopolize or share with the hapless inmates, and the porters stow themselves away under the projecting eaves of the habitations. The main attraction of the place is the plenty of provisions. Grain is so abundant that the inhabitants exist almost entirely upon the intoxicating pombe, or holcus-beer—a practice readily imitated by their visitors. Bhang and the datura plant, growing wild, add to the attractions of the spot. The bhang is a fine large species of the Cannabis Indica, the bang of Persia, the bhang of India, and the benj of Arabia, the fasukh of Northern, and the dakha of Southern Africa. In the low lands of East Africa it grows before every cottage door. As in hot climates generally, the fibre degenerates, and the plant is only valued for its narcotic properties. The Arabs smoke the sun-dried leaf with, and the Africans without tobacco, in huge water-pipes, whose bowls contain a quarter of a pound. Both ignore the more luxurious preparations, momiya and hashish, ganja and sebzi, charas and maajun. Like the "jangli" or jungle (wild)-bhang of Sindh, affected by kalandars, fakirs, and other holy beggars, this variety, contracting the muscle of the throat, produces a violent whooping-cough, ending in a kind of scream, after a few long puffs, when the smoke is inhaled; and if one man sets the example the others are sure to follow. These grotesque sounds are probably not wholly natural; even the boys may be heard practicing them; they appear to be a fashion of "renowning it;" in fact, an announcement to the public that the fast youths are smoking bhang. The Datura stramonium, called by the Arabs and by the Wasawahili "muranhá," grows in the well-watered plains; it bears a large whitish flower and a thorn-apple like that of India. The heathen, as well as their visitors, dry the leaves, the flowers, and the rind of the rootlet, which is considered the strongest preparation, and smoke them in a common bowl or in a water-pipe. This is held to be a sovereign remedy against zik el nafas (asthma) and influenza; it diminishes the cough by loosening the phlegm. The Washenzi never make that horrible use of the plant known to the Indian dhaturiya, or datura-poisoners; many accidents, however, occur from ignorance of its violent narcotism. Meat is scarce: the only cattle are those driven down by the Wanyamwezi to the coast; milk, butter, and ghee are consequently unprocurable. A sheep or a goat will not cost less than a shukkah, or four cubits of domestics, here worth twenty-five cents. The same will purchase only two fowls; and eggs and fruit—chiefly papaws and plantains, cocos and limes—are at fancy prices. For the shukkah, eight rations of unhusked holcus, four measures of rice—which must here be laid in by those traveling up-country—and five cakes of tobacco, equal to about three pounds, are generally procurable. Thus the daily expenditure of a large caravan ranges from one dollar to one dollar fifty cents' worth of cloth in the Zanzibar market. The value, however, fluctuates greatly, and the people will shirk selling even at any price.

The same attractions which draw caravans to Zungomero render it the great rendezvous of an army of touters, who, while watching for the arrival of the ivory traders, amuse themselves with plundering the country. The plague has now spread like a flight of locusts over the land. The Wak'hutu, a timid race, who, unlike the Wazaramo, have no sultan to gather round, are being gradually ousted from their ancient seats. In a large village there will seldom be more than three or four families, who occupy the most miserable hovels, all the best having been seized by the touters or pulled down for firewood. These men—slaves, escaped criminals, and freemen of broken fortunes, flying from misery, punishment, or death on the coast—are armed with muskets and sabres, bows and spears, daggers and knobsticks. They carry ammunition, and thus are too strong for the country people. When rough language and threats fail, the leveled barrel at once establishes the right to a man's house and property, to his wife and children. If money runs short, a village is fired by night, and the people are sold off to the first caravan. In some parts the pattering of musketry is incessant, as it ever was in the turbulent states of independent India. It is rarely necessary to have recourse to violence; the Wak'hutu, believing their tyrants to be emissaries, as they represent themselves, from his highness the sultan, and the chief nobles of Zanzibar, offer none but the most passive resistance, hiding their families and herds in the bush. Thus it happens that toward the end of the year nothing but a little grain can be purchased in a land of marvelous fertility.

As has been mentioned, these malpractices are severely reprobated by his highness the sultan, and when the evil passes a certain point remedial measures are taken. A Banyan, for instance, is sent to the coast with warnings to the diwans concerned. But what care they for his empty words, when they know that he has probably equipped a similar party of black buccaneers himself? and what hope can there be of reform when there is not an honest man in the country to carry it out? Thus the government of Zanzibar is rendered powerless;—improvement can be expected only from the hand of Time. The Wak'hutu, indeed, often threaten a deputation to entreat the Arab sultan for protection in the shape of a garrison at Baloch. This measure has been retarded for sound reasons: no man dares to leave his house for fear of finding it a ruin on his return; moreover, he would certainly be shot if the touters guessed his intention, and, even if he escaped this danger, he would probably be sold, on the way to the coast, by his truculent neighbors the Wazaramo. Finally, if they succeeded in their wishes, would not a Baloch garrison act the part of the man who, in the fable, was called in to assist the horse against the stag? The Arabs, who know the temper of these mercenaries, are too wise ever to sanction such a "dragon-nade."

The reader will readily perceive that he is upon the slave-path, so different from travel among the free and independent tribes of Southern Africa. The traffic practically annihilates every better feeling of human nature. Yet, though the state of the Wak'hutu appears pitiable, the traveler can not practice pity; he is ever in the dilemma of maltreating or being maltreated. Were he to deal civilly and liberally with this people he would starve; it is vain to offer a price for even the necessaries of life; it would certainly be refused, because more is wanted, and so on beyond the bounds of possibility. Thus, if the touter did not seize a house, he would never be allowed to take shelter in it from the storm; if he did not enforce a "corvée," he must labor beyond his strength with his own hands; and if he did not fire a village and sell the villagers, he might die of hunger in the midst of plenty. Such in this province are the action and reaction of the evil.

Party of Wak'hutu Women.

CHAPTER IV.

ON THE GEOGRAPHY AND ETHNOLOGY OF THE FIRST REGION.

BEFORE bidding adieu to the maritime region, it will be expedient to enter into a few details concerning its geography and ethnology.*

The first, or maritime region, extends from the shores of the Indian Ocean in E. long. 39° to the mountain chain forming the land of Usagara in E. long. 37° 28′; its breadth is therefore 92 geographical miles, measured in rectilinear distance, and its mean length, bounded by the waters of the Kingani and the Rufiji Rivers, may be assumed at 110. The average rise is under four feet per mile. It is divided into two basins; that of the Kingani easterly, and westward that of the Mgeta stream, with its many tributaries; the former, which is the principal, is called the land of Uzaramo; the latter, which is of the second order, contains the province of K'hutu, by the Arabs pronounced Kutu, and Uziraha, a minor district. The natives of the country divide it into the three lowlands of Tunda, Dut'humi, and Zungomero.

The present road runs with few and unimportant deviations along the whole length of the fluviatile valleys of the Kingani

* Those who consider the subject worthy of further consideration are referred, for an ampler account of it, to the Journal of the R. Geographical Society, vol. xxix., of 1860.

and the Mgeta. Native caravans, if lightly laden, generally accomplish the march in a fortnight, one halt included. On both sides of this line, whose greatest height above the sea-level was found by B. P. therm. to be 330 feet, rises the rolling ground, which is the general character of the country. Its undulations present no eminences worthy of notice; near the sea they are short and steep, farther inland they roll in longer waves, and every where they are covered with abundant and luxuriant vegetation, the result of decomposition upon the richest soil. In parts there is an appearance of park land; bushless and scattered forests, with grass rising almost to the lower branches of the smaller thorns; here and there clumps and patches of impassable shrubbery cluster round knots and knolls of majestic and thickly-foliaged trees. The narrow foot-paths connecting the villages often plunge into dark and dense tunnels, formed by overarching branch and bough, which delay the file of laden porters; the mud lingering long after a fall of rain in these low grounds fills them with a chilly, clammy atmosphere. Merchants traverse such spots with trembling: in these, the proper places for ambuscade, a few determined men easily plunder a caravan by opposing it in front or by an attack in rear. The ways are often intersected by deep nullahs and water-courses, dry during the hot season, but unfordable when rain falls. In the many clearings, tobacco, maize, holcus, sesamum, and ground-nuts, manioc, beans, pulse, and sweet potatoes flourish; the pine-apple is a weed, and a few cocos and mangoes, papaws, jack-fruit, plantains, and limes are scattered over the districts near the sea. Rice grows abundantly in the lower levels. The villages are hidden deep in the bush or grass; the crowing of the cocks heard all along the road, except in the greater stretches of wilderness, proves them to be numerous; they are, however, small and thinly populated. The versant, as usual in maritime East Africa, trends toward the Indian Ocean. Water abounds even at a distance from the rivers; it springs from the soil in diminutive runnels and lies in "shimo" or pits, varying from surface-depth to ten feet. The monsoon-rains, which are heavy, commence in March, about a month earlier than in Zanzibar, and the duration is similar. The climate of the higher lands is somewhat superior to that of the valley, but it is still hot and oppressive. The formation, after passing from the corallines, the limestones, the calcareous tuffs, and the rude gravelly conglomerates of the coast, is purely primitive and sandstone: erratic blocks of fine black hornblende and hornblendic rock, used by the people as whet-stones and grinding-slabs, abound in the river-beds, which also supply the clay used for pottery. The subsoil is near the sea a stiff blue loam, in the interior a ruddy quartzose gravel; the soil is a rich brown or black humus, here and there coated with, or varied by, clean white sand, and in some parts are seams of reddish loam. Fresh-water shells are scattered over the surface, and land-crabs burrow in the looser earths where stone seldom appears. Black cattle are unknown in the maritime region, but poultry, sheep, and goats are plentiful: near the jungle they are protected from the leopards or ounces by large wooden huts, like cages, raised on piles for cleanliness.

As a rule, the fluviatile valleys resemble in most points the physical features of the coast and Island of Zanzibar: the general aspect of the country, however—the expression of its climate— undergoes some modifications. Near the sea, the basin is a broad winding line, traversed by the serpentine river, whose bed is now too deep for change. About the middle expanse stony ridges and rocky hills crop out from the rolling ground, and the head of the valley is a low continuous plain. In many places, especially near the estuary, river-terraces, like road embankments, here converging, there diverging, indicate by lines and strews of water-worn pebbles and sea-shells the secular uprise of the country and the declension of the stream to its present level. These raised sea-beaches at a distance appear crowned with dwarf rounded cones, which, overgrown with lofty trees, are favorite sites for settlements. In the lower lands the jungle and the cultivation are of the rankest and most gigantic description, the effect of a damp, hot region, where atmospheric pressure is excessive. The grass, especially that produced by the black soils in the swamps and marshes, rises to the height of 12 to 13 feet, and serves to conceal runaway slaves and malefactors: the stalks vary in thickness from a goose-quill to a man's finger. The larger growths, which are so closely planted that they conceal the soil, can not be traversed without paths, and even where these exist the traveler must fight his way through a dense screen, receiving from time to time a severe blow when the reeds recoil, or a painful thrust from some broken and inclined stump. Even the horny sole of the sandal-less African can not tread these places without being cut or staked, and every where a ride through these grass avenues while still dripping with the cold exhalations of night, with the sun beating fiercely upon the upper part of the body, is a severe infliction to any man not in perfect health. The beds of streams and nullahs are sometimes veiled by the growth of the banks. These crops spring up with the rains, and are burned down by hunters, or more frequently by accident, after about a month of dry weather; in the interim fires are dangerous: the custom is to beat down the blaze with leafy boughs. Such is the variety of species that in some parts of the river-valleys each day introduces the traveler to a grass before unseen. Where the inundations lie long, the trees are rare, and those that exist are slightly raised by mounds above the ground to escape the destructive effects of protracted submergence: in these places the decomposed vegetation exhales a fetid odor. Where the waters soon subside there are clumps of tall shrubbery and seams of forest rising on extensive meadows of grassy land, which give it the semblance of a suite of natural parks or pleasure-grounds, and the effect is not diminished by the frequent herds of gnu and antelope prancing and pacing over their pastures.

The climate is hot and oppressive, and the daily sea-breeze, which extends to the head of the Mgeta valley, is lost in the lower levels. About Zungomero rain is constant, except for a single fortnight in the month of January; it seems to the stranger as if the crops must infallibly decay, but they do not. At most times the sun, even at its greatest northern declination, shines through a veil of mist with a sickly blaze and a blistering heat, and the overcharge of electricity is evidenced by frequent and violent thunder-storms. In the western parts cold and cutting breezes descend from the rugged crags of Dut'humi.

The principal diseases of the valley are severe ulcerations and fevers, generally of a tertian type. The "mkunguru" begins with coldness in the toes and finger-tips; a frigid shiver seems to creep up the legs, followed by pains in the shoulders, severe frontal headache, hot eyes, and a prostration and irritability of mind and body. This preliminary lasts for one to three hours, when nausea ushers in the hot stage: the head burns, the action of the heart becomes violent, thirst rages, and a painful weight presses upon the eyeballs: it is often accompanied by a violent cough and irritation. Strange visions, as in delirium, appear to the patient, and the excitement of the brain is proved by unusual loquacity. When the fit passes off with copious perspiration, the head is often affected, the ears buzz, and the limbs are weak. If the patient attempts to rise suddenly, he feels a dizziness, produced apparently by a gush of bile along the liver duct: want of appetite, sleeplessness and despondency, and a low fever, evidenced by hot pulses, throbbing temples, and feet painfully swollen, with eruptions of various kinds, and ulcerated mouth, usher in the cure. This fever yields easily to mild remedies, but it is capable of lasting three weeks.

A multitude of roads, whose point of departure is the coast, form a triangle and converge at the "makutaniro," or junction-place, in Central Uzaramo. The route whose several stations have been described is one of the main lines running from Kaole and Bagamoyo, in a general southwest direction, till it falls into the great trunk-road which leads directly west from Mbuamaji. It is divided into thirteen caravan stages, but a well-girt walker will accomplish the distance in a week.

No apology is offered for the lengthiness of the ethnographical descriptions contained in the following pages. The ethnology of Africa is indeed its most interesting, if not its only interesting feature. Every thing connected with the habits and customs, the moral and religious, the social and commercial state of these new races, is worthy of diligent observation, careful description, and minute illustration.   There is indeed little in the physical features of this portion of the great peninsula to excite the attention of the reader beyond the satisfaction that ever accompanies the victory of truth over fable, and a certain importance which in these " traveling times"—when man appears rapidly rising to the rank of a migratory animal—must attach to discovery.   The subject, indeed, mostly banishes ornament.   Lying under the same parallels with a climate whose thermical variations know no extremes, the succession of alluvial valley, ghaut, table-land, and shelving plain is necessarily monotonous, the soil is the same, the productions are similar, and the rocks and trees resemble one another.   Eastern and central inter-tropical Africa also lacks antiquarian and historic interest; it has few traditions, no annals, and no ruins, the hoary remnants of past splendor so dear to the traveler and to the reader of travels.   It contains not a single useful or ornamental work; a canal or a dam is, and has ever been, beyond the narrow bounds of its civilization.   It wants even the scenes of barbaric pomp and savage grandeur with which the student of Occidental Africa is familiar.   But its ethnography has novelties; it exposes strange manners and customs, its Fetichism is in itself a wonder, its commerce deserves attention, and its social state is full of mournful interest.   The fastidiousness of the age, however, forbidding ampler details, even under the veil of the "learned languages," cripples the physiologist, and robs the subject of its principal peculiarities.   I have often regretted that if Greek and dog-Latin be no longer a sufficient disguise for the facts of natural history, human and bestial, the learned have not favored us with a system of symbols which might do away with the grossness of words.

The present tenants of the first region are the Wazaramo, the Wak'hutu, and their great sub-tribe, the Waziraha; these form the staple of population—the Wadoe and the Wazegura being minor and immigrant tribes.

The Wazaramo are no exception to the rule of barbarian maritime races: they have, like the Somal, the Gallas, the Wangindo, the Wamakua, and the Cape Kafirs, come into contact with a civilization sufficiently powerful to corrupt without subjugating them; and though cultivators of the ground, they are more dreaded by caravans than any tribe from the coast to the lake region.   They are bounded eastward by the thin line of Moslems in the maritime regions, westward by the Wak'hutu, northward by the Kingani River, and on the south by the tribes of the Rufiji. The Wazaramo, or, as they often pronounce their own name, Wazalamo, claim connection with the semi-nomade Wakamba, who have, within the last few years, migrated to the northwest of Mombasah.   Their dialect, however, proves them to be congeners of the Wak'hutu, and distinct from the Wakamba.   As in East Africa generally, it is impossible to form the remotest idea of the number of families or of the total of population.   The Wazaramo number many sub-tribes, the principal of which are the Wákámbá and the Wáp'hangárá.

These negroids are able-bodied men, tall and straight, compared with the coast-clans, but they are inferior in development to most of the inner tribes. The complexion, as usual, varies greatly. The chiefs are often coal-black, and but few are of light color. This arises from the country being a slave-importer rather than exporter; and here, as among the Arabs, black skins are greatly preferred. The Mzaramo never circumcises, except when becoming a "mhájí," or Moslem convert; nor does this tribe generally tattoo, though some adorn the face with three long cicatrized cuts, like the Mashali of Mecca, extending down each cheek from the ear-lobes to the corners of the mouth. Their distinctive mark is the peculiarity of dressing their hair. The thick wool is plastered over with a cap-like coating of ochreish and micaceous clay, brought from the hills, and mixed to the consistency of honey with the oil of the sesamum or the castor-bean. The pomatum, before drying, is pulled out with the fingers to the ends of many little twists, which circle the head horizontally, and the mass is separated into a single or a double line of knobs, the upper being above and the lower below the ears, both look stiff and matted, as if affected with a bad plica polonica. The contrast between these garlands of small red dilberries and the glossy black skin is, however, effective. The clay, when dry, is washed out with great trouble by means of warm water—soap has yet to be invented—and by persevering combing with the fingers. Women wear the hair-thatch like men; there are, however, several styles. It is usually parted in the centre, from the crinal frontline to the nape of the neck, and allowed to grow in a single or double dense thatch, ridging the head breadthwise from ear to ear; this is colored or not colored, according to the wearer's taste. Some of the Wazaramo, again, train lumps of their wool to rise above the region of cautiousness, and very exactly simulate bears' ears. The face is usually lozenge-shaped, the eyes are somewhat oblique, the nose is flat and patulated, the lips tumid and everted, the jaw prognathous, and the beard, except in a few individuals, is scanty. The sebaceous odor of the skin among all these races is overpowering; emitted with the greatest effect during and after excitement either of mind or body, it connects the negroid with the negro, and separates him from the Somal, the Galla, and the Malagash. The expression of countenance is wild and staring, the features are coarse and harsh, the gait is loose and lounging; the Arab strut and the Indian swagger are unknown in East Africa. The Wazaramo tribe is rich in albinos; three were seen by the expedition in the course of a single day. They much resemble Europeans of the leucous complexion; the face is quite bald; the skin is rough, and easily wrinkles in long lines, marked by a deeper pink; the hair is short, sharp-curling, and colored like a silk-worm's cocoon, and the lips are red. The eyes have gray pupils and rosy "whites;" they appear very sensitive to light, and are puckered up so as to distort the countenance. The features are unusually plain, and the stature appears to range below the average. The people, who have no prejudice against them, call these leucœthiops Wazungu, "white men."

The Wazaramo tribe is wealthy enough to dress well: almost every man can afford a shukkah or loin-cloth of unbleached cotton, which he stains a dirty yellow, like the Indian gerua, with a clay dug in the subsoil. Their ornaments are extensive girdles and bead necklaces of various colors, white disks, made from the base of a sea-shell, and worn single on the forehead or in pairs at the neck. A massy ring of brass or zinc encircles the wrist. The decoration peculiar to the tribe, and common to both sexes, is the mgoweko, a tight collar or cravat, 1 to 1.50 inches broad, of red and yellow, white and black beads, with cross-bars of different colors at short intervals. Men never appear in public without an ostentatious display of arms. The usual weapons, when they can not procure muskets, are spears, bows, and arrows, the latter poisoned, and sime, or long knives like the Somali daggers, made by themselves with imported iron. The chiefs are generally seen in handsome attire; embroidered Surat caps bound with a tight snowy turban of a true African shape, which contrasts well with black skins and the short double-peaked beards below. The body-garment is a loin-cloth of showy Indian cotton or Arab check; some prefer the long shirt and the kizbao or waistcoat affected by the slaves at Zanzibar. The women are well dressed as the men—a circumstance rare in East Africa. Many of them have the tibia bowed in front by bearing heavy water-pots at too early an age; when not burdened they have a curious mincing gait; they never veil their faces, and they show no shame in the presence of strangers. The child is carried in a cloth at the back.

The habitations of the Wazaramo are far superior in shape and size to those of K'hutu, and, indeed, to any on this side of Unyamwezi. Their buildings generally resemble the humbler sort of English cow-house, or an Anglo-Indian bungalow. In poorer houses the outer walls are of holcus canes, rudely puddled; the better description are built of long and broad sheets of myombo and mkora bark, propped against strong uprights inside, and bound horizontally by split bamboos, tied outside with fibrous cord. The heavy pent-shaped roof, often provided with a double thatch of grass and reeds, projects eaves, which are high enough to admit a man without stooping; these are supported by a long cross-bar resting on perpendiculars, tree-trunks, barked and smoothed, forked above, and firmly planted in the ground. Along the outer marginal length of this veranda lies a border of large logs polished by long sittings. The interior is dark and windowless, and party-walls of stiff grass-cane divide it into several compartments.

The list of furniture comprises a dwarf cartel about 4 feet long by 16 inches broad, upon which even the married couple manages to make itself comfortable; a stool cut out of a single block, a huge wooden mortar, mtungi or black earthen pots, gourds, ladles of cocoanut, cast-off clothes, whetstones, weapons, nets, and in some places creels for fishing. Grain is ground upon an inclined slab of fine-grained granite or syenite, sometimes loose, at other times fixed in the ground with a mud plaster; the classical Eastern handmill is unknown in this part of Africa. The inner roof and its rafters, shining with a greasy soot, in wet weather admit drenching lines of leakage, and the only artifice applied to the flooring is the tread of the proprietors. The door is a close hurdle of parallel holcus straw bound to five or six cross-bars with strips of bark. In a village there will be from four to twelve "bungalows;" the rest are the normal haycock and beehive hut of Africa. Where enemies are numerous the settlements are palisaded; each has, moreover, but a single entrance, which is approached by a narrow alley of strong stockade, and is guarded by a thick planking that fits into a doorway large enough to admit cattle.

The Wazaramo are an ill-conditioned, noisy, boisterous, violent, and impracticable race. A few years ago they were the principal obstacle to Arab and other travelers entering into East Africa. But the seizure of Kaole and other settlements by the late Sayyid of Zanzibar has now given strangers a footing in the land. After tasting the sweets of gain, they have somewhat relented; but quarrels between them and the caravans are still frequent. The p'házi, or chief of the district, demands a certain amount of cloth for free passage from all merchants on their way to the interior; from those returning he takes cattle, jembe, or iron hoes, shokah or hatchets, in fact, whatever he can obtain. If not contented, his clansmen lie in ambush and discharge a few poisoned arrows at the trespassers: they never have attempted, like the Wagogo, to annihilate a caravan; in fact, the loss of one of their number causes a general panic. They have hitherto successfully resisted the little armies of touters that have almost desolated K'hutu, and they are frequently in hostilities with the coast settlements. The young men sometimes set out on secret plundering expeditions to Bagamoyo and Mbuamaji, and enter the houses at night by mining under the walls. The burghers attempt to defeat them by burying stones and large logs as a foundation, but in vain: their superior dexterity has originated a superstitious notion that they possess a peculiar "medicine," a magic spell called "ugumba," which throws the household into a deep trance. When a thief is caught *in flagrante delicto*, his head soon adorns a tall pole at the entrance of the settlement: it is not uncommon to see half a dozen bloody or bleached fragments of humanity collected in a single spot. When disposed to be friendly the Wazaramo will

act as porters to Arabs, but if a man die his load is at once confiscated by his relatives, who, however, insist upon receiving his
blood-money as if he had been slain in battle. Their behavior
to caravans in their own country depends upon the strangers'
strength; many trading bodies therefore unite into one before beginning the transit, and even then they are never without fear.

The Wazaramo chiefs are powerful only when their wealth or
personal qualities win the respect of their unruly republican subjects. There are no less than five orders in this hereditary mas-
ter-class. The p'hazi is the headman of the village, and the mwene goha is his principal counselor; under these are three ranks of
elders—the kinyongoni, the chúmá, and the káwámbwá. The
headman, unless exceptionally influential, must divide among
his "ministry" the black-mail extorted from travelers. The p'hazi
usually fills a small village with his wives and families; he has
also large estates, and he personally superintends the labor of his
slave-gangs. He can not sell his subjects except for two offenses
—ugoni, or adultery, and uchawi, or black magic. The latter
crime is usually punished by the stake; in some parts of the country the roadside shows at every few miles a heap or two of ashes,
with a few calcined and blackened human bones mixed with bits
of half-consumed charcoal, telling the tragedy that has been enact-
ed there. The prospect can not be contemplated without horror.
Here and there, close to the larger circles where the father and
mother have been burnt, a smaller heap shows that some wretched child has shared their terrible fate, lest growing up he should
follow in his parents' path. The power of conviction is wholly in
the hands of the mgángá or medicine-man, who administers an ordeal, called bága or kyápo, by boiling water. If the hand, after
being dipped, show any sign of lesion, the offense is proven, and
the sentence is instantly carried into execution.

Instinctively conscious of their moral wants, the Washenzi
throughout this portion of East Africa have organized certain customs which have grown to laws. The first is the sáre or brother
oath. Like the "manred" of Scotland, the "munh bola bhai" of
India, and similar fraternal institutions among most of the ancient
tribes of barbarians, in whom sociability is a passion, it tends to
reconcile separate interests between man and man, to modify the
feuds and discords of savage society, and, principally, to strength-
en those that need an alliance. In fact, it is a contrivance for
choosing relations instead of allowing Nature to force them upon
man, and the flimsiness of the tie between brothers born in polygamy has doubtless tended to perpetuate it. The ceremony,
which is confined to adults of the male sex, is differently performed in the different tribes. Among the Wazaramo, the Wazegura,
and the Wasagara, the two "brothers" sit on a hide face to face,
with legs outstretched to the front and overlapping one another;
their bows and arrows are placed across their thighs; while a third

person, waving a sword over their heads, vociferates curses against any one that may "break the brotherhood." A sheep is then slaughtered, and its flesh, or more often its heart, is brought roasted to the pair, who, having made with a dagger incisions in each other's breasts close to the pit of the stomach, eat a piece of meat smeared with the blood. Among the Wanyamwezi and the Wajiji the cut is made below the left ribs or above the knee. Each man receives in a leaf his brother's blood, which, mixed with oil or butter, he rubs into his own wound. An exchange of small presents generally concludes the rite. It is a strong tie, as all men believe that death or slavery would follow its infraction. The Arabs, to whom the tasting of blood is unlawful, usually perform it by proxy. The slave "fundi," or fattori, of the caravans, become brothers, even with the Washenzi, whenever they expect an opportunity of utilizing the relationship.

The second custom is more peculiar. The East African dares not appropriate an article found upon the road, especially if he suspect that it belongs to a fellow-tribeman. He believes that a "kigámbo," an unexpected calamity, slavery or death, would follow the breach of this custom. At Zungomero, a watch, belonging to the expedition, was picked up by the country people in the jungle, and was punctually returned, well wrapped round with grass and leaves. But subsequent experience makes the traveler regret that the superstition is not of a somewhat more catholic and comprehensive character.

The religion of the East African will be treated of in a future page. The Wazaramo, like their congeners, are as little troubled with ceremony as with belief. In things spiritual as in things temporal they listen to but one voice, that of "ádá," or custom. The most offensive scoffer or skeptic in Europe is not regarded with more abomination than the man who in these lands would attempt to touch a jot or tittle of ádá.

There are no ceremonies on birth-occasions and no purification of women among these people. In the case of abortion or of a still-born child they say, "He hath returned," that is to say, to home in earth. When the mother perishes in childbirth, the parents claim a certain sum from "the man that killed their daughter." Neither on the continent nor at Zanzibar do they bind with cloth the head of the new-born babe. Twins, here called wápáchá, and, by the Arabs of Zanzibar, shukúl (شكرل), are usually sold, or exposed in the jungle, as among the Ibos of West Africa. If the child die, an animal is killed for a general feast, and in some tribes the mother does a kind of penance. Seated outside the village, she is smeared with fat and flour, and exposed to the derision of people who surround her, hooting and mocking with offensive jests and gestures. To guard against this calamity, the Wazaramo and other tribes are in the habit of vowing that the babe shall not be shaved till manhood, and the mother wears a number of talismans—bits of wood tied with a thong of snake's skin—round her neck, and beads of different shapes round her head. When carrying her offspring, which she rarely leaves alone, she bears in her hand what is technically called a kirangozi, a "guide" or "guardian," in the form of two sticks a few inches in length, bound with bands of parti-colored beads. This article, made up by the mgángá or medicine-man, is placed at night under the child's head, and is carried about till it has passed the first stage of life. The kirangozi is intended to guard the treasure against the malevolent spirits of the dead. That almost universal superstition, the Evil Eye, though an article of faith among the Arabs, the Wasawahili, and the Wamrima, is unknown to the inner heathen.

A name is given to the child without other celebration than a debauch with pombe: this will sometimes occur at the birth of a male, when he is wanted. The East Africans, having few national prejudices, are fond of calling their children after Arabs and other strangers; they will even pay a sheep for the loan of a merchant's name. There must be many hundred Sayyid Saids and Sayyid Majids now in the country; and as during the eighteen months' peregrination of the East African Expedition every child born on and near the great trunk-line was called Muzungu, the "white," the Englishman has also left his mark in the land. The period of ablactation, as in South Africa, is prolonged to the second or third year. May this account, in part, for the healthiness of the young, and the almost total absence of debility and deformity? Indeed, the nearest approach to the latter is the unsightly protrusion of the umbilical region, sometimes to the extent of several inches, owing to ignorance of proper treatment; but, though conspicuous in childhood, it disappears after puberty. Women retain the power of suckling their children to a late age, even when they appear withered grandams. Until the child can walk without danger, it is carried by the mother, not on the hip, as in Asia, but on the bare back for warmth, a sheet or skin being passed over it and fastened at the parent's breast. Even in infancy it clings like a young simiad, and the peculiar formation of the African race renders the position easier by providing a kind of seat upon which it subsides; the only part of the body exposed to view is the little cocoanut head, with the small, round, beady black eyes in a state of everlasting stare. Finally, the "kigogo," or child who cuts the two upper incisors before the lower, is either put to death, or is given away or sold to the slave-merchant, under the impression that it will bring disease, calamity, and death into the household. The Wasawahili and the Zanzibar Arabs have the same impressions: the former kill the child; the latter, after a khitmah or perlection of the Koran, make it swear, by nodding its head, if unable to articulate, that it will not injure those about it. Even in Europe, it may be remembered, the old prejudice against children born with teeth is not wholly forgotten.

Among the Wazaramo there is no limitation to the number of wives, except the expense of wedding and the difficulty of supporting a large establishment. Divorce is signified by presenting to the wife a piece of holcus-cane; if a sensible woman she at once leaves the house, and, if not, she is forced to leave. There is no more romance in the affair even before marriage than in buying a goat. The marriageable youth sends a friend to propose to the father: if the latter consents, his first step is, not to consult his daughter—such a proceeding would be deemed the act of a madman—but to secure for himself as many cloths as possible, from six to twelve, or even more, besides a preliminary present which goes by the name of kiremba (kilemba), his "turban." This, however, is a kind of settlement which is demanded back if the wife die without issue; but if she bear children, it is preserved for them by their grand-parents. After the father the mother puts in her claim in behalf of the daughter; she requires a kondáví, or broad parti-colored band of beads worn round the waist and next the skin; her mukájyá or loin-cloth, and her wereko, or sheet in which the child is borne upon the back. In the interior the settlement is made in live-stock, varying from a few goats to a dozen cows. This weighty point duly determined, the husband leads his wife to his own home, an event celebrated by drumming, dancing, and extensive drunkenness. The children born in wedlock belong to the father.

When a man or a woman is at the point of death, the friends assemble, and the softer sex sometimes sings, howls, and weeps: the departing is allowed to depart life upon the kitanda, or cartel. There is, however, little demonstrative sorrow among these people, and, having the utmost dread of disembodied spirits, all are anxious to get rid of the corpse and its appertainings. The Wazaramo, more civilized than their neighbors, bury their dead stretched out and in the dress worn during life: their graves have already been described.

The "industry" of Usaramo will occupy but few sentences. Before the great rains of the year set in the land must be weeded, and scratches must be made with a hoe for the reception of seed. The wet season ushers in the period for copal-digging: the proceeds are either sold to traveling traders, or are carried down to the coast in mákándá—mat sacks—of light weight, and are sold to the Banyans. Bargaining and huckstering, cheapening and chaffering, are ever the African's highest intellectual enjoyments, and he does not fail to stretch them to their utmost limits. After the autumnal rains during the azyab, or the northeast monsoon, the grass is fired, when the men seizing their bows, arrows, and spears, indiscriminately slaughter beast and bird—an operation which, yearly repeated, accounts in part for the scarcity of animal life so remarkable in this animal's paradise. When all trades fail, the Mzaramo repairs to the coast, where, despite his bad name, he usually finds employment as a laborer.

Next in order to the maritime Wazaramo are the Wak'hutu, to whom many of the observations upon the subject of their more powerful neighbors equally apply. Their territory extends from the Mgeta River to the mountains of Usagara, and in breadth from the Dut'humi Highlands to the Rufiji River.

The Wak'hutu are physically, and, apparently, mentally a race inferior to the Wazaramo; they are very dark, and bear other marks of a degradation effected by pernicious climatory conditions. They have no peculiar tattoo, although individuals raise complicated patterns in small cicatrices upon their breasts. The popular head-dress is the clay coating of the Wazaramo, of somewhat modified dimensions; and some of them, who are possibly derived from the Wahiao and other southern clans, have a practice—exceptional in these latitudes—of chipping their incisors to sharp points, which imitate well enough the armature of the reptilia. Their eyes are bleared and red with perpetual intoxication, and they seem to have no amusements but dancing and singing through half the night. None but the wealthier can afford to wear cloth; the substitute is a kilt of the calabash fibre, attached by a cord of the same material to the waist. In women it often narrows to a span, and would be inadequate to the purposes of decency were it not assisted by an under-clothing of softened goat-skin; this and a square of leather upon the bosom, which, however, is often omitted, compose the dress of the multitude. The ornaments are like those of the Wazaramo, but by no means so numerous. The Wak'hutu live poorly, and, having no ghee, are contented with the oil of the sesamum and the castor-bean, with their holcus porridge. The rivers supply them with the usual mud-fish; at times they kill game. Their sheep, goats, and poultry they reserve for barter on the coast; and, though bees swarm throughout the land, and even enter the villages, they will not take the trouble to make hives.

As on the Mrima, the proportion of chiefs to subjects seems to increase in the inverse ratio of what is required. Every district in K'hutu has its p'hazi or headman, with his minister the mwene goha, and inferior chiefs, the chándumé, the muwinge, and the mbárá. These men live chiefly upon the produce of their fields, which they sell to caravans; they are too abject and timid to insist upon the black-mail which has caused so many skirmishes in Uzaramo; and the only use that they make of their power is to tyrannize over their villages, and occasionally to organize a little kidnapping. With the aid of slavery and black magic they render their subjects' lives as precarious as they well can: no one, especially in old age, is safe from being burned at a day's notice. They are civil to strangers, but wholly unable to mediate between them and the tribe. The Wak'hutu have been used as porters, but they have proved so treacherous and so determined to desert that no man will trust them in a land where prepayment is the first condition of an agreement. Property among them is insecure: a man has always a vested right in his sister's children, and when he dies his brothers and relations carefully plunder his widow and orphans.

The dirty, slovenly villages of the Wak'hutu are an index of the character of the people. Unlike the comfortable cottages of the coast, and the roomy abodes of the Wazaramo, the settlements of the Wak'hutu are composed of a few straggling hovels of the humblest description, with doors little higher than an English pigsty, and eaves so low that a man can not enter them except on all fours. In shape they differ, some being simple cones, others like European haystacks, and others like our old straw beehives. The common hut is a circle from 12 to 25 feet in diameter; those belonging to the chiefs are sometimes of considerable size, and the first part of the erection is a cylindrical framework composed of tall stakes, or the rough trunks of young trees, interwoven with parallel and concentric rings of flexible twigs and withies, which are coated inside and outside with puddle of red or gray clay. In some a second circle of wall is built round the inner cylinder, thus forming one house within the other. The roof, subsequently added, is of sticks and wattles, and the weight rests chiefly upon a central tree. It has eaves-like projections, forming a narrow veranda, edged with horizontal bars which rest upon forked uprights. Over the sticks interwoven with the frame, thick grass or palm-fronds are thrown, and the whole is covered with a coat of thatch tied on with strips of tree bark. During the first few minutes of heavy rain, this roofing, shrunk by the parching suns, admits water enough to patch the interior with mud. The furniture of the cottages is like that of the Wazaramo; and the few square feet which compose the area are divided by screens of wattle into dark pigeon-holes, used as stores, kitchen, and sleeping-rooms. A thick field of high grass is allowed to grow in the neighborhood of each village, to baffle pursuers in case of need : and some cottages are provided with double doorways for easier flight. In the middle of the settlement there is usually a tall tree, under which the men lounge upon cots scarcely large enough for an English child; and where the slaves, wrangling and laughing, husk their holcus in huge wooden mortars. These villages can scarcely be called permanent: even the death of a chief causes them to be abandoned, and in a few months long grass waves over the circlets of charred stakes and straw.

The only sub-tribe of the Wak'hutu which deserves notice is the Waziráhá, who inhabit the low grounds below the Mabruki Pass, in the first parallel of the Usagara Mountains. They are remarkable only for having beards somewhat better developed than in the other Eastern races: in sickly appearance they resemble their congeners.

Remain for consideration the Wadoe and the Wazegura. The proper habitat of the Wadoe is between the Watondwe or the tribes of Saadani, on the littoral, and the Wak'hwere, near K'hutu, on the west; their northern frontier is the land of the Wazegura, and their southern the Gama and the Kingani Rivers. Their country, irrigated by the waters of the Gama, is plentiful in grain, though wanting in cattle; they export to Zanzibar sorghum and maize, with a little of the chakazi or unripe copal.

The Wadoe once formed a powerful tribe, and were the terror of their neighbors. Their force was first broken by the Wakamba, who, however, so weakened themselves that they were compelled to emigrate in mass from the country, and have now fixed themselves in a region about 14 marches to the northwest of Mombasah, which appears to have been anciently called that of the Meremongao. During this struggle the Wadoe either began or, what is more likely, renewed a practice which has made their name terrible even in African ears. Fearing defeat from the Wakamba, they proceeded, in presence of the foe, to roast and devour slices from the bodies of the fallen. The manœuvre was successful; the Wakamba could dare to die, but they could not face the idea of becoming food. Presently, when the Wazegura had armed themselves with muskets, and the people of Whinde had organized their large plundering excursions, the Wadoe lost all power. About ten years ago Juma Mfumbi, the late Diwan of Saadani, exacted tribute from them, and after his death his sons succeeded to it. In 1857, broken by a famine of long continuance, many Wadoe fled to the south of the Kingani River, and obtained from the Wazaramo lands near Sagesera and Dege la Mhora.

The Wadoe differ greatly in color and in form. Some are tall, well-made, and light-complexioned negroids, others are almost black. Their distinctive mark—in women as well as men—is a pair of long cuts down both cheeks, from the temple to the jaw; they also frequently chip away the two inner sides of the upper central incisors, leaving a small chevron-shaped hole. This, however, is practiced almost throughout the country. They are wild in appearance, and dress in softened skins, stained yellow with the bark and flowers (?) of the mimosa. Their arms are a large hide-shield, spears, bows, and arrows, shokah, or the little battle-axe, the sime-knife, and the rungu or knobstick. They are said still to drink out of human skulls, which are not polished or prepared in any way for the purpose. The principal chief is termed mweme: his privy councilors are called mákungá (?), and the elders m'áná miráo (?). The great headmen are buried almost naked, but retaining their bead-ornaments, sitting in a shallow pit, so that the forefinger can project above the ground. With each

man are interred alive a male and a female slave, the former holding a mundu, or bill-hook, wherewith to cut fuel for his lord in the
cold death-world, and the latter, who is seated upon a little stool,
supports his head in her lap. This custom has been abolished by
some of the tribes: according to the Arabs, a dog is now buried
in lieu of the slaves. The subdivisions of the Wadoe are numerous and unimportant.

The Wazegura, who do not inhabit this line of road, require
some allusion, in consequence of the conspicuous part which they
have played in the evil drama of African life. They occupy the
lands south of the Pangani River to the Cape of Utondwe, and
they extend westward as far as the hills of Nguru. Originally a
peaceful tribe, they have been rendered terrible by the possession
of fire-arms; and their chiefs have now collected large stores of
gunpowder, used only to kidnap and capture the weaker wretches
within their reach. They thus supply the market of Zanzibar
with slaves, and this practice is not of yesterday. About twenty
years ago the Wazegura serfs upon the island, who had been
cheaply bought during a famine for a few measures of grain, rose
against their Arab masters, retired into the jungle, and, re-enforced
by malefactors and malcontents, began a servile war, which raged
with the greatest fury for six months, when the governor, Ahmed
bin Sayf, maternal uncle to his highness the late Sayyid Said,
brought in a body of mercenaries from Hazramaut, and broke the
force of this jacquerie by setting a price upon their heads, and by
giving the captives as prizes to the captors. The exploits of Kisabengo, the Mzegura, have already been alluded to. The Arab
merchants of Unyanyembe declare that the road will never be
safe until that person's head adorns a pole: they speak with bitterness of heart, for he exacts an unconscionable " black-mail."

The Wazegura are, in point of polity, an exception to the rule
of East Africa: instead of owning hereditary sultans, they obey
the loudest tongue, the most open hand, and the sharpest spear.
This tends practically to cause a perpetual blood-feud, and to raise
up a number of petty chiefs, who, aspiring to higher positions,
must distinguish themselves by bloodshed, and must acquire
wealth in weapons, especially fire-arms, the great title to superiority, by slave-dealing. The only occasion when they combine is
an opportunity of successful attack upon some unguarded neighbor. Briefly, the Wazegura have become an irreclaimable race,
and such they will remain until compelled to make a livelihood
by honest industry.

CHAPTER V.

HALT AT ZUNGOMERO, AND FORMATION OF THE CARAVAN.

I HALTED to collect carriage and to await the arrival of the twenty-two promised porters for about a fortnight at that hot-bed of pestilence, Zungomero, where we nearly found "wet graves." Our only lodging was under the closed eaves of a hut built African fashion, one abode within the other. The roof was a sieve, the walls were systems of chinks, and the floor was a sheet of mud. Outside the rain poured pertinaciously, as if K'hutu had been situated in the "black north" of Hibernia; the periodical S. and S.W. winds were raw and chilling, the gigantic vegetation was sopped to decay, and the tangled bank of the Mgeta River, lying within pistol-shot of our hovels, added its quotum of miasma. The hardships of a march in inclement weather had taken effect upon the Baloch guard: expecting every thing to be done for them, they endured seven days of wet and wind before they could find energy to build a shed, and they became almost mutinous because left to make shelter for themselves. They stole the poultry of the villagers like gipsies, they quarreled violently with the slaves, they foully abused their temporal superior, Said bin Salim, and three of the thirteen were accused of grossly insulting the women of the Wak'hutu. The latter charge, after due investigation, was "not proven:" we had resolved, in case of its being brought home, severely to flog the culprits or to turn them out of camp.

On the 27th July, Sayf bin Salim returned to Dut'humi with his gang of thirty slaves, who also had distinguished themselves by laying violent hands on sheep, goats, and hens. Their patroon had offered to carry our baggage half way over the mountains to Ugogo, for a sum of sixty dollars; thinking his conditions exorbitant, I stipulated for conveyance the whole way. He refused, declaring that he was about to organize another journey up-country. I doubted his assertion, as he was known to have audaciously defrauded Musa Mzuri, an Indian merchant, who had intrusted him with a large venture of ivory at Kazeh: yet he spoke truth; nearly a year afterward we met him on his march to the "Sea of Ujiji." During his visit he had begged for drugs, tea, coffee, sugar, spices, every thing, but the stores were already far wasted by the improvidence of the Goanese, who seemed to think that they were living in the vicinity of a bazar. To punish me for not engaging his gang, he caused the desertion of nine porters hired at Dut'humi, by declaring that I was bearing them into slavery. As

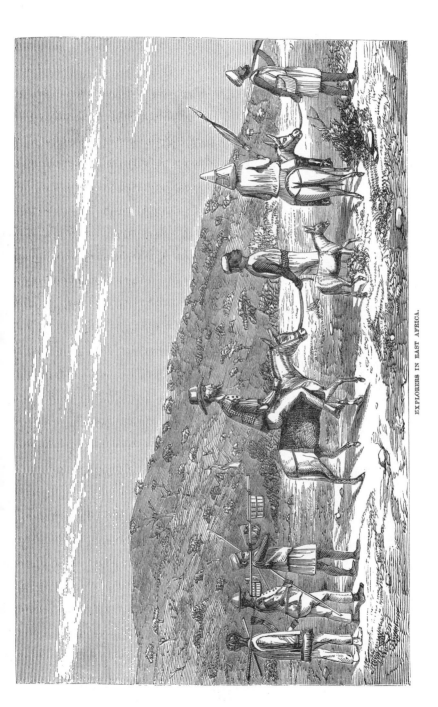

EXPLORERS IN EAST AFRICA.

they carried off, in addition to half their pay, sundry sundries and Muinyi Wazira's sword, I sent three slave-musketeers to recover the stolen goods by force if necessary. With respect to the cloth, Sayf bin Salim wrote back to say that as I could well afford the loss of a few "domestics," he would not compel the fugitives to restore it: at the same time that he did himself the honor to return the sword, which I might want. This man proved himself the sole "base exception" to the hospitality and the courteousness of the Omani Arabs. I forwarded an official complaint to H. M. the Sayyid Majid, but the arm of Zanzibar has not yet reached K'hutu.

At Zungomero five fresh porters were engaged, making up the whole party to a total of 132 souls. They were drafted into the men of Muinyi Wazira, whose open indulgence in stingo had made his society at meals distasteful to Moslem sticklers for propriety. He was an able interpreter, speaking five African dialects, which is not, however, in these lands a remarkable feat, and when sober, he did at first the work of three men. But linguists are a dangerous race, as the annals of old India prove—I doubt a bilingual Eastern man, and if he can speak three languages I do not doubt him at all. Moreover, true to his semi-servile breed—his dam was a Mzaramo slave, and his sire a half-caste Wawahili—he began well and he finished badly. His deep undying fondness for pombe or holcus beer kept him in alternate states of maudlin apathy or of violent pugnacity. He had incurred heavy debts upon the coast. After his arrival at Unyamwezi, letters were sent urging upon the Arabs his instant arrest, but fortunately for him the bailiff and jailer are not, as the venerable saying declares the schoolmaster to be, abroad. Muinyi Wazira, however, did not sight the Sea of Ujiji in my service, and his five messmates, who each received 15 dollars' worth of cloth for the journey thither and back, were not more fortunate.

Before marching from Zungomero into the mountains I will order, for the reader's inspection, a muster of the party, and enlist his sympathies in behalf of the unhappy being who had to lead it.

Said bin Salim may pass on: he has been described in Blackwood (February, 1858), and he scarcely deserves a second notice. He is followed by his four slaves, including the boy Faraj, who will presently desert, and without including his active wife, the Lady Halimah. That young person's pug-dog countenance and bulky charms seem to engross every thought not appropriated to himself. One day, however, my ears detect the loud voice of wail proceeding from the Lady Halimah, accompanying methinks the vigorous performance of a stick; the peccadillo was—but I eschew scandal and request the lady to advance.

My companion's gun-carrier, Seedy Mubarak Bombay, a negro from Uhiao, has twice been sketched in Blackwood (March, 1858, and September, 1859); he also requires no further celebrity. My henchman, Muinyi Mabruki, had been selected by his fellow-tribe-man Bombay at Zanzibar; he was the slave of an Arab shaykh, who willingly let him for the sum of five dollars per mensem. Mabruki is the type of the bull-headed negro, low-browed, pig-eyed, pug-nosed, and provided by nature with that breadth and power, that massiveness and muscularity of jaw, which character-ize the most voracious carnivors. He is at once the ugliest and the vainest of the party; his attention to his toilette knows no limit. His temper is execrable, even in extremes; now wild with spirits, then dogged, depressed, and surly, then fierce and violent. He is the most unhandy of men, he spoils every thing intrusted to him, and presently he will be forbidden to engage in any pur-suit beyond ass-leading and tent-pitching. These worthies com-menced well. They excited our admiration by braving noon-day suns, and by snoring heavily through the rawest night with noth-ing to warm them but a few smouldering embers. In an evil hour compassion-touched, I threw over their shoulders a pair of English blankets, which in the shortest time completely demoral-ized them. They learned to lie abed o' mornings, and when call-ed up their shrugged shoulders and shrinking forms were wrap-ped tightly round, lest the breath of dawn should visit them too roughly. Idleness marked them for her own: messmates and sworn brothers, they made at the halt huts out of hail, lest they should be called to do work. As a rule, however, Englishmen have the art of spoiling Eastern servants; we begin with the ut-most stretch of exertion, and we expect this high-pressure system to last. Of course the men's energies are soon exhausted, their indolence and apathy contrast with their former activity; we con-ceive dislikes to them, and we end by dismissing them. This, however, was not the case with Bombay and Mabruki. They returned with us to Zanzibar, and we parted à l'aimable, especial-ly with the former, who, after a somewhat protracted fit of the "blue devils," became once more, what he before had been, a rara avis in the lands, an active servant and an honest man.

Regard for the Indian perusers of these pages, who know by experience how "banal" a character is the half-caste Oriental Port-uguese, prevents my offering any thing but a sketch of Valentine A. and Gaetano B. I had hired them at Bombay for Co.'s rs. 20 per mensem, besides board and lodging. Scions of that half Pa-riah race which yearly issues from Goa, Daman, and Diu to gather rupees as "cook-boys," dry-nurses, and "buttrels," in wealthy British India, the hybrids had their faults: a pride of caste, and a contempt for Turks and heathen, heretics and infidels, which often brought them to grief; a fondness for acting triton among the minnows; a certain disregard for the seventh commandment, in the matter of cloth and clothes, medicines and provisions; a con-stitutional repugnance to "Signior Sooth;" a wastefulness of other men's goods and a peculiar tenacity of their own; a deficiency of bodily strength and constitutional vigor; a voracity which induced indigestion once a day; and, finally, a habit of frequent phlebotomy which, deferred, made them sick. They had also their merits. Valentine was a good specimen of the neat-handed and ready-witted Indian; in the shortest time he learned to talk Kisawahili sufficiently for his own purposes, and to read a chronometer and thermometer sufficiently for ours; he had, however, one blemish, an addiction to "fudging," which rendered the severest overseeing necessary. A "Davy do a' things," he was as clever at sewing a coat as at cooking a curry. Gaetano had a curious kind of tenderness when acting nurse, and, wonderful to relate, an utter disregard for danger: he would return alone through a night-march of jungle to fetch his forgotten keys, and would throw himself into an excited mob of natives with a fearlessness which, contrasted with his weakly body, never failed to turn their wrath into merriment. He suffered severely from the secondaries of fever, which, in his case, as in his master's, assumed a cerebral form. At Msene he was seized with fits resembling epilepsy; and as he seemed every month to become more addle-headed and scatter-brained, more dirty and untidy, more wasteful and forgetful, more loth to work without compulsion, and more prone to start and feed the fire with ghee when it was the scarcest of luxuries, I could not but attribute many of his delinquencies to disease.

The Baloch are now to appear. My little party were servants of his highness the Sayyd Majid of Zanzibar, who had detached them as an escort upon the usual "deputation-allowance" of ten dollars per mensem. They had received the command of their master to accompany me wherever I might please to march, and they had been rendered responsible to him for the safety of my person and property. As has been mentioned, Lieut. Colonel Hamerton had advanced to them before departure a small sum for outfit, and had promised them, on condition of good conduct, an ample reward on the part of H. M.'s government after return to Zanzibar. These men were armed with the usual matchlock, the Cutch sabre—one or two had Damascus blades—the Indian hide-targe, decorated with its usual tinsel, the long khanjar or dagger, extra matches, flints and steels, and toshdan, or ammunition pouches, sensibly distributed about their persons.

The Jemadar Mallok led from Zanzibar seven warriors of fame, yclept severally, Mohammed, Shahdad, Ismail, Belok, Abdullah, Darwaysh, and the Seedy Jelai; at Kaole he persuaded to follow his fortunes Khudabakhsh, Musa, Gul Mohammed, Riza, and Hudul, a tailor-boy.

The Jemadar Mallok is a monocular, and the Sanscrit proverb declares:

> "Rare a kana (one-eyed man) is a good man and sound,
> Rare a layde gay will be faithful found."

Mallok is no exception to this rule of the "kana." He is a man with fine Italian features, somewhat disfigured by the small-pox; but his one eye never looks you "in the face," and there is an expression about the mouth which forbids implicit trust in his honesty. He proclaims himself to be somewhat fonder of fighting than of feeding, yet suspicious circumstances led me to believe that he was one of those whom the Arabs describe as "first at the banquet, and last at the brawl." He began with a display of zeal and activity which died young; he lapsed, through grumbling and discontent, into open insubordination as we progressed westward, or from home; he became submissive and somewhat servile as we returned to the coast, and when he took leave of me, he shed a flood of crocodile's tears.

Mohammed is the rish safid, or gray-beard of the caravan, and without a gray-beard no Eastern caravan considers itself *en règle*. Of these indispensable veterans I had two specimens; but of what use they were, except to teach hot youth the cold caution of eld, I never could divine—*vieux soldat, vielle bête*. In the civilized regiment age is not venerable in the private, as every gray hair is a proof that he has not merited or has forfeited promotion; so in the East, where there is a paucity of competitors in the race of fortune, the rish safid of humble fortune may be safely set down as a fool or a foolish knave, and though his escort is sought, he generally proves himself to be no better than he should have been.

Mohammed's body is apparently hard as a rock, his mind is soft as putty, and his comrades, disappointed in their hopes of finding brains behind those wrinkles, derisively compare him to a rotten walnut, and say before his face, "What! gray hairs and no wits?" He has invested the fifteen dollars advanced to him as outfit by Lieut. Colonel Hamerton in a slave-boy, whom presently he will exchange for a slave-girl, despite all the innuendoes of his friends. He was at first a manner of peace-maker, but soon my refusal to enlist and pay his slave as a hired porter acted like Ithuriel's spear. This veteran of fractious temper and miserly habits ended, in a question of stinted rations, by drawing his sabre upon and cutting at his jemadar; an offense which I was compelled to visit with a bastinado, inflicted out of the sight of man by the hand of Khudabakhsh.

Shahdad is the chelebi of the party—the fast young man. He is decidedly not handsome. A figure short and *trapu*, a retrussed nose, small pigs' eyes, a beard like a blackberry-bush, and a crop of hair which, projecting its wiry waves in a deep long curtain from beneath a diminutive scarlet fez, makes his head appear top-heavy. Yet he does sad havoc among female hearts by means of his zeze or guitar, half a gourd with an arm to which is attached a single string, and by his lively accompaniment in a squeaking falsetto, which is here as fascinating and emollient to the sex as

ever was the organ of Rubini in Europe. During a lengthened
sojourn at Bombay he has enlarged his mind by the acquisition
of the Hindoostani tongue and of Indian trickery. He is almost
the only Eastern whom I remember that abused the poor letter
H like a thorough-bred Londoner. His familiarity with Anglo-
Europeans, and his experience touching the facility of gulling
them, has induced in him a certain proclivity for peculation,
grumbling, and mutiny. His brother—or rather cousin, for in
these lands all fellow-tribesmen are brethren—"Ismail" is a confirmed invalid, a man with a "broken mouth," deeply-sunken
cheeks, and emaciated frame, who, though earnestly solicited to return eastward, will persist in accompanying the party till he falls
a victim to a chronic malady in Unyamwezi.

Belok is our snob; a youth of servile origin, with coarse features, wide mouth, everted lips, and a pert, or rather an impudent
expression of countenance, which, acting as index to his troublesome character, at once prejudices the physiognomist against him.
Belok's comrades have reason to quote the Arab saw, "Defend
me from the beggar become wealthy, and from the slave become
a freeman!" He has invested his advance of salary in a youth;
and the latter serves and works for the rest of the mess, who must
patiently and passively endure the insolence of the master for fear
of losing the offices of the man. After the fashion of a certain
sort of fools, he applies the whole of his modicum of wit to mis-
chief-making, and he succeeds admirably where better men, whose
thoughts attempt a wider range, would fail. By his exertions the
Baloch became, in point of social intercourse, not unlike the passengers of a ship bound on a long voyage: after the first month
the society divides itself into two separate and adverse cliques;
after the second it breaks up into little knots; and after the third
it is a checker-work of pairs and solitaires. Arrived at the "Pond
of Ugogo," I was compelled to address an official letter to Zanzibar, requesting the recall of Belok and his coadjutor in mischief,
Khudabakhsh.

Abdullah is the type of the respectable, in fact, of the good
young man. It is really pathetic to hear him recount, with ac-
cents broken by emotion, the "tale full of waters of the eye"—the
parting of an only son, who was led away to an African grave,
from the aged widow his mamma; to listen to her excellent advice, and to his no less excellent resolves. He is capable of calling his bride elect, were such article a subject ever to be mentioned among Moslems, "his choicest blessing." With an edifying
mingling of piety and discipline, he never neglects the opportunity of standing in prayer behind the Jemadar Mallok, whose elevation to a superior grade—*honneur oblige!*—has compelled him to
rub up a superficial acquaintance with the forms of devotion.
Virtue in the abstract I revere; in the concrete I sometimes suspect. The good young man soon justified this suspicion by re-

peatedly applying to Said bin Salim for beads, in my name, which he converted to his own purposes.

Of Darwaysh little need be said. He is a youth about twenty-two years old, with a bulging brow, a pair of ferret-eyes, a "peaky" nose, a thin chin; in fact, with a face the quintessence of curiosity. He is the "brother"—that is to say, the spy—of the jemadar, and his principal peculiarity is a repugnance to obeying an order because it is an order. With this individual I had at first many a passage of words. Presently prostrated in body and mind by severe disease, he obtained relief from European drugs; and from that time until the end of the journey, he conducted himself with a certain stiffness and decorum which contrasted pleasantly enough with the exceeding "bounce" of his earlier career.

The Seedy Jelai calls himself a Baloch, though palpably the veriest descendant of Ham. He resents with asperity the name of "nigger," or "nig"—Jupiter Tonans has heard of the offensive dissyllable, which was a household word before the days of the Indian mutiny, but has he heard of the more offensive monosyllable which was forced upon the abbreviating Anglo-Saxon by the fatal necessity of requiring to repeat the word so frequently? Jelai clothes his long lank legs—cucumber-shinned and bony-kneed—in calico tights, which display the full deformity of those members; and taking a pride in the length of his mustaches, which distinguishes him from his African-born brethren, he twists them *en croc* like a hidalgo in the days of Gil Blas. The Seedy, judging from analogy, ought to be brave, but he is not. On the occasion of alarm in the mountains of Usagara, he privily proposed to his comrades to "bolt" and leave us. Moreover, on the "Sea of Ujiji," where he was chosen as an escort, he ignobly deserted me.

Khudabakhsh was formed by nature to be the best man of the party; he has transformed himself into the worst. A man of broad and stalwart frame, with stern countenance, and a quietness of demeanor which usually argues *sang-froid* and persistency, his presence is in all points soldier-like and prepossessing. But his temper is unmanageable: he enters into a quarrel when certain of discomfiture; he is utterly reckless—on one occasion he amused himself by blowing a charge of gunpowder into the calves of African warriors who were dancing in front of him;—and lastly, his innate propensity for backbiting, intrigue, and opposition to all authority, renders him a dangerous member of the expedition. He herds with Belok, whose tastes lie in the same line: he is the head and front of all mischief, and presently his presence will become insupportable.

Musa, a tall, gaunt, and dark-brown old man, is the assistant rish safid, or gray-beard; in fact, the complement of "Gray-beard Mohammed." After a residence of twenty years at Mombasah, he has clean forgotten Persian; he speaks only a debased Mekrani dialect, and the Kisawahili, which, as usual with his tribe, he prefers. An old soldier, he compensates for want of youth and vigor by artfulness; an old traveler—nothing better distinguishes in these lands the veteran of the road from the griffin or greenhorn, than the careful and systematic consideration of his comforts—he carries the lightest matchlock, he starts in the cool of the morning, he presses forward to secure the best quarters, and throughout he thinks only of himself. His character has a want of wrath, which, despite his white hairs, causes him to be little regarded. Gray-beard Mohammed is considered a fool; Gray-beard Musa, an old woman. Yet he troubles himself little about the opinions of his fellows; he looks well after his morning and evening meals, his ghee, his pipe, and his sleeping-mat; and knowing that he will last out all the novices, with enviable philosophy he casts ambition to the winds.

Gul Mohammed is the most civilized man of the party. He has straight and handsome features, of the old Grecian type, a reddish-brown skin—the skin by excellence—and a Central-Asian beard of largest dimensions. His mind is as civilized as his body; he is an adept after the fashion of his tribe, in divinity especially, in medicine and natural history; and when landing at Marka, he actually took the trouble to visit, for curiosity, the Juba River. Unfortunately, "Gul Mohammed" is a mixture of Baloch mountaineer-blood with the Sindhian of the plain, and the cross is, throughout the East, renowned for representing the worst points of both progenitors. Gul Mohammed is brave and treacherous, fair-spoken and detractive, honorable and dishonest, good-tempered and bad-hearted.

Of the Baloch remain Riza, and Hudul, the tailor-boy: the former is a kind of Darwaysh, utterly insignificant, but by no means so disagreeable as his fellows: the only marking corporeal peculiarity of the latter is a deficiency of skin; his mouth appears ever open, and his teeth resemble those of an old rabbit. His mental organization has its *petite pointe*, its little twist; he is under the constant delusion that those who speak in unknown tongues are employed specially in abusing him. His first complaint was against the Goanese: as he could not understand a word of their language, it was dismissed with some derision; he then charged me to his comrades with his normal grievance, and in due time he felt aggrieved by my companion.

A proper regard to precedence induces me now to marshal the "sons of Ramji," who acted as interpreters, guides, and war-men. They were armed with the old "Tower-musket," which, loaded with nearly an ounce of powder, they never allowed to quit the hand, and with those antiquated German cavalry sabres which find their way over all the East: their accoutrements were small leathern boxes, strapped to the waist, and huge cow-horns for ammunition. The most part called themselves muinyi (master), the title of an African freeman, because they had been received in pawn by the Banyan Ramji from their parents or uncles, who had forgotten to redeem the pledge, and they still claimed the honor of noble birth. Of these there were eight men under their mtu mku, or chief man, Kidogo—Anglice, Mr. Little. Kidogo had preceded the expedition, escorting the detachment of thirty-six Wanyamwezi porters to Zungomero, and he possessed great influence over his brother slaves, who all seemed to admire and to be proud of him. He was by no means a common man. "Natione magis quam ratione barbarus;" he had a fixed and obstinate determination: among these puerile, futile African souls he was exceptional as "a sage Sciote or a green horse." His point of honor consisted in the resolve that his words should be held as Median laws, and he had, as the Africans say, a "large head," namely, abundant self-esteem, that blessed quality which makes man independent of his fellows. Muinyi Kidogo is a short, thin, coal-black person, with a something arguing gentle blood in his tribe, the Wadoe cannibals; he has a peaked beard, a bulging brow, close thin lips, a peculiar wall-eyed roll of glance, and a look fixed, when unobserved, with a manner of fascination which men felt. His attitude is always humble and deprecatory, he drops his chin upon the collar of reflection, he rarely speaks, save in dulcet tones, low, plaintive, and modulated; yet agreeing in every conceivable particular, he never fails to introduce a most pertinacious "but," which brings him back precisely to his own starting-point. The vehemence of his manner, and the violence of his temper, win for him the fears of the porters; having a wife and children in Unyamwezi, he knows well the languages, the manners, and the customs of the people; he never hesitates, when necessary, to enforce his mild commands by a merciless application of the staff, or to air his blade and to fly at the recusant like a wild-cat. In such moods, he is always seized by his friends, and led forcibly away as if dangerous. To insure some regularity on the road, I ordered him to meet Said bin Salim and Muinyi Wazira every evening at my tent for a "mashauri," or palaver, about the next day's march and halt. The measure was rendered futile by Kidogo, who soon contrived so to browbeat the others, that they would not venture an opinion in his presence. As a chief, he would have been in the right position; as a slave, he was falsely placed, because determined not to obey. He lost no time in demanding that he and his brethren should be considered askári, soldiers, whose sole duty it was to carry a gun; and he took the first opportunity of declaring that his men should not be under the direction of the jemadar. Having received for answer that we could not all be sultans, he retired with a "ngema"—a "very well," accompanied by a glance that boded little good. From that hour the "sons of Ramji" went wrong. Before, servilely civil, they waxed insolent; they learned their power—without them I must have returned to the coast—and they presumed upon it. They assumed the "swashing and martial outside" of valiant men: they disdained to be " mechanical;" they swore not to carry burdens; they objected to loading and leading the asses; they would not bring up articles left behind in the camp or on the road; they claimed the sole right of buying provisions; they arrogated to themselves supreme command over the porters; and they pilfered from the loads whenever they wanted the luxuries of meat and beer; they drank deep; and on more than one occasion they endangered the caravan by their cavalier proceedings with the fair sex. It was "water-painting" to complain; they had one short reply to all objections, namely, the threat of desertion. Preferring any thing to risking the success of the expedition, I was reduced to the bitter alternative of long-suffering, but it was with the hope of a *revanche* at some future time. The suffering was perhaps not wholly patient. Orientals advise the traveler " to keep his manliness in his pocket for braving it and ruffling at home." Such, however, is not exactly the principle or the practice of an Englishman, who recognizes a primary duty of commanding respect for himself, for his successors, and for the noble name of his nation. On the return of the expedition, Kidogo proved himself a "serviceable villain," but an extortionate; any thing committed to him was, as the Arabs say, in "ape's custody," and the only remedy was to remove him from all power over the outfit.

Under the great Kidogo were the Muinyi Mboni, Buyuni, Hayja, and Jako; these four took precedence as being the sons of diwans, while the commonalty was represented by the Muinyi Shehe, Mbaruko, Wulaydi, and Khamisi.

The donkey-men, five in number, had been hired at the rate of thirty dollars per head for the whole time of exploration. Their names were Musangesi, Sangora, Nasibu, Hasani, and Saramalla. Of their natures little need be said, except that they were a trifle less manageable than the "sons of Ramji:" perfect models of servile humanity, obstinate as asses and vicious as mules, gluttonous and lazy, noisy and overbearing, insolent and quarrelsome as slaves.

Lowest in rank, and little above the asses even in their own estimation, are the thirty-six Wanyamwezi pagazi, or porters, who formed the transport-corps. Concerning these men and their burdens, a few words of explanation will be necessary.

In collecting a caravan the first step is to "make," as the people say, a "khambi," or kraal. The mtongi, or proprietor of the goods, announces, by pitching his tent in the open, and by planting his flag, that he is ready to travel; this is done because among the Wanyamwezi a porter who persuades others to enlist does it under pain of prosecution and fine-paying if a death or an accident ensue. Petty chiefs, however, and their kinsmen, will bring with them in hope of promotion a number of recruits, sometimes all the male adults of a village, who then recognize them as headmen. The next step is to choose a kirangozi or guide. Guides are not a peculiar class; any individual of influence and local knowledge who has traveled the road before is eligible to the post. The kirangozi must pay his followers to acknowledge his supremacy, and his mganga or medicine-man for providing him with charms and prophylactics. On the march he precedes his porters, and any one who breaks this rule is liable to a fine. He often undergoes abuse for losing the way, for marching too far or not far enough, for not halting at the proper place, and for not setting out at the right time. In return he enjoys the empty circumstance of command, and the solid advantage of better food and a present, which, however, is optional, at the end of the journey: he carries a lighter load, and his emoluments frequently enable him to be attended by a slave. The only way of breaking the perverse and headstrong herd into a semblance of discipline, is to support the kirangozi at all conjunctures, and to make him, if possible, dole out the daily rations and portion the occasional presents of meat.

At the preliminary khambi the mtongi superintends the distribution of each muzigo or load. The pagazi or porters are mostly lads, lank and light, with the lean and clean legs of leopards. Sometimes, however, a herculean form is found with the bullet-head, the broad bull-like neck, the deep wide chest, and the large strong extremities that characterize the Hammal of Stamboul. There is usually a sprinkling of gray-beards, who might be expected, as the proverb is, to be "leaning against the wall." Among these races, however, the older men, who have learned to husband their strength, fare better than their juniors, and the Africans, like the Arabs, object to a party which does not contain veterans in beard, age, and experience. In portioning the loads there is always much trouble: each individual has his favorite fancy, and must choose, or, at any rate, must consent to his burden. To load porters properly is a work of skill. They will accept at the hand of a man who knows their nature a weight which, if proposed by a stranger, would be rejected with grunts of disgust. They hate the inconvenience of boxes, unless light enough to be carried at both ends of a "banghi"-pole by one man, or heavy enough to be slung between two porters. The burden must never be under a fair standard, especially when of that description that it decreases by expenditure toward the end of the journey; a lightly-laden man not only becomes lazy, he also makes his fellows discontented. The nature of the load, however, causes an inequality of weight. Cloth is tightly rolled up in the form of a huge bolster, five feet long by eighteen to twenty-four inches in diameter, protected against wear and weather by makanda or coarse matting of brab-leaf, and corded over. This bundle is fastened, for the purpose of preserving its shape and for convenience of stacking, in a cradle of three or more flexible branches, cut from a small tree below the place of junction, barked and trimmed, laid along the length of the load, and confined at the open end by a lashing of fibre-rope. Besides his weapons and marching kit a man will carry a pack of two frasilah or seventy pounds, and this perhaps is the maximum. Beads are placed in long, narrow bags of domestics, matted, corded, and cradled in sticks like cloth; being a less elastic load, they are more difficult to carry, and therefore seldom exceed fifty pounds. Brass and other wires are carried in daur, khata, or circles, lashed to both ends of a pole, which is generally the large midrib of a palm-frond, with a fork cut in its depth at one extremity to form a base for the load when stacked, and provided at the point of junction with a kitambara or pad of grass, rag, or leather. Wire is the lightest, as ivory is the heaviest, of loads. The African porter will carry only the smallest burdens upon his head, and the custom is mostly confined to women and children. The merchants of course carry nothing but themselves, except in extreme cases; but when the sudden sickness or the evasion of a porter endangers the safety of his load, they shoulder it without hesitation. The chief proprietor usually follows his caravan, accompanied by some of his partners and armed slaves, to prevent the straggling which may lead to heavy loss; he therefore often endures the heat and tedium of the road longer than the rest of his party.

The loads of the pagazi, it has appeared, are composed of beads, cloth, and wire, which, in this land of " round trade" or barter, supply the wants of a circulating medium, and they severally represent copper, silver, and gold. For a detailed notice, the reader is referred to the Appendix; in this place a few general remarks will suffice to set before him the somewhat complicated use of the articles.

Of beads there are about 400 varieties, some of which have each three or four different names. The cheapest, which form the staple of commerce, are the hafizi, khanyera, or ushanga waupe, a round white porcelain, the price of which averages at Zanzibar 1 dollar per 5 or 6 lbs. avoirdupois. The most expensive are the samsam or samesame, also called joho (scarlet cloth), kimara-p'hamba (food-finishers), because a man will part with his dinner to obtain them, and kifunjyá-mji (town-breakers), because the women will ruin themselves and their husbands for them: these are the small coral bead, scarlet enameled upon a white ground; they are of fifteen different sizes, and the value at Zanzibar is from 13 to 16 dollars per 35 lbs. Beads are purchased from the Banyan monopolizers unstrung, and are afterward mounted by the merchant upon t'hembe, or threads of palm-fibre; much depends for success in sale upon the regularity and the attractiveness of the line. The principal divisions are the bitil and the khete, which may represent the farthing and the penny. The former is a single length from the tip of the index to the wrist; the latter, which comprises four of the former, is a double length round the thumb to the elbow-bone, or, what is much the same, twice the circumference of the throat. Ten khete compose the fundo or knot, which is used in the larger purchases, and of these from two to three were daily expended in our small expenses by the Goanese servants, while the usual compensation for rations to an African is a single khete. The utmost economy should be exercised in beads: apparently exhaustless, a large store goes but a little way, and a man's load rarely outlasts a month. It is difficult to divine what becomes of these ornaments: for centuries ton after ton has been imported into the country, they are by no means perishable substances, and the people carry, like the Indians, their wealth upon their persons. Yet not a third of the population was observed to wear any considerable quantity. Possibly the excessive demand in the lands outlying direct intercourse with the coast tends to disperse them throughout the vast terra incognita of the central African basin.

The African preserves the instincts of infancy in the higher races. He astonished the enlightened De Gama some centuries ago by rejecting with disdain jewels, gold, and silver, while he caught greedily at beads and other bawbles, as a child snatches at a new plaything. To the present day he is the same. There is something painfully ludicrous in the expression of countenance, the intense and all-absorbing admiration, and the greedy wistfulness with which he contemplates the rubbish. Yet he uses it as a toy: after sacrificing perhaps his goat or his grain to become the happy possessor of a khete, he will hang it round his neck for a few days, and then, child-like, weary of the acquisition, he will do his best to exchange it for another. In all bargains beads must be thrown in, especially where women are concerned: their sisters of civilization would reproach themselves with an unconscious lapse into the "nil admirari" doctrines so hateful to the muscular system of the age, and with a cold indifference to the charms of diamonds and pearls, could they but witness the effect of a string of scarlet porcelains upon the high-born dames of Central Africa.

The cloths imported into East Africa are of three kinds, merkani, kaniki, and "cloths with names."

"Merkani," in which we detect the African corruption of American, is the article of "domestics"—unbleached shirting and sheeting from the mills near Salem. Kaniki is the common Indian indigo-dyed cotton. "Cloths with names," as they are called by the Africans, are Arab and Indian checks, and colored goods, of cotton or silk mixed with cotton. Of these the most common is the barsati, a dark-blue cotton cloth with a broad red stripe, which, representing the dollar in the interior, is useful as presents to chiefs. Of double value is the dabwani, made at Maskat, a small blue and white check, with a quarter breadth of red stripe, crossed with white and yellow; this showy article is invariably demanded by the more powerful sultans for themselves and their wives, while they divide the merkani and kaniki, which composes their honga—" black-mail" or dash—among their followers.

The people of East Africa, when first visited by the Arabs, were satisfied with the coarsest and flimsiest kaniki imported by the Banyans from Cutch. When American merchants settled at Zanzibar, kaniki yielded before the advance of " merkani," which now supplies the markets from Abyssinia to the Mozambique. But the wild men are fast losing their predilection for a stuff which is neither comfortable nor durable, and in many regions the tribes, satisfied with goat-skins and tree-barks, prefer to invest their capital in the more attractive beads and wire. It would evidently be advantageous if England or her colonies could manufacture an article better suited to the wants of the country than that now in general use; but as long as the Indian short-stapled cotton must be used, there is little probability of her competing with the produce of the New World.

In Eastern Africa cotton cloth is used only for wear. The popular article is a piece of varying breadth, but always of four cubits, or six feet in length: the braça of Portuguese Africa, it is called by the Arabs shukkah, by the Wasawahili unguo, and in the far interior upande or lupande. It is used as a loin-wrapper, and is probably the first costume of Eastern Africa and of Arabia. The plate borrowed from Montfaucon's edition of the "Topographia Christiana," by Dr. Vincent (Part I. Appendix to the Periplus), shows the shukkah to be the general dress of Ethiopians, as it was of the Egyptians, and the spear their weapon. The use of the shukkah during the Meccan pilgrimage, when the devotees cast off such innovations as coats and breeches for the national garb of their ancestors, proves its antiquity throughout the regions eastward of the Red Sea. On the African coast the shukkah merkani is worth about 0.25 dollar=1s. 0½d., in the interior it rises to the equivalent of a dollar (4s. 2d.), and even higher. The kaniki is but little cheaper than the merkani, when purchased upon the sea-board; its increase of value in the interior, however, is by no means in proportion to its prime cost, and by some tribes it is wholly rejected. A double length of shukkah, or twelve feet, the article worn by women who can afford it, is called a doti, and corresponds with the tobe of Abyssinia and of the Somali country. The whole piece of merkani, which contains from seven to eleven doti, is termed a jurah or gorah.

After beads and piece-goods, the principal imports into Eastern Africa, especially on the northern lines and in the western portion of the great central route, are masango or brass wires of large sizes, Nos. 4 and 5. They are purchased at Zanzibar, when cheap, at 12, and, when dear, at 16 dollars per frasilah of 35 lbs. When imported up-country the frasilah is divided into three or four large coils, called by the Arabs "daur," and by the Africans "khata:" the object is convenience of attachment to the porters' banghy-poles. Arrived at Unyanyembe they are converted by artisans into the kitindi, or coil-bracelet, a peculiarly African decoration. It is a system of concentric circles extending from the wrist to the elbow; at both extremities it is made to bulge out for grace and for allowing the joints to play, and the elasticity of the wire keeps it in its place. It weighs nearly 3 lbs., yet— "vanity knows no sore"—the women of some tribes will wear four of these bulky decorations upon their arms and legs. It is mostly a feminine ornament. In the lake regions, however, men assume the full-sized armlet, and in the mountains of Usagara their wrists, arms, and ankles are often decorated with half and quarter lengths, which, being without terminal bulges, appear to compress the limbs painfully. At Unyanyembe the value of a kitindi varies from two to four shukkah; at Ujiji, where the ornament is in demand, it rises to four or five.

The remainder of the live stock forming the *personnel* of the caravan is composed of asses. At Zanzibar I had bought five riding animals to mount the chiefs of the party, including Said bin Salim and the Goanese. The price varied from fifteen to forty dollars. Of the twenty-nine asses used for carriage, only twenty remained when the muster was made at Zungomero, and the rapid thinning of their numbers by loss, death, and accident began to suggest uncomfortable ideas.

The following "equipment of the expedition," sent by me to Mr. Francis Galton, the South African traveler, and bearing date, "Camp Zungomero in Khutu, Sunday, 2nd August, 1857," is here republished: it will assist the reader in picturing to himself the mass of material which I am about to drag over the mountains.

Provisions, etc.—1 dozen brandy (to be followed by 4 dozen more); 1 box cigars; 5 boxes tea (each 6 lbs.); a little coffee; 2 bottles curry stuff, besides ginger, rock and common salt, red and black pepper, 1 bottle each, pickles, soap, and spices; 20 lbs. pressed vegetables; 1 bottle vinegar; 2 bottles oil; 20 lbs. sugar (honey is procurable in the country).

Arms and Ammunition, including 2 smooth bores, 3 rifles, a Colt's carbine, and 3 revolvers, spare fittings, etc., and 3 swords. Each gun has its leather bag with three compartments, for powder-flask, ball, caps, patches, etc. 100 lbs. gunpowder (in 2 safety copper magazines and others); 60 lbs. shot; 380 lbs. lead bullets, cast of hardened material at the Arsenal, Bombay, placed in boxes, 40 lbs. each for convenience of carriage, also to serve as specimen boxes, and screwed down to prevent pilfering; 20,000 copper caps; wadding.

The Baloch are armed with matchlocks, shields, swords, daggers, and knives. They have for ammunition—40 lbs. gunpowder (4 kegs); 1000 lead bullets; 1000 flints for slaves' muskets, and are to be followed by about an equal quantity of ammunition.

Camp Furniture.—1 sepoy's rowtie; 1 small (gable-shaped) tent of two sails joined, to cover and shelter property in this land of perpetual rains; 1 table and chair; 1 tin Crimean canteen, with knives and forks, kettle, cooking-pots, etc.; bedding, painted tarpaulin cover, 2 large cotton pillows for stuffing birds, 1 air-pillow, 2 water-proof blankets (most useful), 1 Maltese blanket (remarkably good), and 2 other blankets; 1 cork bed, with two pillows, 3 blankets, and musquito net. The Goanese have thick cotton-padded mattresses, pillows, and blankets, and all the servants have some kind of bedding. 3 solid leather portmanteaus for clothes and books; 1 box, like an Indian petarah, for books; 1 patent-leather bag for books, washing materials, diaries, drawing-books, etc.; 1 small courier's bag for instruments, etc.; 5 canvas bags for kit generally; 3 mats, used as carpets.

Instruments.—1 lever watch; 2 chronometers; 2 prismatic compasses, slings, and stands; 1 ship's azimuth compass; 2 pocket-compasses; 1 pocket-thermometer; 1 portable sun-dial; 1 rain gauge; 1 evaporating dish; 2 sextants and boxes, with canvas bags to be slung over porters' shoulders; 2 artificial horizons (with a little extra mercury, to be followed by more); 1 pocket lens; 1 mountain barometer lent by Bombay Geographical Society (very delicate); 3 thermometers; 1 measuring tape (100 ft.); 1 sounding lead; 2 boiling thermometers; 1 box of mathematical instruments; 1 glass; 1 telescope; 2 ft. rule with brass slide; 1 pocket pedometer by Dixie; 1 parallel ruler.

Stationery.—Foolscap paper; 1 ream common paper; 6 blank books; 3 Letts' diaries; 2 dozen pencils; 6 pieces caoutchouc; 6 metallic note books; 3 memorandum ditto; 1 box wafers and sealing-wax; 2 field-books; steel pens; quill ditto; ink-powder which makes up well without acid; 3 bottles ink; 1 bottle native ink; 2 sets meteorological tables, blank; 4 tin cylinders for papers (very bad, every thing rusts in them); Nautical Almanacs for 1857 and 1858; charts, Mr. Cooley's maps; "Mombas mission map"; skeleton maps; table of stars; account book; portfolio; wooden and tin cylinders for pens, etc.

Tools.—1 large turnscrew; 1 hand-saw; 1 hammer; 20 lbs. nails; 1 hand-vice; 1 hone; 9 hatchets (as a rule every porter carries an axe); 2 files; 9 jembe or native hoe; 9 mas'ha or native dibbles; 1 cold chisel; 1 heavy hammer; 1 pair pincers. To be followed by 1 bench-vice; 1 hand ditto; 12 gimlets of sizes; 1 18-inch stone grinder, with spindle and handle; 6 splitting axes; 12 augers of sizes; 2 sets centre-bits, with stock; 12 chisels; 4 mortise chisels; 2 sets drills; 24 saw-files; 6 files of sorts; 4 gouges of sizes; 50 lbs. iron nails; 2 planes, with 2 spare irons; 3 hand-saws; screws. These things were expected to be useful at the lakes, where carpenters are in demand.

Clothing, Bedding, and Shoes.—Shirts, flannel and cotton; turbans and thick felt caps for the head. (N.B. not looking forward to so long a journey, we left Zanzibar without a new outfit; consequently we were in tatters before the end, and in a climate where flannel fights half the battle of life against death, my companion was compelled to invest himself in overalls of American domestics, and I was forced to cut up blankets into coats and wrappers. The Goanese also had laden themselves with rags which would have been refused by a Jew; they required to be reclothed in kaniki, or blue cotton. African travel is no favorable opportunity for wearing out old clothes; the thorny jungles, and the practice of packing up clothes wet render a double outfit necessary for long journeys. The second should be carried packed up in tin—flannel shirts, trowsers and stocks, at least six of each—not to be opened till required.

The best bedding in this country would be a small horse-hair mattress with two blankets, one thick the other thin, and musquito curtains that would pack into the pillow. A simple carpet-bag, without leathern or other adjuncts, should contain the traveling clothes, and all the bedding should roll up into a single bundle, covered with a piece of water-proof canvas, and tightly bound with stout straps.

As regards shoes, the best would be ammunition-boots for walking and jack-boots for riding. They must be of light color, and at least one size too large in England; they should be carefully protected from external air, which is ruinous to leather, and they must be greased from time to time—with fat, not with oil—otherwise they will soon become so hard and dry, that it is impossible to draw them on unless treated after the Indian plan, viz., dipped in hot water and stretched with a stuffing of straw.)

Books and Drawing Materials.—Norie; Bowditch; Thompson's "Lunar Tables;" Gordon's "Time Tables;" Galton's "Art of Travel;" Buist's "Manual of Observation;" Jackson's "What to Observe;" Jackson's "Military Surveying;" "Admiralty Manual;" Cuvier's "Animal Life;" Prichard's "History of Man;" Keith's "Trigonometry;" Krapf's "Kisuaheli Grammar;" Krapf's "Kinika Testament;" Amharic Grammar (Isenberg's); Belcher's "Mast Head Angles;" Cooley's "Geography of N'yassi;" and other miscellaneous works; 1 paint-box complete, soft water colors; 1 small ditto, with Chinese ink, sepia, and Prussian blue; 2 drawing-books; 1 large drawing-book; 1 camera lucida.

Portable domestic Medicine-chest.—Vilely made. Some medicines for natives in packages. Application was made to Zanzibar for more quinine, some morphia, Warburg's drops, citric acid, and chiretta root.

Miscellaneous.—10 pieces scarlet broadcloth for presents (3 expended); 3 knives for servants; 4 umbrellas; 1 hank salmon gut; 1 dozen twisted gut; 1 lb. beeswax; courier's box with brass clasps to carry sundries on the road; 2 dozen penknives; 2000 fishing-hooks; 42 bundles fishing-line; 2 lanterns (policeman's bull's eye and common horn); 2 iron ladles for casting lead; 1 housewife, with buttons, needles, thread, silk, pins, etc.; 12 needles (sailors') and palms; 2 pair scissors; 2 razors; 1 hone; 2 pipes; 1 tobacco-pouch; 1 cigar-case; 7 canisters of snuff; 1 filter; 1 pocket-filter; 1 looking-glass; 1 small tin dressing-case, with soap, nail-brush, and tooth-brush (very useful); brushes and combs; 1 union jack; arsenical paste for specimens; 10 steels and flints.

Life at Zungomero, I have said, was the acme of discomfort. The weather was, as usual at the base of the mountains, execrable; pelting showers descended in a succession, interrupted only by an occasional burst of fiery sunshine, which extracted steam from the thick covert of grass, bush, and tree. The party, dispersing throughout the surrounding villages—in which, it was said, about 1000 travelers were delayed by the inundations—drank beer, smoked bhang, quarreled among themselves, and, by their insolence and violence, caused continual complaints on the part of the villagers. Both the Goanese being prostrated with mild modifications of "yellow jack," I was obliged to admit them into the hut, which was already sufficiently populated with pigeons, rats, and flies by day, and with musquitoes, bugs, and fleas by night. At length, weary of waiting the arrival of the twenty-two promised porters, we prepared our papers, which I committed

A Village in K'hutu.   The Silk-cotton-tree.

to the confidential slave of a coast diwan, here dwelling as cara-van-touter, for his uncle Ukwere of Kaole. His name was some-what peculiar, Chomwi la Mtu Mku Wambele, or the "Headman Great Man of Precedence." These little Jugurthas have all the titles of emperors, with the actual power of country squires. He never allowed himself to appear in public sober, and, to judge from the list of stations with which he obliged me—of eighteen not one was correct—I hesitated to intrust his slave with reports and specimens. But the Headman Great Man of Precedence did as he promised to do, and as his charge arrived safely, I here make to him the "amende honorable."

THE EAST AFRICAN GHAUTS.

Sycamore in the Dhun of Ugogi.

CHAPTER VI.

WE CROSS THE EAST AFRICAN GHAUTS.

On the 7th of August, 1857, the expedition left Zungomero. We were martyred by miasma; my companion and I were so feeble that we could scarcely sit our asses, and weakness had almost deprived us of the sense of hearing. It was a day of severe toil. We loaded with difficulty; for the slaves and porters did not assemble till past 8 A.M., and, instead of applying for their loads to Said bin Salim, every man ran off with the lightest burden or the easiest ass.

From Central Zungomero to the nearest ascent of the Usagara Mountains is a march of five hours. The route, emerging from the cultivated districts, leaves to the right the Wigo Hills, so called, probably, from the fishing-weirs in the stagnant waters below, and in the Mgeta River, which flows through the plain. On the left, and distant four or five miles, is a straggling line of low cones: at the foot of one, somewhat larger than its neighbors, rises the thermal spring known to the people as the Maji ya W'heta, the geyser, jetting-water, or *fontaine qui bouille*. Its position is a gentle slope between the hill-base and a dwarf savanna which is surrounded by high walls of jungly forest, and the water-shed is from south to north. The hot water boils and bubbles out of a white sand, here and there stained and incrusted with oxyd of iron. Upon the surface lie caked and scaly sheets of calcareous tufa, expressed by the spring, and around it are erratic boulders blackened probably by the thermal fumes. The earth is dark, sometimes sandy, and sprinkled over with fragments of quartzite and sandstone; in other places a screen of brab-tree backs a bold expanse of ground, treacherous, boggy, and unstable as water. The area is about 200 feet in diameter, and the centre of ebullition is unapproachable, owing to the heat and the instability of the soil. According to the guides, it is subject to occasional eruptions, when the water bursts out with violence, and fragments of lime are flung high in the air. Animals are said to refuse it, and tales are told of wild beasts having been bogged in the seething mire.

With the Mgeta thrown on the left hand, we passed, by a path almost invisible, through dense grass and trees, and presently we entered the luxuriant cultivation surrounding the westernmost villages of K'hutu. As the land beyond this point, for three long marches, lies barren, the slaves and porters had comfortably housed themselves. The prospect of another night in the plains made me desperate; I dislodged them, and persuaded them to advance once more. The settlements were of the most miserable description; many were composed of a few sticks lashed together at the top, and loosely covered with a few armfuls of holcus-cane. Here we sighted the cocoa-tree for the last time. The rats were busy in the fields, and the plundered peasants were digging them out for food. At almost every corner of the deeply-pitted path stood a mtego, or trap for small birds, a cage of rush or split bamboo planted in the ground near some corn, where a boy lies waiting till the prey nibbles at the bait, and then creeping up, bars with his hand the little doorway left in one of the sides. Beyond the villages, the path forded six times the sandy bed of the Mgeta, whose steep and slippery banks supported dense screens of shrub and grass. Beyond the sixth passage the road falls into the gravelly river-shoals, with the stream flowing in the other half of the course under well-wooded masses of primitive hill. After again thrice fording the cold and muddy water, which even in the dry season is here ankle, there foot-deep, the road passed some clearings where porcupines and the African red squirrel, a sturdy little animal, with a long thick fur of dark brown, shot with green on the back, and a bright red waistcoat, muzzle, and points, were observed. About noon we diverged a few yards from the Mgeta, and ascended the incline of the first gradient in Usagara, rising about 300 feet from the plain below. This, the frontier of the second region, or ghauts, and the debris encumbering the lowest escarpment, is called Mzizi Mdogo, or the "Little Tamarind," to distinguish it from the "Great Tamarind" station which lies beyond. There was no vestige of building upon the spot—no sight nor sound of man—the blood-feud and the infernal slave-trade had made a howling desert of the land. We found, however, a tattered kraal erected by the last passing caravan, and, spent with fatigue, we threw ourselves on the short grass to rest. The porters and the asses did not appear till the evening, when it became apparent that two of the latter had been lost by their drivers, Hayja and Khamisi, sons of Ramji, who preferred sitting in the shade and chatting with passing caravans, to the sore task of doing their duty. The animals were recovered on the morrow by sundry parties sent in search. During the fordings of the Mgeta, however, they had not been unpacked; our salt and sugar, therefore, had melted away; soap, cigars, mustard, and arsenical paste, were in pulp; the tea was spoiled, the compressed vegetables presently became musty, and the gunpowder in a fire-proof copper magazine was caked like stale bread.

There was a wondrous change of climate at Mzizi Mdogo; strength and health returned as if by magic; even the Goanese shook off the obstinate bilious remittents of Zungomero. Truly delicious was the escape from the nebulous skies, the fog-driving gusts, the pelting rain, the clammy mists veiling a gross growth of fetor, the damp raw cold, rising as it were from the earth, and the alternations of fiery and oppressive heat; in fact, from the cruel climate of the river-valley, to the pure sweet mountain-air, alternately soft and balmy, cool and reviving, and to the aspect of clear blue skies, which lent their tints to highland ridges well wooded with various greens. Dull mangrove, dismal jungle, and monotonous grass, were supplanted by tall solitary trees, among which the lofty tamarind rose conspicuously graceful, and a card-table-like swamp, cut by a net-work of streams, nullahs, and stagnant pools, gave way to dry healthy slopes, with short steep pitches and gently shelving hills. The beams of the large sun of the equator—and nowhere have I seen the rulers of night and day so large—danced gayly upon blocks and pebbles of red, yellow, and dazzling snowy quartz, and the bright sea-breeze waved the summits of the trees, from which depended graceful llianas, and wood-apples large as melons, while creepers, like vine tendrils, rising from large bulbs of brown-gray wood, clung closely to their stalwart trunks. Monkeys played at hide-and-seek, chattering behind the bolls, as the iguana, with its painted scale-armor, issued forth to bask upon the sunny bank; white-breasted ravens cawed when disturbed from their perching-places; doves cooed on the well-clothed boughs, and hawks soared high in the transparent sky. The field-cricket chirped like the Italian cigala in the shady bush, and every where, from air, from earth, from the hill slopes above, and from the marshes below, the hum, the buzz, and the loud continuous voice of insect life, through the length of the day, spoke out its natural joy. Our gipsy encampment lay

> "By shallow rivers, to whose falls
> Melodious birds sing madrigals."

By night, the soothing murmurs of the stream at the hill's base rose mingled with the faint rustling of the breeze, which at times broken by the scream of the night-heron, the bellow of the bull-frog in his swampy home, the cynhyena's whimper, and the fox's whining bark, sounded through the silence most musical, most melancholy. Instead of the cold night rain, and the soughing of the blast, the view disclosed a peaceful scene, the moonbeams lying like sheets of snow upon the ruddy highlands, and the stars hanging like lamps of gold from the dome of infinite blue. I never wearied with contemplating the scene, for, contrasting with the splendors around me, still stretched in sight the Slough of Despond, unhappy Zungomero, lead-colored above, mud-colored below, wind-swept, fog-veiled, and deluged by clouds that dared not approach these delectable mountains.

During a day's halt at this sanitarium fresh diversions agitated the party. The Baloch, weary of worrying one another, began to try their 'prentice hands upon the sons of Ramji, and these fortified by the sturdy attitude of Muinyi Kidogo, manfully resolved to hold their own. The asses fought throughout the livelong night, and, contrary to the custom of their genus, strayed from one another by day. And as,

> "When sorrows come, they come not single spies,
> But in battalions,"

Said bin Salim, who hated and was hated by the Baloch on account of their divided interests, began to hate and to be hated by the sons of Ramji. His four children, the most ignoble of their ignoble race, were to him as the apples of his eyes. He had entered their names as public porters, yet, with characteristic egotism and self-tenderness, he was resolved that they should work for none but their master, and that even in this their labor should as much as possible fall upon the shoulders of others. His tent was always the first pitched and his fire the first built; his slaves were rewarded with such luxuries as ghee, honey, and turmeric, when no one in camp, ourselves included, could procure them. When all wanted clothes he clad his children out of the outfit as if it had been his own, and, till strong remonstrances were made, large necklaces of beads decked their sooty necks. On the return-march he preferred to pay hire for three porters rather than to allow the fat lazy knaves to carry a bed or a few gourds. They became of course insolent and unmanageable—more than once they gave trouble by pointing their muskets at the Baloch and the porters, and they would draw their knives and stab at a man who refused to give up his firewood or his hearth-stones, without incurring a word of blame from their master. Encouraged by impunity, they robbed us impudently; curry-stuff was soon exhausted, the salt-bottles showed great gaps, and cigar-ends were occasionally seen upon the road-side. The Goanese accused the slaves, and the slaves the Goanese; probably both parties for once spoke the truth.

Said bin Salim's silly favoritism naturally aroused the haughty Kidogo's bile; the sons of Ramji, consequently, worked less than before. The two worthies, Arab and African, never, however, quarreled, no harsh word passed between them; with smiles upon their faces, and a bitter hate at heart, they confined themselves to all manner of backbiting and talebearing. Said bin Salim sternly declared to me that he would never rest satisfied until Kidogo's sword was broken and his back was scarified at the flagstaff of Zanzibar; but I guessed that this "wrathful mouse and most magnanimous dove" would, long before his journey's end, have forgotten all his vengeance. Kidogo asserted that the Muárabu or Arab was a greenhorn, and frequently suggested the propriety of "planting" him. At last this continual harping upon the same chord became so offensive, that B'ana Saidi was forbidden to pronounce the name of Muinyi Kidogo, and Muinyi Kidogo was ordered never to utter the words B'ana Saidi before the exasperated leader of the expedition, who could not, like these squabblers, complain, resent, forget and forgive, in the short space of a single hour.

We left Mzizi Mdogo on the 9th August, much cheered by the well-omened appearance of a bird with red bill, white breast, and long tail-feathers. The path ran over a succession of short steep hills with a rufous-brown soil, dotted with blocks and stones, thinly veiled with grass, and already displaying signs of aridity in the growth of aloetic and thorny plants, the cactus and the larger asclepias, the euphorbia, or spurge-wort, and the stunted mimosa. The calabash, however, still rose a stately tree, and there was a sprinkling of the fine tamarinds which have lent their name to the district. The tamarind, called by the Arabs of Zanzibar "subar," extends from the coast to the lake regions: with its lofty stem, its feathery leaflets, and its branches spreading dark cool shade, it is a beautiful feature in African landscape. The acidulated fruit is doubtless a palliative and a corrective to bilious affections. The people of the country merely peel and press it into bark baskets, consequently it soon becomes viscid, and is spoiled by mildew; they ignore the art of extracting from it an intoxicating liquor. The Arabs, who use it extensively in cooking, steam, sun-dry, and knead it, with a little salt and oil to prevent the effects of damp, into balls: thus prepared and preserved from the air, it will keep for years.

On the way we were saddened by the sight of the clean-picked skeletons, and here and there the swollen corpses, of porters who had perished in this place of starvation. A single large body, which had lost fifty of its number by small-pox, had passed us but yesterday on the road, and the sight of their deceased comrades recalled to our minds terrible spectacles; men staggering on blinded by disease, and mothers carrying on their backs infants as loathsome objects as themselves. The wretches would not leave the path, every step in their state of failing strength was precious; he who once fell would never rise again; no village would admit death into its precincts, no relation nor friend would return for them, and they would lie till their agony was ended by the raven and vulture, the fisi and the fox. Near every khambi or kraal I remarked detached tents which, according to the guides, were set apart for those seized with the fell disease. Under these circumstances, as might be expected, several of our party caught the infection; they lagged behind, and probably threw themselves into some jungle, for the path when revisited showed no signs of them.

We spent 4^{hrs.} 30^{m.} in weary marching, occasionally halting to reload the asses that threw their packs. Near the Mgeta River, which was again forded six times, the vegetation became tall and thick, grasses obstructed the path, and in the dense jungle on the banks of the stream the cowhage (*Dolichos pruriens*), and stiff reeds known as the "wild sugar-cane," annoyed the half-naked porters. Thus bounded and approached by muddy and slippery, or by steep and stony inclines, the stream shrank to a mountain torrent, in places hardly fifty feet broad; the flow was swift, the waters were dyed by the soil a ruddy brown, and the bed was sandy and sometimes rocky with boulders of primitive formation, streaked with lines of snow-white quartz. Near the end of the marsh we ascended a short steep staircase of rock and root, with a dwarf precipice overhanging the river on the right, which was dangerous for the laden beasts as they crawled like beetles up the path. At 3 P.M. we arrived at a kraal called Cha K'henge—of the iguana, from the number of these animals found near the stream. It was a delightful spot, equal to Mzizi Mdogo in purity of air, and commanding a fair prospect of the now distant Dut'hu-mi Highlands.

The next day was a forced halt at Cha K'henge. Of two asses that had been left behind one was recovered, the other was abandoned to its fate. The animals purchased at Zanzibar were falling off visibly in condition. Accustomed to a kind of grass which nowhere grows upon these sun-burnt hills, they had regular feeds of holcus, but that, as Said bin Salim expressed himself, was only coffee to them. The Wanyamwezi asses, however, managed to pick a sustenance from the rushes and from the half-burned stubbles, when fortunate enough to find any. Sickness again declared itself. Shahdad the Baloch bellowed like a bull with fever pains, Gaetano complained that he was suffering tortures generally, two of the Wanyamwezi were incapacitated by the symptoms preliminary to small-pox from carrying their packs, and a third was prostrated by ague. We started, however, on the next day for a long march, which concluded the passage of the "Tamarind Hills." Crossing a country broken by dry nullahs, or rather ditches, we traversed a seam of forest with a deep woody ravine on the right, and twice unpacked and reloaded the asses, who lay down instead of breasting the difficulties: a muddy swamp full of water-courses, and the high earth-banks of the Rufuta a fiumara, here dry during the hot season. Thence, winding along a hill-flank to avoid a bend in the bed, the path plunged into the sole of the Rufuta. This main drain of the lower gradients carries off, according to the guides, the waters of the high ground around it into the Mgeta. The bed, which varies from three to sixteen feet in breadth, serpentines abruptly through the hills: its surface is either deep sand or clay, sopped with water, which near the head becomes a thin fillet, ankle-deep, now sweet, then salt: the mud is tinged in places with a solution of iron, showing, when stagnant, prismatic and iridescent tints. Where narrowest, the tall grasses of the banks meet across the gut, which, after a few yards of short, sharp winding, opens out again. The walls are in some parts earth, in others blocks of gray syenite, which here and there encumber the bed: on the right, near the end of the stage, the hills above seem to overhang the fiumara in almost perpendicular masses of sandstone, from whose chinks spring the gnarled roots of tall trees corded with creepers, overgrown with parasites, and hung with fruits like foot-balls, dangling from twines sometimes thirty feet long. The lower banks, where not choked with rush, are overgrown with the brightest verdure, and with the feathery bamboo rising and falling before the wind. The corpses of porters were even more numerous than on the yester: our Muslems passed them with averted faces and with the low "la haul!" of disgust, and a decrepit old Mnyamwezi porter gazed at them and wept for himself. About 2 P.M., turning abruptly from the bed, we crawled up a short stony steep strewed with our asses and their loads; and, reaching the summit of a dwarf cone near the foot of the "Goma Pass," we found the usual outlying huts for porters dying of small-pox, and an old kraal, which we made comfortable for the night. In the extensive prospect around, the little beehive villages of the Wakaguru and the Wakwivi, sub-tribes of the Wasagara, peeped from afar out of the forest nooks on the distant hill-folds. The people are rich in flocks and grain, but a sad experience has taught them to shun intercourse with all strangers, Arabs and Wasawahili, Wamrima and Wanyamwezi. In happier days the road was lined with large villages, of which now not a trace remains.

A boiling-point thermometer by Cox, the gift of Lieut. Colonel Hamerton, and left with him by Captain, now Admiral Smyth, F. R. G. S., who had used it in measuring the Andes, had been accidentally broken by my companion at Cha K'henge. Arrived at Rufuta, I found that a second B. P. by Newman, and a Bath thermometer by the same maker, had been torn so violently from their box that even the well-soldered handles were wrenched off. But a few days afterward our third B. P. was rendered useless by

the carelessness of Gaetano. Thus, of the only three really accurate hypsometrical instruments which we possessed—the barometer had come to grief, and no aneroid had been sent from
Bombay—not one was spared to reach the lake. We saved,
however, two Bath thermometers marked Newman, and Johnson
and Co., Bombay, which did good service, and one of which was
afterward corrected by being boiled at sea-level. I may here observe that on such journeys, where triangulation is impossible,
and where the delicate aneroid and the mountain barometer can
scarcely be carried without accident, the thermometer is at present the traveler's stand-by. It abounds, however, in elements of
error. The elasticity of the glass, especially in a new instrument,
causes the mercury to subside below the graduated scale. The
difference of level in a covered "shaving-pot" and in an open pan
exposed to the wind, will sometimes amount to $1°$ F.$=500$ feet:
they therefore are in error who declare that any vessel suffices
for the purpose of boiling. Finally, in all but the best instruments the air is not thoroughly expelled from the tube; indeed,
some writers, Dr. Buist, for instance, actually advise the error.

Another ass was left at Rufuta unable to stand, and anxiously
eying its stomach, whereby the Baloch conjectured that it was
dying of a poisonous grass. Having to ascend on the 12th August the Gomar Pass of the Rufuta, or the eastern range, I had arranged with Kidogo and the kirangozi, or guide, that the porters
should proceed with their packs, and after topping the hill, should
return, for a consideration, to assist the asses. None, however,
reappearing, when the sun had risen a spear's length we set out,
hugging the hill-flanks, with deep ravines yawning on the right.
Presently, after passing through a clear forest of tall scattered
trees, between whose trunks were visible on both sides in perspective, far below, long rolling tracts of well-wooded land broken
by ravines and cut by water-courses, we arrived at the foot of a
steep hill. The ascent was a kind of ramp, composed of earth-
steps, clods bound by strong tenacious roots, and thickly strewn
with blocks of schiste, micaceous grit, and a sandstone showing
the presence of iron. The summit of this "kloof" was ascertained to rise 2235 feet above sea-level. It led to an easy descent
along the flank of a hill commanding on the left hand, below a
precipitous foreground, a fine bird's-eye view of scattered cone
and wavy ridge rising and falling in a long roll, and on a scale
decreasing till they settled into a line of hazy-blue horizon, which
had all the effect of a circumambient ocean. We reached the remains of a kraal on the summit of a dwarf hill called Mfu'uni,
from the abundance of the mfu'u-tree, which bears an edible apple
externally like the smallest "crab," but containing a stone of inordinate proportions: below the encamping ground the pagazi
found a runnel of pure water, which derived its name from the
station. In former times Mfu'uni was a populous settlement;

the kidnapping parties from the coast, and especially the filibusters of Whinde, have restored it to the fox and the cynhyena, its "old inhabitants." I spent a sleepless night in watching each star as it sank and set in its turn, piercing with a last twinkle the thin silhouette of tall trees that fringed the hilly rim of the horizon, and in admiring the hardness of the bull-headed Mabruki, as he lay half-roasted by the fire and half-frozen by the cold southern gale.

Rations had been issued at K'hutu to all hands for three days, the time in which they expected to make the principal provisioning-place, "Muhama." They had consumed, as usual, their stores with the utmost possible quickness; it was our fifth day, and Muhama was still a long march distant. On the 13th August, therefore, in that hot haste which promises cold speed, we loaded at dawn, and ascended the last step of the pass by an easy path. The summit was thickly wooded; the hills were crowned with trees; the ravines were a mass of tangled verdure; and from the dub (*Cynodon dactylon*, a nutritive and favorite food for cattle in India) and other grasses arose a sickening odor of decay. A Scotch mist, thick and raw, hung over the hill-tops, and about 10 P.M. a fiery outburst of sunshine told severely upon hungry and fever-stricken men. From the level table-summit of the range the route descended rapidly at first, but presently stretching out into gentle slopes, totally unlike the abrupt eastern or seaward face of the mountains: I counted twelve distinct rises and fifteen falls, separated by tree-clad lines of half-dried nullahs, which were choked with ill-savored weeds. We halted every quarter of an hour to raise and reload the asses; when on the ground, they were invariably abandoned by the donkey-men. My companion's bedding was found near the path, where it had been left by its porter, a slave given at Zungomero to Muinyi Wazira by his drunken brother. The fellow had been sworn by his mganga, or medicine-man, not to desert, and he had respected his oath for the long length of a week. A dispute with another man, however, had irritated him; he quietly threw his burden and ran down the nearest steep, probably to fall into the hands of the Wakwivi. As the rain-catching peaks were left behind, the slopes of dry soil began to show sun-burned herbage and tufty grass. Signs of lions appeared numerous, and the cactaceous and aloetic plants that live on arid soil again met the eye. About noon we forded the little Zonhwe River, a stream of sweet water here flowing westward in a bed of mire and grass, under high banks bearing a dense bush. Two hours afterward I suddenly came upon the advance-guard, halted, and the asses unloaded, in a dry watercourse, called in the map, from our misadventure, "Overshot Nullah." A caravan of Wanyamwezi had misdirected them, Muinyi Wazira had in vain warned them of their error, he was overruled by Kidogo, and the Baloch had insisted upon camping at the first place where they expected to find a spring. Like all soft men, they were most impatient of thirst, and nothing caused so much grumbling and discontent as the cry of "Maji mb'hali!" (water is far!) That night, therefore, after a long march of fifteen miles, they again slept supperless.

On the 14th of August we loaded early, and through spitting rains from the southeast hills we marched back for two hours from the Overshot Nullah to Zonhwe, the small and newly-built settlement which we had missed on the preceding day. Several of the porters had disappeared during the night. Men were sent in all directions for provisions, which came in, however, slowly and scantily; and the noise made by the slaves—they were pulling down Said bin Salim's hut, which had accidentally caught fire—frightened away the country people. We were, therefore, detained in this unwholesome spot for two days.

Zonhwe was the turning-point of the expedition's difficulties. Another ass had died, reducing the number to twenty-three, and the Baloch, at first contented with two, doubled their requirements, and on the 14th August took a fifth, besides placing all their powder upon our hard-worked animals. I therefore proposed to the jemadar that the cloth, the beads, and the other similar luggage of his men, should be packed, sealed up, and inserted into the porters' loads, of which several had shrunk to half-weight. He probably thought the suggestion a ruse on my part to discover the means by which their property had almost trebled its quantity; his men, moreover, had become thoroughly weary of a journey where provisions were not always obtainable, and they had persuaded themselves that Lieut. Colonel Hamerton's decease had left me without support from the government of Zanzibar. After a priming with opium, the monocular returned and reported that his men refused to open their baggage, declaring their property to be "on their own heads." While I was explaining the object of the measure, the escort appeared in mass, and, with noise sufficient for a general action, ostentatiously strewed their old clothes upon the ground, declaring that at Zanzibar they were honorable men, and boasting that the Baloch were intrusted with lacs of dollars by the Sayyid Said. Again I offered reasons, which, as is the wont of the world in such cases, served only to make them more hopelessly unreasonable. The jemadar accused me of starving the party. I told him not to eat abominations, upon which, clapping hand to hilt, he theatrically forbade me to repeat the words. Being prostrated at the time by fever, I could only show him how little dangerous he was by using the same phrase half a dozen times. He then turned fiercely upon the timid Said bin Salim, and having safely vented the excess of his wrath, he departed to hold a colloquy with his men.

The debate was purposely conducted in so loud a tone that every word reached my ears. Khudabakhsh, from first to last my evil genius and the main-spring of all mischief, threatened to take "that man's life," at the risk of chains for the remainder of his days. Another opined, that "in all Nazarenes there is no good." All complained that they had no "hishmat" (respect!), no food, and, above every thing, no meat.

Presently Said bin Salim was deputed by them to state that for the future they would require one sheep per diem—men who, when at Zanzibar, saw flesh probably once a year on the Eed. This being inadmissible, they demanded three cloths daily instead of one. I would willingly have given them two, as long as provisions continued scarce and dear, but the shade of concession made them raise the number to four. They declared that in case of refusal they would sleep at the village, and on the next day would return to Zanzibar. Receiving a contemptuous answer, they marched away in a body, noisily declaring that they were going to make instant preparation for departure.

Such a proceeding on the part of several of these mercenaries was inexcusable. They had been treated with kindness and even indulgence. They had hitherto never complained, simply because they had no cause for complaint. One man, Ismail, who suffered from dysentery, had been regularly supplied with food cooked by the Goanese; and even while we dragged along our fevered frames on foot, he was allowed to ride an ass. Yet the recreant never attempted a word of dissuasion, and deserted with the rest.

After the disappearance of the Baloch, the sons of Ramji were summoned. I had privily ascertained from Said bin Salim the opinions of these men concerning their leader: they said but little evil, complaining principally of the Englishman's "heat," and that he was not wholly ruled by their rascalities, whereas the Baloch in their private confabs never failed to indulge in the choicest of Oriental Billingsgate. The slaves, when they heard the state of the case, cheerfully promised to stand by us, but on the same evening, assembled by Kidogo, they agreed to follow the example of the escort on the first justifiable occasion. I did not learn this till some days afterward, and even if I had been told it on the spot it would have mattered little. My companion and I had made up our minds, in case of the escort and the slaves deserting, to bury our baggage, and to trust ourselves in the hands of the Wanyamwezi porters. The storm, however—a *brutum fulmen*—blew over with only noise.

A march was ordered for the next day—the 17th August. As the asses were being loaded, appeared the one-eyed jemadar, with Gray-beard Musa and Darwaysh, looking more crestfallen and foolish than they had ever looked before. They took my hand with a polite violence, begged suppliantly for a paper of dismissal to "cover their shame," and declared that, so far from deserting me, I was deserting them. As this required no reply, I mounted and rode on.

The path fell easily westward down a long grassy and jungly incline, cut by several water-courses. About noon, I lay down half-fainting in the sandy bed of the Muhama Nullah—the "palmetto," or "fan-palm;" and retaining Wazira and Mabruki, I urged the caravan forward, that my companion might send me back a hammock from the halting-place. Suddenly appeared the whole body of deserters shouldering—as porters and asses had been taken from them—their luggage, which outwardly consisted of cloth, dirty rags, green skins, old earthen pots, and greasy gourds and calabashes. They led me to a part of the nullah where stagnant water was found, and showing abundant penitence, they ever and anon attempted excuses, which were reserved for consideration. At 3 P.M., no hammock appearing, I remounted, and pursued a path over rolling ground, with masses of dwarf hill flanking a low bottom, which renewed the scenery of the "Slough of Despond"—Zungomero. Again the land, matted with putrid grass, displayed the calabash and the hyphæna, the papaw and the palmetto; the holcus and maize were of luxuriant dimensions, and deep rat-holes, enlarged by the boy-hunters, broke the grassy path. I found two little villages, inhabited by Wangindo and Mandandu immigrants from the vicinity of Kilwa. Then appeared on a hill-side the kraal in which the caravan had halted; the party had lost the road, and had been dispersed by a swarm of wild bees, an accident even more frequent in East Africa than in India.

Next morning the Baloch were harangued; they professed themselves profoundly penitent, and attributing their unsoldierlike conduct to opium and to the wiswas, the temptations of Sathanas, they promised to reform. The promise was kept till we reached Ugogi. They were, however, always an encumberance; they did no good beyond creating an impression, and "making the careless Æthiopians afraid." I saw them, it is true, in their worst colors. They held themselves to be servants of their prince, and as no Eastern man can or will serve two masters, they forfeited all claim to their sole good quality—manageability. As men, they had no stamina; after a few severe marches they murmured that

> "Famine, despair, thirst, cold, and heat,
> Had done their work on them by turns."

Their constitutions, sapped by long residence at Zanzibar, were subject to many ailments, and in sickness they were softer than Indian Pariahs. Under the slightest attack of fever they threw themselves moaning upon the ground; they were soon deterred by the sun from bringing up the rear, and by night they would not keep watch or ward even when in actual danger of robbery. Notwithstanding their affectation of military carriage their bravery was more than problematical; they were disciplined only by their fears. As men-at-arms, one and all deserved to wear the wooden spoon. I saw the whole garrison of Kaole firing for an hour, without effect, at a shell, stuck on a stick, distant about a dozen paces. Our party expended thirty pounds of gunpowder without bagging a pair of antelope, and it was impossible to trust them with ammunition; when unable to sell it, they wasted it upon small birds. Ever claiming for themselves "hishmat," or respect, they forgot their own proverb that "courtesy hath two heads;" they complained that they were not seated half the day in our tents; and the being "told to depart," when their terribly long visits rendered the measure necessary, was a standing grievance. Like the lower races of Orientals, they were ever attempting to intrude, to thrust themselves forward, to take an ell when an inch was offered. They considered all but themselves fools, ready to be imposed upon by the flimsiest lie, by the shallowest artifices. Gratitude they ignored; with them a favor granted was but an earnest of favors to come, and one refusal obliterated the trace of a hundred largesses. Their objects in life seemed to be eating, and buying slaves; their pleasures, drinking and intrigue. Insatiable beggars were they; noisy, boisterous, foul-mouthed knaves; swearers "with voices like cannons;" rude and forward in manner; low and abusive in language; so slanderous that, for want of other subjects, they would calumniate one another, and requiring a periodical check to their presumption. I might have spent the whole of my day in superintending the food of these thirteen "great eaters and little runners." Repeatedly warned, both by myself and my companion, that their insubordination would prevent our recommending them for recompense at the end of the journey, they could not check repeated ebullitions of temper. Before arrival at the coast they seemed to have made up their minds that they had not fulfilled the conditions of reward. After my departure from Zanzibar, however, they persuaded Lieut. Colonel Hamerton's successor to report officially to the government of Bombay "the claims of these men, the hardships they endured, and the fidelity and perseverance they showed!"

At Muhama I halted three days, a delay which generally occurred before long desert marches for which provisions are required. On the first, Kidogo would bring about sixty pounds of grain; on the second, he would disperse his men throughout the villages, and procure the 300 pounds required for five marches; and on the third, he would cause it to be husked and pounded, so as to be ready for the morrow. Three up-caravans, containing a total of about 150 men, suffering severely from small-pox, here passed us. One was commanded by Khalfan bin Muallim Salim and his brother Id, coast Arabs, whom we afterward met at two places. He told me several deliberate falsehoods about the twenty-two porters that were to follow us; for instance, that he had left them, halted by disease, at Kidunda, in the maritime region, under the command of one Abdullah bin Jumah, and thus he led me to expect them at a time when they had not even been engaged. He and his men also spread reports in Ugogo and other places where the people are peculiarly suspicious, concerning the magical and malignant powers of the "whites;" in fact, he showed all the bad spirit of his bastard blood. At Muhama, the farthest point westward to which the vuli or autumnal rains extend, the climate was still that of the Rufuta Range, foggy, misty mornings, white rags of cloud-bank from the table-cloths outspread upon the heights, clear days, with hot suns and chilling south winds, and raw, dewy nights. I again suffered from fever; the attack, after lasting seven days, disappeared, leaving, however, hepatic complications, which, having lasted uninterruptedly ten months, either wore themselves out, or yielded to the action of acids, narcotics, and stimulants tardily forwarded from Zanzibar. Here, also, over-fatigue, in a fruitless shooting-excursion, combined with the mephitic air of stagnant, weedy waters, caused a return of my companion's fever.

Two other Wanyamwezi porters were laid up with small-pox. One ass died of fatigue; while a second, torn by a hyena, and a third, too weak to walk, were left, together with the animal that had been stung by bees, in charge of Mpambe, headman of the Wangindo. Being now reduced to the number of nineteen beasts, I submitted to Said bin Salim the advisability of leaving behind wire and ammunition, either cached in the jungle, as is the custom of these lands, or intrusted to the headman. The Arab approved. Kidogo, however, dissented. I took the opinion of the latter. He was positive that the effects once abandoned would never be recovered, and that the headman, who appeared a kind of cunning idiot, was not to be trusted. Some months afterward I commissioned an Arab merchant, who was marching toward the coast, to recover the asses left in the charge of Mpambe; the latter refused to give them up, thus proving the soundness of Kidogo's judgment.

Having collected with difficulty—the land was sun-cracked, and the harvest-store had been concealed by the people—some supplies, but scarcely sufficient for the long desert tract, we began, on the 21st of August, to cross the longitudinal plain that, gently shelving westward, separates the Rufuta from the second, or Mukondokwa Range. The plain was inclosed on all sides by low lines of distant hill, and cut by deep nullahs, which gave more than the usual amount of trouble. The tall palmyra (*Borassus flabelliformis*), whose majestic bulging column renders it so difficult to climb, was a novel feature in the scenery. This tree, the mvumo of East Africa, and the deleb-palm of the Upper Nile, is scattered through the interior, extending to the far south. On this line it is more common in Western Unyamwezi, where, and where only, an intoxicating toddy is drawn from the cut-frond, than elsewhere. The country abounded in game, but we were both too weak to work—my companion, indeed, was compelled to lag behind — and the Baloch, to whom the guns were lent, returned empty-handed. Sign of the mbogo (*Bos Caffer*) here appeared; it is general in East Africa, especially upon the river plains where water abounds. These wild cattle are fine animals, somewhat larger than the common-sized English bullock, with uniform dun skins, never parti-colored like the tame herds, and with thick black-brown horns, from twelve to thirteen inches broad at the base, diverging outward, and incurved at the points, which in large specimens are distant about three feet from each other; they are separated by a narrow channel, and this in age becomes a solid mass of bone. The mbogo is as dull of comprehension as it is fierce and powerful; affecting particular spots, it will often afford several chances of a successful shot to the fundi—shikari, or chasseur—of a caravan : the Africans kill it with arrows. The flesh, though considered heating and bilious, is eaten, and the hide is preferred for thongs and reins to that of the tame animal.

The approach to the kraal was denoted by a dead level of dry, caked, and cracked mud, showing the subsidence of an extensive inundation. We passed a large camping-ground, affected by down-caravans, on the near side of the Makata, a long river-like "tank," whose lay is E. by N. The oozy banks of this water, which is said to flow, after rains, into the Mukondokwa River, are fringed with liliaceous and other large aquatic plants; the water, though dark, is potable. After fording the tank, which was then breast-deep, we found on the farther side the kraal used by porters of up-caravans, who sensibly avoid commencing the day with hard labor, and who fear that a sudden fall of rain might compel them to intempestive halts. In such places, throughout the country, there are two distinct khambi, one on each side of the obstacle, whether this be a river, a pass, or a populous clearing; in the latter case, caravans unload at the farther end of the cultivation, prepared to escape from a fray into the jungle, without running the gauntlet of the villages. That evening I tried to reduce the ever-increasing baggage of the sons of Ramji, who added to the heaps piled upon the wretched asses, now burdened with rations for several days, their drums and sleeping-hides, and their cocks and hens, while they left the beds and the cooking utensils of the Goanese upon the ground. They informed me that if our animals could not carry their property they could not drive our animals. The reply was significant. With some exertion of the "rascally virtue"—prudence—I retired.

The night was disturbed only by musquitoes. These piping pests, however, are less troublesome in this part of East Africa than might be expected from the nature and the position of the country, and the bite has little venom compared with those of the Mozambique, or even of Western India. The common culex is a large variety, of brownish or dun color; its favorite breeding-places are the back-waters on the banks of rivers, and the margins of muddy pools, and upon the creeks of the maritime regions, and the central lakes.

Pursuing our march on the next day, I witnessed a curious contrast in this strange African nature, which is ever in extremes, and where extremes ever meet—where grace and beauty are seldom seen without a sudden change to a hideous grotesqueness. A splendid view charmed me in the morning. Above lay a sky of purest azure, flaked with fleecy opal-tinted vapors floating high in the empyrean, and catching the first roseate smiles of the unrisen sun. Long lines, one bluer then the other, broken by castellated crags and towers of most picturesque form, girdled the far horizon; the nearer heights were of a purplish brown, and snowy mists hung like glaciers about their folds. The plain was a park in autumn, burnt tawny by the sun, patched with a darker hue where the people were firing the grass—a party was at work merrily, as if preparing for an English harvest-home—to start the animals, to promote the growth of a young crop, and, such is the popular belief, to attract rain. Calabashes, palmyras, tamarinds, and clumps of evergreen trees were scattered over the scene, each stretching its lordly arms over subject circlets of deep dew-fed verdure. Here the dove cooed loudly, and the guinea-fowl rang its wild cry, while the peewit chattered in the open stubble, and a little martin, the prettiest of its kind, contrasted, by its nimble dartings along the ground, with the condor wheeling slowly through the upper air. The most graceful of animals, the zebra and the antelope, browsed in the distance: now they stood to gaze upon the long line of porters, then, after leisurely pacing, with retrospective glances, in an opposite direction, they halted motionless for a moment, faced about once more to satiate curiosity, and lastly, terrified by their own fancy, they bounded in ricochets over the plain.

About noon the fair scene vanished as if by enchantment. We suddenly turned northward into a tangled mass of tall fetid reeds, rank jungle and forest, with its decaying trunks encroaching upon the hole-pierced goat-track that zigzagged toward the Myombo River. This perennial stream rises, according to the guides, in an elevation opposite to the highlands of Dut'humi. It is about fifty feet broad at the ford, breast-deep, and the swift brown waters swirl under a canopy of the trees whose name it bears. The "myombo" is a fine specimen of African timber, apparently unknown to the people of Zanzibar, but extending almost from the coast to the lake regions. The flower is greenish, with the overpowering smell of the Indian jasmines; the fruit is a large pod, containing ten or twelve long hard acorns, of a brown-black color, set in cups which resemble red sealing-wax. The coarse bark is used for building huts and kraals, the inner fibre for "bast" and ropes, and the wood makes what Easterns call a hot fire, lasting long, and burning well out. After the fiery sun and the dry atmosphere of the plains, the sudden effect of the dank and clammy chill, the result of exceeding evaporation, under the impervious shades that line the river banks, was overpowering. In such places one feels as if poisoned by miasma; a shudder runs through the frame, and a cold perspiration, like the prelude for a fainting-fit, breaks from the brow. Unloading the asses, and fording the stream, we ascended the left bank, and occupied a kraal, with fires still smoking, on its summit. Though another porter was left behind with small-pox, I had little difficulty with the luggage on this march: the more I worked the men the harder they worked. Besides, they seldom fell sick on the road, though often prostrated when halting—a phenomenon which my companion explained by their hard eating and little exercise when stationary, and which Said bin Salim more mercifully attributed to the fatigue and exposure of the journey taking effect when the excitement had passed away.

At dawn on the 23d of August we resumed our journey, and in 4$^{hrs.}$ 30$^{m.}$ concluded the transit of the lateral plain, which separates the Rufuta from the Mukondokwa Range. The path wound over a wintry land, green with vegetation only in the vicinity of water. After struggling through a forest of canes, we heard a ngoma, or large drum, which astonished us, as we had not expected to find a village. Presently, falling into a net-work of paths, we lost our way. After long wandering, we came upon a tobacco-field which the Baloch and the sons of Ramji had finished stripping, and conducted by some Wanyamwezi who had delayed returning to guide us, in order to indulge their love for drumming and plundering, we arrived at the débris of a once flourishing village of Wasagara, called Mbumi, from its headman. A pitiable scene here presented itself. The huts were torn and half-burnt, and the ground was strewed with nets and drums, pestles and mortars, cots and fragments of rude furniture; and though no traces of blood were observed, it was evident that a commando had lately taken place there. Said bin Salim opined this ruin to be the work of Khalfan bin Salim, the youth who had preceded us from Muhama; ever suspicious, he saw in it a plan adopted by the coast Arab in order to raise against us the people of the mountains. Kidogo, observing that the damage was at least ten days old, more acutely attributed it to the Moslem kidnappers of Whinde, who, aided by the terrible Kisabengo, the robber-chief of Ukami, near K'hutu, harry the country with four or five hundred guns. Two of the wretched villagers were seen lurking in the jungle, not daring to revisit the wreck of their homes. Here again the demon of slavery will reign over a solitude of his own creation. Can it be that, by some inexplicable law, where Nature has done her best for the happiness of mankind, man, doomed to misery, must work out his own unhappiness? That night was spent at the deserted village by our men in drumming, singing, and gleaning all that Khalfan's gang had left; they were, moreover, kept awake by fear lest they might be surprised by the remnants of the villagers.

Late in the morning of the 24th of August, after losing another ass, torn by a cynhyena, we followed the path that leads from Mbumi along the right bank of the Mukondokwa River to its ford. The marescent vegetation and the tall, stiff, and thick-stalked grass dripped with dew, which struck cold as a freezing-mixture. The path was slippery with mud, and man and beast were rendered wild by the cruel stings of a small red ant and a huge black pismire. The former cross the road in dense masses like the close columns of an army. They are large-headed, showing probably that they are the defenders of the republic, and that they perform the duties of soldiers in their excursions. Though they can not spring, they show great quickness in fastening themselves to the foot or ankle as it brushes over them. The pismire, known to the people as the " chungu-fundo," or " siyafu," from the Arabic " siyaf," is a horse-ant, about an inch in length, whose bull-dog-like head and powerful mandibles enables it to destroy rats and mice, lizards and snakes. It loves damp places upon the banks of rivers and stagnant waters; it burrows but never raises hills, and it appears scattered for miles over the paths. Like the other species, it knows neither fear nor sense of fatigue; it rushes to annihilation without hesitating, and it can not be expelled from a hut except by fire or boiling water. Its bite, which is the preamble to its meal, burns like a pinch with a red-hot needle; and when it sets to work, twisting itself round and " accroupi" in its eagerness for food, it may be pulled in two without relaxing its hold. The favorite food of this pismire is the termite: its mortal enemy is a large ginger-colored ant, called from its painful wound " maji m'oto," or " hot-water." In this foul jungle our men also suffered severely from the tzetze. This fly, the torment of Cape travelers, was limited, by Dr. Livingstone, to the regions south of the Zambezi River. A specimen brought home by me and submitted to Mr. Adam White, of the British Museum, was pronounced by him to be a true Glossina morsitans, and Mr. Petherick has fixed its limits about eight degrees north of the equator. On the line followed by the expedition, the tzetze was found extending from Usagara westward as far as the central lakes; its usual habitat is the jungle-strip which incloses each patch of cultivated ground, and in the latter it is rarely seen. It has more persistency of purpose even than the Egyptian fly, and when beaten off it will return half a dozen times to the charge; it can not be killed except by a smart blow, and its long sharp proboscis draws blood even through a canvas hammock. It is not feared by the naked traveler; the sting is as painful as that of an English horse-fly, and leaves a lasting trace, but this hard-skinned people expect no evil consequences from it. In the vicinity of Kilwa it was heard of under the name of " kipanga," the " little sword." It is difficult to conceive the purpose for which this plague was placed in a land so eminently fitted for breeding cattle and for agriculture, which without animals can not be greatly extended, except as an exercise for human ingenuity to remove. Possibly at some future day, when the country becomes valuable, the tzetze may be exterminated by the introduction of some insectivorous bird, which will be the greatest benefactor that Central Africa ever knew.

After about an hour's march, the narrow tunnel in the jungle—it was so close that only one ass could be led up and unloaded at a time—debouched upon the Mukondokwa ford. The view was not unpleasing. The swift brown stream was broadened by a branch-islet in its upper bed to nearly a hundred yards, and its margins were fringed with rushes backed by a screen of dense verdure and tall trees which occupied the narrow space between the water and the hills. The descent and the landing-place were equally bad. Slipping down the steep miry bank, the porters sank into the river breast-deep, causing not a little damage to their loads: the ford now wetted the waist, then the knee, and the landing-place was a kind of hippopotamus-run of thick slushy mud, floored with roots and branches, snags and sawyers, and backed by a quagmire rendered passable only by its mat-work of tough grass-canes laid by their own weight. Having crossed over on our men's backs, we ascended a little rise and lay down somewhat in the condition of traveling manes fresh from the transit of the Styx. I ordered back Kidogo with a gang of porters to assist Said bin Salim, who was bringing up the rear; he promised to go, but he went the wrong way—forward. Resuming our march along the river's left or northern bank, we wound along the shoulders and the bases of hills, sometimes ascending the spurs of stony and jungly eminences, where the paths were unusually rough and precipitous, at other times descending into the stagnant lagoons, the reedy and rushy swamps, and the deep bogs which margin the stream. After a total of six hours we reached a kraal situated upon the sloping ground at the foot of the northern walls which limit the grassy river-basin; through this the Mukondokwa flows in a dark turbid stream now narrowed to about forty feet. The district of "Kadetamare" was formerly a provisioning station where even cattle were purchasable, a rare exception to the rule in the smaller settlements of Usagara. I at once sent men to collect rations, none, however, were procurable: meeting a small party that were bringing grain from Rumuma, they learned that there was a famine in the land.

At Kadetamare the only pedometer, a patent watch-shaped instrument, broke down, probably from the effects of the climate. While carried by my companion it gave a steady exaggerative rate, but being set to the usual military pace of 30 inches, when transferred to the person of "Seedy Bombay" and others, it became worse than useless, sometimes showing 25 for 13 miles. I would suggest to future explorers in these regions, as the best and the most lasting means of measuring distances, two of the small wheelbarrow perambulators—it is vain to put trust in a single instrument—which can each be rolled on by one man. And when these are spoilt or stolen, timing with the watch, and a correct estimate of the walking rate combined with compass-bearings, the mean of the oscillations being taken when on the march, would give a " dead-reckoning," which checked by latitudes, as often as the cloudy skies permit, and by a few longitudes at crucial stations, would afford materials for a map approximating as nearly to correctness as could be desired in a country where a " handful of miles" little matters. The other instruments, though carefully protected from the air, fared not better than the pedometer : with three pocket-chronometers and a valuable lever-watch, we were at last reduced to find time by a sixpenny sun-dial. Before the first fortnight after our second landing in Africa had elapsed, all these instruments, notwithstanding the time and trouble devoted to them by my companion at Zanzibar, failed in their ratings and became useless for chronometric longitudes. Two of them (Ed. Baker, London, No. 863, and Barraud, London, No. $\frac{2}{537}$) stopped without apparent reason. A third, a first-rate article (Parkinson and Frodsham, No. 2955), issued to me from the Royal Observatory Greenwich, at the kind suggestion of Capt. Belcher, of the Admiralty, had its glass broken and its second-hand lost by the blunderer Gaetano : we remedied that evil by counting the ticks without other trouble than that caused by the odd number—5 to 2 seconds. This instrument also summarily struck work on the 9th November, 1858, the day before we intended to have " made a night of it" at Jiwe la Mkoa. This may serve as a warning for future travelers to avoid instruments so delicate that a jolt will disorder them—the hair-spring of the lever-watch was broken by my companion in jumping out of a canoe—and which no one but a professional can attempt to repair. A box-chronometer carried in a ".petarah" by a pole swung between two men so as to preserve its horizontality, might outlast the pocket-instruments, yet we read in Capt. Owen's celebrated survey of the African coasts, that out of nine, not one kept rate without fluctuations. The best plan would be to purchase half a dozen sound second-hand watches, carefully inspected and cleaned, and to use one at a time; if gold-mounted, they would form acceptable presents to the Arabs, and ultimately would prove economical by obviating the necessity of parting with more valuable articles.

The break-down of the last chronometer disheartened us for a time. Presently, when our brains, addled by sun and sickness, had recovered tone by a return to the Usagara sanitarium, we remembered a rough and ready succedaneum for instruments. I need scarcely tell the reader that, unhappily for travelers, the only means of ascertaining the longitude of a place is by finding the difference between the local and Greenwich times, and that this difference of time with certain corrections is converted into distance of space. We split a 4 oz. rifle-ball, inserted into it a string measuring 39 inches from the point of suspension to the centre of the weight, and fixed it by hammering the halves together. The loose end of the cord was attached to a three-edged file as a pivot, and this was lashed firmly to the branch of a tree sheltered as much as possible from the wind. Local time was ascertained with a sextant by taking the altitude of a star or a planet; Greenwich time by a distance between the star or planet and the moon, and the vibrations of our rude pendulum did all that a watch could do, by registering the seconds that elapsed between the several observations.

I am somewhat presuming upon the subject, but perhaps it may here be better to chronicle the accidents which happened to the rest of our instruments. We had two Schmalcalder's compasses (H. Barron & Co., 26 Oxenden Street), which, when the pasteboard faces had been acclimatized and no longer curled up against their glasses, did good service; one of them was trodden upon by my companion, the other by a sailor during a cruise on the lake. We returned with a single instrument, the gift of my old friend Lieut. General Monteith; it had surveyed Persia, and outlasting two long excursions into Eastern Africa, it still outlives, and probably will outlive many of the showy articles now supplied by the trade. Finally, a ship's compass, mounted in gimbals for boat-work and indented for upon the engineer's stores, Bombay, soon became lumber, its oscillations were too sluggish to be useful.

We left Kadetamare on the 25th August, to ascend the fluviatile valley of the Mukondokwa. According to the guides this stream is the upper course of the Kingani River, with which it anastomoses in Uzaramo (?) It cuts its way through the chain to which it gives a name, by a transversal valley perpendicular to the lay, and so conveniently disposed that the mountains seem rather to be made for their drain than the drain for its mountains. The fluviatile valley is apparently girt on all sides by high peaks, with homesteads smoking and cattle grazing on all sides. Crippled by the night-cold that rose from the river-bed, and then wet through with the dew that dripped from the tall grass, we traversed, within ear-shot of the frightened villagers who hailed one another from the heights, some fields of grain and tobacco that had been lately reaped. After an hour and a half of marching we arrived at the second ford of the Mukondokwa. Receiving less drainage than in the lower bed, the stream was narrower and only knee-deep; the landing-place of sloppy mud caused, however, many accidents to the asses, and on inspecting our stores a few days afterward we found them all soft and mildewed. The reader will wonder that on these occasions we did not personally inspect the proceedings of our careless followers. The fact is we were physically and morally incapacitated for any exertion beyond balancing ourselves upon the donkeys; at Kadetamare I had laid in another stock of fever, and my companion had not recovered from his second severe attack. After fording the Mukondokwa we followed the right bank, through cultivation, grass, and trees, up a gradually broadening valley peculiarly rich in field-rats. The path then crossing sundry swamps and nullahs, hill-spurs and "neat's tongues," equally rough, thorny, and precipitous, presently fell into a river-reach where pools of water, breast-deep, and hedged in by impassable jungle and long runs of slushy mire festering in a furious sun, severely tried the porters and asses. Thence the road wound under the high hills to the south, whose flanks were smoking with extensive conflagrations, while on the opposite or left bank of the river, the opening valley displayed a forest of palms and tall trees. About 2 P.M. I reached the ground, a hutless circle of thorns, called by our people Muinyi: the rearguard, however, did not straggle in before 6 P.M., and the exhaustion of the asses—seventeen now remained—rendered a day's halt necessary.

During the last two marches the Baloch had been, they declared, without grain; the sons of Ramji and the porters, more provident, had reserved a small store; moreover, they managed to procure a sheep from the next station. On the morrow a party, headed by Muinyi Wazira, set out to forage among the mountain settlements, bearing no arms, in token of peace. About noon they returned, and reported that at the sight of strangers the people had taken to flight, after informing the party that they were in the habit of putting to death all murungwana or freemen found trespassing off the road; however, that on this occasion the lives of the strangers should be spared. But Ambari, a slave belonging to Said bin Salim, presently tattled the true tale. The gallant foragers had not dared to enter the village; when the warcry flew from hamlet to hamlet, and all the Wasagara, even the women and children, seized their spears and stood to arms, they at once threw themselves into the jungle and descended the hill with such unseemly haste that most of them bore the wounds of thorns and stones. Two of the Baloch, Riza and Belok, lit their matches and set out proudly to provide themselves by their prowess; they were derided by Kidogo: "Verily, O my brethren! ye go forth to meet men and not women!" and after a hundred yards' walk they took second thoughts and returned. The Mukondokwa Mountains, once a garden, have become a field for fray and foray; cruelty and violence have brutalized the souls of the inhabitants, and they have learned, as several atrocities committed since our passage through the country prove, to wreak their vengeance upon all weaker than themselves.

On the 27th of August we resumed our way under fresh difficulties. The last march had cost us another ass. Muhinna, a donkey-driver, complaining of fever, had been mounted by Kidogo without my permission, and had summarily departed, thus depriving us of the services of a second, while all were in a state of weakness which compelled them to walk at their slowest pace. On the other hand, the men of the caravan, hungry and suffering from raw southeast wind and the chilly cold, the result not of low temperature but of humidity and extensive evaporation, were for pushing forward as fast as possible. The path was painful, winding along the shoulders of stony and bushy hills, with rough re-entering angles, and sometimes dipping down into the valley of the Mukondokwa, which, hard on their right, spread out in swamps, nearly two miles broad, temporary where they depended upon rain, and permanent where their low levels admitted of free infiltration. On the steep eminences to the left of the path rose tall and thick the thorny aloetic and cactaceous growth of arid Somaliland; the other side was a miniature of the marine lagoons, the creeks, and the bayous of green Zanzibar. After three hours of hard marching, the labor came to its crisis, where the path, breaking off at a right angle from the river, wound up an insecure ladder of loose earth and stones, which caused several porters and one ass to lose their footing, and to roll with their loads through the thorny bushes of the steep slope, near the off side, into the bed of rushes below. Then leaving the river-valley on the right, we fell into a fiumara of deep loose sand, about a hundred yards broad, and occupying the centre of a widening table-land. The view now changed, and the "wady" afforded pleasant glimpses of scenery. Its broad, smooth, and glistening bed, dinted by the footprints of cattle, was bounded by low perpendicular banks of stiff red clay, margined by mighty masses of brilliant green tamarinds, calabashes, and sycamores, which stood sharply out against the yellow stubbles beyond them. The mkuyu or sycamore in Eastern Africa is a magnificent tree; the bole, composed of a pillared mass, averages from eight to ten feet in height, and the huge branches, thatched with thick cool foliage, extend laterally, overshadowing a circle whose perimeter, when the sun is vertical, sometimes attains five hundred feet. The fruit, though eaten by travelers, is a poor berry, all rind and seeds, with a slender title to the name of fig. There are apparently two varieties of this tree, resembling each other in general appearance, but differing in details. The mtamba has a large, heavy, and fleshy leaf; its fruit is not smooth like that of the mkuyu, but knobbed with green excrescences, and the bole is loftier than the common sycamore's trunk. The roots of the older trees, rising above the earth, draw up a quantity of mould which, when the wood is decayed or destroyed, forms the dwarf mounds that in many parts encumber the surface of the country. Traces of extensive cultivation—fields of bajri or panicum, the staple cereal which here supplants

the normal African holcus, or Kafir corn, and plantations of luxuriant maize, of beans, of the vetch known as the voiandzeia sub-
terranea, of tobacco, and other plants—showed that this district is
beyond the reach of the coast-kidnappers. From the rising ground
on the left hand we heard the loud tattoo of the drum. The Baloch, choosing to be alarmed, fired several shots, much to the annoyance of the irascible Kidogo, who had laid down as a law that
waste of powder in this region was more likely to invite than to
prevent an attack. As we ascended the fiumara it narrowed rapidly, and its head was encumbered with heaps of boulders, from
which sprang a runnel of the sweetest water. The camping-
ground was upon the left bank of the bed. The guide called it
Ndábi, probably from a small gnarled tree here abundant, bearing
a fruit like a pale red currant, which tastes like sweetened gum
dissolved in dirty water. I lost no time in sending for provisions,
which were scarce and dear. Bombay failed in procuring a sheep,
though the Baloch, by paying six cloths, were more fortunate.
One of Kidogo's principles of action, in which he was abetted by
Said bin Salim, was to prevent our buying provisions, however
necessary, at high prices, fearing lest the tariff thus established
might become an "ada," a precedent or custom for future travelers, himself and others. We were, therefore, fain to content ourselves and our servants with a little bajri and two eggs.

After a day's halt at Ndabi we resumed the journey on the
29th August. The path crossed a high and stony hill-shoulder,
where the bleak raw air caused one of the porters to lie down torpid like a frozen man. It then stretched over gradually rising
and falling ground to a dense bush of cactaceæ and milk-bush,
aloetic plants and thorns, based upon a surface of brick-dust red.
Beyond this point lay another plateau of wavy surface, producing
dwarfed and wind-wrung calabashes, and showing grain-fields
carefully and laboriously ridged with the hoe. Flocks and herds
now appeared in all directions. The ground was in some places
rust-colored, in others dazzlingly white with a detritus of granite;
mica glittered like silver-filings in the sun, and a fine silky grass
waved in the wind, bleached clean of color by the glowing rays.
This plateau ended in a descent with rapid slopes, over falls and
steps of rock and boulder into the basin of the Rumuma River.
It is a southern influent, or a bifurcation of the Mukondokwa, and
it drains the hills to the southwest of the Rumuma district, whereas
the main stream, arising in the highlands of the Wahumba or
Wamusai, carries off the waters of the lands on the west. Losing
our way, we came upon this mountain torrent, which swirls through
blocks and boulders under stiff banks of red earth densely grown
with brush and reeds; and to find the kraal we were obliged to
travel up the bed-side, through well-hoed fields irrigated by raised
water-courses. The khambi was badly situated in the dwarf hollow between the river and the hills, and having lately been ten-

anted, as the smoking embers showed, it was uncleanly in the extreme. It was heart-breaking to see the asses that day. I left
them to Said bin Salim, who, with many others, did not appear
till eventide.

Rumuma is a favorite resting-place with caravans, on account
of the comparative abundance of its supplies. I halted here two
whole days, to rest and feed the starving porters, and to repair
the sacks, the pack-saddles, and the other appointments of the
asses. Here, for the first time, the country people descended in
crowds from the hills, bringing fowls, hauling along small but
beautifully-formed goats, lank sheep, and fine bullocks—the latter
worth twelve cloths—and carrying on their heads basket-platters
full of the voiandzeia, bajri, beans, and the *Arachis hypogœa*. The
latter is called by the Arabs sumbul el sibal, or "monkey's spike-
nard;" on the coast, njugu ya nyassa; in Unyamwezi, karanga
or k'haranga, and farther west, mayowwa or mwanza. It is the
bhuiphali, or "earth-fruit" of India, and the bik'han of Maharatta
land, where it is used by cheap confectioners in the place of almonds, whose taste it simulates. Our older Cape travelers term
it the pig-nut. The plant extends itself along the surface of the
ground, and puts forth its fruit at intervals below. It is sown before the rains, and ripens after six months—in the interior about
June. The Arabs fry it with cream that has been slightly salted,
and employ it in a variety of rich dishes; it affords them also a
favorite oil. The Africans use it principally on journeys. The
price greatly varies according to the abundance of the article;
when moderate, about two pounds may be purchased for a "khete"
of coral beads.

The Wasagara of Rumuma are short, black, beardless men.
They wear their hair combed off the forehead, and twisted into a
fringe of little pig-tails, which extend to the nape of the neck.
Few boast of cloth, the general body contenting themselves with
a goat-skin flap somewhat like a cobbler's apron tied over one
shoulder, as we sling a game-bag. Their ornaments are zinc and
brass, ear-rings in rolls, which distend the ear-lobe, bangles, or
armlets of similar metal, and iron chains with oblong links as
anklets. Their arms are bows and arrows, assegais with long
lanceated heads, and bull-hide shields three feet long by one broad,
painted black and red in perpendicular stripes. I was visited by
their Sultan Njasa, a small grizzled old man, with eyes reddened
by liquor, a wide mouth, a very thin beard, a sooty skin, and long
straggling hair, "*à la malcontent.*" He was attired in an antiquated barsati, or blue and red Indian cotton, tucked in at the
waist, with another thrown over his shoulders, and his neck was
decked with many strings of beads. He insisted upon making
" sare" or brotherhood with Said bin Salim, who, being forbidden
by his law to taste blood, made the unconscientious Muinyi Wazira his proxy. The two brothers being seated on the ground

opposite each other, with legs well to the fore, one man held over their heads a drawn sword, while another addressed to them alternately a little sermon, denouncing death or slavery as the penalty for proving false to the vow. Then each brother licked a little of the other's blood, taken with the finger from a knife-cut above the heart, or rather where the heart is popularly supposed to be. The sultan then presented to the Muinyi, *in memoriam*, a neat iron chain-anklet, and the Muinyi presented to the sultan a little of our cloth.

The climate of Rumuma was new to me, after the incessant rains of the maritime valley, and the fogs and mists of the Rufuta Range. It was, however, in extremes. At night the thermometer, under the influence of dewy gusts, sank in the tent to 48° F., a killing temperature in these latitudes to half-naked and houseless men. During the day the mercury ranged between 80° and 90° F.; the sun was fiery, while a furious south wind coursed through skies purer and bluer than I had ever seen in Greece or Italy. At times, according to the people, the hill-tops are veiled, especially in the mornings and evenings, with thick nimbus, vapors, and spitting clouds, which sometimes extend to the plain, and discharge heavy showers that invariably cause sickness. Here my companion once more suffered from an attack of "liver," brought on, he supposed, from over-devotion to a fat bullock's hump. Two of the Wanyamwezi porters were seized with preliminary symptoms of small-pox, euphuistically termed by Said bin Salim "shurua," or chicken-pox. Several of the slaves, including the charming Halimah, were laid up; the worst of all, however, was Valentine, who complained of an unceasing racking headache, while his puffed cheeks and dull-yellow skin gave him the look of one newly deceased. At length, divining his complaint, he was cupped by a Mnyamwezi porter, and he recovered after the operation strength and appetite.

The 2d of September saw us *en route* to Márengá Mk'hali, or the "brackish water." Fording the Rumuma above the spot where it receives the thin supplies of the Márengá Mk'hali, we marched over stony hills and thorny bushes, dotted with calabash and mimosa, the castor-shrub and the wild egg-plant, and gradually rising, we passed into scattered fields of holcus and bajri, pulse and beans. Here, for the first time, bee-hives, called by the coast-people mazinga, or cannons, from their shape, hollowed cylindrical logs, closed with grass and puddle at both ends, and provided with an oval opening in the centre, were seen hanging to the branches of the foliaged trees. Cucumbers, watermelons, and pumpkins grew apparently without cultivation. The watermelon, called by the Arabs johh, and by the Wasawahili tikiti, flourishes throughout the interior, where it is a favorite with the people. It is sown before the rainy season, gathered after six months, and placed to ripen upon the flat roofs of the villages. Like the produce of Kafir-land, it is hard, insipid, fleshy, and full of seeds, having nothing but the name in common with the delicious fruit of Egypt and Afghanistan. The junsal, or boga, the pumpkin, is, if possible, worse than the water-melon. Its red meat, simply boiled, is nauseously sweet; it is, however, considered wholesome, and the people enjoy the seeds toasted, pounded, and mixed with the "mboga," or wild vegetables, with which a veritable African can, in these regions, keep soul and body together for six months. About 10 A.M. I found Khalfan's caravan halted in a large kraal among the villages, on the eastern hill above the " brackish water." They were loading for the march, and my men looked wistfully at the comfortable huts; but their halt had been occasioned by small-pox, I therefore hurried forward across the streamlet to a wind-swept summit of an opposite hill. The place was far from pleasant, the gusts were furious; by night the thermometer showed 54° F., by day there was but scanty shelter from the fiery sun, and the " Márengá Mk'hali," which afforded the only supplies of water, was at a considerable distance. Moreover, our umbrellas and bedding suffered severely from a destructive host of white ants, that here became troublesome for the first time. The " chunga mchwa," or termite, abounds throughout the sweet red clay soils and cool damp places, avoiding heat, sand, and stone, and it acts like a clearer and scavenger; without it, indeed, some parts of the country would be impassable, and it is endowed with extraordinary powers of destruction. A hard clay-bench has been drilled and pierced like a sieve by these insects in a single night, and bundles of reeds placed under bedding have in a few hours been converted into a mass of mud; straps were consumed, cloths and umbrellas were reduced to rags, and the mats used for covering the servants' sleeping-gear were, in the shortest possible time, so tattered as to be unserviceable. Man revenges himself upon the white ant, and satisfies his craving for animal food, which in these regions becomes a principle of action —a passion—by boiling the largest and fattest kind, and eating it as a relish with his insipid ugali, or porridge. The termite appears to be a mass of live water. Even in the dryest places it finds no difficulty in making a clay paste for the mud-galleries, like hollow tree-twigs, with which it disguises its approach to its prey. The phenomenon has been explained by the conjecture that it combines by vital force the atmospheric oxygen with the hydrogen evolved by its food. When arrived at the adult state, the little peoples rise ready-winged, like thin curls of pipe-smoke, generally about even-tide, from the ground. After a flight of a few yards, the fine membranes, which apparently serve to disperse the insects into colonies, drop off. In East Africa there is also a semi-transparent brown ant, resembling the termite in form, but differing in habits, and even exceeding it in destructiveness. It does not, like its congener, run galleries up to the point of attack.

Each individual works for itself in the open air, tears the prey with its strong mandibles, and carries it away to its hole. The cellular hills of the termites in this country rarely rise to the height of three feet, whereas in Somaliland they become dwarf towers, forming a conspicuous feature in the view.

No watch was kept by the Baloch at Márengá Mk'hali, though we were then in the vicinity of the bandit Wahumba. On the next day we were harangued by Kidogo, who proceeded to expound the principles that must guide us through the unsafe regions ahead. The caravan must no longer straggle on in its usual disorder, the van must stop short when separated from the main body, and the rear must advance at the double when summoned by the sound of the barghumi, or the koodoo-horn, which acts as bugle in Eastern Africa. I thought, at the time, that Kidogo might as well address his admonitions to the wind, and I thought rightly.

The route lay through the lateral plain which separates the Mukondokwa or second, from the Rubeho or third parallel range of the Usagara Mountains. At Márengá Mk'hali, situated as it is under the lee of the two eastern walls, upon which the humid northeast and southeast trade-winds impinge, the eye no longer falls, as before, upon a sheet of monotonous green, and the nose is not offended by the death-like exhalations of a pestilent vegetation. The dew diminishes, the morning cloud is rare upon the hill-top, and the stratus is not often seen in the valley; rain, moreover, seldom falls heavily, except during its single appointed season. The climate is said to be salubrious, and the medium elevation of the land—2500 feet—raises it high above the fatal fever-level, without attaining the altitudes where dysentery and pleurisy afflict the inhabitants. For many miles beyond Márengá Mk'hali water is rarely found. Caravans, therefore, resort to what is technically called a "tirikeza," or afternoon march. In the Kisawahili, or coast language, "ku tirikeza," or "tilikeza," and in Kinyamwezi "ku witekezea," is the infinitive of a neuter verb signifying "to march after noon-day;" by the Arabs it is corrupted into a substantive. Similarly the verb ku honga, to pay "dash," tribute, passage-money, or black-mail, becomes, in the mouths of the stranger, ku honga, or honga. The tirikeza is one of the severest inflictions that African traveling knows. At 11 A.M. every thing is thrown into confusion, although two or three hours must elapse before departure. Loads are bound up, kitchen-batteries are washed and packed, tents are thrown, and stools are carried off by fidgeting porters and excited slaves. Having drunk for the last time, and filled their gourds for the night, the wayfarers set out when the midday ends. The sun is far more severely felt after the sudden change from shade, than during the morning marches, when its increase of heat is slow and gradual. They trudge under the fire-ball in the firmament, over ground seething with glow and reek, through an air which seems to parch the eye-balls, and they endure the affliction till their shadows lengthen out upon the ground. The tirikeza is almost invariably a lengthy stage, as the porters wish to abridge the next morning's march, which leads to water. It is often bright moonlight before they arrive at the ground, with faces torn by the thorns projecting across the jungly path, with feet lacerated by stone and stub, and occasionally a leg lamed by stumbling into deep and narrow holes, the work of field-rats and of various insects.

We left Márengá Mk'hali at 1 P.M. on the 3d of September, and in order to impressionize a large and well-armed band of the country people that had gathered to stare at, to criticise, and to deride us, we indulged in a little harmless sword-play, with a vast show of ferocity and readiness for fight. The road lay over several rough, steep, and bushy ridges, where the wretched asses, rushing away to take advantage of a yard of shade, caused constant delays. The Wanyamwezi animals having a great persistency of character, could scarcely be dislodged, and, when they were, they threw their loads in pure spite. After topping a little "col," or pass, we came in sight of an extensive basin, bounded by distant blue hills, to which the porters pointed with a certain awe, declaring them to be the haunts of the fierce Wahumba. A descent of the western flank led us to a space partially cleared by burning, when the cry arose that men were lurking about. We then plunged into a thick bush of thorny trees, based upon a red clayey soil caked into the semblance of a rock. Contrary to expectation, when crossing a deep nullah trending northward, we found a little rusty, ochreish water, in one of the cups and holes that dented the sandstone of the soles. Thence the path, gradually descending, fell into a coarse scrub, varied with small open savannas, and broken, like the rest of the road, by deep, narrow water-courses, which carry off the waters of the southern hills to the northern lowlands. About 6 P.M., we came upon a cleared space in a thick thorn-jungle, where we established ourselves for the night. The near whine of the hyena, and the alarm of the asses, made sleep a difficulty. The impatience and selfishness of thirst showed strongly in the Baloch. Belok had five large gourds full of water, perhaps three gallons, yet he would not part with a palmful to the sick Ismail. That day I was compelled to dismiss my usual ass-leader, Shahdad, the zeze-player and fracturer of female hearts, who, preferring the conversation of his fellows, dragged the animal through thorns and alongside of trees so artistically, that my nether garments were soon in strips. I substituted for him Musa the Gray-beard, who, after a few days, begged, with bitter tears, to be excused. It was his habit to hurry on toward the kraal and shade, and the slow hobble of the ass detained him a whole hour in sore discomfort. The task was then committed to the tailor-youth Hudul, who lost no time in declaring that I had

abused him—that he was a Baloch—that he was not an asinego.
Then I tried Abdullah—the good young man. I dismissed him
because every day brought with it a fresh demand for cloth or
beads, gourds or sandals—for a " chit" to the balyuz—the consul
—or a general good character as regards honesty, virtue, and the
et ceteras. Finally, the ass was intrusted to the bull-headed slave
Mabruki, who, thinking of nothing but chat with his " brother,"
Seedy Bombay, and having that curious mania for command which
seems part of every servile nature, hurried my monture so recklessly, that earth-cracks and rat-holes caused us twain many a severe fall. My companion had intrusted himself to Bombay, who,
though he did nothing well, rarely did any thing very badly.

The 4th of September began with an hour's toil through the
dense bush, to a rapid descent over red soil and rocks, which necessitated frequent dismounting—no pleasant exercise after a
sleepless night. Below lay a wide basin of rolling ground, surrounded in front by a rim of hills. It was one of the many views
which, " catching the reflex of heaven," and losing by indistinct-
ness the harshness of defined outline and the deformity of individual feature, assume, viewed from afar, a peculiar picturesqueness. Traces of extensive cultivation, flocks and herds, were descried in the lower levels, which were a net-work of sandy nullahs;
and upon the rises, the regular and irregular square or oblong habitations called " tembe" were seen for the first time. Early September is, in this region, the depth of winter. Under the burning, glaring sun, the grass becomes white as the ground; the
fields, stubbles stiff as harrows, are stained only by the shadow of
passing clouds; the trees, except upon the nullah-banks, are gaunt
and bare, the animals are walking skeletons, and nothing seems to
flourish but flies and white ants, caltrops and grapple-plants. After crossing deep water-cuts trending northeast and north-north-
east, we descended a sharp incline and a rough ladder of boulders,
and found a dirty and confined kraal, on the side of a rocky khad*
or ravine, which drains off the surplus moisture of the westerly
crags and highlands, and which affords sweet springs, that cover
the soil as far as they extend with a nutritious and succulent grass.
As this was to be a halting-place, a more than usually violent
rush was made by the Baloch, the sons of Ramji, and the porters,
to secure the best quarters. The jemadar remaining behind with
three of the Wanyamwezi, who were unable to walk, did not arrive till after noon, and my companion, suffering from a paroxysm
of bilious fever, came in even later. Valentine was weaker than
usual, and Gaetano groaned more frequently, " ang duk'hta"—
body pains! To add other troubles, an ass had been lost, and
" Khamsin"—No. 50—my riding-animal, had, by breaking a tooth

---

* The Indian "khad" is the deep rocky drain in hilly countries, thus differing
from the popular idea of a "ravine," and from the nullah, which is a formation in
more level lands.

in fighting, incapacitated itself for food or drink. Its feebleness compelled me to transfer the saddle to the last of the Zanzibar riding-asses, Siringe—the quarter dollar—and Siringe, sadly back-sore, cowering in the hams, and slipping from under me every few minutes, showed present signs of giving in.

The basin of Inenge lies at the foot of the Rubeho or " Windy Pass," the third and westernmost range of the Usagara Mountains. The climate, like that of Rumuma, is ever in extremes—during the day a furnace, and at night a refrigerator—the position is a funnel, which alternately collects the fiery sunbeams and the chilly winds that pour down from the misty highlands. The villagers of the settlements overlooking the ravine flocked down to barter their animals and grain. Here, for the first time since our departure from the coast, honey, clarified butter, and, greatest boon of all, milk, fresh and sour, were procurable. The man who has been restricted to a diet so unwholesome as holcus and bajri, with an occasional treat of kennel-food—broth and beans—will understand that the first unexpected appearance of milk, butter, and honey formed an epoch in our journey.

The halt was celebrated with abundant drumming and droning, which lasted half the night; it served to cheer the spirits of the men, who had talked of nothing the whole day but the danger of being attacked by the Wahumba. On the next morning arrived a caravan of about 400 Wanyamwezi porters, marching to the coast, under the command of Isa bin Hijji and three other Arab merchants. An interchange of civilities took place. The Arabs, lacking cloth, could not feed their slaves and porters, who deserted daily, imperiling a valuable investment in ivory. The Europeans could afford a small contribution of three gorah or pieces of domestics: they received a present of fine white rice, a few pounds of salt, and a goat, in exchange for a little perfumed snuff and asafœtida, which, after a peculiar infusion, is applied to wounds, and which, administered internally, is considered a remedy for many complaints. I was allured to buy a few yards of rope, indispensable for packing the animals. The number of our asses being reduced from thirty to fifteen, and the porters from thirty-six to thirty, it was necessary to recruit. The Arabs sold two Wanyamwezi animals for ten dollars each, payable at Zanzibar. One proved valuable as a riding-ass, and carried me to the Central Lake, and back to Unyanyembe: the other, though caponized and blind on the off side, had become by bad treatment so obstinate and so cleverly vicious, that the Baloch called him " Shaytan yek-cham," or the " one-eyed fiend:" he carried, besides sundries, four boxes of ammunition, weighing together 160 pounds, and even under these he danced like a deer. Nothing was against him but his character: after a few days he was cast adrift in the wilderness of Mgunda M'khali, because no man dared to load and lead him. Knowing that the Arab merchants upon this line hold it a point of honor to discourage, by refusing a new engagement, the down-porters in their proclivity to desert, and believing that it was a stranger's duty to be even stricter than they are, I gave most stringent orders that any fugitive porter detected in my caravan should be sent back a prisoner to his employers. But the coast Arabs and the Wasawahili ignore this commercial chivalry, and shamelessly offer a premium to "levanters:" moreover, in these lands it is hard to make men understand the *rapport* between sayings and doings. Seven or eight fellows, who secretly left the party, were sent back; one, however, was taken on without my knowledge. Said bin Salim persuaded the merchants to lend us the services of three Wanyamwezi, who, for sums varying from eight shukkah to two cloths, and a coil large enough to make three wire bracelets, undertook to carry packs as far as Unyanyembe. Our Ras Kafilah had increased in Uzaramo his suite by the addition of "Zawada"—the "nice gift," a parting present of the headman Kizaya. She was a woman about thirty, with a black skin shining like a patent-leather boot, a bulging brow, little red eyes, a wide mouth, which displayed a few long, strong, scattered teeth, and a figure considerably too bulky for her thin legs, which were unpleasantly straight, like nine-pins. Her *morale* was superior to her *physique;* she was a patient and hardworking woman, and respectable in the African acceptation of the term. She was at once married off to old Musangesi, one of the donkey-men, whose nose and chin made him a caricature of our dear old friend Punch. After detecting her in a lengthy walk, perhaps not solitary, through the jungle, he was palpably guilty of such cruelty that I felt compelled to decree a dissolution of the marriage. After passing through sundry adventures she returned safely to Zanzibar, where, for aught I know, she may still grace the harem of Said bin Salim. At Inenge another female slave was added to the troop, in the person of the Lady Sikujui, "Don't know," a "mulier nigris dignissima barris," whose herculanean person and virago manner raised her value to six cloths and a large coil of brass wire. The channel of her upper lip had been pierced to admit a disk of bone; her Arab master had attempted to correct the disfigurement by scarification and the use of rock salt, yet the distended muscles insisted upon projecting sharply from her countenance, like a duck's bill, or the beak of an ornithorhyncus. This truly African ornamentation would have supplied another instance to the ingenious author of "Anthropometamorphosis."* "Don't know's" morals were frightful. She was

---

* Anthropometamorphosis: Man-transformed: or the Artificial Changeling, historically presented, In the mad and cruel Gallantry, foolish Bravery, Ridiculous Beauty, filthy Finenesse, and loathsome Loveliness of most NATIONS, fashioning and attiring their Bodies from the mould intended by NATURE; with figures of these Transfigurations. To which artificial and affected Deformations are added, all the Native and National Monstrosities that have appeared to disfigure the Humane Fabrick. With a VINDICATION of the Regular Beauty and Honesty of NATURE.

duly espoused—as the forlorn hope of making her an "honest woman"—to Goha, the sturdiest of the Wak'hutu porters: after a week she treated him with a sublime contempt. She gave him first one, then a dozen rivals; she disordered the caravan by her irregularities; she broke every article intrusted to her charge, as the readiest way of lightening her burden, and—"le moindre dé-faut d'une femme galante est de l'être"—she deserted so shame-lessly that at last Said bin Salim disposed of her at Unyanyembe, for a few measures of rice, to a traveling trader, who came the next morning to complain of a broken head.

Isa bin Hijji did us various good services. He and his com-panions kindly waited some days to superintend our preparations for crossing the Rubeho Range. They supplied useful hints for keeping the caravan together at different places infamous for de-sertion. They gave me valuable information about Ugogo and Ujiji, and they placed at my disposal their house at Unyanyembe. They "wigged" the kirangozi, or guide, for carelessness in not building a kraal-fence every night, and for not bringing in, as the custom is, wood and water. Kidogo was reproved for allowing his men to load our asses with their luggage, and the Baloch for their continual complaints about food. The latter had long for-gotten the promises made at Muhama; they returned at every op-portunity to their old tactic, that of obtaining, by all manner of pretexts, as much cloth and beads as possible, ostensibly for pro-visions, really for trading and buying slaves. At Rumuma they declared that one cloth per diem starved them. Said bin Salim sent them its value, about fifty pounds of beans, and they had abundant rations of beef and mutton, but they could not eat beans. At Inenge they wanted flour, and as the country people sold only grain, they gave themselves up to despair. I sent for the jema-dar and told him, in presence of the merchants, that, as a fitting opportunity had presented itself, I was willing to weed the party by giving official dismissal to Khudabakhsh and Belok, to the in-valid Ismail and his musical "brother" Shahdad. All four, when consulted, declared that they would die rather than blacken their faces by abandoning the "Haji Abdullah;" that same evening, however, as I afterward learned, they wrote, by means of the Arabs, a heart-rending complaint to their chief jemadar at Zanzibar, de-claring that he had thrown them into the fire (of affliction), and that their blood was upon his hands. My companion prepared official papers and maps for the secretary of the Royal Geograph-ical Society, and I again indented upon the consul and the col-lector of customs for drugs, medical comforts, and an extra supply of cloth and beads, to the extent of 400 dollars, for which a check upon my agents in Bombay was inclosed. The Arabs took leave

With an Appendix of the Pedigree of the ENGLISH GALLANT.   Scripsit J. B. Cognomento Chirosophus, M.D.   "In nova fert animus, mutatas dicere formas." London: Printed by William Hunt, Anno Dom. 1653.

of us on the 2d of September. I charged them repeatedly not to spread reports of our illness, and I saw them depart with regret. It had really been a relief to hear once more the voice of civility and sympathy.

The great labor still remained. Trembling with ague, with swimming heads, ears deafened by weakness, and limbs that would hardly support us, we contemplated with a dogged despair the apparently perpendicular path that ignored a zigzag, and the ladders of root and boulder, hemmed in with tangled vegetation, up which we and our starving drooping asses were about to toil. On the 10th September we hardened our hearts, and began to breast the Pass Terrible. My companion was so weak that he required the aid of two or three supporters; I, much less unnerved, managed with one. After rounding in two places wall-like sheets of rock—at their bases green grass and fresh water were standing close to camp, and yet no one had driven the donkeys to feed—and crossing a bushy jungly step, we faced a long steep of loose white soil and rolling stones, up which we could see the Wanyamwezi porters swarming, more like baboons scaling a precipice than human beings, and the asses falling after every few yards. As we moved slowly and painfully forward, compelled to lie down by cough, thirst, and fatigue, the "sayhah" or war-cry rang loud from hill to hill, and Indian files of archers and spearmen streamed like lines of black ants in all directions down the paths. The predatory Wahumba, awaiting the caravan's departure, had seized the opportunity of driving the cattle and plundering the villages of Inenge. Two passing parties of men, armed to the teeth, gave us this information; whereupon the negro "Jelai" proposed, fear-maddened, a *sauve qui peut*—leaving to their fate his employers, who, bearing the mark of Abel in this land of Cain, were ever held to be the head and front of all offense. Khudabakhsh, the brave of braves, being attacked by a slight fever, lay down, declaring himself unable to proceed, moaned like a bereaved mother, and cried for drink like a sick girl. The rest of the Baloch, headed by the jemadar, were in the rear; they leveled their matchlocks at one of the armed parties as it approached them, and, but for the interference of Kidogo, blood would have been shed.

By resting after every few yards, and by clinging to our supporters, we reached, after about six hours, the summit of the Pass Terrible, and there we sat down among the aromatic flowers and bright shrubs—the gift of mountain dews—to recover strength and breath. My companion could hardly return an answer; he had advanced mechanically and almost in a state of coma. The view from the summit appeared eminently suggestive, perhaps unusually so, because disclosing a retrospect of severe hardships, now past and gone. Below the foreground of giant fractures, huge rocks, and detached boulders, emerging from a shaggy growth of mountain vegetation, with forest glens and hanging woods, black with shade gathering in the steeper folds, appeared, distant yet near, the tawny basin of Inenge, dotted with large square villages, streaked with lines of tender green, that denoted the water-courses, mottled by the shadows of flying clouds, and patched with black where the grass had been freshly fired. A glowing sun gilded the canopy of dense smoke which curtained the nearer plain, and in the background the hazy atmosphere painted with its azure the broken wall of hill which we had traversed on the previous day.

Somewhat revived by the *tramontana* which rolled like an ice-brook down the Pass, we advanced over an easy step of rolling ground, decked with cactus and the flat-topped mimosa, with green grass and bright shrubs, to a small and dirty khambi, in a hollow flanked by heights, upon which several settlements appeared. At this place, called the "Great Rubeho," in distinction from its western neighbor, I was compelled to halt. My invalid sub. had been seized with a fever-fit that induced a dangerous delirium during two successive nights; he became so violent that it was necessary to remove his weapons, and, to judge from certain symptoms, the attack had a permanent cerebral effect. Death appeared stamped upon his features, yet the Baloch and the sons of Ramji clamored to advance, declaring that the cold disagreed with them.

On the 12th of September the invalid, who, restored by a cool night, at first proposed to advance, and then doubted his ability to do so, was yet hesitating when the drum-signal for departure sounded without my order. The Wanyamwezi porters instantly set out. I sent to recall them, but they replied that it was the custom of their race never to return; a well-sounding principle against which they never offended except to serve their own ends. At length a hammock was rigged up for my companion, and the whole caravan broke ground.

The path ran along the flank of an eminence, and, ascending a second step, as steep but shorter than the Pass Terrible, placed us at the Little Rubeho, or Windy Pass, the summit of the third and westernmost range of the Usagara Mountains, raised 5700 feet above the sea-level. It is the main water-parting of this ghaut region. At Inenge the trend is still to the S.E.; beyond Rubeho the direction is S.W. Eventually, however, the drainage of both slope and counter-slope finds its way to the Indian Ocean, the former through the Mukondokwa and the Kingani, the latter through the Rwaha and the Rufiji Rivers.

A lively scene awaited my arrival at the "Little Rubeho." From a struggling mass of black humanity, which I presently determined to be our porters, proceeded a furious shouting and yelling. Spears and daggers flashed in the sun, and cudgels played with a threshing movement which promised many a broken head.

At the distance of a few yards, with fierce faces and in motionless martial attitudes, the right hand upon the axe-handle stuck in the waist-belt, and the left grasping the bow and two or three polish- ed assegais, stood a few strong fellows, the forlorn hope of the fray. In the midst of the crowd, like Norman Ramsay's troop begirt by French cavalry—to compare small things with great—rose and fell the chubby, thickset forms of Muinyi Wazira and his four Wak'hutu, who, undaunted by numbers, were dealing death to nose and scalp.   Charge! Mavi ya Gnombe ("Bois de Vache"), charge! On! Mashuzi ("Fish Fry-soup"), on! Bite, Kuffan Kwe- ma ("To die is good"), bite! Smite, Na daka Mali ("I want wealth"), smite!   At length, when

"Blood ('twas from the nose) began to flow,"

a little active interference rescued the five "enfans perdus."   The porters had been fighting upon the question whether the men with small-pox should, or should not, be admitted into the kraal, and Muinyi Wazira and his followers, under the influence of po- tations which prevented their distinguishing friend from foe, had proved themselves, somewhat unnecessarily, heroes.   It is usually better to let these quarrels work themselves out; if prematurely cut short, the serpent, wrath, is scotched, not slain.   A little "pun- ishment" always cools the blood, and secures peace and quiet for the future.   Moreover, the busy peace-maker here often shares the fate of M. Porceaugnac, and earns the reward of those who, accord- ing to the proverb, in quarrels interpose.   It is vain to investigate, where all is lie, the origin of the squabble.   Nothing easier, as the Welsh justice was fond of declaring, than to pronounce judg- ment after listening to one side of the question; but an impartial hearing of both would strike the inquiring mind with a sense of impotence.   Perhaps it is not unadvisable to treat the matter aft- er the fashion adopted by a "police-officer," a certain captain in the X. Y. Z. army, who deemed it his duty to discourage litig- iousness and official complaints among the quarrelsome Sindhi population of Hyderabad.   The story is somewhat out of place; though so being, I will here recount it.

Would enter, for instance, two individuals in an Oriental cos- tume considerably damaged; one has a cloth carefully tied round his head, the other has artificially painted his eye and his ear with a few drops of blood from the nose.   They express their emotions by a loud drumming of the tom-tom accompanying the high- sounding Cri de Haro—Faryad! Faryad! Faryad!—

"I'll 'Faryad' yer, ye"—

After these, the usual appellatives with which the "native" was in those days, on such occasions, received, the plaintiff is thus addressed:

"Well, you—fellow! your complaint, what is it?"

"Oh, sahib! Oh, cherisher of the poor! this man who is, the same hath broken into my house, and made me eat a beating, and called my ma and sister naughty names, and hath stolen my brass pot, and—"

"Bas! bas! enough!" cries the beak; "tie him"—the defend-ant—"up, and give him three dozen with thine own hand."

The wrathful plaintiff, as may be imagined, is nothing loth. After being vigorously performed upon by the plaintiff aforesaid, the defendant is cast loose, and is in turn addressed as follows:

"Well, now, you fellow! what say you?"

"Oh, my lord and master! Oh, dispenser of justice! what lies hath not this man told? What abominations hath he not de-voured? Behold (pointing to his war-paint) the sight! He hath met me in the street; he hath thrown me down; he hath kicked and trampled upon me; he hath—"

"Bas! enough!" again cries the beak; "tie him"—the plain-tiff—"up, and see if you can give *him* a good three dozen."

Again it may be imagined that the three dozen are well applied by the revengeful defendant, and that neither that plaintiff nor that defendant ever troubled that excellent "police-officer" again.

On Rubeho's summit we found a single village of villainous Wasagara; afterward "made clean"—as the mild Hindoo ex-presses the extermination of his fellow-men—by a caravan in re-venge for the murder of a porter. We were delayed on the hill-top a whole day, despite the extreme discomfort of all hands. Water had to be fetched from a runnel that issued from a rusty pool shaded by tilted-up strata of sandstone, at least a mile dis-tant from camp. Rain fell daily, alternating with eruptions of sun; a stream of thick mist rolled down the ravines and hollows, and at night the howling winds made Rubeho their meeting-place. Yet neither would the sons of Ramji carry my companion's ham-mock, nor would Said bin Salim allow his children to be so bur-dened; moreover, whatever measures one attempted with the por-ters, the other did his best to thwart. "Men," say the Persians, "kiss an ass for an object." I attempted with Kidogo that sweet speech which, according to Orientals, is stronger than chains, and administered "goose's oil" in such quantities that I was gracious-ly permitted to make an arrangement for the transport of my companion with the kirangozi.

On the 14th September, our tempers being sensibly cooled by the weather, we left the hill-top and broke ground upon the coun-ter-slope or landward descent of the Usagara Mountains. Follow-ing a narrow footpath that wound along the hill-flanks, on red earth growing thick clumps of cactus and feathery mimosa, after forty-five minutes' march we found a kraal in a swampy green gap, bisected by a sluggish rivulet that irrigated scanty fields of grain, gourds, and watermelons, the property of distant villagers. For the first time since many days I had strength enough to mus-ter the porters and to inspect their loads. The outfit, which was expected to last a year, had been half exhausted in three months. I summoned Said bin Salim, and passed on to him my anxiety. Like a veritable Arab, he declared, without the least emotion, that we had enough to reach Unyanyembe, where we certainly should be joined by the escort of twenty-two porters. "But how do you know that?" I inquired. "Allah is all-knowing," replied Said; "but the caravan *will* come." Such fatalism is infectious. I ceased to think upon the subject.

On the 15th September, after sending forward the luggage, and waiting as agreed upon for the return of the porters to carry my companion, I set out about noon, through hot sunshine tempered by the cool hill-breeze. Emerging from the grassy hollow, the path skirted a well-wooded hill and traversed a small savanna, overgrown with stunted straw and hedged in by a bushy forest. At this point massive trees, here single, there in holts and clumps, foliaged more gloomily than church-yard yews, and studded with delicate pink flowers, rose from the tawny sun-burned expanse around, and defended from the fiery glare braky rings of emerald shrubbery, sharply defined as if by the forester's hand. The savanna extended to the edge of a step, which, falling deep and steep, suddenly disclosed to view, below and far beyond the shaggy ribs and the dark ravines and folds of the foreground, the plateau of Ugogo and its Eastern desert. The spectacle was truly impressive. The vault above seemed "an ample æther," raised by its exceeding transparency higher than it is wont to be. Up to the curved rim of the western horizon, lay, burnished by the rays of a burning sun, plains rippled like a yellow sea by the wavy reek of the dancing air, broken toward the north by a few detached cones rising island-like from the surface, and zebra'd with long black lines, where bush and scrub and strip of thorn jungle, supplanted upon the water-courses, trending in mazy net-work southward to the Rwaha River, the scorched grass and withered cane-stubbles, which seemed to be the staple growth of the land. There was nothing of effeminate or luxuriant beauty, nothing of the flush and fullness characterizing tropical nature, in this first aspect of Ugogo. It appeared, what it is, stern and wild—the rough nurse of rugged men—and perhaps the anticipation of dangers and difficulties ever present to the minds of those preparing to endure the waywardness of its children, contributed not a little to the fascination of the scene. After lingering for a few minutes upon the crest of the step, with feelings which they will understand who, after some pleasant months—oases in the grim deserts of Anglo-Indian life—spent among the tree-clad heights, the breezy lakes, and the turfy valleys of the Himalayas and the Neilgherries, sight from their last vantage-ground the jaundiced and fevered plains below, we scrambled down an irregular incline of glaring red clay and dazzling white chalk, plentifully besprinkled with dark-olive silex in its cherty crust. Below the descent was a level space upon a long ridge, where some small villages of Wasagara had surrounded themselves with dwarf fields of holcus, bajri, and maize. A little beyond this spot, called the "Third Rubeho," we found a comfortless kraal on uneven ground, a sloping ledge sinking toward a deep ravine.

At the third Rubeho we were delayed for a day—as is customary before a "tirikeza"—by the necessity of laying in supplies for a jungle march, and by the quarrels of the men. The Baloch were cross as naughty children, ever their case when cold and hungry: warm and full, they become merry as crickets. The kirangozi in hot wrath brought his flag to Said bin Salim, and threatened to resign, because he had been preceded on the last stage by two of the Baloch: his complaints of this highly irregular proceeding were with difficulty silenced by force of beads. I remarked, however, a few days afterward, when traveling through Ugogo, that the kirangozi, considering himself in danger, applied to me for a vanguard of matchlock men. The sons of Ramji combined with the porters in refusing to carry my companion, and had Bombay and Mabruki not shown good-will, we might have remained a week in the acme of discomfort. The asses, frightened by wild beasts, broke loose at night, and one was lost. The atmosphere was ever in excesses of heat and cold: in the morning, a mist so thick that it displayed a fog-rainbow—a segment of an arch, composed of faint prismatic tints—rolled like a torrent down the ravine in front: the sun, at noon, made us cower under the thin canvas, and throughout the twenty-four hours a gale like a "vent de bise," attracted by the heat of the western plains, swept the encamping-ground.

Sending forward my invalid companion in his hammock, I brought up the rear: Said bin Salim, who had waxed unusually selfish and surly, furtively left to us the task; he wore only sandals—he could not travel by night. Some of the Baloch wept at the necessity of carrying their gourds and skins.

On the 17th September, about 2 P.M., we resumed the descent of the rugged mountains. The path wound to the N.W. down the stony and bushy crest of a ridge with a deep woody gap on the right hand: presently, after alternations of steep and step, and platforms patched with odoriferous plants, it fell into the upper channel of the Mandama or the Dungomaro, the "Devil's Glen." Dungomaro in Kisawahili is the proper name of an evil spirit, not in the European but in the African sense—some unblessed ghost who has made himself unpopular to the general;—perhaps the term was a facetiousness on the part of the sons of Ramji.

It was a "via mala" down this great surface-drain of the western slopes, over boulders and water-rolled stones reposing upon deep sand, and with branches of thorny trees in places canopying the bed. After a march of five hours, I found the porters bivouacking upon a softer spot, and with difficulty persuaded four of the sons of Ramji to return and to assist the weary stragglers: horns were sounded, and shots were fired to guide the Baloch, who did not, however, arrive before 10 P.M.

On the 18th of September, a final march of four hours placed us in the plains of Ugogo. Leaving the place of the last night's bivouac, we pursued the line of the Dungomaro, occasionally quitting it where boulders obstructed progress, and presently we came to its lower bed, where perennial rills, exuding from its earth-walls and trickling down its side, veiled the bottom with a green and shrubby perfumed vegetation. As the plain was neared, the difficulties increased, and the scenery became curious. The Dungomaro appeared a large crevasse in lofty rocks of pink and gray granite, streaked with white quartz, and pudding'd with greenstone and black hornblende; the sole, strewed with a rugged layer of blocks, was side-lined with narrow ledges and terraces of brown humus, supporting dwarf cactus and stunted thorny trees; while high above towered stony wooded peaks, closing in the view on all sides. Farther down the bed huge boulders, sun-burnt, and stained by the courses of rain-torrents, rose, perpendicularly as walls, to the height of one hundred and one hundred and twenty feet, and there the flooring was a sheet or slide of shiny and shelving rock, with broad fissures and steep drops, and cups, "pot-holes," baths, and basins, filed and cut by the friction of the gravelly torrents, regularly as if turned with the lathe. Where water lay, deep mud and thick clumps of grass and reed forced the path to run along the ledges at the sides of the base. Gradually, as the angle of inclination became more obtuse, the bed widened out, the tall stone walls gave way to low earth-banks clad with gum-trees; pits, serving as wells, appeared in the deep loose sand, and the Dungomaro, becoming a broad, smooth fiumara, swept away verging southward into the plain. Before noon, I sighted from a sharp turn in the bed our tent pitched under a huge sycamore, on a level step that bounded the fiumara to the right. It was a pretty spot in a barren scene, grassy and grown with green mimosas, spreading out their feathery heads like parachutes, and shedding upon the ground a filmy shade that fluttered and flickered in the draughty breeze.

The only losses experienced during the scrambling descent were a gun-case, containing my companion's store of boots, and a chair and table. The latter being indispensable on a journey where calculations, composition, and sketching were expected, I sent, during the evening halts, a detachment consisting of Muinyi Wazira, the Baloch, Gray-beard Musa, and a party of slaves, to bring up the articles, which had been cache'd on the torrent bank. They returned with the horripilatory tale of the dangers lately incurred by the expedition, which it appeared from them had been dogged by an army of Wasagara, thirsting for blood and furious for booty:—under such such circumstances, how could they recover the chair and table? Some months afterward an up-caravan commanded by a Msawahili found the articles lying where we had left them, and delivered them, for a consideration, to us at Unyanyembe. The party sent from Ugogo doubtless had passed a quiet, pleasant day, dozing in the shade at the nearest well.

Maji ya W'heta, or the Jetting Fountain in K'hutu.

CHAPTER VII.

THE GEOGRAPHY AND ETHNOLOGY OF THE SECOND REGION.

THE second or mountain region extends from the western frontier of K'hutu, at the head of the alluvial valley, in E. long. 37° 28', to the province of Ugogi, the eastern portion of the flat table-land of Ugogo, in E. long. 36° 14'. Its diagonal breadth is 85 geographical and rectilinear miles; and native caravans, if lightly laden, generally traverse it in three weeks, including three or four halts. Its length can not be estimated. According to the guides, Usagara is a prolongation of the mountains of Nguru, or Ngu, extending southward, with a gap forming the fluviatile valley of the Rwaha or Rufiji River, to the line of highlands of which Njesa in Uhiao is supposed to be the culminating apex: thus the feature would correspond with the Eastern Ghauts of the Indian Peninsula. The general law of the range is north and south; in the region now under consideration, the trend is from north by west to south by east, forming an angle of 10° 12' with the meridian. The Usagara chain is of the first order in East Africa; it is indeed the only important elevation in a direct line from the coast to Western Unyamwezi; it would hold, however, but a low grade in the general system of the earth's mountains. The highest point above sea-level, observed by B. P. therm., was 5700 feet; there are, however, peaks which may rise to 6000 and even to 7000 feet, thus rivaling the inhabited portion of the Neilgherries.

As has appeared, the chain, where crossed, was divided into three parallel ridges by longitudinal plains.

Owing to the lowness of the basal regions at the seaward slope, there is no general prospect of the mountains from the east, where, after bounding the plains of K'hutu on the north by irregular bulging lines of rolling hill, the first gradient of insignificant height springs suddenly from the plain. Viewed from the west, the counterslope appears a long crescent, with the gibbus to the front, and the cusps vanishing into distance; the summit is in the centre of the half-moon, whose profile is somewhat mural and regular. The flanks are rounded lumpy cones, and their shape denotes an igneous and primary origin, intersected by plains and basins, the fractures of the rocky system. Internally the lay, as in granitic formations generally, is irregular; the ridges, preserving no general direction, appear to cross one another confusedly. The slope and the counterslope are not equally inclined. Here, as usual in chains fringing a peninsula, the seaward declivities are the more abrupt; the landward faces are not only more elongated, but they are also shortened in proportion as the plateau into which they fall is higher than the mountain-plains from which they rise. To enter, therefore, is more toilsome than to return.

From the mingling of lively colors, Usagara is delightful to the eye, after the monotonous tracts of verdure which pall upon the sight at Zanzibar and in the river valleys. The subsoil, displayed in the deeper cuts and ravines, is either of granite, greenstone, schiste, or a coarse incipient sandstone, brown or green, and out-cropping from the ground with strata steeply tilted up. In the higher elevations the soil varies in depth from a few inches to thirty feet; it is often streaked with long layers of pebbles, apparently water-rolled. The color is either an ochrish brick-red, sometimes micaceous, and often tinted with oxyd of iron; or it is a dull gray, the debris of comminuted felspar, which, like a mixture of all the colors, appears dazzlingly white under the sun's rays. The plains and depressions are of black earth, which after a few showers becomes a grass-grown sheet of mire, and in the dry season a deeply-cracked, stubbly savanna. Where the elevations are veiled from base to summit with a thin forest, the crops of the greenstone and sandstone strata appear through a brown coat of fertile humus, the decay of vegetable matter. A fossil bulimus was found about 3000 feet above sea-level, and large achatinæ, locally called khowa, are scattered over the surface. On the hill-sides, especially in the lower slopes, are strewed and scattered erratic blocks and boulders, and diminutive pieces of white, dingy-red, rusty-pink, and yellow quartz, with large irregularly-shaped fragments, and small nodules of calcareous kunkur. Where water lies deep below the surface, the hills and hill-plains are clothed with a thin shrubbery of mimosas and other thorny gums. Throughout Eastern Africa these forests are the only spots in which traveling is enjoyable: great indeed is their contrast with the normal features—bald glaring fields, fetid bush and grass, and monotonous expanses of dull dead herbage, concealing swamps and water-courses, hedged in by vegetation whose only varieties are green, greener, and greenest.   In these favored places the traveler appears surrounded by a thick wood which he never reaches, the trees thinning out as he advances.   On clear and sunny days the scenery is strange and imposing.   The dark-red earth is prolonged half way up the tree-trunks by the ascending and descending galleries of the termite: contrasting with this peculiarly African tint, the foliage, mostly confined to the upper branches, is of a tender and lively green, whose open fret-work admits from above the vivid blue or the golden yellow of an unclouded sky.   In the basins where water is nearer the surface, and upon the banks of water-courses and rivulets, the sweet and fertile earth produces a rich vegetation, and a gigantic growth of timber, which distinguishes this region from others farther west. Usagara is peculiarly the land of jungle-flowers, and fruits, whose characteristic is a pleasant acidity, a provision of nature in climates where antiseptics and correctives to bile are almost necessaries of life.   They are abundant, but, being uncultivated, the fleshy parts are undeveloped.   In the plains, the air, heavy with the delicious perfume of the jasmine (*Jasminum Abyssinicum?*), with the strong odor of a kind of sage (*Salvia Africana*, or *Abyssinica?*), and with the fragrant exhalations of the mimosa-flowers, which hang like golden balls from the green-clad boughs, forms a most enjoyable contrast to the fetid exhalations of the great dismal swamps of the lowlands.   The tamarind, every where growing wild, is a gigantic tree.   The myombo, the mfu'u, the ndábi, and the mayágeá, a spreading tree with a large fleshy red flower, and gourds about eighteen inches long and hanging by slender cords, are of unusual dimensions; the calabash is converted into a hut; and the sycamore, whose favorite habitat is the lower counterslope of Usagara, is capable of shading a regiment.   On the steep hill-sides, which here and there display signs of cultivation and clearings of green or sun-burnt grass, grow parachute-shaped mimosas, with tall and slender trunks, and crowned by domes of verdure, rising in tiers one above the other, like umbrellas in a crowd.

The plains, basins, and steps, or facets of table-land found at every elevation, are fertilized by a stripe-work of streams, runnels, and burns, which, anastomosing in a single channel, flow off into the main drain of the country.   Cultivation is found in patches isolated by thick belts of thorny jungle, and the villages are few and rarely visited.   As usual in hilly countries, they are built upon high ridges and the slopes of cones, for rapid drainage after rain, a purer air and fewer musquitoes, and, perhaps, protection from kidnappers.   The country people bring down their supplies

of grain and pulse for caravans. There is some delay and difficulty on the first day of arrival at a station, and provisions for a
party exceeding a hundred men are not to be depended upon after the third or fourth marketing, when the people have exhausted
their stores. Fearing the thievish disposition of the Wasagara,
who will attempt even to snatch away a cloth from a sleeping
man, travelers rarely lodge near the settlements. Kraals of thorn,
capacious circles inclosing straw boothies, are found at every
march, and, when burned or destroyed by accident, they are re-
built before the bivouac. The roads, as usual in East Africa, are
tracks trodden down by caravans and cattle, and the water-course
is ever the favorite pass. Many of the ascents and descents are
so proclivitous that donkeys must be relieved of their loads; and
in fording the sluggish streams, where no grass forms a causeway
over the soft, viscid mire, the animals sink almost to the knees.
The steepest paths are those in the upper regions; in the lower,
though the inclines are often severe, they are generally longer,
and consequently easier. At the foot of each hill there is either
a mud or a water-course dividing it from its neighbor. These
obstacles greatly reduce the direct distance of the day's march.

The mountains are well supplied with water, which tastes sweet
after the brackish produce of the maritime valley, and good when
not rendered soft and slimy by lying long on rushy beds. Upon
the middle inclines the burns and runnels of the upper heights
form terraces of considerable extent, and of a picturesque aspect.
The wide and open sole, filled with the whitest and cleanest sand,
and retaining pools of fresh clear water or shallow wells, is edged
by low steep ledges of a dull red clay, lined with glorious patriarchs of the forest, and often in the bed is a thickly-wooded branch
or shoal-islet, at whose upper extremity heavy drift-wood, arrested
by the gnarled mimosa-clumps and the wall of shrubs, attests the
violence of the rufous-tinted bore of waves, with which a few
showers fill the broadest courses. Lower down the channels
which convey to the plains the surplus drainage of the mountains are heaps and sheets of granite, with long reaches of rough
gravel; their stony walls, overrun with vegetation, tower high
on either hand, and the excess of inclination produces after heavy
rains torrents like avalanches, which cut their way deep into the
lower plains. During the dry season, water is drawn from pits
sunk from a few inches to 20 feet in the re-entering angles of the
beds. Fed by the percolations of the soil, they unite the purity
of springs with the abundance of rain-supplies—a comfort fully
appreciated by down-caravans after the frequent tirikeza, or
droughty afternoon-marches in the western regions.

The versant of the mountains varies. In the seaward and the
central sections streams flow eastward, and swell the Kingani and
other rivers. The southern hills discharge their waters south and
southwest through the Maroro River, and various smaller tributa-

ries, into the " Rwaha," which is the proper name for the upper course of the Rufiji. In the lateral plains between the ridges, and in the hill-girt basins, stagnant pools, which even during the masika, or rainy season, inundate, but will not flow, repose upon beds of porous black earth, and engendering, by their profuse herbage of reeds and rush-like grass, with the luxuriant crops produced by artificial irrigation, a malarious atmosphere, cause a degradation in the people.

The climate of Usagara is cold and damp. It has two distinct varieties, the upper regions being salubrious, as the lower are unwholesome. In the sub-ranges heavy exhalations are emitted by the decayed vegetation, the nights are raw, the mornings chilly and misty, and the days are bright and hot. In the higher levels, near the sources of the Mukondokwa River, the climate suggests the idea of the Mahabaleshwar and the Neilgherry Hills in Western India. Compared with Uzaramo or Unyamwezi, these mountains are a sanatorium, and should Europeans ever settle in Eastern Africa as merchants or missionaries, here they might reside until acclimatized for the interior. The east wind, a local deflection of the southeast trade, laden with the moisture of the Atlantic and the Indian Oceans, and collecting the evaporation of the valley, impinges upon the seaward slope, where ascending, and relieved from atmospheric pressure, it is condensed by a colder temperature; hence the frequent precipitations of heavy rain, and the banks and sheets of morning-cloud which veil the tree-clad peaks of the highest gradients. As the sun waxes hot, the atmosphere acquires a greater capacity for carrying water; and the results are a milky mist in the basins, and in the upper hills a wonderful clearness, broken only by the thin cirri of the higher atmosphere. After sunset, again, the gradual cooling of the air causes the deposit of a copious dew, which renders the nights peculiarly pleasant to a European. The diurnal sea-breeze, felt in the slope, is unknown in the counterslope of the mountains, where, indeed, the climate is much inferior to that of the central and eastern heights. As in the Sawalik Hills and the sub-ranges of the Himalayas, the sun is burning hot during the dry season, and in the rains there is either a storm of thunder and lightning, wind and rain, or a stillness deep and depressing, with occasional gusts, whose distinct moaning shows the highly electrical state of the atmosphere. The masika, here commencing in early January, lasts three months, when the normal easterly winds shift to the north and the northwest. The vuli, confined to the eastern slopes, occurs in August, and, as on the plains, frequent showers fall between the vernal and the autumnal rains.

The people of Usagara suffer in the lower regions from severe ulcerations, from cutaneous disorders, and from other ailments of the plain. Higher up they are healthier, though by no means free from pleurisy, pneumonia, and dysentery. Fever is common;

it is more acute in the range of swamps and decomposed herbage, and is milder in the well-ventilated cols and on the hill-sides. The type is rather a violent bilious attack, accompanied by remittent febrile symptoms, than a regular fever. It begins with cold and hot fits, followed by a copious perspiration, and sometimes inducing delirium; it lasts as a quotidian or a tertian from four to seven days; and though the attacks are slight, they are followed by great debility, want of appetite, of sleep, and of energy. This fever is greatly exacerbated by exposure and fatigue, and it seldom fails to leave behind it a legacy of cerebral or visceral disease.

The mountains of Usagara are traversed from east to west by two main lines; the Mukondokwa on the northern and the Kiringawana on the southern line. The former was closed until 1856 by a chronic famine, the result of such a neighborhood as the Wazegura and the people of Whinde on the east, the Wahumba and the Wamasai northward, and the Warori on the southwest. In 1858 the mountaineers, after murdering by the vilest treachery a young Arab trader, Salim bin Nasir, of the Bu Saidi, or the royal family of Zanzibar, attempted to plunder a large mixed caravan of Wanyamwezi and Wasawahili, numbering 700 or 800 guns, commanded by a stout fellow, Abdullah bin Nasib, called by the Africans " Kisesa," who carried off the cattle, burned the villages, and laid waste the whole of the Rubeho or western chain.

The clans now tenanting these East African ghauts are the Wasagara—with their chief sub-tribe the Wakwivi—and the Wahehe; the latter a small body inhabiting the southwestern corner, and extending into the plains below.

The limits of the Wasagara have already been laid down by the names of the plundering tribes that surround them. These mountaineers, though a noisy and riotous race, are not overblessed with courage: they will lurk in the jungle with bows and arrows to surprise a stray porter; but they seem ever to be awaiting an attack—the best receipt for inviting it. In the higher slopes they are fine, tall, and sturdy men; in the lowlands they appear as degraded as the Wak'hutu. They are a more bearded race than any other upon this line of East Africa, and, probably from extensive intercourse with the Wamrima, most of them understand the language of the coast. The women are remarkable for a splendid development of limb, while the bosom is lax and pendent.

The Wasagara display great varieties of complexion, some being almost black, while the others are chocolate-colored. This difference can not be accounted for by the mere effects of climate —level and temperature. Some shave the head; others wear the Arab's shushah, a kind of skull-cap growth, extending more or less from the poll. Among them is seen, for the first time on this line, the classical coiffure of ancient Egypt. The hair, allowed to attain its fullest length, is twisted into a multitude of the thinnest ringlets, each composed of two thin lengths wound together; the wiry stiffness of the curls keeps them distinct and in position. Behind, a curtain of pigtails hangs down to the nape; in front the hair is either combed off the forehead, or it is brought over the brow and trimmed short. No head-dress has a wilder nor a more characteristically African appearance than this, especially when, smeared with a pomatum of micaceous ochre, and decorated with beads, brass balls, and similar ornaments, it waves and rattles with every motion of the head. Young men and warriors adorn their locks with the feathers of vultures, ostriches, and a variety of bright-plumed jays, and some tribes twist each ringlet with a string of reddish fibre. It is seldom combed out, the operation requiring for a head of thick hair the hard work of a whole day; it is not, therefore, surprising that the pediculus swarms through the land. None but the chiefs wear caps. Both sexes distend the ear-lobe; a hole is bored with a needle or a thorn; it is enlarged by inserting bits of cane, wood, or quills, increasing the latter to the number of twenty, and it is kept open by a disk of brass, ivory, wood, or gum, a roll of leaf or a betel-nut; thus deformed, it serves for a variety of purposes apparently foreign to the member; it often carries a cane snuff-box, sometimes a goat's horn pierced for a fife, and other small valuables. When empty, especially in old age, it depends in a deformed loop to the shoulders. The peculiar mark of the tribe is a number of confused little cuts between the ears and the eyebrows. Some men, especially in the eastern parts of the mountains, chip the teeth to points.

The dress of the Wasagara is a shukkah or loin-cloth, six feet long, passed round the waist in a single fold—otherwise walking would be difficult—drawn tight behind, and with the fore extremities gathered up, and tucked in over the stomach, where it is sometimes supported by a girdle of cord, leather, or brass wire; it is, in fact, the Arab's "uzár." On journeys it is purposely made short and scanty for convenience of running. The material is sometimes indigo-dyed, at other times unbleached cotton, which the Wasagara stain a dull yellow. Cloth, however, is the clothing of the wealthy. The poor content themselves with the calabash-"campestre" or kilt, and with the softened skins of sheep and goats. It is curious that in East Africa, where these articles have from time immemorial been the national dress, and where among some tribes hides form the house, that the people have neither invented nor borrowed the principles of rude tanning, even with mimosa-bark, an art so well known to most tribes of barbarians. Immediately after flaying, the stretched skin is pegged, to prevent shrinking, inside upward, in the sun, and it is not removed till thoroughly cleansed and dried. The many little holes in the margin give it the semblance of ornamentation, and sometimes the hair is scraped off, leaving a fringe two or three inches broad around the edge: the legs and tail of the animal are favorite appendages with "dressy gentlemen." These skins are afterward softened by trampling, and they are vigorously pounded with clubs: after a few days' wear, dirt and grease have almost done the duty of tanning. The garb is tied over either shoulder by a bit of cord, or simply by knotting the corners; it therefore leaves one side of the body bare, and, being loose and ungirt, it is at the mercy of every wind. On journeys it is doffed during rain, and placed between the burden and the shoulder, so that, arrived at the encamping ground, the delicate traveler may have a "dry shirt."

Women of the wealthier classes wear a tobe, or double-length shukkah, tightly drawn under the arms, so as to depress while it veils the bosom, and tucked in at either side. Dark stuffs, indigo-dyed, and Arab checks, are preferred to plain white for the usual reasons. The dress of the general is a short but decorous jupe of greasy skin, and a similar covering for the bosom, open behind, and extending in front from the neck to the middle of the body: the child is carried in another skin upon the back. The poorest classes of both sexes are indifferently attired in the narrow kilt of bark-fibre, usually made in the maritime countries from the ukhindu or brab-tree; in the interior from the calabash. The children wear an apron of thin twine, like the Nubian thong-garments. Where beads abound, the shagele, a small square napkin of these ornaments strung upon thread, is fastened round the waist by a string or a line of beads. There are many fanciful modifications of it: some children wear a screen of tin plates, each the size of a man's finger: most of the very juniors, however, are simply attired in a cord, with or without beads, round the waist.

The ornaments of the Wasagara are the normal beads and wire, and their weight is the test of wealth and respectability. A fillet of blue and white beads is bound round the head, and beads—more beads—appear upon the neck, the arms, and the ankles. The kitindi, or coil of thick brass wire, extends from the elbow to the wrist; some others wear little chains or thick bangles of copper, brass, or zinc, and those who can afford it twist a few circles of brass wire under the knee. The arms of the men are bows and arrows, the latter unpoisoned, but armed with cruelly-barbed heads, and spines like fish-bones, cut out in the long iron shaft which projects from the wood. Their spears and assegais are made from the old hoes which are brought down by the Wanyamwezi caravan; the ferule is thin, and it is attached to the shaft by a cylinder of leather from a cow's tail, drawn over the iron, and allowed to shrink at its junction with the wood: some assegais have a central swell in the shaft, probably to admit of their being used in striking like the rungu or knobstick. Men seldom leave the house without a bill-hook of peculiar shape—a narrow

sharp blade, ending in a right angle, and fixed in a wooden handle, with a projection rising above the blade. The shield is rarely found on this line of East Africa. In Usagara it is from three
to four feet in length, by one to two feet in breadth, composed of
two parallel belts of hardened skin. The material is pegged out
to stretch and dry, carefully cleaned, sometimes doubled, sewn together with a thin thong longitudinally, and stained black down
one side, and red down the other. A stout lath is fastened lengthwise as a stiffener to the shield, and a central bulge is made in the
hide, enabling the hand to grasp the wood. The favorite materials are the spoils of the elephant, the rhinoceros, and the giraffe;
the common shields are of bull's hide, and the hair is generally
left upon the outside as an ornament, with attachments of zebra
and cow's tails. It is a flimsy article, little better than a "wisp
of fern or a herring-net" against an English "clothyard:" it suffices, however, for defense against the puny cane arrows of the
African archer.

As a rule, each of these villages has its headman, who owns,
however, an imperfect allegiance to the mutwa or district chief,
whom the Arabs call "sultan." The mgosi is his wazir, or favorite councilor, and the elders or headmen of settlements collectively are wabáhá. Their principal distinction is the right to wear a
fez, or a surat cap, and the kizbáo, a sleeveless waistcoat. They
derive a certain amount of revenue by trafficking in slaves: consequently many of the Wasagara find their way into the market
of Zanzibar. Moreover, the game-laws as regards elephants are
here strictly in favor of the sultan. An animal found dead in
his district, though wounded in another, becomes his property on
condition of his satisfying his officials with small presents of cloth
and beads: the flesh is feasted upon by the tribe, and the ivory
is sold to traveling traders.

The Wahehe, situated between the Wasagara and Wagogo, par-
take a little of the appearance of both. They are a plain race, but
stout and well grown. Though to appearance hearty and good-
humored, they are determined pilferers; they have more than once
attacked caravans, and only the Warori have prevented them from
cutting off the road to Ugogo. During the return of the expedition in 1858 they took occasion to drive off unseen a flock of
goats; and at night no man, unless encamped in a strong kraal,
was safe from their attempts to snatch his goods. On one occasion, being caught in flagrant delict, they were compelled to restore their plunder, with an equivalent as an indemnity. They
are on bad terms with all their neighbors, and they unite under
their chief, Sultan Bumbumu.

The Wahehe enlarge their ears like the Wagogo, they chip the
two upper incisors, and they burn beauty-spots in their forearms.
Some men extract three or four of the lower incisors: whenever
an individual without these teeth is seen in Ugogo he is at once

known as a Mhehe. For distinctive mark they make two cicatrized incisions on both cheeks from the zygomata to the angles
of the mouth. They dress like the Wagogo, but they have less
cloth than skins. The married women usually wear a jupe, in
shape recalling the old swallow-tailed coat of Europe, with kitindi,
or coil armlets of brass or iron wire on both forearms and above
the elbows. Unmarried girls among the Wahehe are known by
their peculiar attire, a long strip of cloth, like the Indian "languti
or T bandage," but descending to the knees, and attached to waist-
belts of large white or yellow porcelain or blue glass beads. Over
this is tied a kilt of calabash fibre, a few inches deep. The men
wear thick girdles of brass wire, neatly wound round a small cord.
Besides the arms described among the Wasagara, the Wahehe carry "sime," or double-edged knives, from one to two feet long,
broadening out from the heft, and rounded off to a blunt point at
the end. The handle is cut into raised rings for security of grip,
and, when in sheath, half the blade appears outside its rude leathern scabbard. The tembe, or villages of the Wahehe, are small,
ragged, and low, probably to facilitate escape from attack. They
do business in slaves, and have large flocks and herds, which are,
however, often thinned by the Warori, whom the Wahehe dare
not resist in the field.

Ugogo.

CHAPTER VIII.

WE SUCCEED IN TRAVERSING UGOGO.

UGOGO, the reader may remember, was the ultimate period applied to the prospects of the exploration by the worthy Mr. Rush Ramji, in conversation with the respectable Ladha Damha, collector of customs, Zanzibar.

I halted three days at Ugogi to recruit the party and to lay in rations for four long desert marches. Apparently there was an abundance of provisions, but the people at first declined to part with their grain and cattle even at exorbitant prices, and the Baloch complained of "cleanness of teeth." I was visited by Ngoma Mromá, *alias* Sultan Makande, a diwan or headman, from Ugogo, here settled as chief, and well known on the eastern sea-board. He came to offer his good services. But he talked like an idiot; he begged for every article that met his eye; and he wished me —palpably for his own benefit—to follow the most northerly of the three routes leading to Unyamwezi, upon which there were not less than eight "sultans," described by Kidogo as being "one hungrier than the other." At last, an elephant having been found dead within his limits, he disappeared, much to my relief, for the purpose of enjoying a gorge of elephant beef.

Ugogi is the half-way district between the coast and Unyanyembe, and it is usually made by up-caravans at the end of the second month. The people of this "no man's land" are a mongrel race: the Wasagara claim the ground, but they have admitted as settlers many Wahehe and Wagogo, the latter, for the most part, men who have left their country for their country's good. The plains are rich in grain, and the hills in cattle, when not harried, as they had been, a little before our arrival, by the Warori. The inhabitants sometimes offer for sale milk and honey, eggs and ghee; but—only the civilized rogue can improve by adulteration —the milk falls like water off the finger, the honey is in the red stage of fermentation, of the eggs there are few without the rude beginnings of a chicken, and the ghee, from long keeping, is sweet above and bitter below. The country still contains game, kanga, or guinea-fowls, in abundance, the ocelot, a hyrax like the coney of the Somali country, and the beautiful "silver jackal." The elephant and the giraffe are frequently killed on the plains. The giraffe is called by the Arabs jamal el wahshí, a translation of the Kisawahili ngamia ya muytu, "camel of the wild," and, throughout the interior, tiga or twiga. Their sign is often seen in the uncultivated parts of the country; but they wander far, and they are rarely found except by accident. The hides are converted into shields and saddle-bags, the long tufty tails into "chauri," or flyflappers, and the flesh is a favorite food. At Ugogi, however, game has suffered from the frequent haltings of caravans, and from the carnivorous propensities of the people, who, huntsmen all, leave their prey no chance against their nets and arrows, their pitfalls, and their packs of yelping curs.

Ugogi stands 2760 feet above sea-level, and its climate, immediately after the raw cold of Usagara, pleases by its elasticity and by its dry healthy warmth. The nights are fresh and dewless, and the rays of a tropical sun are cooled by the gusts and raffales which, regularly as the land and sea breezes of the coast, sweep down the sinuosities of Dungomaro. As our "gnawing stomachs" testified, the air of Usagara had braced our systems. My companion so far recovered health that he was able to bring home many a brace of fine partridge, and of the fat guinea-fowl that, clustering upon the tall trees, awoke the echoes of the rocks as they called for their young. The Baloch, the sons of Ramji, and the porters began to throw off the effects of the pleurisies and the other complaints, which they attributed to hardship and exposure on the mountain-tops. The only obstinate invalids were the two Goanese. Gaetano had another attack of the mukunguru, or seasoning fever, which, instead of acclimatizing his constitution, seemed, by ever increasing weakness and depression, to pave the way for a fresh visitation. Valentine, with flowing eyes, pathetically pointed to two indurations in his gastric region, and bewailed his hard fate in thus being torn from the dearly-loved shades of Panjim and Margao, to fatten the inhospitable soil of Central Africa.

Immediately before departure, when almost in despair at the rapid failure of our carriage—the asses were now reduced to nine

—I fortunately secured, for the sum of four cloths per man, the services of fifteen Wanyamwezi porters. In all a score, they had left at Ugogi their mtongi, or employer, in consequence of a quarrel concerning *the* sex. They dreaded forcible seizure and sale if found without protection traveling homeward through Ugogo; and thus they willingly agreed to carry our goods as far as their own country, Unyanyembe. Truly is traveling like campaigning—a pennyweight of luck is better than a talent of all the talents! And if marriages, as our fathers used to say, are made in the heavens, the next-door manufactory must be devoted to the fabrication of African explorations. Notwithstanding, however, the large increase of conveyance, every man appeared on the next march more heavily laden than before: they carried grain for six days, and water for one night.

From Ugogi to the Ziwa or Pond, the eastern limits of Ugogo, are four marches, which, as they do not supply provisions, and as throughout the dry season water is found only in one spot, are generally accomplished in four days. The lesser desert, between Ugogi and Ugogo, is called Marenga M'khali, or the brackish water: it must not be confounded with the district of Usagara bearing the same name.

We left Ugogi on the 22d September, at 3 P.M., instead of at noon. As all the caravan hurried recklessly forward, I brought up the rear, accompanied by Said bin Salim, the jemadar, and several of the sons of Ramji, who insisted upon driving the asses for greater speed at a long trot, which, after lasting a hundred yards, led to an inevitable fall of the load. Before emerging from Ugogi, the road wound over a grassy country, thickly speckled with calabashes. Square tembe appeared on both sides, and there was no want of flocks and herds. As the villages and fields were left behind, the land became a dense thorny jungle, based upon a sandy red soil. The horizon was bounded upon both sides by gradually-thinning lines of lumpy outlying hill, the spurs of the Rubeho Range, that extended, like a scorpion's claws, westward; and the plain, gently falling in the same direction, was broken only by a single hill-shoulder and by some dwarf descents. As we advanced through the shades—a heavy cloud-bank had shut out the crescent moon—our difficulties increased; thorns and spiky twigs threatened the eyes; the rough and rugged road led to many a stumble, and the frequent whine of the cynhyena made the asses wild with fear. None but Bombay came out to meet us; the porters were overpowered by their long march under the fiery sun. About 8 P.M., directed by loud shouts and flaring fires, we reached a kraal, a patch of yellow grass, offering clear room in the thorny thicket. That night was the perfection of a bivouac, cool from the vicinity of the hills, genial from their shelter, and sweet as forest-air in these regions ever is.

On the next day we resumed our labor betimes: for a dreary and thirsty stage lay before us. Toiling through the sunshine of the hot waste I could not but remark the strange painting of the land around. At a distance the plain was bright yellow with stubble, and brown-black with patches of leafless wintry jungle based upon a brick-dust soil. A closer approach disclosed colors more vivid and distinct. Over the ruddy plain lay scattered untidy heaps of gray granite boulders, surrounded and capped by tufts of bleached white grass. The copse showed all manner of strange hues, calabashes purpled and burnished by sun and rain, thorns of a greenish coppery bronze, dead trees with trunks of ghastly white, and gums (the blue-gum tree of the Cape?) of an unnatural sky-blue, the effect of the yellow outer pellicle being peeled off by the burning rays, while almost all were reddened up to a man's height, by the double galleries, ascending and descending, of the white ants. Here, too, I began to appreciate the extent of the nuisance, thorns. Some were soft and green, others a finger long, fine, straight, and woody—they serve as needles in many parts of the country—one, a "corking pin," bore at its base a filbert-like bulge, another was curved like a cock's spur; the double thorns placed dos-à-dos, described by travelers in Abyssinia and in the Cape Karroos, were numerous, the "wait-a-bit," a dwarf, sharply-bent spine, with acute point and stout foundation, and a smaller variety, short and deeply crooked, numerous and tenacious as fish-hooks, tore without difficulty the strongest clothing, even our woolen Arab "abas," and our bed-covers of painted canvas.

Traveling through this broom-jungle and crossing grassy plains, over paths where the slides of elephants' feet upon the last year's muddy clay showed that the land was not always dry, we halted after 11 A.M. for about an hour at the base of a steep incline, apparently an offset from the now distant Rubeho Range. The porters would have nighted at the mouth of a small drain, which, too steep for ascent, exposed in its rocky bed occasional sand-patches and deep pools; Kidogo, however, forced them forward, declaring that if the asses drank of this "brackish water," they would sicken and die. His assertion, suspected of being a "traveler's tale," was subsequently confirmed by the Arabs of Unyanyembe, who declared that the country people never water their flocks and herds below the hill; there may be poisonous vegetation in the few yards between the upper and the lower pools, but no one offered any explanation of the phenomenon.

Ascending with difficulty the eastern face of the step, which presented two ladders of loose stones and fixed boulders of gray syenite, hornblende, and greenstone, with colored quartzes, micaceous schistes, and layers of talcose slate glittering like mother-o'-pearl upon the surface, we found a half-way platform some 150 feet of extreme breadth. Upon its sloping and irregular floor, black-green pools, sadly offensive to more senses than one, spring-fed, and forming the residue of the rain-water which fills the torrent, lay in muddy holes broadly fringed with silky grass. Travelers drink without fear this upper Marenga Mk'hali, which, despite its name, is rather soft and slimy than brackish, and sign of wild beasts—antelope and buffalo, giraffe and rhinoceros—appear upon its brink. It sometimes dries up in the heart of the hot season, and then deaths from thirst occur among the porters who, mostly Wanyanwezi, are not wont to practice abstinence in this particular. "Sucking-places" are unknown to them, water-bearing bulbs might here be discovered by the South African traveler; as a rule, however, the East African is so plentifully supplied with the necessary that he does not care to provide for a dry day by unusual means. Ascending another steep incline we encamped upon a small step, the half-way gradient of a higher level.

The 24th September was to be a tirikeza: the Baloch and the sons of Ramji spent the earlier half in blowing away gunpowder at antelope, partridge and parrot, Guinea-fowl and floriken, but not a head of game found its way into camp. The men were hot, tired, and testy, those who had wives beat them, those who had not "let off the steam" by quarreling with one another. Said bin Salim, sick and surly, had words concerning a water-gourd with the brave Khudabakhsh, and the monocular jemadar, who made a point of overloading his porters, bitterly complained because they would not serve him. At 2 P.M. we climbed up the last ladder of the rough and stony incline, which placed us a few hundred feet above the eastern half of the Lesser Desert. We took a pleasant leave of the last of the rises; on this line of road, between Marenga Mk'hali and Western Unyamwezi, the land, though rolling, has no steep ascents nor descents.

From the summit of the Marenga Mk'hali step we traveled till sunset—the orb of day glaring like a fire-ball in our faces—through dense thorny jungle and over grassy plains of black, cracked earth, in places covered with pebbles and showing extensive traces of shallow inundations during the rains; in the lower lands huge blocks of weathered granite stood out abruptly from the surface, and on both sides, but higher on the right hand, rose blue cones, some single, others in pairs like "brothers." The caravan once rested in a thorny coppice, based upon rich red and yellow clay, whence it was hurriedly dislodged by a swarm of wild bees. As the sun sank below the horizon the porters called a halt on a calabash-grown plain, near a block of stony hill veiled with cactus and mimosa, below whose northern base ran a tree-lined nullah, where they declared, from the presence of antelope and other game, that water might be found by digging. Vainly Kidogo urged them forward, declaring that they would fail to reach the Ziwa or Pond in a single march; they preferred "crowing" and scooping up sand till midnight to advancing a few miles, and some gourdfuls of dirty liquid rewarded their industry.

On the morning of the 26th of September, I learned that we

had sustained an apparently irreparable loss. When the caravan was dispersed by bees, a porter took the opportunity of deserting. This man, who represented himself as desirous of rejoining at Unyanyembe, his patron Abdullah bin Musa, the son of the well-known Indian merchant, had been engaged for four cloths by Said bin Salim at Ugogi. The Arab with his usual after-wit found out, when the mishap was announced, that he had from the first doubted and disliked the man so much that he had paid down only half the hire. Yet to the new porter had been committed the most valuable of our packages, a portmanteau containing the Nautical Almanac for 1858, the surveying books, and most of our paper, pens, and ink. Said bin Salim, however, was hardly to be blamed, his continual quarrels with the Baloch and the sons of Ramji absorbed all his thoughts. Although the men were unanimous in declaring that the box never could be recovered, I sent back Bombay Mabruki and the slave Ambari with particular directions to search the place where we had been attacked by bees; it was within three miles, but, as the road was deemed dangerous, the three worthies preferred passing a few quiet hours in some snug neighboring spot.

At 1.30 P.M., much saddened by the disaster, we resumed our road, and, after stretching over a monotonous grassy plain variegated with dry thorny jungle, we arrived about sunset at a waterless kraal, where we determined to pass the night. Our supplies of liquid ran low, the Wanyamwezi porters, who carried our pots and gourds, had drained them on the way, and without drink an afternoon march in this droughty land destroys all appetite for supper. Some of the porters presently set out to fill their gourds with the waters of the Ziwa, thence distant but a few miles; they returned, after a four hours' absence, with supplies, which restored comfort and good-humor to the camp.

Before settling for the night Kidogo stood up, and to loud cries of "Maneno! maneno!"—words! words! equivalent to our parliamentary hear! hear!—delivered himself of the following speech:

"Listen, O ye whites! and ye children of Sayyidi Majidi! and ye sons of Ramji! hearken to my words, O ye offspring of the night! The journey entereth Ugogo—Ugogo (the orator threw out his arm westward). Beware, and again beware (he made violent gesticulations). You don't know the Wagogo, they are ——s and ——s! (he stamped). Speak not to those Washenzi pagans; enter not into their houses (he pointed grimly to the ground). Have no dealings with them, show no cloth, wire, nor beads (speaking with increasing excitement). Eat not with them, drink not with them, and make not love to their women (here the speech became a scream). Kirangozi of the Wanyamwezi, restrain your sons! Suffer them not to stray into the villages, to buy salt out of camp, to rob provisions, to debauch with beer, or to sit by the wells!" And thus, for nearly half an hour, now violently, then composedly, he poured forth the words of wisdom, till the hubbub and chatter of voices which at first had been silenced by surprise, brought his eloquence to an end.

We left the jungle-kraal early on the 26th September, and, after hurrying through thick bush, we debouched upon an open stubbly plain, with herds of gracefully-bounding antelopes and giraffes, who stood for a moment with long outstretched necks to gaze, and presently broke away at a rapid, striding camel's trot, their heads shaking as if they would jerk off, their limbs loose, and their joints apparently dislocated. About 9 P.M. we sighted the much-talked-of Ziwa. The Arabs, fond of "showing a green garden," had described to me at Inenge a piece of water fit to float a man-of-war. But Kidogo, when consulted, had replied simply with the Kisawahili proverb, "Khabari ya mb'hali;" i. e., "news from afar"—a beau mentir qui vient de loin. I was not therefore surprised to find a shallow pool, which in India would barely merit the name of tank.

The Ziwa, which lies 3100 feet above the sea, occupies the lowest western level of Marenga Mk'háli, and is the deepest of the many inundated grounds lying to its north, northeast, and northwest. The extent greatly varies: in September, 1857, it was a slaty sheet of water, with granite projections on one side, and about 300 yards in diameter; the centre only could not be forded. The bottom and the banks were of retentive clay; a clear ring, whence the waters had subsided, margined the pool, and beyond it lay a thick thorny jungle. In early December, 1858, notihng remained but a surface of dry, crumbling, and deeply-cracked mud, and, according to travelers, it had long, in consequence of the scanty rains, been in that state. Caravans always encamp at the Ziwa when they find water there. The country around is full of large game, especially elephants, giraffes, and zebras, who come to drink at night; a few widgeon are seen breasting the little waves; "kata" (sand-grouse), of peculiarly large size and dark plumage, flock there with loud cries; and at eventide the pool is visited by guinea-fowl, floriken, curlews, peewits, wild pigeons, doves, and hosts of small birds. When the Ziwa is desiccated, travelers usually encamp in a thick bush, near a scanty clearing, about one mile to the northwest, where a few scattered villages of Wagogo have found dirty-white water, hard and bad, in pits varying from twenty to thirty feet in depth. Here, as elsewhere in Eastern Africa, the only trough is a small ring sunk in the retentive clayey soil, and surrounded by a little raised dam of mud and loose stones. A demand is always made for according permission to draw water—a venerable custom, dating from the days of Moses. "Ye shall buy meat of them (the Edomites) for money, that ye may eat; and ye shall also buy water of them for money, that ye may drink." —Deut., ii., 6. Yet as thirsty, like hungry men, are not to be trifled with, fatal collisions have resulted from this inhospitable practice. Some years ago a large caravan of Wanyamwezi was annihilated in consequence of a quarrel about water, and lately several deaths occurred in a caravan led by an Arab merchant, Sallum bin Hamid, because the wells were visited before the rate of payment was settled. In several places we were followed upon the march lest a gourd might be furtively filled. To prevent exhaustion, the people throw euphorbia, asclepias, and solanaceous plants into the well after a certain hour, and when not wanted it is bushed over, to keep off animals and to check evaporation.

At the Ziwa the regular system of kuhonga, or black-mail, so much dreaded by travelers, begins in force. Up to this point all the chiefs are contented with little presents; but in Ugogo tribute is taken by force, if necessary. None can evade payment; the porters, fearing least the road be cut off to them in future, would refuse to travel unless each chief is satisfied; and when a quarrel arises they throw down their packs and run away. Ugogo, since the closing of the northern line through the Wahumba and the Wamasai tribes, and the devastation of the southern regions by the Warori, is the only open line, and the sultans have presumed upon their power of stopping the way. There is no regular tariff of taxes: the sum is fixed by the traveler's dignity and outfit, which, by means of his slaves, are as well known to every sultan as to himself. Properly speaking, the exaction should be confined to the up-caravans; from those returning, a head or two of cattle, a few hoes, or some similar trifle, are considered ample. Such, however, was not the experience of the expedition. When first traveling through the country the "Wazungu" were sometimes mulcted to the extent of fifty cloths by a single chief, and the Arabs congratulated them upon having escaped so easily. On their downward march they pleaded against a second demand as exorbitant as the first, adducing the custom of caravans, who are seldom mulcted in more than two cows or a pair of jembe, or iron hoes; the chiefs, however, replied that as they never expected to see white faces again, it was their painful duty to make the most from them.

The kuhonga, however, is not unjust. In these regions it forms the customs-dues of the government: the sultan receives it nominally, but he must distribute the greater part among his family and councilors, his elders and attendants. It takes the place of the fees expected by the Balderabba of the Abyssinians, the Mogasa of the Gallas, the Abban of the Somal, and the Ghafir and Rafik amongst the Bedouin Arabs, which are virtually assertions of supremacy upon their own ground. These people have not the idea which seems prevalent in the south, namely, that any man has a right to tread God's earth gratis as long as he does not interfere with property. If any hesitation about the kuhonga be made, the first question put to the objector will be, "Is this your ground or my ground?" The practice, which is sanctioned by the customs of civilized nations, is, however, vitiated in East Africa by the slave-trade: it becomes the means of intrusion and extortion, of insolence and violence. The Wagogo are an importing people, and they see with envy long strings of what they covet passing through their territory from the interior to the coast. They are strong enough to plunder any caravan; but violence they know would injure them by cutting of communication with the markets for their ivory. Thus they have settled into a silent compromise, and their nice sense of self-interest prevents any transgression beyond the bounds of reason. The sultans receive their kuhonga, and the subjects entice away slaves from every caravan, but the enormous interest upon capital laid out in the trade still leaves a balance in favor of the merchants. The Arabs, however, declaring that the evil is on the increase, propose many remedies—such as large armed caravans, sent by their government, and heavy dues to be exacted from those Wagogo who may visit the coast. But they are wise enough to murmur without taking steps which would inevitably exacerbate the evil. Should it pass a certain point, a new road will be opened, or the old road will be reopened, to restore the balance of interests.

At the Ziwa we had many troubles. One Marema, the sultan of a new settlement situated a few hundred yards to the northwest, visited us on the day of our arrival, and reproving us for "sitting in the jungle," pointed out the way to his village. On our replying that we were about to traverse Ugogo by another route, he demanded his ada or customs, which being newly imposed were at once refused by Kidogo. The sultan, a small man, a "mere thief"—as a poor noble is graphically described in these lands—threatened violence, whereupon the asses were brought in from grazing, and were ostentatiously loaded before his eyes: when he changed his tone from threats to beggary. Kidogo relenting gave him two cloths with a few strings of beads, preferring this slender disbursement to the chance of a flight of arrows during the night. His good judgment was evidenced by the speedy appearance of the country people, who brought with them bullocks, sheep, goats and poultry, watermelons and pumpkins, honey, buttermilk, whey and curded milk, an 'abundance of holcus and calabash-flour. The latter is made from the hard dry pulp surrounding the bean-like seed contained in the ripe gourd: the taste is a not unpleasant agro-dolce, and the people declare it to be strengthening food, especially for children; they convert it into porridge and rude cakes.

This abundance of provaunt caused a halt of four days at the Ziwa, and it was spent in disputes between the great Said and the greater Kidogo. The ostensible "bone of contention" was cloth advanced by the former to the porters—who claimed as their perquisite a bullock before entering Ugogo—without consulting the hard-headed slave, who, wounded in his tenderest place of pride, had influence enough to halt the caravan. The real cause of the dispute was kept from my ears till some months afterward, but secrets in this land are, as the Arabs say, "like musk, murder, and Basrah-garlic," they must out, and Bombay, who could never help blurting forth the tacenda with the dicenda, at last accidentally unveiled the mystery. Said had deferred taking overcharge of the outfit from Kidogo till our arrival at the Ziwa, and the latter felt aggrieved by the sudden yet tardy demand, which deprived him of the dignity and the profits of stewardship. Sickness became rife in camp, the effect of the cold night-winds and the burning suns, and as usual when men are uncomfortable, violent quarrels ensued. Again the officious Wazira shook the torch of discord by ordering Khamisi, an exceedingly drunken and debauched son of Ramji, to carry certain bundles which usually graced the shoulders of Goha, one of the Wak'hutu porters. When words were exhausted Khamisi drew his blade upon Goha and was tackled by Wazira, while Goha brought the muzzle of my elephant-gun to bear upon Khamisi, and was instantly collared by Bombay. Being thus "in chancery," both heroes waxed so "exceedingly brave—particular," that I was compelled to cool their noble bile with a long pole. At length it became necessary to make Kidogo raise his veto against the advance of the caravan. He did not appear before me till summoned half a dozen times: when he at last vouchsafed so to do, I dragged rather than led him to the mat where sat in surly pride Said bin Salim, with the monocular jemadar, and I ordered the trio to quench with the waters of explanation the fire of anger. After an apparently satisfactory arrangement Kidogo started up and disappeared in the huts of his men: it presently proved that he had so done for the purpose of proposing to his party, who were now the sole interpreters, that to Said bin Salim, an ignoramus in such matters, should be committed the weighty task of settling the amount of our black-mail and presents with the greedy chiefs of Ugogo. Had the mischievous project been carried into execution, we should have been sufferers to some extent: lack of unanimity, however, caused the measure to be thrown out. A march was fixed for the next day, when the bullock, on this occasion the scape-grace, broke its tether and plunged into the bush: it was followed by the Baloch and the porters, whose puny arrows, when they alighted upon the beast's stern, only goaded it forward, and at least threescore matchlock balls were discharged before one bullet found its billet in the fugitive. The camp of course then demanded another holiday to eat beef.

The reader must not imagine that I am making a "great cry" about a little matter. Four days are not easily spent when snowed up in a country inn, and that is a feeble comparison for the halt in East Africa, where outfit is leaking away, the valuable traveling-time is perhaps drawing to a close, health is palpably failing, and nothing but black faces, made blacker still by ill-humor and loud squabbles, meet the eye and ear. Insignificant things they afterward appear viewed through the medium of memory, these petty annoyances of travel; yet at the moment they are severely felt, and they must be resented accordingly. The African traveler's fitness for the task of exploration depends more upon his faculty of chafing under delays and kicking against the pricks than upon his power of displaying the patience of a Griselda or a Job.

On the 30th of September, the last day of our detention at the Jiwa, appeared a large caravan headed by Said bin Mohammed of Mbuamaji, with Khalfan bin Khamis, and several other coast Arabs. They brought news from the sea-board, and—wondrous good fortune!—the portmanteau containing books which the porter, profiting by the confusion caused by the swarm of bees, had deposited in the long grass, at the place where I had directed the slaves to seek it. Some difficulty was at first made about restitution: the Arab law of "lakit," or things trove, being variable, complicated, and altogether opposed to our ideas. However, two cloths were given to the man who had charge of it, and the jemadar and Said bin Salim were sent to recover it by any or all means. The merchants were not offended. They consented to sell for the sum of thirty-five dollars a strong and serviceable but an old and obstinate African ass, which, after carrying my companion for many a mile, at last broke its heart when toiling up the steeps from whose summit the fair waters of the Central Lake were first sighted. Moreover, they proposed that for safety and economy the two caravans should travel together under a single flag, and thus combine to form a total of 190 men. These coast Arabs traveled in comfort. The brother of Said Mohammed had married the daughter of Fundikira, Sultan of Unyanyembe, and thus the family had a double home, on the coast and in the interior. All the chiefs of the caravan carried with them wives and female slaves, negroid beauties, tall, bulky, and "plenty of them," attired in tulip-hues, cochineal and gamboge, who walked the whole way, and who when we passed them displayed an exotic modesty by drawing their head-cloths over cheeks which we were little ambitious to profane. They had a multitude of fundi, or managing men, and male slaves, who bore their personal bag and baggage, scrip and scrippage, drugs and comforts, stores and provisions, and who were always early at the ground to pitch, to surround with a "pai," or dwarf drain, and to bush for privacy, with green boughs, their neat and light ridge-tents of American domestics. Their bedding was as heavy as ours, and even their poultry traveled in wicker cages. This caravan was useful to us in dealing with the Wagogo: it always managed, however, to precede us on the march, and to monopolize the best kraals. The Baloch and the sons of Ramji, when asked on these occasions why they did not build a palisade, would reply theatrically, " Our hearts are our fortifications!"—methought a sorry defense.

By Kidogo's suggestion I had preferred the middle line through the hundred miles of dreaded Ugogo: it was the beaten path, and infested only by four sultans, namely: 1. Myandozi of Kifukuru; 2. Magomba of Kanyenye; 3. Maguru-Mafupi of K'hok'ho; and 4. Kibuya of Mdaburu. On the 1st of October, 1857, we left the Ziwa late in the morning, and, after passing through the savannas and the brown jungles of the lower levels, where giraffe again appeared, the path crested a wave of ground and debouched upon the table-land of Ugogo. The aspect was peculiar and unprepossessing. Behind still towered in sight the delectable mountains of Usagara, mist-crowned and robed in the lightest azure, with streaks of a deep plum-color, fronting the hot low land of Marenga Mk'hali, whose tawny face was wrinkled with lines of dark jungle. On the north was a tabular range of rough and rugged hill, above which rose three distant cones pointed out as the haunts of the robber Wahumba: at its base was a deep depression, a tract of brown brush patched with yellow grass, inhabited only by the elephant, and broken by small outlying hillocks. Southward, scattered eminences of tree-crowned rock rose a few yards from the plain which extended to the front, a clearing of deep red or white soil, decayed vegetation based upon rocky or sandy ground, here and there thinly veiled with brown brush and golden stubbles: its length, about four miles, was studded with square villages, and with the stately but grotesque calabash. This giant is to the vegetable what the elephant is to the animal world: the Persians call it the "practice-work of nature"—its disproportionate conical bole rests upon huge legs exposed to view by the washing away of the soil, and displays excrescences which in pious India would merit a coat of vermilion. From the neck extend gigantic gnarled arms, each one a tree, whose thinnest twig is thick as a man's finger, and their weight causes them to droop earthward, giving to the outline the shape of a huge dome. In many parts the unloveliness of its general appearance is varied by the wrinkles and puckerings which, forming by granulation upon the oblongs where the bark has been removed for fibre, give the base the appearance of being chamfered and fluted; and often a small family of trunks, four or five in number, springs from the same root. At that season all were leafless; at other times they are densely foliaged, and, contrasting with their large timber and with their coarse fleshy leaf, they are adorned with the delicatest flowers of a pure virgin white, which, opening at early dawn, fade and fall before eventide. The babe-tree issues from the ground about one foot in diameter: in Ugogo, however, all those observed were of middle age. The young are probably grubbed up to prevent their encumbering the ground, and when decayed enough to be easily felled they are converted into fire-wood. By the side of these dry and leafless masses of dull dead hue, here and there a mimosa or a thorn was beginning to bear the buds of promise green as emeralds. The sun burned like the breath of a bonfire, a painful glare—the reflection of the terrible crystal above—arose from the hot earth; warm siroccos raised clouds of dust, and in front the horizon was so distant that, as the Arabs expressed themselves, "a man might be seen three marches off."

We were received with the drumming and the ringing of bells attached to the ivories, with the yells and frantic shouts of two caravans halted at Kifukuru: one was that of Said Mohammed, who awaited our escort, the other a return "safari," composed of about 1000 Wanyamwezi porters, headed by four slaves of Salim bin Rashid, an Arab merchant settled at Unyanyembe. The country people also flocked to stare at the phenomenon; they showed that excitement which, some few years ago, might have been witnessed in more polished regions, when a "horrible mur-der" roused every soul from Tweed Banks to Land's End; when, to gratify a morbid destructiveness, artists sketched, literati de-scribed, tourists visited, and curio-hunters met to bid for the rope and the murderer's whiskers. Yet I judged favorably of the Wa-gogo by their curiosity, which stood out in strong relief against the apathy and the uncommunicativeness of the races lately vis-ited. Such inquisitiveness is, among barbarians, generally a proof of improvability—of power to progress. One man who had vis-ited Zanzibar could actually speak a few words of Hindoostani, and in Ugogo, and there only, I was questioned by the chiefs concerning Uzungu, "White Land," the mysterious end of the world in which beads are found under ground, and where the women weave such cottons. From the day of our entering to that of our leaving the country, every settlement turned out its swarm of gazers, men and women, boys and girls, some of whom would follow us for miles with explosions of Hi!—i!—i! screams of laughter and cries of excitement, at a long high trot—most un-graceful of motion!—and with a scantiness of toilette which dis-played truly unseemly spectacles. The matrons, especially the aged matrons, realized Madame Pernelle's description of an un-pleasant female:

" Un peu trop forte en gueule et fort impertinente ;"

and of their sex the old men were ever the most pertinacious and intrusive, the most surly and quarrelsome. Vainly the escort attempted to arrest the course of this moving multitude of semi-nude babarity. I afterward learned that the two half-caste Arabs who had passed us at Muhama, Khalfan, and Id, the sons of Mu-allim Salim of Zanzibar, had, while preceding us, spread through Ugogo malevolent reports concerning the Wazungu. They had one eye each and four arms; they were full of "knowledge," which in these lands means magic; they caused rain to fall in advance and left droughts in their rear; they cooked watermelons and threw away the seeds, thereby generating small-pox; they heated and hardened milk, thus breeding a murrain among cattle; and their wire, cloth, and beads caused a variety of misfortunes; they were kings of the sea, and therefore white-skinned and straight-haired—a standing mystery to these curly-pated people—as are all men who live in salt water; and next year they would return and seize the country. Suspicion of our intentions touching "territorial aggrandizement" was a fixed idea: every where the value attached by barbarians to their homes is in inverse ratio to the real worth of the article. Hence mountaineers are proverbially patriotic. Thus the lean Bedouins of Arabia and the lank Somal, though they own that they are starving, never sight a stranger without suspecting that he is spying out the wealth of the land. "What will happen to us?" asked the Wagogo; "we never yet saw this manner of man!" But the tribe can not now forfeit intercourse with the coast: they annoyed us to the utmost, they made the use of their wells a daily source of trouble, they charged us double prices, and when they brought us provisions for sale, they insisted upon receiving the price of even the rejected articles; yet they did not proceed to open outrage. Our timid Arab, the Baloch, the sons of Ramji, and the porters humored them in every whim. Kidogo would not allow observations to be taken with a bright sextant in presence of the mobility. He declined to clear the space before the tent, as the excited starers, some of whom had come from considerable distances, were apt, under disappointment, to wax violent; and though he once or twice closed the tent-flaps, he would not remove the lines of men, women, and children, who stretched themselves, for the greater convenience of peeping and peering, lengthways upon the ground. Whenever a Mnyamwezi porter interfered, he was arrogantly told to begone, and he slunk away, praying us to remember that these men are "Wagogo." Caravan after caravan had thus taught them to become bullies, whereas a little manliness would soon have reduced them to their proper level. They are neither brave nor well-armed, and their prestige rests solely upon their feat in destroying, about one generation ago, a caravan of Wanyamwezi —an event embalmed in a hundred songs and traditions. They seemed to take a fancy to the Baloch, who received from the fair sex many a little souvenir in the shape of a kid or a watermelon. Whenever the Goanese Valentine was sent to a village, he was politely and hospitably welcomed, and seated upon a three-legged stool by the headman; and generally the people agreed in finding fault with their principal sultans, declaring that they unwisely made the country hateful to "wakonongo," or travelers. Fortunately for the expedition, several scions of the race saw the

light safely during our transit of Ugogo : had an accident occurred to a few babies or calves, our return through the country
would have been difficult and dangerous. All received the name
of "Muzungu," and thus there must now be a small colony of
black "white men" in this part of the African interior.

At Kifukuru I was delayed a day while settling the black-mail
of its sultan, Miyandozi. Said bin Salim, the jemadar, and Kidogo called upon him in the morning, and were received in the gateway of a neat "tembe," the great man disdaining to appear on so
trivial an occasion. This sultan is the least powerful of the four;
he is plundered by the Warori tribes living to the southwest, and
by his western neighbor, Magomba; his subjects are poorly clad,
and are little ornamented compared with those occupying the
central regions, where they have the power to detain travelers and
to charge them exorbitantly for grain and water. Yet Miyandozi
demanded four white and six blue shukkahs; besides which, I was
compelled to purchase for him from the sons of Ramji, who of
course charged treble its value, a "sohari," or handsome silk and
cotton loin-cloth. In return he sent—it appeared to be in irony
—one kayla, or four small measures of grain. The slaves of Salim bin Rashid obliged me with a few pounds of rice, for which
I gave them a return in gunpowder, and they undertook to convey to Zanzibar a package of reports, indents, and letters, which
was punctually delivered. An ugly accident had nearly happened that night; the Wanyamwezi porters managed to fire the grass
round a calabash-tree, against which they had stretched their
loads, and a powder magazine—fortunately fire-proof—was blackened and charred by the flames. A traveler can not be too careful about his ammunition in these lands. I have seen a slave
smoking a water-pipe, tied for convenience of carriage to a leaky
keg of powder; and another, in the caravan of Salim bin Sayf of
Dut'humi, resting the muzzle of his musket against a barrel of
ammunition, fired it to try its strength, and blew himself up with
several of his comrades.

On the 3d October we quitted Kifukuru in the afternoon, and
having marched nearly six hours, we encamped in one of the strips
of waterless brown jungles which throughout Ugogo divide the
cultivated districts from one another, and occupy about half the
superficies of the land. The low grounds, inundated during the
rains, were deeply cracked, and my weak ass, led by the purblind
Shahdad, fell with violence upon my knee, leaving a mixture of
pain and numbness which lasted for some months. On the next
day we resumed our journey betimes through a thick rugged jungle and over a rolling grassy plain, which extended to the frontier
of Kanyenye, where Sultan Magomba rules. The 5th October
saw us in the centre of Kanyenye, a clearing about ten miles in
diameter. The surface is a red tamped clayey soil, dotted with
small villages, huge calabashes, and stunted mimosas; water is

found in wells—or rather pits—sunk from ten to twelve feet in the lower lands, or in the sandy beds of the several fiumaras. Flocks and herds abound, and the country is as cultivated and populous as the saline nitrous earth, and the scarceness of the potable element, which often tarnishes silver like sulphur-fumes, permits.

At Kanyenye I was delayed four days to settle black-mail with Magomba, the most powerful of the Wagogo chiefs. He was on this, as on a subsequent occasion, engaged in settling a cause arising from uchawi or black magic; yet all agree that in Ugogo, where, to quote the "Royal Martyr's" words,

"Plunder and murder are the kingdom's laws,"

there is perhaps less of wizardhood and witchcraft, and consequently less of its normal consequences, fiscs and massacres, than in any other region between the Atlantic and the Indian Ocean. "Arrow-heads" employed every art of wild diplomacy to relieve me of as much cloth as possible. I received, when encamped at the Ziwa, a polite message declaring his desire to see white men; but—"the favor of the winds produces dust"—I was obliged to acknowledge the compliment with two cottons. On arrival at his head-quarters, I was waited upon by an oily cabinet of wazirs and elders, who would not depart without their "respects"—four cottons. The next demand was made by his favorite wife, a peculiarly hideous old princess, with more wrinkles than hairs, with no hair black and no tooth white, and attended by ladies in waiting as unprepossessing as herself: she was not to be dismissed without a fee of six cottons. At last, accompanied by a mob of courtiers, who crowded in like an African House of Commons, appeared in person the magnifico. He was the only sultan that ever entered my tent in Ugogo—pride and a propensity for strong drink prevented other visits. He was much too great a man to call upon the Arab merchants, but in our case curiosity had mastered state considerations. Magomba was a black and wrinkled elder, driveling and decrepit, with a half-bald head, from whose back and sides depended a few straggling corkscrews of iron gray; he wore a coat of castor-oil and a "barsati" loin-cloth, which grease and use had changed from blue to black. A few bead strings decorated his neck, large flexible anklets of brass wire adorned his legs, solid brass rings, single and in coils, which had distended his ear-lobes almost to splitting, were tied by a string over his cranium, and his horny soles were defended by single-soled sandals, old, dirty, and tattered. He chewed his quid and he expectorated without mercy; he asked many a silly question, yet he had ever an eye to the main chance. He demanded and received five "cloths with names," which I was again compelled to purchase at an exorbitant price from the Baloch and slaves, one coil of brass wire, four blue cottons, and ten "domestics;" the total amounted to fifty shukkahs, here worth at least fifty dollars, and exhausting nearly two thirds of a porter's load. His return present was the leanest of calves: when it was driven into camp with much parade, his son, who had long been looking out for a fit opportunity, put in a claim for three cottons.

Magomba before our departure exacted from Kidogo an oath that his Wazungu would not smite the land with drought or with fatal disease, declaring that all we had was in his hands. He boasted, and with truth, of his generosity. It was indeed my firm conviction from first to last that, in case of attack or surprise, I had not a soul except my companion to stand by me: all those who accompanied us could, and consequently would, have saved their lives;—*we* must have perished. We should have been as safe with six as with sixty guns; but I would by no means apply to these regions Mr. Galton's opinion, " that the last fatal expedition of Mungo Park is full of warning to travelers who propose exploring with a large body of men." For though sixty guns do not suffice to prevent attack in Ugogo, 600 stout fellows armed with the " hot-mouthed weapon" might march through the length and breadth of Central Africa.

During our four days' detention at Kanyenye, I was compelled to waste string after string of beads in persuading the people to water the porters and asses. Yet their style of proceeding proved that it was greed of gain, not scarcity of the element, which was uppermost in their minds; they would agree to supply us with an unlimited quantity, and then would suddenly gather round the well and push away the Wanyamwezi, bidding them go and fetch more beads. All the caravan took the opportunity of loading itself with salt. While the halt lasted, my companion brought in a fine-flavored pallah and other antelopes, with floriken, guinea-fowl, and partridge. Neither he nor I, however, had strength enough, nor had we time, to attack the herds of elephants that roam over the valley whose deep purple line separates the table-land of Ugogo from the blue hills of the Wahumba to the north. And here, perhaps, a few words concerning the prospects of sportsmen in this part of Africa may save future travelers from the mistake into which I fell. I expected great things, and returned without realizing a single hope. This portion of the peninsula is a remarkable contrast to the line traversed by Dr. Livingstone, where the animals standing within bow-shot were so numerous and fearless, that the burden of provisions was often unnecessary. In the more populous parts game has melted away before the woodman's axe and the hunter's arrows: even where large tracts of jungle abound with water and forage, the note of a bird rarely strikes the ear, and during a long day's march not a single large animal will be seen from the beaten track. It is true that in some places there is

> " Enough
> Of beastes that be chaseable."

The park lands of Dut'humi, the jungles and forests of Ugogi and Mgunda Mk'hali, the barrens of Usukuma, and the tangled thickets of Ujiji, are full of noble game—lions and leopards, elephants and rhinoceroses, wild cattle, giraffes, gnus, zebras, quaggas, and ostriches. But these are dangerous regions, where the sportsman often can not linger for a day. Setting aside the minor considerations of miasma and malaria—the real or fancied perils of the place, and the want of food, or the difficulty of procuring water, would infallibly cause the porters to desert. Here are no Cape-wagons, at once house, store, and transport; no "Ships of the Desert," never known to run away; in fact, there is no vehicle but man, and he is so impatient and headstrong, so suspicious and timorous, that he must be humored in every whim. As sportsmen know, it is difficult to combine surveying operations and collection of specimens with a pursuit which requires all a man's time; in these countries, moreover, no merely hunting-expedition would pay, owing to the extraordinary expense of provisions and carriage. Thus Venator will be reduced to use his "shooting-iron" on halting days and at the several periods of his journey, and his only consolation will be the prospect of wreaking vengeance upon the hippopotamus and the crocodile of the coast, if his return there be entered in the book of Time. Finally, East Africa wants the vast variety of animals, especially the beautiful antelopes, which enrich the lists of the Cape Fauna. The tale of those observed in short: the horns of the oryx were seen, the hartebeest and steinbok, the saltiana and the pallah—the latter affording excellent venison—were shot. The country generally produces the "suiya," a little antelope, with reddish coat and diminutive horns, about the size of an English hare, the swangura, or sungula, an animal somewhat larger than the saltiana, and of which, according to the people, the hind only has horns; and at K'hutu my companion saw a double-horned antelope which he thought resembled the "chouka-singa" (*Tetraceros Quadricornis*) of Nepaul. The species of birds, also, are scarcely more numerous than the beasts; the feathered tribe is characterized by sombreness of plumage, and their song is noisy but not harmonious, unpleasant, perhaps because strange, to the European ear.

On the 8th of October appeared at Kanyenye a large down-caravan headed by Abdullah bin Nasib, a Msawahili of Zanzibar, whose African name is Kisesa. This good man began with the usual token of hospitality, the gift of a goat, and some measures of the fine Unyanyembe rice, of which return-parties carry an ample store: he called upon me at once with several companions—one of them surprised me not a little by an English "good-morning"—and he kindly volunteered to halt a day while we wrote reports and letters, life-certificates, and duplicate indents upon Zanzibar for extra supplies of drugs and medical comforts, cloth and beads. The asses were now reduced to five, and as Magomba refused to part with any of his few animals, at any price—on the coast I had been assured that asses were as numerous as dogs in Ugogo—Abdullah gave me one of his riding-animals, and would take nothing for it except a little medicine, and a paper acknowledging his civility. Several of the slaves and porters had been persuaded by the Wagogo to desert, and Abdullah busied himself to recover them. One man, who had suddenly deposited his pack upon the path and had disappeared in the jungle during the noonday halt, was pointed out by a woman to Kidogo, and was found lurking in a neighboring village, where the people refused to give him up. Abdullah sent for Magomba's four chief "ministers," and persuaded them to render active aid: they seized the fellow, took from him his wire and his nine cloths, appropriated four, and left me five wherewith to engage another porter. The deserter was of course dismissed, but the severity of the treatment did not prevent three desertions on the next day.

The 10th October ushered in an ugly march. Emerging betimes from the glaring white and red plains of Kanyenye, dotted with fields, villages, and calabashes, we unloaded in a thin jungle of mimosa and grass bunches, near sundry pools, then almost dried up, but still surrounded by a straggling growth of chamærops and verdurous thorns. The bush gave every opportunity to the porters, who had dispersed in the halt, to desert with impunity. In our hurried morning tramp, want of carriage had caused considerable confusion, and at 2 P.M., when again the word "load" was given for a tirikeza, every thing seemed to go wrong. Said bin Salim and the jemadar hurried forward, leaving me to manage the departure with Kidogo, who, while my companion lay under a calabash almost unable to move, substituted for his strong Mnyamwezi ass a wretched animal unable to bear the lightest load. The Baloch Belok was asked to carry our only gourd full of water; he pleaded sickness as an excuse. And, when the rear of the caravan was about to march, Kidogo, who alone knew the way, hastened on so fast that he left us to wander through a labyrinth of elephants' tracks, hedged in by thorns and brambly trees, which did considerable damage to clothes and cutis.

Having at length found the way, we advanced over a broad, open, and grassy plain, striped with southward-trending sandy water-courses of easy ascent and descent, and lined with a green aromatic vegetation, in which the tall palm suggested a resemblance to the valley-plains of the Usagara Mountains. As night fell upon us like a pall, we entered the broken red ground that limits the flat westward, and, ascending a dark ridge of broken, stony ground, and a dense thorn-bush, we found ourselves upon a higher level. The asses stumbled, the men grumbled, and the want of water severely tried the general temper.

From this cold jungle—the thermometer showed a minimum

of 54° F.—we emerged at dawn on the 11th October, and, after three hours' driving through a dense bush of various thorns, with calabashes reddened by the intense heat, and tripping upon the narrow broken path that ran over rolling ground, we found the porters halted at some pits full of sweet clear water. Here the caravan preserved a remarkable dead silence. I inquired the cause. The coast Arabs who accompanied us were trying an experiment, which, had it failed, would have caused trouble, expense, and waste of time; they were attempting to pass without blackmail the little clearing of Usek'he, which lay to the south of the desert road, and they knew that its sultan, Ganza Mikono, usually posted a party upon the low masses of bristling hill hard by, to prevent caravans evading his dues. As no provisions were procurable in the jungle, it was judged better to proceed, and the sun was in the zenith before we reached the district of K'hok'ho. We halted under a spreading tree, near the head-quarter village of its villainous sultan, in an open plain of millet and panicum stubbles. Presently Kidogo, disliking the appearance of things—the men, rushing with yells of excitement from their villages, were forming a dense ring around us; the even more unmanageable old women stared like *sages femmes*, and already a Mnyamwezi porter had been beaten at the well—stirred us up and led the way to an open jungle about a mile distant. There we were safe; no assailant would place himself upon the plain, the coast Arabs were close at hand, and in the bush we should have been more than a match for the Wagogo.

The Baloch, fatigued by the tedious marches of the last two days, had surlily refused their escort to our luggage, as well as to ourselves. When the camp was pitched, I ordered a goat to be killed; and, serving out rations to the sons of Ramji and the porters, I gave them none—a cruel punishment to men whose souls centred in their ingesta. The earlier part of the evening was spent by them in enumerating their grievances; they were careful to speak in four dialects, so that all around might understand them, in discussing their plans of desertion, and in silencing the contradiction of their commander, the monocular jemadar, who, having forsworn opium, now headed the party in opposition to the mutineers. They complained that they were faint for want of meat; the fellows were driving a bullock and half a dozen goats, which they had purchased with cloth certainly not their own. I had, they grumbled, given them no ghee or honey, consequently they were obliged to "eat dry;" they knew this to be false, as they had received both at Kanyenye. We had made them march ten "cos" in our eagerness to obtain milk; they were the first to propose reaching a place where provisions were procurable. The unmanageables, Khudabakhsh, Shahdad, and Belok, proposed an immediate departure, but a small majority carried the day in favor of desertion next morning. Kidogo and the sons of Ramji ridiculed, as was their wont, the silly boasters with, "Of a truth, brethren! the coast is far off, and ye are hungry men!" On the ensuing day, when a night's reflection had cooled down their noble bile, they swallowed their words like buttered parsnips. I heard no more of their plans, and in their demeanor they became cringing as before.

The transit of the K'hok'ho clearing, which is also called the Nyika, or wilderness, is considered the nucleus of travelers' troubles in Ugogo. The difficulty is caused by its sultan, M'ana Miaha, popularly known as Maguru Mafupi, or Short-shanks. This petty tyrant, the most powerful, however, of the Wagogo chiefs, is a toothache to strangers, who complain that he can not even plunder à l'aimable. He was described to me as a short elderly man, nearly bald, chocolate-colored, and remarkable for the duck-like conformation which gave origin to his nickname. His dress was an Arab check round his loins, and another thrown over his shoulders. He becomes man, idiot, and beast with clock-work regularity every day; when not disguised in liquor he is surly and unreasonable, and when made merry by his cups he refuses to do business. He is in the habit of detaining Wanyamwezi caravans to hoe his fields, and he often applies them to a corvée of five or six days during the spring-time, before he will consent to receive his black-mail.

We were delayed five days at K'hok'ho to lay in provisions for four marches, and by the usual African pretexts, various and peculiar. On the afternoon of arrival it would have been held indecent haste to trouble his highness. On the first morning his highness's spouse was unwell, and during the day he was "sitting upon pombe," in other words, drinking beer. On the second he received, somewhat scurvily, a deputation headed by Said bin Salim, the coast Arab merchants, and the jemadar. Two wazagira, or chief councilors, did the palaver, which was conducted, for dignity, outside the royal hovel. He declared that the two caravans must compound separately, and that in my case he would be satisfied with nothing under six porters' loads. As about one twelfth of his demand was offered to him, he dismissed them with ignominy, affirming that he held me equal to the Sayyid of Zanzibar, and accordingly that he should demand half the outfit. The third day was spent by the coast Arabs in haggling with the courtiers before his highness, who maintained a solemn silence, certainly the easiest plan; and the present was paraded, as is customary on such occasions, in separate heaps, each intended for a particular person, but her highness, justly offended by the flimsiness of a bit of chintz, seized a huge wooden ladle and hooted and hunted the offenders out of doors. After high words the Arabs returned, and informed me that things were looking desperate. I promised assistance in case of violence being offered to them— a civility which they acknowledged by sending a shoulder of beef. The fourth day was one of dignified idleness. We received a message that the court was again sitting upon pombe, and we too well understood that his highness, with his spouse and cabinet, were drunk as drunk could be. On the morning of the fifth day a similar delaying process was attempted; but as the testy Kidogo, who had taken the place of the tame Said, declared that the morrow should see us march in the afternoon, the present was accepted, and the two or three musket shots usual on such occasions sounded the joyful tidings that we were at liberty to proceed. The unconscionable extortioner had received one coil of brass wire, four "cloths with names," eight domestics, eight blue cottons, and thirty strings of coral beads. Not contented with this, he demanded two Arab checks, and these failing, a double quantity of beads, and another domestic. I compromised the affair with six feet of crimson broadcloth, an article which I had not produced, as the coast Arabs, who owned none, declared that such an offering would cause difficulties in their case. But as they charged me double and treble prices for the expensive cloths which the sultan required, and which, as they had been omitted in our outfit, it was necessary to purchase from them, I at length thought myself justified in economizing by the only means in my power. The fiery-tempered coast Arabs left K'hok'ho with rage in their hearts and curses under their tongues. These men usually think outside their heads, but they know that in Ugogo the merest pretext—the loosing a hot word, touching a woman, offending a boy, or taking in vain the name of the sultan —infallibly leads to being mulcted in cloth.

I was delighted to escape from the foul strip of crowded jungle in which we had halted. A down-caravan of Wanyamwezi had added its quotum of discomfort to the place. Throughout the fiery day we were stung by the tzetze, and annoyed by swarms of bees and pertinacious gadflies. On one occasion an army of large poisonous siyafu, or black pismire, drove us out of the tent by the wounds which it inflicted between the fingers and on other tender parts of the body, before a kettle of boiling water persuaded them to abandon us. These ant-fiends made the thin-skinned asses mad with torture. The nights were cold and raw, and when we awoke in the morning we found some valuable article rendered unserviceable by the termites. K'hok'ho was an ill-omened spot. There my ass "Syringe," sole survoice of the riding-animals brought from Zanzibar, was so torn by a hyena that I was compelled to leave it behind. I was afterward informed that it had soon died of its wounds. The next mishap was the desertion of the fifteen Wanyamwezi porters who had been hired and paid at Ugogi. These men had slept in the same kraal with the somnolent sons of Ramji, and had stealthily disappeared during the night. As usual, though they carried off their own, they had left our loads behind, that they might reach their homes with greater speed. They would choose a jungle road, to avoid the danger of slavery, and, living the while upon roots and edible grasses, would traverse the desert separating them from their country in three or four days. This desertion of fifteen men first suggested to me that my weary efforts and wearing anxiety about carriage were to a certain extent self-inflictions. Expecting to see half the outfit left upon the ground, I was surprised by the readiness with which it disappeared. The men seemed to behave best whenever things were palpably at the worst; besides which, as easily as the baggage of 50 porters was distributed among 100, so easily were the loads of 100 men placed upon the shoulders of 50. Indeed, the original Wanyamwezi gang, who claimed by right extra pay for carrying extra weight, though fiercely opposed to lifting up an empty gourd gratis, were ever docile when a heavier pack brought with it an increase of cloth and beads.

However, the march on the 17th of October had its trifling hardships. My companion rode forward on the ass lately given to us by Abdullah bin Nasib; while I, remaining behind, and finding that no carriage could be procured for two bags of clothes and shoes, placed them upon my animal the Mnyamwezi bought at Inenge, inasmuch as it appeared somewhat stronger than the half dozen wretched brutes that flung themselves upon the ground apparently too fagged to move. I had, however, overrated its powers: it soon became evident that I must walk, or that the valuable cargo must be left behind. Trembling with weakness, I set out to traverse the length of the Mdáburu jungle. The memory of that march is not pleasant: the burning sun and the fiery reflected heat arising from the parched ground; here a rough, thorny, and waterless jungle, where the jasmine flowered and the frankincense was used for fuel; there a grassy plain of black and suncracked earth—compelled me to lie down every half hour. The water-gourds were soon drained by my attendant Baloch; and the sons of Ramji, who, after reaching the resting-place, had returned with ample stores for their comrades, hid their vessels on my approach. Sarmalla, a donkey-driver, the model of a surly negro, whose crumpled brow, tightened eyes, and thick lips which shot out on the least occasion of excitement, showed what was going on within his head, openly refused me the use of his gourd, and—thirst is even less to be trifled with than hunger—found ample reason to repent himself of the proceeding. Near the end of the jungle I came upon a party of the Baloch, who, having seized upon a porter belonging to a large caravan of Wanyamwezi that had passed us on that march, were persuading him, half by promises and half by threats, to carry their sleeping-mats and their empty gourds. The strict and positive orders as regards enticing away deserters which I had issued at Inenge, were looked upon by them, in their all-engrossing egotism, as a mere string of empty words. I could do nothing beyond threatening to report their conduct to their master, and dismissing the man, who obviously stood in fear of death, with his tobacco and hoes duly counted back to him. Toward the end of that long march I saw with pleasure the kindly face of Seedy Bombay, who was returning to me in hot haste, leading an ass, and carrying a few scones and hard-boiled eggs. Mounting, I resumed my way, and presently arrived at the confines of Mdáburu, where, under a huge calabash, stood our tent, amid a kraal of grass boothies, surrounded by a heaped-up ridge of thorns.

Mdáburu is the first important district in the land of Uyanzi, which, beginning from Western K'hok'ho, extends as far as Tura, the eastern frontier of Unyamwezi-land. It is a fertile depression of brick-red earth, bisected by a broad, deep, and sandy fiumara, which, trending southward, supplies from five pits water in plenty even during the dryest season. It is belted on all sides by a dense jungle, over whose dark-brown line appeared the summits of low blue cones, and beyond them long streaks of azure ridge, beautified by distance into the semblance of a sea. We were delayed two days at this, the fourth and westernmost district of Ugogo. It was necessary to lay in a week's provision for the party—ever a tedious task in these regions, but more especially in the dead of winter—moreover, the Sultan Kibuya expected the settlement of his black-mail. From this man we experienced less than the usual incivility. By birth a Mkimbu foreigner, and fearing at that time wars and rumors of wars on the part of his villainous neighbor, Maguru Mafupi, he contented himself with a present which may be estimated at nineteen cloths, whereas the others had murmured at forty and fifty. However, he abated nothing of his country's pretentious pride. A black, elderly man, dressed in a grimy cloth, without other ornament but a broad ivory bracelet covering several inches of his right wrist, he at first refused to receive the deputation because his "ministers" were absent; and, during the discourse about the amount of black-mail, he sat, preserving an apathetic silence, outside his dirty lodging in the huge kraal which forms his capital. The demand concluded with a fine silk-cotton cloth on the part of his wife; and when "ma femme" appears on such occasions in these regions, as in others farther west, it is a sure sign that the stranger is to be taken in. As usual with the East African chiefs, Kibuya was anxious to detain me, not only in order that his people might profitably dispose of their surplus stores, but also because the presence of so many guns would go far to modify the plans of his enemies. His attempts at delay, however, were skillfully out-manœuvred by Said bin Salim, who broke through all difficulties with the hardihood of fear. The little man's vain terrors made him put the ragged kraal which surrounded us into a condition of defense, and every night he might be seen stalking like a troubled spirit among the forms of sleeping men.

At Mdáburu I hired two porters from the caravan that accompanied us, and Said bin Salim began somewhat tardily to take the usual precautions against desertion. He was ordered, before the disappearance of the porters that levanted at K'hok'ho, to pack their hire in our loads, and every evening to chain up the luggage heaped in front of our tent. The accident caused by his neglect rendered him now quasi-obedient. Moreover, two or three Baloch were told off to precede the line, and as many to bring up the rear. The porters, as I have said, hold it a point of honor not to steal their packs; but if allowed to straggle forward, or to loiter behind, they will readily attempt the recovery of their goods by opening their burdens, which they afterward abandon upon the road. The coast Arabs, in return for some small shot, which is here highly prized, assisted me by carrying some surplus luggage. Among other articles, two kegs of gunpowder were committed to them: both were punctually returned at Unyanyembe, where gunpowder sells at two cloths, or half a frasilah (17.5 lbs.) of ivory per lb.; but the bungs had been stove in, and a quarter of the contents had evaporated. The evening of the second day's halt closed on us before the rations for the caravan were collected, and seventeen shukkah, with about a hundred strings of beads, barely produced a sufficiency of grain.

From the Red Vale of Mdáburu three main lines traverse the desert between Ugogo and Unyamwezi. The northernmost, called Njia T'humbi, leads in a west-northwesterly direction to Usukuma. Upon this track are two sultans and several villages. The central "Karangásá," or "Mdáburu," is that which will be described in the following pages. The southernmost, termed Uyánzi, sets out from K'hok'ho, and passes through the settlements known by the name of Jiwe lá Singá. It is avoided by the porters, dreading to incur the wrath of Sultan Kibuyá, who would resent their omitting to visit his settlement, M'dáburu.

These three routes pass through the heart of the great desert and elephant-ground "Mgunda Mk'hali"—explained by the Arabs to mean in Kinyamwezi, the Fiery "Shamba" or Field. Like Marenga Mk'hali, it is a desert, because it contains no running water nor wells, except after rain. The name is still infamous, but its ill-fame rests rather upon tradition than actuality; in fact, its dimensions are rapidly shrinking before the torch and axe. About fifteen years ago it contained twelve long stages, and several tirikeza; now it is spanned in eight marches. The wildest part is the first half from Mdáburu to Jiwe lá Mkoa, and even here, it is reported, villages of Wakimbu are rising rapidly on the north and south of the road. The traveler, though invariably threatened with drought and the death of cattle, will undergo little hardship beyond the fatigue of the first three forced marches through the "Fiery Field;" in fact, he will be agreeably surprised by its contrast with the desert of Marenga Mk'hali.

From east to west the diagonal breadth of Mgunda Mk'hali is 140 miles. The general aspect is a dull uniform bush, emerald-colored during the rains, and in the heats a net-work of dry and broom-like twigs. Except upon the banks of nullahs—"rivers" that are not rivers—the trees, as in Ugogo, wanting nutriment, never afford timber, and even the calabash appears stunted. The trackless waste of scrub, called the "bush" in Southern Africa, is found in places alternating with thin gum-forest; the change may be accounted for by the different depths of water below the level of the ground. It is a hardy vegetation of mimosas and gums mixed with evergreen succulent plants, cactaceæ, aloes, and euphorbias; the grass, sometimes tufty, at other times equally spread, is hard and stiff; when green it feeds cattle, and when dry it is burned in places by passing caravans to promote the growth of another crop.

The ground-work of Mgunda Mk'hali is a detritus of yellowish quartz, in places white with powdered feldspar, and where vegetation decays, brown-black with humus. Water-worn pebbles are sprinkled over the earth, and the vicinity of fiumaras abounds in a coarse and modern sandstone conglomerate. Upon the rolling surface, and towering high above the tallest trees, are based the huge granite and syenitic outcrops before alluded to. The contrast between the masses and the dwarf rises which support them at once attracts the eye. Here and there the long waves that diversify the land appear in the far distance like blue lines bounding the nearer superficies of brown or green. Throughout this rolling table-land the water-shed is to the south. In rare places the rains stagnate in shallow pools, which become systems of mud-cakes during the drought. At this season water is often unprocurable in the fiumaras, causing unaccustomed hardships to caravans, and death to those beasts which, like the elephant and the buffalo, can not long exist without drinking.

On the 20th October we began the transit of the "Fiery Field," whose long broad line of brown jungle, painted blue by the intervening air, had, since leaving K'hok'ho, formed our western horizon. The waste here appeared in its most horrid phase. The narrow goat-path serpentined in and out of a growth of poisonous thorny jungle, with thin, hard grass-straw, growing on a glaring white and rolling ground; the view was limited by bush and brake, as in the alluvial valleys of the maritime region, and in weary sameness the spectacle surpassed every thing that we had endured in Marenga Mk'hali. We halted through the heat of the day at some water-pits in a broken course; and resuming our tedious march early in the afternoon, we arrived about sunset at the bed of a shallow nullah, where the pure element was found in sand-holes about five feet deep.

On the second day we reached the large Mabunguru fiumara, a deep and tortuous gash of fine yellow quartzose sand and sun-

burnt blocks of syenite; at times it must form an impassable torrent; even at this season of severe drought it affords long pools of
infiltrated rain-water, green with weeds and abounding with shell-
fish, and with the usual description of silurus.   In the earlier
morning the path passed through a forest already beautified by
the sprouting of tender green leaves and by the blooming of flowers, among which was a large and strongly perfumed species of jasmine, while young grass sprouted from the fire-blackened remnants of the last year's crop.   Far upon the southern horizon rose
distant hills and lines, blue, as if composed of solidified air, and
mocking us by their mirage-likeness to the ocean.   Nearer, the
ground was diversified by those curious evidences of igneous action, which extend westward through Eastern Unyamwezi, and
northward to the shores of the Nyanza Lake.   These outcrops of
gray granite and syenite are principally of two different shapes,
the hog's back and the turret.   The former usually appears as a
low lumpy dome of various dimensions; here a few feet long,
there extending a mile and a half in diameter: the outer coat
scales off under the action of the atmosphere, and in places it is
worn away by a net-work of paths.   The turret is a more picturesque and changing feature.   Tall rounded blocks and conical
or cylindrical boulders, here single, there in piles or ridges, some
straight and stiff as giant nine-pins, others split as if an alley or a
gateway passed between them, rise abruptly and perpendicularly
almost without foundationary elevation, cleaving the mould of a
dead plain, or—like gypseous formations, in which the highest
boulders are planted upon the lowest and broadest bases—they
bristle upon a wave of dwarfish rocky hill.   One when struck
was observed to give forth a metallic clink, and not a few, balanced upon points, reminded me of the tradition-bearing rocking
stones.   At a distance in the forest, the larger masses might be
mistaken for Cyclopean walls, towers, steeples, minarets, loggans,
dwelling-houses, and ruined castles.   They are often overgrown
with a soft grass, which, decaying, forms with the degradation of
the granite a thin cap of soil; their summits are crowned with
tufty cactus, a stomatiferous plant, which imbibes nourishment
from the oxygen of the air; while huge creepers, imitating trees,
project gnarled trunks from the deeper crevices in their flanks.
Seen through the forest, these rocks are an effective feature in the
landscape, especially when the sunbeams fall warm and bright
upon their rounded summits and their smooth sides, here clothed
with a mildew-like lichen of the tenderest leek-green, there yel-
lowed like Italian marbles by the burning rays, and there streaked with a shining black as if glazed by the rain, which, collecting
in cupfuls upon the steps and slopes, at times overflows, coursing
in mimic cataracts down the heights.

That march was a severe trial; we had started at dawn, we did
not, however, arrive at the Mabunguru fiumara before noon, and

our people straggled in about eveningtide. All our bullet-moulds and three boxes of ammunition were lost. Said bin Salim, the jemadar, and three other men had followed in the rear, driving on the "one-eyed fiend," which, after many a prank, lay down upon the ground, and positively declined to move. The escort, disliking the sun, abandoned it at once to its fate, and the want of provisions, and the inordinate length of the marches, rendered a halt or a return for the valuable load—four boxes of ammunition— out of the question. An article once abandoned in these deserts is rarely if ever recovered; the caravan-porters will not halt, and a small party dares not return to recover it.

The 22d of October saw us at Jiwe la Mkoa, the half-way house of Mgunda Mk'hali. The track, crossing the rough Mabunguru fiumara, passed over rolling ground through a thorny jungle that gradually thinned out into a forest; about 8 A.M. a halt was called at a water in the wilderness. My companion being no longer able to advance on foot, an ass was unloaded, and its burden of ammunition was divided, for facility of porterage, among the sons of Ramji. After noon we resumed our march, and Kirangozi, derided by the rival guide of the coast Arabs' caravan, and urged forward by Kidogo, who was burning to see his wife and children in Unyamwezi, determined "to put himself at the head of himself." The jungle seemed interminable. The shadows of the hills lengthened out upon the plains, the sun sank in the glory of purple, crimson, and gold, and the crescent moon rained a flood of silvery light upon the topmost twig-work of the trees; we passed a dwarf clearing, where lodging and perhaps provisions were to be obtained, and we sped by water near the road where the frogs were chanting their vesper hymn; still far, far ahead we heard the horns and the faint march-cries of the porters. At length, towards the end of the march, we wound round a fantastic mass of cactus-clad boulders, and crossing a low ridge, we found at its base a single tembe or square village of emigrant Wakimbu, who refused to admit us. The little basin beyond it displayed, by "black jacks" and felled tree-trunks, evidences of modern industry, and it extended to the jiwe or rock, which gives its name to the clearing. We were cheered by the sight of the red fires glaring in the kraal, but my companion's ass, probably frightened by some wild beast to us invisible, reared high in the air, bucked like a deer, broke his frail Arab girths, and threw his invalid rider heavily upon the hard earth. Arrived at the kraal, I found every boothy occupied by the porters, who refused shelter, until dragged out like slaughtered sheep. Said bin Salim's awning was, as usual, snugly pitched; ours still lay on the ground. The little Arab's "duty to himself" appeared to attain a higher limit every stage; once comfortably housed, he never thought of offering cover to another, and his children knew him too well even to volunteer such a service to any one but himself. On a late occasion, when our tent had not appeared, Said bin Salim, to whom message had been sent, refused to lend us one half of the awning committed to him, a piece of canvas cut out to serve as a tent and lug-sail. Bombay then distinguished himself by the memorable words—"If you are not ashamed of your master, be ashamed of your servant!" which had the effect of bringing the awning and of making Said bin Salim testily refuse the half returned to him.

Jiwe la Mkoa, or the Round Rock, is the largest of the many hogs'-backs of gray syenite that stud this waste. It measures about two miles in extreme diameter, and the dome rises with a gentle slope to the height of 200 or 300 feet above the dead level of the plain. Tolerable water is found in pits upon a swamp at its northern base, and well-covered mtego or elephant-traps, deep grave-like excavations, like the Indian "ogi," prove dangerous to travelers; in one of these the jemadar disappeared suddenly, as if by magic. The smooth and rounded surface of the rock displays deep hoof-shaped holes, which in a Moslem land would at once be recognized as the asr, or the footprints of those holy quadrupeds, Duldul or Zu'l Jenah. In places the jiwe, overgrown with scattered tufts of white grass, and based upon a dusty surface blackened by torrent rains, forcibly suggested to the Baloch the idea of an elderly negro's purbald poll.

We encamped close to the jiwe, and in so doing we did wrong: however pleasant may be the shadow of a tall rock in a thirsty land by day, way-wise travelers avoid the vicinity of stones which, by diminished radiation, retain their heat throughout the night. All caravans passing through this clearing clamor to be supplied with provisions; our porters, who had received rations for eight days, which they consumed in four, were no exceptions to the rule. As the single little village of Jiwe la Mkoa could afford but one goat-skin of grain and a few fowls, the cattle not being for sale, and no calves having been born to the herds, the porters proposed to send a party with cloth and beads to collect provaunt from the neighboring settlements. But the notable Khalfan bin Khamis, the most energetic of the coast Arabs in whose company we were traveling, would brook no delay: he had issued as usual three days' rations for a long week's march, and thus by driving his porters beyond their speed, he practiced a style of economy usually categorized by us at home as "penny-wise and pound-foolish." His marching was conducted upon the same principle; determining to save time, he pushed on till his men began to flag, presently broke down, and finally deserted.

At Jiwe la Mkoa the neck of the desert is broken: the western portion of the Mgunda Mk'hali has already thinned out. On the 23d October, despite the long march of the preceding day, Khalfan proposed a tirikeza, declaring that the heavy nimbus from the west, accompanied by a pleasant cold, portended rain, and that this rain, like the "choti barsat" of India, announces the approach of the great masika, or vernal wet season. Yielding to his reasons, we crossed the "Round Rock," and passing through an open forest of tall trees, with here and there an undulating break, now yellow with quartz, then black with humus, we reached, after about three hours, another clearing like Jiwe la Mkoa, which owes its origin to the requirements of commerce. "Kirurumo" boasted of several newly-built tembe of Wakimbu, who supplied caravans at an exorbitant rate. The blackness of the ground, and the vivid green of vegetation, evidenced the proximity of water. The potable element was found in pits, sunk in a narrow nullah running northward across the clearing: it was muddy and abundant. On the next day the road led through a thin forest of thorns and gums, which, bare of bush and underwood, afforded a broad path, and pleasant, easy traveling. Signs of elephant and rhinoceros, giraffe and antelope, crossed the path, and, as usual in such places, the asses were tormented by the tzetze. After traveling four hours and thirty minutes, we reached a new settlement upon the western frontier of Uganzi, called "Jiweni," "near the stones," from the heaps of block and boulder scattered round pits of good water, sunk about three feet in the ground. The Mongo Nullah, a deep surface-drain, bisects this clearing, which is palpably modern. Many of the trees are barked previous to felling, and others have fallen prostrate, apparently from the depredations of the white ant. On the 25th, after another desert march of 2$^{hrs.}$ 20$^{m.}$ through a flat country, where the forest was somewhat deformed by bush and brake, which in places narrowed the path to a mere goat-track, we arrived at the third quarter of Mgunda Mk'hali. "Mgongo T'hembo," or the Elephant's Back, derives its name from a long narrow ridge of chocolate-colored syenite, outcropping from the low forest lands around it; the crest of the chain is composed of loose rocks and large detached boulders. Like the other inhabited portions of Mgunda Mk'hali, it is a recent clearing; numerous "black-jacks," felled trees, and pollarded stumps still cumber the fields. The "Elephant's Back" is, however, more extensive and better cultivated than any of its neighbors—Mdáburu alone excepted—and water being abundant and near the surface, it supports an increasing population of mixed Wakimbu and Wataturu, who dwell in large substantial tembe, and live by selling their surplus holcus, maize, and fowls to travelers. They do not, like the Wakimbu of Jiwe la Mkoa, refuse entrance to their villages, but they receive the stranger with the usual niggard guest-rites of the slave-path, and, African-like, they think only of what is to be gained by hospitality. Here I halted for a day to recruit and to lay in rations. The length of the stages had told upon the men; Bombay had stumped himself, several of the sons of Ramji, and two of Said bin Salim's children were unable to walk; the asses, throwing themselves upon the ground, required to be raised with the stick, and all preferred rest even to food. Mboni, one of the sons of Ramji, carried off a slave-girl from the camp of the coast Arabs; her proprietor came armed to recover her, swords were drawn, a prodigious clash and clatter of tongue arose, friends interfered, and blades were sheathed. Khalfan bin Khamis, losing all patience at this delay, bade us adieu, promising to announce our approach at Unyanyembe; about a week afterward, however, we found him in most melancholy plight, halted half way, because his overworked porters had taken "French leave."

We resumed our march on the 27th October, and after a slow and painful progress for seven hours over a rolling country, whose soil was now yellow with argile, then white with feldspar, then black-brown with humus, through thorny bush, and forest here opening out, there densely closing in, we arrived at the "Tura Nullah," the deepest of the many surface-drains winding tortuously to the S.W. The trees lining the margin were of the noblest dimensions; the tall thick grass that hedged them in showed signs of extensive conflagration, and water was found in shallow pools and in deep pits beneath the banks, on the side to which the stream, which must be furious during the rainy season, swings. When halted in a clear place in the jungle, we were passed by a down-caravan of Wanyamwezi; our porters shouted and rushed up to greet their friends, the men raised their right hands about a dozen times, and then clapped palm to palm, and the women indulged in "vigelegele," the African "lulliloo," which rang like breech-loaders in our ears.

On the next day we set out betimes through the forest, which, as usual when nearing populous settlements, spread out, and which began at this season to show a preponderance of green over brown. Presently we reached a large expanse of yellow stover, where the van had halted, in order that the caravan might make its first appearance with dignity. Ensued a clearing, studded with large stockaded villages, peering over tall hedges of dark-green milk-bush, fields of maize and millet, manioc, gourds, and watermelons, and showing numerous flocks and herds, clustering around the shallow pits. The people swarmed from their abodes, young and old hustling one another for a better stare; the man forsook his loom and the girl her hoe, and for the remainder of the march we were escorted by a tail of screaming boys and shouting adults; the males almost nude, the women bare to the waist and clothed only knee-deep in kilts, accompanied us, puffing pipes the while, with wallets of withered or flabby flesh flapping the air, striking their hoes with stones, crying "Beads! beads!" and ejaculating their wonder in strident explosions of "Hi! hi!—Hui! ih!" and "Ha!—a!—a!" It was a spectacle to make an anchorite of a man—it was at once ludicrous and disgusting.

At length the kirangozi fluttered his red flag in the wind, and the drums, horns, and larynxes of his followers began the fearful uproar which introduces a caravan to the admiring "natives." Leading the way, our guide, much to my surprise—I knew not then that such was the immemorial custom of Unyamwezi—entered uninvited and sans ceremony the nearest large village; the long string of porters flocked in with bag and baggage, and we followed their example. The guests at once dispersed themselves through the several courts and compounds into which the interior hollow was divided, and lodged themselves with as much regard for self and disregard for their grumbling hosts as possible. We were placed under a wall-less roof, bounded on one side by the bars of the village palisade, and the mob of starers that relieved one another from morning till night made me feel like the denizen of a menagerie.

Usagara Mountains, seen from Ugogo.

CHAPTER IX.

THE GEOGRAPHY AND ETHNOGRAPHY OF UGOGO—THE THIRD REGION.

The third division of the country visited is a flat table-land extending from the Ugogi "dhun," or valley, at the western base of the Wasagara Mountains, in E. long. 36° 14', to Tura, the eastern district of Unyamwezi, in E. long. 33° 57'; occupying a diagonal breadth of 155 geographical rectilinear miles. The length from north to south is not so easily estimated. The Wahumba and the Watataru in the former, and the Wahehe and Warori in the latter direction, are migratory tribes that spurn a civilized frontier; according to the Arabs, however, the Wagogo extend three long marches on an average to the north and four or five southward. This, assuming the march at 15 miles, would give a total of 120. The average of the heights observed is 3650 feet, with a gradual rise westward to Jiwe la Mkoa, which attains an altitude of 4200 feet (?).

The third region, situated to leeward of a range whose height compels the southeast trades to part with their load of vapors, and distant from the succession of inland seas which, stationed near the centre of the African continent, act as reservoirs to restore the balance of humidity, is an arid, sterile land, a counterpart in many places of the Kalahari and the Karroo, or South African desert-plains. The general aspect is a glaring yellow flat, darkened by long growths of acrid, saline, and succulent plants, thorny bush, and stunted trees, and the coloring is monotonous in the extreme. It is sprinkled with isolated dwarf cones, bristling with rocks and boulders, from whose interstices springs a thin forest of gums, thorns, and mimosas. The power of igneous agency is displayed in protruding masses of granitic formation, which rise from the dead level with little foundationary elevation; and the masses of sandstone, superincumbent upon the primitive base in other parts of the country, here disappear. On the north rises the long tabular range of the Wahumba Hills, separated by a line of lower ground from the plateau. Southward, a plain, imperceptibly shelving, trends toward the Rwaha River. There are no rivers in Ugogo: the periodical rains are carried off by large nullahs, whose clay banks are split and cut during the season of potent heat into polygonal figures like piles of columnar basalt. On the sparkling nitrous salinas and the dull-yellow or dun-colored plains the mirage faintly resembles the effects of refraction in desert Arabia. The roads are mere foot-tracks worn through the fields and bushes. The kraals are small dirty circles inclosing a calabash or other tree, against which goods are stacked. The boothies are made of dried canes and stubble, surrounded by a most efficient *chevaux de frise* of thorn-boughs. At the end of the dry season they are burnt down by inevitable accident. The want of wood prevents their being made solidly, and for the same reason " bois de vache" is the usual fuel of the country.

The formation of the subsoil is mostly sandstone bearing a ruddy sand. The surface is in rare places a brown vegetable humus, extending but a few inches in depth, or more generally a hard yellow-reddish ferruginous clay, covered with quartz nodules of many colors, and lumps of carbonate of lime, or white and silicious sand, rather resembling a well-metalled road or an "untidy expanse of gravel-walk" than the rich moulds which belong to the fertile African belt. In many parts are conical ant-hills of pale red earth; in others iron-stone crops out of the plain; and every where fine and coarse grits abound. The land is in parts condemned to perpetual drought, and nowhere is water either good or plentiful. It is found in the serpentine beds of nullahs, and after rain in ziwa, vleys, tanks, pools, or ponds, filled by a gentle gravitation, and retained, by a strong clay, in deep pits excavated by the people, or in shallow holes "crowed" in the ground. The supplies of this necessary divide the country into three great districts. On the east is Marenga Mk'hali, a thick bush, where a few villages, avoided by travelers, are scattered north and south of the road. The heart of the region is Ugogo, the most populous and the best cultivated country, divided into a number of small and carefully cultivated clearings by tracts of dense bush and timberless woods, a wall of verdure during the rains, and in the hot season a system of thorns and broom-work, which serves merely to impede a free circulation of the air. These seams of waste land appear strange in a country populated of old; the Arabs, however, declare that the land is more thinly inhabited than it used to be. Mgunda Mk'hali, the western division, is a thin forest and a heap of braky jungle. The few hills are thickly clothed with vegetation, probably because they retain more moisture than the plains.

The climate of Ugogo is markedly arid. During the transit of the expedition in September and October, the best water-colors faded and hardened in their pans; India-rubber, especially the prepared article in squares, became viscid, like half-dried bird-lime; "Macintosh" was sticking-plaster, and the best vulcanized elastic bands tore like brown paper. During almost the whole year a violent east wind sweeps from the mountains. There are great changes in the temperature, while the weather apparently remains the same, and alternate currents of hot and cold air were observed. In the long summer the climate much resembles that of Sindh; there are the same fiery suns playing upon the naked surface with a painful dazzle, cool crisp nights, and clouds of dust. The succulent vegetation is shriveled up and carbonized by heat, and the crackling covering of clayey earth and thin sand, whose particles are unbound by dew or rain, rises in lofty whirling columns like water-spouts when the north wind from the Wahumba Hills meets the gusts of Usagara, which are soon heated to a furnace-breath by the glowing surface. These "p'hepo" or "devils" scour the plain with the rapidity of horsemen, and, charged with coarse grain and small pebbles, strike with the violence of heavy hail. The siccity and repercussion of heat produce an atmosphere of peculiar brilliancy in Ugogo: the milky haze of the coast-climate is here unknown. The sowing season, at which time also trees begin to bud and birds to breed, is about the period of the sun's greatest southern declination, and the diminution of temperature displays in these regions the effects of the tepid winds and the warm vernal showers of the European continent. There is no vuli, and thus the climate is unrefreshed by the copious tropical rains. About the middle of November the country is visited by a few preliminary showers, accompanied by a violent tramontana, and the vital principle, which appears extinct, starts once more into sudden and excessive activity. Toward the end of December the masika, or rainy season, commences with the wind shifting from the east to the north and northeast, blowing steadily from the high grounds eastward and westward of the Nyanza Lake, which have been saturated by heavy falls beginning in September. The "winter" seldom exceeds the third month, and the downfall is desultory and uncertain, causing frequent droughts and famine. For this reason the land is much inferior in fertility to the other regions, and the cotton and tobacco, which flourish from the coast to the Tanganyika Lake, are deficient in Ugogo, while rice is supplanted by the rugged sorghum and maize.

Arab and other travelers unaccustomed to the country at first suffer from the climate, which must not, however, be condemned. They complain of the tourbillons, the swarms of flies, and the violent changes from burning heat to piercing cold, which is always experienced in that region when the thermometer sinks below $60°$–$55°$ F. Their thin tents, pitched under a ragged calabash, can not mitigate the ardor of an unclouded sun; the salt-bitter water, whose nitrous and saline deposits sometimes tarnish a silver ring like the fumes of sulphur, affects their health; while the appetite, stimulated by a purer atmosphere and the coolness of the night air, is kept within due bounds only by deficiency in the means of satisfying it. Those who have seen Africa farther west are profuse in their praises of the climate on their return-march from the interior. The mukunguru, or seasoning fever, however, rarely fails to attack strangers. It is, like that of the second region, a violent bilious attack, whose consequences are sleeplessness, debility, and severe headaches: the hot fit, compared with the algid stage, is unusually long and rigorous. In some districts the pyrexia is rarely followed by the relieving perspiration; and when natural diaphoresis appears, it by no means denotes the termination of the paroxysm. Other diseases are rare, and the terrible ulcerations of K'hutu and Eastern Usagara are almost unknown in Ugogo. There is little doubt that the land, if it afforded good shelter, purified water, and regular diet, would be eminently wholesome.

In the uninviting landscape a tufty, straggling grass, like living hay, often raised on little mounds, with bald places between, thinly strewed with bits of quartz and sandstone, replaces the tall luxuriant herbage of the maritime plain and the arboraceous and frutescent produce of the mountains. The dryness of the climate, and the poverty of the soil, are displayed in the larger vegetation. The only tree of considerable growth is the calabash, and it is scattered over the country widely apart. A variety of frankincense overspreads the ground; the bark is a deep burnished bronze, whitened above with an incrustation, probably nitrous, that resembles hoar-frost; and the long woody twigs are bleached by the falling off of the outer integuments. The mukl or bdellium-tree rises like a dwarf calabash from a low copse. The Arabs declare this produce of Ugogo (*Balsamodendron Africanum?*) to be of good quality. Rubbed upon a stone and mixed with water, it is applied with a pledget of cotton to sluggish and purulent sores; and women use it for fumigation. The Africans ignore its qualities, and the Baloch, though well acquainted with the bdellium, gugal, or guggur, in their own country, did not observe it in Ugogo. The succulent plants, cactus, aloe, and euphorbia, will not burn; the air within them expands with heat, and the juices gushing out extinguish the flame. Among various salsolæ, or saltworts, the shrub called by the Arabs arak, the Capparis Sodata of Sindh and Arabia, with its currant-like bunches of fruit, is conspicuous for its evergreen verdure; the ragged and stunted mtungulu rains its apples upon the ground; and the mbembu, in places sheltered from the sun, bears a kind of medlar which is eagerly sought by the hungry traveler. The euphorbiæ here rise to the height of 35 or 40 feet, and the hard woody stem throws out a mass of naked arms, in the shape of a huge cap, impervious to the midday sun.

Wild animals abound through these jungles, and the spoor lasts long upon the crisp gravelly soil. In some districts they visit by night the raised clay water-troughs of the cultivators. The elephant prefers the thick jungle, where he can wallow in the pools and feed delicately upon succulent roots and fruits, bark, and leaves. The rhinoceros loves the dark clumps of trees, which guard him from the noonday sun, and whence he can sally out all unexpected upon the assailant. The mbogo, or bos caffer, driven from his favorite spots, low grassy plains bordering on streams, wanders, like the giraffe, through the thinner forests. As in Unyamwezi, the roar of the lion strikes the ear by night, and the cry of the ostrich by day. The lion upon this line of Eastern Africa is often heard, but rarely seen; on only two occasions its footprints appeared upon the road. The king of beasts, according to the Arabs, is of moderate stature: it seldom attains its maximum of strength, stature, and courage, except in plain countries where game abounds, as in the lands north of the Cape, or in hills and mountains, where cattle can be lifted at discretion, as in Northern Africa. In Unyamwezi its spoils, which are yellow, like those of the Arab lion, with a long mane, said to hang over the eyes, and with a whitish tinge under the jaws, become the property of the sultan. The animal is more common in the high lands of Karagwah than in the low countries; it has, however, attacked the mbogo, or wild bull, and has destroyed cattle within sight of the Arabs at Kazeh in Unyanyembe. The lion is rarely a maneater; this peculiarity, according to some writers, being confined to old beasts, whose worn teeth are unfit for fight.

The "polygamous bird" was first observed on the Ugogo plateau; it extends through Unyamwezi and Usukuma to Ujiji. The eggs are sold, sometimes fresh, but more generally stale. Emptied and dried, they form the principal circulating medium between the Arab merchants and the coffee-growing races near the Nyanza Lake, who cut them up and grind them into ornamental disks and crescents. The young birds are caught, but are rarely tamed. In Usukuma, the bright and glossy feathers of the old male are much esteemed for adorning the hair; yet, curious to say, the bird is seldom hunted. Moreover, these East Africans have never attempted to export the feathers, which, when white and uninjured, are sold, even by the Somal, for eight dollars per lb. The birds are at once wild and stupid, timid and headstrong;

their lengthened strides and backward glances announce terror at the sight of man, and it is impossible to stalk them in the open grounds, which they prefer. The leopard and the cynhyena, the koodoo and the different species of antelope, are more frequently killed in these deserts than in any other part of the line. Hog of reddish color, and hares with rufous fur, are sometimes started by caravans. The hyrax of the Somali country basks upon the rocks and boulders, and the carapace of a small land-turtle, called khasa, fastened to a branch, serves as a road-sign. The k'hwalu, a small green parrot with yellow shoulders, the upupa or hoopoe, a great variety of fly-catchers, larks with jet-black heads and yellow bodies, small bustards, hornbills, nightjars, muscicapæ, green pigeons, sparrow-hawks, and small doves, are seen in every jungle. Near the settlements, the white-necked raven and the common chíl of India (Falco cheela) attest the presence of man, as the monkey does the proximity of water. The nest of the loxia swings to and fro in the fierce simoom; the black bataleur eagle of Somaliland, a‧splendid bird, towering shyly in the air, with his light under-plume gleaming like a silver plate, and large vultures (condors?) flocking from afar, denote the position of a dead or dying animal.

Until late years, the Wagogo, being more numerous than they are now, deterred travelers from traversing their country: in those early days the road to Unyamwezi, running along the left or northern bank of the Rwaha, through the Warori tribe, struck off near Usanga and Usenga. It is related, when the first caravan, led by Jumah Mfumbi, the late Diwan of Saadani, entered Ugogo, that the people, penetrated with admiration of his corpulence, after many experiments to find out whether it was real or not, determined that he was and must be the Deity. Moreover, after coming to this satisfactory conclusion, they resolved that, being the Deity, he could improve their country by heavy rains, and when he protested against both these resolutions, they proposed to put him to death. A succession of opportune showers, however, released him. By degrees the ever-increasing insolence and violence of the Warori drove travelers to this northern line, and the Wagogo learned to see strangers without displaying this Libyan mania for sacrificing them.

Three main roads, leading from Western Usagara westward, cross the desert of Marenga Mk'hali. The most northern is called Yá Nyiká—of the wilderness—a misnomer, if the assertion of the guides be correct that it is well watered, and peopled by the subjects of eight sultans. The central line, described in the preceding pages, is called, from its middle station, Marenga Mk'hali: it is invariably preferred when water is scarce. The southern road is termed Nyá Ngáhá, a continuation of the Kiringwana route, previously alluded to: it has provisions, but the people cause much trouble.

The superiority of climate, and probably the absence of that luxuriant vegetation which distinguishes the eastern region, have proved favorable to the physical development of the races living in and about Ugogo. The Wagogo, and their northern neighbors the Wahumba, are at once distinguishable from the wretched population of the alluvial valleys, and of the mountains of Usagara; though living in lower altitudes, they are a fairer race—and therefore show better blood—than the Wanyamwezi. These two tribes, whose distinctness is established by difference of dialect, will be described in order.

The Wagogo extend from the landward base of Usagara in direct distance to Mdáburu a five days' march. On the north they are bounded by the Watáturu, on the south by the Wabena tribes. The breadth of their country is computed at about eight stages. In the north, however, they are mingled with the Wahumba, in the southeast with the Wahehe, and in the south with the Warori.

The Wagogo display the variety of complexion usually seen among slave-purchasing races: many of them are fair as Abyssinians; some are black as negroes. In the eastern and northern settlements they are a fine, stout, and light-complexioned race. Their main peculiarity is the smallness of the cranium compared with the broad circumference of the face at and below the zygomata: seen from behind, the appearance is that of a small half bowl fitted upon one of considerably larger bias; and this, with the widely-extended ears, gives a remarkable expression to the face. Nowhere in Eastern Africa is the lobe so distended. Pieces of cane an inch or two in length, and nearly double the girth of a man's finger, are so disposed that they appear like handles to the owner's head. The distinctive mark of the tribe is the absence of the two lower incisors; but they are more generally recognized by the unnatural enlargement of their ears. In Eastern Africa the "aures perforatæ" are the signs not of slavery, but of freedom. There is no regular tattoo, though some of the women have two parallel lines running from below the bosom down the abdomen, and the men often extract only a single lower incisor. The hair is sometimes shaved clean, at others grown in mop-shape; more generally it is dressed in a mass of tresses, as among the Egyptians, and the skin, as well as the large bunch of corkscrews, freely stained with ochre and micaceous earths, drips with ghee, the pride of rank and beauty. The Wagogo are not an uncomely race: some of the younger women might even lay claim to prettiness. The upper part of the face is often fine, but the lips are ever thick, and the mouth coarse; similarly the body is well formed to the haunches, but the lean calf is placed peculiarly high up the leg. The expression of the countenance, even in the women, is wild and angry, and the round eyes are often reddened and bleared by drink. The voice is strong, strident, and commanding.

Their superiority of clothing gives the Wagogo, when compared with the Wasagara or the Wanyamwezi, an aspect of civilization;

a skin garment is here as rare as a cotton farther west. Even the children are generally clad. The attire of the men is usually some Arab check or dyed Indian cotton: many also wear sandals of single hide. Married women are clothed in " cloths with names," when wealthy, and in domestics when poor. The dress of the maidens under puberty is the languti of Hindoostan, a kind of T bandage, with the front ends depending to the knees; it is supported by a single or double string of the large blue glass beads called sungomaji. A piece of coarse cotton cloth two yards long and a few inches broad is fastened to the girdle behind, and, passing under the fork, is drawn tightly through the waist-belt in front; from the zone the lappet hangs mid-down to the shins, and when the wearer is in rapid motion it has a most peculiar appearance. The ornaments of both sexes are kitindi, and bracelets and anklets of thick iron and brass wires, necklaces of brass chains, disks and armlets of fine ivory, the principal source of their wealth, and bands of hide-strip with long hair, bound round the wrists, above the elbows, and below the knees: they value only the highest-priced beads, coral and pink porcelains. As usual, the males appear armed. Some import from Unyamwezi and the westward regions the long double-edged knife called sime, a " serviceable dudgeon," used in combat or in peaceful avocations, like the snick-an-snee of the ancient Dutch. Shields are unknown. The bow is long: the handle and the horns are often adorned with plates of tin and zinc, and the string is whipped round the extremities for strength. The spear resembles that used by the Wanyamwezi in the elephant hunt: it is about four feet long, and the head is connected with a stout wooden handle by an iron neck measuring half the length of the weapon. In Eastern Ugogo, where the Masai are near, the Wagogo have adopted their huge shovel-headed spears and daggers, like those of the Somal. It is the fashion for men to appear in public with the peculiar bill-hook used in Usagara; and in the fields the women work with the large hoe of Unyamwezi.

The villages of the Wagogo are square tembe, low and mean-looking for want of timber. The outer walls are thin poles, planted in the ground and puddled with mud. The huts, partitioned off like ships' bunks, are exceedingly dirty, being shared by the domestic animals, dogs and goats. They are scantily furnished with a small stool, a cot of cow's hide stretched to a small frame-work, a mortar for grain, and sundry gourds and bark corn-bins. About sunset all the population retires, and the doors are carefully barricaded for fear of the plundering Wahumba. At night it is dangerous to approach the villages.

The language of Ugogo is harsher than the dialects spoken by their eastern and western neighbors. In the eastern parts the people understand the Masai tongue. Many can converse fluently in the Kisawahili, or coast-tongue. The people, however, despise all strangers except the Warori and the Wahumba, and distinguish the Wanyamwezi by the name of Wakonongo, which they also apply to travelers in general. Within the memory of man, one Kafuke, of Unyamwezi, a great merchant, and a mtongi or caravan-leader, when traversing Ugogo with some thousands of followers, became involved in a quarrel about paying for water. After fifteen days of skirmishing, the leader was slain and the party was dispersed. The effect on both tribes has lasted to the present day. After the death of Kafuke, no rain fell for some years,—a phenomenon attributed by the Wagogo to his powers of magic; and the land was almost depopulated. The Wanyamwezi, on the other hand, have never from that time crossed the country without fear and trembling. In the many wars between the two tribes the Wagogo have generally proved themselves the better men. This superiority has induced a brawling and bullying manner. They call themselves Wáná Wádege, or sons of birds—that is to say, semper parati. The Wanyamwezi studiously avoid offending them; and the porters will obey the command of a boy rather than risk an encounter. "He is a Mgogo," said before the Bobadil's face, makes him feel himself forty times a man; yet he will fly in terror before one of the Warori or the Wahumba.

The strength of the Wagogo lies in their comparative numbers. As the people seldom travel to the coast, their scattered villages are full of fighting-men. Moreover, uchawi or black magic here numbers few believers, consequently those drones of the social hive, the waganga, or medicine-men, are not numerous. The Wagogo seldom sell their children and relations, yet there is no order against the practice. They barter for slaves their salt and ivory, the principal produce of the country. No caravan ever passes through the country without investing capital in the salt-bitter substance which is gathered in flakes efflorescing from the dried mud upon the surface of the mbugu, or swampy hollows; the best and the cheapest is found in the district of Kanyenye. It is washed to clear it of dirt, boiled till it crystallizes, spread upon clean and smoothed ground, and moulded with the hands into rude cones about half a foot in length, which are bought at the rate of 7–10 for a shukkah, and are sold at a high premium after a few days' march. Ugogo supplies Western Usagara and the eastern regions of Unyamwezi with this article. It is, however, far inferior to the produce of the Rusugi pits, in Uvinza, which, on account of its "sweetness," finds its way throughout the centre of Africa. Elephants are numerous in the country: every forest is filled with deep traps, and during droughty seasons many are found dead in the jungle. The country is divided into districts; the tusks become the property of the sultan within whose boundaries the animal falls, and the meat is divided among his subjects. Ivory is given in barter for slaves: this practice assures to caravans a hold upon the people, who, having an active commerce with the coast, can not afford to be shut out from it. The Wagogo are so greedy of serviles that every gang leaves among them some of its live stock—the principal want of the listless and indolent cultivator. The wild captives bought in the interior, wayworn and fond of change, are persuaded by a word to desert; they take the first opportunity of slipping away from their masters, generally stealing a weapon and a little cloth or rations for immediate use. Their new masters send them off the road, lest they should be recognized and claimed: after a time a large hoe is placed in their hands, and the fools feel, when too late, that they have exchanged an easy for a hard life. The Wagago sell their fellow-tribe-men only when convicted of magic; though sometimes parents, when in distress, part with their children. The same is the case among their northern neighbors, the Wamasai, the Wahumba, and the Wakwafi, who, however, are rarely in the market, and who, when there, though remarkable for strength and intelligence, are little prized, in consequence of their obstinate and untamable characters; many of them would rather die under the stick than level themselves with women by using a hoe.

The Wagogo are celebrated as thieves who will, like the Wahehe, rob even during the day. They are importunate beggars, who specify their long list of wants without stint or shame: their principal demand is tobacco, which does not grow in the land; and they resemble the Somal, who never sight a stranger without stretching out the hand for "bori." The men are idle and debauched, spending their days in unbroken crapulence and drunkenness, while the girls and women hoe the fields, and the boys tend the flocks and herds. They mix honey with their pombe, or beer, and each man provides entertainment for his neighbors in turn. After midday it would be difficult throughout the country to find a chief without the thick voice, fiery eyes, and moidered manners, which prove that he is either drinking or drunk.

The Arabs declaim against the Wagogo as a "curst," ill-conditioned and boisterous, a violent and extortionate race. They have certainly no idea of manners: they flock into a stranger's tent, squat before him, staring till their curiosity is satisfied, and unmercifully quizzing his peculiarities. Upon the road a mob of both sexes will press and follow a caravan for miles. The women, carrying their babes in leopard skins bound behind the back, and with unveiled bosoms, stand or run, fiercely shouting with the excitement of delight, and the girls laugh and deride the stranger as impudently as boys would in more modest lands. Yet, as has been said, this curiosity argues to a certain extent improvability; the most degraded tribes are too apathetic to be roused by strange sights. Moreover, the Wagogo are not deficient in rude hospitality. A stranger is always greeted with the "Yambo" salutation. He is not driven from their doors, as among the Wazaramo and Wasagara; and he is readily taken into brotherhood. The host places the stool for his guests, seating himself on the ground: he prepares a meal of milk and porridge, and on parting presents, if he can afford it, a goat or a cow. The African "fundi" or "fattori" of caravans are rarely sober in Ugogo. The women are well disposed toward strangers of fair complexion, apparently with the permission of their husbands. According to the Arabs, the husband of the daughter is also *de jure* the lover of the mother.

The sultan among the Wagogo is called mtemi, a high title. He exercises great authority, and is held in such esteem by his people, that a stranger daring to possess the same name would be liable to chastisement. The ministers, who are generally brothers or blood-relations, are known as wázágíra (in the singular mzágírá), and the councilors, who are the elders and the honorables of the tribe, take the Kinyamwezi title "wányápárá."

The necessaries of life are dear in Ugogo. The people will rarely barter their sheep, goats, and cows for plain white or blue cottons, and even in exchange for milk they demand coral, pink, or blue glass beads. A moderate-sized caravan will expend from six to ten shukkah per diem. The Wanyamwezi traveling-parties live by their old iron hoes, for which grain is returned by the people, who hold the metal in request.

The Wahumba, by some called Wahumpa, is one of the terrible pastoral nations "beyond the rivers of Æthiopia." To judge from their dialect, they are, like the Wakwafi, a tribe or a sub-tribe of the great Masai race, who speak a language partly South African and partly Semitico African, like that of the Somal. The habitat of the Wahumba extends from the north of Usagara to the eastern shores of the Nyanza or Ukerewe Lake; it has been remarked that a branch of the Mukondokwa River rises in their mountains. The blue highlands occupied by this pastoral race, clearly visible, on the right hand, to the traveler passing from Ugogo westward, show where the ancient route from Pangani Town used to fall into the main trunk road of Unyamwezi. Having but little ivory, they are seldom visited by travelers: their country, however, was explored some years ago by an Arab merchant, Hamid bin Salim, for the purpose of buying asses. He set out from Tura, in Eastern Unyamwezi, and, traversing the country of the wild Watatúru, arrived on the eighth day at the frontier district I'ramba, where there is a river which separates the tribes. He was received with civility; but none have since followed his example.

The Wahumba are a fair and comely race, with the appearance of mountaineers, long-legged, and lightly made. They have repeatedly ravaged the lands of Usagara and Ugogo: in the latter country, near Usek'he, there are several settlements of this people, who have exchanged the hide-tent for the hut, and the skin for the cotton-cloth. They stain their garments with ochrish earth, and their women are distinguished by wearing kitindi of full and half size above and below the elbows. The ear-lobes are pierced and distended by both sexes, as among the Wagogo. In their own land they are purely pastoral; they grow no grain, despise vegetable food, and subsist entirely upon meat or milk according to the season. Their habitations are hemispheres of boughs lashed together and roofed with a cow's hide; it is the primitive dwelling-place, and the legs of the occupant protrude beyond the shelter. Their arms, which are ever hung up close at hand, are broad-headed spears of soft iron, long "sine," or double-edged daggers, with ribbed wooden handles fastened to the blade by a strip of cow's tail shrunk on, and "rungu," or wooden knob-kerries, with double bulges that weight the weapon as it whirls through the air. They ignore and apparently despise the bow and arrows, but in battle they carry the pavoise, or large hide-shield, affected by the Kafirs of the Cape. The Arabs, when in force, do not fear their attacks.

The Wahumba, like their congeners the Wakwafi, bandage the infant's leg from ankle to knee, and the ligature is not removed till the child can stand upright. Its object is to prevent the development of the calf, which, according to their physiology, diminishes the speed and endurance of the runner. The specimens of Wahumba seen in different parts of Ugogo showed the soleus and gastrocnemius muscles remarkably shrunken, and the projection of the leg rising close below the knee.

Ladies' Smoking-party.

CHAPTER X.

WE ENTER UNYAMWEZI, THE FAR-FAMED LAND OF THE MOON.

THE district of Tura, though now held, like Jiwe la Mkoa and Mgongo T'hembo, by Wakimbu, is considered the eastern frontier of Unyamwezi proper, which claims superiority over the minor neighboring tribes. Some, however, extend the "Land of the Moon" eastward as far as Jiwe la Mkoa, and the porters, when entering the "Fiery Field," declare that they are setting foot upon their own ground. The word "tura," pronounced by the Wanyamwezi "tula" or "itula," means "put down!" (scil. your pack): as the traveler, whether from the east or from the west, will inevitably be delayed for some days at this border settlement. Tula is situated in S. lat. 5° 2′ and E. lon. 33° 57′, and the country rises 4000 feet above sea-level. After the gloomy and monotonus brown jungles and thorn forests of Mgunda Mk'hali, whose sinu-

VIEW IN UNYAMWEZI.

ous line of thick jungle still girds the northern horizon, the fair champaign, bounded on either hand by low rolling and rounded hills of primary formation, with a succession of villages and many a field of holcus and sesamum, maize, millet, and other cereals, of manioc and gourds, watermelons and various pulses, delights the sight, and appears to the African traveler a Land of Promise.

The pertinacious Kidogo pressed me to advance, declaring the Wakimbu Tura to be a dangerous race : they appeared, however, a timid and ignoble people, dripping with castor and sesamum oil, and scantily attired in shreds of unclean cotton or greasy goat-skins. At Tura the last of the thirty asses bought at Zanzibar paid the debt of nature, leaving us, besides the one belonging to the jemadar, but three African animals purchased on the road. A few extra porters were therefore engaged. Our people, after the discomforts of the bivouac, found the unsavory village a perfect paradise ; they began somewhat prematurely to beg far bakhshish, and Muinyi Wazira requested dismissal on the plea that a slave sent by him on a trading expedition into the interior had, by dying, endangered the safety of the venture. On the morning of the 30th of October Kidogo led us over the plain through cultivation and villages to another large settlement on the western outskirt of the Tura district. As I disappointed him in his hopes of a tirikeza, he passed the night in another tembe, which was occupied by the caravans of coast Arabs and their slave-girls, to one of whom, said Scan. Mag., he had lost his heart, and he punished me by halting through the next day. As we neared the end of the journey the sons of Ramji became more restive under their light loads ; their dignity was hurt by shouldering a pack, and day after day, till I felt weary of life, they left their burdens upon the ground. However, on the 1st of November, they so far recovered temper that the caravan was able to cross the thin jungle, based upon a glaring white soil, which divides the Tura from the Rubuga District. After a march of 6$^{hrs.}$ and 30$^{m.}$, we halted on the banks of the Kwale or "Partridge" Nullah, where, though late in the season, we found several long pools of water. The porters collected edible bivalves and caught a quantity of mud-fish by the "rough and ready" African process, a waist-cloth tied to a pair of sticks, and used by two men as a drag-net. At Rubuga, which we reached in 5$^{hrs.}$ 45$^{m.}$, marching over a plain of black earth thinly garnished with grass and thorn-trees, and then through clearings overgrown with stubble, I was visited by an Arab merchant, Abdullah bin Jumah, who, with a flying caravan, had left Konduchi on the coast 2 months and 20 days after our departure. According to him, his caravan had lately marched thirty miles in the twenty-four hours : it was the greatest distance accomplished in these regions ; but the Arabs are fond of exaggeration ; the party was small and composed of lightly-laden men, and moreover, it required two days' rest after so unusual an exertion. This merchant unwittingly explained a something which had puzzled me; whenever an advance beyond Unyanyembe had been made the theme of conversation, Said bin Salim's countenance fell, and he dropped dark hints touching patience and the power of Allah to make things easy. Abdullah rendered the expression intelligible by asking me if I considered the caravan strong enough to dare the dangers of the road—which he grossly exaggerated—between Unyamwezi-land and Ujiji. I replied that I did, and that even if I did not, such bugbears should not cause delay. Abdullah smiled, but was too polite to tell me that he did not believe me.

A "doux marcher" of 2$^{hrs.}$ 40$^{m.}$ on the 3d of November led us to the western limit of the Rubuga district. During the usual morning halt under a clump of shady milk-bush, I was addressed by Maura or Maula, the sultan of a large neighboring village of Wanyamwezi: being a civilized man and a coast traveler, he could not allow the caravan of the "Wazungu" to pass his quarters without presenting to him a bullock, and extracting from him a little cloth. Like most chiefs in the "Land of the Moon," he was a large-limbed, gaunt, angular, tall old man, with a black oily skin seamed with wrinkles; and long wiry pigtails, thickened with grease, melted butter, and castor-oil, depending from the sides of his purbald head. His dress—an old barsati round the loins, and a grimy subai loosely thrown over the shoulders—was redolent of boiled frankincense; his ankles were concealed by a foot-depth of brass and copper "sambo," thin wires twisted round a little bundle of elephant's, buffalo's, or zebra's hair; and he wore single-soled sandals, decorated with four disks of white shell, about the size of a crown-piece, bound to the thongs that passed between the toes and girt the heel. He recognized the Baloch, greeted all kindly, led the way to his village, ordered lodgings to be cleared and cleaned, caused the cartels or bedsteads—the first seen by us for many months—to be vacated, and left us to look for a bullock. At the village door I had remarked a rude attempt at fashioning a block of wood into what was palpably intended for a form human and feminine; the Moslems of course pronounced it to be an idol, but the people declared that they paid no respect to it. They said the same concerning the crosses and the serpent-like ornaments of white ashes—in this land lime is unknown—with which the brown walls of their houses were decorated.

We made bonne chère at Rubuga, which is celebrated for its milk and meat, ghee and honey. On the wayside were numerous hives, the mazinga or "cannons," before described; here however they were raised out of the reach of the ants, white and black, upon a pair of short forked supports, instead of being suspended from the branches of a tall tree. My companion brought from a neighboring swamp a fine Egyptian, or ruddy goose, and a brace of crane-like water-fowl: these the Wanyamwezi porters, expecting beef, disdained, because rejected by the Baloch, yet at Inenge they had picked the carcass of a way-spent ass. Presently we were presented by the sultan with one of the fattest of his fine bulls; it was indeed

" A grazier's without and a butcher's within;"

withal, so violent and unmanageable that no man could approach, much less secure it: it rushed about the village like a wild buffalo, scattering the people, who all fled except the sultan, till it was stopped dead, in a most determined charge, with a couple of rifle bullets, by my companion. In return, Maula received a crimson cloth and two domestics, after which he begged for every thing, including percussion caps, for which he had no gun. He appeared most anxious to detain the caravan, and in the evening his carefully-concealed reasons leaked out—he wanted me to cure his son of fever, and to "put the colophon" upon a neighboring hostile chief. At 8 P.M. I was aroused by my gun-carrier, Mabruki, who handed to me my Ferrara, and by the Baloch Riza, who reported that the palisade was surrounded by a host of raging blacks. I went out into the village, where the guard was running about in a state of excitement which robbed them of their wits, and I saw a long dark line of men sitting silently and peaceably, though armed for fight, outside the strong stockade. Having caused our cloth to be safely housed, and given orders to be awakened if work began, I returned to the hut, determined to take leave of Sultan Maura and his quarrels on the next day.

The porters were all gorged with beef, and three were "staledrunk" with the consequences of pombe; yet so anxious were they rendered by the gathering clouds and the spitting showers to reach their homes before the setting in of the " sowing rains," that my task was now rather to restrain than to stimulate their ardor: the moon was resplendent, and had I wished it, they would have set out at midnight. On the 4th of November we passed through another jungle-patch, to a village in the fertile slopes of Ukona, where the cannabis and the datura, with its large fetid flowers, disputed the ground with brinjalls and castor-plants, holcus and panicum: tobacco grew luxuriantly, and cotton-plots, carefully hedged round against the cattle, afforded material for the loom, which now appeared in every village.

On the next day, we passed out of the fertile slopes of Ukona, and traversed an open wavy country, streaked with a thin forest of mimosa, the mtogwe or wood-apple, and a large quadrangular cactus. Beyond this point, a tract of swampy low level led to the third district of Eastern Unyamwezi, called Kigwa, or Mkigwa. We found quarters in a tembe which was half-burned and partly pulled down, to be re-erected.

The 6th of November saw us betimes in the ill-omened forest that divided us from the Unyanyembe district; it is a thin growth of gum-trees, mimosas, and bauhinias, with tiers, earth-waves, and long rolling lines of tawny-yellow hill—mantled with umbrella-shaped trees, and sometimes capped with blocks and boulders—extending to a considerable distance on both sides. The Sultan of Kigwa, one Manwa, has taken an active part in the many robberies and murders which have rendered this forest a place of terror, and the Arabs have hitherto confined themselves to threats, though a single merchant complains that his slave-caravans have at different times lost fifty loads of cloths. Manwa is aided and counseled by Mansur, a coast Arab, who, horsewhipped out of the society of his countrymen at Kazeh for drunken and disorderly conduct, has become a notorious traitor. Here also Msimbira, a sultan of the Wasukuma, or Northern Wanyamwezi, who has an old and burning hatred against the Arabs, sends his plundering parties. On the 6th of November the Baloch set out at 1 A.M., we followed at 2.15 A.M.: they had been prevented from obtaining beads on false pretenses, consequently they showed temper, and determined to deny their escort. Their beards were now in my hand; they could neither desert nor refuse to proceed; but they desired to do me a harm, and they did it. During the transit of the forest an old porter, having imprudently lagged behind, was clubbed and cruelly bruised by three black Mohawks, who relieved him of his load, a leathern portmanteau, containing clothes, umbrellas, books, ink, journals, and botanical collections. I afterward heard that the highwaymen had divided their spoils in the forest, and that, separating into two parties, they had taken the route homeward. On the way, however, they were seized by a plundering expedition sent by Kitambi, the Sultan of Uyuwwi, a district half a day's march N.E. from Kazeh. The delict was flagrant; the head of one robber at once decorated the main entrance of Kitambi's village, but the other two escaped Jeddart-justice with their share of the plunder to his mortal enemy Msimbira. A present of a scarlet waistcoat and four domestics recovered our clothes from Kitambi; but Msimbira, threatening all the penalties of sorcery, abused, plundered, and expelled Masud ibn Musullam el Wardi, an old Arab merchant sent to him from Unyanyembe for the purpose of recovering the books, journals, and collections. The perpetual risk of loss discourages the traveler in these lands; he never knows at what moment papers which have cost him months of toil may be scattered to the winds. As regards collections, future explorers are advised to abandon the hope of making them on the march upward, reserving their labor for the more leisurely return. The precautions with which I prefaced our down-march may not be useless as suggestions. My field and sketch books were intrusted to an Arab merchant, who preceded me to Zanzibar; they ran no other danger except from the carelessness of the consul who, unfortunately for me, succeeded Lieut. Col. Hamerton. My companion's maps, papers, and instruments, were

committed to a heavy "petarah," a deal box with pent-lid and
hide-bound, as a defense against rain, to be carried to "Mziga-
ziga," as the phrase is—suspended on a pole between the two porters least likely to desert. I loaded one of the sons of Ramji with
an enameled leathern bag, converted from a dressing-case into a
protection for writing and sketching materials; and a shooting-bag,
hung during the march over the shoulders of Nasiri, a coast Arab
youth engaged as ass-leader at Unyanyembe, contained my vocabularies, ephemeris, and drawing-books.

Considering the conduct of the escort, I congratulated myself
upon having passed through the Kigwa forest without other accident. Two or three days after our arrival at Kazeh several loads
of beads were plundered from a caravan belonging to Abdullah
bin Salih. Shortly afterward Msimbira sent a large foraging party with a view to cutting off the road: they allowed themselves
to be surprised during sleep by Mpagamo's men, who slew twenty-five of their number and dispersed the rest. This accident,
however, did not cure their propensity for pillage; on our return-
march, when halted at a village west of the Kigwa forest, a body
of slaves passed us in hot haste and sore tribulation: they had
that day been relieved by bandits of all their packs.

Passing from the Kigwa forest, and entering the rice-lands of the
Unyanyembe district, we found quarters—a vile cow-house—in a
large dirty village called Hanga. The aspect of the land became
prepossessing: the route lay along a valley bisected by a little
rivulet of sweet water, whose course was marked by a vivid leek-
green line; the slopes were bright with golden stubble upon a
a surface of well-hoed field, while to the north and south ran low
and broken cones of granite blocks and slabs, here naked, there
clothed from base to brow with dwarf parasol-shaped trees, and
cactaceæ of gigantic size.

From this foul village I was urged by Kidogo to conclude by
a tirikeza the last stage that separated the caravan from Kazeh
in Unyanyembe, the place which he and all around him had apparently fixed as the final bourn of the exploration. But the
firmament seemed on fire, the porters were fagged, and we felt
feverish: briefly, an afternoon's march was not judged advisable.
To temper, however, the wind of refusal, I served out to each of
the sons of Ramji five rounds of powder for blowing away on entering the Arab head-quarters. All, of course, had that private
store which the Arabs call "el akibah"—the ending; it is generally stolen from the master, and concealed for emergencies with
cunning care. They had declared their horns to be empty, and,
said Kidogo, "Every peddler fires guns here—shall a great man
creep into his tembe without a soul knowing it?"

On the 7th of November, 1857—the 134th day from the date of
our leaving the coast—after marching at least 600 miles, we prepared to enter Kazeh, the principal bandari of Eastern Unyam-

wezi, and the capital village of the Omani merchants. We left Hanga at dawn. The Baloch were clothed in that one fine suit without which the Eastern man rarely travels: after a few displays the dress will be repacked, and finally disposed of in barter for slaves. About 8 A.M. we halted for stragglers at a little village, and when the line of porters, becoming compact, began to wriggle, snake-like, its long length over the plain, with floating flags, booming horns, muskets ringing like saluting-mortars, and an uproar· of voice which nearly drowned the other noises, we made a truly splendid and majestic first appearance. The road was lined with people who attempted to vie with us in volume and variety of sound: all had donned their best attire, and with such luxury my eyes had been long unfamiliar. Advancing, I saw several Arabs standing by the wayside; they gave the Moslem salutation, and courteously accompanied me for some distance. Among them were the principal merchants, Snay bin Amir, Said bin Majid, a young and handsome Omani of noble tribe, Muhinna bin Sulayman, who, despite elephantiasis, marched every year into Central Africa, and Said bin Ali el Hinawi, whose short, spare, but well-knit frame, pale face, small features, snowy beard, and bald head, surmounted by a red fez, made him the type of an Arab old man.

I had directed Said bin Salim to march the caravan to the tembe kindly placed at my disposal by Isá bin Hijji and the Arabs met at Inenge. The kirangozí and the porters, however, led us on by mistake (?) to the house of "Musa Mzuri"—handsome Moses—an Indian merchant settled at Unyanyembe, for whom I bore an introductory letter, graciously given by H. H. the Sayyid Majid of Zanzibar. As Musa was then absent on a trading journey to Karagwah, his agent, Snay bin Amir, a Harisi Arab, came forward to perform the guest-rites, and led me to the vacant house of Abayd bin Sulayman, who had lately returned to Zanzibar.

After allowing me, as is the custom, a day to rest and to dismiss the porters, who at once separated to their homes, all the Arab merchants, then about a dozen, made the first ceremonious call, and to them was officially submitted the circular addressed by the Prince of Zanzibar to his subjects resident in the African interior. Contrary to the predictions of others, nothing could be more encouraging than the reception experienced from the Omani Arabs; striking, indeed, was the contrast between the open-handed hospitality and the hearty good-will of this truly noble race, and the niggardness of the savage and selfish African—it was heart of flesh after heart of stone. A goat and a load of the fine white rice grown in the country were the normal prelude to a visit and to offers of service which proved something more than a mere *vox et præterea nihil*. Whatever I alluded to, onions, plantains, limes, vegetables, tamarind-cakes, coffee from Karagwah, and similar articles, only to be found among the Arabs, were sent at once, and the very name of payment would have been an insult. Snay bin Amir, determined to surpass all others in generosity, sent two goats to us and two bullocks to the Baloch and the sons of Ramji: sixteen years before, he had begun life a confectioner at Maskat, and now he had risen to be one of the wealthiest ivory and slave dealers in Eastern Africa. As his health forbade him to travel, he had become a general agent at Kazeh, where he had built a village containing his store-houses and his depôts of cloth and beads, slaves and ivory. I have to acknowledge many an obligation to him. Having received a "wakalat-namah," or "power of attorney," he enlisted porters for the caravan to Ujiji. He warehoused my goods, he disposed of my extra stores, and, finally, he superintended my preparations for the down-march. During two long halts at Kazeh he never failed, except through sickness, to pass the evening with me, and from his instructive and varied conversation was derived not a little of the information contained in the following pages. He had traveled three times between Unyamwezi and the coast, besides navigating the great Lake Tanganyika and visiting the northern kingdoms of Karagwah and Uganda. He first entered the country about fifteen years ago, when the line of traffic ended at Usanga and Usenga, and he was as familiar with the languages, the religion, the manners, and the ethnology of the African, as with those of his natal Oman. He was a middle-aged man, with somewhat of the Quixotic appearance, high-featured, sharp and sunken-eyed, almost beardless, light-colored, tall, gaunt, and large-limbed. He had read much, and, like an Oriental, for improvement, not only for amusement: he had a wonderful memory, fine perceptions, and passing power of language. Finally, he was the stuff of which friends are made; brave as all his race, prudent withal, ready to perish for the "Pundonor," and—such is not often the case in the East—he was as honest as he was honorable.

Before proceeding with the thread of my narrative, the reader is requested to bear with the following few lines upon the subject of Unyanyembe.

Unyanyembe, the central and principal province of Unyamwezi, is, like Zungomero in Khutu, the great bandari or meeting-place of merchants, and the point of departure for caravans which thence radiate into the interior of Central Intertropical Africa. Here the Arab merchant from Zanzibar meets his compatriot returning from the Tanganyika Lake and from Uruwwa. Northward well-traveled lines diverge to the Nyanza Lake, and the powerful kingdoms of Karagwah, Uganda, and Unyoro; from the south Urori and Ubena, Usanga and Usenga, send their ivory and slaves; and from the southwest the Rukwa Water, K'hokoro, Ufipa, and Marungu must barter their valuables for cottons, wires, and beads. The central position and the comparative safety of Unyanyembe have made it the head-quarters of the Omani or pure Arabs, who, in many cases, settle here for years, remaining in charge of their depôts, while their factors and slaves travel about the country and collect the items of traffic. At Unyanyembe the merchants expect some delay. The porters, whether hired upon the coast or at the Tanganyika Lake, here disperse, and a fresh gang must be collected—no easy task when the sowing season draws nigh.

Unyanyembe, which rises about 3480 feet above sea-level, and lies 356 miles in rectilinear distance from the eastern coast of Africa, resembles in its physical features the lands about Tura. The plain or basin of Ihárá, or Kwihárá, a word synonymous with the "bondei" or lowland of the coast, is bounded on the north and south by low, rolling hills, which converge toward the west, where, with the characteristically irregular lay of primitive formations, they are crossed almost at right angles by the Mfuto chain. The position has been imprudently chosen by the Arabs: the land suffers from alternate drought and floods, which render the climate markedly malarious. The soil is aluminous in the low levels—a fertile plain of brown earth, with a subsoil of sand and sandstone, from eight to twelve feet below the surface; the water is often impregnated with iron, and the higher grounds are uninhabited tracts covered with bulky granite boulders, bushy trees, and thorny shrubs.

Contrary to what might be expected, this "bandari district" contains villages and hamlets, but nothing that can properly be termed a town. The mtemi or Sultan Fundikira, the most powerful of the Wanyamwezi chiefs, inhabits a tembe, or square settlement, called "Ititenya," on the western slope of the southern hills. A little colony of Arab merchants has four large houses at a neighboring place, "Mawiti." In the centre of the plain lies "Kazeh," another scattered collection of six large hollow oblongs, with central courts, garden-plots, store-rooms, and outhouses for the slaves. Around these nuclei cluster native villages—masses of Wanyamwezi hovels, which bear the names of their founders.

This part of Unyanyembe was first colonized about 1852, when the Arabs who had been settled nearly ten years at Kigandu of P'huge, a district of Usukuma, one long day's march north of Kazeh, were induced by Mpagamo to aid them against Msimbira, a rival chief, who defeated and drove them from their former seats. The details of this event were supplied by an actor in the scenes; they well illustrate the futility of the people. The Arabs, after five or six days of skirmishing, were upon the point of carrying the boma or palisade of Msimbira, their enemy, when suddenly at night their slaves, tired of eating beef and raw groundnuts, secretly deserted to a man. The masters awaking in the morning found themselves alone, and made up their minds for annihilation. Fortunately for them, the enemy, suspecting an ambuscade, remained behind their walls, and allowed the merchants to retire without an attempt to cut them off. Their employer, Mpagamo, then professed himself unable to defend them; when, deeming themselves insecure, they abandoned his territory. Snay bin Amir and Musa Mzuri, the Indian, settled at Kazeh, then a desert, built houses, sunk wells, and converted it into a populous place.

It is difficult to average the present number of Arab merchants at Unyanyembe, who, like the British in India, visit but do not colonize; they rarely, however, exceed twenty-five in number; and during the traveling season, or when a campaign is necessary, they are sometimes reduced to three or four; they are too strong to yield without fighting, and are not strong enough to fight with success. Whenever the people have mustered courage to try a fall with the strangers, they have been encouraged to try again. Hitherto the merchants have been on friendly terms with Fundi-kira, the chief. Their position, however, though partly held by force of prestige, is precarious. They are all Arabs from Oman, with one solitary exception, Musa Mzuri, an Indian Kojah, who is perhaps in these days the earliest explorer of Unyamwezi. In July, 1858, an Arab merchant, Silim bin Masud, returning from Kazeh to his home at Msene, with a slave porter carrying a load of cloth, was, though well armed and feared as a good shot, attack-ed at a water in a strip of jungle westward of Mfuto, and speared in the back by five men, who were afterward proved to be sub-jects of the Sultan Kasanyare, a Mvinza. The Arabs organized a small expedition to revenge the murder, marched out with 200 or 300 slave musketeers, devoured all the grain and poultry in the country, and returned to their homes without striking a blow, because each merchant-militant wished his fellows to guarantee his goods or his life for the usual diyat, or blood-money, 800 dol-lars. This impunity of crime will probably lead to other out-rages.

The Arabs live comfortably, and even splendidly, at Unyan-yembe. The houses, though single-storied, are large, substantial, and capable of defense. Their gardens are extensive and well planted; they receive regular supplies of merchandise, comforts, and luxuries from the coast; they are surrounded by troops of concubines and slaves, whom they train to divers crafts and call-ings; rich men have riding-asses from Zanzibar, and even the poorest keep flocks and herds. At Unyanyembe, as at Msene, and sometimes at Ujiji, there are itinerant fundi, or slave artisans —blacksmiths, tinkers, masons, carpenters, tailors, potters, and rope-makers—who come up from the coast with Arab caravans. These men demand exorbitant wages. A broken matchlock can be repaired, and even bullets cast; good cord is purchasable; and for tinning a set of seventeen pots and plates five shukkah mer-kani are charged. A pair of Arab stirrups are made up for one shukkah besides the material, and chains for animals at about double the price. Fetters and padlocks, however, are usually imported by caravans. Pack-saddles are brought from Zanzibar: in caravans a man may sometimes be found to make them. There is, moreover, generally a pauper Arab who for cloth will make up a ridge-tent; and as most civilized Orientals can use a needle, professional tailors are little required. Provisions are cheap and plentiful; the profits are large; and the Arab, when wealthy, is disposed to be hospitable and convivial. Many of the more prosperous merchants support their brethren who have been ruined by the chances and accidents of trade. When a stranger appears among them, he receives the "hishmat l'il gharíb," or the guest-welcome, in the shape of a goat and a load of white rice; he is provided with lodgings, and is introduced by the host to the rest of the society at a general banquet. The Arabs' great deficiency is the want of some man to take the lead. About fifteen years ago Abdullah bin Salim, a merchant from Zanzibar, with his body of 200 armed slaves, kept the whole community in subjection: since his death, in 1852, the society has suffered from all the effects of disunion where union is most required. The Arab, however, is even in Africa a pantisocrat, and his familiarity with the inferior races around him leads to the proverbial consequences.

The houses of the Arabs are Moslem modifications of the African tembe, somewhat superior in strength and finish. The deep and shady outside veranda, supported by stout uprights, shelters a broad bench of raised earth-work, where men sit to enjoy the morning cool and the evening serenity, and where they pray, converse, and transact their various avocations. A portcullis-like door, composed of two massive planks, with chains thick as a ship's cable—a precaution rendered necessary by the presence of wild slaves—leads into the barzah, or vestibule. The only furniture is a pair of clay benches, extending along the right and left sides, with pillow-shaped terminations of the same material; over these, when visitors are expected, rush-mats and rugs are spread. From this barzah a passage, built at the angle proper to baffle the stranger's curiosity, leads into the interior, a hollow square or oblong, with the several rooms opening upon a court-yard, which, when not built round, is completely closed by a "liwan," a fence of small tree-trunks or reeds. The apartments have neither outward doors nor windows: small bull's-eyes admit the air, and act as loop-holes in case of need. The principal room on the master's side of the house has a bench of clay, and leads into a dark closet, where stores and merchandise are placed. There are separate lodgings for the harem, and the domestic slaves live in barracoons or in their own outhouses. This form of tembe is perhaps the dullest habitation ever invented by man. The exterior view is carefully removed from sight, and the dull, dirty court-yard, often swamped during the rains, is ever before the tenant's eyes. The darkness caused by want of windows painfully contrasts with the flood of sunshine pouring in through the doors, and at night no number of candles will light up its gloomy walls of gray or reddish mud. The breeze is either excluded by careless frontage, or the high and chilling winds pour in like torrents. The roof is never water-tight, and the walls and rafters harbor hosts of scorpions and spiders, wasps and cockroaches. The Arabs, however, will expend their time and trouble in building rather than trust their goods in African huts, exposed to thieves and to the frequent fires which result from barbarous carelessness: every where, when a long halt is in prospect, they send their slaves for wood to the jungle, and superintend the building of a spacious tembe. They neglect, however, an important precaution, a sleeping-room raised above the mean level of malaria.

Another drawback to the Arab's happiness is the failure of his constitution: a man who escapes illness for two successive months boasts of the immunity; and, as in Egypt, no one enjoys robust health. The older residents have learned to moderate their appetites. They eat but twice a day—after sunrise, and at noon. The midday meal concluded, they confine themselves to chewing tobacco or the dried coffee of Karagwah. They avoid strong meats, especially beef and game, which are considered heating and bilious, remaining satisfied with light dishes, omelets and pillaus, harísah, firni, and curded milk; and the less they eat the more likely they are to escape fever. Harísah, in Kisawahili "boko-boko," is the roast-beef—the *plat de résistance*—of the Eastern and African Arab. It is a kind of pudding made with finely-shredded meat, boiled with flour of wheat, rice, or holcus, to the consistence of a thick paste, and eaten with honey or sugar. Firni, an Indian word, is synonymous with the muhallibah of Egypt, a thin jelly of milk and water, honey, rice flour, and spices, which takes the place of our substantial northern rice-pudding. The general health has been improved by the importation from the coast of wheat, and a fine white rice, instead of the red aborigen of the country; of various fruits—plantains, limes, and papaws; and of vegetables—brinjalls, cucumbers, and tomatoes, which relieve the indigenous holcus and maize, manioc and sweet-potato, millet and phaseoli, sesamum and ground-nuts. They declare to having derived great benefit from the introduction of onions—an antifebral, which flourishes better in Central than in Maritime Africa. The onion, so thriving in South Africa, rapidly degenerates upon the Island of Zanzibar into a kind of house-leek. In Unyamwezi it is of tolerable size and flavor. It enters into a variety of dishes, the most nauseous being probably the sugared onion-omelet. In consequence of general demand, onions are expensive in the interior; an indigo-dyed shukkah will purchase little more than a pound. When the bulbs fail, the leaves, chopped into thin circles, and fried in clarified butter with salt, are eaten as a relish with meat. They are also inserted into marak, or soups, to disguise the bitter and rancid taste of stale ghee. Onions may be sown at all seasons except during the wet monsoon, when they are liable to decay. The Washenzi have not yet borrowed this excellent and healthy vegetable from the Arabs. Garlic has also been tried in Unyanyembe, but with less success; moreover, it is considered too heating for daily use. As might be expected, however, among a floating population with many slaves, foreign fruits and vegetables are sometimes allowed to die out. Thus some enterprising merchant introduced into Unyanyembe the date and the mkungu, bidam, or almond-tree of the coast: the former, watered once every third day, promised to bear fruit, when, in the absence of the master, the Wanyamwezi cut up the young shoots into walking-sticks. Sugar is imported: the water-wanting cane will not thrive in arid Unyanyembe, and honey must be used as a succedaneum. Black pepper, universally considered cooling by Orientals, is much eaten with curry-stuffs and other highly-seasoned dishes; whereas the excellent chillies and bird-pepper, which here grow wild, are shunned for their heating properties. Butter and ghee are made by the wealthy; humbler houses buy the article, which is plentiful and good, from the Wanyamwezi. Water is the usual beverage. Some Arabs drink togwa, a sweet preparation of holcus; and others, debauchees, indulge in the sour and intoxicating pombe, or small-beer.

The market at Unyanyembe varies greatly according to the quantity of the rains. As usual in barbarous societies, a dry season, or a few unexpected caravans, will raise the prices, even to trebling; and the difference of value in grain before and after the harvest will be double or half of what it is at par. The price of provisions in Unyamwezi has increased inordinately since the Arabs have settled in the land. Formerly a slave-boy could be purchased for five fundo, or fifty strings of beads: the same article would now fetch three hundred. A fundo of cheap white porcelain beads would procure a milch cow; and a goat, or ten hens, its equivalent, was to be bought for one khete. In plentiful years Unyanyembe is, however, still the cheapest country in East Africa, and, as usual in cheap countries, it induces the merchant to spend more than in the dearest. Paddy of good quality, when not in demand, sells at twenty kayla (120 lbs.) for one shukkah of American domestics; maize, at twenty-five; and sorghum, here the staff of life, when in large stock, at sixty. A fat bullock may be bought for four domestics, a cow costs from six to twelve, a sheep or a goat from one to two. A hen, or its equivalent, four or five eggs, is worth one khete of coral or pink porcelain beads. One fundo of the same will purchase a large bunch of plantains, with which máwá or plantain-wine, and siki or vinegar, are made; and the Wanyamwezi will supply about a pint of milk every morning at the rate of one shukkah per mensem. A kind of mud-fish is caught by the slaves in the frequent pools which, during the cold season, dot the course of the Gombe Nullah, lying three miles north of Kazeh; and return-caravans often bring with them stores of the small fry, called kashwá or daga'a, from the Tanganyika Lake.

From Unyanyembe, twenty marches, which are seldom accomplished under twenty-five days, conduct the traveler to Ujiji, upon the Tanganyika. Of these the fifth station is Msene, the great bandari of Western Unyamwezi. It is usually reached in eight days; and the twelfth is the Malagarazi River, the western limit of the fourth region.

The traveler, by means of introductory letters to the doyen of the Arab merchants at Kazeh, can always recruit his stock of country currency—cloth, beads, and wire—his requirements of powder and ball, and his supply of spices, comforts, and drugs, without which travel in these lands usually ends fatally. He will pay, it is true, about five times their market value at Zanzibar: sugar, for instance, sells at its weight in ivory, or nearly one third more than its weight in beads. But though the prices are exorbitant, they preserve the buyer from greater evils, the expense of porterage, the risk of loss, and the trouble and annoyance of personally superintending large stores in a land where "vir" and "fur" are synonymous terms.

And now comfortably housed within a stone-throw of my new friend Shaykh Snay bin Amir, I bade adieu for a time to the march, the camp, and the bivouac. Perhaps the reader may not be unwilling to hear certain details concerning the "road and the inn" in Eastern Africa; he is familiar from infancy with the Arab kafilah and its host of litters and camels, horses, mules, and asses, but the porter-journeys in Eastern Africa have as yet escaped the penman's pen.

Throughout Eastern Africa made roads, the first test of progress in a people, are unknown. The most frequented routes are foot-tracks, like goat-walks, one to two spans broad, trodden down during the traveling season by man and beast, and during the rains the path, in African parlance, "dies," that is to say, it is overgrown with vegetation. In open and desert places four or five lines often run parallel for short distances. In jungly countries they are mere tunnels in thorns and under branchy trees, which fatigue the porter by catching his load. Where fields and villages abound, they are closed with rough hedges, horizontal tree-trunks, and even rude stockades, to prevent trespassing and pilferage. Where the land is open, an allowance of one fifth must be made for winding: in closer countries this must be increased to two fifths or to one half, and the traveler must exercise his judgment in distributing the marches between these two extremes. In Uzaramo and K'hutu the tracks run through tall grasses, which are laid by their own weight after rains, and are burned down during the hot seasons: they often skirt cultivated lands, which they are not allowed to enter, miry swamps are spanned, rivers breast-deep, with muddy bottoms and steep slippery banks, are forded, while deep holes, the work of rodents and insects, render them perilous to ridden cattle.   In Usagara the gradients are surmounted either by beds of mountain torrents or by breasting steep and stony hills, mere ladders of tree-root and loose stones: laden animals frequently can not ascend or descend them.   The worst paths in this region are those which run along the banks of the many streams and rivulets, and which traverse the broken and thorny ground at the base of the hills.   The former are "thieves' roads," choked with long succulent grass springing from slushy mud; the latter are continued rises and falls, with a small but ragged and awkward water-course at every bottom.   From Usagara to Western Unyamwezi the roads lead through thick thorn-jungle, and thin forests of trees blazed or barked along the track, without hill, but interrupted during the rains by swamps and bogs.   They are studded with sign-posts, broken pots and gourds, horns and skulls of game and cattle, imitations of bows and arrows pointing toward water, and heads of holcus.   Sometimes a young tree is bent across the path and provided with a cross-bar; here is a rush gateway like the yoke of the ancients, or a platform of sleepers supported by upright trunks; there a small tree felled and replanted, is tipped with a crescent of grass twisted round with bark, and capped with huge snail-shells, and whatever barbarous imagination may suggest.   Where many roads meet, those to be avoided are barred with a twig or crossed by a line drawn with the foot.   In Western Uvinza and near Ujiji the paths are truly vile, combining all the disadvantages of bog and swamp, river and rivulet, thorn-bush and jungle, towering grasses, steep inclines, riddled surface, and broken ground.   The fords on the whole line are temporary as to season, but permanent in place: they are rarely more than breast-deep; and they average in dry weather a cubit and a half, the fordable medium.   There are but two streams, the Mgeta and the Ruguvu, which are bridged over by trees; both could be forded higher up the bed; and on the whole route there is but one river, the Malagarazi, which requires a ferry during the dry season.   Cross roads abound in the populous regions.   Where they exist not, the jungle is often impassable, except to the elephant and the rhinoceros: a company of pioneers would in some places require a week to cut their way for a single march through the net-work of thorns and the stockade of rough tree-trunks.   The directions issued to travelers about drawing off their parties for safety at night to rising grounds will not apply to Eastern Africa; it would be far easier to dig for themselves abodes under the surface.

It is commonly asserted in the island of Zanzibar that there are no caravans in these regions.   The dictum is true if the term be limited to the hosts of camels and mules that traverse the deserts and the mountains of Arabia and Persia. It is erroneous if applied to a body of men traveling for commercial purposes. From time immemorial the Wanyamwezi have visited the road to the coast, and though wars and blood-feuds may have temporarily closed one line, another necessarily opened itself. Among a race so dependent for comfort and pleasure upon trade, commerce, like steam, can not be compressed beyond a certain point. Until a few years ago, when the extension of traffic induced the country people to enlist as porters, all merchants traversed these regions with servile gangs hired on the coast or island of Zanzibar, a custom still prevailing on the northern and southern routes from the sea-board to the lakes of Nyanza and Nyassa. Porterage, on the long and toilsome journey, is now considered by the Wanyamwezi a test of manliness, as the Englishman deems a pursuit or a profession necessary to clear him from the charge of effeminacy. The children imbibe the desire with their milk, and at six or seven years old they carry a little tusk on their shoulders—instinctive porters, as pointer-pups are hereditary pointers. By premature toil their shin-bones are sometimes bowed to the front like those of animals too early ridden. "He sits in hut egg-hatching," is their proverbial phrase to express one more elegant—

"Home-keeping youth have ever homely wits."

And they are ever quoting the adage that men who travel not are void of understanding—the African equivalent of what was said by the European sage: "The world is a great book, of which those who never leave home read but a page." Against this traditional tendency reasons of mere hire and rations, though apparently weighty, are found wanting. The porter will bargain over his engagement to the utmost bead, saying that all men are bound to make the best conditions for themselves; yet, after two or three months of hard labor, if he chance upon a caravan returning to his home, a word from a friend, acting upon his innate debility of purpose, will prevail upon him to sacrifice by desertion all the fruits of his toil. On these occasions the porters are carefully watched; open desertion would, it is true, be condemned by the general voice, yet no merchant can so win the affections of his men that some will not at times disappear. Until the gangs have left their homes far behind, their presence seems to hang by a thread; at the least pretext they pack up their goods and vanish in a mass. When approaching their settlements—at the frontier districts of Tura and Mfuto, for instance—their cloth and hire are taken from them, packed in the employer's bales, and guarded by armed slaves, especially at night, and on the line of march. Yet these precautions frequently fail, and, once beyond the camp limits, it is vain to seek the fugitive. In the act of desertion they show intelligence: they seldom run away when caravans first meet, lest their employer should halt and recover them by main force, and, except where thieves and wild beasts are unknown, they will not fly by night. The porter, however, has one point of honor; he leaves his pack behind him. The slave, on the other hand, certainly robs his employer when he runs away, and this, together with his unwillingness to work and the trouble and annoyance which he causes to his owner, counterbalances his superior dexterity and intelligence.

Caravans, called in Kisawahili safári (from the Arab safar, a journey), and by the African rugendo or lugendo, "a going," are rarely wanting on the main trunk-lines. The favorite seasons for the upward-bound are the months in which the greater and the lesser masika or tropical rains conclude—in June and September, for instance, on the coast—when water and provisions are plentiful. Those who delay till the dry weather has set in must expect hardships on the march; the expense of rations will be doubled and trebled, and the porters will frequently desert. The down-caravans set out in all seasons except the rainy; it is difficult to persuade the people of Unyanyembe to leave their fields between the months of October and May. They will abandon cultivation to the women and children, and merrily take the foot-path way if laden with their own ivory, but from the merchant they will demand exorbitant wages, and even then they will hesitate to engage themselves.

Porterage varies with every year and in every caravan. It knows but two limits: the interest of the employer to disburse as little as possible by taking every advantage of the necessities of his employé, and the desire of the employé to extract as much as he can by presuming upon the wants of his employer. In some years there is a glut of porters on the coast; when they are rare, quarrels take place between the several settlements, each attempting a monopoly of enlistment to the detriment of its neighbors, and a little blood is sometimes let. When the Wanyamwezi began to carry, they demanded for a journey from the coast to their own country six to nine dollars' worth of domestics, colored cloths, brass wires, and the pigeon's-egg bead called sungomaji. The rate of porterage then declined; the increase of traffic, however, has of late years greatly increased it. In 1857 it was 10 dollars, and it afterward rose to 12 dollars per porter. In this sum rations are not included; the value of these—which by ancient custom are fixed at 1 kubabah (about 1.5 lbs.) of grain per diem, or, that failing, of manioc, sweet potatoes, and similar articles, with the present of a bullock at the frontier—is subject to greater variations, and is even less reducible to an average than the porter's pay. It is needless to say that the down-journey is less expensive than the up-march, as the carriers rely upon a fresh engagement on the coast. The usual hire from Unyanyembe would be nine cloths, payable on arrival at the sea-port, where each is worth 25 cents, or about 1 shilling. The Arabs roughly calculate—the errors balancing one another—that, rations included, the hire of a porter from the coast to the Tanganyika Lake and back amounts to a total of 20 dollars = £4 3s. From the coast, Wanyamwezi porters will not engage themselves for a journey westward of their own country; at Unyanyembe they break up, and a fresh gang must be enlisted for a march to the Tanganyika or to the Nyanza Lake. It is impossible to average the numbers of an East African caravan, which varies from half a dozen to 200 porters, under a single mundewa or merchant. In dangerous places travelers halt till they form an imposing force; 500 is a frequent figure, and even bodies of 1000 men are not rare. The only limit to the gathering is the incapability of the country to fill more than a certain number of mouths. The larger caravans, however, are slow and cumbrous, and in places they exhaust the provision of water.

Caravans in East Africa are of three kinds. The most novel and characteristic are those composed only of Wanyamwezi; secondly, are the caravans directed and escorted by Wasawahili freemen or funda (slave fattori), commissioned by their patrons; and, lastly, those commanded by Arabs.

The porter, called pagazi or fagazi—the former is the African, the latter the ridiculous Arabized form of the word—corresponds with the carregador of West Africa. The Wanyamwezi make up large parties of men, some carrying their own goods, others hired by petty proprietors, who for union and strength elect a head mtongi, ras kafilah, or leader. The average number of these parties that annually visit the coast is far greater than those commanded by stranger merchants. In the Unyamwezi caravan there is no desertion, no discontent, and, except in certain spots, little delay. The porters trudge from sunrise to 10 or 11 A.M., and sometimes, though rarely, they will travel twice a day, resting only during the hours of heat. They work with a will, carrying uncomplainingly huge tusks, some so heavy that they must be lashed to a pole between two men—a contrivance technically called mziga-ziga. Their shoulders are often raw with the weight, their feet are sore, and they walk half or wholly naked to save their cloth for displays at home. They ignore tent or covering, and sleep on the ground; their only supplies are their country's produce, a few worn-down hoes, intended at times to purchase a little grain, or to be given as black-mail for sultans, and small herds of bullocks and heifers, that serve for similar purposes, if not lost, with characteristic African futility, upon the road. Those who most consult comfort carry, besides their loads and arms, a hide for bedding, an earthen cooking-pot, a stool, a kilindo or bark-box containing cloth and beads, and perhaps a small gourd full of ghee. They sometimes suffer severely from exposure to a climate which forbids long and hard work upon short and hard fare. Malignant epidemics, especially small-pox, often attack caravans as they approach the coast; generally, however, though somewhat lean and haggard, the porters appear in better condition than might be expected. The European traveler will repent accompanying these caravans; as was said of a similar race, the Indians of Guiana, "they will not deviate three steps from the regular path."

Porters engaged by Arab mtajiri or mundewa—the former is the Kisawahili, the latter is the Inner African term for a merchant or traveling trader—are known by their superior condition; they eat much more, work much less, and give far greater trouble to their commanders. They expend part of the cloth and beads which they have received as hire to procure for themselves occasional comforts; and on the down-journey they take with them a few worn-down hoes, to retain the power of desertion without starving. The self-willed wretches demean themselves with the coolest impudence; reply imperiously, lord it over their leaders, regulate the marches and the halts, and though they work, they never work without loud complaints and open discontent. Rations are a perpetual source of heart-burning: stinted at home to a daily mess of grain-porridge, the porters on the line of march devote, in places where they can presume, all their ingenuity to extort as much food as possible from their employers. At times they are seized with a furore for meat. When a bullock is slaughtered, the kirangozi or guide claims the head, leaving the breast and loin to the mtongi or principal proprietor, and the remainder is equally portioned among the khambi or messes into which the gang divides itself. As has been remarked, the Arab merchant, next to the Persian, is the most luxurious traveler in the East; a veteran of the way, he well knows the effects of protracted hardship and scarcity upon a wayfarer's health. The European traveler, however, will not enjoy the companionship of the Arab caravan, which marches by instinct rather than by reason. It begins by dawdling over the preliminaries; it then pushes hurriedly onward, till arrested by epidemic or desertion; and finally, it lingers over the end of the journey, thus losing time twice. This style of progress is fatal to observation; moreover, none but a special caravan, consisting of slaves hired for the purpose in the the island of Zanzibar or on the coast, and accompanied by their own ahbab or patron—without whom they will obey no employer, however generous or energetic—will enable the explorer to strike into an unbeaten path, or to progress a few miles beyond the terminus of a main trunk-road. The most enterprising of porters will desert, leaving the caravan-leader like a water-logged ship.

Between these two extremes are the trading parties directed by the Wasawahili, the Wamrima, and the slave fundi—the Pombeiros of West Africa—kindred souls with the pagazi, understanding their languages, and familiar with their habits, manners, and customs. These "safari" are neither starved like those composed of Wanyamwezi, nor pampered like those headed by the Arabs. There is less fatigue during the march, and more comfort at the halting-place, consequently there are fewer cases of disease and death. These semi-African mtongi, hating and jealousing Arabs and all strangers, throw every obstacle in their way, spread reports concerning their magical and malevolent powers, which are dangerous among the more superstitious barbarians, they offer a premium for desertion, and in fine, they labor hard, though fruitlessly, to retain their ancient monopoly of the profits derived from the interior.

I will now describe the day's march and the halt of the East African caravan.

At 3 A.M. all is silent as the tomb, even the Mnyamwezi watchman nods over his fire. About an hour later the red-faced, apoplectic chanticleer—there are sometimes half a dozen of them—the alarum of the caravan, and a prime favorite with the slaves and porter, who carry him on their banghy-poles by turns, and who drench him with water when his beak opens under the sun —flaps his wings and crows a loud salutation to the dawn; he is answered by every cock and cockerel within ear-shot. I have been lying awake for some time, longing for the light, and, when in health, for an early breakfast. At the first paling of the east, the torpid Goanese are called up to build a fire, they tremble with the cold—thermometrically averaging 60° F.—and they hurry to bring food. Appetite, somewhat difficult at this hour, demands a frequent change of diet; we drink tea or coffee when procurable, or we eat rice-milk and cakes raised with whey, or a porridge not unlike water-gruel. While we are so engaged, the Baloch, chanting the spiritual songs which follow prayers, squat round a caldron placed upon a roaring fire, and fortify the inner man with boiled meat and grain, with toasted pulse and tobacco.

About such time, 5 A.M., the camp is fairly roused, and a little low chatting becomes audible. This is a critical moment. The porters have promised over night to start early, and to make a long wholesome march. But, "uncertain, coy, and hard to please," they change their minds like the fair sex: the cold morning makes them unlike the men of the warm evening, and perhaps one of them has fever. Moreover, in every caravan there is some lazy, loud-lunged, contradictory, and unmanageable fellow, whose sole delight is to give trouble. If no march be in prospect, they sit obstinately before the fire, warming their hands and feet, inhaling the smoke with everted heads, and casting quizzical looks at their fuming and fidgety employer. If all be unanimous, it is vain to attempt them; even soft sawder is but "throwing comfits to cows." We return to our tent. If, however, there be a division, a little active stimulating will cause a march. Then a louder conversation leads to cries of Kwecha! Kwecha! Pakia!

Pakia! Hopa! Hopa! Collect! pack! set out! Safari! Safari leo! a journey, a journey to-day! and some peculiarly African boasts, P'hunda! Ngami! I am an ass!—a camel! accompanied by a roar of bawling voices, drumming, whistling, piping, and the braying of barghumi, or horns. The sons of Ramji come in a body to throw our tents, and to receive small burdens, which, if possible, they shirk; sometimes Kidogo does me the honor to inquire the programme of the day. The porters, however, hug the fire till driven from it, when they unstack the loads piled before our tents, and pour out of the camp or village. My companion and I, when well enough to ride, mount our asses, led by the gunbearers, who carry all necessaries for offense and defense; when unfit for exercise, we are borne in hammocks, slung to long poles, and carried by two men at a time. The Baloch, tending their slaves, hasten off in a straggling body, thinking only of escaping an hour's sun. The jemadar, however, is ordered to bring up the rear with Said bin Salim, who is cold and surly, abusive and ready with his ratan. Four or five packs have been left upon the ground by deserters, or shirkers, who have started empty-handed; consequently our Arab either double-loads more willing men, or persuades the sons of Ramji to carry a small parcel each, or, that failing, he hires from some near village a few porters by the day. This, however, is not easy; the beads have been carried off, and the most tempting promises without prepayment have no effect upon the African mind.

When all is ready, the kirangozi or Mnyamwezi guide rises and shoulders his load, which is ever one of the lightest. He deliberately raises his furled flag, a plain blood-red, the sign of a caravan from Zanzibar, much tattered by the thorns, and he is followed by a privileged pagazi, tom-toming upon a kettle-drum much resembling a European hour-glass. The dignitary is robed in the splendor of scarlet broadcloth, a narrow piece about six feet long, with a central aperture for the neck, and with streamers dangling before and behind: he also wears some wonderful head-dress, the spoils of a white and black "tippet-monkey," or the barred skin of a wildcat, crowning the head, bound round the throat, hanging over the shoulders, and capped with a tall cup-shaped bunch of owl's feathers, or the gorgeous plumes of the crested crane. His insignia of office are the kipungo or fly-flapper, the tail of some beast, which he affixes to his person as if it were a natural growth, the kome, or hooked iron spit, decorated with a central sausage of parti-colored beads, and a variety of oily little gourds containing snuff, simples, and "medicine" for the road, strapped round his waist. He leads the caravan, and, the better to secure the obedience of his followers, he has paid them in a sheep or a goat, the value of which he will recover by fees and superiority of rations —the head of every animal slaughtered in camp and the presents at the end of the journey are exclusively his. A man guilty of preceding the kirangozi is liable to fine, and an arrow is extracted from his quiver to substantiate his identity at the end of the march. Pouring out of the kraal in a disorderly mob, the porters stack their goods at some tree distant but a few hundred yards, and allow the late, the lazy, and the invalids to join the main body. Generally at this conjuncture the huts are fired by neglect or mischievousness. The khambi, especially in winter, burns like tinder, and the next caravan will find a heap of hot ashes and a few charred sticks still standing. Yet, by way of contrast, the pagazi will often take the trouble to denote by the usual sign-posts to those following them that water is at hand. Here and there a little facetiousness appears in these erections; a mouth is cut in the tree-trunk to admit a bit of wood simulating a pipe, with other representations still more waggish.

After the preliminary halt, the caravan, forming into the order of march, winds, like a monstrous land-serpent, over hill, dale, and plain. The kirangozi is followed by an Indian file; those nearest to him—the grandees of the gang—are heavily laden with ivories: when the weight of the tusk is inordinate, it is tied to a pole, and is carried, palanquin fashion, by two men. A large cow-bell, whose music rarely ceases on the march, is attached to the point which is to the fore; to the bamboo behind is lashed the porter's private baggage—his earthen cooking-pot, his water-gourd, his sleeping-mat, and his other necessaries. The ivory-carriers are succeeded by the bearers of cloth and beads; each man poising upon either shoulder, and sometimes raising upon the head for rest, packs that resemble huge bolsters, six feet long by two in diameter, cradled in sticks, which generally have a forked projection for facility of stacking and reshouldering the load. The sturdiest fellows are usually the lightest loaded: in Eastern Africa, as elsewhere, the weakest go to the wall. The maximum of burden may be two farasilah, or seventy pounds avoirdupois. Behind the cloth-bearers straggles a long line of porters and slaves, laden with the lighter stuff, rhinoceros-teeth, hides, salt-cones, tobacco, brass wire, iron hoes, boxes and bags, beds and tents, pots and water-gourds, mats and private stores. With the pagazi, but in separate parties, march the armed slaves, who are never seen to quit their muskets, the women, and the little toddling children, who rarely fail to carry something, be it only of a pound weight, and the asses, neatly laden with saddle-bags of giraffe or buffalo hide. A "mganga" almost universally accompanies the caravan, not disdaining to act as a common porter. The "parson" not only claims, in virtue of his sacred calling, the lightest load; he is also a stout, smooth, and sleek-headed man, because, as usual with his class, he eats much and he works little. The rear is brought up by the master or the masters of the caravan, who often remains far behind for the convenience of walking and to prevent desertion.

All the caravan is habited in its worst attire; the East African derides those who wear upon a journey the cloth which should be reserved for display at home. If rain fall, they will doff the single goat-skin hung round their sooty limbs, and, folding it up, place it between the shoulder and the load. When grain is served out for some days' march, each porter bears his posho or rations, fastened like a large "bussel" to the small of his back. Upon this again he sometimes binds, with its legs projecting outward, the three-legged stool, which he deems necessary to preserve him from the danger of sitting upon the damp ground. As may be imagined, the barbarians have more ornament than dress. Some wear the ngala, a strip of zebra's mane bound round the head, with the bristly parti-colored hair standing out like a saint's "gloria:" others prefer a long bit of stiffened ox-tail, rising like a unicorn's horn at least a foot above the forehead. Other ornaments are the skins of monkeys and ocelots, rouleaus and fillets of white, blue, or scarlet cloth, and huge bunches of ostrich, crane, and jay's feathers, crowning the head like the tufts of certain fowls. Their arms are decorated with massive ivory bracelets, heavy bangles of brass or copper, and thin circlets of the same metal; beads in strings and bands, adorn their necks, and small iron bells, a "knobby" decoration, whose incessant tinkling harmonizes, in African ears, with the regular chime-like "Ti-ti! ti-ti! tang!" of the tusk-bells, and the loud broken "Wa-ta-ta!" of the horns, are strapped below the knee or round the ankle by the more aristocratic. All carry some weapon; the heaviest armed have a bow and a bark quiver full of arrows, two or three long spears and assegais, a little battle-axe borne on the shoulder, and the sime or dudgeon.

The normal recreations of a march are, whistling, singing, shouting, hooting, horning, drumming, imitating the cries of birds and beasts, repeating words which are never used except on journeys —a "chough's language, gabble enough and good enough"— and abundant squabbling; in fact, perpetual noise which the ear, however, soon learns to distinguish for the hubbub of a halt. The uproar redoubles near a village, where the flag is unfurled and where the line lags to display itself. All give vent to loud shouts, "Hopa! hopa!—go on! go on! Mgogolo!—a stoppage! Food! food! Don't be tired! The kraal is here—home is near! Hasten, kirangozi—Oh! We see our mothers! We go to eat!" On the road it is considered prudent as well as pleasurable to be as loud as possible, in order to impress upon plunderers an exaggerated idea of the caravan's strength; for equally good reasons silence is recommended in the kraal. When threatened with attack and no ready escape suggests itself, the porters ground their loads and prepare for action. It is only self-interest that makes them brave; I have seen a small cow, trotting up with tail erect, break a line of 150 men carrying goods not their own. If a hapless hare or antelope cross the path, every man casts his pack, brandishes his spear, and starts in pursuit; the animal never running straight, is soon killed and torn limb from limb, each negroid helluo devouring his morsel raw. Sometimes a sturdy fellow "renowns it" by carrying his huge burden round and round, like a horse being ringed, and starts off at full speed. When two bodies meet, that commanded by an Arab claims the road. If both are Wanyamwezi, violent quarrels ensue, but fatal weapons, which are too ready at hand, are turned to more harmless purposes, the bow and spear being used as whip and cudgel. These affrays are not rancorous till blood is shed. Few tribesmen are less friendly for so trifling an affair as a broken head; even a slight cut or a shallow stab is little thought of; but, if returned with interest, great loss of life may arise from the slenderest cause. When friendly caravans meet, the two kirangozis sidle up with a stage pace, a stride, and a stand, and with sidelong looks prance till arrived within distance; then suddenly and simultaneously "ducking," like boys "giving a back," they come to loggerheads and exchange a butt violently as fighting rams. Their example is followed by all with a rush and a crush, which might be mistaken for the beginning of a faction, but it ends, if there be no bad blood, in shouts of laughter. The weaker body, however, must yield precedence and offer a small present as black-mail.

About 8 A.M., when the fiery sun has topped the trees, and a pool of water, or a shady place appears, the planting of the red flag, the braying of a barghumi, or koodoo's horn, which, heard at a distance in the deep forests, has something of the charm which endears the "cor de chasse" to every woodman's ear, and sometimes a musket-shot or two announces a short halt. The porters stack their loads, and lie or loiter about for a few minutes, chatting, drinking, and smoking tobacco and bhang, with the usual whooping, screaming cough, and disputing eagerly about the resting-place for the day. On long marches we then take the opportunity of stopping to discuss the contents of two baskets which are carried by a slave under the eye of the Goanese.

If the stage be prolonged toward noon, the caravan lags, straggles, and suffers sorely. The heat of the ground, against which the horniest sole never becomes proof, tries the feet like polished leather boots on a quarter-deck in the dog-days near the Line, and some tribulation is caused by the cry M'iba hapa!—thorns here! the Arabs and the Baloch must often halt to rest. The slaves ensconce themselves in snug places; the porters, propping their burdens against trees, curl up, dog-like, under the shade; some malinger; and this, the opportunity preferred for desertion, is an anxious hour to the proprietor; who, if he would do his work "deedily," must be the last in the kraal. Still the men rarely break down. As in Indian marching, the African caravan prefers to end the day, rather than to begin it, with a difficulty—the ascent of a hill or the fording of a stream. They prefer the strip of jungle at the farther end of a district or a plantation, for safety as well as for the comfort of shade. They avoid the vicinity of rocks; and on desert plains they occupy some slightly rising ground, where the night-cold is less severe than in the lower levels.

At length an increased hubbub of voices, blended with bells, drums, fifes, and horns, and sometimes a few musket-shots, announce that the van is lodged, and the hubbub of the halt confirms the pleasing intelligence that the journey is shortened by a stage. Each selfish body then hurries forward to secure the best boothy in the kraal, or the most comfortable hut in the village, and quarrels seem serious. Again, however, the knife returns home guiltless of gore, and the spear is used only as an instrument for sound belaboring. The more energetic at once apply themselves to "making all snug" for the long hot afternoon and the nipping night; some hew down young trees, others collect heaps of leafy boughs; one acts architect, and many bring in huge loads of firewood. The East African is so much accustomed to house-life, that the bivouac in the open appears to him a hardship; he prefers even to cut out the interior of a bush and to squat in it, the portrait of a comfortable cynocephalus. We usually spread our donkey-saddles and carpets in some shade, awaiting the arrival of our tent, and its erection by the grumbling sons of Ramji; if we want a hut, we draw out the man in possession like a badger —he will never have the decency to offer it. As a rule, the villagers are more willing to receive the upward-bound caravans than those who, returning, carry wealth out of instead of into the country. Merchants, on account of their valuable outfits, affect, except in the safest localities, the khambi rather than the village; the latter, however, is not only healthier, despite its uncleanliness, in miasmatic lands, but it is also more comfortable, plenty and variety of provisions being more readily procured inside than outside. The Arab's khaymah is a thin pole or ridge-tent of flimsy domestics, admitting sun and rain, and, like an Irish cabin, permitting at night the occupant to tell time by the stars; yet he prefers it, probably for dignity, to the boothy which, in this land of verdure and cool winds, is a far more comfortable lodging.

The Wamrima willingly admit strangers into their villages; the Wazaramo would do the same, but they are constantly at feud with the Wanyamwezi, who therefore care not to avail themselves of the dangerous hospitality. In K'hutu caravans seize by force the best lodgings. Throughout Eastern Usagara travelers pitch tents in the clear central spaces, surrounded by the round huts of the peasantry, under whose low and drooping eaves the pagazi find shelter. In the western regions, where the tembe or square village prevails, kraals form the nighting-place. In Ugogo strangers rarely enter the hamlets, the hovels being foul, and the people dangerous. Throughout Eastern and Central Unyamwezi caravans defile into the villages without hesitation. Some parties take possession of the iwanza or public-house; others build for themselves tabernacles of leafy boughs, which they are expected to clear away before departure, and the headman provides lodgings for the mtongi. In Western Unyamwezi the doors are often closed against strangers, and in Eastern Uvinza the people will admit travelers to bivouac, but they will not vacate their huts. In Western Uvinza, a desert like Marenga and Mgunda Mk'hali, substantial khambi occur at short intervals. At Ujiji, the sultan, after offering the preliminary magubiko or presents, provides his guests with lodgings, which, after a time sufficient for enabling them to build huts, they must vacate in favor of new-comers. In the other lake regions the reception depends mainly upon the number of muskets in a caravan, and the character of the headman and his people.

The khambi or kraal every where varies in shape and material. In the eastern regions, where trees are scarce, wattle frames of rough sticks, compacted with bark-fibre, are disposed in a circle; the forked uprights, made higher behind and lower in front, to form a sloping roof, support horizontal or cross poles, which are overlaid with a rough thatch of grass or grain-cane. The central space upon which the boothies open is occupied by one or more huts for the chiefs of the party; and the outer circle is a loose fence of thorn branches, flimsy, yet impassable to breechless legs, unshod feet, and thin loose body-garments. When a kraal must be built, rations are not served out till inclosures made round the camp secure the cattle; if the leader be dilatory, or unwilling to take strong measures, he may be a serious loser. The stationary kraals become offensive, if not burned down after a few months. The masika-kraal, as it is called, is that occupied only during the rainy monsoon, when water is every where found. The vicinity and the abundance of that necessary are the main considerations in selecting the situation of encampments. The bark kraals commence in Uvinza, where trees abound, and extend to the Tanganyika Lake; some are substantial, as the temporary villages, and may be a quarter of a mile in circumference. The lakist population carry with them, when traveling, karagwah or stiff mats of reed and rush; these they spread over and fasten to a firmly-planted frame-work of flexible boughs, not unlike a bird's nest inverted, or they build a cone of strong canes, in the shape of piled muskets, with the ends lashed together. It is curious to see the small compass in which the native African traveler can contract himself: two, and even three, will dispose their heads and part of their bodies—leaving their lower limbs to the mercy of the elements—under a matting little more than a yard square.

When lodgings in the kraal have been distributed, and the animals have been off-packed, and water has been brought from the pit or stream, all apply themselves to the pleasant toil of refection. Merrily then sounds the breathless chant of the woman pounding or rubbing down grain, the song of the cook, and the tinkle-tinkle of the slave's pestle, as he bends over the iron mortar from which he stealthily abstracts the coffee. The fireplaces are three stones or clods, placed trivet-wise upon the ground, so that a draught may feed the flame; they are far superior to the holes and trenches of our camps and pic-nics. The tripod supports a small black earthen pot, round which the khambi or little knot of messmates perseveringly squat despite the stinging sun. At home, where they eat their own provisions, they content themselves with a slender meal of flour and water once a day. But like Spaniards, Arabs, and all abstemious races, they must "make up for lost time." When provisions are supplied to them, they are cooking and consuming as long as the material remains; the pot is in perpetual requisition, now filled to be emptied, then refilled to be re-emptied. They will devour in three days the rations provided for eight, and then complain loudly that they are starved. To leave a favorable impression upon their brains, I had a measure nearly double that generally used, yet the perverse wretches pleading hunger, though they looked like aldermen by the side of the lean bony anatomies whom they met on the road, would desert whenever met by a caravan. After a time there will, doubtless, be a reaction; when their beards whiten they will indulge in the garrulity of age; they will recount to wondering youth the prodigality of the muzungu, in filling them with grain, even during the longest marches, and they will compare his loads of cloth and beads with the half dozen "shaggy" cows and the worn-out hoes, the sole outfit for presents and provisions carried by caravans of "Young Africa." If there be any delay in serving out provisions, loud cries of Posho! p'hamba!—rations! food!—resound through the camp; yet when fatigued, the porters will waste hours in apathetic idleness rather than walk a few hundred yards to buy grain. Between their dozen meals they puff clouds of pungent tobacco, cough and scream over their jungle-bhang, and chew ashes, quids, and pinches of red earth, probably the graves of white ants. If meat be served out to them, it is eaten as a relish; it never, however, interferes with the consumption of porridge. A sudden glut of food appears to have the effect of intoxicating them. The Arabs, however, avoiding steady rations, alternately gorge and starve their porters, knowing by experience that such extremes are ever most grateful to the barbarian stomach. The day must be spent in very idleness; a man will complain bitterly if told to bring up his pack for opening; and general discontent, with hints concerning desertion, will arise from the mortification of a muster. On such occasions he and his fellows will raise their voices—when not half choked by food—and declare that they will not be called about like servants, and crouch obstinately round the smoky fire, the pictures of unutterable disgust; and presently enjoy the sweet savor of stick-jaw dough and pearl-holcus like small shot, rat stews, and boiled weeds, which they devour till their "bulge" appears like the crop of a stuffed turkey. Sometimes, when their improvidence has threatened them with a banyan-day, they sit in a melancholy plight, spitefully smoking and wickedly eying our cooking-pots; on these occasions they have generally a goat or a bullock in store, and, if not, they finesse to obtain one of ours. I always avoid issuing an order to them direct, having been warned by experience that Kidogo or the kirangozi is the proper channel, which sorely vexes Valentine and Seedy Bombay, whose sole enjoyment in life is command. I observed that when wanted for extra work, to remove thorns or to dig for water, the false alarm of Posho! (rations!) summons them with a wonderful alacrity. Moreover, I remarked that when approaching their country and leaving ours —the coast—they became almost unmanageable, and *vice versâ* as conditions changed.

My companion and I pass our day as we best can, sometimes in a bower of leafy branches, often under a spreading tree, rarely in the flimsy tent. The usual occupations are the diary and the sketch-book, added to a little business. The cloth must be doled out, and the porters must be persuaded, when rested, to search the country for rations, otherwise—the morrow will be a blank. When a bullock is killed one of us must be present. The porters receive about a quarter of the meat, over which they sit, wrangling and screaming like hyenas, till a fair division according to messes is arrived at. Then, unless watched, some strong and daring hand will suddenly break through the ring, snatch up half a dozen portions, and disappear at a speed defying pursuit; others will follow his example, with the clatter and gesture of a troop of baboons, and the remainder will retire, as might be expected, grumbling and discontented. Dinner at four P.M. breaks the neck of the day. Provisions of some kind are mostly procurable; our diet, however, varies from such common doings as the hard holcus-scone, the tasteless bean-broth, and the leathery goat-steak, to fixings of delicate venison, fatted capon, and young Guineafowl or partridge, with "bread sauce," composed of bruised rice and milk. At first the Goanese declined to cook "pretty food," as pasties and rissoles, on the plea that such things were impossible upon the march; they changed their minds when warned that persistence in such theory might lead to a ceremonious fustigation. Moreover, they used to serve us after their fashion, with a kind of "portion" on plates; the best part, of course, remained in the pots and digesters; these, therefore, were ordered to do duty as dishes. When tea or coffee is required in a drinkable state, we must superintend the process of preparing it, the notions of the Goanese upon such subjects being abominable to the civilized palate. When we have eaten, our servants take their turn; they squat opposite each other over a private "cooking-pot" to which they have paid unremitting attention; the stretch forth their talons and eat till weary, not satiated, pecking, nodding, and cramming like two lank black pigeons. Being "Christians," that is to say, Roman Catholics, they will not feed with the heathenry; moreover a sort of semi-European dignity forbids. Consequently Bombay messes with his "brother" Mabruki, and the other slaves eat by themselves.

When the wells ahead are dry the porters will scarcely march in the morning; their nervous impatience of thirst is such that they would exhaust all their gourds, if they expected a scarcity in front, and then they would suffer severely through the long hot day. They persist, moreover, upon eating before the march, under the false impression that it gives them strength and bottom. In fact, whenever difficulties as regards grain or drink suggest themselves, the African requires the direction of some head-piece made of better stuff than his own. The hardships of the tirikeza have already been described: they must be endured to be realized.

Night is ushered in by penning and pounding the cows, and by tethering the asses—these "careless Æthiopians" lose them every second day—and by collecting and numbering the loads—a task of difficulty where every man shirks the least trouble. When there has been no tirikeza, when provisions have been plentiful, and when there is a bright moonshine, which seems to enliven these people like jackals, a furious drumming, a loud clapping of hands, and a general droning song, summon the lads and the lasses of the neighboring villages to come out and dance and "make love." The performance is laborious, but these Africans, like most men of little game, soon become too tired to work, but not too tired to play and amuse themselves. Their style of saltation is remarkable only for the excessive gravity which it induces; at no other time does the East African look so serious, so full of earnest purpose. Sometimes a single dancer, the village buffoon, foots a *pas seul*, featly, with head, arms, and legs, bearing strips of hair-garnished cow-skin, which are waved, jerked, and contorted, as if dislocation had occurred to his members. At other times, a line or a circle of boys and men is formed near the fire, and one standing in the centre, intones the song solo, the rest humming a chorus in an undertone. The dancers plumbing and tramping to the measure with alternate feet, simultaneously perform a treadmill exercise with a heavier stamp at the end of every period: they are such timists, that a hundred pair of heels sound like one. At first the bodies are slowly swayed from side to side, presently, as excitement increases, the exercise waxes severe: they "cower down and lay out their buttocks," to use pedantic Ascham's words, "as though they would shoot at crows;" they bend and recover themselves, and they stoop and rise to the redoubled sound of the song and the heel-music, till the assembly, with arms waving like windmills, assumes the frantic semblance of a ring of Egyptian Darwayshes. The performance often closes with a grand promenade; all the dancers being jammed in a rushing mass, a *galop infernale*, with the features of satyrs, and gestures resembling aught but the human. When the fun threatens to become too fast and furious, the song dies, and the performers, with loud shouts of laughter, throw themselves on the ground, to recover strength and breath. The gray-beards look on with admiration and sentiment, remembering the days when they were capable of similar feats. Instead of "Bravo," they ejaculate "Nice! nice! verynice!" and they wonder what makes the white men laugh. The ladies prefer to perform by themselves, and, perhaps, in the East ours would do the same, if a literal translation of the remarks to which a ball always gives rise among Orientals happened by misfortune to reach their refined ears.

When there is no dancing, and the porters can no longer eat, drink, and smoke, they sit by their fires, chatting, squabbling, talking, and singing some such "pure nectar" as the following. The song was composed, I believe, in honor of me, and I frequently heard it when the singers knew that it was understood. The cosmopolitan reader will not be startled by the epithet "mbaya," or wicked, therein applied to the muzungu. A "good white man" would indeed, in these lands, have been held an easy-going soul, a natural, an innocent, like the "buona famiglia" of the Italian cook, who ever holds the highest quality of human nature to be a certain facility for being "plucked without 'plaining," and being "flayed without flinching." Moreover, despite my "wickedness," they used invariably to come to me for justice and redress, especially when proximity to the coast encouraged the guide and guards to "bully" them.

> "Muzungu mbaya" (the wicked white man) goes from the shore,
> (*Chorus.*)   Puti! puti!   (I can only translate it by "grub! grub!")
> We will follow "muzungu mbaya."
> Puti! puti!
> As long as he gives us good food!
> Puti! puti!
> We will traverse the hill and the stream,
> Puti! puti!
> With the caravan of this great mundewa (merchant).
> Puti! puti! etc., etc.

The Baloch and the sons of Ramji quarrel, yell, roar, and talk of eating—the popular subject of converse in these lands, as is beer in England, politics in France, law in Normandy, "pasta" at Naples, and, to say no more, money every where—till a late hour. About 8 P.M., the small hours of the country, sounds the cry Lala! lala!—sleep! It is willingly obeyed by all except the women, who must sometimes awake to confabulate even at midnight. One by one the caravan sinks into torpid slumber. At this time, especially when in the jungle bivouac, the scene often becomes truly impressive. The dull red fires flickering and forming a circle of ruddy light in the depths of the black forest, flaming against the tall trunks and defining the foliage of the nearer trees, illuminate lurid groups of savage men, in every variety of shape and posture. Above, the dark purple sky, studded with golden points, domes the earth with bounds narrowed by the gloom of night. And behold! in the western horizon, a resplendent crescent, with a dim, ash-colored globe in its arms, and crowned by Hesperus, sparkling like a diamond, sinks through the vast of space, in all the glory and gorgeousness of Eternal Nature's sublimest works. From such a night, methinks, the Byzantine man took his device, the Crescent and the Star.

The rate of caravan-marching in East Africa greatly varies. In cool moonlit mornings, over an open path, the pagazi will measure perhaps four miles an hour. This speed is reduced by a quarter after a short "spurt," and under normal, perhaps favorable, circumstances, three statute miles will be the highest average. Throughout the journey it is safe to reckon for an Indian file of moderate length—say 150 men—2.25 English miles, or, what is much the same, 1.75 geographical miles per hour, measured by compass from point to point. In a clear country an allowance of 20 per cent. must be made for winding; in closer regions 40 to 50 per cent., and the traveler must exercise his judgment in distributing his various courses between these extremes. Mr. Cooley (Inner Africa Laid Open, p. 6), a "resolute," and, I may add, a most successful "reducer of itinerary distances," estimates that the ordinary day's journey of the Portuguese missionaries in West Africa never exceeded six geographical miles projected in a straight line, and that on rare occasions, and with effort only, it may have extended to 10 miles. Dr. Lacerda's porters in East Africa were terrified at the thought of marching ordinarily 2.50 Portuguese leagues, or about 9.33 statute miles per day. Dr. Livingstone gives the exceedingly high maximum of 2.50 to 3 miles an hour in a straight line; but his porters were lightly laden, and the Makololo are apparently a far "gamer" race, more sober and industrious, than the East Africans. Mr. Petherick, H. M.'s consul at Khartum, estimates his gangs to have marched 3.50 miles per hour, and the ordinary day's march at 8 hours. It is undoubted that the negro races north of the equator far surpass in pedestrian powers their southern brethren; moreover, the porters in question were marching only for a single day; but as no instruments were used, the average may fairly be suspected of exaggeration. Finally, Mr. Galton's observation concerning Cape traveling applies equally well to this part of Africa, namely, that 10 statute or 6 rectilinear geographical miles per diem is a fair average of progress, and that he does well who conducts the same caravan 1000 geographical miles across a wild country in six months.

I will conclude this chapter with a succinct account of the inn, that is to say the village, in East Africa.

The habitations of races form a curious study and no valueless guide to the nature of the climate and the physical conditions to which men are subject.

Upon the East African coast the villages, as has been mentioned, are composed of large tenements, oblongs or squares of wattle and dab, with eaves projecting to form a deep veranda and a thatched pent-roof, approaching in magnitude that of Madagascar.

Beyond the line of maritime land the "nyumba" or dwelling-house assumes the normal African form, the circular hut described by every traveler in the interior. Dr. Livingstone appears to judge rightly that its circularity is the result of a barbarous deficiency in inventiveness. It has, however, several varieties. The simplest is a loose thatch thrown upon a cone of sticks based upon the ground, and lashed together at the apex: it ignores windows, and the door is a low hole in the side. A superior kind is made after the manner of our ancient bee-hives: it is cup-shaped, with bulging sides, and covered with neat thatch, cut in circles which overlap one another tile-fashion; at a distance it resembles an inverted bird's-nest. The common shape is a cylindrical framework of tall staves, or the rough trunks of young trees planted in the earth, neatly interwoven with parallel and concentric rings of flexible twigs and withies. This is plastered inside and outside with a hard coat of red or gray mud; in the poorer tenements the surface is rough and chinked; in the better order it is carefully smoothed, and sometimes adorned with rude imitations of life. The diameter averages from 20 to 25, and the height from 7 to 15 feet in the centre, which is supported by a strong roof-tree, to which all the stacked rafters and poles converge. The roof is subsequently added. It is a structure similar to the walls, interwoven with sticks, upon which thick grass or palm-fronds are thrown, and the whole is covered with thatch, tied on by strips of tree-bark. It has eaves, which, projecting from two to six feet—under them the inhabitants love to sit or sunshade themselves—rest upon horizontal bars, which are here and there supported by forked uprights—trees rudely barked. Near the coast the eaves are broad and high; in the interior they are purposely made so low that a man must creep in on all-fours. The doorway resembles the entrance to an English pig-sty; it serves, however, to keep out heat in the hot season, and to keep in smoke and warmth during the rains and the cold weather. The threshold is garnished with a horizontal log or board that defends the interior from inundation. The door is a square of reeds fastened together by bark or cord, and planted upright at night between the wall and two dwarf posts at each side of the entrance. There is generally a smaller and a secret door opposite that in use, and jealously closed up except when flight is necessary. In the colder and damper regions there is a second wall and roof outside the first, forming, in fact, one house within the other.

About Central Usagara the normal African haystack-hut makes place for the "tembe," which extends westward a little beyond Unyanyembe. The tembe, though of Hamitic origin, resembles the utum of the ancients, and the hishan of the modern Hejaz, those hollow squares of building which have extended through Spain to France, and even to Ireland: it was probably suggested to Africa and to Arabia by the necessity of defense to, as well as lodging for, man and beast. It is, to a certain extent, a proof of civilization in Eastern Africa: the wildest tribes have not progressed beyond the mushroom or circular hut, a style of architecture which seems borrowed from the indigenous mimosa-tree.

Westward of Unyamwezi in Uvinza and about the Tanganyika Lake the round hovel again finds favor with the people; but even there the Arabs prefer to build for themselves the more solid and comfortable tembe.

The haystack-hut has been described by a multitude of travelers: the "tembe," or hollow village, yet awaits that honor.

The "tembe" wants but the addition of whitewash to make it an effective feature in African scenery: as it is, it appears from afar like a short line of raised earth. Provided with a block-house at each angle to sweep dead ground where fire, the only mode of attack practiced in these regions, can be applied, it would become a fort impregnable to the Eastern African. The form is a hollow square or oblong, generally irregular, with curves, projections, and semicircles; in the East African Ghauts, the shape is sometimes round or oval to suit the exigencies of the hill-sides and the dwarf cones upon which it is built. On the mountains and in Ugogo, where timber is scarce, the houses form the continued frontage of the building, which, composed of mimosa-trunks, stout stakes, and wattle and dab, rarely exceeds seven feet in height. In the southern regions of Usagara, where the tembe is poorest, the walls are of clods loosely put together and roofed over with a little straw. About Msene, where fine trees abound, the tembe is surrounded by a separate bomba or palisade of young unbarked trunks, short or tall, and capped here and there with cattle-skulls, blocks of wood, grass-wisps, and similar talismans; this stockade, in damper places, is hedged with a high thick fence, sometimes doubled and trebled, of pea-green milk-bush, which looks pretty and refreshing, and is ditched outside with a deep trench serving as a drain. · The cleared space in front of the main passage through the hedges is often decorated with a dozen poles, placed in a wide semicircle to support human skulls, the mortal remains of ill-conducted boors. In some villages the principal entrance is approached by long, dark, and narrow lanes of palisading. When the settlement is built purely for defense, it is called "kaya," and its headman "muinyi kaya;" the word, however, is sometimes used for "bomo" or "mji," a palisaded village in general. In some parts of Unyamwezi there is a bandani or exterior boothy, where the men work at the forge or sit in the shade, and where the women husk, pound, and cook their grain.

The general roof of the tembe is composed of mud and clay heaped upon grass thickly strewed over a frame-work of rafters supported by the long walls. It has, usually, an obtuse slope to the front and another to the rear, that rain may not lie; it is, however, flat enough to support the bark-bins of grain, gourds, old pots, firewood, watermelons, pumpkins, manioc, mushrooms, and other articles placed there to ripen or dry in the sun. It has no projecting eaves, and it is ascended from the inside by the primitive ladder, the inclined trunk of a tree, with steps formed by the stumps of lopped boughs, acting rings. The roof, during the rains, is a small plot of bright green grass: I often regretted not having brought with me a little store of mustard and cress. In each external side of the square one or two doorways are pierced: they are large enough to admit a cow, and, though public, they often pass through private domiciles. They are jealously closed at sunset, after which hour not a villager dares to stir from his home till morning. The outer doors are sometimes solid planks, more often they are three or four heavy beams suspended to a cross-bar passing through their tops. When the way is to be opened they are raised from below, and are kept up by being planted in a forked tree-trunk inside the palisade: they are let down when the entrance is to be closed, and are barred across with strong poles.

The tenements are divided from one another by party-walls of the same material as the exterior. Each house has, usually, two rooms, a "but" and a "ben," which vary in length from 20 to 50 feet, and in depth from 12 to 15: they are partitioned by a screen of corn-canes supported by stakes, with a small passage left open for light. The "but," used as parlor, kitchen, and dormitory, opens upon the common central square; the "ben" receives a glimmer from the doors and chinks, which have not yet suggested the idea of windows: it serves for a sleeping and a store room; it is a favorite place with hens and pigeons that aspire to be mothers, and the lambs and kids in early infancy are allowed to pass the night there. The inner walls are smeared with mud: lime is not procurable in Eastern Africa, and the people have apparently no predilection for the Indian "gobar:" the floor is of tamped earth, rough, uneven, and unclean. The prism-shaped ceiling is composed of rafters and thin poles gently rising from the long walls to the centre, where they are supported by strong horizontals, which run the whole length of the house, and these again rest upon a proportionate number of pillars, solid forked uprights, planted in the floor. The ceiling is polished to a shiny black with smoke, which winds its way slowly through the door—smoke and grease are the African's coat and small clothes; they contribute so much to his health and comfort that he is by no means anxious to get rid of them—and sooty lines depend from it like negro-stalactites.

The common enceinte formed by the houses is often divided into various courts, intended for different families, by the walls of the tenements or by stout screens, and connected by long wynds and dark alleys of palisade-work. The largest and cleanest square usually belongs to the headman. In these spaces cattle are milked and penned; the ground is covered with a thick coat of the animals' earths, dust in the hot weather, and deep viscid mud during the rains: the impurity must be an efficacious fomite of cutaneous and pectoral disease. The villagers are fond of planting in the central courts trees, under whose grateful shade the loom is plied, the children play, the men smoke, and the women work. Here, also, stands the little mzimu, or fetiss-hut, to receive the oblations of the pious. Places are partioned off from the public ground near the houses by horizontal trunks of trees, resting on forks, forming pens to keep the calves from the cows at night. In some villages huge bolsters of surplus grain, neatly packed in bark and corded round, are raised on tall poles near the interior doors of the tenements. Often, too, the insides of the settlements boast of pigeon-houses, which in this country are made to resemble, in miniature, those of the people. In Unyamwezi the centre is sometimes occupied by the iwanza, or village "public house," which will be described in a future chapter.

In some regions, as in Ugogo, these lodgings become peculiarly offensive if not burned after the first year. The tramping of the owners upon the roof shakes mud and soot from the ceiling, and the rains wash down masses of earth-work heavy enough to do injury. The interior is a menagerie of hens, pigeons, and rats of peculiar impudence. Scorpions and earwigs fall from their nests in the warm or shady rafters. The former, locally termed "nge," is a small yellow variety, and though it stings spitefully, the pain seldom lasts through the day; as many as three have dropped upon my couch in the course of the week. In Ugogo there is a green scorpion from four to five inches long which inflicts a torturing wound. According to the Arabs, the scorpion in Eastern Africa dies after inflicting five consecutive stings, and commits suicide if a bit of stick be applied to the middle of its back. The earwig is common in all damp places, and it haunts the huts on account of the shade. The insect apparently casts its coat before the rainy season, and the Africans ignore the superstition which in most European countries has given origin to its trivial name. A small xylophagus with a large black head rains a yellow dust like pollen from the riddled wood-work; house-crickets chirp from evening to dawn; cockroaches are plentiful as in an Indian steamer; and a solitary mason-wasp, the "kumbharni," or "potter's wife" of Western India—a large hymenopter of several varieties, tender-green, or black and yellow, or dark metallic blue—burrows holes in the wall, or raises plastered nests, and buzzes about the inmates' ears; lizards, often tailless after the duello, tumble from the ceilings; in the darker corners spiders of frightful hideousness weave their solid webs; and the rest of the population is represented by tenacious ticks of many kinds, flies of sorts, bugs, fleas, musquitoes, and small ants, which are, perhaps, the worst plagues of all. The riciniæ in Eastern Africa are locally called papazi, which probably explains the "pazi bug," made by Dr. Krapf a rival in venom to the Argas Persicus, or fatal "bug of Miana." In Eastern Africa these parasites are found of many shapes, round and oval, flat and swollen; after suction they vary in size from microscopic dimensions to three quarters of an inch; the bite can not poison, but the constant irritation caused by it may induce fever and its consequences. A hut infested with papazi must be sprinkled with boiling water and swept clean for many weeks before they will disappear. In the tembe there is no draught to disturb the smaller occupants, consequently they are more numerous than in the circular cottage. Moreover, the people, having an aversion to sleeping in the open air, thus supply their co-inhabitants with nightly rations which account for their fecundity.

The abodes, as might be expected, are poorly furnished. In Unyamwezi they contain invariably one or more "kitanda." This cartel, or bedstead, is a rude contrivance. Two parallel lines of peeled tree-branches, planted at wide intervals, support in their forks horizontal poles: upon these is spread crosswise a layer of thick sticks, which forms the frame. The bedding consists of a bull-hide or two, and perhaps a long, coarse rush-mat. It is impossible for any one but an African to sleep upon these kitanda, on account of their shortness, the hardness of the material, and the rapid slope which supplies the want of pillows, and serves for another purpose which will not be described. When removed, a fractured pole will pour forth a small shower of the foul cimex: this people of hard skins considers its bite an agreeable titillation, and, what may somewhat startle a European, esteems its odor a perfume. Around the walls depend from pegs neatly-plaited slings of fibrous cord, supporting gourds and "vilindo"—neat cylinders, like small band-boxes, of tree-bark, made to contain cloth, butter, grain, or other provisions. In the store-room, propped upon stones, and plastered over with clay for preservation, are lindo, huge corn-bins of the same material; grain is ground upon a coarse granite slab, raised at an angle of 25°, about one foot above the floor, and embedded in a rim of hard clay. The hearth is formed of three "mafiga," or truncated cones of red or gray mud, sometimes two feet high and ten inches in diameter at the base: they are disposed triangularly, with the apex to the wall, and open to the front when the fire is made. The pot rests upon the tripod. The broom, a wisp of grass, a bunch of bamboo splints, or a split fibrous root, usually sticks in the ceiling; its work is left to the ants. From the rafters hang drums and kettle-drums, skins and hides in every process, and hooked twigs dangling from strings support the bows and arrows, the spears and assegais. An arrow is always thrust into the inner thatch for good luck: ivory is stored between the rafters, hence its dark ruddy color, which must be removed by ablution with warm blood; and the ceiling is a favorite place for small articles that require seasoning—bows, quivers, bird-bolts, knob-sticks, walking-canes, reed-nozzles for bellows, and mi'iko or ladles, two feet long, used to stir porridge. The large and heavy water-pots, of black clay, which are filled every morning and evening by the women at the well, lie during the day empty or half empty about the room. The principal article of luxury is the "kiti," or dwarf stool, cut out of a solid block, measuring one foot in height by six inches in diameter, with a concave surface for convenience of sitting: it has usually three carved legs or elbows; some, however, are provided with a fourth, and with a base like the seat to steady them. They are invariably used by the sultan and the mganga, who disdain to sit upon the ground; and the Wamrima ornament them with plates of tin let into the upper concaves. The woods generally used for the kiti are the mninga and the mpingu. The former is a tall and stately tree, which supplies wood of a dark mahogany color, exuding in life a red gum, like dragon's blood: the trunk is converted into bowls and platters, the boughs into rafters, which are, however, weak and subject to the xylophagus, while of the heart are made spears, which, when old and well-greased, resemble teak-wood. The mpingu is the sisam of India (Dalbergia sissoo), here erroneously called by the Arabs abnus—ebony. The tree is found throughout Eastern Africa. The wood is of fine quality, and dark at the core: the people divide it into male and female; the former is internally a dark brick-dust red, while the latter verges upon black: they make from it spears and axe-handles, which soon, however, when exposed to the air, unless regularly greased, become brittle. The massive mortar for husking grain, called by the people "mchi," is shaped exactly like those portrayed in the interior scenes of ancient Egypt; it is hewn out of the trunk of the close-grained mkora-tree. The huge pestle, like a capstan-bar, is made of the mkorongo, a large tree with a fine-grained wood, which is also preferred to others for rafters, as it best resists the attacks of insects.

Such, gentle reader, is the tembe of Central Africa. Concerning village life, I shall have something to say in a future page. The scene is more patent to the stranger's eye in these lands than in the semi-civilized regions of Asia, where men rarely admit him into their society.

African House-building.

CHAPTER XI.

WE CONCLUDE THE TRANSIT OF UNYAMWEZI.

I WAS detained at Kazeh from the 8th of November to the 14th of December, 1857, and the delay was one long trial of patience.

It is customary for stranger-caravans proceeding toward Ujiji to remain six weeks or two months at Unyanyembe for repose and recovery from the labors which they have, or are supposed to have, endured: moreover, they are expected to enjoy the pleasures of civilized society, and to accept the hospitality offered to them by the resident Arabs. In Eastern Africa, I may again suggest, six weeks is as the three days' visit in England.

On the morning after our arrival at Kazeh, the gang of Wanyamwezi porters that had accompanied us from the coast withdrew their hire from our cloth-bales; and not demanding, because they did not expect bakhshish, departed, without a sign of farewell, to their homes in Western Unyamwezi. The kirangozi or guide received a small present of domestics: his family being at Msene, distant five marches ahead, he fixed, after long haggling, the term of fifteen days as his leave of absence, after which he promised to join me with a fresh gang for the journey to Ujiji.

The rest of the party apparently considered Unyanyembe, not Ujiji, the end of the exploration; it proved in effect a second point of departure, easier than Kaole only because I had now gained some experience.

Two days after our arrival, the Baloch, headed by their jema-dar, appeared in full toilette to demand a "hakk el salamah," or reward for safe-conduct. I informed them that this would be given when they had reached the end of the up-march. The pragmatical darwaysh declared that without bakhshish there would be no advance; he withdrew his words, however, when my companion was called in to witness their being committed to paper—a proceeding always unpalatable to the Oriental. The Baloch then subsided into begging for salt and spices, and having received more than they had probably ever possessed in their lives, they privily complained of my parsimony to Said bin Salim. They then sent for tobacco, a goat, gunpowder, bullets—all which they obtained. Their next manœuvre was to extract four cloths for tinning their single copper pot and for repairing the match-dogs and stocks of two old matchlocks. They then sold a keg of gunpowder committed to their charge. They had experienced every kindness from Snay bin Amir, from Sallum bin Hamid—in fact, from all the Arab merchants of Kazeh. They lodged com-fortably in Musa Mzuri's house, and their allowance, one shukkah of domestics per diem, enabled them to buy goats, sheep, and fowls—luxuries unknown in their starving huts at Zanzibar. Yet they did not fail, with their foul tongues, ever ready, as the Per-sians say, for "spitting at Heaven," to charge their kind hosts with the worst crime that the Arab knows—niggardness.

On the 8th of November, I had arranged with Kidogo, as well as with the kirangozi, to resume the march at the end of a fort-night. Ten days afterward I again sent for him to conclude the plans concerning the journey: evidently something lay deep with-in his breast, but the difficulty was to extract it. He began by requiring a present for his excellent behavior—he received, to his astonishment, four cloths. He next demanded leave to visit his Unyamwezi home for a week, and was unpleasantly surprised when it was granted. He then "hit the right nail on the head." The sons of Ramji, declaring that I had promised them a bullock on arrival at Kazeh, had seized, hamstrung, and cut up a fine fat animal sent to me by Sallum bin Hamid; yet Kidogo averred that the alleged promise must be fulfilled to them. When I re-fused, he bluntly informed me that I was quite equal to the task of collecting porters for myself; I replied that this was his work, and not mine. He left the house abruptly, swearing that he would not trouble himself any longer, and, moreover, for the fu-ture, that his men should not carry the lightest load nor assist us even in threading beads. At last, on the 27th of November, I sent for Kidogo, and told him that the march was positively fixed for the next week. After sitting for a time "*cupo concentrato,*" in profound silence, the angry slave arose, delivered a volley of rat-tling words with the most theatrical fierceness, and rushed from the room, leaving the terrified Said bin Salim gazing upon vacancy

like an idiot. Accompanied by his followers, who were shouting
and laughing, he left the house, when—I afterward heard—they
drew their sabres, and waving them round their heads, they shouted, for the benefit of Arabs, "Tume-shinda Wazungu"—"We
have conquered the Whites!" I held a consultation with my
hosts concerning the advisability of disarming the recreant sons
of Ramji. But Sallum bin Hamid, the "papa" of the colony, took
up the word, and, as usual with such deliberative bodies, the council of war advised peace. They informed me that in Unyamwezi
slaves and muskets are the stranger's sole protection, and as they
were unanimous in persuading me to temporize, to "swallow anger" till after return, I felt bound, after applying for it, to be guided
by their advice. At the consultation, however, the real object
which delayed the sons of Ramji at Kazeh oozed out: their patroon, Mr. Rush Ramji, had written to them that his and their
trading outfit was on its way from the coast; consequently, they
had determined to await, and to make us await, its arrival before
marching upon Ujiji.

On the 14th of November, the masika, or wet season, which had
announced its approach by premonitory showers and by a final
burst of dry heat, set in over the Land of the Moon with torrents
of rain and "rain-stones," as hail is here called, and with storms
of thunder and lightning, which made it more resemble the first
breaking of an Indian than the desultory fall of a Zanzibar wet
monsoon. I was still under the impression that we were encoun-
tering the choti barsat or Little Rains of Bengal and Bombay;
and curious to say, the Arabs of Unyanyembe one and all declared, even after the wet monsoon had reached its height, that
the masika in Unyamwezi is synchronous with that of the island
and the coast, namely, in early April.

The rains in Eastern Africa are, like the summer in England,
the only healthy and enjoyable season:· the contrast between the
freshness of the air and the verdure of the scenery after the heat,
dust, and desolation that preceded the first showers, was truly luxurious. Yet the masika has many disadvantages for travelers.
The Wanyamwezi, who were sowing their fields, declined to act
porters, and several Arab merchants, who could not afford the expenditure required to hire unwilling men, were halted perforce in
and near Unyanyembe. The peasants would come in numbers;
offer to accompany the caravan; stand, stare, and laugh their
vacant laughs; lift and balance their packs; chaffer about hire;
promise to return next morning, and definitively disappear. With
the utmost exertion Snay bin Amir could collect only ten men,
and they were all ready to desert. Moreover, the opening of the
masika is ever unhealthy; strangers suffer severely from all sudden changes of temperature; Unyamwezi speedily became

"As full of agues as the sun in March."

Another cause of delay became imminent; my companion was

comparatively strong, but the others were prostrated by sickness. Valentine first gave in; he was nearly insensible for three days and nights, the usual period of the mukunguru or "seasoning" of Unyamwezi—a malignant bilious remittent—which left him weaker and thinner that he had ever been before. When he recovered Gaetano fell ill, and was soon in the happy state of unconsciousness which distinguished all his fevers. The bull-headed slave Mabruki also retired into private life, and Bombay was laid up by a shaking ague, while the Baloch and the sons of Ramji, who had led a life so irregular that the Arabs had frequently threatened them with punishment, also began to pay the penalty of excess.

Snay bin Amir was our principal doctor. An adept in the treatment called by his countrymen "camel-physic," namely, cautery and similar counter-irritants, he tried his art upon me when I followed the example of the party. At length, when the hummah, or hot fit, refused to yield to its supposed specific, a coating of powdered ginger, he insisted upon my seeing a mganga, or witch, celebrated for her cures throughout the country-side. She came, a wrinkled old beldame, with a greasy skin, black as soot, set off by a mass of tin-colored pigtails: her arms were adorned with copper bangles like manacles, and the implement of her craft was, as usual, a girdle of small gourds, dyed red-black with oil and use.

After demanding and receiving her fee in cloth, she proceeded to search my mouth and to inquire anxiously concerning poison. The question showed the prevalence of the practice in the country, and indeed the people, to judge from their general use of "mithridates," seem ever to expect it. She then drew from a gourd a greenish powder, which was apparently bhang, and having mixed it with water, she administered it like snuff, causing a convulsion of sneezing, which she hailed with shouts and various tokens of joy. Presently she rubbed my head with powder of another kind, and promising to return the next day, she left me to rest, declaring that sleep would cause a cure. The prediction, however, was not fulfilled, nor was the promise. Having become wealthy, she absconded to indulge in unlimited pombe for a week. The usual consequences of this "seasoning," distressing weakness, hepatic derangements, burning palms, and tingling soles, aching eyes, and alternate thrills of heat and cold, lasted, in my case, a whole month.

Our departure from Kazeh had now been repeatedly deferred. The fortnight originally fixed for the halt had soon passed in the vain search for porters. Sickness then delayed the journey till the 1st of December, and Snay bin Amir still opined that want of carriage would detain me till the 19th of that month; he would not name the 18th, which was an unlucky day. When they recovered from their ailments, the jemadar and the Baloch again began to be troublesome. All declared that a whole year, the term for which they had been sent by their prince, had elapsed, and therefore that they had now a right to return. The period was wholly one of their own, based perhaps upon an answer which they had received from Lieut. Col. Hamerton touching the probable duration of the expedition, "a year or so." Even of that time it still wanted five months, but nothing from myself or from Said bin Salim could convince men who would not be convinced, of that simple fact. Ismail, the Baloch, who was dying of dysentery, reported himself unable to proceed : arrangements were made to leave him and his "brother" Shahdad—the fearful tinkling of whose sleepless guitar argued that the sweet youth was in love—under the charge of Snay bin Amir, at Kazeh. Gray-beard Mohammed was sulking with his fellows. He sat apart from them; and complaining that he had not received his portion of food, came to me for dismissal, which was granted, but not accepted. The jemadar required for himself and the escort a porter per man. When this was refused he changed his tactics, and began to lament bitterly the unavoidable delay. He annoyed me with ceaseless visits, which were spent in harping upon the one string, "When do we march?" At last I forbade all allusion to the subject. In wrath he demanded leave, declaring that he had not come to settle in Africa, and much "excessiveness" to the same effect. He was at last brought to his senses by being summarily turned out of the house for grossly insulting my companion. A reaction then ensued; the Baloch professed penitence, and all declared themselves ready to march or to halt as I pleased. Yet, simulating impatience to depart, they clung to the pleasures of Kazeh; they secretly caused the desertion of the porters, and they never ceased to spread idle reports, vainly hoping that I might be induced to return to the coast.

Finally, Said bin Salim fulfilled at Kazeh Lieut. Col. Hamerton's acute prophecy. The Bukini blood of his mother—a Malagash slave—got the better of his Omani descent. I had long reformed my opinion concerning his generosity and kindheartedness, hastily concluded during a short cruise along the coast. "Man's heart," say the Arabs, "is known only in the fray, and man's head is known only on the way." But though high-flown sentiment and studied courtesy had disappeared with the first days of hardship and fatigue, he preserved for a time the semblance of respectability and respect. Presently, like the viler orders of Orientals, he presumed upon his usefulness, and his ability to forward the expedition; the farther we progressed from our "*point d'appui*," the coast, the more independent became his manner— of course, it afterward subsided into its former civility—and an overpowering egotism formed the motive of his every action. I had imprudently allowed him to be accompanied by the charming Halimah. True to his servile origin, he never seemed happy except in servile society, where he was "king of his company." At Kazeh, jealous of my regard for Snay bin Amir, and wearied by long evening conversations, where a little "ilm" or knowledge in the shape of history and divinity used to appear—his ignorance and apathy concerning all things but A. bin B., and B. bin C., who married his son D. to the daughter of E., prevented his taking part in them—he became first sulky, and then "contrarious." Formerly he was wont, on the usual occasions, to address a word of salutation to my companion: this ceased, and presently he would pass him as if he had been a bale of cloth. He affected in society the indecorous posture of a European woman stretched upon a sofa, after crouching for months upon his shins—in fact he was, as the phrase is, "trailing his jacket" for a quarrel.

Through timidity he had been profuse in expending the goods intrusted to his charge, and he had been repeatedly reproved for serving out, without permission, cloth and beads to his children. Yet, before reaching Unyanyembe, I never had reason to suspect him of dishonesty or deceit. At Kazeh, however, he was ordered to sell a keg of gunpowder before his slaves could purloin the whole. He reported that he had passed on the commission to Snay bin Amir. I also forbade him to issue hire to porters for a return-march from the Lake, having been informed that such was the best way to secure their desertion; and the information proved true enough, as twenty-five disappeared in a single night. He repeatedly affirmed that he had engaged and paid them for the up-march only. When he stood convicted of a double falsehood, he had *not* spoken about the gunpowder, and he *had* issued whole hire to several of the porters, I improved the occasion with a mild reproach. The little creature became vicious as a weasel, screamed like a hyena, declared himself no tallab or "asker," but an official under his government, and poured forth a torrent of justification. I cut the same short by leaving the room—a confirmed slight in these lands—and left him to rough language on the part of Snay bin Amir. Some hours subsequently he recovered his temper, and observed that "even husband and wife must occasionally have a gird at each other." Not caring, however, for a repetition of such puerilities, I changed the tone of kindness in which he had invariably been addressed for one of routine command, and this was preserved till the day of our final parting on the coast.

The good Snay bin Amir redoubled his attentions. His slaves strung in proper lengths, upon the usual palm-fibre, the beads sent up loose from Zanzibar, and he distributed the bales in due proportions for carriage. Our lights being almost exhausted, he made for us "dips," by ladling over wicks of unraveled "domestics" the contents of a caldron filled with equal parts of hot wax and tallow. My servant, Valentine, who, evincing uncommon aptitude for cooking, had as yet acquired only that wretched art of burlesquing coarse English dishes which renders the table in Western India a standing mortification to man's palate, was apprenticed to Mama Khamisi, a buxom housekeeper in Snay's establishment. There, in addition to his various Goanese accomplishments — making curds and whey, butter, cheese, and ghee; potting fish, pickling onions and limes, and preparing jams and jelly from the pleasant and cooling rosel—he learned the art of yeasting bread with whey or sour bean-flour (his leathery scones of coarse meal were an abomination to us); of straining honey, of preparing the favorite "kawurmeh," jerked or smoked meat chipped up and soused in ghee; of making firni, rice-jelly, and halwa, confectionery, in the shape of "Kazi's luggage," and "handworks:" he was taught to make ink from burnt grain; and last, not least, the trick of boiling rice as it should be boiled. We, in turn, taught him the various sciences of bird-stuffing, of boiling down isinglass and ghee, of doctoring tobacco with plantain, heeart, and tea-leaves, and of making milk punch, cigars, and guraku for the hookah. Snay bin Amir also sent into the country for plantains and tamarinds, then unprocurable at Kazeh, and he brewed a quantity of beer and mawa or plantain-wine. He admonished the Baloch and the sons of Ramji to be more careful as regards conduct and expenditure. He lent me valuable assistance in sketching the outlines of the Kinyamwezi, or language of Unyamwezi, and by his distances and directions we were enabled to lay down the southern limits and the general shape of the Nyanza or Northern Lake as correctly—and the maps forwarded from Kazeh to the Royal Geographical Society will establish this fact—as they were subsequently determined, after actual exploration, by my companion. He took charge of our letters and papers intended for home, and he undertook to forward the lagging gang still expected from the coast: as the future will prove, his energy enabled me to receive the much-wanted reserve in the "nick of time."

At length it became apparent that no other porters were procurable at Kazeh, and that the restiff Baloch and the sons of Ramji, disdaining Cæsar's "ite," required his "venite." I therefore resolved to lead them, instead of expending time and trouble in driving them, trusting that old habit, and that the difficulties attending their remaining behind would induce them to follow me. After much murmuring, my companion preceded me on the 5th of December, and "made a khambi" at Zimbili, a lumpy hill, with a north and south lay, and conspicuous as a landmark from the Arab settlements, which are separated from it by a march of two hours. On the third day I followed him, in truth, more dead than alive—the wing of Azrael seemed waving over my head— even the movement of the manchila was almost unendurable. I found cold and comfortless quarters in a large village at the base of Zimbili; no cartel was procurable, the roof leaked, and every night brought with it a furious storm of lightning, wind, and rain. By slow degrees the Baloch began to drop in, a few of the sons of Ramji, and the donkey-men followed, half a dozen additional porters were engaged, and I was recovering strength to advance once more, when the report that our long-expected caravan was halted at Rubuga in consequence of desertion, rendered a further delay necessary. My companion returned to Kazeh, to await the arrival of the reserve supplies, and I proceeded onward to collect a gang for the journey westward.

At 10 A.M., on the 15th of December, I mounted the manchila, carried by six slaves, hired by Snay bin Amir from Khamis bin Salim, at the rate of three pounds of white beads each, for the journey to Msene. After my long imprisonment, I was charmed with the prospect, a fine open country, with well-wooded hills rolling into blue distance on either hand. A two hours' ride placed me at Yombo, a new and picturesque village of circular tents, surrounded by plantains and wild fruit-trees. The mkuba bears an edible red plum, which, though scanty of flesh, as usual, where man's care is wanting, was found by no means unpalatable. The metrongoma produces a chocolate-colored fruit, about the size of a cherry: it is eaten, but it lacks the grateful acid of the mkuba. The gigantic palmyra, or borassus, which failed in the barren platform of Ugogo, here reappears, and hence extends to the Tanganyika Lake.

I halted two days at Yombo: the situation was low and unhealthy, and provisions were procurable in homeopathic quantities. My only amusement there was to watch the softer part of the population. At eventide, when the labors of the day were past and done, the villagers came home in a body, laden with their implements of cultivation, and singing a kind of "dulce domum" in a simple and pleasing recitative. The sunset hour, in the "Land of the Moon," is replete with enjoyments. The sweet and balmy breeze floats in waves like the draught of a fan; the sky is softly and serenely blue; the fleecy clouds, stationary in the upper firmament, are robed in purple and gold, and the beautiful blush crimsoning the west is reflected by all the features of earth. At this time all is life. The vulture soars with silent flight high in the blue expanse; the small birds preen themselves for the night, and sing their evening hymns; the antelopes prepare to couch in the bush; the cattle and flocks frisk and gambol while driven from their pastures; and the people busy themselves with the simple pleasures that end the day. Every evening there is a smoking-party, which particularly attracts my attention. All the feminine part of the population, from wrinkled grandmother to the maiden scarcely in her teens, assemble together, and, sitting in a circle upon dwarf stools and logs of wood, apply themselves to their long black-bowled pipes.

> " Sæpe illæ long-cut vel short-cut flare tobacco
> Sunt solitæ pipos."

They smoke with an intense enjoyment, slowly and deeply inhaling the glorious weed, and exhaling clouds from their nostrils; at times they stop to cool the mouth with slices of raw manioc, or cobs of green maize roasted in the ashes; and often some earnest matter of local importance causes the pipes to be removed for a few minutes, and a clamor of tongues breaks the usual silence. The pipe also requires remark: the bowl is of imperfect material —the clay being half baked—but the shape is perfect. The African tapering cone is far superior to the European bowl: the former gives as much smoke as possible while the tobacco is fresh and untainted, and as little when it becomes hot and unpleasant; the latter acts on the contrary principle. Among the fair of Yombo there were no less than three beauties—women who would be deemed beautiful in any part of the world. Their faces were purely Grecian; they had laughing eyes, their figures were models for an artist, with—

"Turgide, brune e ritondette mamme,"

like the "bending statue that delights the world" cast in bronze. The dress—a short kilt of calabash fibre—rather set off than concealed their charms, and, though destitute of petticoat or crinoline, they were wholly unconscious of indecorum. It is a question that by no means can be positively answered in the affirmative, that real modesty is less in proportion to the absence of toilette. These "beautiful domestic animals" graciously smiled when, in my best Kinyamwezi, I did my devoir to the sex; and the present of a little tobacco always secured for me a seat in the undress circle.

After hiring twenty porters—five lost no time in deserting— and mustering the Baloch, of whom eleven now were present, I left Yombo on the 18th of December, and passing through a thick green jungle, with low, wooded, and stony hills rising on the left hand to about 4000 feet above sea-level, I entered the little settlement of Pano. The next day brought us to the clearing of Mfuto, a broad, populous, and fertile rolling plain, where the stately tamarind flourished to perfection. A third short march, through alternate patches of thin wood and field studded with granite blocks, led to Irora, a village in Western Mfuto, belonging to Salim bin Salih, an Arab from Mbuamaji, and a cousin of Said bin Mohammed, my former traveling companion, who had remained behind at Kazeh. This individual, a fat, pulpy, and dingy-colored mulatto, appeared naked to the waist, and armed with bow and arrows: he received me surlily, and when I objected to a wretched cow-shed outside his palisade, he suddenly waxed furious: he raved like a madman, shook his silly bow, and declared that he ignored the name of the Sayyid Majid, being himself as good a "sultan" as any other. He became pacified on perceiving that his wrath excited nothing but the ridicule of the Baloch, found a better lodging, sent a bowl of fresh milk wherein to drown differences, and behaved on this and a subsequent occasion more like an Arab shaykh than an African headman.

On the 22d of December my companion rejoined me, bringing four loads of cloth, three of beads, and seven of brass wire: they formed part of the burden of the twenty-two porters who were to join the expedition ten days after its departure from the coast. The Hindoos, Ladha Damha and Mr. Rush Ramji, after the decease of Lieut. Colonel Hamerton, had behaved with culpable neglect. The cloth was of the worst and flimsiest description; the beads were the cheap white and the useless black—the latter I was obliged to throw away; and as they sent up the supply without other guard than two armed slaves, "Mshindo" and "Kirikhota," the consequence was that the pair had plundered *ad libitum*. No letters had been forwarded, and no attention had been paid to my repeated requests for drugs and other stores. My companion's new gang, levied at Kazeh, affected the greatest impatience. They refused to halt for a day—even Christmas-day. They proposed double marches, and they resolved to proceed by the straight road to Msene. It was deemed best to humor them. They arrived, however, at their destination only one day before my party, who traveled leisurely, and who followed the longer and the more cultivated route.

We left Irora on the 23d of December, and marched from sunrise till noon to the district of Eastern Wilyankuru. There we again separated. On the next day I passed alone through the settlement called Muinyi Chandi, where certain Arabs from Oman had built large tembe, to serve as barracoons and warehouses. This district supplies the adjoining countries with turmeric, of which very little grows in Unyanyembe. After this march disappeared the last of the six hammals who had been hired to carry the hammocks. They were as unmanageable as wild asses, ever grumbling and begging for "kitoweyo"—"kitchen;" constitutionally unfitted to obey an order; disposed, as the noble savage generally is, to be insolent; and, like all porters in this part of the world, unable to carry a palanquin. Two men, instead of four, insisted upon bearing the hammock; thus overburdened and wishing to get over the work, they hurried themselves till out of breath. When one was fagged, the man that should have relieved him was rarely to be found; consequently, two or three stiff trudges knocked them up and made them desert. Said bin Salim, the jemadar, and the Baloch, doubtlessly impressed with the belief that my days were numbered, passed me on the last march without a word—the sun was hot, and they were hastening to shade—and left me with only two men to carry the hammock in a dangerous strip of jungle where, shortly afterward, Salim bin Masud, an Arab merchant of Msene, was murdered.

On Christmas-day I again mounted ass, and passing through the western third of the Wilyankuru district, was hospitably received by a wealthy proprietor, Salim bin Said, surnamed, probably on account of his stature, Simba, or the Lion, who had obtained from the Sultan Mrorwa permission to build a large tembe. The worthy and kind-hearted Arab exerted himself strenuously to promote the comfort of his guest. He led me to a comfortable lodging, placed a new cartel in the coolest room, supplied meat, milk, and honey, and spent the evening in conversation with me. He was a large middle-aged man, with simple, kindly manners, and an honesty of look and words which rendered his presence exceedingly prepossessing.

After a short and eventless march, on the 26th of December, to Masenge, I reached on the following day the little clearing of Kirira. I was unexpectedly welcomed by two Arabs, Masud ibn Musallam el Wardi, and Hamid bin Ibrahim el Amuri. The former, an old man of the Beni Bu Ali clan, and personally familiar with Sir Lionel Smith's exploits, led me into the settlement, which was heaped round with a tall green growth of milk-bush, and placed me upon a cartel in the cool and spacious barzah or vestibule of the tembe. From my vantage-ground I enjoyed the pleasant prospect of those many little miseries which Orientals—perhaps not only Orientals—create for themselves by "ceremony" and "politeness." Weary and fagged by sun and dust, the Baloch were kept standing for nearly half an hour before the preliminaries to sitting down could be arranged and the party could be marshaled in proper order—the most honorable man on the left hand of the host, and the "lower class" off the dais or raised step; and, when they commenced to squat, they reposed upon their shins, and could not remove their arms or accoutrements till especially invited to hang them up. Hungry and thirsty, they dared not commit the solecism of asking for food or drink; they waited from nine A.M. till noon, sometimes eying the door with wistful looks, but generally affecting an extreme indifference as to feeding. At length came the meal, a mountain of rice, capped with little boulders of mutton. It was allowed to cool long before precedence round the tray was settled, and ere the grace, "bismillah"—the signal to "set to"—was reverentially asked by Said bin Salim. Followed a preparation of curdled milk, for which spoons being requisite, a wooden ladle did the necessary. There was much bustling and not a little importance about Hamid, the younger host, a bilious subject twenty-four or twenty-five years old, who, for reasons best known to himself, assumed the style and title of sarkal—government servant. The meal concluded with becoming haste, and was followed by that agreeable appearance of repletion which is so pleasing to the Oriental Amphitryon. The Baloch returned to squat upon their shins, and they must have suffered agonies till 5 P.M., when the appearance of a second and a more ceremonious repast enabled them once more to perch upon their heels. It was hard eating this time; the shorwa, or mutton broth, thickened with melted butter, attracted admiration; the guests, however, could only hint at its excellences, because in the East if you praise a man's meat you intend to slight his society. The *plat de résistance* was, as usual, the pillaw, or, as it is here called, pulao—not the conventional mess of rice and fowl, almonds and raisins, onion-shreds, cardamoms, and other abominations, which goes by that name among Anglo-Indians, but a solid heap of rice, boiled after being greased with a handful of ghee—

(I must here indulge in a little digression. For the past century, which concluded with reducing India to the rank of a British province, the proud invader has eaten her rice after a fashion which has secured for him the contempt of the East. He deliberately boils it, and after drawing off the nutritious starch or gluten called "conjee," which forms the perquisite of his Portuguese or his Pariah cook, he is fain to fill himself with that which has become little more nutritious than the prodigal's husks. Great, indeed, is the invader's ignorance upon that point. Peace be to the manes of Lord Macaulay, but listen to and wonder at his eloquent words!—"The Sepoys came to Clive, not to complain of their scanty fare, but to propose that all the grain should be given to the Europeans, who required more nourishment than the natives of Asia. The thin gruel, they said, which was strained away from the rice would suffice for themselves. History contains no more touching instance of military fidelity, or of the influence of a commanding mind." Indians never fail to drink the "conjee." The Arab, on the other hand, mingles with his rice a sufficiency of ghee to prevent the extraction of the "thin gruel," and thus makes the grain as palatable and as nutritious as Nature intended it to be.)

—and dotted over with morsels of fowl, so boiled that they shredded like yarn under the teeth. This repast again concluded with a bowl of sweetened milk and other entremets, for which both hosts amply apologized; the house had lately been burned down, and honey had been used instead of sugar. The day concluded with prayers, with a seance in the veranda, and with drinking fresh milk out of gourds—a state of things which again demanded excuses. A multitude of "Washenzi" thronged into the house, especially during the afternoon, to gaze at the muzungu. I was formally presented to the Sultan Kafrira, a tall and wrinkled elder, celebrated for ready wits and spear. The sons of Ramji had often looked in at the door while preparations for feeding were going on, but they were not asked to sit down: the haughty host had provided them with a lean goat, in return for which they privily expressed an opinion that he was a "dog." Masud, boasting his intimacy with the Sultan Msimbira, whose subjects had plundered our portmanteau, offered on return to Unyanyembe his personal services in ransoming it. I accepted with joy; but the Shaykh Masud, as afterward proved, nearly "left his skin" in the undertaking.

The climate of Kíríra is called by the Arabs a medicine. They vaunt its virtues, which become apparent after the unhealthy air of Kazeh, and, after a delicious night spent in the cool barzah, I had no reason to question its reputation. I arose in the morning wonderfully refreshed, and Valentine, who had been prostrated with fever throughout the day, became another man. Yet the situation was apparently unpropitious; the Gombe Nullah, the main drain of this region, a line of stagnant pools, belted with almost impassable vegetation, lies hard by, and the background is an expanse of densest jungle.

Three short and eventless marches through thick jungle, with scattered clearings, led me, on the 30th of December, to the district of Msene, where the dense wild growth lately traversed suddenly opens out and discloses to the west a broad view of admirable fertility. Before entering the settlements, the caravan halted, as usual, to form up. We then progressed with the usual pomp and circumstance; the noise was terrific, and the streets, or rather the spaces between the houses, were lined with negroid spectators. I was led to the tembe of one Saadullah, a low-caste Msawahili, and there found my companion looking but poorly. Gaetano, his "boy," was so excited by the scene, that he fell down in a fit closely resembling epilepsy.

Msene, the chief bandari of Western Unyamwezi, may be called the capital of the coast Arabs and the Wasawahili, who, having a natural antipathy to their brethren of Oman, have abandoned to them Unyanyembe and its vicinity. Of late years, however, the Omani merchants, having been driven from the neighboring districts by sundry murders into Msene, may at times be met there to the number of four or five. The inhabitants are chiefly Wasumbwá, a sub-tribe of the Wanyamwezi race. There is, however, besides Arabs and Wasawahili, a large floating population of the pastoral clan called Watosi, and fugitives from Uhha. In 1858 the chief of Msene was the Sultan Masanza. Both he and Funza, his brother, were hospitable and friendly to travelers, especially to the Arabs, who but a few years ago beat off with their armed slaves a large plundering party of the ferocious Watuta. This chief has considerable power, and the heads of many criminals elevated upon poles in front of his several villages show that he rules with a firm hand. He is never approached by a subject without the clapping of hands and the kneeling which, in these lands, are the honors paid to royalty. He was a large-limbed, gaunt, and sinewy old man, dressed in a dirty subai or Arab check over a coating of rancid butter, with a broad brass disk, neatly arabesqued, round his neck, with a multitude of little pigtails where his head was not bald, and with some thirty sambo or flexible wire rings deforming, as if by elephantiasis, his ankles.

Like the generality of sultans, he despises beads as an article of decoration, preferring coils of brass or copper. He called several times at the house occupied by the expedition, and on more than one occasion brought with him a bevy of wives, whose deportment was, I regret to say, rather *naïve* than decorous.

Msene, like Unyanyembe, is not a town, but a mass of detached settlements, which are unconscious of a regular street. To the northward lie the villages of the sultan—Kwihángá and Yovu. These are surrounded with a strong stockade, a deep moat, and a thick milk-bush hedge, intended for defense. The interior is occupied by thatched circular huts, divided by open square-like spaces, and wynds and alleys are formed by milk-bush hedges and palisades. There are distinct places for the several wives, families, and slaves. The other settlements—Mbugání ("in the wild") and Mji Mpia ("new town"), the latter being the place affected by the Wasawahili—cluster in a circle, separated by short cross-roads, which after rain are ankle-deep in mud, from Chyámbo, the favorite locale of the coast Arabs. This settlement, which contained in 1858 nine large tembe and about 150 huts, boasts of an African attempt at a soko or bazar, a clear space between the houses, where, in fine weather, bullocks are daily slaughtered for food, and where grain, vegetables, and milk are exposed for sale. At Msene a fresh outfit of cloth, beads, and wire can be procured for a price somewhat higher than at Unyanyembe. The merchants have small stores of drugs and spices, and sometimes a few comforts, as coffee, tea, and sugar. The latter is generally made of granulated honey, and therefore called sukárí zá ásalí. The climate of Msene is damp, the neighboring hills and the thickly-vegetated country attracting an abundance of rain. It is exceedingly unhealthy, the result doubtless of filth in the villages and stagnant waters spread over the land. The Gombe Nullah, which runs through the district, about six hours' march from the settlements, discharges after rain its superfluous contents into the many lakelets, ponds, and swamps of the lowlands. Fertilized by a wet monsoon, whose floods from the middle of October to May are interrupted only by bursts of fervent heat, the fat, black soil, manured by the decay of centuries, reproduces abundantly any thing committed to it. Flowers bloom spontaneously over the flats, and trees put forth their richest raiment. Rice of the red quality —the white is rare and dear—grows with a density and a rapidity unknown in Eastern Unyamwezi. Holcus and millet, maize and manioc, are plentiful enough to be exported. Magnificent palmyras, bauhinias and sycamores, plantains and papaws, and a host of wild fruit-trees, especially the tamarind, which is extensively used, adorn the land. The other produtions are onions, sweet potatoes, and egg-plants, which are cultivated; turmeric, brought from the vicinity; tomatoes and bird-pepper, which grow wild; pulse, beans, pumpkins, watermelons, excellent mushrooms, and edible fungi. Milk, poultry, honey, and tobacco are cheap and plentiful. The currency at Msene in 1858—the date is specified, as the medium is liable to perpetual and sudden change, often causing severe losses to merchants, who, after laying in a large outfit of certain beads, find them suddenly unfashionable, and therefore useless—was the "pipe-stem," white and blue porcelain-beads, called sofi in the string, and individually msaro. Of these ten were sufficient to purchase a pound of beef. The other beads in demand were the sungomaji, or pigeon-egg, the red coral, the pink porcelain, and the shell decorations called kiwangwa. The cheaper varieties may be exchanged for grain and vegetables, but they will not purchase fowls, milk, and eggs. At this place only the palmyra is tapped for toddy; in other parts of East Africa the people are unable to climb it. The market at Msene is usually somewhat cheaper than that of Unyanyembe, but at times the prices become very exorbitant.

The industry of Msene is confined to manufacturing a few cotton cloths, coarse mats, clay pipe-heads, and ironmongery. As might be expected from the constitution of its society, Msene is a place of gross debauchery most grateful to the African mind. All, from sultan to slave, are intoxicated whenever the material is forthcoming, and the relations between the sexes are of the loosest description. The drum is never silent, and the dance fills up the spare intervals of carouse till exhausted nature can no more. The consequence is, that caravans invariably lose numbers by desertion when passing through Msene. Even household slaves, born and bred upon the coast, can not tear themselves from its Circean charms.

There was "cold comfort" at Msene, where I was delayed twelve days. The clay-roof of the tembe was weed-grown like a deserted grave, and in the foul patio or central court-yard only dirty puddles set in black mud met the eye. The weather was what only they can realize who are familiar with a "rainy monsoon." The temptations of the town rendered it almost impossible to keep a servant or a slave within doors; the sons of Ramji vigorously engaged themselves in trading, and Muinyi Wazira in a debauch, which ended in his dismissal. Gaetano had repeated epileptic fits, and Valentine rushed into the room half crying to show a white animalcule—in this country called funza—which had lately issued from his "buff." None of the half-caste Arabs, except I'd and Khalfan, sons of Muallim Salim, the youths who had spread evil reports concerning us in Ugogo and elsewhere, called or showed any civility, and the only Arab at that time resident at Msene was the old Salim bin Masud. I received several visits from the Sultan Masanza. His first greeting was, "White man, what pretty thing hast thou brought up from the shore for me?" He presented a bullock, and received in return several cloths and strings of beads, and he introduced to us a variety of princesses, who returned the salutes of the Baloch and others with a wild effusion. As Christmas-day had been spent in marching, I hailed the opportunity of celebrating the advent of the New Year. Said bin Salim, the jemadar, and several of the guard, were invited to an English dinner on a fair sirloin of beef, and a curious succedaneum for a plum-pudding, where neither flour nor currants were to be found. A characteristic trait manifested itself on this occasion. Among Arabs, the remnants of a feast must always be distributed to the servants and slaves of the guests;—a "brass knocker" would lose a man's reputation. Knowing this, I had ordered the Goanese to do in Rome as the Romans do; and being acquainted with their peculiarities, I paid them an unexpected visit, where they were found so absorbed in the task of hiding under pots and pans every better morsel from a crowd of hungry peerers that the interruption of a stick was deemed necessary.

At length, on the 10th of January, 1858, I left Msene with considerable difficulty. The kirangozi, or guide, who had promised to accompany me, had sent an incompetent substitute, his brother, a raw young lad, who had no power to collect porters. The sons of Ramji positively refused to lend their aid in strengthening the gang. One of Said bin Salim's children, the boy Faraj, had fled to Kazeh. The bull-headed Mabruki was brought back from flight only by the persuasion of his brother "Bombay," and even "Bombay," under the influence of some negroid Neæra, at the time of departure hid himself in his hut. All feared the march westward. A long strip of blue hill lying northward ever keeps the traveler in mind of the robber Watuta, and in places where the clans are mixed, all are equally hostile to strangers. Villages are less frequented and more meanly built, and caravans are not admitted beyond the faubourgs—the miserable huts outlying the fences. The land also is most unhealthy. After the rain, the rich dark loam becomes, like the black soils of Guzerat and the Deccan, a coat of viscid mire. Above is a canopy of cumulus and purple nimbus, that discharge their loads in copious day-long floods. The vegetation is excessive; and where there is no cultivation, a dense matting of coarse grass, laid by wind and water and decayed by mud, veils the earth, and from below rises a clammy chill, like the thaw-cold of England, the effect of extreme humidity. And, finally, the paths are mere lines, pitted with deep holes, and worn by cattle through the jungle.

After an hour and thirty minutes' march I entered Mb'hali, the normal cultivator's village in Western Unyamwezi—a heap of dwarf huts like inverted bird's-nests surrounding a central space, and surrounded by giant heaps of euphorbia or milk-bush. Tall grasses were growing almost up to the doorways, and about the settlement were scattered papaws and plaintains; the mwongo, with its damson-like fruit, the mtogwe or wood-apple-tree, and the tall solitary palmyra, whose high columnar stem, with its grace-ful central swell, was eminently attractive. We did not delay at Mb'hali, whence provisions had been exhausted by the markets of Msene. The 11th of January led us through a dense jungle upon a dead flat, succeeded by rolling ground bordered with low hills and covered with alternate bush and cultivation, to Sengati, another similar verdure-clad village of peasantry, where rice and other supplies were procurable. On the 12th of January, after passing over a dead flat of fields and of the rankest grass, we en-tered rolling ground in the vicinity of the Gombe Nullah, with scattered huts upon the rises, and villages built close to the dense vegetation bordering upon the stream. Sorora or Solola is one of the deadliest spots in Unyamwezi; we were delayed there, however, three long days, by the necessity of collecting a two months' supply of rice, which is rarely to be obtained farther west.

The non-appearance of the sons of Ramji rendered it necessary to take a strong step. I could ill afford the loss of twelve guns, but Kidogo and his men had become insufferable: moreover, they had openly boasted that they intended to prevent my embarking upon the "Sea of Ujiji." Despite, therefore, the persuasions of the jemadar and Said bin Salim, who looked as if they had heard their death-warrants, I summoned the slaves, who first condescend-ed to appear on the 13th of January—three days after my de-parture—informed them that the six months for which they were engaged and paid had expired, and that they had better return and transact their proprietor's business at Kazeh. They changed, it is true, their tone and manner, pathetically pleaded, as an excuse for their ill conduct, that they were slaves, and promised in future to be the most obedient of servants. But they had deceived me too often, and I feared that, if led forward, they might compro-mise the success of the exploration. They were therefore formal-ly dismissed, with a supply of cloth and beads sufficient to reach Kazeh, a letter to their master, and another paper to Snay bin Amir, authorizing him to frank them to their homes. Kidogo departed, declaring that he would carry off perforce, if necessary, the four donkey-drivers who had been engaged and paid for the journey to the "Sea of Ujiji" and back; as two of these men, Nasibu and Hassani, openly threatened to desert, they were at once put in irons and intrusted to the Baloch. They took oaths on the Koran, and, by strong swearing, persuaded Said bin Salim and their guard to obtain my permission for their release. I gave it unwillingly, and on the next march they "levanted," carrying off, as runaway slaves are wont to do, a knife, some cloth, and other necessaries belonging to Sangora, a brother donkey-driver. Sangora returning without leave to recover his goods was seized, tied up, and severely fustigated by the inexorable Kidogo for dar-ing to be retained while he himself was dismissed.

The kirangozi and Bombay having rejoined at Sorora, the expedition left it on the 16th of January. Traversing a fetid marsh, the road plunged into a forest, and crossed a sharp elbow of the Gombe Nullah, upon whose grassy and reedy banks lay a few dilapidated "baumrinden" canoes, showing that at times the bed becomes unfordable. Having passed that night at Ukungwe, and the next at Panda, dirty little villages where the main of the people's diet seemed to be mushrooms resembling ours, and a large white fungus growing over the grassy rises, on the 18th of January we entered Kajjanjeri.

Kajjanjeri appeared in the shape of a circle of round huts. Its climate is ever the terror of travelers: to judge from the mud and vegetation covering the floors, the cultivators of the fields around usually retire to another place during the rainy season. Here a formidable obstacle to progress presented itself. I had been suffering for some days : the miasmatic air of Sorora had sown the seeds of fresh illness. About 3 P.M. I was obliged to lay aside the ephemeris by an unusual sensation of nervous irritability, which was followed by a general shudder as in the cold paroxysm of fevers. Presently the extremities began to weigh and to burn as if exposed to a glowing fire, and a pair of jack-boots, the companions of many a day and night, became too tight and heavy to wear. At sunset the attack had reached its height. I saw yawning wide to receive me

> "Those dark gates across the wild
> That no man knows."

The whole body was palsied, powerless, motionless, and the limbs appeared to wither and die; the feet had lost all sensation, except a throbbing and tingling, as if pricked by a number of needle-points; the arms refused to be directed by will, and to the hands the touch of cloth and stone was the same. Gradually the attack seemed to spread upward till it compressed the ribs; there, however, it stopped short.

This at a distance of two months from medical aid, and with the principal labor of the expedition still in prospect! However, I was easily consoled. Hope, says the Arab, is woman, Despair is man. If one of us was lost, the other might survive to carry home the results of the exploration. I had undertaken the journey in the " nothing-like-leather" state of mind, with the resolve either to do or die. I had done my best, and now nothing appeared to remain for me but to die as well.

Said bin Salim, when sent for, declared by a "la haul!" the case beyond his skill; it was one of partial paralysis, brought on by malaria, with which the faculty in India are familiar. The Arab consulted a Msawahili fundi, or caravan-guide, who had joined us on the road, and this man declared that a similar accident had once occurred to himself and his little party in consequence of eating poisoned mushrooms. I tried the usual reme-

dies without effect, and the duration of the attack presently revealed what it was. The contraction of the muscles, which were
tightened like ligatures above and below the knees, and those
λύτα γούνατα, a pathological symptom which the old Greek loves
to specify, prevented me from walking to any distance for nearly
a year; the numbness of the hands and feet disappeared even
more slowly. The fundi, however, successfully predicted that I
should be able to move in ten days—on the tenth I again mounted my ass.

This unforeseen misfortune detained the caravan at Kajjanjeri
till porters could be procured for the hammock. On the 21st of
January four men were with difficulty persuaded to carry me over
the first march to Usagozi. This gang was afterward increased to
six men, who severally received six cloths for the journey to Ujiji;
they all "bolted" eight days after their engagement, and before
completing half the journey. These men were sturdier than the
former set of hammals, but, being related to the Sultan of Usagozi, they were even more boisterous, troublesome, and insolent.
One of them narrowly escaped a pistol bullet; he ceased, however, stabbing with his dagger at the slave Mabruki before the
extreme measure became necessary.

Usagozi was of old the capital province of Unyamwezi, and is
still one of its principal and most civilized divisions. Some authorities make Usagozi the western frontier of Unyamwezi, others
place the boundary at Mukozimo, a few miles to the westward;
it is certain, however, that beyond Usagozi the Wanyamwezi are
but part-proprietors of the soil. The country is laid out in alternate seams of grassy plains, dense jungle, and fertile field. The
soil is a dark vegetable humus, which bears luxuriant crops of
grain, vegetables, and tobacco; honey-logs hang upon every large
tree, cattle are sold to travelers, and the people are deterred by
the aspect of a dozen discolored skulls capping tall poles, planted
in a semicircle at the main entrance of each settlement, from doing violence to caravans. When I visited Usagozi it was governed by "Sultan Ryombo," an old chief "adorned with much
Christian courtesy." His subjects are Wakalaganza, the noble
tribe of the Wanyamwezi, mixed, however, with the Watosi, a fine-
looking race, markedly superior to their neighbors, but satisfied
with leaky, ragged, and filthy huts, and large but unfenced villages. The general dress of the Wakalaganza is bark-cloth,
stained a dull black.

We halted three days on the western extremity of the Usagozi
district, detained by another unpleasant phenomenon. My companion, whose blood had been impoverished, and whose system
had been reduced by many fevers, now began to suffer from "an
inflammation of a low type affecting the whole of the interior
tunic of the eyes, particularly the iris, the choroid coat, and the
retina;" he describes it as "an almost total blindness, rendering

every object enclouded as by a misty veil." The Goanese Valentine became similarly afflicted, almost on the same day; he complained of a "drop serene" in the shape of an inky blot—probably some of the black pigment of the iris deposited on the front of the lens—which completely excluded the light of day; yet the pupils contracted with regularity when covered with the hand, and as regularly dilated when it was removed. I suffered in a minor degree; for a few days webs of flitting muscæ obscured smaller objects and rendered distant vision impossible. My companion and servant, however, subsequently, at Ujiji, were tormented by inflammatory ophthalmia, which I escaped by the free use of "camel medicine."

Quitting Usagozi on the 26th of January, we marched, through grain fields, thick jungle-strips, and low grassy and muddy savannas, to Masenza, a large and comfortable village of stray Wagara or Wagala, an extensive tribe, limiting Unyamwezi on the S. and S.E., at the distance of about a week's march from the road. On the 27th of January, after traversing cultivation, thick jungles, and low muddy bottoms of tall grass, checkered with lofty tamarinds, we made the large, well-palisadoed villages of the Mukozimo district, inhabited by a mixture of Wanyamwezi, with Wagara from the S.E. and Wawende from the S.W. The headman of one of these inhospitable "kaya," or fenced hamlets, would not house "men who ride asses." The next station was Uganza, a populous settlement of Wawende, who admitted us into their faubourg, but refused to supply provisions. The 29th of January saw us at the populous and fertile clearing of Usenye, where the mixed races lying between the Land of the Moon eastward and Uvinza westward, give way to pure Wavinza, who are considered by travelers even more dangerous than their neighbors.

Beyond Usenye we traversed a deep jungle where still lingered remains of villages which had been plundered and burned down by the Wawende and the Watuta, whose hills rose clearly defined on the right hand. Having passed the night at Rukunda, or Lukundah, on the 31st of January we sighted the plain of the Malagarazi River. Northward of the road ran the stream, and the low level of the country adjoining it had converted the bottoms into permanent beds of soft, deep, and slippery mire. The rest of the march was the usual country—jungle, fields, and grasses—and, after a toilsome stretch, we unpacked at the settlement of Wanyika.

At Wanyika we were delayed for a day by the necessity of settling kuhonga, or black-mail, with the envoys of Mzogera. This great man, the principal sultan of Uvinza, is also the lord of the Malagarazi River. As he can enforce his claims by forbidding the ferrymen to assist strangers, he must be carefully humored. He received about forty cloths, white and blue, six kitindi or coil bracelets, and ten fundo (or 100 necklaces) of coral beads. It is equivalent in these lands to £50 in England. When all the items had been duly palavered over, we resumed our march on the 2d of February. The road, following an incline toward the valley of the river, in which bush and field alternated with shallow pools, black mud, and putrid grass, led to Unyanguruwwe, a miserable settlement, producing, however, millet in abundance, sweet potatoes, and the finest manioc. On the 3d of February we set out betimes. Spanning cultivation and undulating grassy ground, and passing over hill-opens to avoid the deeper swamps, we debouched from a jungle upon the river-plain, with the swift brown stream, then about fifty yards broad, swirling through the tall wet grasses of its banks on our right hand, hard by the road. Upon the off side a herd of elephants, forming Indian file, slowly broke through the reed fence in front of them: our purblind eyes mistook them for buffaloes. Northward lay an expanse of card-table plain, over which the stream, when in flood, debords to the distance of two miles, cutting it with deep creeks and inlets. The flat is bounded in the far offing by a sinuous line of faint blue hills, the haunts of the Watuta; while westward and southward rises the wall-shaped ridge, stony and wooded, which buttresses the left bank of the river for some days' journey down the stream. We found lodgings for the night in a little village, called, from its district, Ugaga. We obtained provisions, and we lost no time in opening the question of ferriage. The Sultan Mzogera had sold his permission to cross the river. The mutware, or mutwale, the lord of the ferry, now required payment for his canoes.

While delayed at Ugaga by the scabrous question of how much was to be extracted from me, I will enter into a few geographical details concerning the Malagarazi River.

The Malagarazi, corrupted by speculative geographers to Mdji-gidgi—the uneuphonious terminology of the "Mombas Mission Map"—to "Magrassie," and to "Magozi," has been wrongly represented to issue from the Sea of Ujiji. According to all travelers in these regions, it arises in the mountains of Urundi, at no great distance from the Kitangure, or River of Karagwah; but while the latter, springing from the upper counterslope, feeds the Nyanza or Northern Lake, the Malagarazi, rising in the lower slope of the equatorial range, trends to the southeast till it becomes entangled in the decline of the Great Central African Depression—the hydrographical basin first indicated, in his Address of 1852, by Sir Roderick I. Murchison, President of the Royal Geographical Society of London.* Thence it sweeps round the south-

* The following notice concerning a discovery which must ever be remembered as a triumph of geological hypothesis, was kindly forwarded to me by the discoverer:

"My speculations as to the whole African interior being a vast watery plateau-land of some elevation above the sea, but subtended on the east and west by much higher grounds, were based on the following data:

"The discovery in the central portion of the Cape colony, by Mr. Bain, of fossil remains in a lacustrine deposit of secondary age, and the well-known existence on

ern base of Urundi, and, deflected westward, it disembogues itself
into the Tanganyika.   Its mouth is in the land of Ukaranga, and
the long promontory behind which it discharges its waters is distinctly visible from Kawele, the head-quarters of caravans in Ujiji.
The Malagarazi is not navigable; as in primary and transition
countries generally, the bed is broken by rapids.   Beyond the ferry
the slope becomes more pronounced, branch and channel islets of
sand and verdure divide the stream, and, as every village near the
banks appears to possess one or more canoes, it is probably unfordable.   The main obstacle to crossing it on foot, over the broken
and shallower parts near the rock-bars, would be the number and
the daring of the crocodiles.

The Lord of the Ferry delayed us at Ugaga, by removing the
canoes, till he had extracted fourteen cloths and one coil bracelet
—half his original demand.   Moreover, for each trip the ferryman
received from one to five khete of beads, according to the bulk,
weight, and value of the freight.   He was as exorbitant when we
returned ; then he would not be satisfied with less than seven
cloths, a large jar of palm oil, and at least three hundred khete.
On the 4th of February we crossed to Mpete, the district on the
right or off bank of the stream.   After riding over the river-plain,
which at that time, when the rains had not supersaturated the soil,
was hard and dry, we came upon the "Ghaut," a muddy run or
clearing in the thicket of stiff grass which crossed the stream.
There we found a scene of confusion.   The Arabs of Kazeh had
described the canoes as fine barges, capable of accommodating fifty
or sixty passengers.   I was not, however, surprised to find wretched "baumrinden"—tree-rind—canoes, two strips of "myombo"
bark, from five to seven feet in length, sown together like a doubled wedge with fibres of the same material.   The keel was sharp,
the bow and stern were elevated, and the craft was prevented
from collapsing by cross-bars—rough sticks about eighteen inches
long, jammed ladder-wise between the sides.   When high and dry
upon the bank, they look not unlike castaway shoes of an unusual

the coast of loftier mountains, known to be of a Palæozoic or primary epoch, and cir-
cling round the younger deposits, being followed by the exploration of the Ngami
Lake, justified me in believing that Africa had been raised from beneath the ocean
at a very early geological period, and that ever since that time the same conditions
had prevailed.   I thence inferred that an interior net-work of lakes and rivers would
be found prolonged northward from Lake Ngami, though at that time no map was
known to me showing the existence of such central reservoirs.   Looking to the west
as well as to the east, I saw no possibility of explaining how the great rivers could
escape from the central plateau-lands and enter the ocean except through deep lateral gorges, formed at some ancient period of elevation, when the lateral chains were
subjected to transverse fractures.   Knowing that the Niger and the Zaire, or Congo,
escaped by such gorges on the west, I was confident that the same phenomenon must
occur upon the eastern coast, when properly examined.   This hypothesis, as sketched out in my 'Presidential Address' of 1852, was afterward received by Dr. Livingstone just as he was exploring the transverse gorges by which the Zambesi escapes to
the east, and the great traveler has publicly expressed the surprise he then felt that
his discovery should have been thus previously suggested."

size. We entered "gingerly." The craft is crankier than the Turkish caïque, and we held on "like grim death" to the gunwale with wetted fingers. The weight of two men causes these canoes to sink within three or four inches of water-level. An extra sheet of stiff bark was placed as a seat in the stern; but the interior was ankle-deep in water, and baling was necessary after each trip. The ferryman, standing amidships or in the fore, poled or paddled according to the depth of the stream. He managed skillfully enough, and on the return-march I had reason to admire the dexterity with which he threaded the narrow, grass-grown, and winding veins of deep water, that ramified from the main trunk over the swampy and rushy plains on both sides. Our riding-asses were thrown into the river, and they swam across without accident. Much to my surprise, none of the bales were lost or injured. The ferrymen showed decision in maintaining, and ingenuity in increasing, their claims. On the appearance of opposition they poled off to a distance, and squatted, quietly awaiting the effect of their decisive manœuvre. When the waters are out, it is not safe to step from the canoe before it arrives at its destination. The boatman will attempt to land his passenger upon some dry mound emerging from deep water, and will then demand a second fee for salvage.

A Village Interior in the Land of the Moon.

Utanta, or Loom.   Iwanza, or Public Houses.

CHAPTER XII.

THE GEOGRAPHY AND ETHNOLOGY OF UNYAMWEZI—THE FOURTH REGION.

THE fourth division is a hilly table-land, extending from the western skirts of the desert Mgunda Mk'hali, in E. long. 33° 57′, to the eastern banks of the Malagarazi River, in E. long. 31° 10′: it thus stretches diagonally over 155 rectilinear geographical miles. Bounded on the north by Usui and the Nyanza Lake, to the southeastward by Ugala, southward by Ukimbu, and south-westward by Uwende, it has a depth of from twenty-five to thirty marches. Native caravans, if lightly laden, can accomplish it in twenty-five days, including four halts. The maximum altitude observed by B. P. therm. was 4050 feet, the minimum 2850. This region contains the two great divisions of Unyamwezi and Uvinza.

The name of Unyamwezi was first heard by the Portuguese, according to Giovanni Botero, toward the end of the sixteenth century, or about 1589. Pigafetta, who, in 1591, systematized the discoveries of the earlier Portuguese, placed the empire of " Mone-mugi," or Munimigi, in a vast triangular area, whose limits were Monomotapa, Congo, and Abyssinia: from his pages it appears that the people of this central kingdom were closely connected by commerce with the towns on the eastern coast of Africa. According to Dapper, the Dutch historian (1671), whose work has

VIEW IN USAGARA.

been the great mine of information to subsequent writers upon Africa south of the equator, about sixty days' journey from the Atlantic is the kingdom of Monemugi, which others call "Nimea-maye," a name still retained under the corrupted form "Nimeaye" in our atlases. M. Malte-Brun, senior, mentioning Mounemugi, adds, "Ou, selon une autographe plus authentique, *Mou-nimougi.*" All the Portuguese authors call the people Monemugi, or Mono-emugi; Mr. Cooley prefers Monomoezi, which he derives from "Munha Munge," or "lord of the world," the title of a great Afri-can king in the interior, commemorated by the historian De Barros. Mr. Macqueen ("Geography of Central Africa"), who also gives Manmoise, declares that "Mueno-muge, Mueno-muize, Monomoise, and Uniamese" relate to the same place and people, comprehend-ing a large extent of country in the interior of Africa: he explains the word erroneously to mean the "great Moises or Movisas." The Rev. Mr. Erhardt asserts that for facility of pronunciation the coast merchants have turned the name "Wanamesi" into "Wania-mesi," which also leads his readers into error. The Rev. Mr. Liv-ingstone thus indorses the mistake of Messrs. Macqueen and Er-hardt: "The names Monomoizes, spelt also Monemuigis, and Monomuizes, and Monomotapistas, when applied to the tribes, are exactly the same as if we should call the Scotch the Lord Doug-lases. . . . Monomoizes was formed from Moiza or Muiza, the singular of the word Babisa or Aiza, the proper name of a large tribe to the north." In these sentences there is a confusion be-tween the lands of the Wanyamwezi, lying under the parallel of the Tanganyika Lake and the Wabisa (in the singular Mbísá, the Wavisa of the Rev. Mr. Rebmann), a well-known commercial tribe dwelling about the Maravi or Nyassa Lake, S.W. of Kilwa, whose name in times of old was corrupted by the Portuguese to Movizas or Movisas. Finally, M. Guillain, in a work already alluded to, states correctly the name of the people to be Oua-nyamouezi, but in designating the country "pays de Nyamouezi," he shows little knowledge of the Zangian dialects. M. V. A. Malte-Brun, junior ("Bulletin de Géographie," Paris, 1856, Part II., p. 295), correctly writes Wanyamwezi.

A name so discrepantly corrupted deserves some notice. Un-yamwezi is translated by Dr. Krapf and the Rev. Mr. Rebmann, "Possessions of the Moon." The initial U, the causal and loca-tive prefix, denotes the land, nya, of, and mwezi, articulated m'ezí with semi-elision of the w, means the moon. The people some-times pronounce their country name Unyamiezi, which would be a plural form, miezi signifying moons or months. The Arabs and the people of Zanzibar, for facility and rapidity of pronunciation, dispense with the initial dissyllable, and call the country and its race Mwezi. The correct designation of the inhabitants of Un-yamwezi is, therefore, Mnyamwezi in the singular, and Wanyam-wezi in the plural: Kinyamwezi is the adjectival form. It is not a little curious that the Greeks should have placed their τῆς σελήνης ὄρος—the mountain of the moon—and the Hindoos their Somo Giri (an expression probably translated from the former), in the vicinity of the African "Land of the Moon." It is impossible to investigate the antiquity of the vernacular term; all that can be discovered is, that nearly 350 years ago the Portuguese explorers of Western Africa heard the country designated by its present name.

There is the evidence of barbarous tradition for a belief in the existence of Unyamwezi as a great empire united under a single despot. The elders declare that their patriarchal ancestor became after death the first tree, and afforded shade to his children and descendants. According to the Arabs, the people still perform pilgrimage to a holy tree, and believe that the penalty of sacrilege in cutting off a twig would be visited by sudden and mysterious death. All agree in relating that during the olden time Unyamwezi was united under a single sovereign, whose tribe was the Wakalaganza, still inhabiting the western district, Usagozi. According to the people, whose greatest chronical measure is a masika, or rainy season, in the days of the grandfathers of their grandfathers the last of the Wanyamwezi emperors died. His children and nobles divided and dismembered his dominions, further partitions ensued, and finally the old empire fell into the hands of a rabble of petty chiefs. Their wild computation would point to an epoch of 150 years ago—a date by no means improbable.

These glimmerings of light thrown by African tradition illustrate the accounts given by the early Portuguese concerning the extent and the civilization of the Unyamwezi empire. Moreover, African travelers in the seventeenth century concur in asserting that, between 250 and 300 years ago, there was an outpouring of the barbarians from the heart of Æthiopia and from the shores of the Central Lake toward the eastern and southern coasts of the peninsula, a general waving and wandering of tribes, which caused great ethnological and geographical confusion, public demoralization, dismemberment of races, and change, confusion, and corruption of tongues. About this period it is supposed the kingdom of Mtándá, the first Kazembe, was established. The Kafirs of the Cape also date their migration from the northern regions to the banks of the Kei about a century and a half ago.

In these days Unyamwezi has returned to the political status of Eastern Africa in the time of the Periplus. It is broken up into petty divisions, each ruled by its own tyrant; his authority never extends beyond five marches; moreover, the minor chiefs of the different districts are virtually independent of their suzerains. One language is spoken throughout the Land of the Moon, but the dialectic differences are such that the tribes in the east with difficulty understand their brethren in the west. The principal provinces are Utakama to the extreme north, Usukuma on the south—in Kinyamwezi sukuma means the north, takama the south, kiya the east, and mwere the west—Unyanyembe in the centre, Ufyoma and Utumbara in the northwest, Unyangwira in the southeast, Usagozi and Usumbwá to the westward. The three normal divisions of the people are into Wanyamwezi, Wasukuma or northern, and Watakama or southern.

The general character of Unyamwezi is rolling ground, intersected with low conical and tabular hills, whose lines ramify in all directions. No mountain is found in the country. The superjacent stratum is clay, overlying the sandstone based upon various granites, which in some places crop out, picturesquely disposed in blocks and boulders, and huge domes and lumpy masses; iron-stone is met with at a depth varying from five to twelve feet, and at Kazeh, the Arab settlement in Unyanyembe, bits of coarse ore were found by digging not more than four feet in a chance spot. During the rains a coat of many-tinted greens conceals the soil; in the dry season the land is gray, lighted up by golden stubbles, and dotted with wind-distorted trees, shallow swamps of emerald grass, and wide sheets of dark mud. Dwarfed stumps and charred " black-jacks" deform the fields, which are sometimes ditched or hedged in, while a thin forest of parachute-shaped thorns diversifies the waves of rolling land and earth-hills spotted with sun-burnt stone. The reclaimed tracts and clearings are divided from one another by strips of primeval jungle varying from two to twelve miles in length. As in most parts of Eastern Africa, the country is dotted with "fairy mounts"—dwarf mounds, the ancient sites of trees now crumbled to dust, and the débris of insect architecture; they appear to be rich ground, as they are always diligently cultivated. The yield of the soil, according to the Arabs, averages sixty-fold, even in unfavorable seasons.

The Land of the Moon, which is the garden of Central Intertropical Africa, presents an aspect of peaceful rural beauty which soothes the eye like a medicine after the red glare of barren Ugogo, and the dark monotonous verdure of the western provinces. The inhabitants are comparatively numerous in the villages, which rise at short intervals above their impervious walls of the lustrous green milk-bush, with its coral-shaped arms, variegating the well-hoed plains; while in the pasture-lands frequent herds of many-colored cattle, plump, round-barreled, and high-humped, like the Indian breeds, and mingled flocks of goats and sheep dispersed over the landscape, suggest ideas of barbarous comfort and plenty. There are few scenes more soft and soothing than a view of Unyamwezi in the balmy evenings of spring. As the large yellow sun nears the horizon, a deep stillness falls upon earth: even the zephyr seems to lose the power of rustling the lightest leaf. The milky haze of midday disappears from the firmament, the flush of departing day mantles the distant features of scenery with a lovely rose-tint, and the twilight is an orange glow that burns like distant horizontal fires, passing upward through an imperceptibly graduated scale of colors—saffron, yellow, tender green, and the lightest azure—into the dark blue of the infinite space above. The charm of the hour seems to affect even the unimaginative Africans, as they sit in the central spaces of their villages, or, stretched under the forest-trees, gaze upon the glories around.

In Unyamwezi water generally lies upon the surface, during the rains, in broad shallow pools, which become favorite sites for rice-fields. These little ziwa and mbuga—ponds and marshes—vary from two to five feet below the level of the land; in the dry season they are betrayed from afar by a green line of livelier vegetation streaking the dead tawny plain. The Arabs seldom dig their wells deeper than six feet, and they complain of the want of "live-water" gushing from the rocky ground, as in their native Oman. The country contains few springs, and the surface of retentive clay prevents the moisture penetrating to the subsoil. The peculiarity of the produce is its decided chalybeate flavor. The versant of the country varies. The eastern third, falling to the southeast, discharges its surplus supplies through the Rwaha River into the Indian Ocean; in the centre, water seems to stagnate; and in the western third, the flow, turning to the north and northwest, is carried by the Gombe Nullah—a string of pools during the dry season, and a rapid and unfordable stream during the rains—into the great Malagarazi River, the principal eastern influent of the Tanganyika Lake. The levels of the country and the direction of the waters combine to prove that the great depression of Central Africa, alluded to in the preceding chapter, commences in the district of Kigwa, in Unyamwezi.

The climate of the island and coast of Zanzibar has, it must be remembered, double seasons, which are exceedingly confused and irregular. The lands of Unyamwezi and Uvinza, on the other hand, are as remarkable for simplicity of division. There eight seasons disturb the idea of year; here but two—a summer and a winter. Central Africa has, as the Spaniards say of the Philippine Isles,

" Seis mezes de polvo,
Seis mezes de lodo."

In 1857 the masika, or rains, commenced throughout Eastern Unyamwezi on the 14th of November. In the northern and western provinces the wet monsoon begins earlier and lasts longer. At Msene it precedes Unyanyembe about a month; in Ujiji, Karagwah, and Uganda, nearly two months. Thus the latter countries have a rainy season which lasts from the middle of September till the middle of May.

The moisture-bearing wind in this part of Africa is the fixed southeast trade, deflected, as in the great valley of the Mississippi and in the Island of Ceylon, into a periodical southwest monsoon. As will appear in these pages, the downfalls begin earlier in Central Africa than upon the eastern coast, and from the latter point they travel by slow degrees, with the northing sun, to the northeast, till they find a grave upon the rocky slopes of the Himalayas.

The rainy monsoon is here ushered in, accompanied, and terminated by storms of thunder and lightning, and occasional hailfalls. The blinding flashes of white, yellow, or rose color play over the firmament uninterruptedly for hours, during which no darkness is visible. In the lighter storms thirty and thirty-five flashes may be counted in a minute: so vivid is the glare that it discloses the finest shades of color, and appears followed by a thick and palpable gloom, such as would hang before a blind man's eyes, while a deafening roar simultaneously following the flash, seems to travel, as it were, to and fro overhead. Several claps sometimes sound almost at the same moment, and as if coming from different directions. The same storm will, after the most violent of its discharges, pass over, and be immediately followed by a second, showing the superabundance of electricity in the atmosphere. When hail is about to fall, a rushing noise is heard in the air, with sudden coolness and a strange darkness from the canopy of brownish purple clouds. The winds are exceedingly variable: perhaps they are most often from the east and northeast during summer, from the northwest and southwest in the rains; but they are answered from all quarters of the heavens, and the most violent storms sail up against the lower atmospheric currents. The Portuguese of the Mozambique attribute these terrible discharges of electricity to the quantity of mineral substances scattered about the country; but a steaming land like Eastern Africa wants, during the rains, no stronger battery. In the rainy season the sensation is that experienced during the equinoctial gales in the Mediterranean, where the sirocco diffuses every where discomfort and disease. The fall is not, as in Western India, a steady downpour, lasting sometimes two or three days without a break. In Central Africa rain seldom endures beyond twelve hours, and it often assumes for weeks an appearance of regularity, reoccurring at a certain time. Night is its normal season; the mornings are often wet, and the torrid midday is generally dry. As in Southern Africa, a considerable decrease of temperature is the consequence of long-continued rain. Westward of Unyanyembe, hail-storms during the rainy monsoon are frequent and violent; according to the Arabs, the stones sometimes rival pigeons' eggs in size. Throughout this monsoon the sun burns with sickly depressing rays, which make earth reek like a garment hung out to dry. Yet this is not considered the unhealthy period: the inundation is too deep, and evaporation is yet unable to extract sufficient poison from decay.

As in India and the southern regions of Africa, the deadly season follows the wet monsoon from the middle of May to the end of June. The kosi or southwest wind gives place to the kaskazi, or northeast, about April, a little later than at Zanzibar. The cold gales and the fervid suns then affect the outspread waters; the rivers, having swollen during the weeks of violent downfall that usher in the end of the rains, begin to shrink, and miry morasses and swamps of black vegetable mud line the low lands whose central depths are still under water. The winds, cooled by excessive evaporation and set in motion by the heat, howl over the country by night and day, dispersing through the population colds and catarrhs, agues and rheumatisms, dysenteries and deadly fevers. It must, however, be remarked, that many cases which in India and Sindh would be despaired of survived in Eastern Africa.

The hot season, or summer, lasting from the end of June till nearly the middle of November, forms the complement of the year. The air now becomes healthy and temperate; the cold, raw winds rarely blow, and the people recover from their transition diseases. At long intervals, during these months, but a few grateful and refreshing showers, accompanied by low thunderings, cool the air and give life to the earth. These phenomena are expected after the change of the moon, and not, as in Zanzibar, during her last quarter. The Arabs declare that here, as in the island, rain sometimes falls from a clear sky—a phenomenon not unknown to African travelers. The drought affects the country severely, a curious exception to the rule in the zone of perpetual rain; and after August whirlwinds of dust become frequent. At this time the climate is most agreeable to the senses; even in the hottest nights a blanket is welcome, especially about dawn, and it is possible to dine at 3 or 4 P.M., when in India the exertion would be impracticable. During the day a ring-cloud, or a screen of vapor, almost invariably tempers the solar rays; at night a halo, or a corona, generally encircles the moon. The clouds are chiefly cumulus, cumulo-stratus, and nimbus; the sky is often overcast with large white masses floating, apparently without motion, upon the milky haze, and in the serenest weather a few threads are seen penciled upon the expanse above. Sunrise is seldom thoroughly clear, and, when so, the clouds, sublimed in other regions and brought up by the rising winds, begin to gather in the forenoon. They are melted, as it were, by the fervent heat of the sun between noon and 3 P.M., at which time also the breezes fall light. Thick mists collect about sunset, and by night the skies are seldom free from clouds. The want of heat to dilate the atmosphere at this season, and the light-absorbing vegetation which clothes the land, causes a peculiar dimness in the galaxy and " Magellan's Clouds." The twilight also is short, and the zodiacal light is not observed. The suffocating sensation of the tropics is unknown, and at noon in the month of September—the midsummer of this region—the thermometer, defended from the wind, in a single-fold Arab tent, never exceeded 113° Fahr. Except during the rains, the dews are not heavy, as in Zanzibar, in the alluvial valleys, and in Usagara and Ujiji: the people do not fear exposure to them, though, as in parts of France, they consider dew-wetted grass unwholesome for cattle. The Arabs stand bathing in the occasional torrents of rain without the least apprehension. The temperature varies too little for the European constitution, which requires a winter. The people, however, scarcely care to clothe themselves. The flies and mosquitoes—those pests of most African countries—are here a minor annoyance.

The principal cause of disease during the summer of Unyamwezi is the east wind, which, refrigerated by the damp alluvial valleys of the first region and the tree-clad peaks and swampy plains of Usagara, sweeps the country, like the tramontanas of Italy, with a freezing cold in the midst of an atmosphere properly tepid. These unnatural combinations of extremes, causing sudden chills when the skin perspires, bring on inevitable disease; strangers often suffer severely, and the influenza is as much feared in Unyamwezi as in England. The east wind is even more dangerous in the hut than in the field: draughts from the four quarters play upon the patient, making one side of the body tremble with cold, while the other, defended by the wall or heated by the fire, burns with fever-glow. The gales are most violent immediately after the cessation of the rains; about the beginning of August they become warmer and fall light. At this time frequent whirlwinds sweep from the sun-parched land clouds of a fine and penetrating clay dust, and slight shocks of earthquakes are by no means uncommon. Three were observed by the expedition—at noon on the 14th of June, 1858; on the morning of the 13th of June; and at 5 P.M. on the 22d of November, 1858. The motion, though mild, was distinctly perceptible; unfortunately, means of ascertaining the direction were wanted. The people of the country call this phenomenon "tetemeka," or the trembling; and the Arabs remember a shock of a serious nature which took place at Unyanyembe in the hot season of 1852. After September, though the land is parched with drought, the trees begin to put forth their leaves; it is the coupling season of beasts, and the period of nidification and incubation for birds. The gradual lowering of the temperature, caused by the southern declination of the sun, acts like the genial warmth of an English spring. As all sudden changes from siccity to humidity are prejudicial to man, there is invariably severe disease at the end of the summer, when the rains set in.

Travelers from Unyamwezi homeward returned often represent that country to be the healthiest in Eastern and Central Africa: they quote, as a proof, the keenness of their appetites and the quantity of food which they consume. The older residents, however, modify their opinions: they declare that digestion does not wait upon appetite; and that, as in Egypt, Mazanderan, Malabar, and other hot-damp countries, no man long retains rude health. The sequelæ of their maladies are always severe; few care to use remedies, deeming them inefficacious against morbific influences to them unknown; convalescence is protracted, painful, and uncertain, and at length they are compelled to lead the lives of confirmed invalids. The gifts of the climate, lassitude and indolence, according to them, predispose to corpulence; and the regular warmth induces baldness, and thins the beard, thus assimilating strangers in body as in mind to the aborigines. They are unanimous in quoting a curious effect of climate, which they attribute to a corruption of the "humors and juices of the body." Men who, after a lengthened sojourn in these regions, return to Oman, throw away the surplus provisions brought from the African coast, burn their clothes and bedding, and for the first two or three months eschew society; a peculiar effluvium rendering them, it is said, offensive to the finer olfactories of their compatriots.

The mukunguru of Unyamwezi is perhaps the severest seasoning-fever in this part of Africa. It is a bilious remittent, which normally lasts three days: it wonderfully reduces the patient in that short period, and in severe cases the quotidian is followed by a long attack of a tertian type. The consequences are severe and lasting, even in men of the strongest nervous diathesis; burning and painful eyes, hot palms and soles, a recurrence of shivering and flushing fits, with the extremities now icy cold, then painfully hot and swollen, indigestion, insomnolency, cutaneous eruptions and fever-sores, languor, dejection, and all the inconveniences resulting from torpidity of liver, or from an inordinate secretion of bile, betray the poison deep-lurking in the system. In some cases this fever works speedily; some even, becoming at once delirious, die on the first or the second day, and there is invariably an exacerbation of symptoms before the bilious remittent passes away.

The fauna of Unyamwezi are similar to those described in Usagara and Ugogo. In the jungles quadrumana are numerous; lions and leopards, cynhyenas and wildcats, haunt the forests; the elephant and the rhinoceros, the giraffe and the Cape buffalo, the zebra, the quagga (?), and the koodoo wander over the plains; and the hippopotamus and crocodile are found in every large pool. The nyanyi or cynocephalus in the jungles of Usukuma attains the size of a greyhound; according to the people, there are three varieties of color—red, black, and yellow. They are the terror of the neighboring districts: women never dare to approach their haunts; they set the leopard at defiance, and when in a large body, they do not, it is said, fear the lion. The Colobus guereza, or tippet monkey, the "polume" of Dr. Livingstone (ch. xvi.), here called mbega, is admired on account of its polished black skin and snowy-white mane. It is a cleanly animal, ever occupied in polishing its beautiful garb, which, according to the Arabs, it tears to pieces when wounded, lest the hunter should profit by it. The mbega lives in trees, seldom descending, and feeds upon the fruit and the young leaves. The Arabs speak of wild dogs in the vicinity of Unyanyembe, describing them as being about eighteen inches in height, with rufous-black and shaggy coats, and long thick tails; they are gregarious, running in packs of from 20 to 200; they attack indiscriminately man and the largest animals, and their only cry is a howl. About the time of our autumn the pools are visited by various kinds of aquatic birds, widgeon, plump little teal, fine snipe, curlew, and crane; the ardea, or white "paddy-bird" of India, and the "lily-trotter" (Parra Africana), are scattered over the country; and sometimes, though rarely, the chenalopex or common Egyptian goose and the gorgeous-crowned crane (Balearica pavonina), the latter a favorite dish with the Arabs, appear. In several parts of Unyamwezi, especially in the north, there is a large and well-flavored species of black-backed goose (Sakidornis melanota): the common wild duck of England was not seen. Several specimens of the buceros, the secretary-bird (Serpentarius reptilivorus), and large vultures, probably the condor of the Cape, were observed in Unyamwezi; the people do not molest them, holding the flesh to be carrion. The Cuculus indicator, called in Kisawahili "tongoe," is common; but, its honey being mostly hived, it does not attract attention. Grillivori, and a species of thrush about the size of common larks, with sulphur-yellow patches under the eyes and two naked black striæ beneath the throat, are here migratory birds; they do good service to the agriculturist against the locust. A variety of the loxia or gross-bill constructs nests sometimes in bunches hanging from the lower branches of the trees. The mtiko, a kind of water-wagtail (Motacilla), ventures into the huts with the audacity of a London sparrow, and the Africans have a prejudice against killing it. Swallows and martins of various kinds, some peculiarly graceful and slender, may be seen migrating at the approach of winter in regular traveling order: of these, one variety resembles the English bird. The Africans declare that a single species of hirundo, probably the sand-martin, builds in the precipitous earth-banks of the nullahs: their nests were not seen, however, as in Southern Africa, under the eaves of houses. There are a few ostriches, hawks, ravens, plovers, nightjars (Caprimulgidæ), red and blue jays of brilliant plume, muscicapæ, blackcaps or mock nightingales (Motacilla atrocapilla?), passerines of various kinds, hoopoes, bulbuls, wrens, larks, and bats. We saw but few poisonous animals. Besides the dendrophis, the only ophidia killed in the country were snakes, with slate-colored backs and silver bellies, resembling the harmless "mas" or "hanash" of Somaliland, the Psammophis sibilaris (L.); C. moniliger Lacépède—according to Mr. Blyth ("Journal of the

As. Soc. of Bengal," vol. xxiv., p. 306), who declares it to be not venomous—they abound in the houses and destroy the rats. The people speak of a yellow and brown-coated snake, eight feet long by five or six inches in diameter; it is probably a boa or rock-snake. Chúrá or frogs are numerous in the swamps, where the frog-concerts resemble those of the New World; and in the regions about the Tanganyika Lake a large variety makes night hideous with its croakings. Of the ranæ there are many species. The largest is probably the "matmalelo" of S. Africa; it is eaten by the Wagogo and other tribes. A smaller kind is of dark color, and with long legs, which enable it to hop great distances. A third is of a dirty yellow, with brownish speckles. There is also a little green tree-frog, which adheres to the broad and almost perpendicular leaves of the thicker grasses. The leech is found in the lakes and rivers of the interior, as well as in Zanzibar and on both coasts of Africa; according to the Arabs, they are of two kinds, large and small. The people neither take precautions against them when drinking at the streams, as the Somal do, nor are they aware of any officinal use for the animals; moreover, it is impossible to persuade a Msawahili to collect them; they are of p'hepo or fiendish nature, and never fail to haunt and harm their captor. Jongo, or huge millepedes, some attaining a length of half a foot, with shiny black bodies and red feet, are found in the fields and forests, especially during the rains: covered with epizoa, these animals present a disgusting appearance, and they seem, to judge from their spoils, to die off during the hot weather. At certain seasons there is a great variety of the papilionaceous family in the vicinity of waters where libellulæ or dragon-flies also abound. The country is visited at irregular times by flights of locusts, here called nzige. In spring the plants are covered in parts with the p'hánzí, a large pink and green variety, and the destructive species depicted and described by Salt: they rise from the earth like a glowing rose-colored cloud, and die off about the beginning of the rains. The black leather-like variety, called by the Arabs "Satan's ass," is not uncommon: it is eaten by the Africans, as are many other edibles upon which strangers look with disgust. The Arabs describe a fly which infests the forest-patches of Unyamwezi: it is about the size of a small wasp, and is so fatal that cattle attacked by it are at once killed and eaten before they become carrion from its venomous effects. In parts the country is dotted with ant-hills, which, when old, become hard as sandstone: they are generally built by the termite under some shady tree, which prevents too rapid drying, and apparently the people have not learned, like their brethren in South Africa, to use them as ovens.

From Tura westward to Unyanyembe, the central district of Unyamwezi, caravans usually number seven marches, making a total of 60 rectilinear geographical miles. As far as Kigwa there is but one line of route; from that point traveling parties diverge far and wide, like ships making their different courses.

The races requiring notice in this region are two, the Wakimbu and the Wanyamwezi.

The Wakimbu, who are immigrants into Unyamwezi, claim a noble origin, and derive themselves from the broad lands running south of Unyanyembe as far westward as K'hokoro. About twenty masika, wet monsoons, or years ago, according to themselves, in company with their neighbors, the Wakonongo and the Wamia, they left Nguru, Usanga, and Usenga, in consequence of the repeated attacks of the Warori, and migrated to Kipiri, the district lying south of Tura; they have now extended into Mgunda Mk'hali and Unyanyembe, where they hold the land by permission of the Wanyamwezi. In these regions there are few obstacles to immigrants. They visit the sultan, make a small present, obtain permission to settle, and name the village after their own chief; but the original proprietors still maintain their rights to the soil. The Wakimbu build firmly-stockaded villages, tend cattle, and cultivate sorghum and maize, millet and pulse, cucumbers and watermelons. Apparently they are poor, being generally clad in skins. They barter slaves and ivory in small quantities to the merchants, and some travel to the coast. They are considered treacherous by their neighbors, and Mapokera, the Sultan of Tura, is, according to the Arabs, prone to commit "*avanies.*" They are known by a number of small lines formed by raising the skin with a needle, and opening it by points laterally between the hair of the temples and the eyebrows. In appearance they are dark and uncomely; their arms are bows and arrows, spears, and knives stuck in the leathern waistbelt; some wear necklaces of curiously-plaited straw, others a strip of white cowskin bound around the brow—a truly savage and African decoration. Their language differs from Kinyamwezi.

The Wanyamwezi tribe, the proprietors of the soil, is the typical race in this portion of Central Africa: its comparative industry and commercial activity have secured to it a superiority over the other kindred races.

The aspect of the Wanyamwezi is alone sufficient to disprove the existence of very elevated lands in this part of the African interior. They are usually of a dark sepia-brown, rarely colored like diluted Indian ink, as are the Wahiao and slave races to the south, with negroid features markedly less Semitic than the people of the eastern coast. The effluvium from their skins, especially after exercise or excitement, marks their connection with the negro. The hair curls crisply, but it grows to the length of four or five inches before it splits; it is usually twisted into many little ringlets or hanks; it hangs down like a fringe to the neck, and is combed off the forehead after the manner of the ancient Egyptians and the modern Hottentots. The beard is thin and short; there are no whiskers, and the mustache—when not plucked out—is scant and straggling. Most of the men, and almost all the women, remove the eyelashes, and pilar hair rarely appears to grow. The normal figure of the race is tall and stout, and the women are remarkable for the elongation of the mammary organs. Few have small waists, and the only lean men in the land are the youths, the sick, and the famished. This race is said to be long-lived, and it is not deficient in bodily strength and savage courage. The clan-mark is a double line of little cuts, like the marks of cupping, made by a friend with a knife or razor, along the temporal fossæ, from the external edges of the eyebrows to the middle of the cheeks or to the lower jaws. Sometimes a third line, or a band of three small lines, is drawn down the forehead to the bridge of the nose. The men prefer a black, charcoal being the substance generally used, the women a blue color, and the latter sometimes ornament their faces with little perpendicular scars below the eyes. They do not file the teeth into a saw-shape, as seen among the southern races, but they generally form an inner triangular or wedge-shaped aperture by chipping away the internal corners of the two front incisors like the Damaras, and the women extract the lower central teeth. Both sexes enlarge the lobes of the ears. In many parts of the country skins are more commonly worn than cloth, except by the sultans and the wealthier classes. The women wear the long tobe of the coast, tightly wrapped round either above or more commonly below the breast; the poorer classes veil the bosom with a square or softened skin; the remainder of the dress is a kilt or short petticoat of the same material, extending from waist to knee. Maidens never cover the breast, and children are rarely clothed; the infant, as usual in East Africa, is carried in a skin fastened by thongs behind the parent's back. The favorite ornaments are beads, of which the red coral, the pink, and the "pigeon-eggs" made at Nuremberg are preferred. From the neck depend strings of beads, with kiwangwa, disks of shell brought from the coast, and crescents of hippopotamus teeth country made, and when the beard is long it is strung with red and parti-colored beads. Brass and copper bangles or massive rings are worn upon the wrists, the forearm bears the ponderous kitindi or coil bracelet, and the arm above the elbow is sometimes decorated with circlets of ivory, or with a razor in an ivory étui; the middle is girt with a coil of wire twisted round a rope of hair or fibre, and the ankles are covered with small iron bells and the rings of thin brass, copper, or iron wire, called sambo. When traveling, a goat's horn, used as a bugle, is secured over the right shoulder by a lanyard and allowed to hang by the left side: in the house many wear a smaller article of the same kind, hollowed inside and containing various articles intended as charms, and consecrated by the mganga or medicine-man. The arms are slender assegais, with the shoulders of the blade rounded off: they are delivered, as by the Somal, with the thumb and fore-finger after a preliminary of vibratory motion, but the people want the force and the dexterity of the Kafirs. Some have large spears for thrusting, and men rarely leave the hut without their bows and arrows, the latter unpoisoned, but curiously and cruelly barbed. They make also the long double-edged knives called sime, and different complications of rungu or knob-kerries, some of them armed with an iron lance-head upon the wooden bulge. Dwarf battle-axes are also seen, but not so frequently as among the western races on the Tanganyika Lake. The shield in Unyamwezi resembles that of Usagara; it is, however, rarely used.

There are but few ceremonies among the Wanyamwezi. A woman about to become a mother retires from the hut to the jungle, and after a few hours returns with a child wrapped in goat-skin upon her back, and probably carrying a load of firewood on her head. The medical treatment of the Arabs with salt and various astringents for forty days is here unknown. Twins are not common as among the Kafir race, and one of the two is invariably put to death; the universal custom among these tribes is for the mother to wrap a gourd or calabash in skins, to place it to sleep with, and to feed it like, the survivor. If the wife die without issue, the widower claims from her parents the sum paid to them upon marriage; if she leave a child, the property is preserved for it. When the father can afford it, a birth is celebrated by copious libations of pombe. Children are suckled till the end of the second year. Their only education is in the use of the bow and arrow; after the fourth summer the boy begins to learn archery with diminutive weapons, which are gradually increased in strength. Names are given without ceremony, and, as in the countries to the eastward, many of the heathens have been called after their Arab visitors. Circumcision is not practiced by this people. The children in Unyamwezi generally are the property not of the uncle but of the father, who can sell or slay them without blame; in Usukuma or the northern lands, however, succession and inheritance are claimed by the nephews or sisters' sons. The Wanyamwezi have adopted the curious practice of leaving property to their illegitimate children by slave-girls or concubines, to the exclusion of their issue by wives; they justify it by the fact of the former requiring their assistance more than the latter, who have friends and relatives to aid them. As soon as the boy can walk he tends the flocks; after the age of ten he drives the cattle to pasture, and, considering himself independent of his father, he plants a tobacco-plot and aspires to build a hut for himself. There is not a boy "which can not earn his own meat."

Another peculiarity of the Wanyamwezi is the position of the wahárá or unmarried girls. Until puberty they live in the father's house; after that period the spinsters of the village, who usually number from seven to a dozen, assemble together and build for themselves at a distance from their homes a hut where they can receive their friends without parental interference. There is but one limit to community in single life; if the mhárá or "maiden" be likely to become a mother, her "young man" must marry her under pain of mulct; and if she die in childbirth, her father demands from her lover a large fine for having taken away his daughter's life. Marriage takes place when the youth can afford to pay the price for a wife: it varies, according to circumstances, from one to ten cows. The wife is so far the property of the husband that he can claim damages from the adulterer; he may not, however, sell her, except when in difficulties. The marriage is celebrated with the usual carouse, and the bridegroom takes up his quarters in his wife's home, not under her father's roof. Polygamy is the rule with the wealthy. There is little community of interests, and apparently a lack of family affection in these tribes. The husband, when returning from the coast laden with cloth, will refuse a single shukkah to his wife, and the wife, succeeding to an inheritance, will abandon her husband to starvation. The man takes charge of the cattle, goats, sheep, and poultry; the woman has power over the grain and the vegetables, and each must grow tobacco, having little hope of borrowing from the other. Widows left with houses, cattle, and fields, usually spend their substance in supporting lovers, who are expected occasionally to make presents in return. Hence, no coast slave in Wanyamwezi is ever known to keep a shukkah of cloth.

The usual way of disposing of a corpse in former times was to carry it out on the head and to throw it into some jungle strip, where the fisi or cynhyena abounds—a custom which accounts for the absence of grave-yards. The Wanyamwezi at first objected to the Arabs publicly burying their dead in their fields, for fear of pollution; they would assemble in crowds to close the way against a funeral party. The merchants, however, persevered till they succeeded in establishing a right. When a Mnyamwezi dies in a strange country, and his comrades take the trouble to inter him, they turn the face of the corpse toward the mother's village—a proceeding which shows more sentiment than might be expected from them. The body is buried standing, or tightly bound in a heap, or placed in a sitting position, with the arms clasping the knees: if the deceased be a great man, a sheep and a bullock are slaughtered for a funeral feast, the skin is placed over his face, and the hide is bound to his back. When a sultan dies in a foreign land his body is buried upon the spot, and his head, or what remains of it, is carried back for sepulture to his own country. The chiefs of Unyamwezi generally are interred by a large assemblage of their subjects with cruel rites. A deep pit is sunk, with a kind of vault or recess projecting from it: in this the corpse, clothed with skin and hide, and holding a bow in the right hand, is placed sitting, with a pot of pombe, upon a dwarf stool, while sometimes one, but more generally three female slaves, one on each side and the third in front, are buried alive to preserve their lord from the horrors of solitude. A copious libation of pombe upon the heaped-up earth concludes the ceremony. According to the Arabs, the Wasukuma inter all their sultans in a jungle north of Unyanyembe, and the neighboring peasants deposit before seed-time small offerings of grain at the mzimo or fetiss-house which marks the spot.

The habitations of the Eastern Wanyamwezi are the tembe, which in the west give way to the circular African hut; among the poorer sub-tribes the dwelling is a mere stack of straw. The best tembe have large projecting eaves supported by uprights: cleanliness, however, can never be expected in them. Having no limestone, the people ornament the inner and outer walls with long lines of ovals formed by pressing the finger-tips, after dipping them into ashes and water for whitewash, and into red clay or black mud for variety of color. With this primitive material they sometimes attempt rude imitations of nature—human beings and serpents. In some parts the cross appears, but the people apparently ignore it as a symbol. Rude carving is also attempted upon the massive posts at the entrances of villages, but the figures, though to appearance idolatrous, are never worshiped. The household furniture of the tembe differs little from that described in the villages generally. The large sloping kitanda, or bedstead of peeled tree-branch, supported by forked sticks, and provided with a bedding of mat and cowhide, occupies the greater part of the outer room. The triangle of clay cones forming the hearth are generally placed for light near the wall-side opposite the front door; and the rest of the supellex consists of large stationary bark corn-bins, of gourds and bandboxes slung from the roof, earthen-pots of black clay, huge ladles, pipes, grass mats, grinding-stones, and arms hung to a trimmed and branchy tree-trunk planted upright in a corner. The rooms are divided by party-walls, which, except when separating families, seldom reach to the ceiling. The fireplace acts as lamp by night, and the door is the only chimney.

The characteristic of the Mnyamwezi village is the "iwánzá"—a convenience resulting probably from the instinct of the sexes, who prefer not to mingle, and for the greater freedom of life and manners. Of these buildings there are two in every settlement, generally built at opposite sides, fronting the normal mrimba-tree, which sheds its filmy shade over the public court-yard. That of the women, being a species of harem, was not visited; as travelers and strangers are always admitted into the male iwánzá, it is more readily described. This public house is a large hut, somewhat more substantial than those adjoining, often smeared with smooth clay, and decorated here and there with broad columns of the ovals before described, and the prints of palms dipped in

ashes and placed flat like the hands in ancient Egyptian buildings. The roof is generally a flying thatch raised a foot above
the walls—an excellent plan for ventilation in these regions.
Outside, the iwánzá is defended against the incursions of cattle by
roughly-barked trunks of trees resting upon stout uprights: in
this space men sit, converse, and smoke. The two doorways are
protected by rude charms suspended from the lintel, hares' tails,
zebras' manes, goats' horns, and other articles of prophylactic
virtue. Inside, half the depth is appropriated to the ubiri, a
huge standing bed-frame, formed, like the planked benches of a
civilized guard-room, by sleepers lying upon horizontal cross-
bars: these are supported by forked trunks about two feet long,
planted firmly in the ground. The floor is of tamped earth.
The furniture of the iwánzá consists of a hearth and grinding-
stone; spears, sticks, arrows, and shillalahs are stuck to smoke in
the dingy rafter ceiling, or are laid upon hooks of crooked wood
depending from the sooty cross-beams: the corners are occupied
by bellows, elephant-spears, and similar articles. In this "public"
the villagers spend their days, and often, even though married, their
nights, gambling, eating, drinking pombe, smoking bhang and tobacco, chatting, and sleeping like a litter of puppies destitute of
clothing, and using one another's backs, breasts, and stomachs as
pillows. The iwánzá appears almost peculiar to Unyamwezi.

In Unyamwezi the sexes do not eat together: even the boys
would disdain to be seen sitting at meat with their mothers. The
men feed either in their cottages or, more generally, in the iwánzá:
they make, when they can, two meals during the day—in the
morning, a breakfast, which is often omitted for economy, and a
dinner about 3 P.M. During the interim they chew tobacco, and,
that failing, indulge in a quid of clay. It probably contains
some animal matter. But the chief reason for using it is apparently the necessity to barbarians of whiling away the time when
not sleeping by exercising their jaws. They prefer the "sweet
earth," that is to say, the clay of ant-hills: the Arabs have tried
it without other effects but nausea. The custom, however, is not
uncommon upon both coasts of Africa: it takes, in fact, the place
of the mastic of Chios, the kat of Yemen, the betel and toasted
grains of India and the farther East, and the ashes of the Somali
country. The Wanyamwezi, and indeed the East African tribes
generally, have some curious food prejudices. Before their closer
intercourse with the Arabs they used to keep poultry, but, like
the Gallas and the Somal, who look upon the fowl as a kind of
vulture, they would not eat it: even in the present day they
avoid eggs. Some will devour animals that have died of disease,
and carrion—the flesh of lions and leopards, elephants and rhinoceroses, asses, wild-cats and rats, beetles and white ants; others
refuse to touch mutton or clean water-fowl, declaring that it is not
their custom. The prejudice has not, however, been reduced to

a system, as among the tribes of Southern Africa. They rarely taste meat except upon the march, where the prospect of gain excites them to an unusual indulgence: when a bullock is killed, they either jerk the meat, or dry it upon a dwarf platform of sticks raised above a slow and smoky fire, after which it will keep for some days. The usual food is the ugali or porridge of boiled flour: they find, however, a variety of edible herbs in the jungle, and during the season they luxuriate upon honey and sour milk. No Mnyamwezi, however, will own to repletion unless he has "sat upon pombe"—in other words, has drunk to intoxication; and the chiefs pride themselves upon living entirely upon beef and stimulants.

The Wanyamwezi have won for themselves a reputation by their commercial industry. Encouraged by the merchants, they are the only professional porters of East Africa; and even among them the Wakalaganza, Wasumbwa, and Wasukuma are the only tribes who regularly visit the coast in this capacity. They are now no longer "honest and civil to strangers"—semi-civilization has hitherto tended to degradation. They seem to have learned but little by their intercourse with the Arabs. Commerce with them is still in its infancy. They have no idea of credit, although in Karagwah and the northern kingdoms payment may be delayed for a period of two years. They can not, like some of their neighbors, bargain: a man names the article which he requires, and if it be not forthcoming he will take no other. The porters, who linger upon the coast or in the Island of Zanzibar, either cut grass for asses, carry stones and mortar to the town, for which they receive a daily hire of from two to eight pice, or they obtain from the larger landholders permission to reclaim and cultivate a plot of ground for vegetables and manioc. They have little of the literature, songs, and tales common among barbarians; and though they occasionally indulge in speeches, they do not, like many kindred tribes, cultivate eloquence. On the march they beguile themselves with chanting for hours together half a dozen words eternally repeated. Their language is copious but confused, and they are immoderately fond of simple and meaningless syllables used as interjections. Their industry is confined to weaving coarse cloths of unbleached cotton, neatly-woven baskets, wooden milk-bowls, saddle-bags for their asses, and arms. They rear asses, and load them lightly when traveling to the coast, but they have not yet learned to ride them. Though they carefully fence and ditch their fields, they have never invented a plow, confining themselves to ridging the land with the laborious hoe. They rarely sell one another, nor do they much encourage the desertion of slaves. The wild bondsman, when running away, is sometimes appropriated by his captor, but a muwallid or domestic slave is always restored after a month or two. The Arabs prefer to purchase men sold under suspicion of magic;

they rarely flee, fearing lest their countrymen should put them
to death.

As has been said, the government of Unyamwezi is conducted
by a multitude of petty chiefs. The ruling classes are thus called: mtemi or mwáme is the chief or sultan, mgáwe (in the plural
wágáwe) the principal councilor, and mánácháro, or mnyapara
(plural wányápárá), the elder. The ryots or subjects, on the other
hand, are collectively styled wasengi. The most powerful chiefs
are Fundikira of Unyanyembe, Masánga of Msene, and Kafrira
of Kiríra. The dignity of mtemi is hereditary. He has power
of life and death over his subjects, and he seldom condescends to
any but mortal punishment. His revenue is composed of additions to his private property by presents from travelers, confisca-
tion of effects in cases of felony or magic, by the sale of subjects,
and by treasure trove. Even if a man kill his own slave, the
slave's effects lapse to the ruler. The villagers must give up all
ivory found in the jungles, although the hunters are allowed to
retain the tusks of the slaughtered animals.

A few brief remarks concerning Fundikira, the chief of Unyamwezi in 1858, may serve to illustrate the condition of the ruling
class in Unyamwezi. This chief was traveling toward the coast
as a porter in a caravan when he heard of his father's death: he
at once stacked his load and prepared to return home and rule.
The rest of the gang, before allowing him to depart, taunted him
severely, exclaiming, partly in jest, partly in earnest, "Ah! now
thou art still our comrade, but presently thou wilt torture and
slay, fine and flog us." Fundikira proceeding to his native country, inherited, as is the custom, all his father's property and widows;
he fixed himself at Ititenya, presently numbered ten wives, who
have borne him only three children, built 300 houses for his slaves
and dependents, and owned 2000 head of cattle. He lived in some
state, declining to call upon strangers, and, though not demanding, still obtaining large presents. Becoming obese by age and
good living, he fell ill in the autumn of 1858, and, as usual, his relations were suspected of compassing his end by uchawi, or black
magic. In these regions the death of one man causes many. The
mganga was summoned to apply the usual ordeal. After admin-
istering a mystic drug, he broke the neck of a fowl, and splitting it
into two lengths inspected the interior. If blackness or blemish
appear about the wings, it denotes the treachery of children, relations and kinsmen; the back-bone convicts the mother and grandmother; the tail shows that the criminal is the wife, the thighs
the concubines, and the injured shanks or feet the other slaves.
Having fixed upon the class of the criminals, they are collected
together by the mganga, who, after similarly dosing a second hen,
throws her up into the air above the heads of the crowd and sin-
gles out the person upon whom she alights. Confession is extorted by tying the thumb backward till it touches the wrist, or by

some equally barbarous mode of question. The consequence of condemnation is certain and immediate death ; the mode is chosen by the mganga. Some are speared, others are beheaded or "ammazati"—clubbed : a common way is to bind the cranium between two stiff pieces of wood which are gradually tightened by cords till the brain bursts out from the sutures. For women they practice a peculiarly horrible kind of impalement. These atrocities continue until the chief recovers or dies : at the commencement of his attack, in one household eighteen souls, male and female, had been destroyed; should his illness be protracted, scores will precede him to the grave, for the mchawi or magician must surely die.

The Wanyamwezi will generally sell their criminals and captives; when want drives, they part with their wives, their children, and even their parents. For economy, they import their serviles from Ujiji and the adjoining regions; from the people lying toward the southeast angle of the Tanganyika Lake, as the Wafipa, the Wapoka, and the Wagara; and from the Nyanza races, and the northern kingdoms of Karagwah, Uganda, and Unyoro.

My Tembe near the Tanganyika.

CHAPTER XIII.

AT LENGTH WE SIGHT THE LAKE TANGANYIKA, THE "SEA OF UJIJI."

THE route before us lay through a howling wilderness, once populous and fertile, but now laid waste by the fierce Watuta. Snay bin Amir had warned me that it would be our greatest trial of patience. The march began badly: Mpete, the district on the right bank of the Malagarazi River, is highly malarious, and the musquitoes feasted right royally upon our life, even during the daytime. We bivouacked under a shady tree within sight of the ferry, not knowing that upon the woody eminences above the valley there are usually fine kraals of dry grass and of mkora or myombo-bark. During the rainy monsoon the best encampments in these regions are made of tree-sheets; two parallel rings are cut in the bole at a distance of six to seven feet; a perpendicular slit then connects them, the bark is easily stripped off, and the trunk, after having been left for a time to season, is filled for use.

On the 5th of February we set out betimes across a route traversing for a short distance swampy ground along the river-side. It then stretched over jungly and wooded hill-spires, with steep rough ascents and descents, divided from neighboring elevations by slippery mire-runs. Exposed to the full break of the rainy monsoon, and the frequent outbursts of fiery sun, I could not but admire the marvelous fertility of the soil; an impervious luxuriance of vegetation veils the lowlands, clothes the hill-sides, and caps their rounded summits. After marching five hours and twenty minutes, we found a large kraal in the district of Kinawani: the encamping-ground—partially cleared of the thick, fetid, and putrescent vegetation around—hugs the right bank of the Malagarazi, and faces the village of Sultan Mzogera on the southern or opposite side. A small store of provisions—grain and sweet potatoes—was purchased from the villagers of Kinawani, who flocked across the stream to trade. They were, however, fanciful in their requirements: beads, especially the coral porcelain, iron wire, salt, and meat. The heaviness of this march caused two of the hammals engaged at Usagozi to levant, and the remaining four to strike work. It was therefore again necessary to mount ass—ten days after an attack of "paraplegia!"

We left Kinawani on the next morning, and striking away from the river we crossed rugged and rolling ground, divided by deep swamps of mire and grass. To the southward ran the stream, rushing violently down a rocky bed, with tall trees lining its banks. Sailing before the morning east wind, a huge mass of nimbus occupied the sky, and presently discharged itself in an unusually heavy downfall: during the afternoon the breeze veered as usual to the west, and the hot sunshine was for once enjoyable. After a weary trudge of five hours and twenty minutes, we entered a large and comfortable kraal, situated near a reach where the swift and turbid river foamed over a discontinuous ledge of rock between avenues of dense and tangled jungle. No provisions were procurable at this place; man appeared to have become extinct.

The 7th of February led us over broken ground, encumbered by forest, and cut by swamps, with higher levels on the right hand, till we again fell into the marshes and fields of the river-valley. The district on the other side of the river, called Jambe-ho, is one of the most flourishing in Uvinza; its villages of small bird-nest huts, and its carefully hoed fields of grain and sweet potato, affected the eye, after the dreary monotony of a jungle-march, like the glimmer of a light at the end of a night-march, or the discovery of land at the conclusion of a long sea-voyage. The village ferry was instantly put into requisition, and the chief, Ruwere, after receiving as his "dash" eight cloths, allowed us to purchase provisions. At that season, however, the harvest of grain and sweet potatoes had not been got in, and for their single old hen the people demanded an exorbitant price. We hastened, despite all difficulties, to escape from this place of pestilence, which clouds of musquitoes rendered as uncomfortable as it was dangerous.

The next day ushered in our departure with drizzling rain, which drenched the slippery paths of red clay; the asses, wild with wind and weather, exposed us to accidents in a country of deep ravines and rugged boulders. Presently diverging from the Malagarazi, we passed over the brow of a low tree-clad hill above the junction of the Rusugi River, and followed the left bank of this tributary as far as its nearer ford. The Rusugi, which drains the northern highlands into the Malagarazi, was then about 100 yards in width : the bottom is a red ochrish soil, the strong stream, divided in the centre by a long low strip of sand and gravel, flowed at that time breast-deep, and its banks—as usual with rivers in these lands—deeply cut by narrow water-courses, rendered traveling unusually toilsome. At the Rusugi Ford the road separates into a northern and a southern branch, a hill-spur forming the line of demarcation. The northern strikes off to the district of Parugerero on the left bank, where a shallower ford is found : the place in question is a settlement of Wavinza, containing from forty to fifty bee-hive huts, tenanted by salt-diggers. The principal pan is sunk in the vicinity of the river, the saline produce, after being boiled down in the huts, is piled up, and hand-made into little cones. The pan affords tripartite revenue to three sultans, and it constitutes the principal wealth of the Wavinza : the salt here sold for one shukkah per masula, or half-load, and far superior to the bitter, nitrous produce of Ugogo, finds its way throughout the heart of Africa, supplying the lands adjoining both the Tanganyika and the Nyanza lakes.

We followed the southern line which crosses the Rusugi River at the branch islet. Fords are always picturesque. The men seemed to enjoy the washing; their numbers protected them from the crocodiles, which fled from their shouting and splashing; and they even ventured into deep water, where swimming was necessary. We crossed, as usual, on a "unicorn" of negroids, the upper part of the body supported by two men, and the feet resting upon the shoulders of a third—a posture somewhat similar to that affected by gentlemen who find themselves unable to pull off their own boots. Then remounting, we ascended the grassy rise on the right of the stream, struggled, slipped, and slided over a muddy swamp, climbed up a rocky and bushy ridge, and found ourselves ensconced in a ragged and comfortless kraal upon the western slopes, within sight of some deserted salt-pans below. As evening drew in, it became apparent that the Goanese Gaetano, the five Wak'hutu porters, and Sarmalla, a donkey-driving son of Ramji, had remained behind, in company with several loads, the tent, two bags of cloths, my companion's elephant-gun, my bedding and that of my servant. It was certain that with this provision in the vicinity of Parugerero they would not starve, and the porters positively refused to halt an hour more than necessary. I found it therefore compulsory to advance. On the 11th of February three "children" of Said bin Salim consented, as usual, for a consideration, to return and to bring up the laggers, and about a week afterward they entered Ujiji without accident. The five Wak'hutu porters, probably from the persuasions of Muinyi Wazira, had, although sworn to fidelity with the strongest oaths, carried into execution a long-organized plan of desertion. Gaetano refused to march on the day of our separation because he was feverish, and he expected a riding-ass to be sent back for him. He brought up our goods safely, but blankets, towels, and many articles of clothing belonging to his companion, had disappeared. This difficulty was, of course, attributed to the Wak'hutu porters; probably the missing things had been sold for food by the Goanese and the son of Ramji: I could not therefore complain of the excuse.

From the Msawahili fundi—fattore, manciple or steward—of a small caravan belonging to an Arab merchant, Hamid bin Sulayyam, I purchased for thirty-five cloths, about thrice its value, a little single-fold tent of thin American domestics, through which sun and rain penetrated with equal facility. Like the cloth-houses of the Arab travelers generally, it was gable-shaped, six or seven feet high, about eight feet long by four broad, and so light that, with its bamboo-poles and its pegs, it scarcely formed a load for a man. On the 9th of February we descended from the ridge upon which the kraal was placed, and traversed a deep swamp of black mud, dotted in the more elevated parts with old salt-pans and pits, where broken pottery and blackened lumps of clay still showed traces of human handiwork. Beyond this lowland, the track, striking off from the river-valley and turning to the right, entered toilsome ground. We crossed deep and rocky ravines, with luxuriant vegetation above, and with rivulets at the bottom trickling toward the Malagarazi, by scrambling down and swarming up the roughest steps of rock, boulder, and knotted tree-root. Beyond these difficulties lay woody and stony hills, whose steep and slippery inclines were divided by half a dozen waters, all more or less troublesome to cross. The porters, who were in a place of famine, insisted upon pushing on to the utmost of their strength: after six hours' march, I persuaded them to halt in the bush upon a rocky hill, where the neighboring descent supplied water. The fundi visited the valley of the Rusugi River, and finding a herd of the mbogo, or bos caffer, brought home a welcome addition to our well-nigh exhausted rations.

The 10th of February saw us crossing the normal sequence of jungly and stony "neat's-tongues," divided by deep and grassy swamps, which, stagnant in the dry weather, drain after rains the northern country to the Malagarazi River. We passed over by a felled tree-trunk an unfordable rivulet, hemmed in by a dense and fetid thicket; and the asses, summarily pitched down the muddy bank into the water, swam across and wriggled up the slimy off-side like cats. Thence a foul swamp of black mire led to the Ruguvu or Luguvu River, the western boundary of Uvinza and the eastern frontier of Ukaranga. This stream, which can be forded during the dry season, had spread out after the rains over its borders of grassy plain; we were delayed till the next morning in a miserable camping-ground, a mud bank thinly veiled with vegetation, in order to bridge it with branching trees. An unusual downfall during the night might have caused serious consequences; provisions had now disappeared, moreover the porters considered the place dangerous.

The 10th of February began with the passage of the Ruguvu River, where again our goods and chattels were fated to be thoroughly sopped. I obtained a few corn-cobs from a passing caravan of Wanyamwezi, and charged them with meat and messages for the party left behind. A desert march, similar to the stage last traveled, led us to the Unguwwe or Uvungwe River, a shallow, muddy stream, girt in, as usual, by dense vegetation; and we found a fine large kraal on its left bank. After a cold and rainy night, we resumed our march by fording the Unguwwe. Then came the weary toil of fighting through tiger and spear grass, with reeds, rushes, a variety of ferns before unseen, and other lush and lusty growths, clothing a succession of rolling hills, monotonous swellings, where the descent was ever a reflection of the ascent. The paths were broken, slippery, and pitted with deep holes; along their sides, where the ground lay exposed to view, a conglomerate of ferruginous red clay—suggesting a resemblance to the superficies of Londa, as described by Dr. Livingstone—took the place of the granites and sandstones of the eastern countries, and the sinking of the land toward the lake became palpable. In the jungle were extensive clumps of bamboo and ratan; the former small, the latter of poor quality; the bauhinia, or blackwood, and the salsaparilla-vine abounded; wild grapes of diminutive size and of the austerest flavor appeared for the first time upon the sunny hill-sides which Bacchus ever loves, and in the lower swamps plantains grew almost wild. In parts the surface was broken into small deep hollows, from which sprang pyramidal masses of the hugest trees. Though no sign of man here met the eye, scattered fields and plantations showed that villages must be somewhere near. Sweet water was found in narrow courses of black mud, which sorely tried the sinews of laden man and beast. Long after noon we saw the caravan halted by fatigue upon a slope beyond a weary swamp: a violent storm was brewing, and while half the sky was purple-black with nimbus, the sun shone stingingly through the clear portion of the empyrean. But these small troubles were lightly borne; already, in the far distance, appeared walls of sky-blue cliff with gilded summits, which were as a beacon to the distressed mariner.

On the 13th of February we resumed our travel through screens of lofty grass, which thinned out into a straggling forest. After about an hour's march, as we entered a small savanna, I saw the fundi before alluded to running forward and changing the direction of the caravan. Without supposing that he had taken upon himself this responsibility, I followed him. Presently he breasted a steep and stony hill, sparsely clad with thorny trees: it was the death of my companion's riding-ass. Arrived with toil—for our fagged beasts now refused to proceed—we halted for a few minutes upon the summit. "What is that streak of light which lies below?" I inquired of Seedy Bombay. "I am of opinion," quoth Bombay, "that that is *the* water." I gazed in dismay; the remains of my blindness, the veil of trees, and a broad ray of sunshine illuminating but one reach of the lake, had shrunk its fair proportions. Somewhat prematurely I began to lament my folly in having risked life and lost health for so poor a prize, to curse Arab exaggeration, and to propose an immediate return, with the view of exploring the Nyanza, or Northern Lake. Advancing, however, a few yards, the whole scene suddenly burst upon my view, filling me with admiration, wonder, and delight. It gave local habitation to the poet's fancy:

> " Tremolavano i rai del Sol nascente
> Sovra l' onde del mar purpuree e d' oro,
> E in veste di zaffiro il ciel ridente
> Specchiar parea le sue bellezze in loro.
> D' Africa i venti fieri e d' Oriente,
> Sovra il letto del mar, prendean ristoro,
> E co' sospiri suoi soavi e lieti
> Col Zeffiro increspava il lembo a Teti."

Nothing, in sooth, could be more picturesque than this first view of the Tanganyika Lake, as it lay in the lap of the mountains, basking in the gorgeous tropical sunshine. Below and beyond a short foreground of rugged and precipitous hill-fold, down which the footpath zigzags painfully, a narrow strip of emerald green, never sere and marvelously fertile, shelves toward a ribbon of glistening yellow sand, here bordered by sedgy rushes, there cleanly and clearly cut by the breaking wavelets. Farther in front stretch the waters, an expanse of the lightest and softest blue, in breadth varying from thirty to thirty-five miles, and sprinkled by the crisp east wind with tiny crescents of snowy foam. The background in front is a high and broken wall of steel-colored mountain, here flecked and capped with pearly mist, there standing sharply penciled against the azure air; its yawning chasms, marked by a deeper plum-color, fall toward dwarf hills of mound-like proportions, which apparently dip their feet in the wave. To the south, and opposite the long low point behind which the Malagarazi River discharges the red loam suspended in its violent stream, lie the bluff headlands and capes of Uguhha, and, as the eye dilates, it falls upon a cluster of outlying islets speckling a sea-horizon. Villages, cultivated lands, the frequent canoes of the fishermen on the waters, and on a nearer approach the murmurs of the waves breaking upon the shore, give a something of variety, of movement, of life to the landscape, which, like all the fairest prospects in these regions, wants but a little of the neatness and finish of art—mosques and kiosks, palaces and villas, gardens and orchards—contrasting with the profuse lavishness and magnificence of nature, and diversifying the unbroken *coup d'œil* of excessive vegetation, to rival, if not to excel, the most admired scenery of the classic regions. The riant shores of this vast crevasse appeared doubly beautiful to me after the silent and spectral mangrove-creeks on the East African sea-board, and the melancholy, monotonous experience of desert and jungle scenery, tawny rock and sun-parched plain or rank herbage and flats of black mire. Truly it was a revel for soul and sight. Forgetting toils, dangers, and the doubtfulness of return, I felt willing to endure double what I had endured; and all the party seemed to join with me in joy. My purblind companion found nothing to grumble at except the "mist and glare before his eyes." Said bin Salim looked exulting—*he* had procured for me this pleasure—the monoculous jemadar grinned his congratulations, and even the surly Baloch made civil salams.

Arrived at Ukaranga, I was disappointed to find there a few miserable grass-huts—used as a temporary shelter by caravans passing to and from the islets fringing the opposite coast—that clustered round a single tembe, then occupied by its proprietor, Hamid bin Sulayyam, an Arab trader. Presently the motive of the rascally fundi in misleading the caravan, which, by the advice of Snay bin Amir, I had directed to march upon the Kawele district in Ujiji, leaked out. The roadstead of Ukaranga is separated from part of Kawele by the line of the Ruche River, which empties itself into a deep hollow bay, whose chord, extending from N.W. to S.E., is five or six miles in length. The strip of shelving plain between the trough-like hills and the lake is raised but a few feet above water-level. Converted by the passage of a hundred drains from the highlands into a sheet of sloppy and slippery mire, breast-deep in select places, it supports with difficulty a few hundred inhabitants: drenched with violent rain-storms and clammy dews, it is rife in fevers, and it is feared by travelers on account of its hippopotami and crocodiles. In the dryest season the land-road is barely practicable; during and after the wet monsoon the lake affords the only means of passage, and the port of Ukaranga contains not a single native canoe. The fundi, therefore, wisely determined that I should spend beads for rations and lodgings among his companions, and be heavily mulcted for a boat by them. Moreover, he instantly sent word to Mnya Mtaza, the principal headman of Ukaranga, who, as usual with the lakist chiefs, lives in the hills at some distance from the water, to come instanter for his honga, or black-mail, as, no fresh fish being procurable, the Wazungu were about to depart. The latter manœuvre, however, was frustrated by my securing a conveyance for the morrow. It was an open solid-built Arab craft, capable of con-

taining thirty to thirty-five men; it belonged to an absent merchant, Said bin Usman; it was in point of size the second on the
Tanganyika, and being too large for paddling, its crew rowed instead of scooping up the water like the natives. The slaves, who
had named four khete of coral beads as the price of a bit of sun-
dried "baccalà," and five as the hire of a foul hovel for one night,
demanded four cloths—at least the price of the boat—for conveying the party to Kawele, a three hours' trip. I gave them ten
cloths and two coil-bracelets, or somewhat more than the market
value of the whole equipage—a fact which I effectually used as
an *argumentum ad verecundiam.*

At eight A.M., on the 14th of February, we began coasting
along the eastern shore of the lake in a northwesterly direction,
toward the Kawele district, in the land of Ujiji. The view was
exceedingly beautiful:

> " . . . the flat sea shone like yellow gold
> Fused in the sun,"

and the picturesque and varied forms of the mountains, rising
above and dipping into the lake, were clad in purplish blue, set
off by the rosy tints of morning. Yet, more and more, as we approached our destination, I wondered at the absence of all those
features which prelude a popular settlement. Passing the low,
muddy, and grass-grown mouth of the Ruche River, I could de-
scry on the banks nothing but a few scattered hovels of miserable
construction, surrounded by fields of sorghum and sugar-cane, and
shaded by dense groves of the dwarf, bright-green plantain, and
the tall, sombre elæis, or Guinea-palm. By the Arabs I had been
taught to expect a town, a ghaut, a port, and a bazar, excelling in
size that of Zanzibar, and I had old, preconceived ideas concerning "die Stadt Ujiji," whose sire was the "Mombas Mission Map."
Presently mammoth and behemoth shrank timidly from exposure,
and a few hollowed logs, the monoxyles of the fishermen, the
wood-cutters, and the market-people, either cut the water singly,
or stood in crowds drawn up on the patches of yellow sand. About
11 A.M. the craft was poled through a hole in a thick welting of
coarse reedy grass and flaggy aquatic plants to a level landing-
place of flat shingle, where the water shoaled off rapidly. Such
was the ghaut or disembarkation quay of the great Ujiji.

Around the ghaut a few scattered huts, in the humblest bee-
hive shape, represented the port-town. Advancing some hundred yards through a din of shouts and screams, tom-toms, and
trumpets, which defies description, and mobbed by a swarm of
black beings, whose eyes seemed about to start from their heads
with surprise, I passed a relic of Arab civilization, the "bazar."
It is a plot of higher ground, cleared of grass, and flanked by a
crooked tree; there, between 10 A.M. and 3 P.M.—weather permitting—a mass of standing and squatting negroes buy and sell,
barter and exchange, offer and chaffer with a hubbub heard for

miles, and there a spear or dagger thrust brings on, by no means unfrequently, a skirmishing faction-fight. The articles exposed for sale are sometimes goats, sheep, and poultry, generally fish, vegetables, and a few fruits, plantains, and melons; palm-wine is a staple commodity, and occasionally an ivory or a slave is hawked about: those industriously disposed employ themselves during the intervals of bargaining in spinning a coarse yarn with the rudest spindle, or in picking the cotton, which is placed in little baskets on the ground. I was led to a ruinous tembe, built by an Arab merchant, Hamid bin Salim, who had allowed it to be tenanted by ticks and slaves. Situated, however, half a mile from, and backed by, the little village of Kawele, whose mushroom-huts barely protruded their summits above the dense vegetation, and placed at a similar distance from the water in front, it had the double advantage of proximity to provisions, and of a view which at first was highly enjoyable. The Tanganyika is ever seen to advantage from its shores: upon its surface the sight wearies with the unvarying tintage—all shining greens and hazy blues—while continuous parallels of lofty hills, like the sides of a huge trough, close the prospect and suggest the idea of confinement.

And now, lodged with comparative comfort in the cool tembe, I will indulge in a few geographical and ethnological reminiscences of the country lately traversed.

The fifth region includes the alluvial valley of the Malagarazi River, which subtends the lowest spires of the highlands of Karagwah and Urundi, the western prolongation of the chain which has obtained, probably from African tradition, the name of "Lunar Mountains." In length, it extends from the Malagarazi Ferry, in E. long. 31° 10', to the Tanganyika Lake, in E. long. 30° 1'. Its breadth, from S. lat. 3° 14', the supposed northern limit of Urundi, to S. lat. 5° 2', the parallel of Ukaranga, is a distance of 108 rectilinear geographical miles. Native caravans pass from the Malagarazi to Ujiji in eight days, usually without halting till arrived within a stone's throw of their destination. To a region of such various elevations it would be difficult to assign an average of altitude; the heights observed by thermometer never exceeded 1850 feet.

This country contains in due order, from east to west, the lands of Uvinza, Ubuha, and Ujiji; on the northern edge is Uhha, and on the southwestern extremity Ukaranga. The general features are those of the alluvial valleys of the Kingani and the Mgeta Rivers. The soil in the vicinity of the Malagarazi is a rich brown or black loam, rank with vegetable decay. This strip along the stream varies in breadth from one to five miles; on the right bank it is mostly desert, but not sterile; on the left it is an expanse of luxuriant cultivation. The northern boundary is a jagged line of hill-spurs of primitive formation, rough with stones and yawning with ravines; in many places the projections assume the form of green "dog's-tails," or "neat's-tongues," projecting, like lumpy ridges, into the card-table-like level of the river-land southward. Each mound or spur is crowned with a tufty clump, principally of bauhinias and mimosas, and often a lone, spreading, and towering tree, a borassus or a calabash, ornamenting the extreme point, forms a landmark for the caravan. The sides of these hills, composed of hornblende and gneissic rock, quartzite, quartz-grit, and ferruginous gritstone, are steep, rugged, and thickly wooded, and one slope generally reflects the other—if muddy, muddy; and if stony, stony. Each "hanger," or wave of ground, is divided from its neighbor by a soft sedgy valley, bisected by a net-work of stagnant pools. Here and there are nullahs, with high stiff earth-banks, for the passage of rain-torrents. The grass stands in lofty screens, and the path leads over a matted mass of laid stalks, which cover so closely the thick mud that loaded asses do not sink; this vegetation is burned down during the hot season, and a few showers bring up an emerald crop of young blades, sprouting phœnix-like from the ashes of the dead. The southern boundary of the valley is more regular; in the eastern parts is an almost tabular wall of rock, covered even to the crest with shrub and tree.

As is proved by the regular course of the Malagarazi River, the westward decline of the country is gentle; along the road, however, the two marches nearest to the Tanganyika Lake appear to sink more rapidly than those preceding them. The main drain receives from the northern hill-spurs a multitude of tributaries, which convey their surplus moisture into the great central reservoir.

Under the influence of the two great productive powers in nature—heat and moisture—the wondrous fertility of the soil, which puts forth, where uncleared, a rank jungle of nauseous odor, renders the climate dangerous. The rains divide the year into two unequal portions of eight and four months, namely, the wet monsoon, which commences with violence in September and ends in May, and the dry hot weather which rounds off the year. The showers fall, as in Zanzibar, uncontinuously, with breaks varying from a few hours to several days; unlike those of Zanzibar, they are generally accompanied by violent discharges of electricity. Lightning from the north, especially at night, is considered a sign of approaching foul weather. It would be vain to seek in these regions of Central Africa the kaskazi and kosi, or regular northeast and southwest monsoons, those local modifications of the trade-winds which may be traced in regular progress from the centre of Equatorial Africa to the Himalayas. The atmospheric currents deflected from the Atlantic Ocean by the coast-radiation and the arid and barren regions of Southern Africa are changed in hydrometric condition, and are compelled by the chilly and tree-clad heights of the Tanganyika Lake, and the low, cold, and river-bearing plains lying to the westward, to part with the moisture which they have collected in the broad belt of extreme humidity lying between the Ngami Lake and the equator. When the land has become super-saturated, the cold, wet wind, driving cold masses, surcharged with electricity, sets continually eastward, to restore the equilibrium in lands still reeking with the torrid blaze, and where the atmosphere has been rarefied by from four to six months of burning suns. At Msene, in Western Unyamwezi, the rains break about October; thence the wet monsoon, resuming its eastward course, crosses the Land of the Moon, and, traveling by slow stages, arrives at the coast in early April. Following the northing sun, and deflected to the northeast by the rarefied atmosphere from the hot, dry surface of the Eastern Horn of Africa, the rains reach Western India in June, and exhaust themselves in frequent and copious downfalls upon the southern versant of the Himalayas. The gradual refrigeration of the ground, with the southing of the sun, produces in turn the inverse process, namely, the northeast monsoon. About the Tanganyika, however, all is variable. The large body of water in the central reservoir preserves its equability of temperature, while the alternations of chilly cold and potent heat, in the high and broken lands around it, cause extreme irregularity in the direction of the currents. During the rains of 1858 the prevalent winds were constantly changing: in the mornings there was almost regularly a cool north breeze drawn by the water from the heights of Urundi; in the course of the day it veered round toward the south. The most violent storms came up from the southeast and the southwest, and as often against as with the gale. The long and rigorous wet monsoon, broken only by a few scattered days of heat, renders the climate exceedingly damp, and it is succeeded by a burst of sunshine which dries the grass to stubble in a few days. Despite these extremes, the climate of Ujiji has the reputation of being comparatively healthy; it owes this probably to the refreshing coolness of the nights and mornings. The mukunguru, or seasoning-fever of this region, is not feared by strangers so much as that of Unyanyembe, yet no one expects to escape it. It is a low bilious and aguish type, lasting from three to four days: during the attack perspiration is induced with difficulty, and it often recurs at regular times once a month.

From the Malagarazi Ferry many lines traverse the desert on the right or northern bank of the river, which is preferred to the southern, whence the Wavinza exclude travelers. Before entering this region caravans generally combine, so as to present a formidable front to possible foes. The trunk-road, called Jambeho, the most southerly of the northern routes, has been described in detail.

The district of Ukaranga extends from the Ruguvu or the Unguwwe River to the waters of the lake: on the south it is bounded by the region of Ut'hongwe, and on the north by the Ruche River. This small and sluggish stream, when near the mouth, is about forty yards in breadth; and, being unfordable at all seasons, two or three ferry-boats always ply upon its waters. The *rauque* bellow of the hippopotamus is heard on its banks, and the adjacent lowlands are infested by musquitoes in clouds. The villages of Ukaranga are scattered in clumps over the plain—wretched hamlets, where a few households live surrounded by rare cultivation in the dryer parts of the swamps. The "port of Ukaranga" is an open roadstead, which seldom shows even a single canoe. . Merchants who possess boats and can send for provisions to the islands across the lake sometimes prefer, for economy, Ukaranga to Kawele; it is also made a halting-place by those *en route* to Uguhha, who would lose time by visiting Ujiji. The land, however, affords no supplies; a bazar is unknown; and the apathetic tribe, who cultivate scarcely sufficient grain for themselves, will not even take the trouble to cast a net. Ukaranga sends bamboos, rafters for building, and firewood, cut in the background of highlands, to Kawele and other parts of Ujiji, at which places, however, workmen must be hired.

Ukaranga signifies, etymologically, the "Land of Groundnuts." This little district may, in earlier ages, have given name to the Mocarangas, Mucarongas, or Mucarangas, a nation which, according to the Portuguese historians, from João dos Sanctos (1586–97) to Don Sebastian Xavier Botelho (1835), occupied the country within the Mozambique, from S. lat. 5° to S. lat. 25°, under subjection to the sovereign and the people of "Monomotapa." In the absence of history, analogy is the only guide. Either, then, the confusion of the Tanganyika and the Nyassa Lakes by the old geographers caused them to extend the "Mocarangas" up to the northern water—and the grammatical error in the word "Mucaranga" justifies some suspicion as to their accuracy—or in the space of three centuries the tribe has declined from its former power and consequence, or the Wakaranga of the Tanganyika are a remnant of the mighty southern nation which, like the Watuta tribe, has of late years been pressed by adverse circumstances to the north. Though Senhor Botelho, in his "Memoria Estatisca," denominates the "Monomoezi country" "Western Mucaranga," it is certain that no Mnyamwezi in the present day owns to connection with a race speaking a different dialect, and distant about 200 miles from his frontier.

The land of Ujiji is bounded on the north by the heights of Urundi, and on the south by the Ukaranga country: eastward it extends to Ubaha, and westward it is washed by the waves of the Tanganyika Lake. On its northeast lies the land of Uhha, now reduced by the predatory Watuta to a luxuriant desert.

The head-quarter village of Ujiji was in 1858 Kawele. To the westward of this settlement was the district of Gungu, facing the islet rock of Bangwe. This place was deserted by travelers on account of the plundering propensities of its former chief. His son "Lurinda," however, labors to recover lost ground by courtesy and attention to strangers. Southeastward of Kawele is the district of Ugoyye, frequented by the Arabs, who find the Sultans Habeyya and Marabu somewhat less extortionate than their neighbors. It is a sandy spot, clear of white ants, but shut out by villages and cultivation from the lovely view of the lake. To one standing at Kawele, all these districts and villages are within two or three miles, and a distant glance discloses the possessions of half a dozen independent tribes.

Caravans entering Ujiji from the land-side usually encamp in the outlying villages on the right or left bank of the Ruche, at considerable inconvenience, for some days. The origin of this custom appears to date from olden time. In East Africa, as a rule, every stranger is held to be hostile before he has proved friendly intentions, and many tribes do not admit him into their villages without a special invitation. Thus, even in the present day, the visitor in the countries of the Somal and Galla, the Wamasai and the Wakwafi, must sit under some tree outside the settlement till a deputation of elders, after formally ascertaining his purpose, escort him to their homes. The modern reason for the custom, which prevails upon the coast as well as on the banks of the Tanganyika, is rather commercial than political. The caravan halts upon neutral ground, and the sultans or chiefs of the different villages send select messengers carrying various presents: in the interior ivory and slaves, and in the maritime regions cloth and provisions, technically called "magubiko," and intended as an earnest of their desire to open trade. Sweet words and fair promises win the day; the mtongi, or head of the caravan, after a week of earnest deliberation with all his followers, chooses his host, temporary lodgings are provided for the guests, and the value of the retaining fees is afterward recovered in hongá and kirembá—blackmail and customs. This custom was known in Southern Africa by the name of "marts;" that is, a "connection with a person belonging to another nation, so that they reside at each other's houses when visiting the place, and make mutual presents." The compulsory guest among the Arabs of Zanzibar and the Somal is called "nezil."

At Ujiji terminates, after twelve stages, which native caravans generally finish in a fortnight, all halts included, the transit of the fifth region. The traveler has now accomplished a total number of 85 long, or 100 short stages, which, with necessary rests, but excluding detentions and long halts, occupy 150 days. The direct longitudinal distance from the coast is 540 geographical miles, which the sinuosities of the road prolong to 955, or in round numbers 950 statute miles. The number of days expended by the expedition in actual marching was 100, of hours 420, which gives a rate of 2.27 miles per hour. The total time was seven and a half months, from the 27th of June, 1857, to the 18th of February, 1858; thus the number of the halts exceeded by one third the number of the marches. In practice Arab caravans seldom arrive at the Tanganyika, for reasons before alluded to, under a total period of six months. Those lightly laden may make Unyanyembe in between two and a half and three months, and from Unyanyembe Ujiji in twenty-five stages, which would reduce their journey to four months.

Dapper ("Beschryving van Africa," Amst., 1671) asserts that the "blacks of Pombo, *i. e.*, the Pombeiros, or native travelers of W. Africa, when asked respecting the distance of the lake, say that it is at least a sixty-days' journey, going constantly eastward." But the total breadth of the continent between Mbuamaji and Loanda being, in round numbers, 1560 geographical miles, this estimate would give a marching rate of twenty-six geographical and rectilinear miles (or, allowing for deviation, thirty-six statute miles) per diem. When Da Couto (1565), quoting the information procured by Francisco Barreto, during his expedition in 1570, from some Moors (Arabs or Wasawahili) at Patta and elsewhere, says that "from Kilwa or Atondo (that is to say, the country of the Watondwe) the other sea of Angola might be reached with a journey of fifteen or twenty (150 or 200 ?) leagues," he probably alludes to the Nyassa Lake, lying southwestward of Kilwa, not to the Tanganyika. Mr. Cooley gives one itinerary, by Mohammed bin Nasur, an old Arab merchant, enumerating seventy-one marches from Buromaji (Mbuamaji) to Oha (Uhha), and a total of eighty-three from the coast to the lake; and a second by a native of Monomoezi, Lief bin Said (a misprint for Khalaf bin Saíd?) sixty-two to Ogara (Ugala), which is placed four or five days from Oha. In another page he remarks that "from Buromaji, near Point Puna, to Oha, in Monomoezi, is a journey of seventy-nine, or, in round numbers, eighty days, the shores of the lake being still six or eight days distant." This is the closest estimate yet made. Mr. Macqueen, from the itinerary of Lief bin Said, estimates the lake from the mouth of the River Pangani at 604 miles, and seventy-one days of total march. It is evident, from the preceding pages, that African authorities have hitherto confounded the Nyanza, the Tanganyika, and the Nyassa Lakes. Still, in the estimate of the distance between the coast and Ujiji there is a remarkable and a most deceptive coherence.

Ujiji—also called Manyofo, which appears, however, peculiar to a certain sultanat or district—is the name of a province, not, as has been represented, of a single town. It was first visited by the Arabs about 1840, ten years after they had penetrated to Unyamwezi; they found it conveniently situated as a mart upon the Tanganyika Lake, and a central point where their depôts might be established, and whence their factors and slaves could navigate the waters and collect slaves and ivory from the tribes upon its banks. But the climate proved unhealthy, the people dangerous, and the coasting-voyages frequently ended in disaster; Ujiji, there-fore, never rose to the rank of Unyanyembe or Msene. At pres-ent it is visited during the fair season, from May to September, by flying caravans, who return to Unyanyembe as soon as they have loaded their porters.

Abundant humidity and a fertile soil, evidenced by the large forest-trees and the abundance of ferns, render Ujiji the most pro-ductive province in this section of Africa: vegetables, which must elsewhere be cultivated, here seem to flourish almost spontaneous-ly. Rice of excellent quality was formerly raised by the Arabs upon the shores of the Tanganyika; it grew luxuriantly, attain-ing, it is said, the height of eight or nine feet. The inhabitants, however, preferring sorghum, and wearied out by the depreda-tions of the monkey, the elephant, and the hippopotamus, have al-lowed the more civilized cereal to degenerate. The principal grains are the holcus and the Indian nagli or nanchni (Eleusine coracano); there is no bajri (panicum or millet) in these regions; the pulses are phaseoli and the voandzeia, ground-nuts, beans, and haricots of several different species. The manioc, egg-plant, and sweet potato, the yam, the cucumber, an edible white fungus growing subterraneously, and the Indian variety of the Jerusalem artichoke, represent the vegetables: the people, however, unlike the Hindoos, despise, and consequently will not be at the pains to cultivate them. Sugar-cane, tobacco, and cotton are always pur-chasable in the bazar. The fruits are the plantain and the Guinea-palm. The mdizi or plantain-tree is apparently an aborigen of these latitudes: in certain parts, as in Usumbara, Karagwah, and Uganda, it is the staff of life: in the hilly countries there are, it is said, about a dozen varieties, and a single bunch forms a load for a man. It is found in the island and on the coast of Zanzibar, at K'hutu in the head of the alluvial valley, and, though rarely, in the mountains of Usagara. The best fruit is that grown by the Arabs at Unyanyembe: it is still a poor specimen, coarse and in-sipid, stringy and full of seeds, and strangers rarely indulge in it, fearing flatulence. Upon the Tanganyika Lake there is a variety called mikono t'hembu, or elephant's-hands, which is considerably larger than the Indian "horse-plantain." The skin is of a brick-dust red, in places inclining to rusty-brown; the pulp is a dull yellow, with black seeds, and the flavor is harsh, strong, and drug-like. The Elæis Guiniensis, locally called mchikichi, which is known by the Arabs to grow in the Islands of Zanzibar and Pemba, and more rarely in the mountains of Usagara, springs ap-parently uncultivated in large dark groves on the shores of the Tanganyika, where it hugs the margin, rarely growing at any dis-tance inland. The bright-yellow drupe, with shiny purple-black point, though nauseous to the taste, is eaten by the people. The mawezi or palm-oil, of the consistency of honey, rudely extracted, forms an article of considerable traffic in the regions about the lake. This is the celebrated extract whose various officinal uses in Europe have already begun to work a social reformation in W. Africa. The people of Ujiji separate by pounding the oily sarcocarpium from the one seed of the drupe, boil it for some hours, allow the floating substance to coagulate, and collect it in large earthern pots. The price is usually about one doti of white cotton for thirty-five pounds, and the people generally demand salt in exchange for it from caravans. This is the "oil of a red color" which, according to Mr. Cooley, is bought by the Wanyamwezi "from the opposite or southwestern side of the lake." Despite its sickly flavor, it is universally used in cooking, and it forms the only unguent and lamp-oil in the country. This fine Guinea-palm is also tapped, as the date in Western India, for toddy; and the cheapness of this tembo—the sura of West Africa—accounts for the prevalence of intoxication, and the consequent demoralization of the lakist tribes.

The bazar at Ujiji is well supplied. Fresh fish of various kinds is always procurable, except during the violence of the rains: the people, however, invariably cut it up and clean it out before bringing it to market. Good honey abounds after the wet monsoon. By the favor of the chief, milk and butter may be purchased every day. Long-tailed sheep and well-bred goats, poultry and eggs—the two latter are never eaten by the people—are brought in from the adjoining countries: the Arabs breed a few Manilla ducks, and the people rear, but will not sell, pigeons. The few herds at Ujiji which have escaped the beef-eating propensities of the Watuta are a fine breed, originally, it is said, derived by the Wahha from the mountains of Karagwah. Their horns in these lands appear unusually large; their stature combines with the smallness of the hump to render them rather like English than Indian or African cattle. They are rarely sold of later days, except for enormous prices, an adult slave being the lowest valuation of a cow. The cattle are never stalled or grain-fed, and the udder is little distended: the produce is about one quarter that of a civilized cow, and the animals give milk only during the few first months after calving. The "tulchan" of Tibet is apparently unknown in Central Africa; but the people are not wanting in barbarous contrivances to persuade a stubborn animal to yield her produce.

The fauna appear rare upon the borders of the Tanganyika: all men are hunters; every human being loves animal food, from white ants to elephants; the tzetze was found there, and probably the luxuriance of the vegetation, in conjunction with the extreme humidity, tends to diminish species and individuals. Herds of elephants exist in the bamboo-jungles which surround the sea, but the heaps of ivory sold in the markets of Ujiji are collected from an area containing thousands of square miles. Hippopotami and crocodiles are common in the waters, wild buffaloes in the plains. The hyenas are bold thieves, and the half-wild "pariah-dogs" that slink about the villages are little inferior as depredators. The people sometimes make pets of them, leading them about with cords; but they do not object to see them shot after a raid upon the Arab's meat, butter, or milk. These animals are rarely heard to bark; they leave noise to the village cocks. The huts are, as usual, haunted by the gray and the musk rat. Of birds there is a fine fish-eagle about the size of a domestic cock, with snowy head and shoulders relieving a sombre chocolate plume: he sits majestically watching his prey upon the tall trees overhanging the waves of the Tanganyika. A larus, or sea-gull, with reddish legs, lives in small colonies upon this lake. At the end of the monsoon in 1858 these birds were seen to collect in troops upon the sands, as they are accustomed to do at Aden when preparing to migrate. The common kingfisher is a large bird with a white and gray plume, a large and strong black bill, and a crest which somewhat resembles that of the Indian bulbul: it perches upon the branches over the waters, and in flight and habits resembles other halcyons. A long and lank black plotus, or diver, is often seen skimming the waters, and sand-pipers run along the yellow sands. The other birds are the white-breasted "parson-crow," partridges, and quails seen in Urundi; swallows in passage, curlews, motacillæ, muscicapæ, and various passerines. Ranæ, some of them noisy in the extreme, inhabit the sedges close to the lake. The termite does great damage in the sweet red soils about Kawele: it is less feared when the ground is dry and sandy. The huts are full of animal life—snakes, scorpions, ants of various kinds, whose armies sometimes turn the occupants out of doors; the rafters are hollowed out by xylophagous insects; the walls are riddled by mason-bees, hideous spiders veil the corners with thick webs, the chirp of the cricket is heard both within and out of doors, cockroaches destroy the provisions, and large brown musquitoes and flies, ticks and bugs, assault the inhabitants.

The rise in the price of slaves and ivory has compelled Arab merchants, as will be seen in another chapter, to push their explorations beyond the Tanganyika Lake. Ujiji is, however, still the great slave-mart of these regions, the article being collected from all the adjoining tribes of Urundi, Uhha, Uvira, and Marungu. The native dealers, however, are so acute, that they are rapidly ruining this, their most lucrative traffic. They sell cheaply, and think to remunerate themselves by aiding and abetting desertion. Merchants, therefore, who do not chain or cord together their gangs till they have reached the east bank of the Malagarazi River, often lose 20 per cent. The prevalence of the practice has already given Ujiji a bad name, and, if continued, will remove the market to another place, where the people are somewhat less clever and more sensible. It is impossible to give any idea of the average price of the human commodity, which varies, under the modifications of demand and supply, from two to ten doti, or tobes of American domestics. Yet, as these purchases sell in Zanzibar for fourteen or fifteen dollars per head, the trade realizes nearly 500 per cent., and will, therefore, with difficulty be put down.

The principal tribes in this region are the Wajiji, the Wavinza, the Wakaranga, the Watuta, the Wabuha, and the Wahha.

The Wajiji are a burly race of barbarians, far stronger than the tribes hitherto traversed, with dark skins, plain features, and straight, sturdy limbs: they are larger and heavier men than the Wanyamwezi, and the type, as it approaches Central Africa, becomes rather negro than negroid.[*] Their feet and hands are large and flat, their voices are harsh and strident, and their looks as well as their manners are independent even to insolence. The women, who are held in high repute, resemble, and often excel, their masters in rudeness and violence; they think little in their cups of entering a stranger's hut, and of snatching up and carrying away an article which excites their admiration. Many of both sexes, and all ages, are disfigured by the small-pox—the Arabs have vainly taught them inoculation—and there are few who are not afflicted by boils and various eruptions; there is also an inveterate pandemic itch, which, according to their Arab visitors, results from a diet of putrid fish.

This tribe is extensively tattooed, probably as a protection against the humid atmosphere and the chills of the Lake Region. Some of the chiefs have ghastly scars raised by fire, in addition to large patterns marked upon their persons—lines, circles, and rays of little cupping-cuts drawn down the back, the stomach, and the arms, like the tattoo of the Wangindo tribe near Kilwa. Both sexes love to appear dripping with oil; and they manifestly do not hold cleanliness to be a virtue. The head is sometimes shaved; rarely the hair is allowed to grow; the most fashionable coiffure is a mixture of the two; patches and beauty-spots in the most eccentric shapes—buttons, crescents, crests, and galeated lines—being allowed to sprout either on the front, the sides, or the back of the head, from a carefully-scraped scalp. Women as well as men are fond of binding a wisp of white tree-fibre round their heads, like the ribbon which confines the European old person's wig. There is not a trace of mustache or whisker in the country; they are removed by the tweezers, and the climate, according to the Arabs, is like

---

[*] My companion observes (in Blackwood, Nov., 1859), "It may be worthy of remark, that I have always found the lighter-colored savages more boisterous and warlike than those of the dingier hue. The *ruddy black*, fleshy-looking Wazaramos and Wagogos are much *lighter* in color (?) than any of the other tribes, and certainly have a far superior, more manly, and warlike independent spirit and bearing than any of the others." The "dingiest" peoples are usually the most degraded, and therefore sometimes the least powerful; but the fiercest races in the land are the Wazaramo, the Wajiji, and the Watuturu, who are at the same time the darkest.

that of Unyamwezi, unfavorable to beards. For cosmetics both sexes apply, when they can procure such luxuries, red earth to the face, and over the head a thick coating of chalk or mountain-meal, which makes their blackness stand out hideously grotesque.

The chiefs wear expensive stuffs, checks, and cottons, which they extract from passing caravans. Women of wealth affect the tobe or coast-dress, and some were seen wearing red and blue broadcloths. The male costume of the lower orders is confined to softened goat, sheep, deer, leopard, or monkey skins, tied at two corners over either shoulder, with the flaps open at one side, and with tail and legs dangling in the wind. Women who can not afford cloth use as a succedaneum a narrow kilt of fibre or skin, and some content themselves with a tassel of fibre or a leafy twig depending from a string bound round the waist, and displaying the nearest approach to the original fig-leaf. At Ujiji, however, the people are observed for the first time to make extensive use of the macerated tree-bark, which supplies the place of cotton in Urundi, Karagwah, and the northern kingdoms. This article, technically termed "mbugu," is made from the inner bark of various trees, especially the mrimba and the mwale, or huge Raphia-palm. The trunk of the full-grown tree is stripped of its integument twice or thrice, and is bound with plantain-leaves till a finer growth is judged fit for manipulation. This bark is carefully removed, steeped in water, macerated, kneaded, and pounded with clubs and battens to the consistency of a coarse cotton. Palm-oil is then spirted upon it from the mouth, and it acquires the color of chamois leather. The Wajiji obtain the mbugu mostly from Urindi and Uvira. They are fond of striping it with a black vegetable mud, so as to resemble the spoils of leopards and wild-cats, and they favor the delusion by cutting the edge into long strips, like the tails and other extremities of wild beasts. The price of the mbugu varies according to size from six to twelve khete or strings of beads. Though durable, it is never washed: after many months' wear the superabundance of dirt is removed by butter or ghee.

Besides the common brass-wire girdles and bracelets, armlets and anklets, masses of white-porcelain, blue-glass, and large pigeon-egg beads, and hundreds of the iron-wire circlets called sambo, which, worn with ponderous brass or copper rings round the lower leg above the foot, suggest at a distance the idea of disease, the Wajiji are distinguished from tribes not on the lake by necklaces of shells—small pink bivalves strung upon a stout fibre. They have learned to make brass from the Arabs, by melting down one third of zinc imported from the coast with two parts of the fine soft and red copper brought from the country of the Kazeembe. Like their lakist neighbors, they ornament the throat with disks, crescents, and strings of six or seven cones, fastened by the apex, and depending to the breast. Made of the whitest ivory or of the teeth, not the tusks, of the hippopotamus, these dazzling ornaments effectively set off the dark and negro-like skin. Another peculiarity among these people is a pair of iron pincers or a piece of split wood ever hanging round the neck; nor is its use less remarkable than its presence. The lakists rarely chew, smoke, or take snuff according to the fashion of the rest of mankind. Every man carries a little half-gourd or diminutive pot of black earthenware nearly full of tobacco; when inclined to indulge, he fills it with water, expresses the juice, and from the palm of his hand sniffs it up into his nostrils. The pincers serve to close the exit, otherwise the nose must be temporarily corked by the application of finger and thumb. Without much practice it is difficult to articulate during the retention of the dose, which lasts a few minutes, and when an attempt is made the words are scarcely intelligible. The arms of the Wajiji are small battle-axes and daggers, spears, and large bows which carry unusually heavy arrows. They fear the gun and the sabre, yet they show no unwillingness to fight. The Arabs avoid granting their demands for muskets and gunpowder, consequently a great chief never possesses more than two or three firelocks.

The lakists are an almost amphibious race, excellent divers, strong swimmers and fishermen, and vigorous ichthyophagists all. At times, when excited by the morning coolness and by the prospect of a good haul, they indulge in a manner of merriment which resembles the gambols of sportive water-fowls: standing upright and balancing themselves in their hollow logs, which appear but little larger than themselves, they strike the water furiously with their paddles, skimming over the surface, dashing to and fro, splashing one another, urging forward, backing, and wheeling their craft, now capsizing, then regaining their position with wonderful dexterity. They make coarse hooks, and have many varieties of nets and creels. Conspicuous on the waters and in the villages is the dewa, or "otter" of Oman, a triangle of stout reeds, which shows the position of the net. A stronger kind and used for the larger ground-fish, is a cage of open basket-work, provided like the former with a bait and two entrances. The fish once entangled can not escape, and a log of wood used as a trimmer, attached to a float-rope of rushy plants, directs the fisherman. The heaviest animals are caught by a rope-net—the likh of Oman—weighted and thrown out between two boats. They have circular lath frames, meshed in with a knot somewhat different from that generally used in Europe; the smaller variety is thrown from the boat by a single man, who follows it into the water—the larger, which reaches six feet in diameter, is lowered from the bow by cords, and collects the fish attracted by the glaring torch-fire. The Wajiji also make large and small drag-nets; some let down in a circle by one or more canoes, the others managed by two fishermen who, swimming at each end, draw them in when ready. They have little purse-nets to catch small fry, hoops thrust into a long stick-handle through the reed walls that line the shore; and by this simple contrivance the fish are caught in considerable quantities. The wigo or crates alluded to as peculiar in the "Periplus," and still common upon the Zanzibar coast, are found at the Tanganyika. The common creel resembles the khún of Western India, and is well-known even to the Bushmen of the South: it is a cone of open bamboo-strips or supple twigs, placed lengthwise, and bound in and out by strings of grass or tree-fibre. It is closed at the top, and at the bottom there is a narrow aperture with a diagonally-disposed entrance like that of a wire rat-trap, which prevents the fish escaping. It is placed upon its side with a bait, embanked with mud, reeds, or sand, and seems to answer the purpose for which it is intended. In Uzaramo and near the coast the people narcotize fish with the juice of certain plants, asclepias and euphorbias: about the Tanganyika the art appears unknown.

There are many varieties of fish in the waters of this lake. The mvoro is a long and bony variety, in shape like a large mackerel; the sangále resembles it, but the head and body are thicker. The mgege, which suggests the pomfret of Western India, is well flavored but full of bones. The mguhe is said to attain the length of five or six feet: it is not unlike the kheri of the Indian rivers, and to a European palate it is the best fish that swims in these waters. The largest is the singá, a scaleless variety, with black back, silvery belly, small fins, and long fleshy cirri: it crawls along the bottom, and is unfit for leaping or for rapid progress. This sluggish and misshapen ground-fish is much prized by the people on account of its rich and luscious fat. Like the pallu of Sindh, it soon palls upon the European palate. Want of flavor is the general complaint made by the Arabs and coast people against the produce of the Tanganyika: they attempt to diminish the wateriness of the fish by exposing it spitted to a slow fire, and by subsequently stowing it for the night in well-closed earthen pots. Besides the five varieties above alluded to, there are dwarf eels of good flavor, resembling the Indian bam; dagá'a, small fish called by the Arabs kashu'a, minnows of many varieties, which, simply sun-dried, or muriated if salt can be afforded, find their way far east; a dwarf shrimp, about one quarter the size of the common English species; and a large bivalve called sinani, and identified as belonging to the genus Iridina. The meat is fat and yellow, like that of a well-fed oyster, but it is so insipid that none but a Mjiji can eat it. The shells collected upon the shores of the Tanganyika and on the land journey have been described by Mr. Samuel P. Woodward, who courteously named the species after the European members of the expedition. To his memoir —quoted in p. 343–345 of this volume—the reader is referred.

The Wajiji are considered by the Arabs to be the most troublesome race in these black regions. They are taught by the example of their chiefs to be rude, insolent, and extortionate; they demand beads even for pointing out the road; they will deride and imitate a stranger's speech and manner before his face; they can do nothing without a long preliminary of the fiercest scolding; they are as ready with a blow as with a word; and they may often be seen playing at "rough and tumble," fighting, pushing, and tearing hair, in their boats. A Mjiji uses his dagger or his spear upon a guest with little hesitation; he thinks twice, however, before drawing blood, if it will cause a feud. Their roughness of manner is dashed with a curious ceremoniousness. When the sultan appears among his people, he stands in a circle and claps his hands, to which all respond in the same way. Women courtesy to one another, bending the right knee almost to the ground. When two men meet, they clasp each other's arms with both hands, rubbing them up and down, and ejaculating for some minutes, "Nama sanga? nama sanga?—art thou well?" They then pass the hands down to the forearm, exclaiming "Wáhke? wáhke?—how art thou?" and finally they clap palms at each other, a token of respect which appears common to these tribes of Central Africa. The children have all the frowning and unprepossessing look of their parents; they reject little civilities, and seem to spend life in disputes, biting and clawing like wildcats. There appears to be little family affection in this undemonstrative race. The only endearment between father and son is a habit of scratching and picking each other, caused probably by the prevalence of a complaint before alluded to; as among the Simiads, the intervals between pugnacity are always spent in exercising the nails. Sometimes, also, at sea, when danger is near, the Mjiji breaks the mournful silence of his fellows, who are all thinking of home, with the exclamation, "Yá mgúri wánje!—O my wife!" They are never sober when they can be drunk; perhaps in no part of the world will the traveler more often see men and women staggering about the village with thick speech and violent gestures. The favorite inebriant is tembo or palm-toddy; almost every one, however, even when on board the canoe, smokes bhang, and the whooping and screaming which follow the indulgence resemble the noise of wild beasts rather than the sounds of human beings. Their food consists principally of holcus, manioc, and fish, which is rarely eaten before it becomes offensive to European organs.

The great Mwami or Sultan of Ujiji in 1858–59 was Rusimba. Under him were several mutware (mutwale) or minor chiefs, one to each settlement, as Kannena in Kawele, and Lurinda in Gungu. On the arrival of a caravan, Rusimba forwards through his relations a tusk or two of ivory, thus mutely intimating that he requires his black-mail, which he prefers to receive in beads and kitindi or coil-bracelets, proportioning, however, his demand to the trader's means. When this point has been settled, the mutware sends his present, and expects a proportionate return. He is, moreover, entitled to a fee for every canoe hired; on each slave the kiremba or excise is about half the price; from one to two cloths are demanded upon every tusk of ivory; and he will snatch a few beads from a man purchasing provisions for his master. The minor headmen are fond of making "sare" or brotherhood with strangers, in order to secure them in case of return. They depend for influence over their unruly subjects wholly upon personal qualifications, bodily strength, and violence of temper. A chief, though originally a slave, may "win golden opinions" by his conduct when in liquor: he assumes the most ferocious aspect, draws his dagger, brandishes his spear, and, with loud screams, rushes at his subjects as intent upon annihilating them. The affairs of the nation are settled by the mwami, the chief, in a general council of the lieges, the wateko (in the singular mteko) or elders presiding. Their intellects, never of the brightest, are invariably fuddled with toddy, and, after bawling for hours together and coming apparently to the most satisfactory conclusion, the word of a boy or of an old woman will necessitate another lengthy palaver. The sultans, like their subjects, brook no delay in their own affairs; they impatiently dun a stranger half a dozen times a day for a few beads, while they patiently keep him waiting for weeks on occasions to him of the highest importance, while they are drinking pombe or taking leave of their wives. Besides the magubiko or preliminary presents, the chiefs are bound, before the departure of a caravan which has given them satisfaction, to supply it with half a dozen masuta or matted packages of grain, and to present the leader with a slave, who generally manages to abscond. The parting gifts are technically called "urangozi," or guidance.

Under the influence of slavery the Wajiji have made no progress in the art of commerce. They know nothing of bargaining or of credit: they will not barter unless the particular medium upon which they have set their hearts is forthcoming; and they fix a price according to their wants, not to the value of the article. The market varies with the number of caravans present at the depôt, the season, the extent of supply, and a variety of similar considerations. Besides the trade in ivory, slaves, bark, cloth, and palm-oil, they manufacture and hawk about iron sickles shaped liked the European, kengere, kiugi, or small bells, and sambo, locally called tambi, or wire circlets, worn as ornaments round the ankles; long double-edged knives in wooden sheaths, neatly whipped with strips of ratan; and jembe or hoes. Of bells a dozen were purchased in March and April of 1858 for two fundo of white beads. Jembe and large sime averaged also two fundo. Of good sambo 100, and of the inferior quality 200, were procurable for a fundo. The iron is imported in a rough state from Uvira. The value of a goat is one shukkah, which here represents, as in Unyamwezi, twelve feet, or double the length of the shukkah in other regions, the single cloth being called lupande, or upande. Sheep, all of a very inferior quality, cost somewhat more than goats. A hen, or from five to six eggs, fetched one khete of samesame, or red coral beads, which are here worth three times the quantity of white porcelain. Large fish, or those above two pounds in weight, were sold for three khete; the small fry—the white bait of this region—one khete per two pounds; and diminutive shrimps one khete per three pounds. Of plantains, a small bunch of fifteen, and of sweet potatoes and yams, from ten to fifteen roots were purchased for a khete; of artichokes, egg-plants, and cucumbers, from fifty to one hundred. The wild vegetables, generically called mboga, are the cheapest of these esculents. Beans, phaseoli, ground-nuts, and the voiandzeia, were expensive, averaging about two pounds per khete. Rice is not generally grown in Ujiji; a few measures of fine white grain were purchased at a fancy price from one Sayfu bin Hasani, a pauper Msawahili, from the Isle of Chole, settled in the country. The sugar-cane is poor and watery; it was sold in lengths of four or five feet for the khete: one cloth and two khete purchased three pounds of fine white honey. Tobacco was comparatively expensive. Of the former a shukkah procured a bag weighing perhaps ten pounds. Milk was sold at arbitrary prices, averaging about three teacups for the khete. A shukkah would procure three pounds of butter, and ghee was not made for the market. It was impossible to find sweet toddy, as the people never smoke nor clean the pots into which it is drawn; of the acid and highly intoxicating drink used by the Wajiji, from five to six teacups were to be bought with a khete. Firewood, being imported, was expensive, a khete being the price of a little fagot containing from fifty to one hundred sticks. About one pound of unclean cotton was to be purchased for three khete of samesame. It must be observed that this list of prices, which represents the market at Kawele, gives a high average, many of the articles being brought in canoes from considerable distances, and even from the opposite coast.

The traveler in the Lake Regions loses by cloth; the people, contented with softened skins and tree-bark, prefer beads, ornaments, and more durable articles: on the other hand, he gains upon salt, which is purchased at half price at the Parugerero Pan, and upon large wires brought from the coast. Beads are a necessary evil to those engaged in purchasing ivory and slaves. In 1858 the Wajiji rejected with contempt the black porcelains, called ububu. At first they would not receive the khanyera, or white porcelains; and afterward, when the expedition had exchanged, at a considerable loss, their large stock for langiyo, or small blues, they demanded the former. The bead most in fashion was the mzizima, or large blue glass, three khete of which were equivalent to a small cloth; the samesame, or red corals, required to be exchanged for mzizima, of which one khete was an equivalent to three of samesame. The maguru nzige, or pink porcelains, were at par. The tobacco-stem bead, called sofi, and current at Msene, was in demand. The reader will excuse the prolixity of these wearisome details, they are necessary parts of a picture of manners and customs in Central Africa. Moreover, a foreknowledge of the requirements of the people is a vital condition of successful exploration. There is nothing to arrest the traveler's progress in this section of the African interior except the failure of his stores.

A serious inconvenience awaits the inexperienced, who find a long halt at and a return from Ujiji necessary. The Wanyamwezi pagazi, or porters, hired at Unyanyembe, bring with them the cloth and beads which they have received as hire for going to and coming from the lake, and lose no time in bartering the outfit for ivory or slaves. Those who prefer the former article will delay for some time with extreme impatience and daily complaints, fearing to cross Uvinza in small bodies when loaded with valuables. The purchasers of slaves, however, knowing that they will inevitably lose them after a few days at Ujiji, desert at once. In all cases, the report that a caravan is marching eastward causes a general disappearance of the porters. As the Wajiji will not carry, the caravan is reduced to a halt, which may be protracted for months, in fact, till another body of men coming from the east will engage themselves as return porters. Moreover, the departure homeward almost always partakes of the nature of a flight, so fearful are the strangers lest their slaves should seize the opportunity to desert. The Omani Arabs obviate these inconveniences by always traveling with large bodies of domestics, whose interest it is not to abandon the master.

South of the Wajiji lie the Wakaranga, a people previously described as almost identical in development and condition, but somewhat inferior in energy and civilization. Little need be said of the Wavinza, who appear to unite the bad qualities of both the Wanyamwezi and the Ujiji. They are a dark, meagre, and ill-looking tribe; poorly clad in skin aprons and kilts. They keep off insects by inserting the chauri, or fly-flap, into the waistband of their kilts: and at a distance they present, like the Hottentots, the appearance of a race with tails. Their arms are spears, bows, and arrows; and they use, unlike their neighbors, wicker-work shields six feet long by two in breadth. Their chiefs are of the Watosi race, hence every stranger who meets with their approbation is called, in compliment, Mtosi. They will admit strangers into their villages, dirty clumps of bee-hive huts, but they refuse to provide them with lodging. Merchants with valuable outfits prefer the jungle, and wait patiently for provisions brought in baskets from the settlements. The Wavinza seldom muster courage to attack a caravan, but stragglers are in imminent danger of being cut off by them. Their country is rich in cattle and poultry, grain and vegetables. Bhang grows every where near the settlements, and they indulge themselves in it immoderately.

The Watuta—a word of fear in these regions—are a tribe of robbers originally settled upon the southern extremity of the Tanganyika Lake. After plundering the lands of Marungu and Ufipa, where they almost annihilated the cattle, the Watuta, rounding the eastern side of the lake, migrated northward. Some years ago they were called in by Ironga, the late Sultan of U'ungu, to assist him against Mui' Gumbi, the powerful chief of the Warori. The latter were defeated, after obstinate fighting for many months. After conquering the Warori, the Watuta settled in Sultan Ironga's lands, rather by might than right, and they were expelled by his son with the greatest difficulty. From U'ungu their next step was to the southern bank of the Malagarazi River. About three years ago this restless tribe was summoned by Mzogera, the present Sultan of Uvinza, to assist him in seizing Uhha, which had just lost T'háre, its chief. The Watuta crossed the Malagarazi, laid waste the lands of Uhha and Ubuha, and desolated the northern region between the river and the lake. Shortly afterward they attacked Msene, and were only repulsed by the matchlocks of the Arabs after a week of hard skirmishing. In the early part of 1858 they slew Ruhembe, the Sultan of Usui, a district north of Unyanyembe, upon the road to Karagwah. In the latter half of the same year they marched upon Ujiji, plundered Gungu, and proceeded to attack Kawele. The Arab merchants, however, who were then absent on a commercial visit to Uviva, returned precipitately to defend their depôts, and with large bodies of slave musketeers beat off the invader. The lands of the Watuta are now bounded on the north by Utumbara, on the south by Msene; eastward by the meridian of Wilyankuru, and westward by the highlands of Urundi.

The Watuta, according to the Arabs, are a pastoral tribe, despising, like the Wamasai and the Somal, such luxuries as houses and fields; they wander from place to place, camping under trees, over which they throw their mats, and driving their herds and plundered cattle to the most fertile pasture-grounds. The dress is sometimes a mbugu or bark-cloth; more generally it is confined to the humblest tribute paid to decency by the Kafirs of the Cape, and they have a similar objection to removing it. On their forays they move in large bodies, women as well as men, with their children and baggage placed upon bullocks, and their wealth in brass wire twisted round the horns. Their wives carry their weapons, and join, it is said, in the fight. The arms are two short spears, one in the right hand, the other in the left, concealed by a large shield, so that they can thrust upward unawares: disdaining bows and arrows, they show their superior bravery by fighting at close quarters, and they never use the spear as an assegai. In describing their tactics, the Arabs call them "manœuvrers like the Franks." Their thousands march in four or five extended lines, and attack by attempting to envelop the enemy. There is no shouting nor war-cry to distract the attention of the combatants: iron whistles are used for the necessary signals. During the battle the sultan, or chief, whose ensign is a brass stool, sits attended by his forty or fifty elders in the rear; his authority is little more than nominal, the tribe priding itself upon autonomy. The Watuta rarely run away, and take no thought of their killed and wounded. They do not, like the ancient Jews, and the Gallas and Abyssinians of the present day, carry off a relic of the slain foe; in fact, the custom seems to be ignored south of the equator. The Watuta have still, however, a wholesome fear of firearms, and the red flag of a caravan causes them to decamp without delay. According to the Arabs they are not inhospitable, and, though rough in manner, they have always received guests with honor. A fanciful trait is related concerning them: their first question to a stranger will be, "Didst thou see me from afar?" which, being interpreted, means, Did you hear of my greatness before coming here? and they hold an answer in the negative to be a casus belli.

Remain for consideration the people of Ubuha and Uhha. The Wabuha is a small and insignificant tribe bounded on the north by Uhha, and on the south by the Malagarazi River: the total breadth is about three marches; the length, from the Rusugi stream of the Wavinza to the frontiers of Ujiji and Ukaranga, is in all a distance of four days. Their principal settlement is Uyonwa, the district of Sultan Mariki: it is a mere clearing in the jungle, with a few pauper huts dotting fields of sweet potatoes. This harmless and oppressed people will sell provisions, but though poor they are particular upon the subject of beads, preferring coral and blue to the exclusion of black and white. They are a dark, curly-headed, and hard-favored race: they wear the shushah or top-knot on the poll, dress in skins and tree-barks, ornament themselves with brass and copper armlets, ivory disks, and beads, and are never without their weapons, spears and assegais, sime or daggers, and small battle-axes. Honorable women wear tobes of red broadcloth and fillets of grass or fibre confining the hair.

Uhha, written by Mr. Cooley Oha, was formerly a large tract of land bounded on the north by the mountains of Urundi, southward and eastward by the Malagarazi River, and on the west by the northern parts of Ujiji. As has been recounted, the Wahha, dispersed by the Watuta, have dispersed themselves over the broad lands between Unyanyembe and the Tanganyika, and their own fertile country, well stocked with the finest cattle, has become a waste of jungle. A remnant of the tribe, under Kano-ni, their present sultan, son of the late T'háre, took refuge in the highlands of Urundi, not far from the principal settlement of the mountain king Mwezí: here they find water and pasture for their herds, and the strength of the country enables them to beat off their enemies. The Wahha are a comparatively fair and a not uncomely race; they are, however, universally held to be a vile and servile people; according to the Arabs they came originally from the southern regions, the most ancient seat of slavery in E. Africa. Their sultans or chiefs are of wahinda or princely origin, probably descendants from the regal race of Unyamwezi. Wahha slaves sell dearly at Msene; an adult male costs from five to six doti merkani, and a full-grown girl one gorah merkani or kaniki.

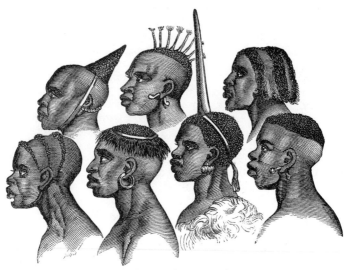

Head-dresses of Wanyamwezi.

CHAPTER XIV.

WE EXPLORE THE TANGANYIKA LAKE.

MY first care after settling in Hamid's tembe, was to purify the floor by pastilles of asafœtida and fumigations of gunpowder; my second was to prepare the roof for the rainy season. Improvement, however, progressed slowly; the "children" of Said bin Salim were too lazy to work; and the Wanyamwezi porters, having expended their hire in slaves, and fearing loss by delay, took the earliest opportunity of deserting. By the aid of a Msawahili artisan, I provided a pair of cartels, with substitutes for chairs and tables. Benches of clay were built round the rooms, but they proved useless, being found regularly every morning occupied in force by a swarming, struggling colony of the largest white ants. The roof, long overgrown with tall grass, was fortified with an extra coat of mud; it never ceased, however, leaking like a colander; presently the floor was covered with deep puddles, then masses of earth dropped from the sopped copings and sides of the solid walls, and, at last, during the violent showers, half the building fell in. The consequence of the extreme humidity was, that every book which had English paste in it was rendered useless by decay; writing was rendered illegible by stains and black mildew; moreover, during my absence while exploring the lake, Said bin Salim having neglected to keep a fire, as was ordered, constantly burning in the house, a large botanical collection was irretrievably lost. This was the more regretable as our return to the coast took place during the dry season, when the woods were bare of leaf, flower, and fruit.

On the second day after my arrival I was called upon by "Kannena," the headman of Kawele, under Rusimba, the mwami, or principal chief of Ujiji. I had heard a bad account of the former. His predecessor, Kabeza, a great favorite with the Arabs, had died about two months before we entered Kawele, leaving a single son, hardly ten years old, and Kannena, a slave, having the art to please the widows of the deceased, and through them the tribe, caused himself to be elected temporary headman during the heir's minority. He was introduced habited in silk turban and broadcloth coat, which I afterward heard he had borrowed from the Baloch, in order to put in a prepossessing first appearance. The effort, however, failed; his aspect was truly ignoble; a short, squat, and broad-backed figure, with natural "plumpers," a black skin cut and carved in various patterns, thick, straight, stumpy legs, and huge splay-feet; his low narrow brow was ever knotted into a peevish frown, his apology for a nose much resembled the pug with which the ancients provided Silenus, and a villainous expression lurked about the depressed corners of his thick-lipped, sensual, liquorish mouth. On this occasion he behaved with remarkable civility, and he introduced, as the envoys commissioned by the great Rusimba to receive his black-mail, two gentlemen a quarter clad in the greasiest and scantiest bark-aprons, and armed with dwarfish battle-axes. The present was finally settled at ten coil-bracelets and two fundi of coral-beads. I had no salt—the first article in demand—to spare, or much valuable merchandise might have been saved. The return was six small bundles of grain, worth, probably, one tenth of what had been received. Then Kannena opened trade by sending us a nominal gift, a fine ivory, weighing at least seventy pounds, and worth, perhaps, one hundred pounds, or nearly two men's loads of the white or blue porcelain beads used in this traffic. After keeping it for a day or two, I returned it, excusing myself by saying that, having visited the Tanganyika as a "sarkal," I could have no dealings in ivory and slaves.

This was right and proper in the character of a "sarkal." But future adventurers are strongly advised always to assume the character of traders. In the first place, it explains the traveler's motives to the people, who otherwise lose themselves in a waste of wild conjecture. Secondly, under this plea, the explorer can push forward into unknown countries; he will be civilly received, and lightly fined, because the hosts expect to see him or his semblables again; whereas, appearing without ostensible motive among them, he would be stripped of his last cloth by recurring confiscations, fines, and every annoyance which greed of gain can suggest. Thus, as the sequel will prove, he loses more by overcharges than by the trifling outlay necessary to support the character of a trader. He travels respectably as a "mundewa" or "tajir," a merchant, which is ever the highest title given by the people to strangers; and he can avoid exciting the jealousy of the Arabs by exchanging his tusks with them at a trifling loss when comforts or provisions are required for the road.

So strange an announcement on my part aroused, as may be supposed, in the minds of the Wajiji marvel, doubt, disbelief, ill-will. "These are men who live by doing nothing!" exclaimed the race commercial as the sons of Hamburg; and they lost no time in requesting me to quit their territory sooner than convenient. To this I objected, offering, however, as compensation for the loss of their octrois and perquisites, to pay for not trading what others paid for trading. Kannena roughly informed me that he had a claim for kiremba, or duties upon all purchases and sales; two cloths, for instance, per head of slave, or per elephant's tusk; and that, as he expected to gain nothing by brokerage from me, he must receive as compensation four coil-bracelets and six cotton cloths. These were at once forwarded to him. He then evidenced his ill-will in various ways, and his people were not slow in showing the dark side of their character. They threatened to flog Sayfu, the old Msawahili of Chole, for giving me hints concerning prices. The two surviving riding-asses were repeatedly wounded with spears. Thieves broke into the outhouses by night, and stole all the clothes belonging to the jemadar and to the bull-headed slave Mabruki. At first the widows of the late Kabeza, to whom the only cows in the district belonged, supplied us plentifully with milk; gradually the quantity shrank; whenever an opportunity offered it was "cut off;" and, at last, we could no longer afford the exorbitant price demanded. My companion having refused a cheese to Kannena, the dowager ladies, who owned the cows, when applied to for milk threw away the vessel, and swore that by boiling what ought to be drunk unboiled, we were manifestly bewitching and killing their cattle. On one occasion, a young person related to Rusimba went to the huts of the Baloch, and, snatching up a fine cloth, which she clasped to her bosom, defied them to recover it by force, and departed, declaring that it was a fine for bringing "whites" into the country. At first our heroes spoke of much slaughter likely to arise from such procedure, and with theatrical gesture made "*rapière au vent;*" presently second thoughts suggested how beautiful is peace, and thirdly, they begged so hard that I was compelled to ransom for them the article purloined. I had unwittingly incurred the animosity of Kannena. On the day after his appearance in rich clothing he had entered unannounced with bare head, a spear or two in hand, and a bundle of wild-cats' skins by way of placket; not being recognized, he was turned out, and the ejectment mortally offended his dignity. Still other travelers fared even worse than we did. Said bin Majid, who afterward arrived at Ujiji to trade for ivory and slaves, had two followers wounded by the Wajiji, one openly speared in the bazar, and the other at night by a thief who was detected digging through the wall of the store-hut.

After trade was disposed of, ensued a general bakhshish. Nothing of the kind had been contemplated or prepared for at Zanzibar, but before leaving Unyanyembe I had found it necessary to offer an inducement, and now the promise was to be fulfilled. Moreover, most of the party had behaved badly, and in these exceptional lands bad behavior always expects a reward. In the first place, says the Oriental, no man misconducts himself unless he has power to offend you and you are powerless to punish him. Secondly, by "petting" the offender, he may be bribed to conduct himself decently. On the other hand, the Eastern declares, by rewarding, praising, or promoting a man who has already satisfied you, you do him no good, and you may do him great harm. The boy Faraj, who had shamelessly deserted his master, Said bin Salim, was afterward found at Unyanyembe, in Snay bin Amir's house, handsomely dressed and treated like a guest; and his patron, forgetting all his stern resolves of condign punishment, met him with a peculiar kindness. I gave to the Baloch forty-five cloths, and to each slave, male and female, a pair. The gratification, however, proved somewhat like that man's liberality who, according to the old satirist, presented fine apparel to those whom he wished to ruin. Our people recklessly spent all their bakhshish in buying slaves, who generally deserted after a week, leaving the unhappy ex-proprietor tantalized by all the torments of ungratified acquisitiveness.

At first the cold damp climate of the Lake Regions did not agree with us; perhaps, too, the fish diet was over-rich and fat, and the abundance of vegetables led to little excesses. All energy seemed to have abandoned us. I lay for a fortnight upon the earth, too blind to read or write except with long intervals, too weak to ride, and too ill to converse. My companion, who when arriving at the Tanganyika Lake was almost as "groggy" upon his legs as I was, suffered from a painful ophthalmia, and from a curious distortion of face, which made him chew sideways, like a ruminant. Valentine was nearly blind; and he also had a wry mouth, by no means the properest for the process of mastication. Gaetano, who arrived at Ujiji on the 17th of February, was half starved, and his anxiety to make up for lost time brought on a severe attack of fever. The Baloch complained of influenzas and catarrhs: too lazy to build huts after occupying Kannena's "Traveler's Bungalow" for the usual week, they had been turned out in favor of fresh visitors, and their tempers were as sore as their lungs and throats.

But work remained undone; it was necessary to awake from this lethargy. Being determined to explore the northern extremity of the Tanganyika Lake, whence, according to several informants, issued a large river flowing northward, and seeing scanty chance of success, and every prospect of an accident if compelled to voyage in the wretched canoes of the people, I at first resolved to dispatch Said bin Salim across the water, and, by his intervention, to hire from an Arab merchant, Hamid bin Sulayyam, the only dow or sailing craft then in existence. But the little Arab evidently shirked the mission, and he shirked so artistically that, after a few days, I released him, and directed my companion to do his best about hiring the dow, and stocking it with provisions for a month's cruise.

Then arose the preliminary difficulties of the trip. Kannena and all his people, suspecting that my only object was economy in purchasing provisions, opposed the project; they demanded exorbitant sums, and often when bargained down and apparently satisfied, they started up and rushed away, declaring that they washed their hands of the business. At length Lurinda, the neighboring headman, was persuaded to supply a nakhoda and a crew of twenty men. An Arab pays on these occasions, besides rations, ten per cent. upon merchandise; the white men were compelled to give four coil-bracelets and eight cloths for the canoe; besides which, the crew received as hire six coil-bracelets, and to each individual provisions for eight days, and twenty khete of large blue-glass beads and small blue porcelains were issued. After many delays, my companion set out on the 2d of March, in the vilest weather, and spent the first stormy day near the embouchure of the Ruche River, within cannon-shot of Kawele. This halt gave our persecutors time to change their minds once more, and again to forbid the journey. I was compelled to purchase their permission by sending to Kannena an equivalent of what had been paid for the canoe to Lurinda, viz., four coil-bracelets and eight cloths. Two days afterward my companion, supplied with an ample outfit, and accompanied by two Baloch and his men — Gaetano and Bombay — crossed the Bay of Ukaranga, and made his final departure for the islands.

During my twenty-seven days of solitude the time sped quickly; it was chiefly spent in eating and drinking, smoking and dozing. Awaking at 2 or 3 A.M., I lay anxiously expecting the gray light creeping through the door-chinks and making darkness visible; the glad tidings of its approach were announced by the cawing of the crows and the crowing of the village cocks. When the golden rays began to stream over the red earth, the torpid Valentine was called up; he brought with him a mess of suji, or rice-flour boiled in water, with a little cold milk as a relish. Then entered Muhabanya, the "slavey" of the establishment, armed with a leafy branch to sweep the floor, and to slay the huge wasps that riddled the walls of the tenement. This done he lit the fire—the excessive damp rendered this precaution necessary—and sitting over it he bathed his face and hands—luxurious dog!—in the pungent smoke. Ensued visits of ceremony from Said bin Salim and the jemadar, who sat, stared, and, somewhat disappointed at seeing no fresh symptoms of approaching dissolution, told me so with their faces, and went away. From 7 A.M. till 9 A.M., the breakfast hour, Valentine was applied to tailoring, gun-cleaning, and similar light work, over which he groaned and grumbled, while I settled down to diaries and vocabularies, a process interrupted by sundry pipes. Breakfast was again a mess of suji and milk—such civilized articles as tea, coffee, and sugar, had been unknown to me for months. Again the servants resumed their labor, and they worked, with the interval of two hours for sleep at noon, till 4 P.M. During this time the owner lay like a log upon his cot, smoking almost uninterruptedly, dreaming of things past, and visioning things present, and sometimes indulging himself in a few lines of reading and writing.

Dinner was an alternation of fish and fowl, game and butchers' meat being rarely procurable at Ujiji. The fish were in two extremes, either insipid and soft, or so fat and coarse that a few mouthfuls sufficed; most of them resembled the species seen in the seas of Western India, and the eels and small shrimps recalled memories of Europe. The poultry, though inferior to that of Unyanyembe, was incomparably better than the lean stringy Indian chicken. The vegetables were various and plentiful, tomatoes, Jerusalem artichokes, sweet potatoes, yams, and several kinds of beans, especially a white haricot, which afforded many a *purée;* the only fruit procurable was the plantain, and the only drink— the toddy being a bad imitation of vinegar—was water.

As evening approached I made an attempt to sit under the broad eaves of the tembe, and to enjoy the delicious spectacle of this virgin Nature and the reveries to which it gave birth.

> " A pleasing land of drowsihed it was,
> Of dreams that wave before the half-shut eye,
> And of gay castles in the clouds that pass,
> Forever flushing round a summer sky."

It reminded me of the loveliest glimpses of the Mediterranean; there were the same " laughing tides," pellucid sheets of dark blue water borrowing their tints from the vinous shores beyond; the same purple light of youth upon the cheek of the earlier evening, the same bright sunsets, with their radiant vistas of crimson and gold opening like the portals of a world beyond the skies; the same short-lived grace and loveliness of the twilight; and, as night closed over the earth, the same cool flood of transparent moonbeam pouring on the tufty heights and bathing their sides with the whiteness of virgin snow.

At 7 P.M., as the last flush faded from the occident, the lamp— a wick in a broken pot full of palm-oil—was brought in; Said bin Salim appeared to give the news of the day—how A. had abused B., and how C. had nearly been beaten by D., and a brief conversation led to the hour of sleep.   A dreary, dismal day, you will exclaim, gentle reader; a day that

> "Lasts out a night in Russia,
> When nights are longest there."

Yet it had its enjoyments.   There were no post-offices, and this African Eden had other advantages which, probably, I might vainly attempt to describe.

On the 29th of March the rattling of matchlocks announced my companion's return.   The masika had done its worst upon him.   I never saw a man so thoroughly moist and mildewed; he justified even the French phrase "wet to the bone."   His paraphernalia were in a similar state; his guns were grained with rust, and his fire-proof powder-magazine had admitted the monsoon-rain.   I was sorely disappointed: he had done literally nothing. About ten days before his return I had been visited by Khamis bin Jumah, an Arab merchant, who, on the part of the proprietor of the dow, gave the gratifying message that we could have it when we pleased.   I can not explain where the mismanagement lay; it appears, however, that the wily "son of Sulayyam" detained the traveler simply for the purpose of obtaining from him gratis a little gunpowder.   My companion had rested content with the promise that after three months the dow should be let to us for a sum of 500 dollars! and he had returned without boat or provisions to report ill success.   The faces of Said bin Salim and the jemadar, when they heard the period mentioned, were indeed a study.   I consoled him and myself as I best could, and applied myself to supplying certain deficiencies as regards orthography and syntax in a diary which appeared in Blackwood, of September, 1859, under the title "Journal of a Cruise in the Tanganyika Lake, Central Africa."   I must confess, however, my surprise at, among many other things, the vast horseshoe of lofty mountain placed by my companion in the map attached to that paper near the very heart of Sir R. Murchison's Depression.   As this wholly hypothetical, or rather inventive feature—I had seen the mountains growing upon paper under my companion's hand from a thin ridge of hill fringing the Tanganyika to the portentous dimensions given in Blackwood (Sept., 1589) and Dr. Petermann's Mittheilungen (No. 9, of 1859)—wore a crescent form, my companion gravely published, with all the pomp of discovery, in the largest capitals, "This mountain range I consider to be THE TRUE MOUNTAINS OF THE MOON." * * * Thus men *do* geography! and thus discovery is stultified.

When my companion had somewhat recovered from his wetness, and from the effects of punching in with a pen-knife a beetle which had visited his tympanum,* I began seriously to seek some

---

* My companion gives in Blackwood, Sept., 1859, the following description of his untoward accident: "This day (that of his arrival at the Isle of Kivira) passed in rest and idleness, recruiting from our late exertions.   At night a violent storm of

means of exploring the northern head of the Tanganyika. Hamid bin Sulayyam had informed his late guest that he had visited the place, where, although attacked by an armada of thirty or forty hostile canoes, he had felt the influence of a large river, which drains the water northward: in fact, he told the "lie with circumstance." By a curious coincidence, Sayfu, the Mswahili of Chole, declared that he also had sighted a stream issuing from the northern extremity of the lake—this was the "lie direct"—and he offered to accompany me as guide and interpreter. When we compared statements, we saw what was before us—a prize for which wealth, health, and life were to be risked.

It now became apparent that the masika or rains, which the Arabs, whose barbarous lunar year renders untrustworthy in measurements of time, had erroneously represented as synchronous with the wet monsoon of Zanzibar, was drawing to a close, and that the season for navigation was beginning.* After some

rain and wind beat on my tent with such fury that its nether parts were torn away from the pegs, and the tent itself was only kept upright by sheer force. On the wind's abating, a candle was lighted to rearrange the kit, and in a moment, as though by magic, the whole interior became covered with a host of small black beetles, evidently attracted by the glimmer of the candle. They were so annoyingly determined in their choice of place for peregrinating, that it seemed hopeless my trying to brush them off the clothes or bedding; for as one was knocked aside another came on, and then another, till at last, worn out, I extinguished the candle, and with difficulty—trying to overcome the tickling annoyance occasioned by these intruders crawling up my sleeves and into my hair, or down my back and legs—fell off to sleep. Repose that night was not destined to be my lot. One of these horrid little insects awoke me in his struggles to penetrate my ear, but just too late: for, in my endeavor to extract him, I aided his immersion. He went his course, struggling up the narrow channel, until he got arrested by want of passage-room. This impediment evidently enraged him, for he began with exceeding vigor, like a rabbit at a hole, to dig violently away at my tympanum. The queer sensation this amusing *measure* excited in me is past description. I felt inclined to act as our donkeys once did when beset by a swarm of bees, who buzzed about their ears and stung their heads and eyes until they were so irritated and confused that they galloped about in the most distracted order, trying to knock them off by treading on their heads, or by rushing under bushes, into houses, or through any jungle they could find. Indeed, I do not know which was worst off. The bees killed some of them, and this beetle nearly did for me. What to do I knew not. Neither tobacco, oil, nor salt could be found: I therefore tried melted butter; that failing, I applied the point of a penknife to his back, which did more harm than good; for though a few thrusts kept him quiet, the point also wounded my ear so badly that inflammation set in, severe suppuration took place, and all the facial glands extending from that point down to the point of the shoulder became contorted and drawn aside, and a string of buboes decorated the whole length of that region. It was the most painful thing I ever remember to have endured; but, more annoying still, I could not open my mouth for several days, and had to feed on broth alone. For many months the tumor made me almost deaf, and ate a hole between that orifice and the nose, so that when I blew it, my ear whistled so audibly that those who heard it laughed. Six or seven months after this accident happened, bits of the beetle, a leg, a wing, or parts of its body, came away in the wax."

* Not unmindful of the instructions of the Bombay Geographical Society, which called especial attention to the amount of rain-fall and evaporation in a region which abounding in lakes and rivers yet sends no supplies to the sea, I had prepared at Zanzibar a dish and a gauge for the purpose of comparing the hygrometry of the African with that of the Indian rainy monsoon. The instruments, however, were fated to do no work. The first portion of the masika was spent in a journey; ensued

preliminaries with Said bin Salim, Kannena, who had been preparing for a cruise northward, was summoned before me. He
agreed to convey me; but when I asked him the conditions on
which he would show me the mtoni, or river, he jumped up, discharged a volley of oaths, and sprang from the house like an enraged baboon.   I was prepared for this difficulty, having had
several warnings that the tribes on the northern shores of the
Tanganyika allow no trade.   But fears like Kannena's may generally be bought over.   I trusted, therefore, to fate, and resolved
that at all costs, even if reduced to actual want, we should visit
this mysterious stream.   At length the headman yielded every
point.   He received, it is true, an exorbitant sum.   Arabs visiting Uvira, the "ultima thule" of lake navigation, pay one cloth to
each of the crew; and the fare of a single passenger is a brace of
coil-bracelets.   For two canoes, the larger sixty feet by four, and
the lesser about two thirds that size, I paid thirty-three coil-bracelets, here equal to sixty dollars, twenty cloths, thirty-six khete of
blue glass beads, and 770 ditto of white porcelains and green glass.
I also promised to Kannena a rich reward if he acted up to his
word; and as an earnest I threw over his shoulders a six-foot
length of scarlet broadcloth, which caused his lips to tremble with
joy, despite his struggles to conceal it.   The nakhoda (captain)
and the crew in turn received, besides rations, eighty cloths, 170
khete of blue glass beads, and forty of coral porcelains, locally
three times more valuable than whites or greens.   Sayfu, the interpreter, was as extravagantly paid in eight cloths and twenty-
seven pounds of white and blue porcelains.   After abundance of
dispute it was settled that the crews should consist of fifty-five
men, thirty-three to the larger and twenty-two to the smaller
canoe.   It was an excess of at least one half, who went for their
own profit, not for our pleasure.   When this point was conceded,
we were kindly permitted to take with us the two Goanese, the
two black gun-carriers, and three Baloch as an escort.   The latter
were the valiant Khudabakhsh, whom I feared to leave behind;
Jelai, the mestiço-mekrani; and, thirdly, Riza, the least mutinous
and uncivil of the party.

Before departure it will be necessary to lay before the reader a
sketch of our conveyance.   The first aspect of these canoes made
me lament the loss of Mr. Francis's iron boat: regrets, however,
were of no avail.   *Quocumque modo—rem!* was the word.

The baumrinden are unknown upon the Tanganyika Lake,
where the smaller craft are monoxyles, generally damaged in the
bow by the fishermen's fire.   The larger are long, narrow "matumbi," or canoes, rudely hollowed with the axe—the application

<hr>

severe sickness, and the end of the rains happened during a voyage to the north of
the Tanganyika. A few scattered observations might have been registered, but it
was judged better to bring home no results, rather than imperfections which could
only mislead the meteorologist.

of fire being still to be invented—in fact, a mere log of mvule, or some other large tree which abound in the land of the Wagoma, opposite Ujiji. The trunks are felled, scooped out in loco, dragged and pushed by man-power down the slopes, and finally launched and paddled over to their destination. The most considerable are composed of three parts—clumsy, misshapen planks, forming, when placed side by side, a keel and two gunwales, the latter fastened to the centre-piece by cords of palm-fibre passing through lines of holes. The want of calking causes excessive leakage: the crew take duty as balesmen in turns. The cry Senga!—bale out!—rarely ceases, and the irregular hollowing of the tree-trunks makes them lie slopsided in the water. These vessels have neither masts nor sails; artifices which now do not extend to this part of the African world. An iron ring fixed in the stern is intended for a rudder, which, however, seldom appears except in the canoes of the Arabs; steering is managed by the paddle, and a flag-staff or a fishing-rod projects jib-like from the bow. Layers of palm-ribs, which serve for fuel, are strewed over the interior to raise the damageable cargo—it is often of salt—above the bilge-water. The crew sit upon narrow benches extending across the canoe and fastened with cords to holes in the two side-pieces; upon each bench, despite the narrowness of the craft, two men place themselves side by side. The "karagwah," stout stiff mats used for hutting and bedding, are spread for comfort upon the seats; and for convenience of paddling, the sailors, when at work, incline their bodies over the sides. The space under the seats is used for stowage. In the centre there is a square place, about six feet long, left clear of benches; here also cargo is stored, passengers, cattle, and slaves litter down, the paddles, gourds, and other furniture of the crew are thrown, and the baling is carried on by means of an old gourd. The hold is often ankle-deep in water, and affords no convenience for leaning or lying down; the most comfortable place, therefore, is near the stern or the bow of the boat. The spears are planted upright amidships, at one or two corners of the central space, so as to be ready at a moment's notice; each man usually has his dagger stuck in his belt, and on long trips all are provided with bows and arrows. These Africans can not row; indeed, they will not use oars. The paddle on the Tanganyika is a stout staff about six feet long, and cut out at the top to admit a trefoil-shaped block the size of a man's hand: it was described in South Africa by Captain Owen. The block, adorned with black paint in triangular patches, is lashed to the staff by a bit of whip-cord, and it seldom lasts through the day without breaking away from its frail tackling. The paddler, placing one hand on the top and the other about the middle of the staff, scoops up, as it were, the water in front of him, steadying his paddle by drawing it along the side of the canoe. The eternal splashing keeps the boat wet. It is a laborious occupation, and an excessive waste of power.

The lake people derive their modern practice of navigation, doubtless, from days of old; the earliest accounts of the Portuguese mention the traffic of this inland sea. They have three principal beats from Ujiji: the northern abuts at the ivory and slave marts of Uvira; the western conducts to the opposite shores of the lake and the island depôts on the southwest; and the southern leads to the land of Marunga. Their canoes creep along the shores like the hollowed elders of thirty bygone centuries, and, waiting till the weather augurs fairly, they make a desperate push for the other side. Nothing but their extreme timidity, except when emboldened by the prospect of a speedy return home, preserves their cranky craft from constant accidents. The Arabs, warned by the past, rarely trust themselves to this lake of storms, preferring the certain peculation incurred by deputing for trading purposes agents and slaves to personal risk. Those who must voyage on the lake build, by means of their menials and artisans, dows, or sailing-vessels, and teach their newly-bought gangs to use oars instead of paddles. This is rather an economy of money than of time: they expend six months upon making the dow, whereas they can buy the largest canoe for a few farasilah of ivory.

As my outfit was already running low, I persuaded, before departure, two of the Baloch to return with a down-caravan westward, and, arrived at Unyanyembe, to communicate personally with my agent, Snay bin Amir. They agreed so to do, but the mtongi, or head of the African kafilah, with true African futility, promised to take them on the next day, and set out that night on his journey. As Said bin Majid was about dispatching a large armed party to the north of the lake, I then hurried on my preparations for the voyage. Provisions and tobacco were laid in, the tent was repaired, and our outfit, four half loads of salt—of these, two were melted in the canoe—six gorah, or one load of domestics, nine coil-bracelets, the remainder of our store, one load of blue porcelain beads, and a small bag of the valuable red coral, intended for private expenses, and "el akibah" (the reserve), was properly packed for concealment. Meanwhile, some trifling disputes occurred with Kannena, who was in the habit of coming to our tembe drunk and surly, with eyes like two gouts of blood, knitted front, and lips viciously shot out: when contradicted or opposed, he screamed and gesticulated as if haunted by his p'hepo —his fiend—and when very evilly disposed, he would proceed to the extreme measure of cutting down a tent. This slave-sultan was a "son of noise:" he affected *brusquerie* of manner and violence of demeanor the better to impressionize his unruly subjects; and he frightened the timid souls around us, till at last the jemadar's phrase was, "Strength is useless here." Had I led, however, three hundred instead of thirty matchlocks, he would have crouched and cowered like a whipped cur.

At 4 P.M. on the 9th of April, appeared before the Kannena in a tattered red turban, donned for the occasion. He was accompanied by his ward, who was to perform the voyage as a training to act sultan, and he was followed by his sailors bearing salt, in company with their loud-voiced wives and daughters performing upon the wildest musical instruments. Of these, the most noisy was a kind of shaum, a straight, long, and narrow tube of wood, bound with palm-fibre, and provided with an open mouth like a clarionet; a distressing bray is kept up by blowing through a hole pierced in the side. The most monotonous was a pair of foolscap-shaped plates of thin iron, joined at the apices and connected at the bases by a solid cross-bar of the same metal; this rude tom-tom is performed upon by a muffled stick with painful perseverance; the sound—how harshly it intruded upon the stilly beauty of the scenes around!—still lingers and long shall linger in my tympanum. The canoe had been moved from its usual position opposite our tembe to a place of known departure —otherwise not a soul could have been persuaded to embark— and, ignoring the distance, I condemned myself to a hobble of three miles over rough and wet ground. The night was comfortless; the crew, who were all "half-seas over," made the noise of bedlamites; and two heavy falls of rain drenching the flimsy tent, at once spoiled the tobacco and flour, the grain and the vegetables prepared for the voyage.

Early on the next morning we embarked on board the canoes: the crews had been collected, paid, and rationed; but as long as they were near home it was impossible to keep them together. Each man thinking solely of his own affairs, and disdaining the slightest regard for the wishes, the comfort, or the advantage of his employers, they objected systematically to every article which I had embarked. Kannena had filled the canoes with his and his people's salt, consequently he would not carry even a cartel. Various points settled, we hove anchor, or rather hauled up the block of granite doing anchoral duty, and, with the usual hubbub and strife, the orders which every man gives and the advice which no man takes, we paddled in half an hour to a shingly and grassy creek defended by a sand-pit and backed by a few tall massive trees. Opposite, and but a few yards distant, rose the desert islet of Bangwe, a quoin-shaped mass of sandstone and red earth, bluff to the north, and gradually shelving toward the water at the other extremity: the prolific moisture above and around had covered its upper ledge with a coat of rich thick vegetation. Landward the country rises above the creek, and upon its earth-waves, which cultivation shares with wild growth, appear a few scattered hamlets.

Boats generally waste some days at Bangwe Bay, the stage being short enough for the usual scene being encored. They load and reload, trim cargo, complete rations, collect crews, and take leave of friends and relatives, women and palm-wine. We pitched a tent, and halted in a tornado of wind and rain. Kannena would not move without the present of one of our three goats. At 4 P.M., on the 11th of April, the canoes were laden and paddled out to and back from Bangwe Islet, when those knowing in such matters pronounced them so heavily weighted as to be unsafe; whereupon the youth Riza, sorely against my will, was sent back to the Kawele. On that night a furious gale carried away my tent, while the Goanese were, or pretended to be, out of hearing. I slept, however, comfortably enough upon the crest of a sand-wave higher than the puddles around it, and—blessings on the name of Mackintosh!—escaped the pitiless pelting of the rain.

The next morning showed a calm sea, leveled by the showers, and no pretext or desire for longer detention lingered in the hearts of the crew. At 7.20 A.M., on the 12th of April, 1858, my canoe —bearing for the first time on those dark waters

"The flag that braved a thousand years
The battle and the breeze—"

stood out of Bangwe Bay, and, followed by my companions, turned the land-spit separating the bight from the main, and made directly for the cloudy and storm-vexed north. The eastern shore of the lake, along which we coasted, was a bluff of red earth puddinged with separate blocks of sandstone. Beyond this headland the coast dips, showing lines of shingle, or golden-colored quartzose sand, and on the shelving plain appear the little fishing-villages. They are usually built at the mouths of the gaps, combes, and gullies, whose deep gorges, winding through the background of hill-curtain, become, after rains, the beds of mountain-torrents. The wretched settlements are placed between the tree-clad declivities and the shore on which the waves break. The sites are far from comfortable: the ground is here veiled with thick and fetid grass, there it is a puddle of black mud, and there a rivulet trickles through the villages. The hamlet consists of half a dozen beehive huts, foul, flimsy, and leaky; their only furniture is a hearth of three clods or stones, with a few mats and fishing implements. The settlements are distinguished from a distance by their plantations of palm and plantain, and by large spreading trees, from whose branches are suspended the hoops and the drag-nets not in actual use, and under whose shade the people sit propped against their monoxyles, which are drawn high up out of danger of the surf. There was no trade, and few provisions were procurable at Kigari. We halted there to rest, and, pitching a tent in the thick grass, we spent a night loud with wind and rain.

Rising at black dawn on the 13th of April, the crews rowed hard for six hours between Kigari and another dirty little fishing-village called Nyasanga. The settlement supplied fish-fry, but neither grain nor vegetables were offered for sale. At this place, the frontier district between Ujiji and Urundi, our Wajiji took

leave of their fellow-clansmen and prepared with serious countenances for all the perils of expatriation.

This is the place for a few words concerning boating and voy-
aging upon the Tanganyika Lakes. The Wajiji, and indeed all
these races, never work silently or regularly. The paddling is
accompanied by a long monotonous melancholy howl, answered
by the yells and shouts of the chorus, and broken occasionally by
a shrill scream of delight from the boys which seems violently to
excite the adults. The bray and clang of the horns, shaums, and
tom-toms, blown and banged incessantly by one or more men in
the bow of each canoe, made worse by brazen-lunged imitations
of these instruments in the squeaking trebles of the younger pad-
dlers, lasts throughout the livelong day, except when terror induces a general silence. These " Wáná Máji"—sons of water—
work in " spirts," applying lustily to the task till the perspiration
pours down their sooty persons. Despite my remonstrances, they
insisted upon splashing the water in shovelfuls over the canoe.
They make terribly long faces, however, they tremble like dogs
in a storm of sleet, and they are ready to whimper when compelled
by sickness or accident to sit with me under the endless cold wave-
bath in the hold. After a few minutes of exertion, fatigued and
worn, they stop to quarrel, or they progress languidly till recruited
for another effort. When two boats are together they race continually till a bump—the signal for a general grin—and the difficulty of using the entangled paddles afford an excuse for a little
loitering, and for the loud chatter and violent abuse, without
which apparently this people can not hold converse. At times
they halt to eat, drink, and smoke: the bhang-pipe is produced
after every hour, and the paddles are taken in while they indulge
in the usual screaming convulsive whooping-cough. They halt
for their own purposes but not for ours; all powers of persuasion
fail when they are requested to put into a likely place for collecting shells or stones.* For some superstitious reason they allow
no questions to be asked, they will not dip a pot for water into

---

* The following Paper by S. P. Woodward, F. G. S., communicated by
Prof. Owen, appeared in the Proceedings of the Zoological Society of
London, June 28, 1859.

The four shells which form the subject of the present note were collected by Captain Speke in the great fresh-water lake Tanganyika in Central Africa.

The large bivalve belongs to the genus *Iridina*, Lamarck—a group of river-mus-
cles, of which there are nine reputed species, all belonging to the African continent.
This little group has been divided into several sub-genera. That to which the new
shell belongs is distinguished by its broad and deeply-wrinkled hinge-line, and is
called *Pleiodon* by Conrad. The posterior slope of this shell is incrusted with tufa,
as if there were limestone rocks in the vicinity of its habitat.

The small bivalve is a normal *Unio*, with finely sculptured valves.

The smaller univalve is concave beneath, and so much resembles a *Nerita* or *Calyp-
traea* that it would be taken for a sea-shell if its history were not well authentica-
ted. It agrees essentially with *Lithoglyphus*—a genus peculiar to the Danube; for
the American shells referred to it are probably, or, I may say, certainly distinct. It
agrees with the Danubian shells in the extreme obliquity of the aperture, and differs

the lake, fearing to be followed and perhaps boarded by crocodiles, which are hated and dreaded by these black navigators,

in the width of the umbilicus, which in the European species is nearly concealed by
the callous columellar lip.

In the Upper Eocene Tertiaries of the Isle of Wight there are several estuary shells,
forming the genus *Globulus*, Sow., whose affinities are uncertain, but which resemble
Lithoglyphus.

The Lake Tanganyika (situated in lat. 3° to 8° S., and long. 30° E.), which is
several hundred miles in length, and 30 to 40 in breadth, seems entirely disconnect-
ed with the region of the Danube : but the separation may not always have been so
complete, for there is another great lake, Nyanza, to the northward of Tanganyika,
which is believed by Speke to be the principal source of the Nile.

The other univalve is a *Melania*, of the sub-genus *Melanella* (Swainson), similar in
shape to *M. hollandi* of S. Europe, and similar to several Eocene species of the Isle
of Wight. Its color, solidity, and tuberculated ribs give it much the appearance of
a small marine whelk (*Nassa*); and it is found in more boisterous waters, on the
shores of this great inland sea, than most of its congeners inhabit.

1. IRIDINA (PLEIODON) SPEKII, n. sp. (Pl. XLVII., fig. 2.)

Shell oblong, ventricose, somewhat attenuated at each end : base slightly concave ;
epidermis chestnut-brown, deepening to black at the margin ; anterior slope obscurely radiated ; hinge-line compressed in front and tuberculated, wider behind and
deeply wrinkled.

Length 4¾, breadth 2, thickness 1¾ inches.

*Testa oblonga, tumida, extremitatibus fere attenuata, basi subarcuata ; epidermide cas-
taneo-fusca, marginem versus nigricante ; linea cardinali antice compressa tubercu-
lata, postice latiore, paucis rugis arata.*

2. UNIO BURTONI, n. sp. (Pl. XLVII., fig. 1.)

Shell small, oval, rather thin, somewhat pointed behind ; umbones small, not erod-
ed ; pale olive, concentrically furrowed, and sculptured more or less with fine divar-
icating lines ; anterior teeth narrow, not prominent ; posterior teeth laminar ; pedal
scar confluent with anterior adductor.

Length 12, breadth 8½, thickness 5½ lines.

*Testa parva, ovalis, tenuiuscula, postice subattenuata ; umbonibus parvis, acuminatis ;
epidermide pallide olivacea ; valvis lineolis divaricatis, decussatum exaratis ; denti-
bus cardinalibus angustis, haud prominentibus.*

3. LITHOGLYPHUS ZONATUS, n. sp. (Pl. XLVII., fig. 3.)

Shell orbicular, hemispherical ; spire very small ; aperture large, very oblique ;
umbilicus wide and shallow, with an open fissure in the young shell ; lip continuous
in front with the umbilical ridge ; columella callous, ultimately covering the fissure ;
body-whirl flattened, pale olivaceous, with two brown bands, darker at the apex ;
lines of growth crossed by numerous oblique, interrupted striæ.

Diameter 5–6, height 3 lines.

*Testa orbicularis, hemisphœrica, late umbilicata (apud juniores rimata), spira minuta ;
apertura magna, valde obliqua ; labio calloso (in testa adulta rimam tegente) ; pallide olivacea, fasciis duabus fuscis zonata ; lineis incrementi striolis interruptis oblique decussatis.*

4. MELANIA (MELANELLA) NASSA, n. sp. (Pl. XLVII., fig. 4.)

Shell ovate, strong, pale brown, with (sometimes) two dark bands ; spire shorter
than the aperture ; whirls flattened, ornamented with six brown spiral ridges crossed
with a variable number of white, tuberculated, transverse ribs ; base of body-whirl
eight, with tuberculated spiral ridges variegated with white and brown ; aperture sinuated in front ; outer lip simple ; inner lip callous.

Length 8½, breadth 5½ lines.

*Testa ovata, solida, pallide fusca, zonis 2 nigricantibus aliquando notata ; spira aper-
tura breviore ; anfractibus planulatis, lineis 6 fuscis spiralibus et costis tuberculatis
ornatis ; apertura antice sinuata ; labro simplici ; labio calloso.*

P.S. July 27th.—In addition to the foregoing shells, several others were collected much as is the shark by our seamen, and for the same cause not a scrap of food must be thrown overboard—even the offal must be cast into the hold. "Whittling" is here a mortal sin: to chip or break off the smallest bit of even a condemned old tub drawn up on the beach causes a serious disturbance. By the advice of a kind and amiable friend,* I had supplied myself with the desiderata for sounding and ascertaining the bottom of the lake: the crew would have seen me under water rather than halt for a moment when it did not suit their purpose. The wild men lose half an hour, when time is most precious, to secure a dead fish as it floats past the canoe entangled in its net. They never pass a village without a dispute; some wishing to land, others objecting because some wish it. The captain, who occupies some comfortable place in the bow, stern, or waist, has little authority; and if the canoe be allowed to touch the shore, its men will spring out, without an idea of consulting aught beyond their own inclinations. Arrived at the halting-place they pour on shore; some proceed to gather firewood, others go in search of rations, and others raise the boothies. A dozen barked sticks of various lengths are planted firmly in the ground; the ends are bent and

by Capt. Speke, when employed, under the command of Capt. Burton, in exploring Central Africa in the years 1856–9; these were deposited in the first instance with the Geographical Society, and are now transferred to the British Museum.

A specimen of *Ampullaria (Lanistes) sinistrorsa*, Lea, and odd valves of two species of *Unio*, both smooth and olive-colored, were picked up in the Ugogo district, an elevated plateau in lat. 6° to 7° S., long. 34° to 35° E.

A large *Achatina*, most nearly related to *A. glutinosa*, Pfr., is the "common snail" of the region between Lake Tanganyika and the east coast. Fossil specimens were obtained in the Usagara district, at a place called Marora, 3000 feet above the sea, overlooking the Lufiji River, where it intersects the coast range (lat. 7° to 8° S., long. 35° to 36° E.).

Another common land-snail of the same district is the well-known "*Bulimus caillaudi*, Pfr.," a shell more nearly related to *Achatina* than *Bulimus*.

Captain Speke also found a solitary example of *Bulimus ovoideus*, Brug., in a musjid on the Island of Kiloa (lat 9° S., long. 39° to 40° E.). This species is identical with *B. grandis*, Desh., from the Island of Nosse Bé, Madagascar, and very closely allied to *B. liberianus*, Lea, from Guinea.

* Captain Balfour, H. M. I. N., who kindly supplied me with a list of necessaries for sail-making and other such operations on the lake. I had indented upon the engineers' stores, Bombay, for a Massey's patent or self-registering log, which would have been most useful had the people allowed it to be used. Prevented by stress of business from testing it in India, I found it at sea so thoroughly defective, that it was returned from whence it came by the good aid of Captain Frushard, then commanding the H. E. I. C.'s sloop of war *Elphinstone*. I then prepared at Zanzibar a line and a lead, properly hollowed to admit of its being armed, and this safely reached the Tanganyika Lake. It was not useless but unused: the crew objected to its being hove, and moreover—lead and metal are never safe in Central Africa—the line, which was originally short, was curtailed of one half during the first night after our departure from Kawele. It is by no means easy to estimate the rate of progress in these barbarous canoes barbarously worked. During the "spirts" when the paddler bends his back manfully to his task, a fully-manned craft may attain a maximum of 7 to 8 miles per hour: this exertion, however, rarely exceeds a quarter of an hour, and is always followed by delay. The usual pace, when all are fresh and cool, is about 4 to 5 miles, which declines through 4 and 3 to 2½, when the men are fatigued, or when the sun is high. The medium, therefore, may be assumed at 4 miles for short, and a little more than two miles an hour for long trips, halts deducted.

lashed together in the shape of half an orange by strips of tree-fibre; they are then covered with the karagwah—the stiff reed mats used as cushions when paddling; these are tightly bound on, and thus a hut is made capable of defending from rain the bodies of four or five men, whose legs, which project beyond the shelter, are apparently not supposed to require covering. Obeying only impulse, and wholly deficient in order and purpose, they make the voyage as uncomfortable as possible; they have no regular stages and no fixed halting-places; they waste a fine cool morning, and pull through the heat of the day, or after dozing throughout the evening, at the loud cry of "Pakírá bábá!"—pack up, hearties!—they scramble into their canoes about midnight. Outward bound they seek opportunities for delay; when it is once "up anchor for home," they hurry with dangerous haste.

On the 14th of April, a cruise of four hours conducted us to Wafanya, a settlement of Wajiji mixed with Warundi. Leaving this wretched mass of hovels on the next day, which began with a solemn warning from Sayfu—a man of melancholic temperament,—we made in four hours Wafanya, the southern limit of Urundi, and the only port in that inhospitable land still open to travelers. Drawing up our canoes upon a clear narrow sand-strip beyond the reach of the surf, we ascended a dwarf earth-cliff, and, pitching our tents under a spreading tree upon the summit, we made ourselves as comfortable as the noisy, intrusive, and insolent crowd, assembled to stare and to laugh at the strangers, would permit. The crew raised their boothies within a stone-throw of the water, flight being here the thought ever uppermost in their minds.

The people of this country are a noisy insolent race, addicted, like all their lakist brethren, to drunkenness, and, when drunk, quarrelsome and violent. At Wafanya, however, they are kept in order by Kanoni, their mutware or minor chief, subject to "Mwezi," the mwami or sultan of Urundi. The old man appeared, when we reached his settlement, in some state, preceded by an ancient carrying his standard, a long wisp of white fibre attached to a spear, like the Turkish "horse-tail," and followed by a guard of forty or fifty stalwart young warriors armed with stout lance-like spears for stabbing and throwing, straight double-edged daggers, stiff bows, and heavy, grinded arrows. Kanoni began by receiving his black-mail—four cloths, two coil-bracelets, and three fundo of coral beads: the return was the inevitable goat. The climate of Wafanya is alternately a damp-cold and a "muggy" heat; the crews, however, if numerous and well armed, will delay here to feed when northward bound, and to lay in provisions when returning to their homes. Sheep and fine fat goats vary in value from one to two cloths; a fowl, or five to six eggs, costs a khete of beads; sweet potatoes are somewhat dearer than at Ujiji; there is no rice, but holcus and manioc are cheap and abundant, about

5 lbs. of the latter being sold for a single khete. Even milk is at times procurable. A sharp business is carried on in chikichi or palm-oil, of which a large earthen pot is bought for a cloth; the best paddles used by the crews are made at Wafanya; and the mbugu, or bark-cloth, is bought for four to ten khete, about one third of the market-price at Ujiji. Salt, being imported from Uvinza, is dear and scarce: it forms the first demand for barter, and beads the second. Large fish is offered for sale, but the small fry is the only article of the kind which is to be purchased fresh. The country owes its plenty, according to the guides, to almost perennial showers.

The inhospitality of the Warundi and their northern neighbors, who would plunder a canoe or insist upon a black-mail equivalent to plunder, allows neither traffic nor transit to the north of Wafanya. Here, therefore, the crews prepare to cross the Tanganyika, which is divided into two stages by the Island of Ubwari.

In Ubwari I had indeed discovered "an island far away." It is probably the place alluded to by the Portuguese historian, De Barros, in this important passage concerning the great lake in the centre of Africa: "It is a sea of such magnitude as to be capable of being navigated by many sail; and among the islands in it there is one capable of sending forth an army of 30,000 men." Ubwari appears from a distance of two days bearing northwest; it is then somewhat hazy, owing to the extreme humidity of the atmosphere. From Wafanya it shows a clear profile about eighteen to twenty miles westward, and the breadth of the western channel between it and the main land averages from six to seven miles. Its north point lies in south lat. 4° 7', and the lay is N. 17° E. (corrected). From the northern point of Ubwari the eastern prolongation of the lake bears N. 3° W., and the western N. 10° W. It is the only island near the centre of the Tanganyika —a long, narrow lump of rock, twenty to twenty-five geographical miles long, by four or five of extreme breadth, with a high longitudinal spine, like a hog's back, falling toward the water— here shelving, there steep, on the sea-side—where it ends in abrupt cliffs, here and there broken by broad or narrow gorges. Green from head to foot, in richness and profuseness of vegetation it equals, and perhaps excels, the shores of the Tanganyika, and in parts it appears carefully cultivated. Mariners dare not disembark on Ubwari except at the principal places; and upon the wooded hill-sides wild men are, or are supposed to be, ever lurking in wait for human prey.

We halted two miserable days at Wafanya. The country is peculiarly rich, dotted with numerous hamlets, which supply provisions and even milk, and divided into dense thickets, palm-groves, and large clearings of manioc, holcus, and sweet potatoes, which mantle like a garment the earth's brown body. Here we found Kannena snugly ensconced in our sepoy's pal, or ridge-tent. He had privily obtained it from Said bin Salim, with a view to add to his and his ward's comfort and dignity. When asked to give it up—we were lodging, I under a lug-sail brought from the coast and converted into an awning, and my companion in the wretched flimsy article purchased from the fundi—he naively refused. Presently having seen a fat sheep, he came to me declaring that it was his perquisite: moreover, he insisted upon receiving the goat offered to us by the Sultan Kanoni. I at first demurred. His satisfactory rejoinder was: "Ngema, ndugu yango! —Well, my brother, here we remain!" I consulted Bombay about the necessity of humoring him in every whim. "What these jungle niggers want," quoth my counsel, "that they will have, or they will see the next month's new moon!"

The morning of the 18th of April was dark and menacing. Huge purpling clouds deformed the face of the northern sky. Having loaded the canoes, however, we embarked to cross the channel which separated us from the Ubwari Island. As the paddles were in hand, the crew, starting up from their benches, landed to bring on board some forgotten manioc. My companion remained in his boat, I in mine. Presently, hearing an unusual uproar, I turned round and saw the sailors arming themselves, while the "curtain-lion," Khudabakhsh, was being hustled with blows, and pushed up the the little cliff by a host of black spearmen; a naked savage the while capering about, waving the Baloch's bare blade in one hand and its scabbard in the other. Kannena joined majestically in the "row," but the peals of laughter from the mob showed no signs of anger. A Mjiji slave belonging to Khudabakhsh had, it appears, taken flight, after landing unobserved with the crowd. The brave had redemanded him of Kannena, whom he charged, moreover, with aiding and abetting the desertion. The slave sultan offered to refer the point to me, but the valiant man, losing patience, out with his sword, and was instantly disarmed, assaulted, and battered, as above described, by forty or fifty sailors. When quiet was restored, I called to him from the boat. He replied by refusing to "budge an inch," and by summoning his "brother" Jelai to join him with bag and baggage. Kannena also used soft words, till at last, weary of waiting, he gave orders to put off, throwing two cloths to Khudabakhsh, that the fellow might not return home hungry. I admired his generosity till compelled to pay for it.

The two Baloch were like mules; they disliked the voyage, and as it was the ramazan, they added to their discomforts by pretending to fast. Their desertion was inexcusable; they left us wholly in the power of the Wajiji, to dangers and difficulties which they themselves could not endure. Prudent Orientals, I may again observe, never commit themselves to the sole custody of Africans, even of the "muwallid," namely, those born and bred in their houses. In Persia the traveler is careful to mix the black blood with that of the higher race; formerly, whenever the member of a family was found murdered, the serviles were all tortured as a preliminary to investigation, and many stories like the following are recounted. The slaves had left their master in complete security, and were sitting, in early night, merrily chatting round the camp fire. Presently one began to relate the list of their grievances; another proposed to end them by desertion; and a third seconded the motion, opining, however, that they might as well begin by murdering the patroon. No sooner said than done. These children of passion and instinct, in the shortest interim, act out the "dreadful thing," and as readily repent when reflection returns. The Arab, therefore, in African lands, seldom travels with Africans only; he prefers collecting as many companions and bringing as many hangers-on as he can afford. The best escort to a European capable of communicating with and commanding them, would be a small party of Arabs fresh from Hazramaut and untaught in the ways and tongues of Africa. They would, by forming a kind of balance of power, prevent that daring pilfering for which slaves are infamous; in the long run they would save money to the explorer, and perhaps save his life.

Khudabakhsh and his comrade-deserter returned safely by land to Kawele; and when derided by the other men, he repeated, as might he expected, notable griefs. Both had performed prodigies of valor; they had, however, been mastered by millions. Then they had called upon "Haji Abdullah" for assistance, to which he had replied, "My power does not extend here!" Thus heartlessly refused aid by the only person who could and should have afforded it, they were reduced, sorely against their will, to take leave of him. Their tale was of course believed by their comrades till the crews brought back the other version of the affair, the "camel-hearts" then once more became the laugh and gibe of man and woman.

After a short consultation among the men concerning the threatening aspect of the heavens, it was agreed by them to defer crossing the lake till the next day. We therefore passed on to the northern side of the point which limits the Bay of Wafanya, and anchoring the craft in a rushy bayou, we pitched tents in time to protect us against a violent thunderstorm with its wind and rain.

On the 19th of April we stretched westward toward Ubwari, which appeared a long strip of green directly opposite Urundi, and distant from eighteen to twenty miles. A little wind caused a heavy chopping swell; we were wet to the skin, and as noon drew nigh, the sun shone stingingly, reflected by a mirrory sea. At 10 A.M. the party drew in their paddles and halted to eat and smoke. About 2 P.M. the wind and waves again arose—once more we were drenched, and the frail craft was constantly baled out to prevent water-logging. A long row of nine hours placed the canoes at a roadstead, with the usual narrow line of yellow sand, on the western coast of Ubwari Island. The men landed to dry themselves, and to cook some putrid fish which they had caught as it floated past the canoe, with the reed triangle that buoyed up the net. It was "strong meat" to us, but to them its staleness was as the "taste in his butter" to the Londoner, the pleasing toughness of the old cock to the Arab, and the savory "fumet" of the aged he-goat to the Baloch. After a short halt we moved a little northward to Mzimu, a strip of low land dividing the waters from their background of grassy rise, through which a swampy line winds from the hills above. Here we found canoes drawn up, and the islanders flocked from their hamlets to change their ivory and slaves, goats and provisions, for salt and beads, wire and cloth. The Wabwari are a peculiar, and by no means a comely race. The men are habited in the usual mbugu, tigered with black stripes, and tailed like leopard-skins: a wisp of fine grass acts as fillet, and their waists, wrists, and ankles, their knob-sticks, spears, and daggers, are bound with ratan-bark, instead of the usual wire. The women train their frizzly locks into two side-bits resembling bear's ears; they tie down the bosom with a cord, apparently for the purpose of distorting nature in a way that is most repulsive to European eyes; and they clothe themselves with the barbarous goat-skin, or the scantiest kilts of bark cloth. The wives of the chiefs wear a load of brass and bead ornaments; and, like the ladies of Wafanya, they walk about with patriarchal staves five feet long, and knobbed at the top.

We halted for a day at Mzimu in Ubwari, where Kannena demanded seventy khete of blue-porcelain beads as his fee for safe conduct to the island. Suddenly, at 6 P.M., he informed me that he must move to other quarters. We tumbled into the boats, and after enjoying two hours of pleasant progress with a northerly current, and a splendid moonshine, which set off a scene at once wild and soft as any

"That savage Rosa dashed, or learned Poussin drew,"

we rounded the bluff northern point of the island, put into "Mtuwwa," a little bay on its western shore, pitched the tent, and slept at ease.

Another halt was required on the 22d of April. The Sultan Kisesa demanded his black-mail, which amounted to one coil-bracelet and two cloths; provisions were hardly procurable, because his subjects wanted white beads, with which, being at a discount at Ujiji, we had not provided ourselves; and Kannena again successfully put in a tyrannical claim for 460 khete of blue porcelains to purchase rations.

On the 23d of April we left Mtuwwa, and made for the opposite or western shore of the lake, which appeared about fifteen miles distant; the day's work was nine hours. The two canoes paddled far apart; there was therefore little bumping, smoking, or quarreling, till near our destination. At Murivumba the malaria, the musquitoes, the crocodiles, and the men are equally feared. The land belongs to the Wabembe, who are correctly described in the "Mombas Mission Map" as "Menschenfresser—anthropophagi." The practice arises from the savage and apathetic nature of the people, who devour, besides man, all kinds of carrion and vermin, grubs and insects, while they abandon to wild growths a land of the richest soil and of the most prolific climate. They prefer man raw, whereas the Wadoe of the coast eat him roasted. The people of a village which backed the port assembled as usual to "sow gape-seed;" but though

"A hungry look hung upon them all"—

and among cannibals one always fancies one's self considered in the light of butcher's meat—the poor devils, dark and stunted, timid and degraded, appeared less dangerous to the living than to the dead. In order to keep them quiet, the bull-headed Mabruki, shortly before dusk, fired a charge of duck-shot into the village; ensued loud cries and deprecations to the "murungwana," but happily no man was hurt. Sayfu the melancholist preferred squatting through the night on the bow of the canoe to trusting his precious person on shore. We slept upon a reed-margined spit of sand, and having neglected to pitch the tent, were rained upon to our heart's content.

We left Murivumba of the man-eaters early on the morning of the 24th of April and stood northward along the western shore of the lake: the converging trend of the two coasts told that we were fast approaching our destination. After ten hours' paddling, halts included, we landed at the southern frontier of Uvira, in a place called Mamaletua, Ngovi, and many other names. Here the stream of commerce begins to set strong; the people were comparatively civil, they cleared for us a leaky old hut with a floor like iron—it appeared to us a palace—and they supplied, at moderate prices, sheep and goats, fish-fry, eggs, and poultry, grain, manioc, and bird-pepper.

After another long stretch of fifteen rainy and sunny hours, a high easterly wind compelled the hard-worked crews to put into Muikamba (?) of Uvira. A neighboring hamlet, a few hovels built behind a thick wind-wrung plantain-grove, backed a reed-locked creek where the canoes floated in safety, and a strip of clean sand on which we passed the night as pleasantly as the bright moonlight and the violent gusts would permit. On the 26th of April, a paddle of three hours and a half landed us in the forenoon at the sandy baystand, where the trade of Uvira is carried on.

Great rejoicings ushered in the end of our outward-bound voyage. Crowds gathered on the shore to gaze at the new merchants arriving at Uvira, with the usual concert, vocal and instrumental, screams, shouts, and songs, shaums, horns, and tom-toms. The captains of the two canoes performed with the most solemn gravity a bear-like dance upon the mat-covered benches which form the "quarter-decks," extending their arms, pirouetting upon both heels, and springing up and squatting down till their hams touched the mats. The crews, with a general grin which showed all their ivories, rattled their paddles against the sides of their canoes in token of greeting, a custom derived probably from the ceremonious address of the lakists, which is performed by rapping their elbows against their ribs. Presently Majid and Bekkari, two Arab youths sent from Ujiji by their chief, Said bin Majid, to collect ivory, came out to meet me; they gave me, as usual, the news, and said that having laid in the store of tusks required, they intended setting out southward on the morrow. We passed half the day of our arrival on the bare landing-place, a strip of sand foully unclean, from the effect of many bivouacs. It is open to the water and backed by the plain of Uvira; one of the broadest of these edges of gently-inclined ground which separate the lake from its trough of hills. Kannena at once visited the Mwami or Sultan Maruta, who owns a village on a neighboring elevation; this chief invited me to his settlement, but the outfit was running low and the crew and party generally feared to leave their canoes. We therefore pitched our tents upon the sand, and prepared for the last labor, that of exploring the head of the lake.

We had now reached the "ne plus ultra," the northernmost station to which merchants have as yet been admitted. The people are generally on bad terms with the Wavira, and in these black regions a traveler coming direct from an enemy's territory is always suspected of hostile intentions—no trifling bar to progress. Opposite us still rose, in a high broken line, the mountains of inhospitable Urundi, apparently prolonged beyond the northern extremity of the waters. The head, which was not visible from the plain, is said to turn north-northwestward, and to terminate after a voyage of two days, which some informants, however, reduce to six hours. The breadth of the Tanganyika is here between seven and eight miles. On the 28th of April all my hopes—which, however, I had hoped against hope—were rudely dashed to the ground. I received a visit from the three stalwart sons of the Sultan Maruta: they were the noblest type of negroid seen near the lake, with symmetrical heads, regular features, and pleasing countenances; their well-made limbs and athletic frames of a shiny jet black, were displayed to advantage by their loose aprons of red and dark-striped bark cloth, slung, like game-bags, over their shoulders, and were set off by opal-colored eyeballs, teeth like pearls, and a profusion of broad massive rings of snowy ivory round their arms, and conical ornaments like dwarf marling-spikes of hippopotamus-tooth suspended from their necks. The subject of the mysterious river issuing from the lake was at once brought forward. They all declared that they had visited it, they offered to forward me, but they unanimously asserted, and every man in the host of bystanders confirmed their words, that the "Rusizi" enters into, and does not flow out of the Tanganyika. I felt sick at heart. I had not, it is true, undertaken to explore the Coy Fountains by this route; but the combined assertions of the cogging shaykh and the false Msawahili had startled me from the proprieties of reason, and—this was the result!

Bombay, when questioned, declared that my companion had misunderstood the words of Hamid bin Sulayyam, who spoke of a river falling into, not issuing *from* the lake; and added his own conviction that the Arab had never sailed north of Ubwari Island. Sayfu, who at Ujiji had described, as an eye-witness, the mouth of the déversoir and its direction for two days, now owned that he had never been beyond Uvira, and that he never intended to do so. Briefly, I had been deceived by a strange coincidence of deceit.

On the 28th of April we were driven from the strip of land which we originally occupied by a southeast gale; here a "blat," or small hurricane, which drives the foaming waters of the tideless sea up to the green margin of the land. Retiring higher up, where the canoes were careened, we spread our bedding on the little muddy mounds that rise a few inches above the surface of grass-closed gutter which drains off the showers daily falling among the hills. I was still obliged to content myself with the lug-sail, thrown over a ridge-pole supported by two bamboo uprights, and pegged out like a tent below; it was too short to fall over the ends and to reach the ground, it was therefore a place of passage for mizzle, splash, and draught of watery wind. My companion inhabited the tent bought from the fundi; it was thoroughly rotted, during his first trip across the lake, by leakage in the boat, and by being "bushed" with mud instead of pegs on shore. He informed me that there was "good grub" at Uvira, and that was nearly the full amount of what I heard from or of him. Our crews had hutted themselves in the dense mass of grass near our tents; they lived as it were under arms, and nothing would induce them to venture away from their only escape, the canoes, which stood ready for launching whenever required. Sayfu swore that he would return to Ujiji rather than venture a few yards inland to buy milk, while Bombay and Mabrukí, who ever labored under the idea that every brother African of the jungle thirsted for their blood, upon the principle that wild birds hate tame birds, became, when the task was proposed to them, almost mutinous. Our nine-days' halt at Uvira had therefore unusual discomforts. The air, however, though damp and raw with gust, storm, and rain, must have been pure in the extreme; appetite and sleep—except when the bull-frogs were "making a night of it"—were rarely wanting, and provisions were good, cheap, and abundant.

I still hoped, however, to lay down the extreme limits of the lake northward. Majid and Bekkari, the Arab agents of Said bin Majid, replied to the offer of an exorbitant sum, that they would not undertake the task for ten times that amount. The sons of Maruta had volunteered their escort; when I wanted to close with them, they drew off. Kannena, when summoned to perform his promise and reminded of the hire that he had received, jumped up and ran out of the tent; afterward at Ujiji he declared that he had been willing to go, but that his crews were unanimous in declining to risk their lives, which was perhaps true. Toward the end of the halt I suffered so severely from ulceration of the tongue that articulation was nearly impossible, and this was a complete stopper to progress. It is a characteristic of African travel that the explorer may be arrested at the very bourn of his journey, on the very threshold of success, by a single stage, as effectually as if all the waves of the Atlantic or the sands of Arabia lay between.

Maruta and his family of young giants did not fail to claim their black-mail; they received a total of twelve cloths, five kitindi, and thirty khete of coral beads. They returned two fine goats, here worth about one cloth each, and sundry large gourds of fresh milk—the only food I could then manage to swallow. Kannena, who had been living at Maruta's village, came down on the 5th of May to demand 460 khete of blue porcelains, wherewith to buy rations for the return-voyage. Being heavily in debt, all his salt and coil-bracelets had barely sufficed for his liabilities: he had nothing to show for them but masses of sambo—iron-wire rings—which made his ankles resemble those of a young hippopotamus. The slaves and all the fine tusks that came on board were the property of the crew.

Our departure from Uvira was finally settled for the 6th of May: before taking leave of our "farthest point," I will offer a few details concerning the commerce of the place.

Uvira is much frequented on account of its cheapness; it is the great northern depôt for slaves, ivory, grain, bark cloth, and iron-ware, and, in the season, hardly a day elapses without canoes coming in for merchandise or provisions. The imports are the kitindi, salt, beads, tobacco, and cotton cloth. Rice does not grow there, holcus and maize are sold at one to two fundo of common beads per masuta or small load—perhaps sixteen pounds—and one khete is sufficient during the months of plenty to purchase five pounds of manioc, or two and even three fowls. Plantains of the large and coarse variety are common and cheap, and one cloth is given for two goodly earthen pots full of palm-oil. Ivory

fetches its weight in brass wire: here the merchant expects for
every 1000 dollars of outfit to receive 100 farasilah (3500 lbs.) of
large tusks, and his profit would be great were it not counterbal-
anced by the risk and by the expense of transport. The prices
in the slave-mart greatly fluctuate. When business is dull, boys
under ten years may be bought for four cloths and five fundo of
white and blue porcelains, girls for six shukkah, and as a rule, at
these remote places, as Uvira, Ujipa, and Marungu, slaves are
cheaper than in the market of Ujiji. Adults fetch no price, they
are notoriously intractable, and addicted to desertion. Bark
cloths, generally in the market, vary from one to three khete of
coral beads. The principal industry of the Wavira is ironware,
the material for which is dug in the lands lying at a little distance
westward of the lake. The hoes, dudgeons, and small hatchets,
here cost half their usual price at Ujiji. The people also make
neat baskets and panniers, not unlike those of Normandy, and
pretty bowls cut out of various soft woods, light and dark: the
latter are also found, though rarely, at Ujiji and in the western
islets.

A gale appeared to be brewing in the north—here the place of
storms—and the crews, fearing wind and water, in the afternoon
insisted upon launching their canoes and putting out to sea at 10
A.M. on the 6th of May. After touching at the stages before described—Muikamba, Ngovi, and Murivumba of the anthropophagi—we crossed without other accidents but those of weather—the
rainy monsoon was in its last convulsions—the western branch or
supplementary channel separating the lake from the Island of
Ubwari. Before anchoring at Mzimu, our former halting-place,
we landed at a steep ghaut, where the crews swarmed up a ladder
of rock, and presently returned back with pots of the palm-oil,
for which this is the principal depôt.

On the 10th of May the sky was dull and gloomy, the wind
was hushed, the "rain-sun" burnt with a sickly and painful heat:
the air was still and sultry, stifling and surcharged, while the
glimmerings of lurid lightning and low mutterings from the sable cloud-banks lying upon the northern horizon, cut by light
masses of mist in a long unbroken line, and from the black arch
rising above the Acroceraunian hills to the west, disturbed at
times the death-like silence. Even the gulls on the beach fore-
felt a storm. I suggested a halt, but the crews were now in a
nervous hurry to reach their homes—impatience mastered even
their prudence.

We left Mzimu at sunset, and for two hours coasted along the
shore. It was one of those portentous evenings of the tropics—
a calm before a tempest—unnaturally quiet; we struck out, however, boldly toward the eastern shore of the Tanganyika, and the
western mountains rapidly lessened on the view. Before, however, we reached the mid-channel, a cold gust—in these regions

the invariable presage of a storm—swept through the deepening shades cast by the heavy rolling clouds, and the vivid nimble lightning flashed, at first by intervals, then incessantly, with a ghastly and blinding glow, illuminating the "vast of night," and followed by a palpable obscure and a pitchy darkness, that weighed upon the sight. As terrible was its accompaniment of rushing, reverberating thunder, now a loud roar, peal upon peal, like the booming of heavy batteries, then breaking into a sudden crash, which was presently followed by a rattling discharge like the sharp pattering of musketry. The bundles of spears planted upright amidships, like paratonnerres, seemed to invite the electric fluid into the canoes. The waves began to rise, the rain descended, at first in warning drops, then in torrents, and had the wind steadily arisen, the cockle-shell craft never could have lived through the short, chopping sea which characterizes the Tanganyika in heavy weather. The crew, though blinded by the showers and frightened by the occasional gusts, held their own gallantly enough; at times, however, the moaning cry, " Oh, my wife!" showed what was going on within. Bombay, a noted Voltairian in fine weather, spent the length of that wild night in reminiscences of prayer. I sheltered myself from the storm under my best friend, the Mackintosh, and thought of the far-famed couplet of Hafiz—with its mystic meaning I will not trouble the reader:

"This collied night, these horrid waves, these gusts that sweep the whirling deep!
What reck they of our evil plight, who on the shore securely sleep?"

Fortunately the rain beat down wind and sea, otherwise nothing short of a miracle could have preserved us for a dry death.

That night, however, was the last of our " sea-sorrows." After floating about during the latter hours of darkness, under the land, but uncertain where to disembark, we made at 7 A.M., on the 11th of May, Wafanya, our former station in ill-famed Urundi. Tired and cramped by the night's work, we pitched tents, and, escaping from the gaze of the insolent and intrusive crowd, we retired to spend a few hours in sleep.

I was suddenly aroused by Mabruki, who, rushing into the tent, thrust my sword into my hands, and exclaimed that the crews were scrambling into their boats. I went out and found every thing in dire confusion. The sailors, hurrying here and there, were embarking their mats and cooking-pots, some were in violent parley with Kannena, while a little knot was carrying a man, mortally wounded, down to the waters of the lake. I saw at once that the affair was dangerous. On these occasions the Wajiji, whose first impulse is ever flight, rush for safety to their boats and push off, little heeding whom or what they leave behind. We therefore hurried in without delay.

When both crews had embarked, and no enemy appeared, Kannena persuaded them to reland, and, proving to them their superior force, induced them to demand, at the arrow's point, satisfaction of Kanoni, the chief, for the outrage committed by his subjects. During our sleep a drunken man—almost all these disturbances arise from fellows who have the "*vin méchant*"—had rushed from the crowd of Warundi, and, knobstick in hand, had commenced dealing blows in all directions. Ensued a general mêlée. Bombay, when struck, called to the crews to arm. The Goanese, Valentine, being fear-crazed, seized my large "Colt" and probably fired it into the crowd; at all events, the cone struck one of our own men below the right pap, and came out two inches to the right of the backbone. Fortunately for us he was a slave, otherwise the situation would have been desperate. As it was, the crowd became violently excited; one man drew his dagger upon Valentine, and with difficulty I dissuaded Kannena from killing him. As the crew had ever an eye to the "main chance," food, they at once confiscated three goats, our store for the return voyage, cut their throats, and spitted the meat upon their spears: thus the lamb died and the wolf dined, and the innocent suffered and the plunderer was joyed, the strong showed his strength and the weak his weakness, according to the usual formula of this sublunary world.

While Kannena was absent, on martial purposes intent, I visited the sole sufferer in the fray, and after seeing his wound washed, I forbade his friends to knead the injured muscles, as they were doing, and to wrench his right arm from side to side. A cathartic seemed to have a beneficial effect. On the second day of his accident he was able to rise. But these occurrences in wild countries always cause long troubles. Kannena, who obtained from Sultan Kanoni, as blood-money, a small girl and a large sheep, declared that the man might die, and insisted upon my forthwith depositing, in case of such contingency, eight cloths, which, should the wound not prove fatal, would be returned. The latter clause might have been omitted; in these lands, *nescit* cloth *missa reverti*. As we were about to leave Ujiji, Kannena claimed for the man's subsistence forty cloths—or, as equivalent, three slaves and six cloths—which also it was necessary to pay. A report was afterward spread that the wretch had sunk under his wound. Valentine heard the intelligence with all that philosophy which distinguishes his race when mishaps occur to any but self. His prowess, however, cost me forty-eight dollars, here worth at least £100 in England. Still I had reason to congratulate myself that matters had not been worse. Had the victim been a Mjiji freeman, the trouble, annoyances, and expense would have been interminable. Had he been a Mrundi, we should have been compelled to fight our way, through a shower of arrows, to the boats; war would have extended to Ujiji, and "England," as usual, would have had to pay the expenses. When Said bin Salim heard at Kazeh a distorted account of this mishap—of course it was reported that "Haji Abdullah" killed the man—he hit upon a notable device. Lurinda, the headman of Gungu, had often begged the Arab to enter into "blood brotherhood" with him, and this had Said bin Salim pertinaciously refused, on religious grounds, to do. When informed that battle and murder were in the wind, he at once made fraternity with Lurinda, hoping to derive protection from his spear. His terrors afterward persuaded him to do the same with Kannena: indeed, at that time he would have hailed a slave as "ndugu yango" (my brother).

When Kannena returned successful from his visit to Kanoni, we prepared to leave Wafanya. The fierce rain and the nightly drizzle detained us, however, till the next morning. On the 11th of May we paddled round the southern point of Wafanya Bay to Makimoni, a little grassy inlet, where the canoes were defended from the heavy surf.

After this all was easy. We rattled paddles on the 12th of May, as we entered our "patrie," Nyasanga. The next night was spent in Bangwe Bay. We were too proud to sneak home in the dark; we had done something deserving a certain cross, we were heroes, braves of braves; we wanted to be looked at by the fair, to be howled at by the valiant. Early on the morning of the 13th of May we appeared with shots, shouts, and a shocking noise, at the reed-lined gap of sand that forms the ghaut of Kawele. It was truly a triumphal entrance. All the people of that country-side had collected to welcome the crew; women and children, as well as men, pressed waist-deep into the water to receive friend and relative with becoming affection: the gestures, the clamor, and the other peculiarities of the excited mob, I must really leave to the reader's imagination; the memory is too much for me.

But true merit is always modest; it aspires to honor, not honors. The Wagungu, or whites, were repeatedly "called for." I broke, however, through the sudant, strident, hircine throng, and regaining, with the aid of Riza's strong arm, the old tembe, was salamed to by the expectant Said bin Salim and the jemadar. It felt like a return home. But I had left, before my departure, with my Arab chargé d'affaires, four small loads of cloth, and on inspecting the supplies there remained only ten shukkah. I naturally inquired what had become of the 110 others which had thus prematurely disappeared. Said bin Salim replied by showing a small pile of grain-bags, and by informing me that he had hired twenty porters for the down-march. He volunteered, it is true, in case I felt disposed to finish the periplus of the lake, to return to Kazeh and to superintend the transmission of our reserve supplies; as, however, he at the same time gave me to understand that he could not escort them back to Ujiji, I thanked him for his offer, and declined it.

We had expended upward of a month—from the 10th of April to the 13th of May, 1858—in this voyage of fifteen days outward bound, nine at Uvira, and nine in returning. The boating was rather a severe trial. We had no means of resting the back; the holds of the canoes, besides being knee-deep in water, were disgracefully crowded: they had been appropriated to us and our four servants by Kannena, but by degrees he introduced, in addition to the sticks, spears, broken vases, pots, and gourds, a goat, two or three small boys, one or two sick sailors, the little slavegirl and the large sheep. The canoes were top-heavy with the number of their crew, and the shipping of many seas spoiled our tents, and, besides, wetted our salt and soddened our grain and flour; the gunpowder was damaged, and the guns were honeycombed with rust. Besides the splashing of the paddles and the dashing of waves, heavy showers fell almost every day and night, and the intervals were bursts of burning sunshine.

The discomfort of the halt was not less than that of the boat. At first we pitched tents near the villages, in tall fetid grass, upon ground never level, where stones were the succedanea for tentpegs stolen for fuel, and where we slept literally upon mire. The temperature inside was ever in extremes, now a raw rainy cold, then a steam-bath that damped us like an April shower. The villagers, especially in the remoter districts, were even more troublesome, noisy, and inquisitive than the Wagogo. A "notable passion of wonder" appeared in them. We felt like baited bears: we were mobbed in a moment, and scrutinized from every point of view by them; the inquisitive wretches stood on tiptoe, they squatted on their hams, they bent sideways, they thrust forth their necks like hissing geese to vary the prospect. Their eyes, "glaring lightning-like out of their heads," as old Homer hath it, seemed to devour us; in the ecstasy of curiosity they shifted from one muzungu to his "brother," till, like the well-known ass between the two bundles of hay, they could not enjoy either. They were pertinacious as flies; to drive them away was only to invite a return, while—worst grief of all—the women were plain, and their grotesque salutations resembled the "encounter of two dog-apes." The Goanese were almost equally honored, and the operation of cooking was looked upon as a miracle. At last my experience in staring enabled me to categorize the infliction as follows. Firstly is the stare furtive, when the starer would peep and peer under the tent, and its reverse, the stare open. Thirdly is the stare curious or intelligent, which is generally accompanied with irreverent laughter regarding our appearance. Fourthly is the stare stupid, which denoted the hebete incurious savage. The stare discreet is that of sultans and great men; the stare indiscreet at unusual seasons is affected by women and children. Sixthly is the stare flattering: it was exceedingly rare, and equally so was the stare contemptuous. Eighthly is the stare greedy; it was denoted by the eyes restlessly bounding from one object to another, never tired, never satisfied. Ninthly is the stare peremp-

tory and pertinacious, peculiar to crabbed age. The dozen concludes with the stare drunken, the stare fierce or pugnacious, and,
finally, the stare cannibal, which apparently considered us as articles of diet. At last, weary of the stare by day and the tent by
night, I preferred inhabiting a bundle of clothes in the wet hold
of the canoe; this, at least, saved the trouble of wading through
the water, of scrambling over the stern, and of making a way between the two close lines of grumbling and surly blacks that
manned the paddle-benches, whenever, after a meaningless halt,
some individual thought proper to scream out "Safári!" (journey!)

Curious to say, despite all these discomforts our health palpably improved. My companion, though still uncomfortably deaf,
was almost cured of his blindness. When that ulcerated mouth,
which rendered it necessary for me to live by suction—generally
milk and water—for seventeen days, had returned to its usual
state, my strength gradually increased. Although my feet were
still swollen by the perpetual wet and by the painful funza or entozoon, my hands partially lost their numbness, and the fingers
which before could hold the pen only for a few minutes were
once more able freely to write and sketch. In fact, I date a slow
but sensible progress toward a complete recovery of health from
the days and nights spent in the canoe and upon the mud of the
Tanganyika Lake. Perhaps mind had also acted upon matter;
the object of my mission was now effected, and this thought enabled me to cast off the burden of grinding care with which the
imminent prospect of a failure had before sorely laden me.

The rainy monsoon broke up on the 14th of May, the day after
my return to Kawele, and once more, after six months of incessant storm-wind and rain, clouds and mists, we had fine, cool
mornings, clear warm sun, and deliciously cold nights. The climate became truly enjoyable, but the scenery somewhat lost its
earlier attractions. The faultless, regular, and uniform beauty,
and the deep stillness of this evergreen land did not fail to produce that strange, inexplicable melancholy of which most travelers in tropical countries complain. In this Nature all is beautiful
that meets the eye, all is soft that affects the senses; but she is a
siren whose pleasures soon pall upon the enjoyer. The mind, en-
feebled perhaps by an enervating climate, is fatigued and wearied
by the monotony of the charms which haunt it; cloyed with
costly fare, it sighs for the rare simplicity of the desert. I have
never felt this sadness in Egypt and Arabia, and was never without it in India and Zanzibar.

Our outfit, as I have observed, had been reduced to a minimum.
Not a word from Snay bin Amir, my agent at Kazeh, had arrived
in reply to my many missives, and old Want began to stare at us
with the stare peremptory. "Wealth," say the Arabs, "hath one
devil, poverty a dozen," and nowhere might a caravan more easi-

ly starve than in rich and fertile Central Africa. Travelers are agreed that in these countries "baggage is life:" the heartless and inhospitable race will not give a handful of grain without return, and to use the Moslem phrase, "Allah pity him who must beg of a beggar!" As usual on such occasions, the Baloch began to clamor for more rations—they received two cloths per diem—and to demand a bullock wherewith to celebrate their Eed, or greater festival. There were several Arab merchants at Kawele, but they had exhausted their stock in purchasing slaves and ivory. None, in fact, were so rich as ourselves, and we were reduced to ten shukkah, ten fundo of coral beads, and one load of black porcelains, which were perfectly useless. With this pittance we had to engage hammals for the hammock, to feed seventy-five mouths, and to fee several sultans; in fact, to incur the heavy expenses of marching back 260 miles to Unyanyembe.

Still, with an enviable development of hope, Said bin Salim determined that we should reach Kazeh unfamished. We made the necessary preparations for the journey, patched tents and umbrella, had a grand washing and scouring day, mended the portmanteaus, and ground the grain required for a month's march, hired four porters for the manchil, distributed ammunition to Said bin Salim and the Baloch, who at once invested it in slaves, and exchanged with Said bin Majid several pounds of lead for palm-oil, which would be an economy at the Malagarazi Ferry. For some days past rumors had reached here that a large caravan of Wanyamwezi porters, commanded by an Arab merchant, was approaching Kawele. I was not sanguine enough to expose myself to another disappointment. Suddenly, on the 22d of May, frequent musket-shots announced the arrival of strangers, and at noon the tembe was surrounded with boxes and bales, porters, slaves, and four "sons of Ramji," Mbaruko, Sangora, Khamisi, and Shehe. Shahdad the Baloch, who had been left behind at Kazeh in love, and in attendance upon his "brother" Ismail, who presently died, had charge of a parcel of papers and letters from Europe, India, and Zanzibar. They were the first received after nearly eleven months, and of course they brought with them evil tidings—the Indian mutinies. *En revanche*, I had a kindly letter from M. Cochet, consul of France, and from Mr. Mansfield, of the United States, who supplied me with the local news, and added, for my edification, a very "low-church" tract, the first of the family, I opine, that has yet presented itself in Central Africa. Mr. Frost reported that he had sent at once a letter apprising me of Lieut. Colonel Hamerton's death, and had forwarded the medical supplies for which I indented from K'hutu: these, as has been explained, had not reached me. Snay bin Amir also informed me that he had retained all the packages for which he could find no porters; that three boxes had been stolen from his "godown;" and finally, that the second supply, 400 dollars' worth of cloth and beads, for which I had written at Inenge, and had rewritten at Ugogo and other places, was hourly expected to arrive.

This was an unexpected good fortune, happening at a crisis when it was really wanted. My joy was somewhat damped by inspecting the packs of the fifteen porters. Twelve were laden with ammunition which was not wanted, and with munitions *de bouche*, which were: nearly half the bottles of curry-powder, spices, and cognac were broken, tea, coffee, and sugar had been squeezed out of their tin canisters, and much of the rice and coffee had disappeared. The three remaining loads were one of American domestics—sixty shukkahs—and the rest contained fifteen coral bracelets and white beads. All were the refuse of their kind: the good Hindoos at Zanzibar had seized this opportunity to dispose of their flimsy, damaged, and unsalable articles. This outfit was sufficient to carry us comfortably to Unyanyembe. I saw, however, with regret that it was wholly inadequate for the purpose of exploring the two southern thirds of the Tanganyika Lake, much less for returning to Zanzibar, *viâ* the Nyassa or Maravi Lake, and Kilwa, as I had once dreamed.

I received several visits from our old companion, Muhinna bin Sulayman, of Kazeh, and three men of his party. He did not fail to improve the fact of his having brought up my supplies in the nick of time. He required five coil-bracelets and sixteen pounds of beads as my share of the toll taken from him by the lord of the Malagarazi ferry. For the remaining fifteen coil-bracelets he gave me forty cloths, and for the load and a half of white beads he exchanged 880 strings of blue porcelains—a commercial operation by which he cleared without trouble 35 per cent. Encouraged by my facility, he proposed to me the propriety of paying part of the kuhonga or black-mail claimed from new-comers by Rusimba and Kannena. But facility has its limits: I quietly objected, and we parted on the best of terms.

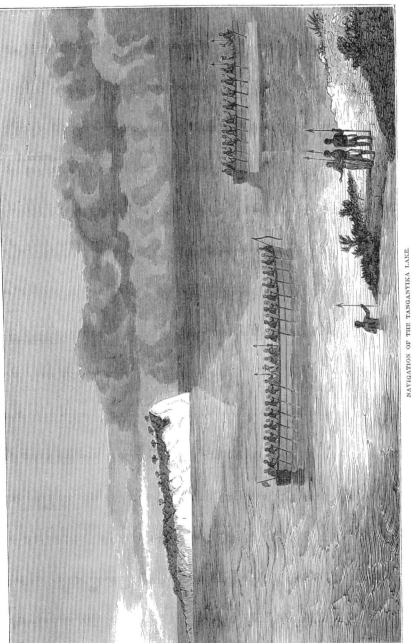

NAVIGATION OF THE TANGANYIKA LAKE.

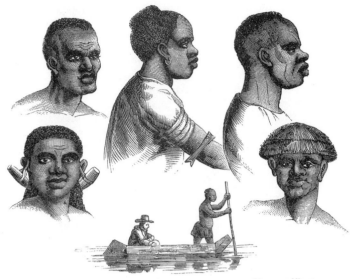

A Mnyamwezi. A Mjiji. Mugungu Mbaya,
"the wicked white man."

A Mgogo. Ferry-boat
on the Malagarazi River. A Mzaramo.

CHAPTER XV.

THE TANGANYIKA LAKE AND ITS PERIPLUS.

THE Tanganyika Lake, though situated in the unexplored centre of Intertropical Africa, and until 1858 unvisited by Europeans,
has a traditionary history of its own, extending through more than
three centuries.

"Accounts of a great sea in the interior of Africa obtained
(partially from native travelers) at Congo and Sofala," reached the
Portuguese settlements on both shores of the continent.* The
details of De Barros (first printed in 1852), while affording sub-
stantially correct details, such as the length of the lake—100
leagues—the capability of navigation, and the one large island—
Ubwari—are curiously intermingled with the errors of theoretical
conclusion. Subsequently Pigafetta (1591) writing upon the authority of Portuguese inquirers, affirms that there is but one lake

* Mr. Cooley's "Memoir on the Geography of N'yassi" p. 1 (vol. xv., of 1845,
Journal of the Royal Geographical Society). The extracts from Portuguese history
in the text are entirely taken from that learned paper, which, in describing actualities, wanted nothing but a solid foundation of data. The geographer's principal informant in 1834 was one "Khamisi bin Tani," civilized into "Khamis bin Osman,"
a Msawahili of Lamu, who, having visited the Nyassa, Maravi, or Kilwa Lake, pretended that he had traveled to the Tanganyika Lake. I can not allow this opportunity to pass without expressing my gratitude to Mr. Cooley for his courtesy in supplying me with references and other information.

(the N'yassa) on the confines of Angola and Monomotapa, but that there are two lakes (the Nyassa and the Tanganyika), not lying east and west, as was supposed by Ptolemy of Alexandria, but north and south of each other, and about 400 miles asunder, which give birth to the Nile. From that epoch dates the origin of our modern misconceptions concerning the Lake Region of Central Intertropical Africa. The Nyassa and the Tanganyika were now blended, then separated, according to the theories or the information of the geographer; no explorer ventured to raise from the land of mystery the veil that invested it; and the "Mombas Mission" added the colophon by confounding with the old confusion the Nyanza or Ukerewe, a third lake, of which they had heard at Mombasah and elsewhere. It is not wonderful then that Dr. Vincent suspected the existence or the place of the central lake, or that the more ignorant popularizers of knowledge confounded the waters of the Nyassa and the Ngami.*

The earliest name given by theoretical writers to the hypothetical single lake appears to have been Zembére, Zémbere, Zambre, Zambri, or Zembre, probably a corruption or dialectic variety of Zambesi, that river being supposed, like the Nile, the Zaire, the Manisa, and others, to be derived from it. The word Moravi or Maravi, which still deforms our maps, is the name of a large tribe or a lordly race like the Wahinda, dwelling to the southeast and southwest of the Nyassa. In the seventeenth century Luigi Mariano, a missioner residing at the Rios de Sena, calls the central sea the Lake of Hemosura: his description, however, applies to the Nyassa, Maravi, or Kilwa Lake, and the word is probably a corruption of Rusuro or Lusuro, which, in the language of Uhiao, signifies a river or flowing water. In the "Mombas Mission Map"

* In the "Westminster Review" (New Series, No. XX.) occurs the following passage, which sufficiently illustrates the assertion in the text; the critic is discussing Mr. C. Andersson's "Lake Ngami," etc., etc. (London, 1856): "African missionaries, penetrating some little distance inland from the southeast, recently brought information which they received second-hand from Arab travelers of a vast fresh-water lake far in the interior, described as being of enormous dimensions—as nothing less than a great inland sea. Frequenters of the Geographical Society's meetings in Whitehall Place have observed, in consequence, on the site which used to be marked in the maps as a sandy desert, a blue spot about the size of the Caspian and the shape of a hideous inflated leech. We trusted that a more accurate survey would correct the extreme frightfulness of the supposed form. Mr. Andersson has spared us further excitement. The lake turns out to be a mirage—a mythus with the smallest conceivable nucleus of fact. On the very spot occupied by this great blue leech—long. E. from Greenwich 23° and lat. S. 20° 21'—he found a small speck of bitter water, something more than twenty miles across, or the size of Lake Corrib, in Galway. So perishes a phantom which has excited London geographers for a whole season."

Had the learned reviewer used his eyes or his judgment in Whitehall Place, he would not thus have confounded the hypothetic sea of the "Mombas Mission Map" —a reservoir made to include the three several waters of Nyanza, Tanganyika, and Nyassa—in E. long. 24° to 29°, and S. lat. 0° 13'—with the little Ngami explored by Dr. Livingstone and a party of friends in August, 1849, and placed by him in E. long. 23°, and in S. lat. 20° 20' 21''. The nearest points of the two waters are separated by an interval, in round numbers, of 700 miles.

the lake is called "See von Uniamesi," a mere misnomer, as it is separated by hundreds of miles from the Land of the Moon: the northern part is termed Ukerewe, by a confusion with the Nyanza Lake and the southern N'hánjá, for Nyassa, the old Maravi water near Kilwa. It is not a little curious, however, that Messrs. Cooley and Macqueen should both have recorded the vernacular name of the northern Lake Tangenyika, so unaccountably omitted from the "Mombas Mission Map." The words Tanganyenka and Tanganyenko used by Dr. Livingstone, who in places appears to confound the Lake with the Nyanza and the Nyassa, are palpable mispronunciations.

The African name for the central lake is Tanganyika, signifying an anastomosis, or a meeting-place (sc. of waters), from ku tanganyika, the popular word, to join, or meet together: the initial t being changed to ch—ku changanyika for ku tanganyika—in the lingua Franca of Zanzibar, doubtless gave rise to Mr. Cooley's "Zanganyika." The word Tanganyika is universally used by the Wajiji and other tribes near and upon the lake. The Arabs and African strangers, when speaking loosely of it, call it indifferently the Bahari or Sea, the Ziwa or Pond, and even the Mtoni or River. The "Sea of Ujiji" would, after the fashion of Easterns, be limited to the waters in the neighborhood of that principal depôt.

The Tanganyika occupies the centre of the length of the African continent, which extends from 32° N. to 33° S. latitude, and it lies on the western extremity of the eastern third of the breadth. Its general direction is parallel to the inner African line of volcanic action drawn from Gondar southward through the regions about Kilima-ngáo (Kilimanjáro) to Mount Njesa, the eastern wall of the Nyassa Lake. The general formation suggests, as in the case of the Dead Sea, the idea of a volcano of depression—not, like the Nyanza or Ukerewe, a vast reservoir formed by the drainage of mountains. Judging from the eye, the walls of this basin rise in an almost continuous curtain, rarely waving and infracted, to 2000 or 3000 feet above the water-level. The lower slopes are well wooded: upon the higher summits large trees are said not to grow; the deficiency of soil, and the prevalence of high fierce winds would account for the phenomena. The lay is almost due north and south, and the form a long oval, widening in the central portions and contracting systematically at both extremities. The length of the bed was thus calculated: From Ujiji (in S. lat. 4° 55′) to Uvira (in S. lat. 3° 25′), where the narrowing of the breadth evidences approach to the northern head, was found by exploration a direct distance of 1° 30′ = 90 miles, which, allowing for the interval between Uvira and the River Rusizi, that forms the northernmost limit, may be increased to 100 rectilinear geographical miles. According to the Arab voyagers, who have frequently rounded the Lake Ujiji in eight stages from the northern and twelve from the southern end of the lake, the extent from Ujiji to the Marungu River, therefore, is roughly computed at 150 miles. The total of length, from Uvira, in S. lat. 3° 25', to Marungu, in S. lat. 7° 20', would then be somewhat less than 250 rectilinear geographical miles. About Ujiji the water appears to vary in breadth from 30 to 35 miles, but the serpentine form of the banks, with a succession of serrations and indentations of salient and re-entering angles—some jutting far and irregularly into the bed— render the estimate of average difficult. The Arabs agree in correctly stating, that opposite Ujiji the shortest breadth of the lake is about equal to the channel which divides Zanzibar from the main land, or between 23 and 24 miles. At Uvira the breadth narrows to eight miles. Assuming, therefore, the total length at 250, and the mean breadth at 20 geographical miles, the circumference of the Tanganyika would represent, in round numbers, a total of 550 miles; the superficial area, which seems to vary little, covers about 5000 square miles; and the drainage from the beginning of the great Central African depression in Unyamwezi, in E. long. 33° 58', numbers from the eastward about 240 miles.

By B. P. thermometer the altitude of the Tanganyika is 1850 feet above the sea-level, and about 2000 feet below the adjacent plateau of Unyamwezi and the Nyanza, or northern lake. This difference of level, even did not hill ranges intervene, would preclude the possibility of that connection between the waters which the Arabs, by a conjecture natural to inexpert geographers, have maintained to the confusion of the learned. The topographical situation of the Tanganyika is thus the centre of a deep synclical depression in the continent, a long narrow trough in the southern spurs of Urundi, which, with its mountain-neighbor Karagwah, situated upon the equator, represents the inner African portion of the Lunar Mountains. It may be observed, that the parallel of the northern extremity of the Tanganyika nearly corresponds with the southern creek of the Nyanza, and that they are separated by an arc of the meridian of about 343 miles.

The water of the Tanganyika appears deliciously sweet and pure after the salt and bitter, the putrid and slimy produce of the wells, pits, and pools on the line of march. The people, however, who drink it willingly when afloat, prefer, when on shore, the little springs which bubble from its banks. They complain that it does not satisfy thirst, and contrast it unfavorably with the waters of its rival, the Nyanza: it appears, moreover, to corrode metal and leather with exceptional power. The color of the pure and transparent mass has apparently two normal varieties: a dull sea-green—never, however, verdigris-colored, as in the shoals of the Zanzibar seas, where the reflected blue of the atmosphere blends with the yellow of the sandy bottom; the other, a clear, soft blue—by day rarely deep and dark, like the ultramarine of the Mediterranean, but resembling the light and milky tints of tropical seas. Under a strong wind the waves soon rise in yeasty lines, foaming up from a turbid greenish surface, and the aspect becomes menacing in the extreme.

It was found impracticable to take soundings of the Tanganyika: the Arabs, however, agreed in asserting that with lines of several fathoms they found bottom only near the shores. The shingly sole shelves rapidly, without steps or overfalls, into blue water. Judging from the eye, the bottom is sandy and profusely strewn with worn pebbles. Reefs and washes were observed near the shores; it is impossible to form an idea of their position or extent, as the crews confine themselves to a few well-known lines, from which they can not be persuaded to diverge. No shoals or shallows were seen at a distance from the coast, and though islets are not unfrequent upon the margin, only one was observed or heard of near the centre.

The affluents of this lake are neither sufficiently numerous nor considerable to alter by sedimentary deposit the depth or the shape of the bed. The borders are generally low : a thick fringe of rush and reed, obviating erosion by the element, conceals the watery margin. Where the currents beat, they cut out a short and narrow strip of quartzose sand, profusely strewn with large shingle, gravel, comminuted shells, and marine exuviæ, with a fringe of drift formed by the joint action of wind and wave. Beyond this is a shelving plain—the principal locality for cultivation and settlements. In some parts it is a hard clay conglomerate; in others, a rich red loam, apparently stained with oxyd of iron ; and in others sandy, but every where coated with the thickest vegetation extending up to the background of mountains. The coast is here and there bluff, with miniature cliffs and headlands, whose formation is of sandstone strata tilted, broken, and distorted, or small blocks imbedded in indurated reddish earth. From the water appeared piles of a dark stone resembling angular basalt, and among the rock-crevices the people find the float-clay, or mountain-meal, with which they decorate their persons and the sterns of their canoes. The uncultivated hill-summits produce various cactaceæ; the sides are clothed with giant trees, the mvule, the tamarind, and the bauhinia. On the declines, more precipitous than the Swiss terraces, manioc and cereals grow luxuriantly, while the lowest levels are dark with groves of plantains and Guinea-palms.

A careful investigation and comparison of statements leads to the belief that the Tanganyika receives and absorbs the whole river-system—the net-work of streams, nullahs, and torrents—of that portion of the Central African depression whose water-shed converges toward the great reservoir. Geographers will doubt that such a mass, situated at so considerable an altitude, can maintain its level without an effluent. Moreover, the freshness of the water would, under normal circumstances, argue the escape of saline matter washed down by the influents from the area of drainage. But may not the Tanganyika, situated, like the Dead Sea, as a reservoir for supplying with humidity the winds which have parted with their moisture in the barren and arid regions of the south, maintain its general level by the exact balance of supply and evaporation? And may not the saline particles deposited in its waters be wanting in some constituent which renders them evident to the taste? One point concerning the versant has been proved by these pages, namely, that the Tanganyika can not be drained eastward by rents in a subtending mountain ridge, as was supposed by Dr. Livingstone from an indiscriminately applied analogy with the ancient head basin of the Zambezi. Dr. Livingstone (chap. xxiv., xxvi., et passim) informs his readers, from report of the Arabs, that the Tanganyika is a large shallow body of water; in fact, the residuum of a mass anciently much more extensive. This, however, is not and can not be the case. In theorizing upon the eastern versant and drainage of the Tanganyika, Dr. Livingstone seems to have been misled by having observed that the vast inland sea of geological ages, of which Lake Ngami and its neighbor Kumadau are now the principal remains, had been desiccated by cracks and fissures, caused in the subtending soils by earthquakes and sudden upheavals, which thus opened for the waters an exit into the Indian Ocean. This may have happened to the Nyassa, or southern lake; it must not, however, be generalized and extended to the Nyanza and the Tanganyika.

As in Zanzibar, there is little variety of temperature upon the Tanganyika. The violent easterly gales, which, pouring down from the cold heights of Usagara, acquire impetus sufficient to carry the current over Ugogo, Unyamwezi, and Uvinza, are here less distinctly defined. The periodical winds over the lake—regular but not permanent—are the southeast and the southwest, which also bring up the foulest weather. The land and sea breezes are felt almost as distinctly as upon the shores of the Indian Ocean. The breath of the morning, called by the Arabs el barad, or the zephyr, sets in from the north. During the day are light variable breezes, which often subside, when the weather is not stormy, into calms. In the evenings a gentle afflatus comes up from the waters. Throughout the dry season the lake becomes a wind-trap, and a heavy ground-sea rolls toward the shore. In the rains there is less sea, but accidents occur from sudden and violent storms. The mountainous breakers of Arab and African informants were not seen; in fact, with a depth of three feet from ridge to dell, a wave would swamp the largest laden canoe. Wind-currents are common. Within a few hours a stream will be traversed, setting strongly to the east, and crossed by a southerly or southwesterly current. High gales, in certain localities where the waves set upon a flush, flat shore, drive the waters fifteen to twenty feet beyond the usual mark. This circumstance may partly explain the Arab's belief in a regular madd wa jarr—ebb and flow—which Eastern travelers always declare to have observed upon the Tanganyika and Nyassa Lakes, and which Mr. Andersson believes to exist in the little Ngami. A mass of water so large must be, to a certain extent, subject to tidal influences; but the narrowness of the bed from east to west would render their effect almost unobservable. Mr. Francis Galton referred me for the explanation of this phenomenon to a paper, "On the Seiches of Lakes," by Colonel J. R. Jackson, F. R. G. S., published in the "Journal of the R. G. S.," Vol. III. of 1833, in which the learned author refers the ebb and flow of the waters of Lake Leman, or of Geneva (and of the lakes of Zurich, Annecy, and Constance), to "an unequal pressure of the atmosphere on different parts of the lake at the same time; that is, to the simultaneous effect of columns of air of different weight or different elasticity, arising from temporary variations of temperature, or from mechanical causes."

The scenery and the navigation of the Tanganyika have been illustrated in the last chapter. Remains only a succinct account of the physical and ethnological features of its periplus, carefully collected from authorities on the spot.

According to the Wajiji, from their country to the Runangwa or Marungu River, which enters the lake at the southern point, there are twelve stages; this periplus numbers 120 khambi or stations, at most of which, however, provisions are not procurable. An extended list of fifty-three principal points was given by the guides; it is omitted, as it contains nothing beyond mere names. There are, however, sixteen tribes and districts which claim attention; of these, Ukaranga and Ujiji have already been described.

The kingdom of Urundi, which lies north of Ujiji, has a seaface of about fifty miles; a low strip of exceeding fertility, backed at short distances by a band of high green hill. This region, rising from the lake in a northeasterly direction, culminates into the equatorial mass of highlands which, under the name of Karagwah, forms the western spinal prolongation of the Lunar Mountains. The residence of the mwami, or chief sultan, Mwezi, is near the head-stream of the Kitangure (Kitangule) or River of Karagwah, which rises at a place distant six days' march (sixty miles), and bearing northeast from the Tanganyika. His settlement, according to the Arabs, is of considerable extent; the huts are built of ratan, and lions abound in the vicinity.

Urundi differs from the lake regions generally in being a strictly monarchical country, locally governed by watware or headmen, who transmit the customs and collections at stated periods to their suzerain. The mwame, it is said, can gather in a short time a large host of warriors, who are the terror of the neighboring tribes. The Warundi are evidently natives of a high cold country; they are probably the "white people resembling Abyssinians," and dwelling near the lake, of whom European geographers have heard from Zanzibar. The complexion varies from a tawny yellow, the color of the women, to a clear dark brown, which is so brightened by the daily use of ochre mixed with palm-oil that in few cases the real tint is discernible. The men tattoo with circles and lines like cupping-cuts; some burn up alti relievi of large shining lumps an inch in diameter, a decoration not a little resembling large boils; others chip the fore-teeth like the Wanyamwezi. Their limbs are stout and well proportioned, many stand upward of six feet high, and they bear the appearance of a manly and martial race. Their dress is the mbugu, worn in the loosest way; their arms are heavy spears, sime, and unusually strong arrows; their ornaments are beads, brass wire, and streaks of a carmine-colored substance, like the red farinaceous powder called in India gulal, drawn across the head and forehead. The waganga, or priests of Urundi, wear a curious hood, a thatch of long white grass or fibre, cut away at the face and allowed to depend behind over the shoulders; their half-naked figures, occasionally rattling wooden clappers, and capering causelessly like madmen, present a savage and horrid appearance. Honorable women wear long tobes of American domestics from below the arms to the ankles; they are followed by hosts of female slaves, and preserve an exceptionally modest and decorous demeanor. Their features are of the rounded African type of beauty. Their necks and bosoms support a profusion of sofi and other various-colored beads; their foreheads are bound with frontlets, fillet-like bands of white and coral porcelain, about three fingers deep, a highly becoming ornament, probably derived from Karagwah; and those who were seen by the expedition invariably walked about with thin staves five or six feet long, pointed and knobbed as the walking-sticks of ancient Egypt.

At the northern extremity of the Urundi sea-face, and at the head of the Tanganyika, lies the land of Uzige; it is rarely visited except by the lakist traders. This people, who, like their neighbors, can not exist without some form of traffic, have, it is said, pursued the dows of the earlier Arab explorers with a flotilla of small canoes; it is probable that negro traders would be better received. In their country, according to the guides, six rivers fall into the Tanganyika in due order from the east: the Kuryama-venge, the Molongwe, the Karindira, the Kariba, the Kibaiba, and westernmost the Rusizi or Lusizi. The latter is the main drain of the northern countries, and the best authorities, that is to say, those nearest the spot, unanimously assert that it is an influent.

The races adjoining Uzige, namely, the Wavira on the north-western head of the Tanganyika, and their southern neighbors, the Wabembe cannibals, have already been mentioned. The Wasenze inhabit the hills within or westward of the Wabembe.

Farther southward, and opposite Kawele in Ujiji, are the Wagoma highlanders. The lower maritime lands belonging to the Wagoma supply the gigantic mvule trees required for the largest canoes. These patriarchs of the forest are felled and shaped with little axes on the spot; when finished they are pushed and dragged down the slopes by the workmen, and are launched and paddled over to the shores of Ujiji.

South of the Wagoma are the Waguhha, who have been mentioned as the proprietors of the islets southwest of Ujiji. In their lands, according to the Arabs, is a lake or large water called Mikiziwá, whence the tribe upon its banks derives its name Wamikiziwá. Through the country of the Waguhha lies the route to Uruwwa, at present the western terminus of the Zanzibar trade. The merchant, crossing the sea-arm which separates Kasenge from the main land of the Tanganyika, strikes toward Uruwwa; the line runs over low levels shelving toward the lake, cut by a reticulation of streams unfordable after rain, and varied by hilly and rolling ground. Provisions are every where procurable, but the people, like the Wavinza, are considered dangerous. At Uruwwa the khete, or string of beads, is half the size of that current in other countries. The price of ivory per frasilah is 15 miranga, or 150 large khete of white, small blue, and coarse red porcelain beads, the latter called lungenga; besides which, a string of sungomaji (pigeon-egg beads) and a few sámesáme, or coral beads, are thrown in. The route numbers nine long or sixteen short stages; the general direction is southwesterly. Kiyombo, the sultan of Uruwwa, is at present friendly with the Arabs; he trades in ivory, slaves, and a little copper from Katata or Katanga, a district distant fifteen marches northwest of Usenda, the now well-known capital of the great chief Kazembe. The grandfather of the present Kazembe, the " viceroy" of the country lying southwest of the Tanganyika, and feudatory to Mwátá yá Nvo, the sovereign of " Uropua," was first visited by Dr. Lacerda, governor of the Rhios de Sena, in 1798–99. The traveler died, however, after being nine months in the country, without recording the name and position of the African capital; the former was supplied by the expedition sent under Major Monteiro and Captain Gamitto in 1831–32; it is variously pronounced Lucenda, Luenda, and by the Arabs Usenda, the difference being caused probably by dialect or inflexion. According to the Arabs, the Kazembe visited by the Portuguese expedition in 1831 died about 1837, and was succeeded by his son the present chief. He is described as a man of middle age, of light-colored complexion, handsomely dressed in a Surat cap, silk coat, and embroidered loin-cloth; he is rich in copper, ivory, and slaves, cloth and furniture, muskets and gunpowder. Many Arabs, probably half castes, are said to be living with him in high esteem, and the medium of intercourse is the Kisawahili. Though he has many wives, he allows his subjects but one each, puts both adulterer and adulteress to death, and generally punishes by gouging out one or both eyes.

On the Uruwwa route caravans are composed wholly of private slaves; the races of the Tanganyika will not carry loads, and the Wanyamwezi, unmaritime savages like the Kafirs, who have a mortal dread and abhorrence of water, refuse to advance beyond Ujiji. On account of its dangers, the thriving merchants have hitherto abandoned this line to debtors and desperate men.

South of Uguhha lies the unimportant tribe of Wat'hembwe, whose possessions are within sight of Kawele in Ujiji. The race adjoining them is the Wakatete or Wakadete, and the country is called by the Arabs Awwal Marungu, on the northern frontier of Marungu. Marungu is one of the most important divisions of the lands about the Tanganyika. Amayr bin Said el Shaksi, a sturdy old merchant from Oman, who, wrecked about twelve years ago on that part of the coast, had spent five months with the people, living on roots and grasses, divides the region generically termed Marungu into three distinct provinces—Marungu to the north, Karungu in the centre, and Urungu on the south. Others mention a western Marungu, divided from the eastern by the Runangwa River, and they call the former in contradistinction Marungu Tajuna, from its sultan.

Western Marungu extends, according to the Arabs, in depth from Ut'hembwe to the Wabisa, a tribe holding extensive lands westward of the Nyassa Lake. Travelers from Unyamwezi to K'hokoro meet near Ufipa caravans of the Northern Wabisa *en route* to Kilwa. Between Marungu and Usenda, the capital of the Kazembe, the road lies through the district of Kavvire, distant seven marches; thence nine stages conduct them to the end of the journey. There is an upper land route through Uruwwa for those traveling from Ujiji to Usenda, and many caravans have passed from Unyanyembe direct through K'hokoro and Ufipa, to the country of the Kazembe. Mr. Cooley ("Geography of N'yassi," p. 7) conjectures that the Ambios or Imbies, Zimbas or Muzimbas, celebrated by the old Portuguese historians of Africa on account of an irruption, in 1570, from the north as far as the Zambezi River, "were no other than the M'Biza, or Moviza, as they are called by the Portuguese who still occupy its (the Nyassa's) southwestern banks." The proper name of this well-known tribe is Wábísá (in the sing. Mbísá), not Wábíshá, as it is pronounced at Zanzibar, where every merchant knows "Bisha ivory." The Wábísá extend, according to the Arabs, from the west of the Nyassa or Kilwa Lake toward the south of the Tanganyika. They dress in bark cloth, carry down their fine ivory to Tete and Kilimani (Quillimane); and every four or five years a caravan appears at Kilwa, where, confounding their hosts with the Portuguese, they call every Arab "muzungu," or white man. They are a semi-pastoral tribe, fond of commerce, and said to be civil and hospitable to strangers. It must be observed that those geographers are in error who connect the Wabisa with the Wanyamwezi; they are distinct in manners and appearance, habits and language. Mr. Cooley has, for instance, asserted that "the 'Moviza' and the 'Monomoezi' are similar in physical character and national marks." The only mark known to the Wabisa is the kishshah, or crest of hair; not, as Khamisi Wa Tani asserted to Mr. Cooley ("Inner Africa laid Open," p. 61), a dotted line on the nose and forehead; whereas the Wanyamwezi, as has been seen, puncture the skin. Thus Lacerda calls the "Moviza" a frizzled and periwigged people. The Arabs deny the assertion of Pereira, recorded by Bowdich, that the Moviza, like the Wahiao, file their teeth.

Marungu is described by the Arabs as a hilly country like Ujiji and Uvira: the precincts of the lake, however, are here less bold than the opposite shore. Off the coast lie four or five islands, two of which, according to the Arabs, are of considerable size; the only name given is Ukungwe, which appears, however, to be rather the name of the farthest point visible from Kasenge, and bearing S. 58° E. On the northwestern frontier of Marungu, and about three marches from the lake, is the district called Utumbara, from Mtumbara, its sultan. This Utumbara, which must not be confounded with the district of the same name in Northern Unyamwezi, is said by the Arabs to be fifteen to twenty days' march from Usenda.

Marungu, though considered dangerous, has often been visited by Arab merchants. After touching at Kasenge they coast along Uguhha for four days, not daring to land there in consequence of an event that happened about 1841–42. A large Arab caravan of 200 armed slaves, led by Mohammed bin Salih and Sulayman bin Nasir, and with four coadjutors, Abd el Al and Ibn Habib, Shiahs of Bahrayn, Nasir and Rashid bin Salim el Harisi (who soon afterward died at Marungu), took boat to Marungu, and in due time arrived at Usenda. They completed their cargo, and were returning in a single boat, when they were persuaded by the Sultan Mtumbara to land, and to assist him in annihilating a neighbor, Sámá or Kipyoká, living at about one day's march from the lake. The Arabs, aided by Africans, attacked a boma, or palisade, where, bursting in, they found Sámá's brother sitting upon pombe, with his wife. The villagers poured in a shower of arrows, to which the Arabs replied by shooting down the happy couple over their cups. Sámá's people fled, but presently returning they massacred the slaves of the Arabs, who were obliged to take refuge in the grass till aid was afforded by their employer Mtumbara. Sámá, thus victorious, burned the Arab boat, and, compelling the merchants to return to Usenda, seized the first opportunity of slaying his rival. The Arabs have found means of sending letters to their friends, but they appear unable to leave the country. Their correspondence declares them to be living in favor with the kazembe, who has presented them with large rice-shambas, that they have collected ivory and copper in large quantities, but are unable to find porters. This being highly improbable in a land where in 1807 a slave cost five, and a tusk of ivory six or seven squares of Indian piece-goods, and as, moreover, several merchants, deluded by exaggerated accounts of the kazembe's wealth and liberality, intrusted these men with considerable ventures, of which no tidings have as yet reached the creditors' ears, the more acute Arabs suspect that their countrymen are living from hand to mouth about Usenda, and are cultivating the land with scant prospect of quitting it.

The people of Marungu are called Wámbozwá by the Arabs; they are subject to no king, but live under local rulers, and are ever at war with their neighbors. They are a dark and plain, a wild and uncomely race. Among these people is observed a custom which connects them with the Wangindo, Wahiao, and the slave races dwelling inland from Kilwa. They pierce the upper lip and gradually enlarge the aperture till the end projects in a kind of bill beyond the nose and chin, giving to the countenance a peculiar duck-like appearance. The Arabs, who abhor this hideous vagary of fashion, scarify the sides of the hole and attempt to make the flesh grow by the application of rock-salt. The people of Marungu, however, are little valued as slaves; they are surly and stubborn, exceedingly depraved, and addicted to desertion.

Crossing the Runangwa or Marungu River, which, draining the southern countries toward the Tanganyika, is represented to equal the Malagarazi in volume, the traveler passes through the districts of Marungu Tafuna, Ubeyya, and Iwemba. Thence, turning to the north, he enters the country of the Wapoka, between whom and the lake lie the Wasowwa and the Wafipa. This coast is divided from the opposite shore by a voyage of fourteen hours; it is a hilly expanse, divided by low plains, where men swarm, according to the natives, like ants. At a short distance from the shore lies the Mvuma group, seven rocks or islets, three of which are considerable in size, and the largest, shaped like a cone, breeds goats in plenty, while the sea around is rich in fish. There are other islets in the neighborhood, but none are of importance.

Ufipa is an extensive district, fertilized by many rivers. It produces grain in abundance, and the wild rice is of excellent flavor. Cattle abounded there before the Watuta, who held part of the country, began a system of plunder and waste, which ended in their emigration to the north of Uvinza; cows, formerly purchased for a few strings of cheap white beads, are now rare and dear. The Wafipa are a wild but kindly people, who seldom carry arms: they have ever welcomed the merchants that visited them for slaves and ivory, and they are subject to four or five principal chiefs. The servile specimens seen at Unyanyembe were more like the jungle races of the Deccan than Africans—small and short, sooty and shrunken men, so timid, ignorant, and suspicious, that it was found impossible to obtain from them the simplest specimen of their dialect. Some of them, like the Wanyoro, had extracted all the lower incisors.

North of the Wafipa, according to the Arabs, lies another tribe, called Wat'hembe (?), an offshoot from the people on the opposite side of the Tanganyika. Here the lake receives a small river, called the Murunguru (?). The circuit of the Tanganyika concludes with the Wat'hongwe, called, from their sultan or their founder, Wat'hongwe Kapana. In clear weather their long promontory is the farthest point visible from Kawele in Ujiji; and their lands extend northward to Ukaranga and the Malagarazi River.

Such are the most important details culled from a mass of Arab oral geography: they are offered, however, to the reader without any guarantee of correctness. The principal authorities are the Shaykh Snay bin Amir el Harisi and Amayr bin Said el Shaksi; the latter was an eye-witness. All the vague accounts noted down from casual informants were submitted to them for an imprimatur. Their knowledge and experience surpassing those of others, it was judged better to record information upon trust from them only, rather than to heap together reliable and unreliable details, and, as some travelers do, by striking out a medium, inevitably to confuse fact with fiction. Yet it is the explorer's unpleasant duty throughout these lands to doubt every thing that has not been subjected to his own eyes. The boldest might look at the "Mombas Mission Map" and tremble.

Mganga, or
Medicine-man.   The Porter.   The Kirangozi, or
                                            Guide.
      Muinyi Kidogo.   Mother and Child.

CHAPTER XVI.

WE RETURN TO UNYANYEMBE.

IMMEDIATELY after the arrival of our caravan, I made preparations for quitting Ujiji. The 26th of May, 1858, was the day appointed for our departure, which was fated to resemble a flight
more than the march of a peaceful expedition. Said bin Salim,
who had received as "urangozi" or retaining-fee from his two
African "brothers," Lurinda and Kannena, a boy-slave and a
youth, thought only of conveying them safely out of the country.
The Baloch, especially the jemadar, who had invested every cubit
of cloth and every ounce of powder in serviles, were also trembling at the prospect of desertion. As usual, when these barbarians see preparations for departure, the Wajiji become more extortionate and troublesome than before. A general drinking-bout
had followed the return of the crews from Uvira: Kannena had
not been sober for a fortnight. At last his succession of violent
and maudlin fits ended, fortunately for us, in a high fever, which
somewhat tamed his vice. Shortly after our disappearance his
territory was attacked by the predal Watuta; and had not the
Arabs assisted in its defense, it would doubtless have been converted into a grizzly solitude, like the once fertile and populous Uhha. Kannena, of course, fled into the mountains from
the attack of the gallant rascals: he had courage enough to
bully but not to fight. I heard of him no more: he showed

SNAY BIN AMIR'S HOUSE.

no pity to the homeless stranger—may the world show none to him!

I shall long remember the morning of the 26th of May, which afforded me the last sunrise spectacle of the Tanganyika Lake. The charm of the scenery was perhaps enhanced by the reflection that my eyes might never look upon it again. Masses of brown-purple clouds covered the quarter of the heavens where the sun was about to rise. Presently the mists, ruffled like ocean billows and luminously fringed with Tyrian purple, were cut by filmy rays, while, from behind their core, the internal living fire shot forth its broad beams, like the spokes of a huge aërial wheel, rolling a flood of gold over the light blue waters of the lake. At last Dan Sol, who at first contented himself with glimmering through the cloud-mass, disclosed himself in his glory and dispersed with a glance the obstacles of the vaporous earth: breaking into long strata and little pearly flakes, they soared high in the empyrean, while the all-powerful luminary assumed undisputed possession of earth, and a soft breeze—the breath of the morn, as it is called in the East—awoke the waters into life.

But I am not long to enjoy this mighty picture. A jarring din sings in my ears, contrasting strangely with the beautiful world before my eyes. A crowd of newly-engaged pagazi are standing before me in the ecstasy of impatience: some poised like cranes upon the right foot, with the left sole placed against the knee; others with their arms thrown in a brotherly fashion round neighbors' necks; while others, squatted in the usual Asiatic and African position, with their posteriora resting upon their calves and heels, their elbows on their thighs, and their chins propped upon their hands, gazed at me with that long longing look which in these lands evidences a something sorely wanted. Presently, from Said bin Majid's home-bound caravan, with which I had consented to travel, shots and a popping of muskets rang through the air: the restless crowd that still watched me appeared at the sound of this signal to lose their wits. In a moment the space before the tembe was cleared. After a few moments Said bin Salim ran up, violently excited, declaring that his orders were of no avail, that some parties were starting with, and others without, their loads, and that no man would take up the burden assigned to him on the yesterday. I directed him to compose himself, and since he could not remain, to precede me with the headstrong gang as far as the Ruche River—the first stage—whence he would send back, as soon as possible, a few men bribed to carry my hammock and to remove the loose loads scattered upon the ground. These, as usual on such occasions, were our own. He departed greatly delighting in the opportunity of escaping further trouble, and of driving off his six wild slaves in safety: true to his inconsequential Arabo-African blood, however, neglecting the appointed station in the eagerness of hurry, he marched on with Said bin Majid's men to at least double the distance, thus placing himself out of Kannena's reach, and throwing all my arrangements into direst confusion.

Meanwhile, having breakfasted, we sat till the afternoon in the now empty and deserted tembe, expecting the return of the slaves. As none appeared, I was induced by the utter misery depicted in the countenances of the Baloch, and trusting that the return-porters would meet us on the way, to give orders for a march about 4 P.M., to mount my manchil, and to set out carried by only two men. Scarcely had I left the tembe when a small party, headed by Said bin Salim's four children, passed by me at speed. Though summoned to halt, they sped onward, apparently intending to fetch the loads from the house, and thus to relieve those left behind as a guard; it proved afterward that they were bound for the bazar to buy plantains for their patroon. Meanwhile, hurrying on with one Baloch, the astute Gul Mohammed, Valentine, and three sons of Ramji, as the shades of evening closed around us, we reached, without guide or direction from the surly villagers, the ferry of the Ruche River. Disappointed at not finding the camp at the place proposed, we were punted across the Styx-like stream; and for what reason no man could say, the party took the swampy road along the Bay of Ukaranga. The musquitoes stung like wasps; the loud spoutings and the hollow bursts of bellow, snort, and grunt of the hippopotami—in these lands they are brave as the bulls of the Spanish sierras—and the roar of the old male crocodile startled the party, while the porters had difficulty in preserving their balance as they waded through water waist-deep, and crept across plains of mud, mire, and sea-ooze.

As the darkness rendered the march risky, I gave the word, when arrived at a bunch of miserable huts, for a bivouac; the party, had I permitted it, would have wandered through the outer glooms without fixed purpose till permanently bogged. We spread our bedding upon the clear space between the cane-cones acting hovels, and we snatched, under a resplendent moon, and a dew that soaked through the blankets, a few hours of sleep, expecting to be aroused by a guide and porters before the end of night. Gaetano had preceded us with the provisions and the *batterie de cuisine;* we were destitute even of tobacco, and we looked forward expectantly to the march. But the dawn broke, and morning flashed over the canopy above, and the sun poured his hot rays through the cool, clear air, still we found ourselves alone. The sons of Ramji, and the others composing our party, had gradually disappeared, leaving with us only Gul Mohammed. Taking heart of grace, we then cleared out a hut, divided the bedding, lay down in the patience of expectation, and dined on goat. Our neighbor afforded us some food for the mind. Apparently an Androgyne, she had the voice, the look, and the thorax of a man, while the dress and the manner argued her to be a woman; it was the only approach to the dubious sex seen by me in East Africa.

About 2 P.M. appeared Ramazan and Salman, children of Said bin Said, with four porters, an insufficient supply for the long and trying march which they described. They insisted upon our enduring the heat and labor of the day so energetically, that they were turned with ignominy out of the village, and were told to send their master to escort us in the evening or on the morning of the next day. Accordingly at 9 A.M. of the 28th of May appeared Said bin Salim and the jemadar, escorted by a full gang of bearers. The former, bursting with irritation, began that loud speaking which in the East is equivalent to impertinence; he was easily silenced by a more explosive and an angrier tone of voice. Having breakfasted, we set out leisurely, and after rejoining Said bin Majid's party we advanced until evening fell·upon us at the end of the first day's stage.

I have related the tale of our departure from the Tanganyika somewhat circumstantially: it was truly characteristic of Arab traveling in Eastern Africa. Said bin Salim had scant cause for hurry: slaves rarely desert on the day of departure; knowing themselves to be watched, they wait their opportunity, and find it perhaps—as our caravan discovered to its loss—a week or two afterward. The Arab was determined to gain a few miles by passing the appointed station; he did so, and he lost two days. In his haste and dread of delay, he had neglected to lay in salt, ghee, or any other stores for the road but grain: consequently he was detained at half a dozen places to procure them. Finally, his froward children, who had done their utmost to waste time in the bazar, were not reproved, much less punished. Truly the half-caste Arab of Zanzibar is almost as futile as the slavish moiety of his ancestry.

There was little novelty in our return-march to Unyanyembe. We took the northerly route, crossing and skirting the lower spurs of the mountains which form the region of Uhha. During the first few stages, being still within the influence of that bag of Æolus, the Tanganyika trough, we endured tornadoes of wind and heavy rain, thunder and lightning. After the 5th of March the threatening clouds drew off, the dank heavy dew diminished, and the weather became clear and hot, with a raw cold eastern wind pouring through the tepid temperature, and causing general sickness. On the 29th of May we pitched at Uyonwa, a little settlement of Wabuha, who have already raised crops of sweet potatoes; if they have the sense to avoid keeping cattle, the only attraction to the robber Watuta, they may once more convert the sad waste of Uhha, a wilderness where men are now wolves to one another, into a land smiling with grains and fruits. Beyond Uyonwa we hurried over " neat-tongue" hills, separated by green swamps and black rivulets with high woody banks, over jungle-paths thick

with spear and tiger grass, brambly bush and tall growths of wild
arrow-root, and over a country for the most part rough and rugged,
with here and there an acacia-barren, a bamboo-clump, or a lone
palmyra. Approaching the Rusugi River, which we forded on
the 1st of June at the upper or Parugerero passage, the regular
succession of ridge and swamp gave way to a dry, stony, and
thorny slope, rolling with an eastward decline. We delayed for
an hour at the Salt-pass to lay in a supply of the necessary, and
the temptation to desert became irresistible. Muhabanya, the
"slavey" of the establishment, ran away, carrying off his property
and my hatchet. The jemadar was rendered almost daft by the
disappearance of half of his six slaves. A Mnyamwezi porter
placed his burden—it was a case of Cognac and vinegar, deeply
regretted!—upon the ground, and levanted. Two other porters
lost their way, and disappeared for some days; their comrades,
standing in awe of the Wavinza, would not venture in search of
them. The kirangozi or Mnyamwezi guide, who had accompanied the expedition from the coast, remained behind, because
his newly-purchased slave girl had become foot-sore, and unable
to advance; finding the case hopeless, he cut off her head, lest
his evil good might come to another. The party gave the usual
amount of trouble. The bull-headed Mabruki had invested his
capital in a small servile, an infant phenomenon, who, apparently
under six years, trotted manfully alongside the porters, bearing
his burden of hide-bed and water-gourd upon his tiny shoulder.
For some days he was to his surly master as her first doll to a
young girl: when tired he was mounted upon the back, and after
crossing every swamp his feet were carefully wiped. When the
novelty, however, wore off, the little unfortunate was so savagely
beaten that I insisted upon his being committed to the far less
hard-hearted Bombay. The hammals who carried my manchil
were the most annoying of their kind. Wanyamwezi veterans
of the way (their chief man wore a kizbao or waistcoat, and carried an old Tower-musket), originally five in number, and paid in
advance as far as Unyanyembe, they deserted slowly and surely,
till it was necessary to raise a fresh gang. For a short time they
worked well, then they fell off. In the mornings when their
names were called they hid themselves in the huts, or they squatted pertinaciously near the camp-fires, or they rushed ahead of the
party. On the road they hurried forward, recklessly dashing the
manchil, without pity or remorse, against stock and stone. A man
allowed to lag behind never appeared again on that march, and
more than once they attempted to place the hammock on the
ground and to strike for increase of wages, till brought to a sense
of their duty by a sword-point applied to their ribs. They would
halt for an hour to boil their sweet potatoes, but if I required the
delay of five minutes, or the advance of five yards, they became
half mad with fidgetiness; they were as loud-voiced, noisy, and

insolent, as turbulent and irritable, as grumbling, importunate, and greedy specimens of the genus *homo*, species *Africanus*, as I have ever seen, even among the "sons of water" in the canoes of Ujiji. In these lands, however, the traveler who can not utilize the raw material that comes to hand will make but little progress.

On the 2d of June we fell into our former route at Jambeho, in the alluvial valley of the Malagarazi River. The party was pitched in two places by the mismanagement of Said bin Salim; already the porters began to raise loud cries of Posho! (provaunt!) and their dread of the Wavinza increased as they approached the Malagarazi Ferry. The land in the higher levels was already drying up, the vegetation had changed from green to yellow, and the strips of grassy and tree-clad rock, buttressing the left bank of the river, afforded those magnificent spectacles of conflagration which have ever been favorite themes with the Indian muse:

> "Silence profound
> Enwraps the forest, save where bubbling springs
> Gush from the rock, or where the echoing hills
> Give back the tiger's roar, or where the boughs
> Burst into crackling flame and wide extends
> The blaze the dragon's fiery breath has kindled."
> WILSON'S *Uttara Rama Cheritra*, Act 2.

A sheet of flame, beginning with the size of a spark, overspread the hill-side, advancing on the wings of the wind, with the roaring rushing sound of many hosts where the grass lay thick, shooting huge forky tongues high into the dark air, where tall trees, the patriarchs of the forest, yielded their lives to the blast, smouldering and darkening, as if about to be quenched where the rock afforded scanty fuel, then flickering, blazing up and soaring again till, topping the brow of the hill, the sheet became a thin line of fire, and gradually vanished from the view, leaving its reflection upon the canopy of lurid smoke studded with sparks and bits of live braise, which marked its descent on the other side of the buttress. Resuming our march along the cold and foggy vale of the Malagarazi, and crossing on the third day the stony slabby hills that bound the fluviatile plain northward, we reached on the 4th of June the dreaded ferry-place of the river.

The great Malagarazi, still swollen, though the rains had ceased, by the surplus moisture of the sopped earth, had spread its wide heart of shallow waters, variegated with narrow veins—a deeper artery in the centre showing the main stream—far over the plain. Thus offering additional obstacles to crossing, it was turned to good account by the mutware, the Lord of the Ferry. On arrival at the kraal overlooking the river, I summoned this Charon, who demanded as his preliminary obolus one pot of oil, seven cloths, and 300 khete of blue porcelains. Said bin Majid, our companion, paid about one fifth the sum. But the kraal was uncomfortable, we were stung out by armies of ants; a slight earthquake, at 11.15 A.M., on the 4th of June, appeared a bad omen to Said bin Salim:

briefly, I was compelled to countenance the extortion. On the next morning we set out, having been cannily preceded by Said bin Majid. Every difficulty was thrown in the way of our boxes and baggage. Often, when I refused the exorbitant sum of four and even five khete per load, the fellows quietly poled off, squatted in their canoes, and required to be summoned back by Said bin Salim with the abjectest concessions. They would not take on board a Goanese or a Baloch without extra pay, and they landed, under some pretext, Said bin Salim and the jemadar upon a dry knoll in the waste of waters, and demanded and received a cloth before they would rescue them. In these and kindred manœuvres nearly seven hours were expended; no accidents, however, occurred, and at 4 P.M. we saw ourselves, with hearts relieved of some load, once more at Ugogo, on the left bank of the river. I found my companion, who had preceded me, in treaty for the purchase of a little pig; fortunately the beads would not persuade the porters to part with it, consequently my pots escaped pollution.

An eventless march of twelve days led from the Malagarazi Ferry to Unyanyembe. Avoiding the *détour* to Msene we followed this time the more direct southern route. I had expected again to find the treacle-like surface over which we had before crept, and perhaps even in a worse state; but the inundations compelled the porters to skirt the little hills bounding the swamps. Provisions—rice, holcus, and panicum, manioc, cucumbers, and sweet potatoes, pulse, ground-nuts, and tobacco—became plentiful as we progressed; the arrow-root and the bhang-plant flourished wild, and plantains and palmyras were scattered over the land. On the 8th of June, emerging from inhospitable Uvinza into neutral ground, we were pronounced to be out of danger, and on the next day, when in the meridian of Usagozi, we were admitted for the first time to the comfort of a village. Three days afterward we separated from Said bin Majid. Having a valuable store of tusks, he had but half loaded his porters; he also half fed them: the consequence was that they marched like madmen, and ours followed like a flock of sheep. He would not incur the danger and expense of visiting a settlement, and he pitched in the bush, where provisions were the least obtainable. When I told him that we must part company, he deprecated the measure with his stock statement, viz., that at the distance of an hour's march there was a fine safe village full of provisions and well fitted for a halt. The hour's march proved a long stage of nearly sixteen miles, over a remarkably toilsome country, a foul jungle with tsetse-haunted thorn-bushes, swamps, and inundated lands, ending at a wretched cluster of huts, which could supply nothing but a tough old hen. I was sorry to part with the Arab merchant, a civil man and a well-informed, yet somewhat addicted to begging like all his people. His marching-freaks, however, were unendurable, dawdling at the beginning of the journey, rushing through the middle, and lagging at the end. We afterward passed him on the road, of course he had been delayed, and subsequently, during a long halt at Unyanyembe, he frequently visited me.

On the 17th of June the caravan, after sundry difficulties caused by desertion, passed on to Irora, the village of Salim bin Salih, who this time received us hospitably enough. Thence we first sighted the blue hills of Unyanyembe, our destination. The next day saw us at Yombo, where, by good accident, we met a batch of seven cloth-bales and one box *en route* to Ujiji, under charge of our old enemy Salim bin Sayf of Dut'humi. My complaint against " Msopora," forwarded from Zungomero, had, after Lieut. Col. Hamerton's decease, on the 5th of July 1857, been laid by M. Cochet, consul de France, before H. M. the Sayyid Majid—a fact which accounts for the readiness with which our effects were on this occasion delivered up, and for the non-appearance of the individual in person. We also received the second packet of letters which reached us during that year: as usual, they were full of evil news. Almost every one had lost some relation or friend near and dear to him: even Said bin Salim's hearth had been spoiled of its chief attraction, an only son, who, born it was supposed in consequence of my "barakat" (propitious influence), had been named Abdullah. Such tidings are severely felt by the wanderer who, living long behind the world, and unable to mark its gradual changes, lulls, by dwelling upon the past, apprehension into a belief that his home has known no loss, and who expects again to meet each old familiar face ready to smile upon his return as it was to weep at his departure.

After a day's halt to collect porters at Yombo, we marched from it on the 20th of June, and passing the scene of our former miseries, the village under the lumpy hill, " Zimbili," we re-entered Kazeh. There I was warmly welcomed by the hospitable Snay bin Amir, who, after seating us to coffee, as is the custom, for a few minutes in his barzah or ante-room, led us to the old abode, which had been carefully repaired, swept, and plastered. There a large metal tray bending under succulent dishes of rice and curried fowl, giblets and manioc boiled in the cream of the ground-nut, and sugared omelets flavored with ghee and onion shreds, presented peculiar attractions to half-starved travelers.

Our return from Ujiji to Unyanyembe was thus accomplished in twenty-two stations, which, halts included, occupied a total of twenty-six days, from the 26th of May to the 20th of June, 1858, and the distance along the road may be computed at 265 statute miles.

After a day's repose at Kazeh, I was called upon, as " etiquette" directs, by the few Arab merchants there present. Musa Mzuri, the Indian, was still absent at Karagwah, and the greater part of the commercial body was scattered in trading-trips over the country. I had the satisfaction of finding that my last indent on Zanzibar for 400 dollars' worth of cloth and beads had arrived under the charge of Tani bin Sulayyam, who claimed four gorah or pieces for safe conduct. I also recovered, though not without some display of force, the table and chair left by the escort and the slaves in the Dungomaro Nullah. The articles had been found by one Muinyi Khamisi, a peddling and not over-honest Msawahili, who demanded an unconscionable sum for porterage, and whose head-piece assumed the appearance of a coal-scuttle when rewarded with the six cloths proposed by Snay bin Amir. The debauched Wazira, who had remained behind at Msene, appeared with an abundance of drunken smiles sideling in at the doorway, which he scratched *more Africano* with one set of five nails, while the other was applied to a similar purpose *à posteriori*. He was ejected, despite his loud asseverations that he, and he only, could clear us through the dangerous Wagogo. The sons of Ramji, who, traveling from Msene, had entered Kazeh on the day preceding our arrival, came to the house *en masse*, headed by Kidogo, with all the jaunty and *sans-souci* gait and manner of yore. I had imagined that by that time they would have found their way to the coast. I saw no reason, however, for re-engaging them, and they at once returned to the gayeties of their capital.

During the first week following the march all paid the inevitable penalty of a toilsome trudge through a perilous jungly country, in the deadliest season of the year, when the waters are drying up under a fiery sun, and a violent *vent de bise* from the east, which pours through the tepid air like cold water into a warm bath. Again I suffered severely from swelling and numbness of the extremities, and strength returned by tantalizingly slow degrees. My companion was a martyr to obstinate deafness and to a dimness of vision which incapacitated him from reading, writing, and observing correctly. Both the Goanese were prostrated by fever, followed by severe rheumatism and liver pains. In the case of Valentine, who after a few hours lay deprived of sense and sensation, quinine appearing useless — the malady only changed from a quotidian to a tertian type — I resolved to try the Tinctura Warburgii, which had been used with such effect by Lieut. Colonel Hamerton at Zanzibar. "Oh true apothecary!" The result was quasi-miraculous. The anticipated paroxysm did not return; the painful emetism at once ceased; instead of a death-like lethargy, a sweet childish sleep again visited his aching eyes, and, chief boon of all to those so affected, the corroding thirst gave way to an appetite, followed by sound if not strong digestion. Finally, the painful and dangerous consequences of the disease were averted, and the subsequent attacks were scarcely worthy of notice. I feel bound in justice, after a personal experiment which ended similarly, to pay this humble tribute of gratitude to Dr. Warburg's invaluable discovery. The Baloch, in their turn, yielded to the effects of malaria, many complained of ulcerations and prurigo, and their recovery was protracted by a surfeit of food and its consequences. But, under the influence of narcotics, tonics, and stimulants, we presently progressed toward convalescence; and stronger than any physical relief, in my case, was the moral effect of success, and the cessation of the ghastly doubts and cares, and of the terrible wear and tear of mind which, from the coast to Uvira, had never been absent. I felt the proud consciousness of having done my best, under conditions from beginning to end the worst and the most unpromising, and that whatever future evils Fate might have in store for me, it could not rob me of the meed won by the hardships and sufferings of the past.

Several Arab merchants were preparing to return coastward for the "mausim" (monsoon), or Indian trading-season, which, at Zanzibar, includes the months of December, January, and February, and they were not unwilling to avail themselves of my escort. But several reasons detained me at Kazeh. Some time was required to make preparations for the long down-march. I had not given up the project of returning to the sea-board *viâ* Kilwa. Moreover, it was judged advisable to collect from the Arabs details concerning the interesting countries lying to the north and south of the line traversed by the expedition. As has been mentioned in Chapter XI., the merchants had detailed to me, during my first halt at Kazeh, their discovery of a large bahr—a sea or lake—lying fifteen or sixteen marches to the north; and from their descriptions and bearings, my companion had laid down the water in a hand-map forwarded to the Royal Geographical Society. All agreed in claiming for it superiority of size over the Tanganyika Lake. I saw at once that the existence of this hitherto unknown basin would explain many discrepancies promulgated by speculative geographers, more especially the notable and deceptive differences of distances, caused by the confusion of the two waters.* Remained only to ascertain if the Arabs had not, with the usual Oriental hyperbole, exaggerated the dimensions of the northern lake.

My companion, who had recovered strength from the repose and the comparative comfort of our head-quarters, appeared a fit person to be detached upon this duty; moreover, his presence at Kazeh was by no means desirable. To associate at the same time with Arabs and Anglo-Indians, who are ready to take offense when it is least intended, who expect servility as their due, and whose morgue of color induces them to treat all skins a shade

* Mr. Erhardt, for instance, "Memoir on the Chart of East and Central Africa, compiled by J. Erhardt and J. Rebmann, London, 1856," announces the "existence of a great lake, called in the south Niandsha (Nyassa), in the north Ukerewe, and on the coast Niasa and Bahari ya Uniamesi," making the distance through Dschaga (Chhaga) and the Masai plains only fifty-nine marches.

darker than their own as "niggers," is even more difficult than to avoid a rupture when placed between two friends who have quarreled with each other. Moreover, in this case, the difficulty was exaggerated by the Anglo-Indian's complete ignorance of Eastern manners and customs, and of any Oriental language beyond, at least, a few words of the debased Anglo-Indian jargon.

I have dwelt upon this subject because my companion has thought proper to represent (in Blackwood, Oct., 1859) that I was "most unfortunately quite done up, but most graciously consented to wait with the Arabs and recruit health." This is far from being the fact. I had other and more important matter to work out. Writing from the spot (Unyanyembe, 2d July, 1858, and published in the Proceedings of the Royal Geographical Society, 24th January, 1859) my companion represents the case somewhat differently. "To diminish the disappointment, caused by the short-coming of our cloth, in not seeing the whole of the Sea Uji-ji, I have proposed to take a flying trip to the unknown lake, while Captain Burton prepares for our return homeward."

On the 30th of June the subject was brought forward in the presence of Said bin Salim and the Baloch. The former, happily lodged at Kazeh, felt loth to tear himself from the massive arms of his charmer Halimah. He finessed as usual, giving an evasive answer, viz., that he could not decide till the last day, and he declined to influence the escort, who afterward declared that he had done all in his power to deter them from the journey. In vain my companion threatened him with forfeiture of his reward after he returned to Zanzibar; in vain my companion told him that it was forfeited.* He held firm, and I was not over-anxious in influencing him, well knowing that though the Baloch, a stolid race, might prove manageable, the brain of the Machiavellian Arab, whose egregious selfishness never hesitated at any measure calculated to insure its gratification, was of a somewhat too heavy metal for the article opposed to it. That Said bin Salim attempted to thwart the project I have no doubt. The kirangozi, and the fifteen porters hired from his village with the tempting offer of five cloths per man, showed an amount of fear and shirking hardly justified by the real risks of treading so well known a tract. The jemadar and his men at first positively refused their escort, but the meaning word "bakhshish" slipping in reassured me. After informing them that in case of recusancy their rations should be stopped, I inquired the amount of *largesse* expected. The ten efficient men composing the guard demanded fifteen cloths apiece, besides one porter each to carry their matchlocks and pervants.

* I transcribe the following words from my companion's paper (Blackwood, October, 1859): "I urged that it was as much his (Said bin Salim's) duty as mine to go there; and said, unless he changed his present resolution, I should certainly recommend the government not to pay the gratuity which the consul had promised him on condition that he worked entirely to our satisfaction in assisting the expedition to carry out the government's plans."

The number of the porters was reduced, the cloth was procured from an Arab merchant, Sayf bin Said el Wardi, at an expense of one hundred dollars, made payable by draught upon Ladha Damha of Zanzibar: at the same time, the Baloch were warned that they must option between this and the reward conditionally promised to them after return.* Their bad example was followed by the old and faithful servant "Bombay," who required instant dismissal unless he also received cloth before the journey: he was too useful to my companion as interpreter and steward to be lightly parted with. But the granting his claim led to a similar strike and menace on the part of the bull-headed slave Mabruki, who, being merely a "headache" to me, at once "got the sack" till he promised, if pardoned, to shake off his fear and not to be naughty in future. By dint of severe exertion my companion was enabled to leave Kazeh on the 10th of July.

I proceed to recount the most important portion of the information—for ampler details the reader is referred to the Journal of the Royal Geographical Society—collected during my halt at Kazeh from various sources, Arab and African, especially from Snay bin Amir, concerning—

THE NORTHERN KINGDOMS: KARAGWAH, UGANDA, AND UNYORO.

The extensive and hitherto unknown countries described in this chapter, being compact despotisms, resembling those of Ashanti and Dahomey more than the semi-monarchies of Unyamwezi and Urundi, or the barbarous republics of Uvinza and Ujiji, are designated the Northern Kingdoms. It is regretable that oral information, and not the results of actual investigation, are offered to the reader concerning regions so interesting as the Southern Tanganyika, the Northern Kingdoms, and the provinces south of Unyanyembe. But absolute obstacles having interfered, it was judged advisable to use the labors of others rather than to omit all notice of a subject which has the importance of novelty, because it lacked the advantages of a regular exploration.

Informants agree in representing the northern races as superior in civilization and social constitution to the other tribes of Eastern and Central Africa. Like the subjects of the Kazembe, they have built extensive and regular settlements, and they reverence even to worship a single despot, who rules with a rigor which in Europe would be called barbarity. Having thrown off the rude equality of their neighbors, they recognize ranks in society; there is order among men, and some idea of honor in women; they add

* So my report printed in the Proceedings Roy. Geog. Soc., loco cit. "Our asses, thirty in number, all died, our porters ran away, our goods were left behind; our black escort became so unmanageable as to require dismissal; the weakness of our party invited attacks, and our wretched Baloch deserted us in the jungle, and throughout have occasioned an infinity of trouble."

to commerce credit, without which commerce can hardly exist; and they hospitably entertain strangers and guests. These accounts are confirmed by the specimens of male and female slaves from Karagwah and Uganda seen at Unyanyembe: between them and the southern races there is a marked physical difference. Their heads are of a superior cast; the regions where the reflective faculties and the moral sentiments, especially benevolence, are placed, rise high; the nose is more of the Caucasian type; the immoderate masticating apparatus, which gives to the negro and the lower negroid his peculiar aspect of animality, is greatly modified, and the expression of the countenance is soft, kindly, and not deficient in intelligence.

From Unyanyembe to Kibuga, the capital of Uganda, are fifty-three stages, which are distributed into four crucial stations of Usui, Karagwah, dependent Unyoro, and Uganda. A few remarks concerning each of these divisions may not be unacceptable.

Between Unyanyembe and Usui are sixteen long, or nineteen short stages. Though the road is for the most part rough and hilly, the marches can scarcely be reduced below ten statute, or six rectilinear geographical miles per diem; in fact, the geographer's danger when making these estimates is that of falling, through fear of exaggeration, into the opposite and equally incorrect extreme. The general direction of the line leading from Kazeh, in Unyanyembe, to Karagwah, pointed out by Snay bin Amir, bore 345° (corrected 332°); the length of the nineteen marches would be about 115 geographical miles. The southern frontier of Usui may, therefore, be safely placed in S. lat. 3° 10'.

The route from Kazeh to Usui falls at once westward of the line leading to the Nyanza Lake; it diverges, however, but little at first, as they both traverse the small districts of Ulikampuri, Unyambewa, and Ukuni. Usonga, crossed in five short marches, is the first considerable district north of Unyanyembe. Thence the road enters the province of Utumbara, which is flanked on the east by Usambiro, and on the west by Uyungu, governed by the Muhinda Sultan Kanze. Utumbara, as has been mentioned, was lately plundered, and Ruhembe, its chief, was slain by the predatory Watuta. In Utumbara and Usambiro the people are chiefly the Wafyoma, a tribe of Wanyamwezi: they are a commercial race, like the Wajiji—trafficking in hoes and ivory; and their present sultan, Mutawazi, has often been visited by the Arabs. Uyofu, governed by Mnyamurunda, is the northern boundary of Unyamwezi, after which the route enters the ill-famed territory of Usui.

Usui is traversed in seven marches, making a sum of twenty-six from Kazeh. According to the former computation, a total march of about 156 geographical miles would place the southern frontier of Karagwah in S. lat. 2° 40'. The road in several parts discloses a view of the Nyanza Lake. Usui is described as a kind of neutral ground between the rolling plateau of Unyamwezi and the highlands of Karagwah: it is broken by ridges in two places —Nyakasene the fourth, and Ruhembe the seventh stage, where mention is also made of a small stream. From this part of the country a wild nutmeg is brought to Kazeh by caravans: the Arabs declare that it grows upon the well-wooded hills, and the only specimen shown was heavy and well flavored, presenting a marked contrast to the poor produce of Zanzibar Island.

The Wasúí, according to the Arabs, are not Wanyamwezi. They are considered dangerous, and they have frequently cut off the route to caravans from Karagwah. Their principal sultan, a Muhinda named Suwarora, demands extraordinary black-mail, and is described as troublesome and overbearing: his bad example has been imitated by his minor chiefs.

The kingdom of Karagwah, which is limited on the north by the Kitangure or Kitangule River, a great western influent of the Nyanza Lake, occupies twelve days in traversing. The usual estimate would thus give it a depth of 72, and place the northern limit about 228 rectilinear geographical miles from Kazeh, or in S. lat. 1° 40'. But the Kitangure River, according to the Arabs, falls into the Nyanza diagonally from southwest to northeast. Its embouchure will, therefore, not be distant from the equator. The line of road is thus described: After ascending the hills of Ruhembe, the route, deflecting eastward, pursues for three days the lacustrine plain of the Nyanza. At Tenga, the fourth station, the first gradient of the Karagwah mountains is crossed, probably at low levels, where the spur falls toward the lake. Kafuro is a large district where merchants halt to trade, in the vicinity of Weranhánjá, the royal settlement, which commands a distant view of the Nyanza. Nyakahanga, the eighth stage, is a gradient similar to that of Tenga; and Magugi, the tenth station, conducts the traveler to the northernmost ridge of Karagwah. The mountains are described as abrupt and difficult, but not impracticable for laden asses: they are compared by the Arabs to the Rubeho chain of Usagara. This would raise them about 4000 feet above the mean level of the Unyamwezi plateau and the Nyanza water, and about 8000 feet above this sea. Their surface, according to the Arabs, is alternately earth and stone, the former covered with plantains and huge timber-trees, the latter bare, probably by reason of their altitude. There are no plains, bush, or jungle, but the deep ravines and the valleys intersecting the various ridges drain the surface of the hills, and are the sites of luxuriant cultivation. The people of Karagwah, averse to the labor of felling the patriarchs of the forest, burn "*bois de vache*," like the natives of Usukuma. North of Magugi, at Katanda, a broad flat extends eastward: the path thence descends the northern counterslope, and falls into the alluvial plain of the Kitangure River.

Karagwah is thus a mass of highlands, bounded on the north by dependent Unyoro, on the south by Usui, eastward by the tribes of Wahayya and Wapororo, upon the lacustrine plain of the Nyanza; on the southwest it inosculates with Urundi, which has been described as extending from the northeastern extremity of the Tanganyika Lake. Its equatorial position and its altitude enable it to represent the Central African prolongation of the Lunar Mountains. Ptolemy describes this range, which he supposes to send forth the White Nile, as stretching across the continent for a distance of 10° of longitude. For many years this traditional feature has somewhat fallen into discredit: some geographers have changed the direction of the line, which, like the Himalayas, forms the base of the South African triangle, from east and west to north and south, thus converting it into a formation akin to the ghauts or lateral ranges of the Indian peninsula; while others have not hesitated to cast ridicule upon the mythus. From the explorations of the "Mombas Mission" in Usumbara, Chhaga, and Kitui, and from the accounts of Arab visitors to the lands of Umasai and the kingdom of Karagwah, it appears that from the fifth parallel of S. lat. to the equator, an elevated mass of granite and sandstone formation crosses from the shores of the Indian Ocean to the centre of tropical Africa. The vast limestone band which extends from the banks of the Burramputra to those of the Tagus appears to be prolonged as far south as the Eastern Horn, and near the equator to give place to sandstone formations. The line is not, however, as might be expected from analogy with the Himalayan, a continuous unbroken chain; it consists of insulated mountains, apparently volcanic, rising from elevated plains, and sometimes connected by barren and broken ridges. The southeastern threshold of the Lunar cordillera is the highland region of Usumbara, which may attain the height of 3000 or 4000 feet above sea-level. It leads by a succession of mountain and valley to Chhaga, whose apex is the "Æthiopian Olympus," Kilima-Ngao. From this corner-pillar the line trends westward, and the rout to Burkene passes along the base of the principal elevations, Doengo Engai and Endia Siriani. Beyond Burkene lies the Nyanza Lake, in a huge gap which, breaking the continuity of the line, drains the regions westward of Kilima-Ngao, while those to the eastward, the Pangani and other similar streams, discharge their waters to the southeast into the Indian Ocean. The kingdom of Karagwah prolongs the line to Urundi upon the Tanganyika Lake, where the southwestern spurs of the Lunar Mountains form a high continuous belt. Mr. Petherick, of Kkartum, traveling twenty-five marches, each of twenty miles (?), in a south-southwestern and due southerly direction from the Bahr el Ghazal, found a granitic ridge rising, he supposes, 2000 to 2500 feet above the plain, near the equator, and lying nearly upon the same parallel of latitnde, and in about 27° E. long. Beyond that point the land is still unexplored. Thence the mountains may sink into the great depression of Central Africa, or, deflected northward of the kingdom of Uropua, they may inosculate with the ridge which, separating the northern negroid races of Islamized Africa from their negro brethren to the south, is popularly known, according to Denham and Clapperton, as el-Gibel Gumhr—Jebel Kamar— or Mons Lunæ.

The high woody hills of Karagwah attract a quantity of rain. The long and copious wet monsoon divides the year into two seasons—a winter of seven or eight, and a summer of four or five months. The vuli, or lesser rains, commence, as at Zanzibar, with the nayruz (29th of August); and they continue with little intermission till the burst of the masika, which lasts in Karagwah from October to May or June. The winds, as in Unyamwezi, are the kaskazi, or north and northeast gales, which shift during the heavier falls of rain to the kosi, the west and southwest. Storms of thunder and lightning are frequent, and the Arabs compare the down-pour rather to that of Zanzibar Island than to the scanty showers of Unyamwezi. The sowing season at Karagwah, as at Msene and Ujiji, begins with the vuli, when maize and millet, the voiandzeia, various kinds of beans and pulse, are committed to the well-hoed ground. Rice being unknown, the people depend much upon holcus: this cereal, which is sown in October to prepare for the masika in November, has, in the mountains, a short cane and a poor insipid grain of the red variety. The people convert it into pombe; and they make the wine called mawa from the plantains, which in several districts are more abundant than the cereals. Karagwah grows according to some, according to others, imports from the northern countries along the western margin of the Nyanza Lake, a small wild coffee, locally called mwámí. Like all wild productions, it is stunted and undeveloped, and the bean, which, when perfect, is about the size of a corking-pin's head, is never drunk in decoction. The berry, gathered unripe, is thrown into hot water to defend it from rot, or to prevent its drying too rapidly—an operation which converts the husk to a dark chocolate color: the people of this country chew it like tobacco, and, during visits, a handful is invariably presented to the guest. According to the Arabs, it has, like the kishr of Yemen, stimulating properties, affects the head, prevents somnolency, renders water sweet to the taste, and forms a pleasant refreshing beverage, which the palate, however, never confounds with the taste of the Mocha berry. In Karagwah a single khete of beads purchases a kubabah (from 1 lb. to 2 lbs.) of this coffee; at Kazeh and Msene, where it is sometimes brought by caravans, it sells at fancy prices. Another well-known production of all these regions is the mt'hí-pít'hípí, or Abrus precatorius, whose scarlet seeds are converted into ornaments for the head.

The cattle is a fine variety, with small humps and large horns, like that of Ujiji and Uviva. The herds are reckoned by gundu, or stallions, in the proportion of 1 to 100 cows. The late Sultan Ndagara is said to have owned 200 gundu, or 20,000 cows, which late civil wars have reduced to 12,000 or 13,000. In Karagwah cattle forms wealth, and every where in Africa wealth, and wealth only, secures defenders and dependents. The surplus males are killed for beef; this meat, with milk in its various preparations, and a little of the fine white hill-honey, forms the food of the higher classes.

The people of Karagwah, who are not, according to South African fashion, called Wakaragwah, are divided into two orders—Wahuma and Wanyambo—who seem to bear to each other the relation of patron and client, patrician and plebeian. The Wahuma comprises the rich, who sometimes possess 1000 head of cattle, and the warriors, a militia paid in the milk of cows allotted to their temporary use by the king. The Wanyambo—fellahs or ryots—are, it is said, treated by the nobles as slaves. The men of Karagwah are a tall stout race, doubtless from the effect of pure mountain air and animal food. Corpulence is a beauty: girls are fattened to a vast bulk by drenches of curds and cream thickened with flour, and are duly disciplined when they refuse. The Arabs describe them as frequently growing to a monstrous size, like some specimens of female Boers mentioned by early travelers in Southern Africa. Fresh milk is the male, sour the female beverage. The complexion is a brown yellow, like that of the Warundi. The dress of the people, and even of the chiefs, is an apron of close-grained mbugu, or bark cloth, softened with oil, and crimped with fine longitudinal lines made with a batten or pounding-club. In shape it resembles the flap of an English saddle, tied by a prolongation of the upper corners round the waist. To this scarcely decent article the chiefs add a languti, or Indian T bandage of goat's skin. Nudity is not uncommon, and nubile girls assume the veriest apology for clothing, which is exchanged after marriage for short kilts and breast-coverings of skin. Both sexes wear tiara-shaped and cravat-formed ornaments of the crimson abrus-seed, pierced and strung upon mondo, the fine fibre of the mwale or raphia-palm. The weapons are bows and arrows, spears, knobsticks, and knives; the ornaments are beads and coil-bracelets, which, with cattle, form the marriage settlement. The huts are of the conical and circular African shape, with walls of stakes and roofs so carefully thatched that no rain can penetrate them: the villages, as in Usagara, are scattered upon the crests and ridges of the hills.

The Mkámá or Sultan of Karagwah, in 1858, was Armanika, son of Ndagara, who, although the dignity is in these lands hereditary, was opposed by his younger brother Rumanika. The rebel, after an obstinate attack, was routed by Suna, the late despot of Uganda, who, bribed by the large present of ivory which was advanced by Musa Mzuri of Kazeh, then trading with Armanika, threw a large force into the field. Rumanika was blinded and pensioned, and about four years ago peace was restored. Armanika resides in the central district, Weranhanja, and his settlement, inhabited only by the royal family, contains from forty to fifty huts. He is described as a man about thirty to thirty-five years old, tall, sturdy, and sinewy-limbed, resembling the Somal. His dress is, by preference, the mbugu, or bark cloth, but he has a large store of fine raiment presented by his Arab visitors: in ornaments he is distinguished by tight gaiters of beads extending from knee to ankle. His diet is meat and milk, with sometimes a little honey, plantains, and grain: unlike his subjects, he eschews mawa and pombe. He has about a dozen wives—an unusually moderate allowance for an African chief—and they have borne him ten or eleven children. The royal family is said to be a race of centagenarians; they are buried in their garments, sitting and holding their weapons: when the king dies there is a funeral feast.

Under the mkama is a single minister, who takes the title of muhinda, and presides over the wakungu, elders and headmen, whose duty it is to collect and to transmit to the monarch, once every month, his revenues, in the shape of slaves and ivory, cattle and provisions. Milk must be forwarded by proprietors of cows and herds, even from a distance of three days' march. Armanika is an absolute ruler, and he governs without squeamishness. Adulterers are punished by heavy fines in cattle, murderers are speared and beheaded, rebels and thieves are blinded by gouging out the eyes with the finger-joints of the right hand and severing the muscles. Subjects are forbidden to sell milk to those who eat beans or salt, for fear of bewitching the animals. The mkama, who lives without state or splendor, receives travelers with courtesy. Hearing of their approach, he orders his slaves to erect four or five tents for shelter, and he greets them with a large present of provisions. He demands no black-mail, but the offerer is valued according to his offerings: the return gifts are carefully proportioned, and for beads which suit his taste he has sent back an acknowledgment of fifty slaves and forty cows. The price of adult male slaves varies from eight to ten fundo of white, green, or blue-porcelain beads: a woman in her prime costs two kitindi (each equal to one dollar on the coast), and five or six fundo of mixed beads. Some of these girls, being light-colored and well favored, sell for sixty dollars at Zanzibar. The merchants agree in stating that a European would receive in Karagwah the kindest welcome, but that to support the dignity of the white face a considerable sum would be required. Arabs still visit Armanika to purchase slaves, cattle, and ivory, the whitest and softest, the largest and heaviest in this part of Central Africa. The land is rich in iron, and the spears of Karagwah, which are, to some extent, tempered, are preferred to the rude work of the Wafyoma. Sulphur is found, according to the Arabs, near hot springs among the mountains.   A species of manatus (?) supplies a fine skin used for clothing.   The simbi, or cowrie (cypræa), is the minor currency of the country: it is brought from the coast by return-caravans of Wanyamwezi.

The country of Karagwah is at present the head-quarters of the Watosi, a pastoral people who are scattered throughout these lake regions. They came, according to tradition, from Usingo, a mountain district lying to the north of Uhha. They refuse to carry loads, to cultivate the ground, or to sell one another. Harmless, and therefore unarmed, they are often plundered, though rarely slain, by other tribes, and they protect themselves by paying fees in cattle to the chiefs. When the Wahinda are sultans, the Watosi appear as councilors and elders; but whether this rank is derived from a foreign and superior origin, or is merely the price of their presents, can not be determined. In appearance they are a tall, comely, and comparatively fair people; hence in some parts every "distinguished foreigner" is complimented by being addressed as "Mtosi." They are said to derive themselves from a single ancestor, and to consider the surrounding tribes as serviles, from whom they will take concubines, but to whom they refuse their daughters. Some lodges of this people were seen about Unyanyembe and Msene, where they live by selling cattle, milk, and butter. Their villages are poor, dirty, and unpalisaded; mere scatters of ragged round huts. They have some curious practices: never eat out of their own houses, and, after returning from abroad, test, by a peculiar process, the fidelity of their wives before anointing themselves and entering their houses. The Arabs declare that they are known by their black gums, which they consider a beauty.

The last feature of importance in Karagwah is the Kitangure River on its northern frontier. This stream, deriving its name from a large settlement on its banks, according to some travelers flows through a rocky trough, according to others it traverses a plain. Some, again, make it thirty yards, others 600, and even half a mile in breadth. All these statements are reconcilable. The river issues from Higher Urundi, not far from the Malagarazi; but while the latter, engaged in the depression of Central Africa, is drawn toward the Tanganyika, the former, falling into the counterslope, is directed to the northeast into the Nyanza Lake. Its course would thus lie through a mountain valley, from which it issues into a lacustrine plain, the lowlands of Unyoro and Uganda.   The dark and swift stream must be crossed in canoes even during the dry season, but, like the Malagarazi, about June or at the end of the rains, it debords over the swampy lands of its lower course.

From the Kitangure River fifteen stations conduct the traveler to Kibuga, the capital district of Uganda, and the residence of its powerful despot. The maximum of these marches would be six daily, or a total of ninety rectilinear geographical miles. Though there are no hills, the rivers and rivulets—said to be upward of a hundred in number—offer serious obstacles to rapid traveling. Assuming, then, the point where the Kitangure River is crossed to be in S. lat. 1° 14′, Kibuga may be placed in S. lat. 0° 10′. Beyond Weranhanja no traveler with claims to credibility has seen the Nyanza water. North of Kibuga all is uncertain; the Arabs were not permitted by Suna, the last despot, to penetrate farther north.

The two first marches from the Kitangure River traverse the territory of "dependent Unyoro," so called because it has lately become subject to the Sultan of Uganda. In former times, Unyoro, in crescent shape, with the cusps fronting eastward and westward, almost encompassed Uganda. From dependent Unyoro the path, crossing a tract of low jungle, enters Uganda in the concave of the crescent. The tributary Wahayya, under Gaetawa, their sultan, still extend to the eastward. North of the Wahayya, of whose territory little is known, lies "Kittara," in Kinyoro (or Kiganda?), a word interpreted to mean "mart" or "meeting-place." This is the region which supplies Karagwah with coffee. The shrub is propagated by sowing the bean. It attains the height of five feet, branching out about half way; it gives fruit after the third, and is in full vigor after the fifth year. Before almost every hut-door there is a plantation, forming an effective feature in the landscape of rolling and wavy hill, intersected by a net-work of rivers and streams: the foliage is compared to a green tapestry veiling the ground; and at times, when the leaves are stripped off by wind and rain, the plant appears decked with brilliant crimson cherry-like berries. The Katonga River, crossed at Kitutu, is supposed to fall into the Nyanza, the general recipient of the net-work of streams about Karagwah. This diagonality may result from the compound incline produced by the northern counterslope of the mountains of Karagwah and the southwestward depression necessary to form and to supply the lake. The Katonga is a sluggish and almost stagnant body of considerable breadth, and when swollen it arrests the progress of caravans. Some portions of the river are crossed, according to the Arabs, over a thick growth of aquatic vegetation, which forms a kind of mat-work, capable of supporting a man's weight, and cattle are towed over in the more open parts by cords attached to their horns. Four stations lead from the Katonga River to Kibuga, the capital district of Uganda.

Kibuga is the residence of the great mkámá or chief of Uganda. Concerning its population and peculiarities the Arabs must be allowed to tell their own tale. "Kibuga, the settlement, is not less than a day's journey in length; the buildings are of cane and ratan. The sultan's palace is at least a mile long, and the circular huts, neatly ranged in line, are surrounded by a strong fence which has only four gates. Bells at the several entrances announce the approach of strangers, and guards in hundreds attend there at all hours. They are commanded by four chiefs, who are relieved every second day: these men pass the night under hides raised upon uprights, and their heads are forfeited if they neglect to attend to the summons of the king. The harem contains about 3000 souls—concubines, slaves, and children. No male or adult animal may penetrate, under pain of death, beyond the barzah, a large vestibule or hall of audience where the king dispenses justice and receives his customs. This palace has often been burned down by lightning: on these occasions the warriors must assemble and extinguish the fire by rolling over it. The chief of Uganda has but two wants with which he troubles his visitors—one, a medicine against death; the other, a charm to avert the thunderbolt; and immense wealth would reward the man who could supply either of these desiderata."

Suna, the great despot of Uganda, a warlike chief, who wrested dependent Unyoro from its former possessor, reigned till 1857. He perished in the prime of life and suddenly, as the Arabs say, like Namrud; while riding "pickaback"—the state carriage of Central Africa—upon a minister's shoulders, he was struck by the shaft of the destroyer in the midst of his mighty host. As is the custom of barbarous and despotic races, the event was concealed for some months. When the usual time had expired, one of his many sons, exchanging his heir-elective name "Sámunjú" for Mtesa, became king. The court usage compels the newly-elected chief to pass two years in retirement, committing state affairs to his ministers; little, therefore, is yet known of him. As he will certainly tread in the footsteps of his sire, the Arabs may again be allowed to describe the state and grandeur of the defunct Suna; and as Suna was in fact the whole kingdom of Uganda, the description will elucidate the condition of the people in general.

"The army of Uganda numbers at least 300,000 men; each brings an egg to muster, and thus something like a reckoning of the people is made. Each soldier carries one spear, two assegais, a long dagger, and a shield, bows and swords being unknown. When marching the host is accompanied by women and children carrying spare weapons, provisions, and water. In battle they fight to the sound of drums, which are beaten with sticks like those of the Franks: should this performance cease, all fly the field. Wars with the Wanyoro, the Wasoga, and other neighbors are rendered almost chronic by the policy as well as the pleasure of the monarch, and there are few days on which a foraging party does not march from or return to the capital. When the king has no foreign enemies, or when the exchequer is indecently deficient, he feigns a rebellion, attacks one of his own provinces, massacres the chief men, and sells off the peasantry. Executions are frequent, a score being often slain at a time: when remonstrated with concerning this barbarity, Suna declared that he had no other secret for keeping his subjects in awe of him, and for preventing conspiracies. Sometimes the king would accompany his army to a battue of game, when the warriors were expected to distinguish themselves by attacking the most ferocious beasts without weapons: even the elephant, borne down by numbers, yielded to the grasp of man. When passing a village he used to raise a shout, which was responded to by a loud flourish of horns, reed-pipes, iron whistles, and similar instruments. At times he decreed a grand muster of his soldiery: he presented himself sitting before his gate, with a spear in the right hand, and holding in the left the leash of a large and favorite dog resembling an Arab suluki or greyhound. The master of the hounds was an important personage. Suna took great pleasure in witnessing trials of strength, the combatants contending with a mixture of slapping and pushing till one fell to the ground. He had a large menagerie of lions, elephants, leopards, and similar beasts of disport, to whom he would sometimes give a criminal as a 'curée:' he also kept for amusement fifteen or sixteen albinos; and so greedy was he of novelty that even a cock of peculiar or uniform color would have been forwarded by its owner to feed his eyes."

Suna when last visited by the Arabs was a "red man," aged about forty-five, tall, robust, and powerful of limb, with a right kingly presence and a warrior carriage. His head was so shaven as to leave what the Omani calls "el kishshah," a narrow crest of hair like a cock's comb, from nape to brow; nodding and falling over his face under its weight of strung beads, it gave him a fierce and formidable aspect. This tonsure, confined to those about the palace, distinguishes its officers and inmates, servile as well as free, from the people. The ryots leave patches of hair where they please, but they may not shave the whole scalp under pain of death, till a royal edict unexpectedly issued at times commands every head to shed its honors. Suna never appeared in public without a spear; his dress was the national costume, a long piece of the fine crimped mbugu or bark cloth manufactured in these regions, extending from the neck to the ground. He made over to his women the rich clothes presented by the Arabs, and allowed them to sew with unraveled cotton thread, whereas the people under severe penalties were compelled to use plaintain fibre. No commoner would wear domestics or similar luxuries; and in the presence, the accidental exposure of a limb led, according to the merchants, to the normal penalty—death.

Suna, like the northern despots generally, had a variety of names, all expressing something bitter, mighty, or terrible, as, for instance, Lbare, the Almighty (?); Mbidde and Purgoma, a lion. He could not understand how the Sultan of Zanzibar allowed his subjects treasonably to assume the name of their ruler; and, besides mortifying the Arabs by assuming an infinite superiority over their prince, he shocked them by his natural and unaffected impiety. He boasted to them that he was the god of earth, as their Allah was the Lord of Heaven. He murmured loudly against the abuse of lightning; and he claimed from his subjects divine honors, which were as readily yielded to him as by the facile Romans to their emperors. No Mgándá would allow the omnipotence of his sultan to be questioned, and a light word concerning him would have imperiled a stranger's life. Suna's domestic policy reminds the English reader of the African peculiarities which form the ground-work of "Rasselas." His sons, numbering more than one hundred, were removed from the palace in early youth to separate dungeons, and so secured with iron collars and fetters fastened to both ends of a long wooden bar that the wretches could never sit, and without aid could neither rise nor lie. The heir-elective was dragged from his chains to fill a throne, and the cadets will linger through their dreadful lives, unless wanted as sovereigns, until death release them. Suna kept his female children under the most rigid surveillance within the palace: he had, however, a favorite daughter named Nasuru, whose society was so necessary to him that he allowed her to appear with him in public.

The principal officers under the despot of Uganda are, first, the kimara vyona (literally, the "finisher of all things"): to him, the chief civilian of the land, the city is committed; he also directs the kabaka or village headmen. The second is the sakibobo, or commander-in-chief, who has power over the sáwágánzí, the life-guards and slaves, the warriors and builders of the palace. Justice is administered in the capital by the sultan, who, though severe, is never accused of perverting the law, which here would signify the ancient custom of the country. A mhozi—Arabized to hoz, and compared with the kazi of el Islam—dispenses in each town criminal and civil rights. The only punishments appear to be death and mulcts. Capital offenders are beheaded or burned; in some cases they are flayed alive; the operation commences with the face, and the skin, which is always much torn by the knife, is stuffed as in the old torturing days of Asia. When a criminal absconds, the males of his village are indiscriminately slain and the women are sold—blood and tears must flow for discipline. In money suits each party begins by placing before the mhozi a sum equivalent to the disputed claim; the object is to prevent an extensive litigiousness. Suna used to fine by fives or tens, dozens or scores, according to the offender's means; thus from a wealthy man he would take twenty male and twenty female slaves, with a similar number of bulls and cows, goats and kids, hens and even eggs. One of his favorites, who used constantly to sit by him on guard, matchlock in hand, was Isa bin Hosayn, a Baloch merce-

nary of H. H. Sayyid Said of Zanzibar. He had fled from his debtors, and had gradually wandered to Uganda, where the favor of
the sovereign procured him wealth in ivory, and a harem containing from 200 to 300 women. "Mzagayya"—the hairy one, as he
was locally called, from his long locks and bushy beard—was not
permitted, nor probably did he desire, to quit the country; after
his patron's death he fled to independent Unyoro, having probably raised up, as these adventurers will, a host of enemies at
Uganda.

Suna greatly encouraged, by gifts and attention, the Arab merchants to trade in his capital; the distance has hitherto prevented
more than half a dozen caravans traveling to Kibuga; all, however, came away loudly praising his courtesy and hospitality. To
a poor trader he has presented twenty slaves, and an equal number of cows, without expecting any but the humblest return.
The following account of a visit paid to him in 1852 by Snay bin
Amir may complete his account of the despot of Uganda. When
the report of arrival was forwarded by word of mouth to Suna,
he issued orders for the erection of as many tents as might be
necessary. The guest was welcomed with a joyful tumult by a
crowd of gazers, and was conducted to the newly-built quarters,
where he received a present of bullocks and grain, plaintains and
sugar-canes. After three or four days for repose, he was summoned to the barzah or audience-hall, outside of which he found
a squatting body of about 2000 guards armed only with staves.
Allowed to retain his weapons, he entered with an interpreter and
saluted the chief, who, without rising, motioned his guest to sit
down in front of him. Suna's only cushion was a mbugu; his
dress was of the same stuff; two spears lay close at hand, and his
dog was as usual by his side. The Arab thought proper to assume the posture of homage, namely, to sit upon his shins, bending his back, and, with eyes fixed on the ground—he had been
cautioned against staring at the "god of earth"—to rest his hands
upon his lap. · The levee was full; at a distance of fifty paces between the king and the guards sat the ministers; and inside the
palace, so placed that they could see nothing but the visitor's back,
were the principal women, who are forbidden to gaze at or to be
gazed at by a stranger. The room was lit with torches of a gum-
my wood, for Suna, who eschewed pombe, took great pleasure in
these audiences, which were often prolonged from sunset to midnight.

The conversation began with a string of questions concerning
Zanzibar, the route, the news, and the other staple topics of barbarous confabulation; when it flagged, a minister was called up
to enliven it. No justice was administered nor present offered
during the first audience; it concluded with the despot rising, at
which signal all dispersed. At the second visit Snay presented
his black-mail, which consisted of ten cotton cloths, and one hund-

red fundo of coral and other porcelain beads. The return was an offering of two ivories and a pair of serviles; every day, moreover, flesh and grain, fruit and milk were supplied without charge; whenever the wish was expressed, a string of slave-girls presently appeared, bending under loads of the article in question; and it was intimated to the "king's stranger" that he might lay hands upon whatever he pleased, animate or inanimate. Snay, however, was too wise to avail himself of this truly African privilege. During the four interviews which followed, Suna proved himself a man of intelligence: he inquired about the Wazungu or Europeans, and professed to be anxious for a closer alliance with the Sultan of Zanzibar. When Snay took leave he received the usual present of provisions for the road, and 200 guards prepared to escort him, an honor which he respectfully declined: Suna offered to send with him several loads of elephants' tusks as presents to H. H. the Sayyid; but the merchant declined to face with them the difficulties and dangers of Usúí. Like all African chiefs, the despot considered these visits as personal honors paid to himself; his pride therefore peremptorily forbade strangers to pass northward of his capital, lest the lesser and hostile chiefs might boast a similar brave. According to Snay, a European would be received with distinction, if traveling with supplies to support his dignity. He would depend, however, upon his ingenuity and good fortune upon farther progress; and perhaps the most feasible plan to explore the water-shed north of the Nyanza Lake would be to buy or to build, with the permission of the reigning monarch, boats upon the nearest western shore. Suna himself, had, according to Snay, constructed a flotilla of matumbi or undecked vessels, similar in shape to the mtope or muntafiyah—the modern "ploiaria rhapta" of the Sawahili coast from Lamu to Kilwa.

Few details were given by the Arabs concerning the vulgar herd of Waganda: they are, as has been remarked, physically a finer race than the Wanyamwezi, and they are as superior in character; more docile and better disciplined, they love small gifts, and show their gratitude by prostrating themselves before the donor. The specimens of slaves seen at Kazeh were, however, inferior to the mountaineers of Karagwah; the complexion was darker, and the general appearance more African. Their language is, to use an Arab phrase, like that of birds, soft and quickly spoken; the specimens collected prove without doubt that it belongs to the Zangian branch of the great South African family. Their normal dress is the mbugu, under which, however, all wear the "languti" or Indian T bandage of goat-skin; women appear in short kilts and breast-coverings of the same material. Both sexes decorate their heads with the tiara of abrus-seeds alluded to when describing the people of Karagwah. As sumptuary laws impede the free traffic of cloth into Uganda, the imports are represented chiefly by beads, cowries, and brass and copper wires. The wealth of the country is in cattle, ivory, and slaves, the latter often selling for ten fundo of beads, and the same sum will purchase the Wasoga and Wanyoro captives from whom the despot derives a considerable portion of his revenues. The elephant is rare in Uganda; tusks are collected probably by plunder from Usoga, and the alakah of about ninety Arab pounds is sold for two slaves, male or female. The tobacco, brought to market in leaf, as in Ujiji, and not worked, as among the other tribes, is peculiarly good. Flesh, sweet potatoes, and the highly nutritious plantain, which grows in groves a whole day's march long, are the chief articles of diet; milk is drunk by women only, and ghee is more valued for unction than for cookery. The favorite inebrients are mawa and pombe; the latter is served in neatly carved and colored gourds, and the contents are imbibed, like sherry cobbler, through a reed.

From Kibuga the Arabs have heard that between fifteen and twenty marches lead to the Kivira River, a larger and swifter stream than the Katonga, which forms the northern limit of Uganda, and the southern frontier of Unyoro. They are unable to give the names of stations. South of Kivira is Usoga, a low alluvial land, cut by a multitude of creeks, islets, and lagoons; in their thick vegetation the people take refuge from the plundering parties of the Waganda, whose chief built, as has been told, large boats to dislodge them. The Wasoga have no single sultan, and their only marketable commodity is ivory.

On the north, the northwest, and the west of Uganda lies, according to the Arabs, the land of independent Unyoro. The slaves from that country vaguely describe it as being bounded on the northwest by a tribe called Wakede, who have a currency of cowries, and wear tiaras of the shell; and the Arabs have heard that on the northeast there is a "people with long daggers like the Somal," who may be Gallas (?). But whether the Nyanza Lake extends north of the equator is a question still to be decided. Those consulted at Kazeh ignored even the name of the Nyamnyam; nor had they heard of the Bahri and Barri, the Shilluks on the west, and the Dinkas east of the Nile, made familiar to us by the Austrian Mission at Gondokoro, and other explorers.

The Wanyoro are a distinct race, speaking a language of the Zangian family; they have suffered from the vicinity of the more warlike Waganda, who have affixed to the conquered the opprobrious name of widdu or "serviles;" and they have lost their southern possessions, which formerly extended between Karagwah and Uganda. Their late despot, Chawambi, whose death occurred about ten years ago, left three sons, one of whom, it is reported, has fallen into the power of Uganda, while the two others still rule independently. The country is rich and fertile, and magnificent tales are told concerning the collections of ivory, which in some parts are planted in the ground to pen cattle. Slaves are cheap; they find their way to the southern markets *viâ* Uganda and Karagwah. Those seen at Kazeh and Kirira, where the Arab traders had a large gang, appeared somewhat inferior to the other races of the northern kingdoms, with a dull dead black color, flattish heads, brows somewhat retreating, prominent eyes, and projecting lower jaws. They were tattooed in large burnt blotches encircling the forehead, and in some cases the inferior excisors had been extracted. The price of cattle in Unyoro varies from 500 to 1000 cowries. In this country ten simbi (cypræa) represent one khete of beads; they are the most esteemed currency, and are also used as ornaments for the neck, arms, and legs, and decorations for stools and drums.

During my companion's absence much of my spare time was devoted to collecting specimens of the multitudinous dialects into which the great South African family here divides itself. After some months of desultory work I had learned the Kisawahili or coast language, the lingua Franca of the South African coast: it is the most useful, because the most generally known, and because, once mastered, it renders its cognates as easy of acquirement as Bengali or Maharatti after Hindoostani. The principal obstacle is the want of instructors and books—the Kisawahili is not a written language; and the elementary publications put forth in Europe gave me the preliminary trouble of composing a grammar and a vocabulary. Said bin Salim, though bred and born among the Wasawahili, knew but little of the tongue, and his peculiarities of disposition rendered the task of instruction as wearisome to himself as it was unsatisfactory to me. My best tutor was Snay bin Amir, who had transferred to the philology of East Africa his knowledge of Arabic grammar and syntax. With the aid of the sons of Ramji and other tame slaves, I collected about 1500 words in the three principal dialects upon this line of road, namely, the Kisawahili, the Kizaramo — which includes the Kik'hutu—and the Kinyamwezi. At Kazeh I found a number of wild captives, with whom I began the dreary work of collecting specimens. In the languages of least consideration I contented myself with the numerals, which are the fairest test of independence of derivation, because the most likely to be primitive vocables. The work was not a labor of love. The savages could not guess the mysterious objects of my inquiry into their names for 1, 2, and 3; often they started up and ran away, or they sat in dogged silence, perhaps thinking themselves derided. The first number was rarely elicited without half an hour's "talkee-talkee" somewhat in this style:

"Listen, O, my brother! in the tongue of the shores (Kisawahili) we say 1, 2, 3, 4, 5"—counting the fingers to assist comprehension.

"Hu! hu!" replied the wild man, "*we* say fingers."

"By no means; that's not it.   This white man wants to know how thou speakest 1, 2, 3."

"One, two, three what? sheep, or goats, or women?" expressing the numerals in Kisawahili.

"By no means; only 1, 2, 3 sheep in thine own tongue—the tongue of the Wapoka."

"Hi! hi! what wants the white man with the Wapoka?"

And so on, till patience was almost impossible. But, like the Irish shay-horse of days gone by; their tongues once started often hobbled on without halting. The tame slaves were more tractable, yet even in their case ten minutes sufficed to weary out the most intellectual; when the listless and incoherent reply, the glazed eye gazing at vacancy, and the irresistible tendency to gape and yawn, to nod and snooze, evidenced a feeble brain soon overworked. Said bin Salim would sit staring at me with astonishment, and ejaculate, like Abba Gregorius, the preceptor of Ludolph, the grammarian philologist, and historian of Æthiopia, "Verily, in the coast-tongue words never take root, nor do they bear branches."

The rest of my time was devoted to preparations for journeying. The fundi's tent, which had accompanied us to Uvira, was provided with an outer cover. The Sepoy's "pal," brought from Zanzibar, having been destroyed by the ill treatment of the villain Kannena, I made up, with the aid of a blackguard Baghdadi, named 'Brahim, a large tent of American domestics, which having, however, but one cloth, and that of the thinnest, proved a fiery purgatory on the down-march eastward. The canvas lug-sail was provided with an extra double cloth, sewn round the top to increase its dimensions: it thus became a pent-shaped affair, twelve feet long, eight broad, and six feet high—seven would have been better—buttoned at the foot, which was semicircular, and in front provided with blue cotton curtains, most useful against glare and stare. Its lightness, combined with impenetrability, made it the model of a tent for rapid marching. It was not, however, pegged down close to the ground, as some explorers advise, without the intervention of ropes; in these lands, a tent so pitched would rot in a week. The three tents were fitted with solid male bamboos, and were provided with skin bags for their pegs, which, unless carefully looked after, disappear almost daily. The only furniture was a kitanda or cartel: some contrivance of the kind, a "Biddulph," or an iron bed-frame, without joints, nuts, or screws, which are sure to break or to be lost, is absolutely necessary in these lands, where, from Kaole to Uvira, every man instinctively attempts to sit and to sleep upon something that raises him above the ground. Moreover, I have ever found the cartel answer the threefold purpose of bed, chair, and table; besides saving weight by diminishing the quantity of bedding required.

To the task of tent-making succeeded tailoring. We had neg-

lected to provide ourselves with the loose blanket suits served out
to sailors on board men-of-war in the tropics: they are most useful in passing through countries where changes of climate are sudden and marked. Besides these, the traveler should carry with
him an ample store of flannels: the material must be shrunk before making up shirts, otherwise it will behave as did the Little
Boy's mantle when tried by the frail fair Guinever. A red color
should moreover be avoided, the dye soon turns dark, and the appearance excites too much attention. Besides shirt and trowsers,
the only necessary is a large "stomach-warmer" waistcoat, with
sleeves and back of similar material, without collar—which renders sleeping in it uneasy—and provided with four flapped pockets, to contain a compass and thermometer, a note-book, and a
sketch-book, a watch, and a moderate-sized knife of many uses.
The latter should contain scissors, tweezers, tooth-pick, and ear-
pick, needle, file, picker, steel for fire, turnscrew, watch-spring
saw, clasp-blade, and pen-blade: it should be made of moderate
dimensions, and for safety be slung by a lanyard to the button-
hole. For the cold mornings and the noonday heats I made up a
large padded hood, bound round the head like the Arab kufiyah.
Too much can not be said in favor of this article, which in eastward travel defends the eyes from the fiery glare, protects, when
wending westward, the carotids against the solar blaze, and at all
times checks the intrusive staring of the crowd. I reformed my
umbrella, ever an invaluable friend in these latitudes, by removing the rings and wires from the worm-eaten stick, and by mounting them on a spear, thus combining with shelter a staff and a
weapon. The traveler should have at least three umbrellas, one
large and water-proof—white, not black—in the shape of those
used by artists; and two others of moderate size, and of the best
construction, which should be covered with light-colored calico, as
an additional defense against the sun. At Kazeh I was somewhat
deficient in material: my lazy "Jack of all trades," Valentine,
made, however, some slippers of green baize, soled with leather,
for me, overalls of American domestics for my companion, and
various articles of indigo-dyed cotton for himself and his fellow-
servant, who presently appeared tastefully rigged out like Paul
and Virginia in "Bengal blue."

The minor works were not many. The two remaining portmanteaus of the three that had left the coast were cobbled with
goat-skins, and were bound with stout thongs. The hammocks,
of which half had disappeared, were patched and provided with
the nara, or Indian cotton-tape, which in these climates is better
than either reims or cord. To save my eyes the spectacle of mor-
ibund fowls suspended to a porter's pole, two light cages were
made, after the fashion of the country, with bent and bound withes.
The metal plates, pots, and pans were furbished, and a damaged
kettle was mended by a traveling tinker: the asses' saddles and

halters were repaired, and, greatest luxury of all, a brace of jembe or iron hoes was converted into two pairs of solid stirrups under the vigilant eye of Snay bin Amir. A party of slaves sent to Msene brought back fifty-four jembe, useful as return presents and black-mail on the down-march; they paid, however, one cloth for two instead of four. Sallum bin Hamid, the "papa" of the Arabs, sold for the sum of forty dollars a fine half-bred Zanzibar she-ass and foal—there is no surer method of procuring a regular supply of milk on Eastern journeys. My black and white beads being almost useless, he also parted with, as a peculiar favor, seventeen or eighteen pounds of pink porcelains for forty dollars, and with a frasibah of coffee and a similar quantity of sugar for eighty dollars, equal to sixteen pounds sterling. On the 14th of July the last Arab caravan of the season left Unyanyembe, under the command of Sayf bin Said el Wardi. As he obligingly offered to convey letters and any small articles which I wished to precede me, and knowing that under his charge effects were far safer than with our own people, I forwarded the useless and damaged surveying instruments, certain manuscripts, and various inclosures of maps, field and sketch books, together with reports to the Royal Geographical Society.

This excitement over I began to weary of Kazeh. Snay bin Amir and most of the Arabs had set out on an expedition to revenge the murder of old Silim—an event alluded to in a former page, and the place had become dull as a mess-dinner. Said bin Salim, who was ill, who coughed and expectorated, and sincerely pitied himself because he had a cold, became more than usually unsociable: he could enjoy nothing but the society of Brahim, the bawling Baghdadi, and the crowd of ill-favored slavery that flocked into the vestibule. My Goanese servant, who connected my aspect with hard labor, avoided it like a pestilence. Already I was preparing to organize a little expedition to K'hokoro and the southern provinces, when unexpectedly—in these lands a few cries and gun-shots are the only credible precursors of a caravan—on the morning of the 25th of August reappeared my companion.

At length my companion had been successful, his "flying trip" had led him to the northern water, and he had found its dimensions surpassing our most sanguine expectations. We had scarcely, however, breakfasted, before he announced to me the startling fact that he had discovered the sources of the White Nile. It was an inspiration perhaps: the moment he sighted the Nyanza, he he felt at once no doubt but that the "lake at his feet gave birth to that interesting river which has been the subject of so much speculation and the object of so many explorers." The fortunate discoverer's conviction was strong; his reasons were weak—were of the category alluded to by the damsel Lucetta, when justifying her penchant in favor of the "lovely gentleman," Sir Proteus:

> "I have no other but a woman's reason,
> I think him so because I think him so;"*

and probably his sources of the Nile grew in his mind as his Mountains of the Moon had grown under his hand.

The main argument in favor of the lake representing the great reservoir of the White River was, that the "principal men" at the southern extremity ignored the extent northward. "On my

---

* The following extract from the Proceedings of the Royal Geographical Society, May 9, 1859, will best illustrate what I mean:

Mr. MACQUEEN, F. R. G. S., said the question of the sources of the Nile had cost him much trouble and research, and he was sure there was no material error either in longitude or latitude in the position he had ascribed to them, namely, a little to the eastward of the meridian of 35°, and a little northward of the equator. That was the principal source of the White Nile. The mountains there were exceedingly high, from the equator north to Kaffa Enarea. All the authorities, from east, west, north, or south, now perfectly competent to form judgments upon such a matter, agreed with him; and among them were the officers commanding the Egyptian commission. It was impossible they could all be mistaken. Dr. Krapf had been within a very short distance of it; he was more than 180 miles from Mombas, and he saw snow upon the mountains. He conversed with the people who came from them, and who told him of the snow and exceeding coldness of the temperature. The line of perpetual congelation, it was well known, was 17,000 feet above the sea. He had an account of the navigation of the White Nile by the Egyptian expedition. It was then given as 3° 30' N. lat. and 31° E. long. At this point the expedition turned back for want of a sufficient depth of water. Here the river was 1370 feet broad, and the velocity of the current *one quarter* of a mile per hour. The journals also gave a specific and daily current, the depth and width of the river, and every thing, indeed, connected with it. Surely, looking at the current of the river, the height of the Cartoom above the level of the sea, and the distance thence up to the equator, the sources of the Nile must be 6000 or 8000 feet above the level of the sea, and still much below the line of the snow, which was 6000 or 8000 feet farther above them. He deeply regretted he was unable to complete the diagram for the rest of the papers he had given to the Society, for it was more important than any others he had previously given. It contained the journey over Africa from sea to sea, second only to that of Dr. Livingstone. But all the rivers coming down from the mountains in question, and running southeastward, had been clearly stated by Dr. Krapf, who gave every particular concerning them. He should like to know what the natives had said was to the northwrad of the large lake? Did they say the rivers ran out from or into the lake? How could the Egyptian officers be mistaken?

CAPTAIN SPEKE replied. They were not mistaken; and if they had pursued their journey 50 miles farther, they would have undoubtedly found themselves at the northern borders of this lake.

Mr. MACQUEEN said that other travelers, Don Angelo, for instance, had been within one and a half degree of the equator, and saw the mountain of Kimborat under the line, and persisted in the statement, adding, that travelers had been up the river until they found it a mere brook. He felt convinced that the large lake alluded to by Captain Speke was not the source of the Nile: it was impossible it could be so, for it was not at a sufficiently high altitude.

The paper presented to the Society, when fully read in conjunction with the map, will clearly show that the Bahr-el-Abied has no connection with Kilimanjaro, that it has no connection whatever with any lake or river to the south of the equator, and that the swelling of the River Nile proceeds from the tropical rains of the northern torrid zone, as was stated emphatically to Julius Cæsar by the chief Egyptian priest Amoreis 2000 years ago.

In nearly 3° N. lat. there is a great cataract which boats can not pass. It is called Gherba. About half way (50 miles) above, and between this cataract and Robego, the capital of Kuenda, the river becomes so narrow as to be crossed by a bridge formed by a tree thrown across it. Above Gherba no stream joins the river either from the south or southwest.

inquiring about the lake's length, the man (the greatest traveler in the place) faced to the north, and began nodding his head to it; at the same time he kept throwing forward his right hand, and making repeated snaps of his fingers endeavored to indicate something immeasurable; and added, that nobody knew, but he thought it probably extended to the end of the world." Strongly impressed by this valuable statistical information, my companion therefore placed the northern limit about 4°–5° north lat., whereas the Egyptian expedition sent by the late Mohammed Ali Pacha, about twenty years ago, to explore the Coy Sources, reached 3° 22′ north lat. It therefore ought to have sailed fifty miles upon the Nyanza Lake. On the contrary, from information derived on the spot, that expedition placed the fountains at one month's journey—300 to 350 miles—to the southeast, or upon the northern counterslope of Mount Kenia. While marching to the coast, my companion—he tells us—was assured by a "respectable Sowahili merchant, that when engaged in traffic some years previously to the northward of the line, and the westward of this lake, he had heard it commonly reported that large vessels frequented the northern extremity of these waters, in which the officers engaged in navigating them used sextants and kept a log, precisely similar to what is found in vessels on the ocean. Query, could this be in allusion to the expedition sent by Mohammed Ali up the Nile in former years?" (Proceedings of Royal Geographical Society, May 9, 1859.) Clearly, if Abdullah Bin Nasib, the Msawahili alluded to, had reported these words, he merely erred; the Egyptian expedition, as has been shown, not only did not find, they never even heard of a lake. But not being present at the conversation I am tempted to assign further explanation. My companion, wholly ignorant of Arabic, was reduced to depend upon "Bombay," who spoke an even more debased dialect than his master, and it is easy to see how the blunder originated. The Arabic bahr and the Kisawahili bahari are equally applicable in vulgar parlance to a river or sea, a lake or a river. Traditions concerning a western sea—the to them now unknown Atlantic —over which the white men voyage, are familiar to many East Africans. I have heard at Harar precisely the same report concerning the log and sextants. Either, then, Abdullah Bin Nasib confounded, or my companion's "interrupter" caused him to confound the Atlantic and the lake. In the maps forwarded from Kazeh by my companion, the River Kivira was, after ample inquiry, made a western *influent* of the Nyanza Lake. In the map appended to the paper in Blackwood, before alluded to, it has become an *effluent*, and the only minute concerning so very important a modification is, "This river (although I must confess at first I did not think so) is the Nile itself!"

Beyond the assertion, therefore, that no man had visited the north, and the appearance of sextants and logs upon the waters, there is not a shade of proof *pro.* Far graver considerations lie on the *con.* side: the reports of the Egyptian expedition, and the dates of the several inundations which—as will presently appear —alone suffice to disprove the possibility of the Nyanza causing the flood of the Nile. It is doubtless a satisfactory thing to disclose to an admiring public, of "statesmen, churchmen, missionaries, merchants, and more particularly geographers," the "solution of a problem, which it has been the first geographical desideratum of many thousand years to ascertain, and the ambition of the first monarchs in the world to unravel." (Blackwood's Magazine, October, 1859.) But how many times since the days of a certain Claudius Ptolemæius surnamed Pelusiota, have not the fountains of the White Nile been discovered and rediscovered after this fashion?

What tended at the time to make me the more skeptical was the substantial incorrectness of the geographical and other details brought back by my companion. This was natural enough. Bombay, after misunderstanding his master's ill-expressed Hindoostani, probably mistranslated the words into Kisawahili to some traveled African, who in turn passed on the question in a wilder dialect to the barbarian or barbarians under examination. During such a journey to and fro words must be liable to severe accidents. The first thing reported to me was the falsehood of the Arabs at Kazeh, who had calumniated the good Sultan Muhayya, and had praised the bad Sultan Machunda: subsequent inquiries proved their rigid correctness. My companion's principal informant was one Mansur bin Salim, a half-caste Arab, who had been flogged out of Kazeh by his compatriots; he pronounced Muhayya to be a "very excellent and obliging person," and of course he was believed. I then heard a detailed account of how the caravan of Salim bin Rashid had been attacked, beaten, captured, and detained at Ukerewe, by its Sultan Machunda. The Arabs received the intelligence with a smile of ridicule, and in a few days Salim bin Rashid appeared in person to disprove the report. These are but two cases of many. And what knowledge of Asiatic customs can be expected from the writer of these lines? "The Arabs at Unyanyembe had advised my donning their habit for the trip in order to attract less attention; a vain precaution, which I believe they suggested more to gratify their own vanity in *seeing an Englishman lower himself to their position*, than for any benefit that I might receive by doing so." (Blackwood, *loço cit.*) This galamatias of the Arabs!—the haughtiest and the most clannish of all Oriental peoples.

But difference of opinion was allowed to alter companionship. After a few days it became evident to me that not a word could be uttered upon the subject of the lake, the Nile, and his *trouvaille* generally without giving offense. By a tacit agreement it was, therefore, avoided, and I should never have resumed it had my companion not stultified the results of the expedition by putting forth a claim which no geographer can admit, and which is at the same time so weak and flimsy that no geographer has yet taken the trouble to contradict it.

I will here offer to the reader a few details concerning the lake in question—they are principally borrowed from my companion's diary, carefully corrected, however, by Snay bin Amir, Salim bin Rashid,* and other merchants of Kazeh.

This fresh-water sea is known throughout the African tribes as Nyanza, and the similarity of the sound to "Nyassa," the indigenous name of the little Maravi or Kilwa Lake, may have caused in part the wild confusion in which speculative geographers have involved the lake regions of Central Africa. The Arabs, after their fashion of deriving comprehensive names from local and minor features, call it Ukerewe, in the Kisukuma dialect meaning the "place of kerewe" (kelewe), an islet. As has been mentioned, they sometimes attempt to join by a river, a creek, or some other theoretical creation, the Nyanza with the Tanganyika, the altitude of the former being 3750 feet above sea-level, or 1900 feet above the latter, and the mountain regions which divide the two having been frequently traveled over by Arab and African caravans. Hence the name Ukerewe has been transferred in the "Mombas Mission Map" to the northern waters of the Tanganyika. The Nyanza, as regards name, position, and even existence, has hitherto been unknown to European geographers; but, as will presently appear, descriptions of this sea by native travelers have been unconsciously transferred by our writers to the Tanganyika of Ujiji, and even to the Nyassa of Kilwa.

M. Brun-Rollet ("Le Nil Blanc et le Soudan," p. 209) heard that on the west of the Padongo tribe, whom he places to the S. of Mount Kambirah, or below 1° S. lat., lies a great lake, from whose northern extremity issues a river whose course is unknown. In the map appended to his volume this water is placed between 1° S. and 3° N. lat., and about 25° 50' E. long. (Greenwich), and the déversoir is made an influent of the White Nile.

---

* When my companion returned to Kazeh, he represented Ukerewe and Mazita to be islands, and, although in sight of them, he had heard nothing concerning their connection with the coast. This error was corrected by Salim bin Rashid, and accepted by us. Yet I read in his discovery of the supposed sources of the Nile: "Mansur and a native, the greatest traveler of the place, kindly accompanied and gave me every obtainable information. This man had traversed the island, as he called it, of Ukerewe from north to south. *But by his rough mode of describing it, I am rather inclined to think that instead of its being an actual island, it is a connected tongue of land, stretching southward from a promontory lying at right angles to the eastern shore of the lake,* which being a wash, affords a passage to the main land during the fine season, but during the wet becomes submerged and thus makes Ukerewe temporarily an island." The information, I repeat, was given, not by the "native," but by Salim bin Rashid. When, however, the latter proceeded to correct my companion's confusion between the well-known coffee-mart Kitara and "the Island of Kitiri occupied by a tribe called Watiri," he gave only offense—consequently Kitiri has obtained a local habitation in Blackwood and Petermann.

Bowdich ("Discoveries of the Portuguese" p. 131, 132), when speaking of the Maravi Lake (the Nyassa), mentions that the "negroes or the Moors of Melinde" have mentioned a great water which is known to reach Mombaca, which the Jesuit missionaries conjectured to communicate with Abyssinia, and of which Father Lewis Marianna, who formerly resided at Tete, recommended a discovery, in a letter addressed to the government at Goa, which is still preserved among the public archives of that city. Here the confusion of the Nyanza, to which there was of old a route from Mombasah, with the Nyassa, is apparent.

At the southern point, where the Muingwira River falls into the tortuous creek, whose surface is a little archipelago of brown rocky islets crowned with trees, and emerging from the blue waters, the observed latitude of the Nyanza Lake, is 2° 24' S.; the longitude by dead reckoning from Kazeh is E. long. 33° and nearly due north, and the altitude by B. P. thermometer 3750 feet above sea-level. Its extent to the north is unknown to the people of the southern regions, which rather denotes some difficulty in traveling than any great extent. They informed my companion that from Mwanza to the southern frontier of Karagwah is a land journey of one month, or a sea voyage of five days toward the N.N.W. and then to the north. They also pointed out the direction of Unyoro N. 20° W. The Arab merchants of Kazeh have seen the Nyanza opposite Weranhanja, the capital district of Armanika, king of Karagwah, and declare that it receives the Kitangure River, whose mouth has been placed about the equator. Beyond that point all is doubtful. The merchants have heard that Suna, the late despot of Uganda, built matumbi, or undecked vessels, capable of containing forty or fifty men, in order to attack his enemies the Wasoga, upon the creeks which indent the western shores of the Nyanza. This, if true, would protract the lake to between 1° and 1° 30' of N. lat., and give it a total length of about 4° or 250 miles. This point, however, is still involved in the deepest obscurity. Its breadth was estimated as follows. A hill, about 200 feet above the water-level, shows a conspicuous landmark on the eastern shore, which was set down as forty miles distant. On the southwestern angle of the line from the same point ground appeared; it was not, however, perceptible on the northwest. The total breadth, therefore, has been assumed at eighty miles—a figure which approaches the traditions unconsciously chronicled by European geographers. In the vicinity of Usoga the lake, according to the Arabs, broadens out: of this, however, and in fact of all the formation north of the equator, it is at present impossible to arrive at certainty.

The Nyanza is an elevated basin or reservoir, the recipient of the surplus monsoon-rain which falls in the extensive regions of the Wamasai and their kinsmen to the east, the Karagwah line of the Lunar Mountains to the west, and to the south Usukuma or

Northern Unyamwezi. Extending to the equator in the central length of the African peninsula, and elevated above the limits of the depression in the heart of the continent, it appears to be a gap in the irregular chain which, running from Usumbara and Kilima-ngao to Karagwah, represents the formation anciently termed the Mountains of the Moon. The physical features, as far as they were observed, suggest this view. The shores are low and flat, dotted here and there with little hills; the smaller islands also are hill-tops, and any part of the country immediately on the south would, if inundated to the same extent, present a similar aspect. The lake lies open and elevated, rather like the drainage and the temporary deposit of extensive floods than a volcanic creation like the Tanganyika, a long narrow mountain-girt basin. The waters are said to be deep, and the extent of the inundation about the southern creek proves that they receive during the season an important accession. The color was observed to be clear and blue, especially from afar in the early morning; after 9 A.M., when the prevalent southeast wind arose, the surface appeared grayish, or of a dull milky white, probably the effect of atmospheric reflection. The tint, however, does not, according to travelers, ever become red or green like the waters of the Nile. But the produce of the lake resembles that of the river in its purity; the people living on the shores prefer it, unlike that of the Tanganyika, to the highest and the clearest springs; all visitors agree in commending its lightness and sweetness, and declare that the taste is rather of river or of rain-water than resembling the soft slimy produce of stagnant muddy bottoms, or the rough harsh flavor of melted ice and snow.

From the southern creek of the Nyanza, and beyond the archipelago of neighboring islets, appear the two features which have given to this lake the name of Ukerewe. The Arabs call them "jezirah"—an ambiguous term, meaning equally insula and peninsula—but they can scarcely be called islands. The high and rocky Mazita to the east, and the comparatively flat Ukerewe on the west, are described by the Arabs as points terminating seaward in bluffs, and connected with the eastern shore by a low neck of land, probably a continuous reef, flooded during the rains, but never so deeply as to prevent cattle fording the isthmus. The northern and western extremities front deep water, and a broad channel separates them from the southern shore, Usukuma. The Arabs, when visiting Ukerewe or its neighbor, prefer hiring the canoes of the Wasukuma, and paddling round the southeastern extremity of the Nyanza, to exposing their property and lives by marching through the dangerous tribes of the coast.

Mazita belongs to a people called Makwiya. Ukerewe is inhabited, according to some informants, by Wasukuma; according to others, the Wakerewe are marked by their language as ancient emigrants from the highlands of Karagwah. In Ukerewe, which

is exceedingly populous, are two brother sultans: the chief is
"Machunda;" the second, "Ibanda," rules at Wiru, the headland
on the western limit.   The people collect ivory from the races on
the eastern main land and store it, awaiting an Arab caravan.
Beads are in most request; as in Usukuma generally, not half a
dozen cloths of native and foreign manufacture will be found upon
a hundred men.   The women are especially badly clad; even the
adult maidens wear only the languti of India, or the Nubian apron
of aloe-fibre, strung with the pipe-stem bead called sofi, and blackened, like India-rubber, by use; it is fastened round the waist, and
depends about one foot by six or seven inches in breadth.

The Arabs who traffic in these regions generally establish themselves with Sultan Machunda, and send their slaves in canoes
round the southeast angle of the lake to trade with the coast people.   These races are successively from the south; the Washaki,
at a distance of three marches, and their inland neighbors the
Watataru; then the Warudi, a wild tribe, rich in ivory, lying
about a fortnight's distance; and beyond them the Wahumba, or
Wamasai.   Commercial transactions extend along the eastern
shore as far as T'hiri, or Ut'hiri, a district between Ururu and
Uhumba.   This is possibly the origin of the Island of Tiri or
Kittiri, placed in my companion's map near the northwest extremity of the Nyanza Lake, off the coast of Uganda, where there
is a province called Kittara, peculiarly rich in coffee.   The explorer heard from the untrustworthy country people that, after a
long coasting voyage, they arrived at an island where the inhabitants, a poor and naked race, live on fish, and cultivate coffee for
sale.   The information appears suspicious.   The Arabs know of
no islands upon the Nyanza which produce coffee.   Moreover, if
the people had any traffic, they would not be without clothing.

The savagery of the races adjacent to the Nyanza has caused
accidents among traveling traders.   About five years ago a large
caravan from Tanga, on the eastern coast, consisting of 400 or 500
guns, and led by Arab merchants, at the end of a journey which
had lasted nearly two years, happened to quarrel with the Wahumba or Wamasai near the lake.   The subject was the burning
down of some grass required for pasture by the wild men.   Words
led to blows; the caravan, having but two or three pounds of
gunpowder, was soon dispersed; seven or eight merchants lost
their lives, and a few made their escape to Unyanyembe.   Before
our departure from Kazeh, the slaves of Salim bin Rashid, having
rescued one of the wounded survivors, who had been allowed by
the Wamasai to wander into Urudi, brought him back to Kazeh.
He described the country as no longer practicable.   In 1858, also,
the same trading party, the principal authority for these statements, were relieved of several bales of cloth during their sleep
when bivouacking upon an inhabited island near the eastern shore.
The altitude, the conformation of the Nyanza Lake, the argilla-

ceous color and the sweetness of its waters, combine to suggest that it may be one of the feeders of the White Nile. In the map appended to M. Brun-Rollet's volume before alluded to, the large water west of the Padongo tribe, which clearly represents the Nyanza or Ukerewe, is, I have observed, made to drain northward into the Fitri Lake, and eventually to swell the main stream of the White River. The details supplied by the Egyptian expedition, which, about twenty years ago, ascended the White River to 3° 22' N. lat., and 31° 30' E. long., and gave the general bearing of the river from that point to its source as southeast, with a distance of one month's journey, or from 300 to 350 miles, would place the actual sources 2° S. lat. and 35° E. long., or in 2° eastward of the southern creek of the Nyanza Lake. This position would occupy the northern counterslope of the Lunar Mountains, the upper water-shed of the high region whose culminating apices are Kilima-Ngao, Kénia, and Doengo Engai. The distance of these peaks from the coast, as given by Dr. Krapf, must be considerably reduced, and little authority can be attached to his river Tumbiri.* The site, supposed by Mr. Macqueen ("Proceedings of the Geographical Society of London," January 24th, 1859) to be at least 21,000 feet above the level of the sea, and consequently 3000 or 4000 feet above the line of perpetual congelation, would admirably explain the two most ancient theories concerning the source of the White River, namely, that it arises in a snowy region, and that its inundation is the result of tropical rains.

It is impossible not to suspect that between the upper portion of the Nyanza and the water-shed of the White Nile there exists a longitudinal range of elevated ground, running from east to west —a "furca" draining northward into the Nile, and southward into the Nyanza Lake—like that which separates the Tanganyika from the Maravi or Nyassa of Kilwa. According to Don Angelo Vinco, who visited Loquéck in 1852, beyond the cataract of Garbo— supposed to be in N. lat. 2° 40'—at a distance of sixty miles lie Robego, the capital of Kuenda, and Lokoya (Logoja), of which the latter receives an affluent from the east. Beyond Lokoya the White Nile is described as a *small and rocky mountain river*, presenting none of the features of a stream flowing from a broad expanse of water like the great Nyanza reservoir.

The periodical swelling of the Nyanza Lake, which, flooding a considerable tract of land on the south, may be supposed—as it

---

* The large river Tumbiri, mentioned by Dr. Krapf as flowing toward Egypt from the northern counterslope of Mount Kenia, rests upon the sole authority of a single wandering native. As, moreover, the word t'humbiri or t'humbili means a monkey, and the people are peculiarly fond of satire in a small way, it is not improbable that the very name had no foundation of fact. This is mentioned, as some geographers—for instance, Mr. Macqueen ("Observations on the Geography of Central Africa:" "Proceedings of the R. G. S. of London," May 9, 1859)—have been struck by the circumstance that the Austrian missionaries and Mr. Werne ("Expedition to discover the sources of the White Nile, in 1840–41") gave Tubirih as the Bari name of the White Nile at the southern limit of their exploration.

lies flush with the basal surface of the country—to inundate extensively all the low lands that form its periphery, forbids belief in the possibility of its being the head-stream of the Nile, or the reservoir of its periodical inundation. In Karagwah, upon the western shore, the masika or monsoon lasts from October to May or June, after which the dry season sets in. The Egyptian expedition found the river falling fast at the end of January, and they learned from the people that it would again rise about the end of March, at which season the sun is vertical over the equator. About the summer solstice (June), when the rains cease in the regions south of and upon the equator, the White Nile begins to flood. From March to the autumnal equinox (September) it continues to overflow its banks till it attains its magnitude, and from that time it shrinks through the winter solstice (December) till March. The Nile is, therefore, full during the dry season and low during the rainy season south of and immediately upon the equator. And as the northern counterslope of Kenia will, to a certain extent, be a lee-land like Ugogo, it can not have the superfluity of moisture necessary to send forth a first-class stream. The inundation is synchronous with the great falls of the northern equatorial regions, which extend from July to September, and is dependent solely upon the tropical rains. It is, therefore, probable that the true sources of the "Holy River" will be found to be a net-work of runnels and rivulets of scanty dimensions, filled by monsoon torrents, and perhaps a little swollen by melted snow on the northern water-parting of the Eastern Lunar Mountains.

Of the tribes dwelling about the Nyanza, the western have been already described. The Washaki and the Warudi are plundering races on the east, concerning whom little is known. Remain the Wahinda, a clan or class alluded to in this and a former chapter, and the Watataru, an extensive and once powerful tribe, mentioned when treating of the regions about Tura.

The Wahinda (in the singular Muhinda) are, according to some Arabs, a foreign and ruling family, who, coming from a distant country, probably in the neighborhood of Somaliland, conquered the lands and became sultans. This opinion seems to rest upon physical peculiarities—the superiority of the Wahinda in figure, stature, and complexion to their subjects suggesting a difference of origin. Others explain the word muhinda to mean a cadet of royal family, and call the class Bayt el Saltanah, or the Kingly House. Thus, while Armanika is the mkámá or sovereign of Karagwah, his brother simply takes the title of muhinda. These conflicting statements may be reconciled by the belief, general in the country, that the families of the sultans are a foreign and a nobler race, the date of whose immigration has long fallen into oblivion. This may be credited without difficulty; the physique of the rulers—approximating more to the northern races of Africa—is markedly less negroid than that of their subjects, and the difference is too great to be explained by the effects of climate or of superior diet, comfort, and luxury.

The Wahinda are found in the regions of Usui, Karagwah, Uh-ha, Uvinza, Uyungu, Ujiji, and Urundi, where they live in boma—stockades—and scattered villages. Of this race are the sultans Suwarora of the Wasui, Armanika of Karagwah, Kanoni of Uhha, Kanze of Uyungu, Mzogera of Uvinza, Rusimba of Ujiji, Mwezi of Urundi, Mnyamurunde of Uyofo, Gaetawa of Uhayya, and Mutawazi of Utumbara. The Wahinda affect a milk diet, which is exceedingly fattening, and anoint themselves plentifully with butter and ghee, to soften and polish the skin. They never sell their fellow-clansmen, are hospitable and civil to strangers, seldom carry arms, fear nothing from the people, and may not be slain even in battle. Where the Wahinda reign, their ministers are the Watosi, a race which has been described when treating of their head-quarters Karagwah.

The Wataturu extend from the Mángewá district, two marches northward of Tura in a north-northwesterly diagonal, to Usmáo, a district of Usukuma, at the southeast angle of the Nyanza Lake. On the north and east they are limited by the Wahumba, on the south by the people of Iramba, and there is said to be a connection between these three tribes. This wild pastoral people were formerly rich in flocks and herds; they still have the best asses in the country. About five years ago, however, they were persuaded by Msimbira, a chief of Usukuma, to aid him against his rival Mpagamo, who had called in the Arabs to his assistance. During the long and bitter contest which ensued, the Arabs, as has been related, were worsted in the field, and the Wataturu suffered severe losses in cattle. Shortly before the arrival of the expedition at Kazeh the foreign merchants had dispatched to Utaturu a plundering party of sixty slave-musketeers, who, however, suddenly attacked by the people, were obliged to fly, leaving behind eighteen of their number. This event was followed by a truce, and the Wataturu resumed their commerce with Tura and Unyanyembe, where, in 1858, a caravan numbering about 300 men came in. Two small parties of this people were also met at Tura; they were small, dark, and ugly savages, almost beardless, and not unlike the "Thakur" people in Maharatta-land. Their asses, provided with neat saddle-bags of zebra-skin, were better dressed than the men, who wore no clothing except the simplest hide-sandals. According to the Arabs, this clan affects nudity; even adult maidens dispense with the usual skin kilt. The men ignored bows and arrows, but they were efficiently armed with long spears, double-edged sime, and heavy hide shields. They brought calabash or monkey-bread flour—in this country, as in Ugogo, a favorite article of consumption—and a little coarse salt, collected from the dried mud of a mbuga or swamp in the land of Iramba, to be bartered for holcus and beads. Their language sounded to the unpracticed ear peculiarly barbarous, and their savage suspiciousness rendered it impossible to collect any specimens.

At Kazeh, sorely to my disappointment, it was finally settled, in a full conclave of Arabs, that we must return to the coast by the tedious path with which we were already painfully familiar. At Ujiji the state of our finances had been the sole, though the sufficient obstacle to our traversing Africa from east to west; we might—had we possessed the means—by navigating the Tanganyika southward, have debouched, after a journey of three months, at Kilwa. The same cause prevented us from visiting the northern kingdoms of Karagwah and Uganda; to effect this exploration, however, we should have required not only funds but time. The rains there setting in about September render traveling impossible; our two years' leave of absence was drawing to a close, and even had we commanded a sufficient outfit, we were not disposed to risk the consequences of taking an extra twelve months. No course, therefore, remained but to regain the coast. We did not, however, give up hopes of making our return useful to geography, by tracing the course of the Rwaha or Rufijí River, and of visiting the coast between the Usagara Mountains and Kilwa, an unknown line not likely to attract future travelers.

SAYDUMI, A NATIVE OF UGANDA.

Mgongo Thembo, or the Elephant's Back.

CHAPTER XVII.

THE DOWN-MARCH TO THE COAST.

On the 5th of November, 1858, Musa Mzuri—Handsome Moses, as he was called by the Africans—returned with great pomp to Kazeh after his long residence at Karagwah. Some details concerning this merchant, who has played a conspicuous part in the eventful "*peripéties*" of African discovery, may be deemed well placed.

About thirty-five years ago, Musa, a Moslem of the Kojah sect, and then a youth, was driven by poverty from his native Surat to follow his eldest brother "Sayyan," who having sought fortune at Zanzibar, and having been provided with an outfit by the Sayyid el Laghbari, then governor of the island, made sundry journeys into the interior. About 1825 the brothers first visited the Land of the Moon, preceding the Arab travelers, who in those days made their markets at Usanga and Usenga, distant about a dozen marches to the S.S.E. of Kazeh. Musa describes Unyamwezi as richly cultivated, and he has not forgotten the hospitable reception of the people. The brothers bought up a little venture of forty farasilah or twenty men's loads of cloth and beads, and returned with a joint stock of 800 farasilah ($800 \times 35 = 28,000$ lbs. avoirdupois) in ivory; as Sayyan died on the road, all fell to Musa's share. Since that time he has made five journeys to the coast and several to the northern kingdoms. About four years ago Armanika, the present sultan of Karagwah, was besieged in a palisaded village by a rebel brother, Rumanika. On this occasion Musa, in company with the king, endured great hardships, and incurred no little risk; when both parties were weary of fighting, he persuaded by a large bribe of ivory, Suna, the powerful despot of the neighboring kingdom of Uganda, to raise the siege, by throwing a strong force into the field. He has ever since been fraternally received by Armanika, and his last journey to Karagwah was for the purpose of recovering part of the ivory expended in the king's cause. After an absence of fifteen months he brought back about a score of splendid tusks, one weighing, he declared, upward of 200 lbs. During his detention, Salim bin Sayf, of Dut'humi, who had been intrusted by Musa with sixty-five farasilah of ivory to barter for goods on the coast, arrived at Unyanyembe, when, hearing the evil tidings, the wily Harisi appropriated the property, and returned to whence he came. Like most merchants in East Africa, Musa's business is extensive, but his gains are principally represented by outlying debts; he can not, therefore, leave the country without an enormous sacrifice. He is the recognized doyen of the commercial body, and he acts agent and warehouseman; his hall is usually full of buyers and sellers, Arab and African, and large investments of wires, beads, and cotton cloths, some of them valuable, are regularly forwarded to him with comforts and luxuries from the coast.

Musa Mzuri is now a man of the uncertain "certain age" between forty-five and fifty, thin-bearded, tall, gaunt, with delicate extremities, and with the regular and handsome features of a high-caste Indian Moslem. Like most of his compatriots, he is a man of sad and staid demeanor, and he is apparently faded by opium, which so tyrannizes over him that he carries pills in every pocket, and stores them, lest the hoard should run short, in each corner and cranny of his house. His clean new dress, perfumed with 'jasmine-oil and sandal-wood, his snowy skull-cap and well-fitting sandals, distinguish him in appearance from the Arabs; and his abode, which is almost a village, with its lofty gates and its spacious courts, full of slaves and hangers-on, contrasts with the humility of the Semite tenements.

On arrival at Kazeh I forwarded to Musa the introductory letter with which H. H. the Sayyid Majid had honored me. Sundry civilities passed between his housekeeper, Mama Khamisi, and ourselves; she supplied the Baloch with lodgings and ourselves with milk, for which we were careful to reward her. After returning from Ujiji we found Abdullah, the eldest of Musa's two sons by different slave girls, resting at Kazeh after his down-march from Karagwah. He knew a few words of English, but he had learned no Hindoostani from his father, who, curious to say, after an expatriation of thirty-five years, still spoke his mother-tongue purely and well. The youth would have become a greater favorite had he not been so hard a drinker and so quarrelsome in his cups; on more than one occasion he had dangerously cut or stabbed his servile boon companions. Musa had spared the rod, or had used it upon him to very little purpose; after intruding himself repeatedly into the hall and begging for handsome clothes, with more instance of freedom than consisted with decorum, he was warned that if he staid away it might be the better for his back, and he took the warning.

Musa, when rested after his weary return-march, called upon me with all due ceremony, escorted by the principal Arab merchants. I was not disappointed in finding him wholly ignorant concerning Africa and things African; Snay bin Amir had told me that such was the case. He had, however, a number of slaves fresh from Karagwah and Uganda, who confirmed the accounts previously received from Arab travelers in those regions. Musa displayed even more hospitality than his fellow-travelers. Besides the mbogoro or skinful of grain and the goat usually offered to fresh arrivals, he was ever sending those little presents of provisions which in the East can not be refused without offense. I narrowly prevented his killing a bullock to provide us with beef, and at last I feared to mention a want before him. During his frequent visits he invariably showed himself a man of quiet and unaffected manners, dashed with a little Indian reserve, which in process of time would probably have worn off.

On the 6th of September, Said bin Salim, nervously impatient to commence the march homeward, "made a khambi," that is to say, pitched our tents under a spreading tree outside and within sight of Kazeh. Although he had been collecting porters for several days, only two came to the fore; a few refreshing showers were falling at the autumnal equinox, and the black peasantry so miscalculated the seasons that they expected the immediate advent of the great Masika. Moreover, when informed that our route would debouch at Kilwa, they declared that they must receive double pay, as they could not expect there to be hired by return-caravans. That the "khambi" might assume an appearance of reality, the Baloch were dispatched into "country quarters." As they followed their usual tactic, affecting eagerness to depart, but privily clinging to the pleasures of Kazeh, orders were issued definitively to "cut" their rations in case of necessity. The sons of Ramji, who had returned from Msene, without, however, intrusion or swagger, were permitted to enter the camp. Before the march I summoned them, and in severe terms recapitulated their misdeeds, warned them that they would not be re-engaged, and allowed them provisions and protection only on condition of their carrying, as the slaves of Arab merchants are expected to do, our lighter valuables, such as the digester, medicine-chest, gun-cases, camp-table, and chair. They promised with an edifying humility to reform. I was compelled, however, to enliven their murmuring by a few slight floggings before they would become amenable to a moral rule, and would acquire those habits of regularity which are as chains and fetters to the African man. The five Wak'hutu porters, who, after robbing and deserting us on the road to Ujiji, had taken service with my old acquaintance, Salim bin Rashid—the well-informed coast Arab merchant, originally named by H. H. the Sayyid Majid as my guide and caravan leader—begged hard to be again employed. I positively refused to see them. If at this distance from home they had perjured themselves and had plundered us, what might be expected when they arrived near their native country?

As the time of departure approached, I regretted that the arrival of several travelers had not taken place a month earlier. Salim bin Rashid, while collecting ivory in Usukuma and to the eastward of the Nyanza Lake, had recovered a Msawahili porter, who, falling sick on the road, had been left by a caravan from Tanga among the wildest of the East African tribes, the Wamasai or Wahumba. From this man, who spent two years among those plunderers and their rivals in villainy the Warudi, I derived some valuable information concerning the great northern route which spans the countries lying between the coast and the Nyanza Lake. I was also called upon by Amayr bin Said el Shaksi, a strong-framed and stout-hearted gray-beard, who, when his vessel foundered in the waters of the Tanganyika, saved his life by swimming, and, as he had no goods, and but few of his slaves had survived, lived for five months on roots and grasses, till restored to Ujiji by an Arab canoe. A garrulous senior, fond of "venting his travels," he spent many hours with me, talking over his past adventures, and his ocular knowledge of the Tanganyika enabled me to gather many, perhaps, reliable details concerning its southern extremity. A few days before departure Hilal bin Nasur, a well-born Harisi, returned from K'hokoro; he supplied me with a list of stations and a lengthy description of his various excursions to the southern provinces.*

Said bin Salim, in despair that the labors of a whole fortnight spent in the jungle had produced the slenderest of results, moved from under the tree in Kazeh plain to Masui, a dirty little village distant about three miles to the east of our head-quarters. As he reported on the 25th of September that his gang was nearly completed, I sent forward all but the personal baggage. The Arab had, however, secured but three hammals or bearers for my hammock; one a tottering old man, the other a knock-kneed boy, and the third a notorious skulk. Although supplied with meat to strengthen them, as they expressed it, they broke down after a single march. From that time, finding it useless to engage bear-

* For this and other purely geographical details concerning the southern provinces, the reader is referred to the Journal of the Royal Geographical Society, vol. xxix., 1860.

ers for a long journey in these lands, I hired men from district to district, and dismissed them when tired. The only objection to this proceeding was its inordinate expense—three cloths being generally demanded by the porter for thirty miles. A little calculation will give an idea of the relative cost of traveling in Africa and in Europe. Assuming each man to receive one cloth, worth one dollar, for every ten miles, and that six porters are required to carry the hammock, we have in Africa an expenditure on carriage alone of nearly half a crown per mile: in most parts of Europe travel on the iron road has been reduced to one penny.

Our return from Unyanyembe to the coast was to take place during the dead season, when provisions are most expensive and are not unfrequently unprocurable. But being "Wazungu," and well provided with "African money," we might expect the people to sell to us their grain and stores, which they would have refused at tariff prices to Arabs or Wasawahili. We carried as stock fourteen porters' loads of cloth, viz., 645 domestics, 653 blue cottons, and 20 colored cloths, principally debwani, barsati, and subai, as presents to chiefs. The supply of beads was represented by one load of ububu or black porcelains—afterward thrown away as useless—half a frasilah (17.5 pounds) of "locust-legs," or pink porcelains, purchased from Sallum bin Hamid, and eight kartasat or papered bundles of the heavy and expensive "town-breakers," vermilion or coral porcelains, amounting to seventy fundo, each of which covered as a rule the day's minor expenses. The other stores were the fifty-four jembe purchased at Msene, besides a few brought from Usukuma by my companion. These articles are useful in making up kuhonga or black-mail; in Ugogo and Usagara, which is their western limit, they double in value, and go even farther than a white cotton cloth. Finally, we had sixteen cows, heifers, and calves, bought in Usukuma by my companion, at the rate of six domestics per head. We expected them to be serviceable as presents, and meanwhile to add materially to our comfort by a more regular supply of milk than the villages afford. But, alas! having neglected to mark the animals, all were changed —a fact made evident by their running dry after a few days: the four calves presently died of fatigue; whenever an animal lay down upon the road its throat was summarily cut, others were left to stray and be stolen, and the last bullock preserved for a sirloin on Christmas-day was prematurely lost. A small percentage proved useful as tribute to the chiefs of Ugogo, and served as rations when grain was unprocurable. The African, however, looks upon meat, not as "posho"—daily bread—but as kitoweyo —kitchen: two or three pounds of beef merely whet his teeth for the usual ugali or porridge of boiled flour. It is almost needless to state that, despite the best surveillance and the strictest economy, we arrived at the coast almost destitute; cloth and beads, hoes and cattle, all had disappeared, and had we possessed treble the quantity, it would have gone the same way.

The 26th of September, 1858, saw us on foot betimes. The hospitable Snay bin Amir, freshly recovered from an influenza which had confined him for some days to his sleeping-mat, came personally to superintend our departure. As no porters had returned for property left behind, and as all the "cooking-pots" had preceded us on the yester, Snay supplied us with his own slaves, and provided us with an Arab breakfast, well cooked, and, as usual, neatly served on porcelain plates, with plaited and colored straw dish-covers, pointed like Chinese caps. Then, promising to spend the next day with me, he shook hands and followed me out of the compound. After a march of three miles under a white-hot sun and through a chilling wind, to which were probably owing our subsequent sufferings, we entered the dirty little village of Masui, where a hovel had been prepared for us by Said bin Salim. There we were greeted by the caravan, and we heard with pleasure that it was ready, after a fashion, to break ground.

Early on the next morning appeared Snay bin Amir and Musa Mzuri: as I was suffering from a slight attack of fever, my companion took my place as host. The paroxysm passing off, allowed me to settle all accounts with Snay bin Amir, and to put a finishing touch to the names of stations in the journal. I then thanked these kind-hearted men for their many good deeds, and promised to report to H. H. the Sayyid Majid the hospitable reception of his Arab subjects generally, and of Snay and Musa in particular. About evening-time I shook hands with Snay bin Amir—having so primed the dear old fellow with a stirrup-cup of burnt punch, that his gait and effusion of manner were by no means such as became a staid and stately Arab shaykh.

On the 4th of October, after a week of halts and snail's marches —the insufficiency of porterage compelled me to send back men for the articles left behind at the several villages—we at last reached Hanga, our former quarters on the eastern confines of the Unyanyembe district. As long as we were within easy distance of Kazeh it was impossible to keep the sons of Ramji in camp, and their absence interfered materially with the completion of the gang. Several desertions took place; a slave given by Kannena of Ujiji to Said bin Salim, old Musangesi the Asinego, and two new purchases, male and female, made by the Baloch at Kazeh, disappeared after the first few marches. The porters were troublesome. They had divided themselves as usual into khambi, or crews, but no regular kirangozi having been engaged, they preferred, through mutual jealousy, following Shehe, one of the sons of Ramji. On the road, also, some heads had been broken, because the cattle-drivers had attempted to precede the line, and I feared that the fall of a chance shower might make the whole squad desert, under the impression that the sowing season had set in. In their idleness and want of excitement, they had determined to secure at Hanga the bullock claimed by down caravans at Rubuga. After four days' halt, without other labor but that of cooking, they arose under pretext of a blow given by one of the children of Said bin Salim, and packing up their goods and chattels, poured in mass, with shouts and yells, from the village, declaring that they were going home. In sore tribulation, Said bin Salim and the jemadar begged me to take an active part, but a short experience of similar scenes among the bashi-buzuks at the Dardanelles had made me wiser than my advisers: the African, like the Asiatic, is naturally averse to the operation proverbially called " cutting off one's own nose;" but if begged not to do so, he may wax, like pinioned men, valorous exceedingly, and dare the suicidal deed. I did not move from my hut, and in half an hour every thing was *in statu quo ante*. The porters had thrown the blame of the proceeding upon the blow, consequently a flogging was ordered for Said bin Salim's " child," who, as was ever the case, had been flagrantly in the wrong; but after return, evading the point, the plaintiffs exposed the true state of affairs by a direct reference to the bullock. Thus the " child" escaped castigation, and the bullock was not given till we reached Rubuga.

At Hanga my companion was taken seriously ill. He had been chilled on the line of march by the cruel easterly wind, and at the end of the second march from Kazeh he appeared trembling as if with ague. Immediately after arrival at the foul village of Hanga—where we lodged in a kind of cow-house, full of vermin, and exposed directly to the fury of the cold gales—he complained, in addition to a deaf ear, an inflamed eye, and a swollen face, of a mysterious pain which often shifted its seat, and which he knew not whether to attribute to liver or to spleen. It began with a burning sensation, as by a branding-iron, above the right breast, and then extended to the heart with sharp twinges. After ranging around the spleen, it attacked the upper part of the right lung, and finally it settled in the region of the liver. On the 10th of October, suddenly waking about dawn from a horrible dream, in which a close pack of tigers, leopards, and other beasts, harnessed with a net-work of iron hooks, were dragging him like the rush of a whirlwind over the ground, he found himself sitting up on the side of his bedding, forcibly clasping both sides with his hands. Half stupefied by pain, he called Bombay, who, having formerly suffered from the " kichyomachyoma"—the " little irons"—raised his master's right arm, placed him in a sitting position, as lying down was impossible, and directed him to hold the left ear behind the head, thus relieving the excruciating and torturing twinges by lifting the lung from the liver. The next spasm was less severe, but the sufferer's mind had begun to wander, and he again clasped his sides, a proceeding with which Bombay interfered.

Early on the next morning, my companion, supported by Bombay and Gaetano, staggered toward the tent. Nearing the doorway, he sent in his Goanese to place a chair for sitting, as usual, during the toils of the day, outside. The support of an arm being thus removed, ensued a second and violent spasm of cramps and twinges, all the muscles being painfully contracted. After resting for a few moments, he called his men to assist him into the house. But neglecting to have a chair previously placed for him, he underwent a, third fit of the same epileptic description, which more closely resembled those of hydrophobia than aught I had ever witnessed. He was once more haunted by a crowd of hideous devils, giants, and lion-headed demons, who were wrenching, with superhuman force, and stripping the sinews and tendons of his legs down to the ankles. At length, sitting, or rather lying upon the chair, with limbs racked by cramps, features drawn and ghastly, frame fixed and rigid, eyes glazed and glassy, he began to utter a barking noise, and a peculiar chopping motion of the mouth and tongue, with lips protruding—the effect of difficulty of breathing—which so altered his appearance that he was hardly recognizable, and completed the terror of the beholders. When this, the third and the severest spasm, had passed away, he called for pen and paper, and fearing that increased weakness of mind and body might presently prevent any exertion, he wrote an incoherent letter of farewell to his family. That, however, was the crisis. He was afterward able to take the proper precautions, never moving without assistance, and always ordering a resting-place to be prepared for him. He spent a better night, with the inconvenience, however, of sitting up, pillow-propped, and some weeks elapsed before he could lie upon his sides. Presently the pains were mitigated, though they did not entirely cease: this he expressed by saying that "the knives were sheathed." Such, gentle reader, in East Africa, is the kichyoma-chyoma: either one of those eccentric after-effects of fever, which perplex the European at Zanzibar, or some mysterious manifestation of the Protean demon miasma.

I at once sent an express to Snay bin Amir for the necessary drugs. The Arabs treat this complaint by applying to the side powdered myrrh mixed with yolk of egg, and converted into a poultice with flour of mung (Phaseolus mungo). The material was duly forwarded, but it proved of little use. Said bin Salim meanwhile, after sundry vague hints concerning the influence of the Father of Hair, the magnificent comet then spanning the western skies, insisted, as his people invariably do on such conjunctures, upon my companion being visited by the mganga, or medicine-man of the caravan. That reverend personage, after claiming and receiving the usual fee, a fat goat, anointed with its grease two little bits of wood strung on to a tape of tree-fibre, and contented himself with fastening this mpigi—the negroid's elixir vitæ—round my companion's waist. The ligature, however, was torn off after a few minutes, as its only effect was to press upon and pain the tenderest part.

During the forced halt which followed my companion's severe attack, I saw that, in default of physic, change of air was the most fitting restorative. My benumbed legs and feet still compelling me to use a hammock, a second was rigged up for the invalid; and by good fortune thirteen unloaded porters of a down-caravan consented to carry us both for a large sum to Rubuga. The sons of Ramji were imperatively ordered to leave Kazeh under pain of dismissal, which none would incur, as they had a valuable investment in slaves: with their aid the complement of porters was easily and speedily filled up.

Seedy Mubarak Bombay—in the interior the name became Mamba (a crocodile) or Pombe (small beer)—had long before returned to his former attitude, that of a respectful and most ready servant. He had, it is true, sundry uncomfortable peculiarities. A heaven-born "pagazi," he would load himself on the march with his "t'haka-t'haka," or "chow-chow," although a porter had been especially hired for him. He had no memory: an article once taken by him was always thrown upon the ground and forgotten: in a single trip he broke my elephant-gun, killed my riding-ass, and lost its bridle. Like the Eastern Africans generally, he lacked the principle of immediate action; if beckoned to for a gun in the field he would probably first delay to look round, then retire, and lastly advance. He had a curious inverted way of doing all that he did. The water-bottle was ever carried on the march either uncorked or inverted; his waistcoat was generally wound round his neck, and it appeared fated not to be properly buttoned; while he walked bareheaded in the sun, his fez adorned the tufty poll of some comrade; and at the halt he toiled like a char-woman to raise our tents and to prepare them for habitation, while his slave, the large lazy Maktubu, a boy-giant from the mountains of Urundi, sat or dozed under the cool shade. Yet with all his faults and failures, Bombay, for his unwearied activity, and especially from his undeviating honesty—there was no man, save our "negro rectitude," in the whole camp who had not proved his claim to the title triliteral—was truly valuable. Said bin Salim had long forfeited my confidence by his carelessness and extravagance; and the disappearance of the outfit committed to him at Ujiji, in favor, as I afterward learned, of an Arab merchant-friend, rendered him unfit for the responsibilities of stewardship.

Having summoned Said bin Salim, I told him with all gentleness, in order to spare his "shame"—the Persian proverb says, fell not the tree which thou hast planted—that being now wiser in Eastern African travel than before, I intended to relieve him of his troublesome duties. He heard this announcement with the wryest of faces; and his perturbation was not diminished when informed that the future distribution of cloth should be wholly in the hands of Bombay, checked by my companion's superintendence. The loads were accordingly numbered and registered; the pagazi were forbidden, under pain of punishment, to open or to change them without permission; and Said bin Salim received, like the Baloch, a certain monthly amount of beads, besides rations of rice for the consumption of his children. This arrangement was persevered in till we separated upon the sea-board: it acted well, saving outfit, time, and a host of annoyances; moreover, it gave us command, as the African man, like the lower animals, respects only, if he respects any thing, the hand that gives— that feeds him. It was wonderful to see how, the "bone of contention," cloth, having been removed, the fierceness of those who were formerly foes melted and merged into friendship and fraternization. The triad of bitter haters, Said bin Salim, the monocular jemadar, and Muinyi Kidogo, now marched and sat and ate together as if never weary of such society; they praised one another openly and without reserve, and if an evil tale ever reached my ear its subject was the innocent Bombay—its object was to ruin him in my estimation.

Acutely remembering the trouble caused by the feuds between Said bin Salim and Kidogo upon the subject of work, I directed the former to take sole charge of the porters, to issue their rations, and to superintend their loads. The better to assist him, two disorderly sons of Ramji were summarily flogged, and several others who refused to carry our smaller valuables were reduced to order by the usual process of stopping rations. "Shehe," though chosen as kirangozi or guide from motives of jealousy by the porters, was turned out of office; he persisted in demanding cloth for feeing an Unyamwezi medicine-man, in order to provide him, a Moslem! with charms against the evil eye, a superstition unknown to this part of Eastern Africa. The pagazi, ordered to elect one of their number, named the youth Twánígáná, who had brought with him a large gang. But the plague of the party, a hideous, puckered, and scowling old man who had called himself "Muzungu Mbaya," or the "Wicked White," so far prevailed that at the first halt Twanigana, with his blushing honors in the shape of a scarlet waistcoat fresh upon him, was found squatting solus under a tree, the rest of the party having mutinously preceded him. I halted at once and recalled the porters, who, after a due interval of murmuring, reappeared. And subsequently, by invariably siding with the newly-made kirangozi, and by showing myself ready to enforce obedience by any means and every means, I gave the long-legged and weak-minded youth, who was called "Gopa-Gopa"— "Funkstick"—on account of his excessive timidity, a little confidence, and reduced his unruly followers to all the discipline of which their race is capable.

As we were threatened with want of water on the way, I prepared for that difficulty by packing a box with empty bottles, which, when occasion required, might be filled at the best springs. The zemzemiyah or traveling canteen of the East African is every where a long-necked gourd, slung to the shoulder by a string. But it becomes offensive after a short use, and it can never be intrusted to a servant, slave, or porter without its contents being exhausted before a mile is measured.

By these arrangements, the result of that after-wisdom which some have termed fools' wit, I commenced the down-march under advantages, happy as a "*bourgeois*" of trappers in the joyous *pays sauvage*. I have detailed, perhaps to a wearisome length, the preparations for the march. But the success of such expeditions mainly depends upon the measures adopted before and immediately after departure, and this dry knowledge may be useful to future adventurers in the great cause of discovery.

The stages now appeared shorter, the sun cooler, the breeze warmer; after fourteen months of incessant fevers, the party had become tolerably acclimatized; all were now loud in praise, as they had been violent in censure, of the "water and air." Before entering the Fiery Field, the hire for carrying the hammocks became so exorbitant that I dismissed the bearers, drew on my jack-boots, mounted the half-caste Zanzibari ass, and appeared once more as the mtongi of a caravan. After a fortnight my companion had convalesced so rapidly that he announced himself ready to ride. The severe liver pains had disappeared, leaving behind them, however, for a time, a harassing heart-ache and nausea, with other bilious symptoms, which developed themselves when exposed to the burning sun of the several tirikeza. Gradually these sequelæ ceased, sleep and appetite returned, and at K'hok'ho, in Ugogo, my companion had strength enough to carry a heavy rifle, and to do damage among the antelope and the Guinea-fowl. Our Goanese servants also, after suffering severely from fever and face-ache, became different men; Valentine, blessed with a more strenuous diathesis, carried before him a crop like a well-crammed capon. As the porters left this country, and the escort approached their homes, there was a notable change of demeanor. All waxed civil, even to servility, grumbling ceased, and smiles mantled every countenance. Even Muzungu Mbaya, who, in Unyamwezi, had been the head and front of all offense, was to be seen in Ugogo meekly sweeping out our tents with a bunch of thorns.

We left Hanga, the dirty cow-village, on the 13th of October. The seven short marches between that place and Taura occupied fifteen days, a serious waste of time and cloth, caused by the craving of the porters for their homes. It was also necessary to march with prudence, collisions between the party and the country-people, who are unaccustomed to see the articles which they most covet carried out of the country, were frequent: in fact we flew

to arms about every second day, and, after infinite noise and chatter, we quitted them to boast of the deeds of "derring do," which
had been consigned to the limbo of things uncreate by the fainé-
ance of the adversary.   At Eastern Tura, where we arrived on
the 28th of October, a halt of six days was occasioned by the necessity of providing and preparing food, at that season scarce and
dear, for the week's march through the Fiery Field.   The caravan
was then mustered, when its roll appeared as follows.   We numbered in our own party two Europeans, two Goanese, Bombay
with two slaves—the child-man Nasibu and the boy-giant Maktubu — the bull-headed Mabruki, Nasir, a half-caste Mazrui Arab,
who had been sent with me by the Arabs of Kazeh to save his
morals, and Taufiki, a Msawahili youth, who had taken service as
gun-carrier to the coast: they formed a total of 10 souls.   Said
bin Salim was accompanied by 12—the charmers Halimah and
Zawada, his five children, and a little gang of five fresh captures,
male and female.   The Baloch, 12 in number, had 15 slaves and
11 porters, composing a total of 38.   The sons of Ramji, and the
ass-drivers under Kidogo their leader, were in all 24, including
their new acquisitions.   Finally, 68 Wanyamwezi porters, carrying the outfit and driving the cattle, completed the party to 152
souls.

On the 3d of November, the caravan issuing from Tura plunged
manfully into the Fiery Field, and after seven marches in as many
days, halted for breath and forage at Jiwe la Mkoa, the Round
Stone.   A few rations having been procured in its vicinity, we

Jiwe la Mkoa, the Round Rock.

resumed our way on the 12th of November, and in two days exchanged, with a sensible pleasure, the dull expanse of dry brown

bush and brushwood, dead thorn-trees, and dry nullahs, for the fertile red plain of Mdaburu. After that point began the transit of Ugogo, where I had been taught to expect accidents; they resolved themselves, however, into nothing more than the disappearance of cloth and beads in inordinate quantities. We were received by Magomba, the Sultan of Kanyenye, with a charge of magic, for which, of course, it was necessary to pay heavily. The Wanyamwezi porters seemed even more timid on the down-journey than on the up-march. They slank about like curs, and the fierce look of a Mgogo boy was enough to strike a general terror. Twanigana, when safe in the mountains of Usagara, would frequently indulge me in a dialogue like the following, and it may serve as a specimen of the present state of conversation in East Africa:

" The state, Mdula?" (*i. e.*, Abdullah, a word unpronounceable to negroid organs).

" The state is very! (well) and thy state?"

" The state is very! (well) and the state of Spikka?" (my companion).

" The state of Spikka is very! (well)."

" We have escaped the Wagogo (resumes Twanigana), white man O!"

" We have escaped, O my brother!"

" The Wagogo are bad."

" They are bad."

" The Wagogo are very bad."

" They are very bad."

" The Wagogo are not good."

" They are not good."

" The Wagogo are not at all good."

" They are not at all good."

" I greatly feared the Wagogo, who kill the Wanyamwezi."

" Exactly so!"

" But now I don't fear them. I call them ——s and ——s, and I would fight the whole tribe, white man O!"

" Truly so, O my brother!"

And thus for two mortal hours, till my ennui turned into marvel. Twanigana however was, perhaps, in point of intellect somewhat below the usual standard of African young men. Older and more experienced was Muzungu Mbaya, and I often listened with no small amusement to the attempts made by the Baloch to impress upon this truly African mind a respect for their revelation. Gul Mohammed was the missionary of the party: like Moslems generally, however, his thoughts had been taught to run in one groove, and if disturbed by startling objections, they were all abroad. Similarly I have observed in the European old lady, that on such subjects all the world must think with her, and I have been suspected of drawing the long bow when describing the worship of gods with four arms, and goddesses with two heads.

Muzungu Mbaya, as the old hunks calls himself, might be sitting deeply meditative, at the end of the march, before the fire, warming his inner legs, smoking his face, and ever and anon casting pleasant glances at a small black earthen pipkin, whence arose the savory steam of meat and vegetables. A concatenation of ideas induces Gul Mohammed to break into his favorite theme.

" And thou, Muzungu Mbaya, thou also must die!"

" Ugh! ugh!" replies the Muzungu personally offended, " don't speak in that way! Thou must die too."

" It is a sore thing to die," resumes Gul Mohammed.

" Hoo! hoo!" exclaims the other, " it is bad, very bad, never to wear a nice cloth, no longer to dwell with one's wife and children, not to eat and drink, snuff, and smoke tobacco. Hoo! hoo! it is bad, very bad!"

"But we shall eat," rejoins the Moslem, "the flesh of birds, mountains of meat, and delicate roasts, and drink sugared water, and whatever we hunger for."

The African's mind is disturbed by this tissue of contradictions. He considers birds somewhat low feeding, roasts he adores, he contrasts mountains of meat with his poor half pound in pot, he would sell himself for sugar; but again he hears nothing of tobacco; still he takes the trouble to ask,

" Where, O my brother?"

" There," exclaims Gul Mohammed, pointing to the skies.

This is a "choke-pear" to Muzungu Mbaya. The distance is great, and he can scarcely believe that his interlocutor has visited the firmament to see the provision; he therefore ventures upon the query,

" And hast thou been there, O my brother?"

"Astaghfar ullah (I beg pardon of Allah)!" ejaculates Gul Mohammed, half angry, half amused. "What a mshenzi (pagan) this is! No, my brother, I have not exactly been there; but my Mulungu (Allah) told my apostle,* who told his descendants, who told my father and mother, who told me, that when we die we shall go to a shamba (a plantation), where—"

"Oof!" grunts Muzungu Mbaya, "it is good of you to tell us all this upumbafu (nonsense) which your mother told you. So there are plantations in the skies?"

"Assuredly," replies Gul Mohammed, who expounds at length the Moslem idea of paradise to the African's running commentary of "Nenda we!" (be off!) "Mama-e!" (O my mother!) and "Tumbanina," which may not be translated.

---

* Those who translate rasul, meaning, literally, "one sent," by prophet instead of apostle, introduce a notable fallacy into the very formula of Moslem faith. Mohammed never pretended to prophesy in our sense of foretelling future events.

Muzungu Mbaya, who for the last minute has been immersed in thought, now suddenly raises his head, and, with somewhat of a goguenard air, inquires—

"Well, then, my brother, thou knowest all things! answer me, is thy Mulungu black like myself, white like this muzungu, or whity-brown as thou art?"

Gul Mohammed is fairly floored: he ejaculates sundry la haul! to collect his wits for the reply,

"Verily, the Mulungu hath no color."

"To-o-oh! Tuh!" exclaims the Muzungu, contorting his wrinkled countenance, and spitting with disgust upon the ground. He was now justified in believing that he had been made a laughing-stock. The mountain of meat had, to a certain extent, won over his better judgment: the fair vision now fled, and left him to the hard realities of the half pound. He turns a deaf ear to every other word; and, devoting all his assiduity to the article before him, he unconsciously obeys the advice which many an Eastern philosopher has inculcated to his disciples—

> "Hold fast the hour, though fools say nay,
>   The spheres revolve, they bring thee sorrow;
> The wise enjoys his joy to-day,
>   The fool shall joy his joy to-morrow."

The transit of Ugogo occupied three weeks, from the 14th of November to the 5th of December. In Kanyenye we were joined by a large down-caravan of Wanyamwezi, carrying ivories; the musket-shots which announced the conclusion of certain brotherly ties between the sons of Ramji and the porters, sounded in my ears like minute-guns announcing the decease of our hopes of a return to the coast viâ Kilwa. At Kanyenye, also, we met the stout Msawahili Abdullah bin Nasib, alias Kisesa, who was once more marching into Unyamwezi: he informed me that the slaughter of Salim bin Nasir, the Bu-Saidi, and the destruction of the Rubeho settlements, after the murder of a porter, had closed our former line through Usagara. He also supplied me with valuable tea and sugar, and my companion with a quantity of valueless, or perhaps misunderstood, information, which I did not deem worth sifting. On the 6th of December, arrived at our old ground in the Ugogi Dhun, we were greeted by a freshly-arrived caravan, commanded by Jumah bin Mbwana and his two brothers, half-caste Hindi or Indian Moslems, from Mombasah.

The Hindis, after receiving and returning news with much solemnity, presently drew forth a packet of letters and papers, which as usual promised trouble. This time, however, the post was to produce the second manner of annoyance—official "wigging"— the first being intelligence of private misfortune. Imprimis, came a note from Captain Rigby, the newly-appointed successor to Lieut. Col. Hamerton at Zanzibar, and that name was not nice in the nostrils of men. Secondly, the following pleasant announcement. I give the whole letter:

"DEAR BURTON,—Go ahead! Vogel and Macguire dead—murdered. Write often to yours truly,   N. S."

And thirdly came the inevitable official wig.

Convinced, by sundry conversations with Arabs and others at Suez and Aden, during my last overland journey to India, and by the details supplied to me by a naval officer who was thoroughly conversant with the Red Sea, that, in consequence of the weakness and insufficiency of the squadron then employed, slavery still flourished, and that the numerous British subjects and protegés were inadequately protected, I had dared, after arrival at Zanzibar, privately to address on the 15th of December, 1856, a letter upon the subject to the Secretary of the Royal Geographical Society. It contained an "Account of Political Affairs in the Red Sea"—to quote the words of the paper, and expressed a hope that it might be "deemed worthy to be transmitted to the Court of Directors, or to the Foreign Office."* The only acknowledgment which I received was the edifying information that the secretary to government, Bombay, was directed by the right honorable the governor in council, Bombay, to state that my "want of discretion and due regard for the authorities to whom I am subordinate, has been regarded with displeasure by the government."

This was hard. I have perhaps been Quixotic enough to attempt a suggestion that, though the Mediterranean is fast becoming a French lake, by timely measures the Red Sea may be prevented from being converted into a Franco-Russo-Austrian lake. But an Englishman in these days must be proud, very proud of his nation, and withal somewhat regretful that he was not born of some mighty mother of men—such as Russia and America—who has not become old and careless enough to leave her bairns unprotected, or cold and crusty enough to reward a little word of wisdom from her babes and sucklings with a scolding or a buffet.

The sore, however, had its salve. The official wig was dated the 23d of July, 1857. Posts are slow in Africa. When received on the 5th of December, 1858, it was accompanied by a copy of a Bombay newspaper, which reported that on the 30th of June, 1858, "a massacre of nearly all the Christians took place at Juddah, on the Red Sea," and that "it was apprehended that the news from Juddah might excite the Arab population of Suez to the commission of similar outrages."

At Ugogi, which, it will be remembered, is considered the halfway station between Unyanyembe and the coast, the sons of Ramji and the porters detained us for a day, declaring that there was a famine upon the Mukondokwa road which we had previously traversed. At the same time they warned us that we should find

* The whole correspondence, with its reply and counter-reply, are printed in Appendix.

the great chief, who has given a name to the Kiringawana route, an accomplished extortioner, and one likely to insist upon our calling upon him in person. Having given their ultimatum, they would not recede from it: for us, therefore, nothing remained but to make a virtue of necessity. We loaded on the 7th of December, and commenced the passage of the Usagara Mountains by the Kiringawana line.

I must indent upon the patience of the reader by a somewhat detailed description of this southern route, which is separated from the northern by a maximum interval of forty-three miles. The former being the more ancient, contains some settlements, like Maroro and Kisanga, not unknown by report to European geographers. It is preferred by down-caravans, who have no store of cloth to be demanded by the rapacious chiefs: the up-country travelers, who have asses, must frequent the Mukondokwa, on account of the severity of the passes on the Kiringawana.

The Kiringawana numbers nineteen short stages, which may be accomplished without hardship in twelve days, at the rate of about five hours per diem. Provisions are procurable in almost every part, except when the Warori are "out;" and water is plentiful, if not good. Travel is rendered pleasant by long stretches of forest land without bush or fetid grass. The principal annoyances are the thievish propensities of the natives and the extortionate demands of the chief. A minor plague is that of musquitoes, that haunt the rushy banks of the hill rivulets, some of which are crossed nine or ten times in the same day; moreover, the steep and slippery ascents and descents of black earth and mud, or rough blocks of stone, make the porters unwilling to work.

Breaking ground at 6 A.M. on the 7th of December, we marched to Murundusi, the frontier of Usagara and Uhehe. The path lay over a rolling thorny jungle, with dottings of calabash, at the foot of the Rubeho Mountains, and lumpy outliers falling on the right of the road. After three hours' march, the sound of the horses announced the vicinity of a village, and the country opening out displayed a scene of wonderful fertility, the effect of subterraneous percolations from the highlands. Nowhere are the tamarind, the sycamore, and the calabash seen in such perfection; of unusual size also are the perfumed myombo and the mkora, the myongo, the ndabi, the chamvya, with its edible yellowish-red berries, and a large sweet-smelling acacia. Amid these piles of verdure, troops of paroquets, doves, jays, and bright fly-catchers find a home, and frequent flocks and herds a resting-place beneath the cool shade. The earth is still sprinkled with "black-jacks," the remains of trees which have come to an untimely end. In the fields near the numerous villages rise little sheds to shelter the guardians of the crops, and cattle wander over the commons or unreclaimed lands. Water, which is here pure and good, lies in pits from fifteen to twenty feet deep, staged over with tree-trunks, and the people draw it in large shallow buckets, made of gourds sewn together and strengthened with sticks. Toward the evening a cold east wind brought up with it a storm of thunder and rain, which was pronounced by the experts to be the opening of the rainy monsoon in Usagara.

The next day led us over an elevated undulation cut by many jagged water-courses, and still flanked by the outlying masses which fall westward into the waste of Mgunda M'khali. After an hour's march we turned abruptly eastward, and crossing a rugged stony fork, presently found a dwarf basin of red soil which supplied water. The Wahehe owners of the land have a chronic horror of the Warori; on sighting our peaceful caravan, they at once raised the war-cry, and were quieted only by the certainty that we were even more frightened than they were. At Kinganyuku the night was again wild and stormy; in fact, after leaving Ugogi we were regularly rained upon till we had crossed the mountains.

On the 9th of December we marched in six hours from Kinganyuku to Rudi, the principal district of Uhehe. It was an ascent plunging into the hills, which, however, on this line are easy to traverse, compared with those of the northern route; the paths were stony and rugged, and the earth was here white and glaring, there of a dull red color. Water pure and plentiful was found in pits about fifteen feet deep, which dented the sole of a picturesque fiumara. The people assembled to stare with the stare pertinacious; they demanded large prices for their small reserves of provisions, but they sold tobacco at the rate of two or three cakes, each weighing about one pound and a half, for a shukkah.

Passing from the settlements of Rudi, on the next morning we entered a thorn jungle, where the handiwork of the fierce Warori appeared in many a shell of smoke-stained village. We then crossed two fiumaras exactly similar to those which attract the eye in the Somali country, broad white sandy beds, with high stiff earth-banks deeply water-cut, and with huge emerald-foliaged trees rising from a hard bare red plain. After a short march of three hours we pitched under a tamarind, and sent our men abroad to collect provisions. Tobacco was cheap as at Rudi, grain and milk, whether fresh or sour, were expensive, and two shukkahs were demanded for a lamb or a young goat. The people of Mporota are notorious pilferers. About noon-tide a loud " hooroosh" and the scampering of spearmen over the country announced a squabble; presently our people reappeared driving before them a flock which they had seized in revenge for a daring attempt at larceny. I directed them to retain one fine specimen —the *lex talionis* is ever the first article of the penal code in the East—and to return the rest. Notwithstanding these energetic measures, the youth Taufiki, awaking in the night with a shriek like one affected by nightmare, found that a Mhehe robber had snatched his cloth, and favored by the shades had escaped with impunity. The illness of Said bin Salim detained us for a day in this den of thieves.

The 12th of December carried us in three hours from Mporota to Ikuka of Uhehe. The route wound over red steps among low stony hills, the legs of the spider-like system, and the lay of the heights was in exceeding confusion. Belted by thorny scrub and forests of wild fruit-trees—some edible, others poisonous— were several villages surrounded by fields especially rich in ground-nuts. Beyond Ikuka the road entered stony and rugged land, with a few sparse cultivations almost choked by thick bushy jungle; the ragged villages contained many dogs, and a few peculiarly hideous human beings. Thence it fell into a fine fiumara, with pure sweet water in pools, breaking the surface of loose white sand; upon the banks, red soil, varying from a few inches to 20 feet in depth, overlay bands and lines of rounded pebbles, based on beds of granite, schiste, and sandstone. After ascending a hill we fell into a second water-course, whose line was almost choked with wild and thorny vegetation, and we raised the tents in time to escape a pitiless pelting, which appeared to spring from a gap in the southern mountains. The time occupied in marching from Ikuka to Inena of Usagara was four hours, and, as usual in these short stages, there was no halt.

Two porters were found missing on the morning of the 14th of December—they had gone for provisions, and had slept in the villages—moreover, heavy clouds hanging on the hill-tops threatened rain: a tirikeza was therefore ordered. At 11 A.M. we set out over rises, falls, and broken ground, at the foot of the neighboring highlands which inclose a narrow basin, the seat of villages and extensive cultivation. Small cascades flashing down the walls that hemmed us in showed the copiousness of the last night's fall. After five hours' heavy marching, we forded a rapid fiumara, whose tall banks of stiff red clay, resting upon tilted-up strata of green-stone, inclosed a stream calf-deep, and from 10 to 12 feet broad. At this place, called Ginyindo, provisions were hardly procurable; consequently the caravan, as was its wont on such occasions, quarreled for disport, and the Baloch, headed by "Gray-beard Musa," began to abuse and to beat the pagazis.

The morning of the 15th of December commenced with a truly African scene. The men were hungry, and the air was chill. They prepared, however, to start quietly betimes. Suddenly a bit of rope was snatched, a sword flashed in the air, a bow-horn quivered with nocked arrow, and the whole caravan rushed frantically with a fearful row to arms. As no one dissuaded the party from "fighting it out," they apparently became friends, and took up their loads. My companion and I rode quietly forward: scarcely, however, had we emerged from the little basin in which the camp had been placed, than a terrible hubbub of shouts and yells announced that the second act had commenced. After a few minutes, Said bin Salim came forward in trembling haste to announce that the jemadar had again struck a pagazi, who, running into the nullah, had thrown stones with force enough to injure his assailant, consequently that the Baloch had drawn their sabres and had commenced a general massacre of porters. Well understanding this misrepresentation, we advanced about a mile, and thence sent back two of the sons of Ramji to declare that we would not be delayed, and that if not at once followed, we would engage other porters at the nearest village. This brought on a denouement: presently the combatants appeared, the Baloch in a high state of grievance, the Africans declaring that they had not come to fight but to carry. I persuaded them both to defer settling the business till the evening, when both parties, well crammed with food, listened complacently to that gross personal abuse, which, in these lands, represents a reprimand.

Resuming our journey, we crossed two high and steep hills, the latter of which suddenly disclosed to the eye the rich and fertile basin of Maroro. Its principal feature is a perennial mountain stream, which, descending the chasm which forms the northern pass, winds sluggishly through the plain of muddy black soil and patches of thick rushy grass, and, diffused through watercourses of raised earth, covers the land with tobacco, holcus, sweet potato, plantains, and maize. The cereals stood five feet high, and were already in ear: according to the people, never less than two, and often three and four crops are reaped during the year. This hill-girt district is placed at one month's march from the coast. At the southern extremity there is a second opening like the northern, and through it the "River of Maroro" sheds into the Rwaha, distant in direct line two marches west with southing.

Maroro, or Malolo, according to dialect, is the "Marorrer town" of Lieut. Hardy (Transactions of the Bombay Geographical Society, from Sept., 1841, to May, 1844), who in 1811–12 was dispatched with Capt. Smee by the government of Bombay to collect information at Kilwa and its dependencies, and the East African coast generally. Mr. Cooley (Inner Africa Laid Open, p. 56) writes the word Marora, and explains it to mean "trade:" the people, however, ignore the derivation. It is not a town, but a district, containing as usual on this line a variety of little settlements. The confined basin is by no means a wholesome locality, the air is warm and "muggy," the swamp vegetation is fetid, the musquitoes venomous, and the population, afflicted with fevers and severe ulceration, is not less wretched and degraded than the Wak'hutu. Their habitations are generally tembe, but small and poor, and their fields are dotted with dwarf platforms for the

THE BASIN OF MAROBO.

guardians of the crops. Here a cow costs twelve cloths, a goat three, while two fowls are procurable for a shukkah. Maroro is the westernmost limit of the touters from the Mrima; there are seldom less than 150 muskets present, and the Wasagara have learned to hold strangers in horror.

In these basins caravans endeavor, and are forced by the people, to encamp upon the farther end after marching through. At the end of a short stage of three hours, we forded three times the river bed, a muddy bottom, flanked by stiff rushes, and encamped under a mkamba-tree, above and to windward of the fetid swamp. The night was hot and rainy, clouds of musquitoes rose from their homes below, and the cynhyenas were so numerous that it was necessary to frighten them away with shots. The labor of laying in provisions detained us for a day at Maroro.

On the 17th of December we left the little basin by its southern opening, which gradually winds eastward. The march was delayed by the distribution of the load of a porter who had fled to the Warori. After crossing a fourth rise, the road fell into the cultivated valley of the Mwega River. This is a rush-girt stream of pure water, about 20 feet broad, and knee-deep at the fords in dry weather; its course is S.W. to the stream of Maroro. Like the Mukondokwa, it spreads out, except where dammed by the correspondence of the salient and the re-entering angles of the hill spurs. The road runs sometimes over this rocky and jungly ground, horrid with thorn and cactus, fording the stream where there is no room for a path, and at other times it traverses lagoon-like back-waters, garnished with grass, rush, and stiff shrubs, based upon sun-cracked or miry beds. After a march of four hours we encamped in the Mwega Basin, where women brought down grain in baskets: cattle were seen upon the higher grounds, but the people refused to sell milk or meat.

The next stage was Kiperepeta; it occupied about 2 hours 30 min. The road was rough, traversing the bushy jungly spurs on the left bank of the rushy narrow stream; in many places there were steps and ladders of detached blocks and boulders. At last passing through a thick growth, where the smell of jasmine loads the air, we ascended a steep and rugged incline, whose summit commanded a fine back view of the Maroro Basin. A shelving counterslope of earth deeply cracked and cut with water-courses led us to the encamping-ground, a red patch dotted with tall calabashes, and boasting a few pools of brackish water. We had now entered the land of grass kilts and bee-hive huts, built for defense upon the ridges of the hills: while cactus, aloe, and milk-bush showed the diminished fertility of the soil. About Kiperepeta it was said a gang of nearly 400 touters awaited with their muskets the arrival of caravans from the interior.

On the 19th of December, leaving Kiperepeta, we toiled up a steep incline, cut by the sinuated channels of water-courses, to a

col or pass, the water-parting of this line in Usagara: before southwesterly, the versant thenceforward trends to the southeast.   Having topped the summit, we began the descent along the left bank
of a mountain burn, the Rufita, which, forming in the rainy season
a series of rapids and cascades, casts its waters into the Yovu, and
eventually into the Rwaha River.   The drainage of the hill-folds
cuts, at every re-entering angle, a ragged irregular ditch, whose
stony depths are impassable to heavily-laden asses.   After a toilsome march of three hours, we fell into the basin of Kisanga,
which, like others on this line, is an enlarged punch-bowl, almost
surrounded by a mass of green hills, cone rising upon cone, with
tufted cappings of trees, and long lines of small haycock-huts
ranged along the acclivities and ridge-lines.   The floor of the
basin is rough and uneven; a rich cultivation extends from the
hill-slopes to the stream which drains the sole, and fine trees,
among which are the mparamusi and the sycamore, relieve the
uniformity of the well-hoed fields.   Having passed through huts
and villages, where two up-caravans of Wanyamwezi were halted,
displaying and haggling over the cloths intended as tribute to the
Sultan Kiringawana, we prudently forded the Yovu, and placed
its bed between ourselves and the enemy.   The Yovu, which bisects the basin of Kisanga from N. to S., and passes by the S.E.
into the Rwaha, was then about four feet deep; it flowed down a

Rufita Pass in Usagara.

muddy bed laced with roots, and its banks, whence a putrid smell
exhaled, were thick lines of sedgy grass, which sheltered myriads
of musquitoes.   Ascending an eminence to the left of the stream,
we obtained lodgings, and at once proceeded to settle kuhonga
with the chief, Kiringawana.

The father, or, according to others, the grandfather of the present chief, a Mnyamwezi of the ancient Wakalaganza tribe, first emigrated from his home in Usagozi, and, being a mighty elephant-hunter and a powerful wizard, he persuaded by arts and arms the Wasagara, who allowed him to settle among them, to constitute him their liege lord. The actual Kiringawana, having spent his heir-apparent days at Zanzibar, returned to Kisanga on the death of his sire, and reigned in his stead. His long residence among the Arabs has so far civilized him that he furnishes his several homes comfortably enough; he receives his tributary visitors with ceremony, affects amenity of manner, clothes his short, stout, and sooty person in rainbow-colored raiment, carries a Persian blade, and is a cunning diplomatist in the art of choosing cloth.

On the day of arrival I was visited by Msimbiri, the heir apparent—kingly dignity prevented Kiringawana wading the Yovu—who gave some information about the Rwaha River, and promised milk. The 20th of December was expended in the palaver about "dash." After abundant chaffering, the chief accepted from the expedition, though passing through his acres on the return-march, when presents are poor, three expensive colored cloths and eight shukkah of domestics and kaniki, wondering the while that the wealthy muzungu had neglected to reserve for him something more worthy of his acceptance. He returned a fat bullock, which was instantly shot and devoured. In their indolence the caravan-men again began to quarrel; and Wulaydi, a son of Ramji, speared a porter, an offense for which he was ordered, if he failed to give satisfaction for the assault, to be turned out of camp. A march was anticipated on the next day, when suddenly, as the moon rose over the walls of the basin, a fine bonfire on the neighboring hill and a terrible outcry announced an accident in the village occupied by the sons of Ramji. Muinyi Buyuni had left in charge of the hearth the object of his affections, a fine strapping slave-girl, whom, for certain reasons, he expected to sell for a premium at Zanzibar, and she had made it over to some friend, who probably had fallen asleep. The hut was soon in flames—in these lands fires are never extinguished—and the conflagration had extended to the nearer hovels, consuming the cloth, grain, and furniture of the inmates. Fortunately, the humans and the cattle escaped, but a delay was inevitable. The elder who owned the chief hut demanded only eighty-eight cloths, one slave, thirteen fundo of beads, and other minor articles: a lesser sum would have purchased the whole household. His cupidity was restrained by Kiringawana, who named as indemnity thirty cloths, here worth thirty dollars, which I gave with extreme unwillingness, promising the sons of Ramji, who appeared rather to enjoy the excitement, that they should pay for their carelessness at Zanzibar.

During the second day's halt I attempted to obtain from Kiringawana a permission to depart from the beaten track. The noble descent of this chief gives him power over the guides of the Wan-yamwezi caravans. In consequence of an agreement with the diwans of the Mrima, he has lately closed the direct route to Kil-wa, formerly regularly traversed, and he commands a little army of touters. He returned a gracious reply, which in East Africa, however, means no gracious intentions.

Resuming our march on the 22d of December, we descended from the eminence into the basin of the Yovu River, and fought our way through a broad "wady," declining from east to west, with thick lines of tree and bush down the centre, and every where else an expanse of dark and unbroken green, like a plate of spinach. Passing along the southern bank among wild anno-nas and fine palmyras, over a good path where there was little mud, we presently ascended rising ground through an open forest of the rainbow hues before described, where sweet air and soft filmy shade formed, while the sun was low and the breath of the morning was pure and good, most enjoyable traveling. After about five hours we descended into the basin of the Ruhembe riv-ulet, which seems to be the "Rohambi people" of Mr. Cooley's Itin-erary (Geography of N'yassi, p. 22). The inhabitants are Wasa-gara; they supply travelers with manioc, grain, and bitter egg-plants, of a scarlet color resembling tomatoes. Cultivation flour-ishes upon the hill-sides and in the swampy grounds about the sole of the basin, which is bisected by a muddy and apparently stagnant stream ten feet broad. We pitched tents in the open central space of a village, and met a caravan of Wasawahili from Zanzibar, who reported to Said bin Salim the gratifying intelli-gence that, in consequence of a rumor of his decease, his worthy brother, Ali bin Salim, had somewhat prematurely laid violent hands upon his goods and chattels.

The porters would have halted on the next day, but the excited Said exerted himself manfully; at 2 P.M. we were once more on the road. Descending from the village eminence, we crossed in a blazing sun the fetid Ruhembe; and, after finding with some dif-ficulty the jungly path, we struck into a pleasant forest like that traversed on the last march. It was cut by water-courses drain-ing south, and at these places it was necessary to dismount. At 6 P.M. appeared a clearing, with sundry villages and clumps of the mgude-tree, whose tufty summits of the brightest green, gilt by the last rays of the sun, formed a lovely picture. The porters would have rested at this spot, but they were forced forward by the sons of Ramji. Presently we emerged upon the southern ex-tremity of the Makata Plain, a hideous low level of black vegeta-ble earth, peaty in appearance, and bearing long puddles of dark scummy and stagnant rain-water, mere horse-ponds, with the ad-ditional qualities of miasma and musquitoes. The sons of Ramji had determined to reach the Makata Nullah, still distant about two hours. I called a halt in favor of the fatigued pagazi, who heard it with pleasure, and sent to recall Wulaydi, Shehe, and Nasibu, who were acting bell-wethers. The worthies returned after a time, and revenged themselves by parading, with many grimaces, up and down the camp.

On the morning of the 24th of December we resumed the transit of the Makata Plain, and crossed the tail of its nullah. It was here bone-dry; consequently, had we made it last night, the thirsty caravan would have suffered severely. Ensued a long slope garnished with the normal thin forest; in two places the plots of ashes, which denote the deaths of wizard and witch, apprised us that we were fast approaching benighted K'hutu. A skeleton caravan of touters, composed of six muskets and two flags, met us on the way. Presently we descended into the basin of Kikoboga, which was occupied in force by gentry of the same description. After wading four times the black, muddy, and rushy nullah which bisects the lake, we crossed a lateral band of rough high ground, whence a further counterslope bent down to a khambi in a diminutive hollow, called Mwimbi. It was the ideal of a bad encamping-ground. The kraal stood on the bank of a dark, miry water at the head of a narrow gap, where heat was concentrated by the funnel-shaped hill-sides, and where the dark ground, strewed with rotting grass and leaves, harbored hosts of cockroaches, beetles, and musquitoes. The supplies, a little grain, poor sugar-cane, good wild vegetables, at times plantains, were distant, and the water was vile. Throughout this country, however, the Wasagara cultivators, fearing plunder should a caravan encamp near their crops, muster in force; the traveler, therefore, must not unpack except at the kraals on either edge of the cultivation.

The dawn of Christmas-day, 1858, saw us toiling along the Kikoboga River, which we forded four times. We then crossed two deep affluents, whose banks were thick with fruitless plantains. The road presently turned up a rough rise, from whose crest began the descent of the Mabruki Pass. This col may be divided into two steps: the first winds along a sharp ridge-line, a chain of well-forested hills, whose heights, bordered on both sides by precipitous slopes of earth overgrown with thorns and thick bamboo-clumps, command an extensive view of spur and sub-range, of dhun and champaign, sprinkled with villages and dwarf cones, and watered by streamlets that glisten like lines of quicksilver in the blue-brown of the hazy distant landscape. Ensues, after a succession of deep and rugged water-courses, with difficult slopes, the second step; a short but sharp steep of red earth, corded with the tree-roots that have been bared by the heavy rains. Beyond this the path, spanning rough ground at the hill-base, debouches upon the course of a streamlet flowing southward from the last heights of Usagara to the plains of Uziraha in K'hutu.

The bullock reserved for the occasion having been lost in Uhehe,

I had ordered the purchase of half a dozen goats wherewith to celebrate the day; the porters, however, were too lazy to collect them. My companion and I made good cheer upon a fat capon, which acted as roast-beef, and a mess of ground-nuts sweetened with sugar-cane, which did duty as plum-pudding. The contrast of what was with what might be now, however, suggested only pleasurable sensations; long odds were in favor of our seeing the Christmas-day of 1859, compared with the chances of things at Msene on the Christmas-day of 1857.

From Uziraha sixteen hours distributed into fourteen marches conducted us from Uziraha, at the foot of the Usagara Mountains, to Central Zungomero. The districts traversed were Eastern Mbwiga, Marundwe, and Kirengwe. The road again realizes the European idea of Africa in its most hideous and grotesque aspect. Animals are scarce amid the portentous growth of herbage, not a head of black cattle is seen, flocks and poultry are rare, and even the beasts of the field seem to flee the land. The people admitted us into their villages, whose wretched straw hovels, contrasting with the luxuriant jungle which hems them in, look like birds'-nests torn from the trees: all the best settlements, however, were occupied by parties of touters. At the sight of our passing caravan the goatherd hurried off his charge, the peasant prepared to rush into the grass, the women and children slunk and hid within the hut, and no one ever left his home without a bow and a sheath of arrows, whose pitchy-colored bark-necks denoted a fresh layer of poison.

We entered Zungomero on the 29th of December, after sighting on the left the cone at whose base rises the Maji ya W'heta, or Fontaine qui bouille. The village on the left bank of the Mgeta, which we had occupied about eighteen months before, had long been level with the ground; we were therefore conducted with due ceremony into another settlement on the right of the stream. An army of black musketeers, in scanty but various and gaudy attire, came out to meet us, and with the usual shots and shouts conducted us to the headman's house, which had already been turned into a kind of barrack by these irregulars. They then stared as usual for half a dozen consecutive hours, which done they retired to rest.

After a day's repose, sending for the kirangozi, and personally offering a liberal reward, I opened to him the subject then nearest my heart, namely, a march upon Kilwa. This proceeding probably irritated the too susceptible Said bin Salim, and caused him, if not actually to interfere, at any rate to withhold all aid toward furthering the project. Twanigana, after a palaver with his people, returned with a reply that he himself was willing, but that his men would not leave the direct track. Their reasons were various. Some had become brothers with the sons of Ramji, and expected employment from their "father." Others declared that it would be necessary to march a few miles back, which was contrary to their custom, and said that they ought to have been warned of the intention before passing the makutaniro, or junction of the two roads. But none expressed any fear, as has since been asserted, of being sold off into slavery at Kilwa. Such a declaration would have been ridiculous. Of the many Wanyamwezi caravans that have visited Kilwa none has ever yet been seized and sold; the coast people are two well acquainted with their own interests to secure for themselves a permanent bad name. Seeing, however, that energetic measures were necessary to open the road, I allowed them two days for consideration, and warned them that after that time posho or rations should be withdrawn.

On the next day I was privately informed by the mnfumo or parson of the caravan, that his comrades intended to make a feint of desertion, and then to return, if they found us resolved not to follow them. The reverend gentleman's sister-in-law, who had accompanied us from Unyamwezi as cook and concubine to Seedy Bombay, persuaded our managing man that there was no danger of the porters traversing Uzaramo without pay, escort, or provisions. On the first of January, 1859, however, the gang rose to depart. I sent for the kirangozi, who declared that, though loth to leave us, he must head his men: in return for which semi-fidelity I made him name his own reward; he asked two handsome cloths, a gorah or piece of domestics, and one fundo of coral beads —it was double his pay, but I willingly gave it, and directed Said bin Salim to write an order to that effect upon Mr. Rush Ramji, or any other Hindoo who might happen to be at Kaole. But I rejected the suggestion of my companion, who proposed that half the sum agreed upon in Unyanyembe as payment to the porters —nine cloths each—should be given to them. In the first place, this donation would have been equivalent to a final dismissal. Secondly, the Arabs at Kazeh had warned me that it was not their custom to pay in part those who will not complete the journey to the coast; and I could see no reason for departing from a commercial precedent evidently necessary to curb the Africans' alacrity in desertion.

On the day following the departure of the gang I set out to visit the Jetting Spring, and found when returning to the village shortly before noon that my companion had sent a man to recall the "pagazi," who were said to be encamped close to the river, and to propose to them a march upon Mbuamaji. The messenger returned and reported that the Wanyamwezi had already crossed the river. Unwilling that the wretches should lose by their head-strongness, I at once ordered Said bin Salim to mount ass and to bring back the porters by offers which they would have accepted. Some time afterward, when I fancied that he was probably haranguing the men, he came to me to say that he had not eaten and the sun was hot. With the view of shaming him I directed Kidogo to do the work, but as he also made excuses, Khamisi and Shehe, two sons of Ramji, were dispatched with cloths to buy rations for the pagazi, and, *coûte qui coûte*, to bring them back. They set out on the 2d of January, and returned on the 7th of January, never having, according to their own account, seen the fugitives.

This was a regretable occurrence: it gave a handle to private malice under the specious semblance of public duty. But such events are common on the slave-path in Eastern Africa; of the seven gangs of porters engaged on this journey only one, an unusually small proportion, left me without being fully satisfied, and that one deserved to be disappointed.

We were detained at K'hutu till the 20th of January. The airiest of schemes were ventilated by Said bin Salim and my companion. Three of the Baloch eye-sores, the " Gray-beard Mohammed," the mischief-maker Khudabakhsh, and the mulatto Jelai, were sent to the coast with letters, reports, and officials for Zanzibar and home. The projectors then attempted to engage Wak'hutu porters, but after a long palaver, P'hazi Madenge, the principal chief of Uziraha, who at first undertook to transport us in person to Dut'humi, declared that he could not assist us. It was then proposed to trust for porterage to the Wazaramo; that project also necessarily fell to the ground. Two feasible plans remained: either to write to the coast for a new gang, or to await the transit of some down-caravan. As the former would have caused an inevitable delay I preferred the latter, justly thinking that during this, the traveling season, we should not long be detained.

On the 11th of January, 1859, a large party of Wanyamwezi, journeying from the interior to the coast, bivouacked in the village. I easily persuaded Muhembe, the mtongi or leader, to make over to me the services of nine of his men, and lest the African mind might conceive that in dismissing the last gang cloth or beads had been an object, I issued to these new porters seventy-two cloths, as much as if they had carried packs from Unyamwezi to the coast. On the 14th of January, 1859, we received Mr. Apothecary Frost's letters, drugs, and medical comforts, for which we had written to him in July, 1857. The next day saw us fording the warm muddy waters of the Mgeta, which was then 100 feet broad: usually knee-deep, it rises after a few showers to the breast, and during the heavy rains which had lately fallen it was impassable. We found a little village on the left bank, and there we sat down patiently to await, despite the trouble inflicted by a host of diminutive ants, who knew no rest by day or night, the arrival of another caravan to complete our gang. The medical comforts so tardily received from Zanzibar fortified us, however, to some extent against enemies and inconveniences; we had ether-sherbet and ether-lemonade, formed by combining a wine-glass of the spirit with a *quant. suff.* of citric acid; and when we wanted a change the villagers supplied an abundance of pombe or small beer.

On the 17th of January a numerous down-caravan entered the settlement which we occupied, and it proved after inquiry to be one of which I had heard often and much. The chiefs, Sulayman bin Rashid el Riami, a coast Arab, accompanied by a Msawahili, Mohammed bin Gharib, and others, called upon me without delay, and from them I obtained a detailed account of their interesting travel.

The merchants had left the coast for Ubena in June, 1857, and their up-march had lasted six months. They set out with a total of 600 free men and slaves, armed with 150 guns, hired on the sea-board for eight to ten dollars per head, half being advanced: they could not persuade the Wanyamwezi to traverse these regions. The caravan followed the Mbuamaji trunk-road westward as far as Maroro in Usagara, thence deflecting southward it crossed the Rwaha River, which at the ford was knee-deep. The party traveled through the Wahehe and the Wafaji, south of and far from the stream, to avoid the Warori, who hold both banks. The sultan of these freebooters, being at war with the Wabena, would not have permitted merchants to pass on to his enemies, and even in time of peace he fines them, it is said, one half of their property for safe conduct. On the right hand of the caravan, or to the south from Uhehe to Ubena, was a continuous chain of highlands, pouring affluents across the road into the Rwaha River, and water was procurable only in the beds of these nullahs and fiumaras. If this chain be of any considerable length, it may represent the water-parting between the Tanganyika and the Nyassa Lakes, and thus divide by another and a southerly lateral band the great depression of Central Africa. The land was dry and barren; in fact, Ugogo without its calabashes. Scarcely a blade of grass appeared upon the whity-brown soil, and the travelers marveled how the numerous herds obtained their sustenance. The masika or rainy monsoon began synchronously with that of Unyamwezi, but it lasted little more than half its period in the north. In the sparse cultivation, surrounded by dense bush, they were rarely able to ration oftener than once a week. They were hospitably received by Kimanu, the Jyari or Sultan of Ubena. His people, though fierce and savage, appeared pleased by the sight of strangers. The Wabena wore a profusion of beads, and resembled in dress, diet, and lodging the Warori; they were brave to recklessness, and strictly monarchical, swearing by their chief. The Warori, however, were the cleaner race; they washed and bathed, while the Wabena used the same fluid to purify teeth, face, and hands.

At Ubena the caravan made considerable profits in slaves and ivory. The former, mostly captured or kidnapped, were sold for four to six fundo of beads, and, merchants being rare, a large stock was found on hand. About 800 were purchased, as each pagazi or porter could afford one at least. On the return-march, however, half of the property deserted. The ivory, which rather resembled the valuable article procured at Karagwah than the poor produce of Unyanyembe, sold at 35 to 70 fundo of yellow and other colored beads per frasilah of 35 lbs. Cloth was generally refused, and the kitindi or wire armlets were useful only in purchasing provisions.

On its return the caravan, following for eighteen stages the right bank of the Rwaha River, met with an unexpected misfortune. They were nighting in a broad fiumara called Bonye, a tributary from the southern highlands to the main artery, when suddenly a roar and rush of waters fast approaching and the cries of men struck them with consternation. In the confusion which ensued 150 souls, for the most part slaves, and probably ironed or corded together, were carried away by the torrent, and the porters lost a great part of the ivory. A more dangerous place for encampment can scarcely be imagined, yet the East African every where prefers it because it is warm at night and the surface is soft. In the neighborhood of the Rwaha they entered the capital district of Mui' Gumbi, the chief, after a rude reception on the frontier, where the people, mistaking them for a plundering party of Wabena, gathered in arms to the number of 4000. When the error was perceived, the Warori warmly welcomed the traders, calling them brothers, and led them to the quarters of their sultan. Mui' Gumbi was apparently in his 70th year, a man of venerable look, tall, burly, and light-colored, with large ears, and a hooked nose like a "moghrebi." His sons, about thirty in number, all resembled him, their comeliness contrasting strongly with the common clansmen, who are considered by their chiefs as slaves. A tradition derives the origin of this royal race from Madagascar or one of its adjoining islets. Mui' Gumbi wore a profusion of beads, many of them antiquated in form and color, and now unknown in the market of Zanzibar: above his left elbow he had a lumpy bracelet of ivory, a decoration appropriated to chieftains. The Warori expressed their surprise that the country had not been lately visited by caravans, and, to encourage others, the sultan offered large gangs of porters without pay to his visitors. These men never desert; such disobedience would cost them their lives. From the settlement of Mui' Gumbi to the coast the caravan traveled without accident, but under great hardships, living on roots and grasses for want of means to buy provisions.

The same caravan-traders showed me divers specimens of the Warori, and gave me the following description, which tallied with the details supplied by Snay bin Amir and the Arabs of Kazeh.

The Warori extend from the western frontier of the Wahehe, about forty marches along principally the northern bank of the

Rwaha River, to the meridian of Eastern Unyanyembe. They are a semi-pastoral tribe, continually at war with their neighbors. They never sell their own people, but attack the Wabena, the Wakimbu, the Wahehe, the Wakonongo, and the races about Unyangwira, and drive their captives to the sea, or dispose of them to the slavers in Usagara. The price is of course cheap; a male adult is worth from two to six shukkah merkani. Some years ago a large plundering party, under their chief, Mbangera, attacked Sultan Kalala of the Wasukuma; they were, however, defeated, with the loss of their leader, by Kafrira of Kivira, the son-in-law of Kalala. They also ravaged Unyanyembe, and compelled the people to take refuge on the summit of a natural rock-fortress between Kazeh and Yombo, and they have more than once menaced the dominions of Fundikira. Those mighty boasters the Wagogo hold the Warori in awe; as the Arabs say, they shrink small as a cubit before foes fiercer than themselves. The Warori have wasted the lands of Uhehe and Unyangwira, and have dispersed the Wakimbu and the Wamia tribes. They have closed the main road from the sea-board by exorbitant black-mail and charges for water, and about five years ago they murdered two coast Arab traders from Mbuamaji. Since their late defeat by the Watuta, they have been comparatively quiet. When the E. African Expedition, however, entered the country they had just distinguished themselves by driving the herds from Ugogi, and thus prevented any entrance into their country from that district. Like the pastoral races generally of this portion of the peninsula, the object of their raids is cattle: when a herd falls into their hands, they fly at the beasts like hyenas, pierce them with their assegais, hack off huge slices, and devour the meat raw.

The Warori are small and shriveled black savages. Their diminutive size is doubtless the effect of scanty food, continued through many generations: the sultans, however, are a peculiarly fine large race of men. The slave specimens observed had no distinguishing mark on the teeth; in all cases, however, two short lines were tattooed across the hollow of the temples. The male dress is a cloak of strung beads, weighing ten or twelve pounds, and covering the shoulders like a European cape. Some wind a large girdle of the same material round the waist. The women wear a bead kilt extending to the knees, or, if unable to afford it, a wrapper of skin. The favorite weapon is a light, thin, and pliable assegai; they carry a sheath of about a dozen, and throw them with great force and accuracy. The bow is unknown. They usually press to close quarters, each man armed with a long heavy spear. Iron is procured in considerable quantities both in Ubena and Urori. The habitations are said to be large tembe, capable of containing 400 to 500 souls. The principal articles of diet are milk, meat, and especially fattened dog's flesh—of which the chiefs are inordinately fond—maize, holcus, and millet. Rice is not grown in these arid districts. They manage their intoxication by means of pombe made of grain and the bhang, which is smoked in gourd-pipes; they also mix the cannabis with their vegetable food. The Warori are celebrated for power of abstinence; they will march, it is said, six days without eating, and they require to drink but once in the twenty-four hours. In one point they resemble the Bedouins of Arabia: the chief will entertain his guests hospitably as long as they remain in his village, but he will plunder them the moment they leave it.

On the 19th of January the expected down-caravan of Wan-yamwezi arrived, and I found no difficulty in completing our car-riage—a fair proof, be it remarked, that I had not lost the confi-dence of the people. The mtongi, however, was, or perhaps pre-tended to be ill; we were, therefore, delayed for another day in a place which had no charms for us.

The 21st of January enabled us to bid adieu to Zungomero and merrily to take the foot-path way. We made Konduchi on the 3d of February, after twelve marches, which were accomplished in fifteen days. There was little of interest or adventure in this return-line, of which the nine first stations had already been visit-ed and described. As the yegea mud, near Dut'humi, was throat-deep, we crossed it lower down: it was still a weary trudge of several miles through thick slabby mire, which admitted a man to his knees. In places, after toiling under a sickly sun, we crept under the tunnels of thick jungle-growth veiling the Mgazi and other streams; the dank and fetid cold caused a deadly sensation of faintness, which was only relieved by a glass of ether-sherbet, a pipe or two of the strongest tobacco, and half an hour's repose. By degrees it was found necessary to abandon the greater part of the remaining outfit and the luggage: the Wanyamwezi, as they neared their destination, became even less manageable than before, and the sons of Ramji now seemed to consider their toils at an end. On the 25th of January we forded the cold, strong, yellow stream of the Mgeta, whose sandy bed had engulfed my elephant-gun, and we entered with steady hearts the formerly-dreaded Uzaramo. The 27th of January saw us pass safely by the village where M. Maizan came to an untimely end. On that day Rama-zan and Salman, children of Said bin Salim, returned from Zanzi-bar Island, bringing letters, clothing, and provisions for their mas-ter, who, by way of small revenge, had dispatched them secretly from Zungomero. On the 28th of January we reached the maku-taniro or anastomosis of the Kaole and Mbuamaji roads, where on our ingress the Wazaramo had barred passage in force. No one now ventured to dispute the way with well-armed paupers. That evening, however, the mtongi indulged his men with "maneno," a harangue. Reports about fatal skirmishes between the Waza-ramo and a caravan of Wanyamwezi that had preceded us had flown about the camp; consequently the mtongi recommended prudence. "There would be danger to-morrow—a place of ambuscade—the porters must not rise and be off too early nor too late—they must not hasten on, nor lag behind—they had with them Wazungu, and in case of accidents they would lose their name!" The last sentence was frequently repeated with ever-increasing emphasis, and each period of the discourse was marked by a general murmur, denoting attention.

As I have said, there was no danger. Yet on the next day a report arose that we were to be attacked in a dense thicket—where no archer, be it observed, could bend his bow—a little beyond the junction of the Mbuamaji road with that of Konduchi, our destination. In the afternoon Said bin Salim, with important countenance, entered my tent and disclosed to me the doleful tidings. The road was cut off. He knew it. A great friend of his —a slave—had told him so. He remembered warning me that such was the case five days ago. I must either delay till an escort could be summoned from the coast, or—I must fee a chief to precede me and to reason with the enemy. It was in vain to storm, I feared that real obstacles might be placed by the timid and wily little man in our way, and I consented most unwillingly to pay two colored cloths and one ditto of blue cotton, as hire to guard that appeared in the shape of four clothless varlets, that left us after the first quarter of an hour. The Baloch, headed by the jemadar, knowing that all was safe, distinguished themselves on that night, for the first time in eighteen months, by uttering the shouts which prove that the Oriental soldier is doing "zam," *i.e.*, is on the *qui vive*. When requested not to make so much noise they grumbled that it was for our sake, not for theirs.

On the 30th of January our natives of Zanzibar screamed with delight at the sight of the mango-tree, and pointed out to one another, as they appeared in succession, the old familiar fruits, jacks and pine-apples, limes and cocos. On the 2d of February we greeted, with doffed caps and three times three and one more, as Britons will do on such occasions, the kindly smiling face of our father Neptune, as he lay basking in the sunbeams between earth and air. Finally, the 3d of February, 1859, saw us winding through the poles decorated with skulls—they now grin in the Royal College of Surgeons, London—a negro Temple-bar which pointed out the way into the little maritime village of Konduchi.

Our entrance was attended with the usual ceremony, now familiar to the reader: the warmen danced, shot, and shouted, a rabble of adults, youths, and boys crowded upon us, the fair sex lulliloo'd with vigor, and a general procession conducted their strangers to the hut swept, cleaned, and garnished for us by old Premji, the principal Banyan of the head-quarter village, and there stared and laughed till they could stare and laugh no more.

On the evening of the same day an opportunity offered of transferring the jemadar, the Baloch, and my *bête noire*, Kidogo, to their homes in Zanzibar Island, which lies within sight of Konduchi: as may be imagined, I readily availed myself of it. After begging powder and *et ceteras* to the last, the monocular insisted upon kissing my hand, and departed weeping bitterly with the agony of parting. By the same boat I sent a few lines to H. M. consul, Zanzibar, inclosing a list of necessaries, and requesting that a battela, or coasting-craft, might be hired, provisioned, and dispatched without delay, as I purposed to explore the delta and the unknown course of the Rufiji River. In due time Said bin Salim and his " children," including the fair Halima and Zawada —the latter was liberally rewarded by me for services rendered to my companion—and shortly afterward the sons of Ramji, or rather the few who had not deserted or lagged behind, were returned to their master, and were, I doubt not, received with all the kindness which their bad conduct deserved.

We were detained at Konduchi for six days between the 3d and 10th of February. There is nothing interesting in this little African village-port: instead of describing it, I will enter into a few details concerning African matters of more general importance.

THE BASIN OF KISANGA.

The Ivory Porter, the Cloth Porter, and Woman, in Usagara.

CHAPTER XVIII.

VILLAGE LIFE IN EAST AFRICA.

THE assertion may startle the reader's preconceived opinions concerning the savage state of Central Africa and the wretched condition of the slave-races, negroid and negro; but it is not less true that the African is in these regions superior in comforts, better dressed, fed, and lodged, and less worked than the unhappy ryot of British India. His condition, where the slave-trade is slack, may, indeed, be compared advantageously with that of the peasantry in some of the richest of European countries.

The African rises with the dawn from his couch of cow's hide. The hut is cool and comfortable during the day, but the barred door impeding ventilation at night causes it to be close and disagreeable. The hour before sunrise being the coldest time, he usually kindles a fire, and addresses himself to his constant companion, the pipe. When the sun becomes sufficiently powerful, he removes the reed-screen from the entrance, and issues forth to bask in the morning beams. The villages are populous, and the houses touching one another enable the occupants, when squatting outside and fronting the central square, to chat and chatter without moving. About 7 A.M., when the dew has partially disappeared from the grass, the elder boys drive the flocks and herds to pasture with loud shouts and sounding applications of the quarter-staff. They return only when the sun is sinking behind the western horizon. At 8 P.M. those who have provisions at home enter the hut to refection with ugali or holcus-porridge; those who have not, join a friend. Pombe, when procurable, is drunk from the earliest dawn.

After breaking his fast the African repairs, pipe in hand, to the iwánzá—the village "public," previously described. Here, in the society of his own sex, he will spend the greater part of the day, talking and laughing, smoking, or torpid with sleep. Occasionally he sits down to play. As with barbarians generally, gambling in him is a passion. The normal game is our "heads and tails," its implement a flat stone, a rough circle of tin, or the bottom of a broken pot. The more civilized have learned the "bao" of the coast, a kind of "tables," with counters and cups hollowed in a solid plank. Many of the Wanyamwezi have been compelled by this indulgence to sell themselves into slavery: after playing through their property, they even stake their aged mothers against the equivalent of an old lady in these lands—a cow or a pair of goats. As may be imagined, squabbles are perpetual; they are almost always, however, settled among fellow-villagers with bloodless weapons. Others, instead of gambling, seek some employment which, working the hands and leaving the rest of the body and the mind at ease, is ever a favorite with the Asiatic and the African; they whittle wood, pierce and wire their pipe-sticks—an art in which all are adepts—shave one another's heads, pluck out their beards, eyebrows, and eyelashes, and prepare and polish their weapons.

At about 1 P.M. the African, unless otherwise employed, returns to his hut to eat the most substantial and the last meal of the day, which has been cooked by his women. Eminently gregarious, however, he often prefers the iwánzá as a dining-room, where his male children, relatives, and friends meet during the most important hour of the twenty-four. With the savage and the barbarian food is the all-in-all of life: food is his thought by day, food is his dream by night. The civilized European, who never knows hunger or thirst without the instant means of gratifying every whim of appetite, can hardly conceive the extent to which his wild brother's soul is swayed by stomach; he can scarcely comprehend the state of mental absorption in which the ravenous human animal broods over the carcass of an old goat, the delight which he takes in superintending every part of the cooking process, and the jealous eye with which he regards all who live better than himself.

The principal articles of diet are fish and flesh, grain and vegetables; the luxuries are milk and butter, honey, and a few fruits, as bananas and Guinea-palm dates; and the inebriants are pombe or millet-beer, toddy, and mawa or plantain-wine.

Fish is found in the lakes and in the many rivers of this well-watered land; it is despised by those who can afford flesh, but it is a "godsend" to travelers, to slaves, and to the poor. Meat is the diet most prized; it is, however, a luxury beyond the reach of peasantry, except when they can pick up the orts of the chiefs. The Arabs assert that in these latitudes vegetables cause heartburn and acidity, and that animal food is the most digestible. The Africans seem to have made the same discovery: a man who can afford it almost confines himself to flesh, and he considers fat the essential element of good living. The crave for meat is satisfied by eating almost every description of living thing, clean or unclean; as a rule, however, the East African prefers beef, which strangers find flatulent and heating. Like most people, they reject game when they can command the flesh of tame beasts. Next to the bullock the goat is preferred in the interior; as indeed it is by the Arabs of Zanzibar Island; whereas those of Oman and of Western Arabia abandon it to the Bedouins. In this part of Africa the cheapest and vilest meat is mutton, and its appearance — pale, soft, and braxy — justifies the prejudice against it. Of late years it has become the fashion to eat poultry and pigeons; eggs, however, are still avoided. In the absence of history and tradition, it is difficult to decide whether this aversion to eggs arises from an imported or an indigenous prejudice. The mundane egg of Hindoo mythology probably typified the physiological dogma "omne vivum ex ovo," and the mystic disciples would avoid it as representing the principle of life. In remote ages the prejudice may have extended to Africa, although the idea which gave birth to it was not familiar to the African mind. Of wild flesh, the favorite is that of the zebra; it is smoked or jerked, despite which it retains a most savory flavor. Of the antelopes a few are deliciously tender and succulent; the greater part are black, coarse, and indigestible. One of the inducements for an African to travel is to afford himself more meat than at home. His fondness for the article conquers at times even his habitual improvidence. He preserves it by placing large lumps upon a little platform of green reeds erected upon uprights about eighteen inches high, and by smoking it with a slow fire. Thus prepared, and with the addition of a little salt, the provision will last for several days, and the porters will not object to increase their loads by three or four pounds of the article, disposed upon a long stick like gigantic kababs. They also jerk their stores by exposing the meat upon a rope, or spread upon a flat stone for two or three days in the sun; it loses a considerable portion of nutriment, but it packs into a conveniently small compass. This jerked meat, when dried, broken into small pieces, and stored in gourds or in pots full of clarified and melted butter, forms the celebrated traveling provision in the East called kavurmeh: it is eaten as a relish with rice and other boiled grains. When meat is not attainable and good water is scarce, the African severs one of the jugulars of a bullock and fastens upon it like a leech. This custom is common in Karagwah and the other northern kingdoms, and some tribes, like the Wanyika, near Mombasah, churn the blood with milk.

The daily food of the poor is grain, generally holcus, maize, or bajri (panicum); wheat is confined to the Arabs, and rice grows locally, as in the Indian peninsula. The inner Africans, like the semi-civilized Arabs of Zanzibar, the Wasawahili, and the Wamrima, ignore the simple art of leavening bread by acidulated whey, sour bean-paste, and similar contrivances universally practiced in Oman. Even the rude Indian chapati or scone is too artificial for them, and they have not learned to toast grain. Upon journeys the African boils his holcus unhusked in an earthen basin, drinks the water, and devours the grain, which in this state is called masango; at home he is more particular. The holcus is either rubbed upon a stone—the mill being wholly unknown—or pounded with a little water in a huge wooden mortar; when reduced to a coarse powder, it is thrown into an earthen pot containing boiling water sufficient to be absorbed by the flour; a little salt, when procurable, is added; and after a few stirrings with a ladle, or rather with a broad and flat-ended stick, till thoroughly saturated, the thick mass is transferred into a porous basket, which allows the extra moisture to leak out. Such is the ugali, or porridge, the staff of life in East Africa.

During the rains vegetables are common in the more fertile parts of East Africa; they are within reach of the poorest cultivator. Some varieties, especially the sweet potato and the mushroom, are sliced and sun-dried to preserve them through the year. During the barren summer they are boiled into a kind of broth.

Milk is held in high esteem by all tribes, and some live upon it almost exclusively during the rains, when cattle find plentiful pasture. It is consumed in three forms—"mabichi," when drunk fresh; or converted into mabivu (buttermilk), the rubb of Arabs; or in the shape of mtindi (curded milk), the laban of Arabia, and the Indian dahi. These Africans ignore the dudh-pinda, or ball of fresh milk boiled down to hardness by evaporation of the serum, as practiced by the Indian halwaí (confectioner); the indurated sour-clot of Arabia, called by the Bedouins el igt, and by the Persians, the Baloch, and the Sindhians kurut, is also unknown; and they consider cheese a miracle, and use against it their stock denunciation, the danger of bewitching cattle. The fresh produce, moreover, has few charms as a poculent among barbarous and milk-drinking races: the Arabs and the Portuguese in Africa avoid it after the sun is high, believing it to increase bile, and eventually to cause fever: it is certain that, however pleasant the draught may be in the cool of the morning, it is by no means so much relished during the heat of the day. On the other hand, the curded milk is every where a favorite on account of its cooling and thirst-quenching properties, and the people accustomed to it from infancy have for it an excessive longing. It is procurable in every village where cows are kept, whereas that newly drawn is generally half-soured from being at once stored in the earthen pots used for curding it. These East Africans do not, however, make their dahi, like the Somal, in lumps floating upon the tartest possible serum; nor do they turn it, like the Arabs, with kid's rennet, nor like the Baloch with the solanaceous plant called panir.   The best is made, as in India, by allowing the milk to stand till it clots in a pot used for the purpose, and frequently smoked for purity.   Buttermilk is procurable only in those parts of the country where the people have an abundance of cattle.

Butter is made by filling a large gourd, which acts as churn, with partially-soured milk, which is shaken to and fro: it is a poor article, thin, colorless, and tainted by being stored for two or three months, without preliminary washing, in the bark boxes called vilindo.   In the Eastern regions it is converted into ghee by simply melting over the fire: it is not boiled to expel the remnant of sour milk, impurities are not removed by skimming, and finally it becomes rancid and bitter by storing in pots and gourds which have been used for the purpose during half a generation.   Ths Arabs attempt to do away with the nauseous taste by throwing into it when boiling a little water, with a handful of flour or of unpowdered rice.   Westward of Unyamwezi, butter is burned instead of oil in lamps.

The common oil in East Africa is that of the karanga, bhuiphali, or ground-nut (Arachis hypogæa): when ghee is not procurable, the Arabs eat it, like cocoanut-oil, with beans, manioc, sweet potato and other vegetables.   A superior kind of cooking is the "uto" extracted from the ufuta, simsim or sesamum, which grows every where upon the coast, and extends far into the interior. The process of pressing it is managed by pounding the grain dry in a huge mortar; when the oil begins to appear, a little hot water is poured in, and the mass is forcibly squeezed with huge pestles; all that floats is then ladled out into pots and gourds.   The viscid chikichi (palm-oil) is found only in the vicinity of the Tanganyika Lake, although the tree grows in Zanzibar and its adjacent islets.   Oil is extracted from the two varieties of the castor-plant; and, in spite of its unsavory smell, it is extensively used as an unguent by the people.   At Unyanyembe and other places where the cucumber grows almost wild, the Arabs derive from its seed an admirable salad-oil, which in flavor equals, and perhaps surpasses, the finest produce of the olive.   The latter tree is unknown in East Africa to the Arabs, who speak of it with a religious respect, on account of the mention made of it in the Koran.

In East Africa every man is his own maltster; and the "iwánzá," or public house of the village, is the common brewery.   In some tribes, however, fermentation is the essential occupation of the women.   The principal inebriant is a beer without hops, called pombe.   This ποτος θειος of the negro and negroid races dates from the age of Osiris: it is the buzah of Egypt and the farther East, and the merissa of the Upper Nile, the ξιθον and xythum of the West, and the oala or boyaloa of the Kafirs and the South African races.   The taste is somewhat like soured wort of the smallest description, but strangers, who at first dislike it exceedingly, are soon reconciled to it by the pleasurable sensations to which it

gives rise. Without violent action, it affects the head, and produces an agreeable narcotism, followed by sound sleep and heaviness in the morning—as much liked by the barbarian, to whom
inebriation is a boon, as feared by the civilized man. Being, as
the Arabs say, a "cold drink," causing hydrocele and rheumatism,
it has some of the after-effects of gin, and the drunkard is readily
recognized by his red and bleared eyes. When made thick with
the grounds or sediment of grain, it is exceedingly nutritious.
Many a gallon must be drunk by the veteran malt-worm before
intoxication; and individuals of both sexes sometimes live almost
entirely upon pombe. It is usually made as follows: half of the
grain—holcus, panicum, or both mixed—intended for the brew is
buried or soaked in water till it sprouts; it is then pounded and
mixed with the other half, also reduced to flour, and sometimes
with a little honey. The compound is boiled twice or thrice in
huge pots, strained, when wanted clear, through a bag of matting,
and allowed to ferment: after the third day it becomes as sour as
vinegar. The "togwa" is a favorite drink, also made of holcus.
At first it is thick and sickly, like honeyed gruel; when sour it
becomes exceedingly heady. As these liquors consume a quantity of grain, they are ever expensive; the large gourdful never
fetches less than two khete or strings of beads, and strangers must
often pay ten khete for the luxury. Some years ago, an Arab
taught the Wanyamwezi to distill: they soon, however, returned
to their favorite fermentation.

The use of pombe is general throughout the country: the other inebriants are local. At the island and on the coast of Zanzibar, tembo, or toddy, in the West African dialects tombo, is drawn
from the cocoa-tree; and in places a pernicious alcohol, called
mvinyo, is extracted from it. The Wajiji and other races upon
the Tanganyika Lake tap the Guinea-palm for a toddy, which,
drawn in unclean pots, soon becomes acid and acrid as the Silesian
wine that serves to mend the broken limbs of the poor. The use
of bhang and datura-seed has already been alluded to. "Máwá,"
or plantain-wine, is highly prized because it readily intoxicates.
The fruit, when ripe, is peeled and hand-kneaded with coarse
green grass, in a wide-mouthed earthen pot, till all the juice is
extracted: the sweet must is then strained through a *cornet* of
plantain-leaf into a clean gourd, which is but partially stopped.
To hasten fermentation a handful of toasted or pounded grain is
added: after standing for two days in a warm room the wine is
ready for drinking.

The East Africans ignore the sparkling berille or hydromel of
Abyssinia and Harar, and the mead of the Bushman race. Yet
honey abounds throughout the country, and near the villages log
hives, which from their shape are called mazinga or cannons by
the people, hang from every tall and shady tree. Bees also
swarm in the jungles, performing an important part in the veg-

etable economy by masculation or caprification, and the conveyance of pollen. Their produce is of two kinds. The cheaper resembles wasp-honey in Europe; it is found in the forest and
stored in gourds. More than half filled with dirt and wood bark,
it affords but little wax; the liquid is thin and watery, and it has
a peculiarly unpleasant flavor. The better variety, the hive-hon-
ey, is as superior to the produce of the jungle as it is inferior to
that of India and of more civilized lands. It is tolerable until
kept too long, and it supplies a good yellow wax, used by the
Arabs to mix with tallow in the manufacture of "dips." The
best honey is sold after the rains; but the African hoards his
store till it reddens, showing the first stage of fermentation: he
will eat it after the second or third year, when it thins, froths, and
becomes a rufous-brown fluid of unsavory taste; and he rarely
takes the trouble to remove the comb, though the Arabs set him
the example of straining the honey through bags of plantain-
straw or matting. Decomposition, moreover, is assisted by softening the honey over the fire to extract the wax instead of placing
it in the sun. The price varies from one to three cloths for a
large gourdful. When cheap, the Arabs make from it "honey-
sugar:" the material, after being strained and cleaned, is stored
for two or three weeks in a cool place till surface-granulation takes
place; the produce resembles, in taste and appearance, coarse
brown sugar. The "siki," a vinegar of the country, is also made
of one part honey and four of water, left for a fortnight to acetize:
it is weak and insipid. Honey is the only sweetener in the country, except in the places where the sugar-cane grows, namely, the
maritime and the lakist regions. The people chew it, ignoring
the simple art of extracting and inspissating the juice; nor do
they, like the natives of Usumbara, convert it into an inebriant.
Yet sugar attracts them like flies; they clap their hands with
delight at the taste; they buy it for its weight of ivory; and if a
thimbleful of the powder happen to fall upon the ground, they
will eat an ounce of earth rather than lose a grain of it.

After eating, the East African invariably indulges in a long fit
of torpidity, from which he awakes to pass the afternoon as he
did the forenoon, chatting, playing, smoking, and chewing "sweet-
earth." Toward sunset all issue forth to enjoy the coolness: the
men sit outside the iwánzá, while the women and the girls, after
fetching water for household wants from the well, collecting in a
group upon their little stools, indulge in the pleasures of gossiped
and the pipe. This hour in the more favored parts of the country is replete with enjoyment, which even the barbarian feels,
though not yet indoctrinated into æsthetics. As the hours of
darkness draw nigh, the village doors are carefully closed, and,
after milking his cows, each peasant retires to his hut, or passes
his time squatting round the fire with his friends in the iwánzá.
He has not yet learned the art of making a wick, and of filling

a bit of pottery with oil. When a light is wanted, he ignites a stick of the oleaginous mtata, or msásá-tree—a yellow, hard, close-grained, and elastic wood, with few knots, much used in making spears, bows, and walking-staves—which burns for a quarter of an hour with a brilliant flame. He repairs to his hard couch before midnight, and snores with a single sleep till dawn. For thorough enjoyment, night must be spent in insensibility, as day is in inebriety; and, though an early riser, he avoids the "early to bed," in order that he may be able to slumber through half the day.

It is evident that these barbarians lead rather a "fast" life; there are, however, two points that modify its evil consequences. The "damned distillation" is unknown, consequently they do not suffer from delirium tremens, its offspring.   Their only brain-work is that necessitated by the simple wants of life, and by the unartificial style of gambling which they affect.   Among the civilized, the peculiar state of the nervous system in the individual, and in society, the abnormal conditions induced by over-crowding in cities and towns, has engendered a cohort of dire diseases which the children of nature ignore.

Such is the African's idle day, and thus every summer is spent. As the wintry rains draw nigh, the necessity of daily bread suggests itself. The peasants then leave their huts at 6 or 7 A.M., often without provision, which now becomes scarce, and labor till noon, or 2 P.M., when they return home, and find food prepared by the wife or the slave-girl. During the afternoon they return to work, and sometimes, when the rains are near, they are aided by the women.   Toward sunset all wend homeward in a body, laden with their implements of cultivation, and singing a kind of "dulce domum" in a simple and pleasing recitative.

When the moon shines bright the spirits of the East African are raised like the jackal's, and a furious drumming and a droning chorus summon the maidens to come out and enjoy the spectacle of a dance.   The sexes seldom perform together, but they have no objection to be gazed at by each other.   Their style of saltation is remarkable only for the extreme gravity which it induces: at no other time does the East African look so serious and so full of earnest purpose. Yet with all this thoughtfulness, "poor human nature can not dance of itself."   The dance has already been described as far as possible: as may be imagined, the African Thalia is by no means free from the reproach which caused Mohammed to taboo her to his followers.

Music is at a low ebb.   Admirable timists, and no mean tunists, the people betray their incapacity for improvement by remaining contented with the simplest and the most monotonous combinations of sounds.   As in every thing else, so in this art, creative talent is wanting.   A higher development would have produced other results; yet it is impossible not to remark the delight which they take in harmony. The fisherman will accompany his paddle, the porter his trudge, and the housewife her task of rubbing down grain with song; and for long hours at night the peasants will sit in a ring repeating, with a zest that never flags, the same few notes and the same unmeaning line. Their style is the recitative, broken by a full chorus, and they appear to affect the major rather than the interminable minor key of the Asiatic. Their singing also wants the strained upper notes of the cracked-voiced Indian performer, and it ignores the complicated raga and ragini or Hindoo modes, which appear rather the musical expression of high mathematics than the natural language of harmony and melody.

The instruments of the East African are all of foreign invention, imported from various regions, Madagascar, and the coast. Those principally in use are the following. The zeze, or banjo, resembles in sound the monochord Arabian rubabah, the rude ancestor of the Spanish guitar. The sounding-board is a large hollow gourd, open below; on the upper part, fastened by strings that pass through drilled holes, is a conical piece of gourd, cleft longitudinally to admit the arm or handle, which projects at a right angle. The arm is made of light wood, from 18 inches to 2 feet in length; the left-hand extremity has three frets formed by two notches, with intervals, and thus the total range is of six notes. A single string, made of "mondo," the fibre of the mwale

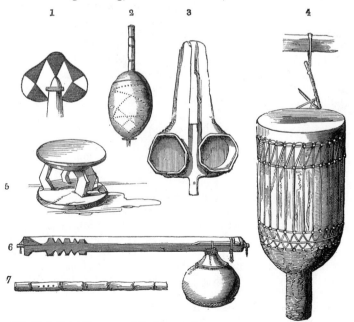

1   2   3   4

1 Paddle in East Africa.   2 The Sange or Gourd.   3 Bellows.   4 Drum.
     5 Stool.   6 The Zeze (Guitar).   7 The D'hete or Kidete.

or raphia palm, is tied to a knob of wood projecting from the dexter extremity of the handle, thence it passes over a bridge of bent quill, which for tuning is raised or depressed, and lastly it is secured round another knob at the end beyond the frets. Sometimes, to form a bass or drone, a second string is similarly attached along the side of the arm, while the treble runs along the top.

The kinanda, a prototype of the psaltery and harp, the lute and lyre, and much used by the southern races in the neighborhood of Kilwa, is of two kinds. One is a shallow box cut out of a single plank, thirteen inches long by five or six in breadth, and about two inches in depth: eleven or twelve strings are drawn tightly over the hollow. The instrument is placed in the lap, and performed upon with both hands. The other is a small bow-guitar, with an open gourd attached to the part about the handle: sometimes the bow passes through the gourd. This instrument is held in the left hand, while the "tocador" strikes its single cord with a thin cane plectrum about one foot long. As in the zeze, the gourd is often adorned with black tattoo, or bright brass tacks, disposed in various patterns, among which the circle and the crescent figure conspicuously. A third form of the kinanda appears to be a barbarous ancestor of the Grecian lyre, which, like the modern Nubian "kisirka," is a lineal descendant from the Egyptian oryx-horn lute with the transverse bar. A combination of the zeze and kinanda is made by binding a dwarf hollow box with its numerous strings to the open top of a large circular gourd, which then acts as a sounding-board.

The wind-instruments are equally rude, though by no means so feeble as their rivals. The nai or sackbut of India, and the siwa, a huge bassoon of black wood, at least five feet long, are known only to the coast people. The tribes of the interior use the d'hete or kidete, called by the Wasawahili zumari. It is literally the bucolic reed, a hollowed holcus cane, pierced with four holes at the farther end: the mouth-piece is not stopped in any way, and the instrument is played upon solely by the lips, a drone being sometimes supplied by the voice. Thus simple and ineffective, it has nevertheless a familiar sound to European ears. The barghumi is made by cutting an oblong hole, about the size of a man's nail, within two or three inches of the tip of a koodoo, an oryx, or a goat's horn, which, for effect and appearance, is sometimes capped with a bit of cane, whence projects a long zebra's or giraffe's tail. Like the det'he, it is played upon by the lips; and without any attempt at stops or keys, four or five notes may be produced. Its sound, heard from afar, especially in the deep silence of a tropical night, resembles not a little the sad, sweet music of the French *cor-de-chasse;* and when well performed upon, it might be mistaken for a regimental bugle. There are smaller varieties of the barghumi, which porters carry slung over the shoulder, and use as signals on the line of march. Another curious instrument is a gourd, a few inches in circumference, drilled with many little apertures: the breath passes through one hole, and certain notes are produced by stopping others with the fingers—its loud, shrill, and ear-piercing quavers faintly resemble the European "piccolo." The only indigenous music of the pastoral African—the Somal, for instance—is whistling, a habit acquired in youth when tending the flocks and herds. This "mu-'unzi" is soft and dulcet; the ear, however, fails to detect in it either phrase or tune. For signals the East Africans practice the ki-k'horombwe, or blowing between the fore and the middle fingers with a noise like that of a railway whistle. The Wanyamwezi also blow over the edge of the hollow in a small antelope's horn, or through an iron tube; and the Watuta are said to use metal whistles as signals in battle.

The drum is ever the favorite instrument with the African, who uses it as the alarum of war, the promise of mirth, the token of hospitality, and the cure of diseases: without drumming his life would indeed be a blank. The largest variety, called "ngoma ku," is the hollowed bole of a mkenga or other soft tree, with a cylindrical solid projection from the bottom, which holds it upright when planted in the ground. The instrument is from three to five feet in length, with a diameter of from one to two feet: the outside is protected with a net-work of strong cord. Over the head is stretched a rough parchment made of calf's-skin; and a cap of green hide, mounted when loose, and afterward shrunken by exposure to fire, protects the bottom. It is vigorously beaten with the fists, and sometimes with coarse sticks. There are many local varieties of this instrument, especially the timbrel or tabret, which is about a foot long, shaped like an hour-glass or a double "darabukkah," and provided with a head of iguana skin. The effect of tom-toming is also produced by striking hollow gourds and similar articles. The only cymbal is the upatu, a flat-bottomed brass pot turned upside down, and tapped with a bit of wood. The "sanje," a gourd full of pebbles, is much affected in parts of the country by women, children, and especially by the mganga or rain-maker; its use being that of the babe's rattle among Europeans.

The insipidity of the African's day is relieved by frequent drinking bouts, and by an occasional hunt. For the former the guests assemble at early dawn, and take their seats in a circle, dividing into knots of three or four to facilitate the circulation of the bowl. The mwandázi, or cup-bearer, goes round the assembly, giving scrupulous precedence to the chiefs and elders, who are also provided with larger vessels. The sonzo, or drinking-cup, which also serves as a traveling canteen, is made generally by the women, of a kind of grass called mávú, or of wild palm-leaf: the split stalks are neatly twisted into a fine cord, which is rolled up, beginning from the bottom, in concentric circles, each joined to its neighbor by a binding of the same material: it is sometimes stained and ornamented with red and black dyes. The shape when finished is a truncated cone, somewhat like a Turk's fez; it measures about six inches in diameter by five in depth, and those of average size may contain a quart. This cup passes around without delay or heel-taps, and the topers stop occasionally to talk, laugh, and snuff, to chew tobacco and to smoke bhang. The scene of sensuality lasts for three or four hours—in fact, till the pombe prepared for the occasion is exhausted—when the carousers, with red eyes, distorted features, and the thickest of voices, stagger home to doze through the day. Perhaps in no European country are so many drunken men seen abroad as in East Africa. Women also frequently appear intoxicated; they have, however, private "pombe," and do not drink with the men.

The East African, who can seldom afford to gratify his longing for meat by slaughtering a cow or a goat, looks eagerly forward to the end of the rains, when the grass is in a fit condition for firing; then, armed with bows and arrows, and with rungu or knob-kerries, the villagers have a battue of small antelopes, hares, and birds. During the hot season also, when the waters dry up, they watch by night at the tanks and pools, and they thus secure the larger kinds of game. Elephants especially are often found dead of drought during the hot season; they are driven from the springs which are haunted by the hunters, and, according to the Arabs, they fear migrating to new seats where they would be attacked by the herds in possession. In many parts the huntsmen suspend by a cord from the trees sharpened blocks of wood, which, loosened by the animal's foot, fall and cause a mortal wound. This "suspended spear," sprung by a latch, has been described by a host of South African travelers. It has been sketched by Lieut. Boteler ("Narrative of a Voyage of Discovery to Africa and Arabia," chap. iv.); and Major Monteiro ("O Muata Cazembe," chap. v.); and described by Mr. Galton, Mr. Gordon Cumming, and Dr. Livingstone (chap. xxviii.). Throughout Ugogo and upon the maritime regions large game is caught in pitfalls, here called mtego, and in India ogi: in some places travelers run the risk of falling into these traps. The mtego is an oblong excavation like a great grave, but decreasing in breadth below the surface of the ground, and it is always found single, not in pairs as in South Africa. The site generally chosen is near water, and the hole is carefully masked with thin layers of small sticks and leaves. The Indian "surrounds" and the hopo or V-shaped trap of the Bakwens are here unknown. The distribution of treasure-trove would seem to argue ancient partitions and lordships, and, in dividing the spoils of wild or tame animals, the chief claims, according to ancient right, the breast. This custom, apparently borrowed by the Hebrews from Africa (Leviticus, chap. vii., 30, 31), is alluded to by almost all South African travelers.

The elephant roams in herds throughout the country, affecting the low grounds where stagnating water produces a plentiful vegetation: with every human being its foe, and thousands living by its destruction, the animal is far from becoming scarce; indeed, the greatest number of footprints appeared near Chogwe and Tongwe, stations of Baloch garrisons close to the town of Pangani. The elephant-hunt is with the African a solemn and serious undertaking. He fortifies himself with periapts and prophylactics given by the mganga, who also trains him to the use of his weapon. The elephant-spear resembles our boarding-pike rather than the light blunt arm employed in war; it is about six feet long, with a broad tapering head cut away at the shoulders, and supported by an iron neck, which is planted in a thick wooden handle, the junction being secured by a cylinder of raw hide from a cow's tail passed over it, and shrunk on by drying: a specimen was deposited with the Royal Geographical Society. The spear is invariably guarded by a mpigi or charm, the usual two bits of wood bound together with a string or strip of skin. It is not a little curious that the East African, though born and bred a hunter, is, unlike almost all barbarians, as skill-less as a European in the art of el asr, the "spoor" or "sign."

The hunting-party, consisting of fifteen to twenty individuals, proceeds before departure to sing and dance, to drink and drum for a consecutive week. The women form line and perambulate the village, each striking an iron jembe or hoe with a large stone, which forms an appropriate accompaniment to the howl and the vigelegele, "lullilooing," or trills of joy. At every step the dancer sways herself elephant-like from side to side, and tosses her head backward with a violence threatening dislocation of the atlas. The line, led by a fugle-woman by the right, who holds two jembe in one hand, but does not drum, stops facing every Arab house where beads may be expected, and performs the most hideous contortions, whirling the arms round the shoulder-socket, kneeling, and imitating the actions of various animals. The labor done, the ladies apply to their pombe, and reappear after four or five hours with a tell-tale stagger and a looseness of limb which adds a peculiar charm to their gesticulations. The day concludes with a "fackeltanz" of remarkable grotesqueness. This merry-making is probably intended as a consolation for the penance which the elephant-hunter's wife performs during the absence of her mate; she is expected to abstain from good food, handsome cloth, and fumigation: she must not leave the house, and for an act of infidelity the blame of failure in the hunt will fall heavily upon her. Meanwhile the men—at least as "far gone" as the women—encircle with a running jumping gait, and with the grace and science of well-trained bears, a drum or a kilindo—the normal bark bandbox—placed with open mouth upon the ground, and violently beaten with sticks and fists or rubbed and scraped with stones. It forms also a sounding-board for a kinanda or bow-guitar, one end of which is applied to it, while a shrill fife or goat's horn gives finish and completeness to the band. Around the drum are placed several elephants' tails, possibly designed to serve the purpose of the clay corpse introduced into the feasts of ancient Egypt.

When thoroughly drenched with drink, the hunters set out early in the morning, carrying live brands lest fire should fail them in the jungle, and applying them to their mouths to keep out the cold air. These trampers are sometimes dangerous to stragglers from caravans, especially in countries where the robber or the murderer expects to escape with impunity. In some places hunting-huts have been erected; they are, however, seldom used when elephants are sought, as a herd once startled does not readily return to the same pasture-grounds. The great art of the African muinzi, or elephant-hunter, is to separate a tusker from the herd without exciting suspicion, and to form a circle round the victim. The mganga, then rising with a shout, hurls or thrusts the first spear, and his example is followed by the rest. The weapons are not poisoned: they are fatal by a succession of small wounds. The baited beast rarely breaks, as might be expected, through the frail circle of assailants: its proverbial obstinacy is excited; it charges one man, who slips away, when another, with a scream, thrusts the long stiff spear into its hind quarters, which makes it change intention and turn fiercely from the fugitive to the fresh assailant. This continues till the elephant, losing breath and heart, attempts to escape; its enemies then redouble their efforts, and at length the huge prey, overpowered by pain and loss of blood trickling from a hundred gashes, bites the dust. The victors, after certain preliminaries of singing and dancing, carefully cut out the tusks with small, sharp axes, and the rich marrow is at once picked from the bamboo and devoured upon the spot, as the hare's liver is in Italy. The hunt concludes with a grand feast of fat and garbage, and the hunters return home in triumph, laden with ivory, with ovals of hide for shields, and with festoons of raw and odorous meat spitted upon long poles.

Throughout East Africa the mouse, as the saying is, travels with a staff: the education of youth and the exercises of manhood are confined to the practice of weapons. Yet the people want the expertness of the Somal of the North and the Kafirs of the South; their internal feuds perpetuate the necessity of offensive measures, and of the presence of arms, but their agricultural state, rendering them independent of the chase, prevents their reliance upon their skill for daily food. In consequence of being ever armed, the African like the Asiatic is nothing without his weapons; he can not use his strength, and when he comes to blows he fights like a woman. Thus the habitual show of arms is a mere substitute for courage; in dangerous countries, as in Ugogo, the Wanyamwezi do not dare to carry them for fear of provocation, whereas at home and in comparative safety they never appear without spear or knobstick.

The weapons universally carried are the spear and the assegai. The bow and arrow, the knobkerry, the dagger, and the battle-axe are confined to certain tribes, while the musket and the sword are used beyond the coast only by strangers. The shield is seldom seen.

The lance of the European, Arab, and Indian is unknown to these unequestrian races. The bravest tribes prefer the stabbing-spear, which brings them to close quarters with the enemy. The weapon indeed can not make the man, but by reaction it greatly modifies his manliness. Thus the use of short weapons generally denotes a gallant nation; the old Roman gladius, the French briquet, and the Afghan charay would be useless in the hands of a timid people. Under the impression that the farther men stand from their enemies the less is to be expected from them, the French knights not inaptly termed the "villainous saltpetre" the "grave of honor," while their English rivals called the gun a "hell-born murderer," and an "instrument hateful in the sight of God and man." The Africans have also acted upon this idea. A great Kafir chief did what Plutarch relates of Camillus: he broke short the assegais of his "magnificent savages" when he sent them to war, and forbade each warrior to return without having stained his stick with blood: the consequence was that, instead of "dumb-shooting" at a distance, they rushed in and won.

The mkuki, farárá, or spear, is more generally used for stabbing than throwing. It has a long narrow blade of untempered iron, so soft that it may be bent with the fingers; it is capable, however, of receiving a fine edge. The shoulders are rounded off, and one or two lines extend lengthwise along the centre from socket to point. At the socket where the shaft is introduced, it is covered with a bit of skin from the tail of some animal drawn on like a stocking, and sometimes the iron is forced on when heated, so as to adhere by contraction of the metal. The shaft, which is five to six feet long, is a branch of the dark-brown mkole or the light-yellow mtata-tree, chosen because close-grained, tough, pliable, and free from knots; it is peeled, straightened in hot ashes, pared down to the heart, smoothed with a knife, carefully oiled or greased, without which it soon becomes brittle, and polished with the leaves of the mkuba-tree. The wood is mostly ornamented with twists of brass and copper wire; it is sometimes plated with zinc or tin, and it is generally provided with an iron heel for planting in the ground. Some tribes—the northern Wagogo and their neighbors the Wamasai, for instance—have huge spear-heads like shovels, unfit for throwing. The best weapons for war are made in Karagwah.

The kikuki, assegai, or javelin, is much used by the Warori and other fighting tribes, who enter action with a sheaf of those weapons. Nowhere, however, did the East African appear possessed of the dexterity described by travelers among the southern races. The assegai resembles the spear in all points, except that the head is often barbed, and it is more lightly timbered; the shaft is rarely more than four feet in length, and it tapers to the thinness of a man's little finger. It is laid upon the palm of the right hand, and balanced with a vibratory motion till the point of equilibrium is found, when it is delivered with little exertion of the muscles beyond the run or spring, and as it leaves the hand it is directed by the forefinger and thumb. Sometimes, to obviate breaking, the assegai is made like the Indian "sang," wholly of iron.

The East African is a "good archère and a fayre." The cubit-high Armiger begins as soon as he can walk with miniature weapons, a cane bow and reed bird-bolts tipped with wood, to practice till perfect at gourds and pumpkins; he considers himself a man when he can boast of iron tips. With many races "pudor est nescire sagittas." The bravest, however, the Wamasai and the Wakwafi, the Warori and the Watuta, ignore the practice; with them,

> "No proof of manhood, none
> Of daring courage, is the bow;"

and the Somali abandons it to his midgan or servile. The bow in East Africa is invariably what is called a "self-bow," that is to say, made of a single piece, and backed weapons are unknown. It is uncommonly stiff, and the strongest archer would find it difficult to "draw up a yard;" of this nature probably was the bow sent to Cambyses by the Æthiopian monarch, with the taunting message that he had better not attack men who could bend such weapons. When straight it may measure five feet from tip to tip. It is made with the same care as the spear, from a branch of the mumepweke or the mtata-tree, laboriously cut and scraped so as to taper off toward the horns, and smeared with oil or grease, otherwise it is easily sprung, and it is sometimes adorned with plates of tin and zinc, with copper or brass wire and tips. The string is made of hide, gut, the tendons of a bullock's neck or hock, and sometimes of tree-fibre; it is nearly double the bow in length, the extra portion being whipped for strength as well as contingent use round the upper horn. In shooting the bow is grasped with the left hand, but the thumb is never extended along the back; the string is drawn with the two bent forefingers, though sometimes the shaft is held after the Asiatic fashion with the thumb and index. The bow is pulled with a jerk as among the Somal, and not let fly as by Europeans with a long steady loose. The best bows are made by the tribes near the Rufiji River.

The arrow is about two feet in length; the stele or shaft is made of some light wood, and often of reed. Its fault is want of weight: to inflict damage upon an antelope it must not be used beyond point-blank, fifteen to twenty paces: and a score will be shot into a bullock before it falls. The musketeer, despising the arrow at a distance, fears it at close quarters, knowing that for his one shot the archer can discharge a dozen. From the days of Franklin to the era of Silistria, Citate, and Kars, fancy tacticians have advocated the substitution of the bow or the addition of it to the "queen of weapons," the musket. Their reasons for a revival of the obsolete arm are its lightness, its rapidity of discharge, and its silent action. They forget, however, the saying of Xenophon, that it is impiety in a man who has not learned archery from his childhood to ask such boon of the easy gods.

The East Africans ignore the use of red-hot arrows; and the poisoned shaft, an unmanly weapon, unused by the English and French archers even in their deadliest wars, is confined to the Wanyika of Mombasah, the Wazaramo, the Wak'hutu, the Western Wasagara, and the people of Uruwwa. The Wazaramo and Wak'hutu call the plant from which the poison is extracted mkandekande. They sold at somewhat an exorbitant price a leaf full of the preparation, but avoided pointing out to the expedition the plant, which from their description appears to be a variety of euphorbia. M. Werne ("Sources of the White Nile," chap. viii.) says that the river tribe prepare their arrow-poison from a kind of asclepias, whose milky sap is pressed out between two stones and allowed to thicken. Dr. Livingstone (chap. viii.) mentions the use of the n'gwa caterpillar among the Bushmen, who also poison waters with the Euphorbia arborescens; and Mr. Andersson (chap. vii.) specifies the Euphorbia candelabrum among the Ovaherero and the Hill Damaras. In East Africa the poison-leaves are allowed to distill their juices into a pot, which for inspissation is placed over a slow fire; becoming thick and slab, the contents are applied with a stick to the arrow, and are smoothed between the hands. When finished, the part behind the barb is covered with a shiny brown-black coat, not unlike pitch, to the extent of four or five inches. After drying it is renewed by the application of a fresh layer, the old being removed by exposure to the fire. The people fear this poison greatly; they wash their hands after touching it, and declare that a wounded man or beast loses sense, "moons about," and comes to the ground before running a quarter of a mile. Much exaggeration, however, must be expected upon the subject of toxicology among barbarians: it acts like the Somali arrow-poison, as a strong narcotic, and is, probably, rarely fatal, even when freshly applied.

Fearing the action of the wind upon such light shafts if unfledged, the archer inserts into the cloven end three or four feathers, the cock-feather being, as in Europe, perpendicular when the ar-

row is nocked. The pile or iron head is curiously and cruelly
barbed with long waving tails; the neck is toothed and edged by
dinting the iron when hot with an axe, and it is sometimes half
sawed that it may break before extraction. The East Africans
also have forkers or two-headed shafts, and bird-bolts or blunt
arrows tipped with some hard wood, used when the weapon is
likely to be lost. Before loosing an arrow the archer throws into
the air a pinch of dust, not to find out the wind, but for good luck,
like the Tartars of Tibet before discharging their guns. In battle
the heavy-armed man holds his spear and a sheaf of spare arrows
in the bow-hand, while a quiver slung to the left side contains reserve missiles, and a little axe stuck in the right side of the girdle
is ready when the rest fail. The ronga or quiver is a bark case,
neatly cut and stained. It is of two forms, full length, and provided with a cover for poisoned, and half length for unpoisoned,
arrows.

The rungu or knobkerry is the African club or mace; it extends from the Cape to the negroid and the Somal tribes north of
the equator. The shape varies in almost every district; the head
is long or round, oval or irregular, and sometimes provided on one
side with an edge; it is cut out of the hardest wood, and generally
from one piece. In some cases the knob is added to the handle,
and in others it is supplied with a spear-head. The handle is
generally two feet long, and it is cut thin enough to make the
weapon top-heavy. The Mnyamwezi is rarely seen abroad without this weapon; he uses it in the chase, and in battle against
the archer: he seems to trust it in close quarters rather than the
feather-weight arrow or the spear that bends like gutta-percha,
and most murders are committed with it. The East people do
not, like the Kafirs, use the handle of the knobkerry as a dibble.

The sime or dudgeon is the make-shift for the Arab jambiyah
and the Persian khanjar. The form of this weapon differs in almost every tribe. The Wahumba or Wamasai use blades about
four feet long by two fingers in breadth; the long, round, and
guardless hilt is ribbed for security of grasp, and covered with
leather; their iron is of excellent quality, and the shape of the
weapon has given rise to the report that "they make swords on
the model of those of the Knights Templars." The Wazegura
and the Wagogo use knives not unlike the poniard of the Somal.
In some tribes it is 3.5 feet long, with a leathern sheath extending half way up the blade. Generally it is about half that size,
straight, pointed, and double-edged, or jagged with teeth. The
regions about the lake manufacture and export great numbers of
these weapons, varying from a finger's length to full dimensions.

The shoka or battle-axe is much used by the tribes around the
Tanganyika. It has a blade of triangular shape, somewhat longer
and thinner than that used as a working-tool, which is passed
through the bulging head of a short handle cut out of the bau-

hinia or some other hard tree. Among the Wasagara the peculiar mundu or bill often serves for the same purpose.

The targes of the Wasagara and the Wanyamwezi have already been described; the Wavinza make a shield of basket-work six feet by two, and much resembling that of the southern Kafirs, and the Wa'ungu carry large pavoises of bull's hide. It is probable that the exceeding humidity of the climate, so ruinous to leather, prevents the general adoption of the shield; on the march it is merely an encumbrance, and the warrior must carry it on his head beyond the reach of the dewy grass.

The maritime races, the Wazegura and others opposite the Island of Zanzibar, have been imprudently allowed to purchase fire-arms, which they employ in obstructing caravans and in kidnapping-commandos against their weaker neighbors. A single German house has, it is said, sold off 13,000 Tower-muskets in one year. The arms now preferred are those exported by Hamburg and America; they fetch 4 dollars each; the French single-barrel is somewhat cheaper, averaging 3 dollars 50 cents. In the interior fire-arms are still fortunately rare—the Arabs are too wise to arm the barbarians against themselves. In Unyamwezi an old gun is a present for a chief, and the most powerful rulers seldom can boast of more than three. Gunpowder is imported from Zanzibar in kegs of 10 and 25 lbs., bearing the American mark; it is of the description used in blasting, and fouls the piece after a few discharges. The price varies at Zanzibar from 3 dollars 50 cents to 7 dollars, and upon the coast from 5 to 10 dollars per small keg; in Unyamwezi ammunition is exchanged for ivory and slaves, and some Arab merchants keep as many as thirty kegs in the house, which they retail to factors and traders at the rate of 1-to 2 shukkahs per lb.

Swords in East Africa are used only by strangers. The Wasawahili and the slave-factors prefer the kittareh, a curved sabre made in Oman and Hazramaut, or, in its stead, an old German cavalry-blade. The Arabs carry as a distinction the "faranji," a straight, thin, double-edged, guardless, and two-handed sword, about four feet long, and sharp as a carving-knife; the price varies from 10 to 100 dollars.

The negroid is an unmechanical race; his industry has scarcely passed the limits of savage invention. Though cotton abounds in the interior, the Wanyamwezi only have attempted a rude loom; and the working of iron and copper is confined to the Wafyoma and the lakist races. The gourd is still the principal succedaneum for pottery. The other branches of industry which are necessary to all barbarians are mats and baskets, ropes and cords.

Carpentering among the East Africans is still in its rudest stage; no Dædalus has yet taught them to jag their knives into saws. It is limited to making the cots and cartels upon which the people invariably sleep, and to carving canoes, mortars, bowls, rude platters, spoons, stools, and similar articles of furniture. The tree, after being rung and barked to dry the juices, is felled by fire or the axe; it is then cut up into lengths of the required dimensions, and hacked into shape with slow and painful toil. The tools are a shoka, or hatchet of puerile dimensions, perhaps one fifth the size of our broad-axes, yet the people can use it to better advantage than the admirable implement of the backwoodsman. The mbizo or adze is also known in the interior, but none except the fundi and the slaves trained upon the coast have ever seen a hand-saw, a centre-bit, or a chisel.

Previous to weaving, cotton is picked and cleaned with the hand; it is then spun into a coarse thread. Like the Paharis of India, the East Africans ignore the distaff; they twist the material round the left wrist. The mlavi, or spindle, is of two forms; one is a short stick, inserted in a hole practiced through a lump of lead or burnt clay, like the Indian bhaunri; the other is a thin bit of wood, about 1.5 ft. long, with a crescent of the same material on the top, and an iron hook to hold the thread. The utanda, or loom-frame, differs from the vertical-shaped article of West Africa. Two side-poles about twelve feet long, and supported at the corners by four uprights, are placed at an angle, enabling the workman to stand to his work; and the oblong is completed by two cross-bars, round which the double line of the warp, or longitudinal threads of the woven tissue are secured. The dimensions of the web vary from five to six feet in length, by two to three broad. The weft, or transverse thread, is shot with two or three thin laths, or spindles, round which the white and colored yarns are wound through the doubled warp, which is kept apart by another lath passing between the two layers, and the spindle is caught with the left hand as it appears at the left side. Lastly, a lath, broader and flatter than the others, is used to close the work and to beat the thread home. As the workman deems three hours per diem ample labor, a cloth will rarely be finished under a week. Taste is shown in the choice of patterns: they are sometimes checks with squares, alternately black and white, or in stripes of black variegated with red dyes upon a white ground: the lines are generally broad in the centre, but narrow along the edges, and the texture not a little resembles our sacking. The dark color is obtained from the juice of the mzima-tree; it stains the yarn to a dull brown, which becomes a dark mulberry, or an Indian-ink black, when buried for two or three days in the vegetable mud of the ponds and pools. The madder-red is produced by boiling the root and bark of a bush called mda'a; an ochrish tint is also extracted from the crimson matter that stains the cane and the leaves of red holcus. All cloths have the tambua or fringe, indispensable in East Africa. Both weaving and dyeing are men's not women's work in these lands.

The cloth is a poor article: like the people of Ashanti, who from time immemorial have woven their own cottons, the East African ever prefers foreign fabrics. The loose texture of his own produce admits wind and rain; when dry it is rough and unpleasant, when wet, heavy, comfortless as leather, and it can not look clean, as it is never bleached. According to the Arabs, the yarn is often dipped into a starch made from grain, for the purpose of thickening the appearance of the texture: this disappears after the first washing, and the cloth must be pegged down to prevent its shrinking to half size. The relative proportion of warp and weft is unknown, and the woolly, fuzzy quality of the half-wild cotton now in use impoverishes the fabric. Despite the labor expended upon these cloths, the largest size may be purchased for six feet of American domestics, or for a pair of iron hoes: there is therefore little inducement to extend the manufacture.

Iron is picked up in the state called utundwe, or gangue, from the sides of low sandstone hills: in places the people dig pits from two to four feet deep, and, according to the Arabs, they find tears, nodules, and rounded lumps. The pisolithic iron, common in the maritime regions, is not worked. The mhesi or blacksmith's art is still in its infancy. The iron-stone is carried to the smithy, an open shed, where the work is done: the smelting-furnace is a hole in the ground filled with lighted charcoal, upon which the utundwe is placed, and, covered with another layer of fire, it is allowed to run through the fuel. The blast is produced by mafukutu (bellows): they are two roughly-rounded troughs, about three inches deep by six in diameter, hewn out of a single bit of wood and prolonged into a pair of parallel branches, pierced for the passage of the wind through two apertures in the walls of the troughs. The troughs are covered with skin, to which are fixed two long projecting sticks for handles, which may be worked by a man sitting. A stone is placed upon the bellows for steadiness, and clay nozzles, or holcus-canes with a lateral hole, are fixed on to the branches to prevent them from charring. Sometimes as many as five pairs are worked at once, and great is the rapidity required to secure a continuous outdraught. Mr. Andersson ("Lake Ngami," chap. xvi.) gives a sketch of a similar contrivance among the South Africans: the clay tubes, however, are somewhat larger than those used in Unyamwezi by "blacksmiths at work." The ore is melted and remelted several times, till pure; tempering and case-hardening are unknown, and it is stored for use by being cast in clay moulds, or made up into hoes. The hammer and anvil are generally smooth stones. The principal articles of ironmongery are spears, assegais, and arrow-heads, battle-axes, hatchets, and adzes, knives and daggers, sickles and razors, rings and sambo, or wire circlets. The kinda is a large bell hung by the ivory-porter to his tusk on the line of the march; the kengere or kiugi, a smaller variety which he fastens to his legs. Pipes, with iron bowls and stems, are made by the more ingenious, and the smoker manufactures for himself small pincers or pliers, which, curious to say, are unknown even by name to the more civilized people of Zanzibar.

Copper is not found upon this line in East Africa. From the country of the Kazembe, however, an excellent red and heavy, soft and bright variety, not unlike that of Japan, finds its way to Ujiji, and sometimes to the coast. It is sold in bars from one to two feet long. At Ujiji, where it is cheap, four to five pounds are procurable for two doti, there worth about four dollars. Native copper, therefore, is almost as expensive as that imported from Europe. It is used in making the rude and clumsy bangles affected by both sexes, sambo, and ornaments for the spear and bow, the staff and the knobkerry.

The art of ceramics has made but little progress in East Africa; no Anacharsis has yet arisen to teach her sons the use of the

Gourds.

wheel. The figuline, a grayish-brown clay, is procured from river-beds, or is dug up in the country; it is subjected to the preliminary operations of pounding, rubbing dry upon a stone, pulverizing, and purifying from stones and pebbles. It is then worked into a thick mass with water, and the potter fashions it with the hand, first shaping the mouth; he adds an inch to it when dry, hardens it in the sun, makes another addition, and thus proceeds till it is finished. Lines and other ornaments having been traced, the pots are baked in piles of seven or eight by burning grass—wood-fire would crack them—consequently the material always remains half raw. Usually the color becomes lamp-black; in Usagara, however, the potter's clay turns red, like the soil—the effect of iron. A cunning workman will make in a day four of these pots, some of them containing several gallons, and their perfect regularity of form, and often their picturesqueness of shape, surprise the stranger. The best are made in Ujiji, Karagwah, and Ugunda: those of Unyamwezi are inferior, and the clay of Zanzibar is of all the worst.

There are many kinds of pots which not a little resemble the glazed jars of ancient Egypt. The ukango, which acts as vat in fermenting liquor, is of the greatest dimensions. The mtungi is a large water-vessel with a short and narrow neck, and rounded at the bottom so as to be conveniently carried on the head. The chungu, or cooking-pot, has a wide and open mouth; it is of several varieties, large and small. The mkungu is a shallow bowl, precisely like those made at the tomb of Moses, and now familiar to Europe. At Ujiji and on the lake they also manufacture smaller vessels, with and without spouts.

In a country where pottery is scarce and dear, the buyu or Cucurbita lagenaria supplies every utensil except those used for cooking; its many and various adaptations render it a valuable production. The people train it to grow in the most fantastic shapes, and ornament it by tatooing with dark paint, and by patterns worked in brass tacks and wires; where it splits it is artistically sewn together. The larger kinds serve as well-buckets, water-pots, traveling-canteens, churns, and the sounding-boards of musical instruments: a hookah, or water-pipe, is made by distorting the neck, and the smaller varieties are converted into snuff-boxes, medicine-cases, and unguent-pots. The fruit of the calabash-tree is also called buyu: split and dried, it is used as ladles, but it is too small to answer all the purposes of the gourd.

The East Africans excel in the manufacture of mtemba or bori —pipe-heads. These are of two kinds. One is made from a soft stone, probably steatite, found in Usonga, near Utumbara, and on the road to Karagwah: it is, however, rare, and about ten times the price of the clay bowls, because less liable to break. The other is made of a plastic or pipe clay, too brittle to serve for pots, and it invariably cracks at the shank unless bound with wire. Both are hand-made, and are burned in the same rough way as the pottery. At Msene, where the clay pipe is cheapest, the price of the bowl is a khete, or double string of white or blue beads. The pipe of Unyamwezi is of graceful shape, a cone with the apex downward; this leaves but little of the hot, oily, and high-smelling tobacco at the bottom, whereas in Europe the contrary seems to be the rule. In Ujiji the bowl is small, rounded, and shallow; it is, moreover, very brittle. The most artful "mtemba" is made by the people of Uvira: black inside, like other pottery, its exterior is colored a grayish white, and is adorned with red by means of the Indian geru (colcothar or crocus martis). Bhang is always, and tobacco is sometimes, smoked in a water-pipe; the bowl is of huge size, capable of containing at least half a pound, and its upper half is made to incline toward the smoker's face. The lakist tribes have a graceful variety, like the Indian "chillam," very different from the awkward, unwieldy, and distorted article now fashionable in Unyamwezi and the Eastern countries. The usual pipe-stem is a tube of about 1.5 feet long, generally a hollow twig of the dwarf melewele-tree. As it is rudely bored with hot wire, it must be made air-tight by wax and a coating of brass or copper wire; a strap of hairy skin prevents the pipe-shank parting from the stick. Iron and brass tubes are rare and highly prized; the fortunate possessor will sometimes ask for a single specimen two shukkahs.

Basket-making and mat-weaving are favorite occupations in East Africa for both sexes and all ages; even the Arabs may frequently be seen absorbed in an employment which in Oman would be considered derogatory to manliness. The sengo, or common basket, from the coast to the lake, is an open, shallow, and pan-shaped article, generally made of mwanzi, or bamboo-bark, reddened in parts and stained black in others by the root of the mkuruti and other trees, and white where the outer coat has been removed from the bamboo. The body, which resembles a popular article in ancient Egypt, is neatly plaited, and the upper ends are secured to a stout hoop of the same material. The kanda (in the plural makanda) acts in the interior as matting for rooms, and is converted into bags for covering bales of cloth, beads, and similar articles. It is made from the myara (myala) or Chamærops humilis; the leaf is peeled, sun-dried, and split with a bit of iron into five or six lengths, joined at the base, which is trimmed for plaiting. The karagwah, the only mat made in the interior of Africa, is used as bedding and carpeting; on journeys the porters bivouac under it; it swells with the wet, and soon becomes impervious to rain or heavy dew. It is of two kinds; one of rushes growing in the vicinity of water, the other of grass rolled up into little bundles. A complicated stitch runs along the whole length in double lines. The best description of mat is called mkeke. It is made at Zanzibar and the coast, from the young fronds of the ukhindu or brab, neatly stained with various dyes. Women of family pride themselves upon their skill in making the mkeke, which still attains a price of four dollars. Among the maritime races none but the chiefs have a right to sit upon it; there are no such distinctions in the interior, where these mats are carried for sale by the slaves. From the brab also are made neat strainers to purify honey, pombe, and similar articles. They are open-mouthed cylinders, from one to two feet long, and varying in diameter from three to six inches. The bottom is narrowed by whipping fibre round the loose ends of the leaves. The fishing-nets have been described when treating of the Tanganyika. The luávo or hand-net is made of calabash or other fibre, with coarse wide meshes; it is affixed to two sticks firmly planted in the ground, and small animals are driven into it by beaters.

The basts or barks and fibrous substances in East Africa are cheap and abundant, but labor and conveyance being difficult and expensive, they would require to be shipped from Zanzibar in the condition of half-stuff. The best and most easily divisible into pliant and knot-tying fibres are, upon the coast the pine-apple, and in the interior the plantain. The next in value are the integuments of the calabash and the myombo-tree. These fibres would produce a good article were it not for the artlessness of African manipulation. The bark is pounded or chewed, and, in lieu of spinning, is twisted between the hands; the largest ropes are made in half an hour, and break after a few minutes of hard work. A fine silky twine, used for fishing, is made from the aloetic plants called by the Wasawahili mkonge, and by the Arabs bag, masad, and kideh: it is the hig or haskul of Somaliland, where it affects the poorest ground, can not be burnt down, and is impassable to naked legs and cattle. The leaves are stripped of their coats, and the ends being tightly bound between two pieces of wood, the mass of fibre is drawn out like a sword from its sheath. Fatilah, or matchlock matches, are made in Zanzibar of cotton, and in the interior of calabash-fibre.

As might be expected among a sparse population leading a comparatively simple life, the vast variety of diseases which afflict more civilized races, who are collected in narrow spaces, are unknown in East Africa, even by name. Its principal sporadic is fever, remittent and intermittent, with its multitudinous secondaries, concerning which notices have been scattered through the preceding pages. The most dangerous epidemic is its aborigen, the small-pox, which, propagated without contact or fomites, sweeps at times like a storm of death over the land. For years it has not left the Arab colony at Kazeh, and, shortly before the arrival of the expedition, in a single month 52 slaves died out of a total of 800. The ravages of this disease among the half-starved and over-worked gangs of caravan-porters have already been described; as many as a score of these wretches have been seen at a time in a single caravan; men staggering along blinded and almost insensible, jostling and stumbling against every one in their way; and mothers carrying babes, both parent and progeny in the virulent stage of the fell disease. The Arabs have partially introduced the practice of inoculating, anciently known in South Africa; the pus is introduced into an incision in the forehead between the eyebrows. The people have no remedy for small-pox: they trust entirely to the vis medicatrix. There is a milder form of the malady, called shúrúá, resembling the chicken-pox of Europe; it is cured by bathing in cold water and smearing the body with ochrish earth. The Arab merchants of Unyanyembe declare that, when they first visited Karagwah, the people were decimated by the táún, or plague. They describe correctly the bubo under the axillæ, the torturing thirst, and the rapid fatality of the disease. In the early part of 1859 a violent attack of cholera, which extended from Maskat along the eastern coast of Arabia and Africa, committed terrible ravages in the Island of Zanzibar and throughout the maritime regions. Of course no precautions of quarantine or cordon militaire were taken, yet the contagion did not extend into the interior.

Strangers in East Africa suffer from dysenteries and similar disorders consequent upon fever; and, as in Egypt, few are free from hemorrhoids, which in Unyamwezi are accompanied by severe colics and umbilical pains. Rheumatism and rheumatic fever, severe catarrhs and influenzas, are caused by the cold winds, and, when crossing the higher altitudes, pneumonia and pleuritis abound in the caravan. On the coast many settlers, Indian and Arab, show upon the skin whitish leprous spots, which are treated with various unguents. In the interior, though well provided with fresh meat and vegetables, travelers are attacked by scurvy, even in the absence of its normal exciting causes, damp, cold, and poor diet. This phenomenon has often been observed upon the upper course of the Nile; Europeans have been prostrated by it even in the dry regions westward of the Red Sea, and the Portuguese officers who explored Usenda of the Kazembe suffered tortures from the complaint.

Common diseases among the natives are umbilical hernia and prolapsus: the latter is treated by the application of powdered bhang, dry or mixed with ghee. They are subject to kihindu-hindu—in Arabic, sara—the epilepsy, which they pretend to cure by the marrow of rhinoceros' shank. Of the many fits and convulsions which affect them, the kichyoma-chyoma is the most dreaded. The word, which means the "little irons," describes the painful sensations, the cramps and stitches, the spasms and lancinations, which torment the sufferer. Many die of this disease. It is not extraordinary that the fits, convulsions, and contortions which it suddenly induces, should lead the people to consider it in the light of possession, and the magician to treat it with charms. Madness and idiocy are not uncommon: of the patient it is said, "Ana wazimo"—"he has fiends." In most parts the people, after middle age, are tender-eyed from the effects of smoke within, glare without, exposure and debauchery. Not a few samples of acute ophthalmic disease were seen.

In the lower and more malarious spots, desquamations, tumors, and skin diseases, are caused by suddenly suppressed perspiration. The terrible kidonda or helcoma of the maritime regions and the prurigo of Ujiji have already been alluded to. The "chokea" is a hordeolum or large boil, generally upon the upper eyelid. The "funza" is supposed to result from the bite of a large variety of fly. It begins with a small red and fiery swelling, which bursts after a time and produces a white entozoon about half an inch in length. "Kumri" are common blains, and "p'hambazi" malignant blind boils, which leave a deep discolored scar; when the parts affected are distant from the seat of circulation, the use of the limb is sometimes lost. For most of these sores, tutiya or murtutu, blue-stone, is considered a specific.

As might be expected among an ignorant and debauched race coming in direct contact with semi-civilization, the lues has found its way from the Island of Zanzibar to Ujiji, and into the heart of Africa. It is universally believed both by the natives and by the

Arabs, who support the assertion with a host of proofs, to be propagated without contact. Such, indeed, is the general opinion of the Eastern world, where perhaps its greater virulence may assimilate it to the type of the earlier attacks in Europe. The disease, however, dies out, and has not taken root in the people as among the devoted races of North America and the South Sea Islands. Although a malignant form was found extending throughout the country, mutilation of the features and similar secondaries were not observed beyond the maritime region. Except bluestone, mineral drugs are unknown, and the use of mercury and ptyalism have not yet exasperated the evil. The minor form of lues is little feared, and yields readily to simples; the consequences, however, are strangury, cystitis, chronic nephritic disease, and rheumatism.

"Polypharmacy" is not the fault of the profession in East Africa, and the universal belief in possession tends greatly to simplify the methodus modendi. The usual cathartic is the bark of a tree called kalákalá, which is boiled in porridge. There is a great variety of emetics, some so violent, that several Arabs who have been bold enough to swallow them barely escaped with life. The actual cautery—usually a favorite counter-irritant among barbarous people—is rarely practiced in East Africa; in its stead, powder of blue-stone is applied to the sore or wound, which has been carefully scraped, and the patient howls with pain for twenty-four hours. They bleed frequently as Italians, who even after being startled resort to a mild phlebotomy, and they cut down straight upon the vein with a sharp knife. They prefer the cucurbitula cruenta, like the Arabs, who say,

> "Few that cup repent;
> Few that bleed rejoice."

A favorite place is the crown of the head. The practitioner, after scarifying the skin with a razor or a dagger, produces a vacuum by exhausting the air through a horn applied with wetted edges; at the point is a bit of wax, which he closes over the aperture with his tongue or teeth, as the hospital "singhi" in India uses a bit of leather. Cupping—called ku hu míká or kumíká—is made highly profitable by showing strange appearances in the blood. They cure by excision the bite of snakes, which, however, are not feared nor often fatal in these lands. They can not reduce dislocations, and they never attempt to set or splint a broken bone.

The mganga or medicine-man, in his character of "doctor," is a personage of importance. He enters the sick-room in the dignity of antelope-horn, grease, and shell necklace, and he sits with importance upon his three-legged stool. As the devil saves him the trouble of diagnosis, he begins by a prescription, invariably ordering something edible for the purpose, and varying it according to the patient's means, from a measure of grain to a bullock. He asserts, for instance, that a pound of fat is required for medicine; a goat must be killed, and his perquisite is the head or breast—a preliminary to a more important fee. Then the price of prescription—a *sine quâ non* to prescribing—is settled upon and paid in advance. After certain questions, invariably suggesting the presence of poison, the medical practitioner proceeds to the cure; this is generally a charm or periapt bound round the part affected. In common diseases, however, like fever, the mganga will condescend to such profane processes as adhibiting sternutatories and rubbing the head with vegetable powders. If the remedies prove too powerful or powerless, he at once decamps; under normal circumstances, he incapacitates himself for performing his promise of calling the next day by expending his fee in liquor. The Africans have in one point progressed beyond Europeans: there are as many women physicians as men.

A Mnyamwezi.   A Mheha.

CHAPTER XIX.

THE CHARACTER AND RELIGION OF THE EAST AFRICANS; THEIR GOVERNMENT, AND SLAVERY.

THE study of psychology in Eastern Africa is the study of man's rudimental mind, when, subject to the agency of material nature, he neither progresses nor retrogrades. He would appear rather a degeneracy from the civilized man than a savage rising to the first step, were it not for his apparent incapacity for improvement. He has not the ring of the true metal; there is no rich nature, as in the New Zealander, for education to cultivate. He seems to belong to one of those childish races which, never rising to man's estate, fall like worn-out links from the great chain of animated nature. He unites the incapacity of infancy with the unpliancy of age; the futility of childhood, and the credulity of youth, with the skepticism of the adult and the stubbornness and bigotry of the old. He has "beaten lands" and seas. For centuries he has been in direct intercourse with the more advanced people of the eastern coast, and though few have seen a European, there are not many who have not cast eyes upon an Arab. Still he has stopped short at the threshold of progress; he shows no signs of development; no higher and more varied orders of intellect are called into being. Even the simple truths of El Islam have failed to fix the thoughts of men who can think, but who, absorbed in providing for their bodily wants, hate the trouble of thinking. His mind, limited to the object seen, heard, and felt, will not, and apparently can not, escape from the circle of sense, nor will it occupy itself with aught but the present. Thus he is cut off from the pleasures of memory, and the world of fancy is altogether unknown to him. Perhaps the automaton which we call spiritual suffers from the inferiority of the mechanism by which it acts.

The East African is, like other barbarians, a strange mixture of good and evil: by the nature of barbarous society, however, the good element has not, while the evil has, been carefully cultured.

As a rule, the civilized or highest type of man owns the sway of intellect, of reason; the semi-civilized—as are still the great nations of the East—are guided by sentiment and propensity in a degree incomprehensible to the more advanced races; and the barbarian is the slave of impulse, passion, and instinct, faintly modified by sentiment, but ignorant of intellectual discipline. He appears, therefore, to the civilized man a paralogic being—a mere mass of contradictions; his ways are not our ways, his reason is not our reason. He deduces effects from causes which we ignore; he compasses his ends by contrivances which we can not comprehend; and his artifices and polity excite, by their shallowness and "inconsequence," our surprise and contempt. Like that Hindoo race that has puzzled the plain-witted Englishman for the century closing with the massacres of Delhi and Cawnpore, he is calculated to perplex those who make conscience an instinct which elevates man to the highest ground of human intelligence. He is at once very good-tempered and hard-hearted, combative and cautious; kind at one moment, cruel, pitiless, and violent at another; sociable and unaffectionate; superstitious and grossly irreverent; brave and cowardly, servile and oppressive; obstinate, yet fickle and fond of changes; with points of honor, but without a trace of honesty in word or deed; a lover of life, though addicted to suicide; covetous and parsimonious, yet thoughtless and improvident; somewhat conscious of inferiority, withal unimprovable. In fact, he appears an embryo of the two superior races. He is inferior to the active-minded and objective, the analytic and perceptive European, and to the ideal and subjective, the synthetic and reflective Asiatic. He partakes largely of the worst characteristics of the lower Oriental types—stagnation of mind, indolence of body, moral deficiency, superstition, and childish passion; hence the Egyptians aptly termed the Berbers and negroes the "perverse race of Kush."

The main characteristic of this people is the selfishness which the civilized man strives to conceal, because publishing it would obstruct its gratification. The barbarian, on the other hand, displays his inordinate egotism openly and recklessly; his every action discloses those unworthy traits which in more polished races chiefly appear on public occasions, when each man thinks solely of self-gratification. Gratitude with him is not even a sense of prospective favors; he looks upon a benefit as the weakness of his benefactor and his own strength; consequently he will not recognize even the hand that feeds him. He will, perhaps, lament for a night the death of a parent or a child, but the morrow will find him thoroughly comforted. The name of hospitality, except for interested motives, is unknown to him: "What will you give me?" is his first question. To a stranger entering a village the worst hut is assigned, and, if he complain, the answer is that he can find encamping-ground outside. Instead of treating him like a guest, which the Arab Bedouin would hold to be a point of pride, of honor, his host compels him to pay and prepay every article, otherwise he might starve in the midst of plenty. Nothing, in fact, renders the stranger's life safe in this land except the timid shrinking of the natives from the "hot-mouthed weapon" and the necessity of trade, which induces the chiefs to restrain the atrocities of their subjects. To travelers the African is, of course, less civil than to merchants, from whom he expects to gain something. He will refuse a mouthful of water out of his abundance to a man dying of thirst; utterly unsympathizing, he will not stretch out a hand to save another's goods, though worth thousands of dollars. Of his own property, if a ragged cloth or a lame slave be lost, his violent excitement is ridiculous to behold. His egotism renders him parsimonious even in self-gratification; the wretched curs, which he loves as much as his children, seldom receive a mouthful of food, and the sight of an Arab's ass feeding on grain elicits a prolonged "Hi! hi!" of extreme surprise. He is exceedingly improvident, taking no thought for the morrow—not from faith, but rather from carelessness as to what may betide him; yet so greedy of gain is he that he will refuse information about a country or the direction of a path without a present of beads. He also invariably demands prepayment: no one keeps a promise or adheres to an agreement, and, if credit be demanded for an hour, his answer would be, "There is nothing in my hand." Yet even greed of gain can not overcome the levity and laxity of his mind. Despite his best interests, he will indulge the mania for desertion caused by that mischievous love of change and whimsical desire for novelty that characterize the European sailor. Nor can even lucre prevail against the ingrained indolence of the race—an indolence the more hopeless as it is the growth of the climate. In these temperate and abundant lands nature has cursed mankind with the abundance of her gifts; his wants still await creation, and he is contented with such necessaries as roots and herbs, game, and a few handfuls of grain—consequently improvement has no hold upon him.

In this stage of society truth is no virtue. The "mixture of a lie" may "add to pleasure" among Europeans; in Africa it enters where neither pleasure nor profit can arise from the deception. If a Mnyamwezi guide informs the traveler that the stage is short he may make up his mind for a long and weary march, and *vice versâ*. Of course, falsehood is used as a defense by the weak and oppressed; but beyond that, the African desires to be lied to, and one of his proverbs is, "'Tis better to be deceived than to be undeceived." The European thus qualifies the assertion,

> " For sure the pleasure is as great
> In being cheated as to cheat."

Like the generality of barbarous races, the East Africans are willful, headstrong, and undisciplinable: in point of stubbornness and restiveness they resemble the lower animals. If they can not obtain the very article of barter upon which they have set their mind, they will carry home things useless to them; any attempt at bargaining is settled by the seller turning his back, and they ask according to their wants and wishes, without regard to the value of goods. Grumbling and dissatisfied, they never do business without a grievance. Revenge is a ruling passion, as the many rancorous fratricidal wars that have prevailed between kindred clans, even for a generation, prove. Retaliation and vengeance are, in fact, their great agents of moral control. Judged by the test of death, the East African is a hard-hearted man, who seems to ignore all the charities of father, son, and brother. A tear is rarely shed, except by the women, for departed parent, relative, or friend, and the voice of the mourner is seldom heard in their abodes. It is most painful to witness the complete inhumanity with which a porter seized with small-pox is allowed by his friends, comrades, and brethren to fall behind in the jungle, with several days' life in him. No inducement—even beads—can persuade a soul to attend him. Every village will drive him from its doors; no one will risk taking, at any price, death into his bosom. If strong enough, the sufferer builds a little bough-hut away from the camp, and, provided with his rations—a pound of grain and a gourdful of water—he quietly expects his doom, to feed the hyena and the raven of the wild. The people are remarkable for the readiness with which they yield to fits of sudden fury; on these occasions they will, like children, vent their rage upon any object, animate or inanimate, that presents itself. Their temper is characterized by a nervous, futile impatience; under delay or disappointment they become madmen. In their own country, where such displays are safe, they are remarkable for a presumptuousness and a violence of manner which elsewhere disappears. As the Arabs say, there they are lions, here they become curs. Their squabbling and clamor pass description: they are never happy except when in dispute. After a rapid plunge into excitement, the brawlers alternately advance and recede, pointing the finger of threat, howling and screaming, cursing and using terms of insult which an inferior ingenuity—not want of will—causes to fall short of the Asiatic's model vituperation. After abusing each other to their full, both "parties" usually burst into a loud laugh or a burst of sobs. Their tears lie high; they weep like Goanese. After a cuff, a man will cover his face with his hands and cry as if his heart would break. More furious shrews than the women are nowhere met with. Here it is a great truth that "the tongues of women can not be governed." They work off excitement by scolding, and they weep little compared with the men. Both sexes delight in "argument," which here, as elsewhere, means two fools talking foolishly. They will weary out of patience the most loquacious of the Arabs. This development is characteristic of the East African race, and "Maneno marefu!"—long words!—will occur as a useless reproof half a dozen times in the course of a single conversation. When drunk, the East African is easily irritated; with the screams and excited gestures of a maniac he strides about, frantically flourishing his spear and agitating his bow, probably with notched arrow; the spear-point and the arrow-head are often brought perilously near, but rarely allowed to draw blood. The real combat is by pushing, pulling hair, and slapping with a will, and a pair thus engaged require to be torn asunder by half a dozen friends. The settled tribes are, for the most part, feeble and unwarlike barbarians; even the bravest East African, though, like all men, a combative entity, has a valor tempered by discretion and cooled by a high development of cautiousness. His tactics are of the Fabian order: he loves surprises and safe ambuscades; and in common frays and forays the loss of one per cent. justifies a *sauve qui peut.* This people, childlike, is ever in extremes. A man will hang himself from a rafter in his tent, and kick away from under him the large wooden mortar upon which he has stood at the beginning of the operation with as much sang-froid as an Anglo-Saxon in the gloomy month of November: yet he regards annihilation, as all savages do, with loathing and ineffable horror. "He fears death," to quote Bacon, "as children fear to go in the dark; and as that natural fear in children is increased with tales, so is the other." The African mind must change radically before it can "think upon death, and find it the least of all evils." All the thoughts of these negroids are connected with this life. "Ah!" they exclaim, "it is bad to die! to leave off eating and drinking! never to wear a fine cloth!" As in the negro race generally, their destructiveness is prominent; a slave never breaks a thing without an instinctive laugh of pleasure; and however careful he may be of his own life, he does not value that of another, even of a relative, at the price of a goat. During fires in the town of Zanzibar, the blacks have been seen adding fuel, and singing and dancing, wild with delight. On such occasions they are shot down by the Arabs like dogs.

It is difficult to explain the state of society in which the civilized "social evil" is not recognized as an evil. In the economy of the affections and the intercourse between the sexes, reappears that rude stage of society in which ethics were new to the mind of now enlightened man. Marriage with this people—as among all barbarians, and even the lower classes of civilized races—is a mere affair of buying and selling. A man must marry because it is necessary to his comfort, consequently the woman becomes a marketable commodity. Her father demands for her as many cows, cloths, and brass-wire bracelets as the suitor can afford; he thus virtually sells her, and she belongs to the buyer, ranking with his other live-stock. The husband may sell his wife, or, if she be taken from him by another man, he claims her value, which is ruled by what she would fetch in the slave-market. A strong inducement to marriage among the Africans, as with the poor in Europe, is the prospective benefit to be derived from an adult family; a large progeny enriches them. The African— like all barbarians, and, indeed, semi-civilized people—ignores the dowry by which, inverting Nature's order, the wife buys the husband, instead of the husband buying the wife. Marriage, which is an epoch among Christians, and an event with Moslems, is with these people an incident of frequent recurrence. Polygamy is unlimited, and the chiefs pride themselves upon the number of their wives, varying from twelve to three hundred. It is no disgrace for an unmarried woman to become the mother of a family; after matrimony there is somewhat less laxity. The mgoni or adulterer, if detected, is punishable by a fine of cattle, or, if poor and weak, he is sold into slavery; husbands seldom, however, resort to such severities, the offense, which is considered to be against vested property, being held to be lighter than petty larceny. Under the influence of jealousy, murders and mutilations have been committed, but they are rare and exceptional. Divorce is readily effected by turning the spouse out of doors, and the children become the father's property. Attachment to home is powerful in the African race, but it regards rather the comforts and pleasures of the house, and the unity of relations and friends, than the fondness of family. Husband, wife, and children have through life divided interests, and live together with scant appearance of affection. Love of offspring can have but little power among a people who have no preventive for illegitimacy, and whose progeny may be sold at any time. The children appear undemonstrative and unaffectionate, as those of the Somal. Some attachment to their mothers breaks out, not in outward indications, but by surprise, as it were: "Mámá! mámá!"—mother! mother!—is a common exclamation in fear or wonder. When childhood is passed, the father and son become natural enemies, after the manner of wild beasts. Yet they are a sociable race, and the sudden loss of relatives sometimes leads from grief to hypochondria and insanity, resulting from the inability of their minds to bear any unusual strain. It is probable that a little learning would make them mad, like the widad, or priest of the Somal, who, after mastering the reading of the Koran, becomes unfit for any exertion of judgment or common sense. To this over-development of sociability must be ascribed the anxiety always shown to shift, evade, or answer blame. The "ukosa," or transgression, is never accepted; any number of words will be wasted in proving the worse the better cause. Hence also the favorite phrase, " Mbáyá we!"—thou art bad!—a pet mode of reproof which sounds simple and uneffective to European ears.

The social position of the women—the unerring test of progress toward civilization—is not so high in East Africa as among the more highly organized tribes of the south. Few parts of the country own the rule of female chiefs. The people, especially the Wanyamwezi, consult their wives, but the opinion of a brother or a friend would usually prevail over that of a woman.

The deficiency of the East African in constructive power has already been remarked. Contented with his hay-stack or bee-hive hut, his hemisphere of boughs, or his hide acting tent, he hates and has a truly savage horror of stone walls. He has the conception of the " Madeleine," but he has never been enabled to be delivered of it. Many Wanyamwezi, when visiting Zanzibar, can not be prevailed upon to enter a house.

The East African is greedy and voracious; he seems, however, to prefer light and frequent to a few regular and copious meals. Even the civilized Kisawahili has no terms to express the breakfast, dinner, and supper of other languages. Like most barbarians, the East African can exist and work with a small quantity of food, but he is unaccustomed, and therefore unable, to bear thirst. The daily ration of a porter is 1 kubabah (=1.5 lbs.) of grain; he can, with the assistance of edible herbs and roots, which he is skillful in discovering in the least likely places, eke out this allowance for several days, though generally, upon the barbarian's impulsive principle of mortgaging the future for the present, he recklessly consumes his stores. With him the grand end of life is eating; his love of feeding is inferior only to his propensity for intoxication. He drinks till he can no longer stand, lies down to sleep, and awakes to drink again. Drinking-bouts are solemn things, to which the most important business must yield precedence. They celebrate with beer every event—the traveler's return, the birth of a child, and the death of an elephant—a laborer will not work unless beer is provided for him. A guest is received with a gourdful of beer, and, among some tribes, it is buried with their princes. The highest orders rejoice in drink, and pride themselves upon powers of imbibing: the proper diet for a king is much beer and a little meat. If a Mnyamwezi be asked after eating whether he is hungry, he will reply yea, meaning that he is not drunk. Intoxication excuses crime in these lands. The East African, when in his cups, must issue from his hut to sing, dance, or quarrel, and the frequent and terrible outrages which occur on these occasions are passed over on the plea that he has drunk beer. The favorite hour for drinking is after dawn—a time as distasteful to the European as agreeable to the African and Asiatic. This might be proved by a host of quotations from the poets, Arab, Persian, and Hindoo. The civilized man avoids early potations because they incapacitate him for necessary labor, and he attempts to relieve the headache caused by stimulants. The barbarian and the semi-civilized, on the other hand, prefer them, because they relieve the tedium of his monotonous day; and they cherish the headache because they can sleep the longer, and, when they awake, they have something to think of. The habit once acquired is never broken: it attaches itself to the heart-strings of the idle and unoccupied barbarian.

In morality, according to the more extended sense of the word, the East African is markedly deficient. He has no benevolence, but little veneration—the negro race is ever irreverent—and, though his cranium rises high in the region of firmness, his futility prevents his being firm. The outlines of law are faintly traced upon his heart. The authoritative standard of morality, fixed by a revelation, is in him represented by a vague and varying custom, derived traditionally from his ancestors; he follows in their track for old-sake's sake. The accusing conscience is unknown to him. His only fear after committing a treacherous murder is that of being haunted by the angry ghost of the dead; he robs as one doing a good deed, and he begs as if it were his calling. His depravity is of the grossest: intrigue fills up all the moments not devoted to intoxication.

The want of veneration produces a savage rudeness in the East African. The body politic consists of two great members, masters and slaves. Ignoring distinctions of society, he treats all men, except his chief, as his equals. He has no rules for visiting: if the door be open, he enters a stranger's house uninvited; his harsh, barking voice is ever the loudest; he is never happy except when hearing himself speak; his address is imperious, his demeanor is rough and peremptory, and his look "sfacciato." He deposits his unwashed person, in his greasy and tattered goatskin or cloth, upon rug or bedding, disdaining to stand for a moment, and he always chooses the best place in the room. When traveling he will push forward to secure the most comfortable hut: the chief of a caravan may sleep in rain or dew, but if he attempt to dislodge his porters, they lie down with the settled purpose of mules—as the Arabs say, they "have no shame." The curiosity of these people, and the little ceremony with which they gratify it, are at times most troublesome. A stranger must be stared at; total apathy is the only remedy: if the victim lose his temper, or attempt to dislodge them, he will find it like disturbing a swarm of bees. They will come for miles to "sow gape-seed:" if the tent-fly be closed, they will peer and peep from below, complaining loudly against the occupant, and, if further prevented, they may proceed to violence. On the road hosts of idlers, especially women, boys, and girls, will follow the caravan for hours; it is a truly offensive spectacle—these uncouth figures, running at a "gymnastic pace," half clothed except with grease, with pendent bosoms shaking in the air, and cries that resemble the howls of beasts more than any effort of human articulation.   This offensive ignorance of the first principles of social intercourse has been fostered in the races most visited by the Arabs, whose national tendency, like the Italian and the Greek, is ever and essentially republican.   When strangers first appeared in the country they were received with respect and deference.   They soon, however, lost this vantage-ground: they sat and chatted with the people, exchanged pleasantries, and suffered slights, till the Africans found themselves on an equality with their visitors.   The evil has become inveterate, and no greater contrast can be imagined than that between the manners of an Indian ryot and an East African mshenzi.

In intellect the East African is sterile and incult, apparently unprogressive and unfit for change.   Like the uncivilized generally, he observes well, but he can deduce nothing profitable from his perceptions.   His intelligence is surprising when compared with that of an uneducated English peasant; but it has a narrow bound, beyond which apparently no man may pass.   Like the Asiatic, in fact, he is stationary, but at a much lower level.   Devotedly fond of music, his love of tune has invented nothing but whistling and the whistle: his instruments are all borrowed from the coast-people.   He delights in singing, yet he has no metrical songs: he contents himself with improvising a few words without sense or rhyme, and repeats them till they nauseate: the long, drawling recitative generally ends in " Ah! ha^n!" or some such strongly-nasalized sound.   Like the Somal, he has tunes appropriated to particular occasions, as the elephant-hunt or the harvest-home.   When mourning, the love of music assumes a peculiar form: women weeping or sobbing, especially after chastisement, will break into a protracted threne or dirge, every period of which concludes with its own particular groan or wail: after venting a little natural distress in a natural sound, the long, loud improvisation, in the highest falsetto key, continues as before. As in Europe the "laughing-song" is an imitation of hilarity somewhat distressing to the spirits of the audience, so the " weeping-song" of the African only tends to risibility.   His wonderful loquacity and volubility of tongue have produced no tales, poetry, nor display of eloquence; though, like most barbarians, somewhat sententious, he will content himself with squabbling with his companions, or with repeating some meaningless word in every different tone of voice during the weary length of a day's march. His language is highly artificial and musical: the reader will have observed that the names which occur in these pages often consist entirely of liquids and vowels, that consonants are unknown at the end of a word, and that they never are double except at the beginning.   Yet the idea of a syllabarium seems not to have occurred to the negroid mind.   Finally, though the East African delights in the dance, and is an excellent timist—a thousand heels striking the ground simultaneously sound like one—his performance is as uncouth as perhaps was ever devised by man. He delights in a joke, which manages him like a Neapolitan; yet his efforts in wit are of the feeblest that can be conceived.

Though the general features of character correspond throughout the tribes in East Africa, there are also marked differences. The Wazaramo, for instance, are considered the most dangerous tribe on this line: caravans hurry through their lands, and hold themselves fortunate if a life be not lost, or if a few loads be not missing. Their neighbors, the Wasagara of the hills, were once peaceful and civil to travelers: the persecutions of the coast-people have rendered them morose and suspicious; they now shun strangers, and, never knowing when they may be attacked, they live in a constant state of agitation, excitement, and alarm. After the Wazaramo, the tribes of Ugogo are considered the most noisy and troublesome, the most extortionate, quarrelsome, and violent on this route: nothing restrains these races from bloodshed and plunder but fear of retribution and self-interest. The Wanyamwezi bear the highest character for civilization, discipline, and industry. Intercourse with the coast, however, is speedily sapping the foundations of their superiority: the East African Expedition suffered more from thieving in this than in any other territory, and the Arabs now depend for existence there not upon prestige, but sufferance, in consideration of mutual commercial advantage. In proportion as the traveler advances into the interior, he finds the people less humane, or rather less human. The Wavinza, the Wajiji, and the other lakist tribes much resemble one another: they are extortionate, violent, and revengeful barbarians; no Mnyamwezi dares to travel alone through their territories, and small parties are ever in danger of destruction.

In dealing with the East African the traveler can not do better than to follow the advice of Bacon—"Use savages justly and graciously, with sufficient guard nevertheless." They must be held as foes; and the prudent stranger will never put himself in their power, especially where life is concerned. The safety of a caravan will often depend upon the barbarian's fear of beginning the fray: if the onset once takes place, the numbers, the fierce looks, the violent gestures, and the confidence of the assailants upon their own ground, will probably prevail. When necessary, however, severity must be employed; leniency and forbearance are the vulnerable points of civilized policy, as they encourage attack by a suspicion of fear and weakness. They may be managed as the Indian saw directs, by a judicious mixture of the "narm" and "garm"—the soft and hot. Thus the old traders remarked in Guinea, that the best way to treat a black man was to hold out one hand to shake with him, while the other is doubled ready to knock him down. In trading with, or even when dwelling among this people, all display of wealth must be avoided. A man who would purchase the smallest article avoids showing any thing beyond its equivalent.

The ethnologist who compares this sketch with the far more favorable description of the Kafirs, a kindred race, given by travelers in South Africa, may suspect that only the darker shades of the picture are placed before the eye. But, as will appear in a future page, much of this moral degradation must be attributed to the working, through centuries, of the slave-trade: the tribes are no longer as nature made them; and from their connection with strangers they have derived nothing but corruption. Though of savage and barbarous type, they have been varnished with the semi-civilization of trade and commerce, which sits ridiculously upon their minds, as a rich garment would upon their persons.

Fetissism—the word is derived from the Portuguese feitiço, "a doing"—scil. of magic, by euphuism—is still the only faith known in East Africa. Its origin is easily explained by the aspect of the physical world, which has colored the thoughts and has directed the belief of man: he reflects, in fact, the fantastical and monstrous character of the animal and vegetable productions around him. Nature, in these regions rarely sublime or beautiful, more often terrible and desolate, with the gloomy forest, the impervious jungle, the tangled hill, and the dread uniform waste tenanted by deadly inhabitants, arouses in his mind a sensation of utter feebleness, a vague and nameless awe. Untaught to recommend himself for protection to a Superior Being, he addresses himself directly to the objects of his reverence and awe: he prostrates himself before the sentiment within him, hoping to propitiate it as he would satisfy a fellow-man. The grand mysteries of life and death, to him unrevealed and unexplained, the want of a true interpretation of the admirable phenomena of creation, and the vagaries and misconceptions of his own degraded imagination, awaken in him ideas of horror, and people the invisible world with ghost and goblin, demon and spectrum, the incarnations, as it were, of his own childish fears. Deepened by the dread of destruction, ever strong in the barbarian breast, his terror causes him to look with suspicion upon all around him: "How," inquires the dying African, "can I alone be ill when others are well, unless I have been bewitched?" Hence the belief in magical and supernatural powers in man, which the stronger minded have turned to their own advantage.

Fetissism is the adoration, or rather the propitiation of natural objects, animate and inanimate, to which certain mysterious influences are attributed. It admits neither god, nor angel, nor devil; it ignores the very alphabet of revealed or traditionary religion—a creation, a resurrection, a judgment-day, a soul or a spirit, a heaven or a hell. A modified practical atheism is thus the prominent feature of the superstition. Though instinctively conscious

of a being above them, the Africans have as yet failed to grasp
the idea: in their feeble minds it is an embryo rather than a conception—at the best a vague god, without personality, attributes,
or providence.   They call that being Mulungu, the Uhlunga of
the Kafirs, and the Utika of the Hottentots.   The term, however,
may mean a ghost, the firmament, or the sun; a man will frequently call himself Mulungu, and even Mulungu Mbaya, the latter word signifying bad or wicked.   In the language of the Wamasai, "Ai," or with the article "Engai"—the Creator—is feminine, the god and rain being synonymous.

The fetiss superstition is African, but not confined to Africa.
The faith of ancient Egypt, the earliest system of profane belief
known to man, with its triad denoting the various phases and
powers of nature, was essentially fetissist; while in the Syrian
mind dawned at first the idea of "Melkart," a god of earth, and
his Baalim, angels, vice-regents, or local deities.   But generally the
history of religions proves that when man, whether degraded from
primal elevation or elevated from primal degradation, has progressed a step beyond atheism—the spiritual state of the lowest
savagery—he advances to the modification called fetissism, the condition of the infant mind of humanity.   According to the late Col.
Van Kennedy, "such expressions as the love and fear of God
never occur in the sacred books of the Hindoos."   The ancient
Persians were ignicolists, adoring ethereal fire.   Confucius owned that he knew nothing about the gods, and therefore preferred
saying as little as possible upon the subject.   Men, still without
tradition or training, confused the Creator with creation, and ventured not to place the burden of providence upon a single deity.
Slaves to the agencies of material nature, impressed by the splendors of the heavenly bodies, comforted by fire and light, persuaded by their familiarity with the habits of wild beasts that the brute
creation and the human claimed a mysterious affinity, humbled by
the terrors of elemental war, and benefited by hero and sage,

> "Quicquid humus, pelagus, cœlum mirabile gignunt,
> Id duxere deos."

The barbarian worshiped these visible objects not as types,
myths, divine emanations, or personifications of a deity: he adored
them for themselves.   The modern theory, the mode in which
full-grown man explains away the follies of his childhood, making the interpretation precede the fable, fails when tested by experience.   The Hindoo, and, indeed, the ignorant Christian, still
adore the actual image of man and beast; it is unreasonable to
suppose that they kneel before and worship with heart and soul
its metaphysics; and an attempt to allegorize it, or to deprive it
of its specific virtues, would be considered, as in ancient Greece
and Rome, mere impiety.

By its essence, then, fetissism is a rude and sensual superstition,
the faith of an abject fear, and of infant races that have not ris-

en, and are, perhaps, incapable of rising to theism—the religion of love and the belief of the highest types of mankind. But old creeds die hard, and error founded upon the instincts and feelings of human nature borrows the coherence and uniformity of truth. That fetissism is a belief common to man in the childhood of his spiritual life, may be proved by the frequent and extensive remains of the faith which the cretinism of the Hamitic race has perpetuated among them to the present day, still sprouting like tares even in the fair field of revealed religion. The dread of ghosts, for instance, which is the mainstay of fetissism, is not inculcated in any sacred book, yet the belief is not to be abolished. Thus the Rakshasa of the Hindoos is a disembodied spirit, doing evil to mankind; and the ghost of the prophet Samuel, raised by the familiar of the Witch of Endor, was the immortal part of a mortal being, still connected with earth and capable of returning to it. Through the manes, the umbra, and the spectrum of the ancients, the belief has descended to the moderns, as the household words ghost, goblin, and bogle, revenant, polter-geist, and spook, duh, dusha, and dukh attest. Precisely similar to the African ghost-faith is the old Irish belief in banshees, pookas, and other evil entities; the corporeal frame of the dead forms other bodies, but the spirit hovers in the air, watching the destiny of friends, haunting houses, killing children, injuring cattle, and causing disease and destruction. Every where, too, their functions are the same: all are malevolent to the living, and they are seldom known to do good. The natural horror and fear of death which may be observed even in the lower animals has caused the dead to be considered vindictive and destructive.

Some missionaries have detected in the habit, which prevails throughout Eastern and Western Africa, of burying slaves with the deceased, of carrying provisions to graves, and of lighting fires on cold nights near the last resting-places of the departed, a continuation of relations between the quick and the dead which points to a belief in a future state of existence. The wish is father to that thought: the doctrine of the soul, of immortality, belongs to a superior order of mind, to a more advanced stage of society. The belief, as its operations show, is in presentity, materialism, not in futurity, spiritualism. According to the ancients, man is a fourfold being:

"Bis duo sunt homini, manes, caro, spiritus, umbra:
Quatuor hæc loci bis duo suscipiunt
Terra tegit carnem, tumulum circumvolitat umbra,
Manes Orcus habet, spiritus astra petit."

Take away the manes and the astral spirit, and remains the African belief in the εἴδωλον or umbra, spiritus, or ghost. When the savage and the barbarian are asked what has become of the "old people" (their ancestors), over whose dust and ashes they perform obsequies, these veritable secularists only smile and reply Wámekwisha, "they are ended." It proves the inferior organization of the race. Even the North American aborigines, a race which Nature apparently disdains to preserve, decided that man hath a future, since even Indian corn is vivified and rises again. The East African has created of his fears a ghost which never attains the perfect form of a soul. This inferior development has prevented his rising to the social status of the Hindoo, and other anciently civilized races, whom a life wholly wanting in purpose and occupation drove from the excitement necessary to stimulate the mind toward a hidden or mysterious future. These wild races seek otherwise than in their faith a something to emotionize and to agitate them.

The East African's credenda—it has not arrived at the rank of a system, this vague and misty dawning of a creed—are based upon two main articles. The first is demonology, or, rather, the existence of koma, the spectra of the dead; the second is uchawi, witchcraft or black magic, a corollary to the principal theorem. Few, and only the tribes adjacent to the maritime regions, have derived from El Islam a faint conception of the one Supreme. There is no trace in this country of the ancient and modern animal-worship of Egypt and India, though travelers have asserted that vestiges of it exist among the kindred race of Kafirs. The African has no more of sabæism than what belongs to the instinct of man: he has a reverence for the sun and moon; the latter is for evident reasons in higher esteem, but he totally ignores star-worship. If questioned concerning his daily bread, he will point with a devotional aspect toward the light of day; and if asked what caused the death of his brother, will reply Jua, or Rimwe, the sun. He has not, like the Kafir, a holiday at the epoch of new moon: like the Moslem, however, on first seeing it, he raises and claps his hands in token of obeisance. The mzimo, or fetiss hut, is the first germ of a temple, and the idea is probably derived from the kurban of the Arabs. It is found throughout the country, especially in Uzaramo, Unyamwezi, and Karagwah. It is in the shape of a dwarf house, one or two feet high, with a thatched roof, but without walls. Upon the ground, or suspended from the roof, are handfuls of grain and small pots full of beer, placed there to propitiate the ghosts, and to defend the crops from injury.

A prey to base passions and melancholy godless fears, the fetiss-ist, who peoples with malevolent beings the invisible world, animates material nature with evil influences. The rites of his dark and deadly superstition are all intended to avert evils from himself, by transferring them to others: hence the witchcraft and magic which flow naturally from the system of demonology. Men rarely die without the wife or children, the kindred or slaves, being accused of having compassed their destruction by "throwing the glamour over them;" and, as has been explained, the trial and the conviction are of the most arbitrary nature. Yet witchcraft is practiced by thousands with the firmest convictions in their own powers; and though frightful tortures await the wizard and the witch who have been condemned for the destruction of chief or elder, the vindictiveness of the negro drives him readily to the malevolent practices of sorcery. As has happened in Europe and elsewhere, in the presence of torture and the instant advance of death, the sorcerer and sorceress will not only confess, but even boast of and believe in, their own criminality. "Verily I slew such a one! I brought about the disease of such another!" these are their demented vaunts, the offspring of mental imbecility, stimulated by traditional hallucination.

In this state of spiritual death there is, as may be imagined, but little of the fire of fanaticism: polemics are as unknown as politics to them; their succedaneum for a god is not a jealous god. But upon the subjects of religious belief and revelation all men are equal: Davus becomes Œdipus, the fool is as the sage. What the "I" believes, that the "Thou" must acknowledge, under the pains and penalties of offending self-esteem. While the African's faith is weakly catholic, he will not admit that other men are wiser on this point than himself. Yet he will fast like a Moslem, because doing something seems to raise him in the scale of creation. His mind, involved in the trammels of his superstition, and enchained by custom, is apparently incapable of receiving the impressions of El Islam. His fetissism, unspiritualized by the philosophic pantheism and polytheism of Europe and Asia, has hitherto unfitted him for that belief which was readily accepted by the more Semitic maritime races, the Somal, the Wasawahili, and the Wamrima. To a certain extent, also, it has been the policy of the Arab to avoid proselytizing, which would lead to comparative equality: for sordid lucre the Moslem has left the souls of these Kafirs to eternal perdition. According to most doctors of the saving faith, an ardent proselytizer might convert by the sword whole tribes, though he might not succeed with individuals, who can not break through the ties of society. The "Mombas Mission," however, relying upon the powers of persuasion, unequivocally failed, and pronounced their flock to be "not behind the greatest infidels and scoffers of Europe: they blaspheme, in fact, like children." With characteristic want of veneration they would say, "Your Lord is a bad master, for he does not cure his servants." When an early convert died, the Wanyika at once decided that there is no Savior, as he does not prevent the decease of a friend. The sentiment generally elicited by a discourse upon the subject of the existence of a Deity is a desire to see him, in order to revenge upon him the deaths of relatives, friends, and cattle.*

---

* That the Western African negro resembles in this point his negroid brother, the following extract from an amusing and truthful little volume, entitled "Trade and

Fetissism supplies an abundance of professionally holy men.
The "mfumo" is translated by the Arabs bassar, a seer or clairvoyant. The mchawi is the sahhar, magician, or adept in the
black art. Among the Wazegura and the Wasagara is the mgo-
nezi, a word Arabized into rammal, or geomantist. He practices

Travels in the Gulf of Guinea and Western Africa" (London, Simpkin and Marshall, 1851), will prove:

Always anxious—says Mr. J. Smith, the author—to get any of them (the Western
Africans) to talk about God and religion, I said, "What have you been doing, King
Pepple?"

"All the same as you do—I tank God."

"For what?"

"Every good ting God sends me."

"Have you seen God?"

"Chi! no; suppose man see God, he must die one minute." (He would die in a
moment.)

"When you die won't you see God?"

With great warmth, "I know no savvy. (I don't know). How should I know?
Never mind. I no want to hear more for that palaver." (I want no more talk on
that subject.)

"What way?" (Why?)

"It no be your business, you come here for trade palaver."

I knew—resumes Mr. Smith—it would be of no use pursuing the subject at that
time, so I was silent, and it dropped for the moment.

In speaking of him dying, I had touched a very tender and disagreeable chord,
for he looked very savage and sulky, and I saw by the rapid changes in his countenance that he was the subject of some intense internal emotion. At length he broke
out, using most violent gesticulations, and exhibiting a most inhuman expression
of countenance, "Suppose God was here, I must kill him, one minute!"

"You what? you kill God?" followed I, quite taken aback, and almost breathless
with the novel and diabolical notion; "you kill God? why, you talk all some fool"
(like a fool); "you can not kill God; and suppose it possible that God could die,
every thing would cease to exist. He is the Spirit of the universe. But he can kill
you."

"I know I can not kill him; but suppose I could kill him, I would."

"Where does God live?"

"For top."

"How?" He pointed to the zenith.

"And suppose you could, why would you kill him?"

"Because he makes men to die."

"Why, my friend," in a conciliatory manner, "you would not wish to live forever,
would you?"

"Yes, I want to stand" (remain forever).

"But you will be old by and by, and if you live long enough, will become very
infirm, like that old man," pointing to a man very old for an African and thin, and
lame, and almost blind, who had come into the court during the foregoing conversation to ask for some favor (I wonder he had not been destroyed), "and like him
you will become lame, and deaf, and blind, and will be able to take no pleasure;
would it not be better, then, for you to die when this takes place, and you are in pain
and trouble, and so make room for your son, as your father did for you?"

"No, it would not; I want to stand all same I stand now."

"But supposing you should go to a place of happiness after death and—"

"I no savvy nothing about that, I know that I now live, and have too many
wives, and niggers (slaves), and canoes" (he did not mean what he said, in saying
he had too many wives, etc., it is their way of expressing a great number), "and
that I am king, and plenty of ships come to my country. I know no other ting,
and I want to stand."

I offered a reply, but he would hear no more, and so the conversation on that subject ceased; and we proceeded to discuss one not much more agreeable to him—the
payment of a very considerable debt which he owed me.

the miramoro, or divination and prediction of fray and famine, death and disease, by the relative position of small sticks, like spilikins, cast at random on the ground. The "rain-maker," or "rain-doctor" of the Cape, common throughout these tribes, and extending far north of the equator, is called in East Africa mganga, in the plural waganga: the Arabs term him tabib, doctor or physician.

The mganga, in the central regions termed mfumo, may be considered as the rude beginning of a sacerdotal order. These drones, who swarm throughout the land, are of both sexes: the women, however, generally confine themselves to the medical part of the profession. The calling is hereditary, the eldest or the cleverest son begins his neoteric education at an early age, and succeeds to his father's functions. There is little mystery in the craft, and the magicians of Unyamwezi have not refused to initiate some of the Arabs. The power of the mganga is great: he is treated as a sultan, whose word is law, and as a giver of life and death. He is addressed by a kingly title, and is permitted to wear the chieftain's badge, made of the base of a conical shell. He is also known by a number of small greasy and blackened gourds, filled with physic and magic, hanging round his waist, and by a little more of the usual grime—sanctity and dirt being connected in Africa as elsewhere. These men are sent for from village to village, and receive as obventions and spiritual fees sheep and goats, cattle and provisions. Their persons, however, are not sacred, and for criminal acts they are punished like other malefactors. The greatest danger to them is an excess of fame. A celebrated magician rarely, if ever, dies a natural death: too much is expected from him, and a severer disappointment leads to consequences more violent than usual. The Arabs deride their pretensions, comparing them depreciatingly to the workers of simiya, or conjuration, in their own country. They remark that the wizard can never produce rain in the dry, or avert it in the wet season. The many, however, who, to use a West African phrase, have "become black" from a long residence in the country, acquire a sneaking belief in the waganga, and fear of their powers. The well-educated classes in Zanzibar consult these heathen, as the credulous of other Eastern countries go to the astrologer and geomantist, and in Europe to the clairvoyant and the tireuse de cartes. In one point this proceeding is wise: the wizard rarely wants wits; and whatever he has heard secretly or openly will inevitably appear in the course of his divination.

It must not be supposed, however, that the mganga is purely an impostor. To deceive others thoroughly a man must first deceive himself, otherwise he will be detected by the least discerning. This is the simple secret of so many notable successes, achieved in the most unpromising causes by self-reliance and enthusiasm, the parents of energy and consistence. These barbarians are more often sinned against by their own fears and fooleries of faith, than sinners against their fellow-men by fraud and falsehood.

The office of uganga includes many duties. The same man is a physician by natural and supernatural means, a mystagogue or medicine-man, a detector of sorcery, by means of the judicium Dei or ordeal, a rain-maker, a conjurer, an augur, and a prophet.

As a rule, all diseases, from a boil to a marasmus senilis, are attributed by the fetissist to p'hepo, hubub, or afflatus. The three words are synonymous. P'hepo, in Kisawahili, is the plural form of upepo (a zephyr), used singularly to signify a high wind, a whirlwind ("devil"), and an evil ghost, generally of a Moslem. Hubub, the Arabic translation, means literally the blowing of wind, and metaphorically "possession." The African phrase for a man possessed is "ana p'hepo," "he has a devil." The mganga is expected to heal the patient by expelling the possession. Like the evil spirit in the days of Saul, the unwelcome visitant must be charmed away by sweet music; the drums cause excitement, and violent exercise expels the ghost, as saltation nullifies in Italy the venom of the tarantula. The principal remedies are drumming, dancing, and drinking, till the auspicious moment arrives. The ghost is then enticed from the body of the possessed into some inanimate article, which he will condescend to inhabit. This, technically called a keti, or stool, may be a certain kind of bead, two or more bits of wood bound together by a strip of snake's skin, a lion's or a leopard's claw, and other similar articles worn round the head, the arm, the wrist, or the ankle. Paper is still considered great medicine by the Wasukuma and other tribes, who will barter valuable goods for a little bit: the great desideratum of the charm, in fact, appears to be its rarity, or the difficulty of obtaining it. Hence also the habit of driving nails into and hanging rags upon trees. The vegetable itself is not worshiped, as some Europeans who call it the "devil's tree" have supposed: it is merely the place for the laying of ghosts, where by appending the keti most acceptable to the spectrum, he will be bound over to keep the peace with man. Several accidents in the town of Zanzibar have confirmed even the higher orders in their lurking superstition. Mr. Peters, an English merchant, annoyed by the slaves who came in numbers to hammer nails and to hang iron hoops and rags upon a "devil's tree" in his courtyard, ordered it to be cut down, to the horror of all the black beholders, of whom no one would lay an axe to it. Within six months five persons died in that house—Mr. Peters, his two clerks, his cooper, and his ship's carpenter. This superstition will remind the traveler of the Indian pipul (Ficus religiosa), in which fiends are supposed to roost, and suggest to the Orientalist an explanation of the mysterious Moslem practices common from Western Africa to the farthest East. The hanging of rags upon trees by pilgrims and travelers is probably a relic of Arab fetissism, derived in the days of ignorance from their congeners in East Africa. The custom has spread far and wide: even the Irish peasantry have been in the habit of suspending to the trees and bushes near their "holy wells" rags, halters, and spancels, in token of gratitude for their recovery, or that of their cattle.

There are other mystical means of restoring the sick to health; one specimen will suffice. Several little sticks, like matches, are daubed with ochre, and marks are made with them upon the patient's body. A charm is chanted, the possessed one responds, and at the end of every stave an evil spirit flies from him, the signal being a stick cast by the mganga upon the ground. Some unfortunates have as many as a dozen haunting ghosts, each of which has his own periapt: the mganga demands a distinct honorarium for the several expulsions. Wherever danger is, fear will be; wherever fear is, charms and spells, exorcisms and talismans of portentous powers will be in demand; and wherever supernaturalisms are in requisition, men will be found, for a consideration, to supply them.

These strange rites are to be explained upon the principle which underlies thaumaturgy in general: they result from conviction in a gross mass of exaggerations heaped by ignorance, falsehood, and credulity upon the slenderest foundation of fact—a fact doubtless solvable by the application of natural laws. The African temperament has strong susceptibilities, combined with what appears to be a weakness of brain, and great excitability of the nervous system, as is proved by the prevalence of epilepsy, convulsions, and hysteric disease. According to the Arab, el sara, epilepsy, or the falling sickness, is peculiarly common throughout East Africa; and, as we know by experience in lands more civilized, the sudden prostration, rigidity, contortions, etc., of the patient, strongly suggest the idea that he has been taken and seized ($\epsilon\pi\iota\lambda\eta\phi\theta\epsilon\iota\varsigma$) by, as it were, some external and invisible agent. The negroid is, therefore, peculiarly liable to the epidemical mania called "phantasmata," which, according to history, has at times of great mental agitation and popular disturbance broken out in different parts of Europe, and which, even in this our day, forms the base-work of "revivals." Thus in Africa the objective existence of spectra has become a tenet of belief. Stories that stagger the most skeptical are told concerning the phenomenon by respectable and not unlearned Arabs, who point to their fellow-countrymen as instances. Salim bin Rashid, a half-caste merchant well known at Zanzibar, avers, and his companions bear witness to his words, that on one occasion, when traveling northward from Unyanyembe, the possession occurred to himself. During the night two female slaves, his companions, of whom one was a child, fell, without apparent cause, into the fits which denote the approach of a spirit. Simultaneously, the master became as one intoxicated; a dark mass, material, not spiritual, entered the tent, and he felt himself pulled and pushed by a number of black figures, whom he had never before seen. He called aloud to his companions and slaves, who, vainly attempting to enter the tent, threw it down, and presently found him in a state of stupor, from which he did not recover till the morning. The same merchant circumstantially related, and called witnesses to prove, that a small slave-boy, who was produced on the occasion, had been frequently carried off by possession, even when confined in a windowless room, with a heavy door carefully bolted and padlocked. Next morning the victim was not found, although the chamber remained closed. A few days afterward he was met in the jungle wandering absently like an idiot, and with speech too incoherent to explain what had happened to him. The Arabs of Oman, who subscribe readily to transformation, deride these tales; those of African blood believe them. The transformation-belief, still so common in Maskat, Abyssinia, Somaliland, and the Cape, and anciently an almost universal superstition, is, curious to say, unknown among these East African tribes. The Wahiao, lying between Kilwa and the Nyassa Lake, preserve, however, a remnant of the old creed in their conviction that a malevolent magician can change a man after death into a lion, a leopard, or a hyena. On the Zambezi the people, according to Dr. Livingstone (chap. xxx.), believe that a chief may metamorphose himself into a lion, kill any one he chooses, and then return to the human form. About Tete (chap. xxxi.) the negroids hold that, "while persons are still living, they may enter into lions and alligators, and then return again to their own bodies." Travelers determined to find in Africa counterparts of European and Asiatic tenets, argue from this transformation a belief in the "transmigration of souls." They thus confuse material metamorphosis with a spiritual progress, which is assuredly not an emanation from the Hamitic mind. The Africans have hitherto not bewildered their brains with metaphysics, and, ignoring the idea of a soul, which appears to be a dogma of the Caucasian race, they necessarily ignore its immortality.

The second, and perhaps the most profitable occupation of the mganga, is the detection of uchawi, or black magic. The fatuitous style of conviction, and the fearful tortures which, in the different regions, await those found guilty, have already been described, as far as description is possible. Among a people where the magician is a police detector, ordeals must be expected to thrive. The baga or kyapo of East Africa—the Arabs translate it el halaf, or the oath—is as cruel, absurd, and barbarous as the red-water of Ashanti, the venoms of Kasanji (Cassange), the muavi of the Banyai tribes of Monomotapa, the tangina poison of the Malagash, the bitter-water of the Jews, the "saucy-water" of West Africa, and the fire tests of medieval Europe. The people of Usumbara thrust a red-hot hatchet into the mouth of the accused. Among the southeastern tribes a heated iron spike, driven into some tender part of the person, is twice struck with a log of wood. The Wazaramo dip the hand into boiling water, the Waganda into seething oil, and the Wazegura prick the ear with the stiffest bristles of a gnu's tail. The Wakwafi have an ordeal of meat that chokes the guilty. The Wanyamwezi pound with water between two stones and infuse a poisonous bark called "mwavi:" it is first administered by the mganga to a hen, who, for the nonce, represents the suspected. If, however, all parties be not satisfied with such trial, it is duly adhibited to the accused.

In East Africa, from Somaliland to the Cape, and throughout the interior, among the negroids and negroes north as well as south of the equator, the rain-maker or rain-doctor is a personage of consequence; and he does not fail to turn the hopes and fears of the people to his own advantage. A season of drought causes dearth, disease, and desolation among these improvident races, who therefore connect every strange phenomenon with the object of their desires, a copious wet monsoon. The enemy has medicines which disperse the clouds. The stranger who brings with him heavy showers is regarded as a being of good omen; usually, however, the worst is expected from the novel portent; he will, for instance, be accompanied and preceded by fertilizing rains, but the wells and springs will dry up after his departure, and the result will be drought or small-pox. These rumors, which may account for the Libyan stranger-sacrifices in the olden time, are still dangerous to travelers. The mganga must remedy the evil. His spells are those of fetissists in general, the mystic use of something foul, poisonous, or difficult to procure, such as the album græcum of hyenas, snakes' fangs, or lions' hair; these and similar articles are collected with considerable trouble by the young men of the tribe for the use of the rain-maker. But he is a weather-wise man, and rains in tropical lands are easily foreseen. Not unfrequently, however, he proves himself a false prophet; and when all the resources of cunning fail he must fly for dear life from the victims of his delusion.

The mganga is also a predictor and a soothsayer. He foretells the success or failure of commercial undertakings, of wars, and of kidnapping-commandos; he foresees famine and pestilence, and he suggests the means of averting calamities. He fixes, also, before the commencement of any serious affair, fortunate conjunctions, without which a good issue can not be expected. He directs expiatory offerings. His word is ever powerful to expedite or to delay the march of a caravan, and in his quality of augur he considers the flight of birds and the cries of beasts, like his prototype of the same class in ancient Europe and in modern Asia.

The principal instrument of the mganga's craft is one of the dirty little buyu or gourds which he wears in a bunch round his waist; and the following is the usual programme when the oracle is to be consulted. The magician brings his implements in a bag of matting; his demeanor is serious as the occasion; he is carefully greased, and his head is adorned with the diminutive antelope-horns fastened by a thong of leather above the forehead. He sits like a sultan upon a dwarf stool in front of the querist, and begins by exhorting the highest possible offertory. No pay, no predict. Divination by the gourd has already been described; the mganga has many other implements of his craft. Some prophesy by the motion of berries swimming in a cup full of water, which is placed upon a low stool surrounded by four tails of the zebra or the buffalo lashed to sticks planted upright in the ground. The kasanda is a system of folding triangles not unlike those upon which plaything soldiers are mounted. Held in the right hand, it is thrown out, and the direction of the end points to the safe and auspicious route; this is probably the rudest appliance of prestidigitation. The shero is a bit of wood about the size of a man's hand, and not unlike a pair of bellows, with a dwarf handle, a projection like a nozzle, and in the circular centre a little hollow. This is filled with water, and a grain or fragment of wood, placed to float, gives an evil omen if it tends toward the sides, and favorable if it veers toward the handle or the nozzle. The mganga generally carries about with him to announce his approach a kind of rattle called "sánje." This is a hollow gourd of pine-apple shape, pierced with various holes, prettily carved and half filled with maize, grains, and pebbles; the handle is a stick passed through its length and secured by cross-pins.

The mganga has many minor duties. In elephant-hunts he must throw the first spear and endure the blame if the beast escapes. He marks ivory with spots disposed in lines and other figures, and thus enables it to reach the coast without let or hindrance. He loads the kirangozi or guide with charms and periapts, to defend him from the malice which is ever directed at a leading man, and sedulously forbids him to allow precedence even to the mtongi, the commander and proprietor of the caravan. He aids his tribe by magical arts in wars, by catching a bee, reciting over it certain incantations, and loosing it in the direction of the foe, when the insect will instantly summon an army of its fellows, and disperse a host, however numerous. This belief well illustrates the easy passage of the natural into the supernatural. The land being full of swarms, and man's body being wholly exposed, many a caravan has been dispersed like chaff before the wind by a bevy of swarming bees. Similarly in South Africa the magician kicks an ant-hill, and starts wasps which put the enemy to flight. And in the books of the Hebrews we read that the hornet sent before the children of Israel against the Amorite was more terrible than sword or bow. (Joshua, xxiv.)

The several tribes in East Africa present two forms of government, the despotic and the semi-monarchical.

In the despotic races, the Wakilima, or mountaineers of Chhaga, for instance, the subjects are reduced to the lowest state of servility. All, except the magicians and the councilors, are "wasoro" —soldiers and slaves to the sultan, mangi, or sovereign. The reader will bear in mind that the word "sultan" is the Arabic term applied generically by traders to all the reguli and roitelets, the chiefs and headmen, whose titles vary in every region. In Uzaramo the sultan is called p'hazi; in Khutu, p'hazi or mundewa; in Usagara, mundewa; in Ugogo, mteme; in Unyamwezi, mwami; in Ujiji and Karagwah, mkama. "Wazir" is similarly used by the Arabs for the principal councilor or minister, whose African name in the several tribes is mwene goha, mbáhá, mzágírá, magáwe, mhángo, and muhinda. The elders are called throughout the country wagosi and wányáp'hárá; they form the council of the chief. All male children are taken from their mothers, are made to live together, and are trained to the royal service, to guarding the palace, to tilling the fields, and to keeping the watercourses in order. The despot is approached with fear and trembling; subjects of both sexes must stand at a distance, and repeatedly clap their palms together before venturing to address him. Women always bend the right knee to the earth, and the chief acknowledges the salutation with a nod. At times the elders and even the women inquire of the ruler what they can do to please him : he points to a plot of ground which he wishes to be cleared, and this *corvée* is the more carefully performed, as he fines them in a bullock if a weed be left unplucked. In war female captives are sold by the king, and the children are kept to swell the number of his slaves. None of the wasoro may marry without express permission. The king has unlimited power of life and death, which he exercises without squeamishness, and a general right of sale over his subjects; in some tribes, as those of Karagwah, Uganda, and Unyoro, he is almost worshiped. It is a capital offense to assume the name of a sultan; even a stranger so doing would be subjected to fines and other penalties. The only limit to the despot's power is the ada, or precedent, the unwritten law of ancient custom, which is here less mutable than the codes and pandects of Europe. The African, like the Asiatic, is by nature a conservative, at once the cause and the effect of his inability to rise higher in the social scale. The king lives in a manner of barbarous state. He has large villages crowded with his families and slaves. He never issues from his abode without an armed mob, and he disdains to visit even the wealthiest Arabs. The monarchical tribes are legitimists of the good old school, disdaining a *novus homo ;* and the consciousness of power invests their princes with a certain dignity and majesty of demeanor. As has been mentioned, some of the sultans whose rule has the greatest prestige appear, from physical peculiarities, to be of a foreign and a nobler origin.

In the aristocratical or semi-monarchical tribes, as the Wanyam-wezi, the power of the sultan depends mainly upon his wealth, importance, and personal qualifications for the task of rule. A chief enabled to carry out "fist-right" policy will raise himself to the rank of a despot, and will slay and sell his subjects without mercy. Though surrounded by a council varying from two to a score of chiefs and elders, who are often related or connected with him, and who, like the Arab shaykhs, presume as much as possible in ordering this and forbidding that, he can disregard and slight them. More often, however, his authority is circumscribed by a rude balance of power; the chiefs around him can probably bring as many warriors into the field as he can. When weak, the sultan has little more authority than the patell of an Indian village or the shaykh of a Bedouin tribe. Yet even when the chief can not command in his own clan, he is an important personage to traveling merchants and strangers. He can cause a quarrel, an advance, or an assassination, and he can quiet brawls even when his people have been injured. He can open a road by providing porters, or bar a path by deterring a caravan from proceeding, or by stopping the sale of provisions. Thus it is easy to travel among races whose chiefs are well disposed to foreigners, and the utmost circumspection becomes necessary when the headmen are grasping and inhospitable. Upon the whole, the chiefs are wise enough to encourage the visits of traders.

A patriarchal or purely republican form of government is un-known in East Africa. The Wasagara, it is true, choose their chief like the Banyai of "Monomotapa," but, once elected, he becomes a monarch. Loyalty—or, to reduce it to its elements, veneration for the divinity that hedges in a king—is a sentiment innate in the African mind. Man, however, in these regions is not a political animal; he has a certain instinctive regard for his chief and a respect for his elders. He ignores, however, the blessings of duly limited independence and the natural classification of humanity into superior and inferior, and honors—the cheap pay of nations—are unknown. He acknowledges no higher and lower social strata. His barbarism forbids the existence of a learned oligarchy, of an educated community, or of a church and state, showing the origin of the connection between the soul and body of society. Man being equal to man, force being the only law and self the sole consideration, mutual jealousy prevents united efforts and deadens all patriotic spirit. No one cares for the public good; the welfare of the general must yield to the most contemptible individual interests; civil order and security are therefore unknown, and foreign relations can not exist.

In the lowest tribes the chieftain is a mere nonentity, "a sultan," as the Arabs say, "within his own walls." His subjects will boast, like the Somal, that he is "*tanquam unus ex nobis;*" and they are so sensible of restraint that "girdles and garters would be to them bonds and shackles" metaphorically as well as literally. The position of these sultans is about equal to that of the diwans of the Mrima; their dignity is confined to sitting upon a dwarf three-legged stool, to wearing more brass wire than beads, and to possessing clothes a little better than those of their subjects. The "regulus" must make a return present to strangers after receiving their offerings, and in some cases must begin with gifts. He must listen to the words of his councilors and elders, who, being without salary, claim a portion of the presents and treasure-trove, interfere on all occasions of black-mail, fines, and penalties, demand from all petitioners gifts and bribes to secure interest, and exert great influence over the populace.

Legitimacy is the rule throughout the land, and the son, usually the eldest, succeeds to the father, except among the Wasukuma of N. Unyamwezi, where the line of descent is by the sister's son —the "surer side"—for the normal reason, to secure some of the blood royal for ruling. Even the widows of the deceased become the property of the successor. This truly African practice prevails also among the Bachwana, and presents another of those curious points of resemblance between the Hamite and Semite races which have induced modern ethnologists to derive the Arab from Africa. The curious custom among the Wanyamwezi of devising property to illegitimate children is not carried out in the succession to power. Where there are many sons, all, as might be expected, equally aspire to power; sometimes, however, of two brothers, one will consent to hold authority under the other. In several tribes, especially in Usukuma, the widow of a chief succeeds to his dignity in default of issue.

Punishments are simple in East Africa. The sar, vendetta or blood-feud, and its consequence, the diyat or weregeld, exist in germ, unreduced, as among the more civilized Arabs, to an artful and intricate system. But these customs are founded, unlike ours, upon barbarous human nature. Instinct prompts a man to slay the slayer of his kith and kin; the offense is against the individual, not the government or society. He must reason to persuade himself that the crime, being committed against the law, should be left to the law for notice; he wants revenge, and he cares naught for punishment or example for the prevention of crime. The sultan encourages the payment of blood-money to the relatives of the deceased, or, if powerful enough, claims it himself, rather than that one murder should lead to another, and eventually to a chronic state of bloodshed and confusion. Thus, in some tribes the individual revenges himself, and in others he commits his cause to the chief. Here he takes an equivalent in cattle for the blood of a brother or the loss of a wife; there he visits the erring party with condign punishment. The result of such deficiency of standard is a want of graduation in severity; a thief is sometimes speared and beheaded, or sold into slavery after all his property has been extorted by the chief, the councilors, and the elders, while a murderer is perhaps only fined.

The land in East Africa is every where allodial; it does not belong to the ruler, nor has the dawn of the feudal system yet arisen there.   A migratory tribe gives up its rights to the soil, contrary to the mortmain system of the Arab Bedouins, and, if it would return, it must return by force.   The sultan, however, exacts a fee from all immigrants settling in his territory.

The sources of revenue in East Africa are uncertain, desultory, and complicated.   The agricultural tribes pay yearly a small percentage of grain; this, however, is the office of the women, who are expert in fraud.   Neither sowing nor harvest can take place without the chief's permission, and the issue of his order is regulated by his own interests.   Among the hunting-tribes, slain elephants become the hunter's property, but the sultan claims as treasure-trove a tusk of any animal found wounded or dead in his dominions, and in all cases the spoils of dead lions are crown property.   The flesh of game is distributed among the elders and the ruling family, who also assert a claim to the cloth or beads purchased by means of the ivory from caravans.   Some have abditaria and considerable stores of the articles most valued by barbarians.   Throughout the slave-paths the chiefs have learned to raise revenue from the slaves, who thus bribe them to forbear from robbery.   But while the stronger require large gifts without return, the weaker make trifling presents, generally of cattle or provisions, and expect many times the value in brass wire, cloth, and beads.   The stranger may refuse these offerings; it is, however, contrary to custom, and as long as he can afford it he should submit to the imposition.   Fiscs and fines are alarmingly frequent.   If the monsoon rains delay, the chief summons a mganga to fix upon the obstructor; he is at once slain, and his property is duly escheated.   The sultan claims the goods and chattels of all felons and executed criminals, even in the case of a servant put to death by his master.   In the more republican tribes the chief lives by the sweat of his slaves.   Briefly, East Africa presents an instructive study of human society in its first stage after birth.

I will conclude this uninteresting chapter—attribute its dullness, gentle reader, to the effects of the climate and society of Konduchi—with a subject which strikes home to the heart of every Englishman, slavery.

The origin of slavery in East Africa is veiled in the glooms of the past.   It is mentioned in the Periplus (chap. iii.) as an institution of the land, and probably it was the result of the ancient trade with southern Arabia.   At present it is almost universal: with the exceptions of the Wahinda, the Watosi, and the Wagogo, all the tribes from the eastern equatorial coast to Ujiji and the regions lying westward of the Tanganyika Lake may be called slave-races. An Arab, Msawahili, and even a bondsman from Zanzibar, is every where called murungwana or freeman. Yet in many parts of the country the tribes are rather slave-importers than exporters. Although they kidnap others, they will not sell their fellows, except when convicted of crime—theft, magic, murder, or cutting the upper teeth before the lower. In times of necessity, however, a man will part with his parents, wives, and children, and when they fail he will sell himself without shame. As has been observed, among many tribes the uncle has a right to dispose of his nephews and nieces.

Justice requires the confession that the horrors of slave-driving rarely meet the eye in East Africa. Some merchants chain or cord together their gangs for safer transport through regions where desertion is at a premium. Usually, however, they trust rather to soft words and kind treatment; the fat lazy slave is often seen stretched at ease in the shade, while the master toils in the sun and wind. The "property" is well fed and little worked, whereas the porter, belonging to none but himself, is left without hesitation to starve upon the road-side. The relationship is rather that of patron and client than of lord and bondsman; the slave is addressed as ndugu-yango, "my brother," and he is seldom provoked by hard words or stripes. In fact, the essence of slavery, compulsory unpaid labor, is perhaps more prevalent in independent India than in East Africa; moreover, there is no adscriptus glebæ, as in the horrid thraldom of Malabar. To this general rule there are terrible exceptions, as might be expected among a people with scant regard for human life. The kirangozi, or guide, attached to the expedition on return from Ujiji, had loitered behind for some days because his slave girl was too footsore to walk. When tired of waiting he cut off her head, for fear lest she should become gratis another man's property.

In East Africa there are two forms of this traffic, the export and the internal trade. For the former slaves are collected like ivories throughout the length and breadth of the land. They are driven down from the principal depôts, the Island of Kasenge, Ujiji, Unyanyembe, and Zungomero to the coast by the Arab and Wasawahili merchants, who afterward sell them in retail at the great mart Zanzibar. The internal trade is carried on between tribe and tribe, and therefore will long endure.

The practice of slavery in East Africa, besides demoralizing and brutalizing the race, leads to the results which effectually bar increase of population and progress toward civilization. These are commandos, or border wars, and intestine confusion.

All African wars, it has been remarked, are for one of two objects, cattle-lifting or kidnapping. Some of the pastoral tribes—as the Wamasai, the Wakwafi, the Watuta, and the Warori—assert the theory that none but themselves have a right to possess herds, and that they received the gift directly from their ancestor who created cattle; in practice they covet the animals for the purpose of a general gorge. Slaves, however, are much more frequently the end and aim of feud and foray. The process of kidnapping, an inveterate custom in these lands, is in every way agreeable to the mind of the man-hunter. A "*multis utile bellum,*" it combines the pleasing hazards of the chase with the exercise of cunning and courage; the battue brings martial glory and solid profit, and preserves the barbarian from the listlessness of life without purpose. Thus men date from foray to foray, and pass their days in an interminable blood-feud and border war. A poor and powerful chief will not allow his neighbors to rest wealthier than himself; a quarrel is soon found, the stronger attacks the weaker, hunts and harries his cattle, burns his villages, carries off his subjects and sells them to the first passing caravan. The inhabitants of the land have thus become wolves to one another; their only ambition is to dispeople and destroy, and the blow thus dealt to a thinly-populated country strikes at the very root of progress and prosperity.

As detrimental to the public interests as the border wars is the intestine confusion caused by the slave-trade. It perpetuates the vile belief in uchawi or black magic: when captives are in demand, the criminal's relations are sold into slavery. It affords a scope for the tyranny of a chief, who, if powerful enough, will enrich himself by vending his subjects in wholesale and retail. By weakening the tie of family, it acts with deadly effect in preventing the increase of the race.

On the coast and in the Island of Zanzibar the slaves are of two kinds—the muwallid or domestic, born in captivity, and the wild slave imported from the interior.

In the former case the slave is treated as one of the family, because the master's comfort depends upon the man being contented; often also his sister occupies the dignified position of concubine to the head of the house. These slaves vary greatly in conduct. The most tractable are those belonging to the diwans and the Wasawahili generally, who treat them with the utmost harshness and contempt. The Arabs spoil them by a kinder usage; few employ the stick, the salib, or cross—a forked pole to which the neck and ankles are lashed—and the makantale or stocks, for fear of desertion. Yet the slave, if dissatisfied, silently leaves the house, lets himself to another master, and returns after perhaps two years' absence as if nothing had occurred. Thus he combines the advantages of freedom and slavery. Moreover, it is a proverb among the Arabs that a slave must desert once in his life, and he does so the more readily as he betters his condition by so doing. The worst in all points are those belonging to the Banyans, the Indians, and other European subjects; they know their right to emancipation, and consult only their own interests and inclinations. The muwallid or domestic slave is also used like the pombeiro of West Africa. From Unyamwezi and Ujiji he is sent to traffic in the more dangerous regions — the master meanwhile dwelling among his fellow-countrymen in some comfortable tembe. This proceeding has greatly injured the commerce of the interior, and necessitates yearly lengthening journeys. The slave intrusted with cloth and beads suddenly becomes a great man; he is lavish in supporting the dignity of a fundi or fattore, and consulting nothing but his own convenience, he will loiter for six months at a place where he has been sent for a week. Thus it is that ivory sold in Unyamwezi but a dozen years ago at 10 lbs. for 1 lb. of beads now fetches nearly weight for weight. And this is a continually increasing evil. No caravan, however, can safely traverse the interior without an escort of slave-musketeers. They never part with their weapons, even when passing from house to house, holding that their lives depend upon their arms; they beg, borrow, or steal powder and ball; in fact, they are seldom found unready. They will carry nothing but the lightest gear, the master's writing-case, bed, or praying-mat; to load them heavily would be to insure desertion. Contrary to the practice of the free porter, they invariably steal when they run away; they are also troublesome about food, and they presume upon their weapons to take liberties with the liquor and the women of the heathen.

The imported slaves again are of two different classes. Children are preferred to adults; they are Islamized and educated so as to resemble the muwallid, though they are even somewhat less tame. Full-grown serfs are bought for predial purposes; they continue indocile, and alter little by domestication. When not used by the master they are left to plunder or to let themselves out for food and raiment, and when dead they are cast into the sea or into the nearest pit. These men are the scourge of society; no one is safe from their violence; and to preserve a garden or an orchard from the depredations of the half-starved wretches, a guard of musketeers would be required. They are never armed, yet, as has been recounted, they have caused at Zanzibar servile wars, deadly and lasting as those of ancient Rome.

Arabs declare that the barbarians are improved by captivity — a partial theory open to doubt. The servum pecus retain in thraldom that wildness and obstinacy which distinguish the people and the lower animals of their native lands; they are trapped, but not tamed; they become captives, but not civilized. However trained, they are probably the worst servants in the world; a slave household is a model of discomfort. The wretches take a trouble and display an ingenuity in opposition and disobedience, in perversity, annoyance, and villainy, which, rightly directed, would make them invaluable. The old definition of a slave still holds good — " An animal that eats as much and does as little as possible." Clumsy and unhandy, dirty and careless, he will never labor unless ordered to do so, and so futile is his nature that even the inducement of the stick can not compel him to continue his exertions; a whole gang will barely do the work of a single servant. He "has no end," to use the Arab phrase: that is to say, however well he may begin, he will presently tire of his task; he does not, and apparently he will not, learn; his first impulse, like that of an ass, is not to obey; he then thinks of obeying, and if fear preponderate he finally may obey. He must deceive, for fraud and foxship are his force; when detected in some prodigious act of rascality he pathetically pleads, "Am I not a slave?" So wondrous are his laziness and hate of exertion, that, despite a high development of love of life, he often appears the most reckless of mortals. He will run away from the semblance of danger, yet on a journey he will tie his pipe to a leaky keg of gunpowder, and smoke it in that position rather than take the trouble to undo it. A slave belonging to Musa, the Indian merchant at Kazeh, unwilling to rise and fetch a pipe, opened the pan of his musket, filled it with tobacco and fire, and, beginning to inhale it from the muzzle, blew out his brains. Growing confident and impudent from the knowledge of how far he may safely go, the slave presumes to the utmost. He steals instinctively, like a magpie: a case is quoted in which the gold spangles were stripped from an officer's sword-belt while dining with the Prince of Zanzibar. The slave is almost always half naked; whatever clothes he obtains from the master are pawned or sold in the bazar; hence he must pilfer and plunder almost openly for the means of gratifying his lowest propensities, drinking and intrigue. He seems to acquire from captivity a greater capacity for debauchery than even in his native wilds; he has learned irregularities unknown to his savage state: it is the brutishness of negroid nature brought out by the cheap and readily-attainable pleasures of semi-civilization. Whenever on moonlight nights the tapping of the tom-tom responds to the vile squeaking of the fife, it is impossible to keep either a male or female slave within doors. All rendezvous at the place, and, having howled and danced themselves into happiness, conclude with a singularly disorderly scene. In the town of Zanzibar these "ngoma" or dances were prohibited for moral reasons by the late Sayyid. The attachment of a slave to his master is merely a development of selfishness; it is a greater insult to abuse the ahbab (patroon) than, according to Eastern fashion, the father and mother, the wife and sister. No slave-owner, however, praises a slave or relies upon his fidelity. The common expression is, "There is no good in the bondsman."

Like the Somal, a merry and light-hearted race in foreign countries, but rendered gloomy and melancholy by the state of affairs at home, the negroid slaves greatly improve by exportation: they lose much of the surliness and violence which distinguish them at Zanzibar, and are disciplined into a kind of respect for superiors. Thus, "Seedy Mubarak" is a prime favorite on board an Indian steamer; he has also strength and courage enough to make himself respected. But "Seedy Mubarak" has tasted the intoxicating draught of liberty, he is in high good-humor with himself and with all around him, he is a slave merely in origin, he has been adopted into the great family of free men, and with it he has identified all his interests. Eastern history preserves instances of the valor and faithfulness of bondsmen, as the annals of the West are fond of recording the virtues of dogs. Yet all the more civilized races have a gird at the negro. In the present day the Persians and other Asiatics are careful, when bound on distant or dangerous journeys, to mix white servants with black slaves; they hold the African to be full of strange childish caprices, and to be ever at heart a treacherous and bloodthirsty barbarian. Like the "bush-negroes" of Surinam, once so dangerous to the Dutch, the runaway slaves from Zanzibar have formed a kind of East African Liberia, between Mount Yombo and the Shimba section of the Eastern Ghauts. They have endangered the direct caravan road from Mombasah to Usumbara; and though trespassing upon the territory of the Mwasagnombe, a sub-clan of the Wadigo, and claimed as subjects by Abdullah, the son of Sultan Kimwere, they have gallantly held their ground. According to the Arabs, there is another servile republic about Gulwen, near Brava. Travelers speak with horror of the rudeness, violence, and cruelty of these self-emancipated slaves; they are said to be more dangerous even than the Somal, who for wanton mischief and malice can be compared with nothing but the naughtiest schoolboys in England.

The serviles at Zanzibar have played their Arab masters some notable tricks. Many a severe lord has perished by the hand of a slave. Several have lost their eyes by the dagger's point during sleep. Curious tales are told of ingenious servile conspiracy. Mohammed bin Sayf, a Zanzibar Arab, remarkable for household discipline, was brought to grief by Kombo, his slave, who stole a basket of nutmegs from the prince, and, hiding them in his master's house, denounced him of theft. Fahl bin Nasr, a traveling merchant, when passing through Ugogo, nearly lost his life in consequence of a slave having privily informed the people that his patroon had been killing crocodiles and preserving their fat for poison. In both these cases the slaves were not punished; they had acted, it was believed, according to the true instincts of servile nature, and chastisement would have caused desertion, not improvement.

As regards the female slaves, the less said about them, from regard to their sex, the better: they are as deficient in honor as in honesty, in modesty and decorum as in grace and beauty. No man, even an Arab, deems the mother of his children chaste, or believes in the legitimacy of his progeny till proved.

Extensive inquiries into the subject lead to a conviction that it is impossible to offer any average of the price of slaves. Yet the question is of importance, as only the immense profit causes men thus to overlook all considerations of humanity. A few general rules may be safely given. There is no article, even horseflesh, that varies so much in market value as the human commodity: the absolute worth is small compared with the wants of the seller and the requirements and means of the purchaser. The extremes range from six feet of unbleached domestics, or a few pounds of grain in time of famine, to seventy dollars, equal to £15. The slaves are cheapest in the interior, on account of the frequency of desertion: about Unyamwezi they are dearer, and most expensive in the Island of Zanzibar. At the latter place, during the last few years they have doubled in price: according to the Arabs, who regard the abolition of slavery with feelings of horror, this increase results from the impediments thrown in the way by the English; a more probable explanation may be found in the greater cheapness of money. At Zanzibar the price of a boy under puberty is from fifteen to thirty dollars. A youth till the age of fifteen is worth a little less. A man in the prime of life, from twenty-five to forty, fetches from thirteen to twenty dollars; after that age he may be bought from ten to thirteen. Educated slaves, fitted for the work of factors, are sold from twenty-five to seventy dollars, and at fancy prices. The price of females is every where about one third higher than that of males. At Zanzibar the ush-ur or custom-dues vary according to the race of the slave: the Wahiao, Wangindo, and other serviles imported from Kilwa, pay one dollar per head, from the Mrima or maritime regions two dollars, and from Unyamwezi, Ujiji, and the rest of the interior three dollars. At the central depôt, Unyanyembe, where slaves are considered neither cheap nor dear, the value of a boy ranges between eight and ten doti or double cloths; a youth, from nine to eleven; a man in prime, from five to ten; and past his prime, from four to six. In some parts of the interior men are dearer than children under puberty. In the cheapest places, as in Karagwah and Urori, a boy costs three shukkahs of cloth and three fundo or thirty strings of coral beads; a youth, from ten to fifteen fundo; a man in prime, from eight to ten; and no one will purchase an old man. These general notes must not, however, be applied to particular tribes: as with ivory and other valuable commodities, the amount and the description of the circulating medium vary at almost every march.

It was asserted by the late Colonel Hamerton, whose local knowledge was extensive, that the average of yearly import into the Island of Zanzibar was 14,000 head of slaves, the extremes being 9000 and 20,000. The loss by mortality and desertion is 30 per cent. per annum; thus the whole gang must be renewed between the third and fourth year.

By a stretch of power slavery might readily be abolished in the

Island of Zanzibar, and in due time, after the first confusion, the measure would doubtless be found as profitable as it is now unpalatable to the landed proprietors and to the commercial body. A "sentimental squadron," like the West African, would easily, by means of steam, prevent any regular exportation to the Asiatic continent. But these measures would deal only with effects, leaving the causes in full vigor; they would strike at the bole and branches, the root retaining sufficient vitality to resume its functions as soon as relieved of the pressure from without. Neither treaty nor fleet would avail permanently to arrest the course of slavery upon the sea-board, much less would it act in the far realms of the interior. At present the African will not work: the purchase of predial slaves to till and harvest for him is the great aim of his life. When a more extensive intercourse with the maritime regions shall beget wants which compel the barbarian, now contented with doing nothing and having nothing, to that individual exertion and that mutual dependency which render serfdom a moral impossibility in the more advanced stages of human society—when man, now valueless except to himself, shall become more precious by his labor than by his sale, in fact an article so expensive that strangers can not afford to buy him—then we may expect to witness the extinction of the evil. Thus and thus only can "Rachel, still weeping for her children," in the evening of her days, be made happy.

Meanwhile, the philanthropist, who after sowing the good seed has sense and patience to consign the gathering of the crop to posterity, will hear with pleasure that the extinction of slavery would be hailed with delight by the great mass throughout the length and breadth of Eastern Africa. This people, "robbed and

The Bull-headed Mabruki.   African standing Position.

spoiled" by their oppressors, who are legionary, call themselves "the meat," and the slave-dealers "the knife:" they hate and fear their own demon Moloch, but they lack unanimity to free their necks from his yoke. Africa still "lies in her blood," but the progress of human society, and the straiter bonds which unite man with man, shall eventually rescue her from her old pitiable fate.

CONCLUSION.

On the 9th of February the battela and the stores required for our trip arrived at Konduchi from Zanzibar, and the next day saw us rolling down the coast, with a fair fresh breeze, toward classic Kilwa, the Quiloa of De Gama, of Camoens, and of the Portuguese annalists. I shall reserve an account of this most memorable shore for a future work, devoted especially to the sea-board of Zanzibar—coast and island: in the present tale of adventure the details of a *cabotage* would be out of place. Suffice it to say that we lost nearly all our crew by the cholera, which, after ravaging the eastern coast of Arabia and Africa, and the islands of Zanzibar and Pemba, had almost depopulated the southern settlements on the main land. We were unable to visit the course of the great Rufiji River, a counterpart of the Zambezi in the south, and a water-road which appears destined to become the highway of nations into Eastern equatorial Africa. No man dared to take service on board the infected vessel; the Hindoo Banyans, who directed the copal trade of the river regions, aroused against us the chiefs of the interior; moreover, the stream was in flood, overflowing its banks, and its line appeared marked by heavy purple clouds, which discharged a deluge of rain. Convinced that the traveling season was finished, I turned the head of the battela northward, and on the 4th of March, 1859, after a succession of violent squalls and pertinacious calms, we landed once more upon the Island of Zanzibar.

Sick and way-worn, I entered the house connected in memory with an old friend, not without a feeling of sorrow for the change —I was fated to regret it even more. The excitement of travel was succeeded by an utter depression of mind and body: even the labor of talking was too great, and I took refuge from society in a course of French novels *à vingt sous la pièce.*

Yet I had fallen upon stirring times: the little state, at the epoch of my return, was in the height of confusion. His highness the Sayyid Suwayni, suzerain of Maskat, seizing the pretext of a tribute owed to him by his cadet brother of Zanzibar, had embarked, on the 11th of February, 1859, a host of Bedouin brigands upon four or five square-rigged ships and many Arab craft: with this power he was preparing a hostile visit to the island. The Baloch stations on the main land were drained of mercenaries, and 7000 muskets, with an amount of ammunition which rendered the town dangerous, were served out to slaves and other

ruffians. Dows from Hadramaut brought down armed adventurers, who were in the market to fight for the best pay. The
turbulent Harisi chiefs of Zanzibar were terrified into siding with
his highness the Sayyid Majid by the influence of H. M. consul,
Captain Rigby. But the representatives of the several Christian
powers could not combine to preserve the peace, and M. Ladislas
Cochet, consul de France, an uninterested spectator of the passing events, thought favorably of his highness the Sayyid Suwayni's claim, he believed that the people if consulted would prefer
the rule of the elder brother, and he could not reconcile his conscience to the unscrupulous means—the *force majeure*—which his
opponent brought into the field. The Harisi, therefore, with their
thousands of armed retainers—in a single review I saw about
2200 of them—preserved an armed neutrality, which threatened
mischief to the weaker of the rival brothers : trade was paralyzed,
the foreign merchants lost heavily, and no less than eighty native
vessels were still at the end of the season due from Bombay and
the north. To confuse confusion, several ships collecting negro
"emigrants" and "free laborers," *per fas et nefas*, even kidnapping
them when necessary, were reported by the Arab local authorities
to be anchored and to be cruising off the coast of Zanzibar.

After a fortnight of excitement and suspense, during which the
wildest rumors flew through the mouths of men, it was officially reported that H. M.'s steamer *Punjaub*, Captain Fullerton, H. M. I. N.,
commanding, had, under orders received from the government of
Bombay, met his highness the Sayyid Suwayni off the eastern
coast of Africa and had persuaded him to return.

Congratulations were exchanged, salutes were fired, a few buggalows belonging to the enemy's fleet, which was said to have
been dispersed by a storm, dropped in and were duly captured,
the negroes drank, sang, and danced for a consecutive week, and
with the least delay armed men poured in crowded boats from the
island toward their several stations on the main land. But the
blow had been struck, the commercial prosperity of Zanzibar
could not be retrieved during the brief remnant of the season, and
the impression that a renewal of the attempt would at no distant
time insure similar disasters seemed to be uppermost in every
man's mind.

His highness the Sayyid Majid had honored me with an expression of desire that I should remain until the expected hostilities
might be brought to a close. I did so willingly, in gratitude to a
prince to whose good-will my success was mainly indebted. But
the consulate was no longer what it was before. I felt myself too
conversant with local politics, and too well aware of what was going on to be a pleasant companion to its new tenant. At last, on
the 15th of March, when concluding my accounts with Ladha
Damha, the collector of customs at Zanzibar, that official requested me, with the usual mystery, to be the bearer of dispatches, pri-

vately addressed by his prince, to the home government. I could easily guess what they contained. Unwilling, however, to undertake such a duty when living at the consulate, and seeing how totally opposed to official *convenance* such a procedure was, I frankly stated my objections to Ladha Damha, and repeated the conversation to Captain Rigby. As may be imagined, this little event did not diminish his desire to see me depart.

Still I was unwilling to leave the field of my labors while so much remained to be done. As my health appeared gradually to return under the influence of repose and comparative comfort, I would willingly have delayed at the island till the answer to an application for leave of absence, and to a request for additional funds could be received from the government of Bombay and the Royal Geographical Society. But the evident anxiety of my host to disembarrass himself of his guest, and the nervous impatience of my companion—who could not endure the thought of losing an hour—compelled me, sorely against my wish, to abandon my intentions.

Said bin Salim, the ras kafilah, called twice or thrice at the consulate. I refused, however, to see him, and explained the reason to Captain Rigby. That gentleman agreed with me at the time that the Arab had been more than sufficiently rewarded by the sum advanced to him by Lieut. Colonel Hamerton: but—perhaps he remembers the cognomen by which he was known in days of yore among his juvenile *confrères* at Addiscombe—he has since thought proper to change his mind. The jemadar and the Baloch attended me to the doorway of the prince's darbar: I would not introduce them to their master or to the consul, as such introduction would have argued myself satisfied with their conduct, nor would I recommend them for promotion or reward. Ladha Damha put in a faint claim for salary due to the sons of Ramji; but when informed of the facts of the case he at once withdrew it, and I heard no more of it at Zanzibar. As regards the propriety of these severe but equitable measures, my companion was, I believe, at that time of the same opinion as myself: perhaps Captain Speke's prospect of a return to East Africa, and of undertaking a similar exploration, have caused him since that epoch to think, and to think that he then thought, otherwise.

The report of the success of the *Punjaub's* mission left me at liberty to depart. With a grateful heart I bade adieu to a prince whose kindness and personal courtesy will long dwell in my memory, and who, at the parting interview, had expressed a hope to see me again, and had offered me a passage homeward in one of his ships of war. At the time, however, a clipper-built bark, the *Dragon of Salem*, Captain M'Farlane commanding, was discharging cargo in the harbor, preparatory to sailing with the S.W. monsoon for Aden. The captain consented to take us on board: Captain Rigby, however, finding his boat too crowded, was compelled to omit accompanying us—a little mark of civility not unusual in the East. His place, however, was well filled up by Seedy Mubarak Bombay, whose honest face appeared at that moment, by contrast, peculiarly attractive.

On the 22d of March, 1859, the clove-shrubs and the cocoa-trees of Zanzibar again faded from my eyes. After crossing and recrossing three times the tedious line, we found ourselves anchored, on the 16th of April, near the ill-omened black walls of the Aden crater.

The crisis of my.African sufferings had taken place during my voyage upon the Tanganyika Lake: the fever, however, still clung to me like the shirt of Nessus. Mr. Apothecary Frost, of Zanzibar, had advised a temporary return to Europe: Dr. Steinhaeuser, the civil surgeon, Aden, also recommended a lengthened period of rest. I bade adieu to the coal-hole of the East on the 28th of April, 1859, and in due time greeted with becoming heartiness the shores of my native land.

FINIS CORONAT OPUS!

The Elephant Rock ('Ακρωτήριον 'Ελέφας, Periplus II. راس الفيل), seen from fifteen miles at sea, direction S.W.

APPENDICES.

APPENDIX I.

COMMERCE, IMPORTS, AND EXPORTS.

COMMERCE has for ages been a necessity to the East African, who can not be contented without his clothing and his ornaments, which he receives in barter for the superfluity of his country. Against its development, however, serious obstacles have hitherto interposed. On the sea-board and in the island the Banyans, by monopolizing the import traffic, do injury to the internal trade. In the interior the Wasawahili excite, with all the animosity of competition, the barbarians against Arab interlopers, upon the same sordid and short-sighted principle that the latter display when opposing the ingress of Europeans. Finally the Arabs, according to their own confession, have by rapacity and imprudence impoverished the people without enriching themselves. Their habit of sending fundi on trading trips is, as has been explained, most prejudicial both to seller and buyer; the prices of provisions as well as of merchandise increase almost visibly; and though the evil might be remedied by a little combination, solidarity of interests being unknown, that little is nowhere found. All, Banyans, Wasawahili, and Arabs, like semi-civilized people generally, abhor and oppose a free trade, which they declare would be as injurious to themselves as doubtless advantageous to the country. Here, as in Europe, the battle of protection has still to be fought; and here, unlike Europe, the first step toward civilization, namely, the facility of intercourse between the interior and the coast, has yet to be created.

The principal imports into East Africa are domestics and piece goods, plain and unbleached cotton cloths, beads, and brass wire. The minor items for the native population are prints, colored cloths, Indian and Arabian, broadcloth, calicoes, caps, ironware, knives and needles, iron and copper wires for ornaments, and in some regions trinkets and ammunition. A small trade, chiefly confined to the Arabs, is done in provisions, spices, drugs, and other luxuries.

The people of East Africa, when first visited, were satisfied with the worst and flimsiest kaniki or indigo-dyed Indian cotton. This they presently gave up for the "merkani," American "domestics," or unbleached shirting and sheeting, which now supplies the markets from Abyssinia to the Mozambique. But the wild men are losing predilection for a stuff which is neither comfortable nor durable, and in many regions the tribes, satisfied with goat-skins and tree-barks, prefer to invest their capital in the more attractive and durable beads and wire. It would evidently be advantageous if England or her Indian colonies would manufacture an article better suited to the wants of the country than that at present in general use; but, under existing circumstances, there is little probability of this being done.

The "domestics" from the mills near Salem, Lawrence, Manchester, and others, called in the Island of Zanzibar wilaiti ("foreign"), or khami (the "raw"), is known throughout the inner country as "merkani," or American. These unbleached cottons are of two kinds: the wilaiti mpana (broad) or sheeting, sold in pieces about 30 yards long and 36 to 38 inches broad, and the wilaiti kabibu (narrow) or shirting, of the same length but less in breadth, from 32 to 34 inches. In the different mills the lengths vary, the extremes being 24 and 36 yards. The cloth measures in use throughout the country are the following:

2¼ Fitr (short spans)	= 1 Mukono, Ziraá, or cubit.
2 Mikono, or Ziraá (cubits)	= 1 Half-Shukkah (*i. e.*, 3 feet of domestics).
2 Half-Shukkah	= 1 Shukkah, Mwenda, Upande, or Lupande, the Portuguese Braça (*i. e.*, 6 feet of domestics).
2 Shukkahs	= 1 Tobe (Ar. Saub), Doti, Unguo ya ku shona (washing-cloth), or simply Unguo (12 ft.).
2 Doti	= 1 Takah.
7 to 11 Doti	= 1 Jurah or Gorah, the piece.

The fitr or short span is from the extended end of the forefinger to the thumb; the shibr or long span is from the thumb to the little finger; of these, two go to that primitive measure the cubit or elbow-length. Two cubits in long measure compose the wár or yard, and two wár the ba'a or fathom.

The price of domestics greatly varies in dear years and cheap years. At Zanzibar it sometimes falls to 2 doll. per gorah or piece, and it often rises to 2.75 doll. When the dollar is alluded to, the Maria Theresa crown is always meant. The price in Bombay is from 213 to 215 Co.'s rs. per cent. At Zanzibar the crown is divided, like the rupee, into 16 annas, and each anna into 9 or 8 pice; of these the full number is 128 to the dollar, but it is subject to incessant fluctuations. Merchants usually keep account in dollars and cents. The Arabs divide the dollar as follows:

4 Ruba baisah (the " pie")' = Baisah (in the plur. Biyas), the Indian Paisa.
8 Biyas = 1 Anna.
2 Annas, or 16 Pice = 1 Tumun or eighth.
4 Annas, or 32 Pice, or 25 cents = 1 Ruba, Rubo or Quarter-dollar, the Indian Paola.
2 Ruba, or 64 Pice, or 50 Cents = 1 Nusu or Half-dollar.
2 Nusu = Dollar.

The Spanish or pillar-dollar is called by the Arabs abu madfa, and by the Wasawahili riyal mazinga (the "cannon-dollar"). In the East generally it is worth from 6 to 8 per cent. more than the Maria Theresa, but at Zanzibar, not being a legal tender, the value is unfixed. The only subdivision of this coin generally known is the seringe, pistoline, or "small quarter-dollar," which is worth only 10 pice and 2 pies, whereas the Ruba, or quarter of the Maria Theresa, is 32 pice. The French 5 franc piece, raised in value by a somewhat arbitrary process from 114 to 110 per 100 "piastres d'Espagne" by M. Guillain in 1846, has no currency, though the Banyans attempt to pass them off upon strangers at 108 for 100 Maria Theresas. In selling, the price ranges from 15 to 22 shukkahs, each of which, assuming the dollar or German crown to be worth 4s. 2d., will be worth upon the island from 6d. to 8d. The shukkah is, as has been said, the shilling and florin of East Africa, and it is assuredly the worst circulating medium ever invented by mankind. The progress of its value as it recedes from the sea-board, and other details concerning it, which may be useful to future travelers, have been treated of in the preceding pages.

First in importance among the cloths is the kaniki or kiniki; its names and measures are made to differ by the traders according to the fashion of semi-civilized people, who seek in confusion and intricacy facilities for fraud and chicanery. The popular divisions are—

4 Mikono, Ziraá or cubits = 1 Shukkah.
2 Shukkah = 1 Doti or Tobe.
2 Doti = 1 Jurah, Gorah, or Takah.
2 Takah = 1 Korjah, Kori, or score.

Of this indigo-dyed cotton there are three kinds: the best, which is close and neatly made, is seldom exported from Zanzibar. The gorah or piece of 16 cubits, 45 inches in breadth, is worth about 1 dollar. The common variety, 40 inches broad, supplied to the markets of the interior, costs about half that sum; and the worst kind, which averages in breadth 36 inches, represents a little less. The value of the korjah or score fluctuates between 8 and 13 dollars. Assuming, therefore, the average at 10 dollars, and the number of shukkahs contained in the gorah at 80, the price of each will represent 6d. Thus it is little inferior in price to the merkani or domestics when purchased upon the sea-board: its progress of value in the interior, however, is by no means in proportion, and by some tribes it is wholly rejected.

The lucrative bead trade of Zanzibar is now almost entirely in the hands of the Banyan capitalists, who, by buying up ships' cargoes, establish their own prices, and produce all the inconveniences of a monopoly. In laying in a stock the traveler must not trust himself to these men, who seize the opportunity of palming off the waste and refuse of their warehouses: he is advised to ascertain from respectable Arab merchants, on their return from the interior, the varieties requisite on the line of march. Any neglect in choosing beads, besides causing daily inconvenience, might arrest an expedition on the very threshold of success: toward the end of these long African journeys, when the real work of exploration commences, want of outfit tells fatally. The bead monopolizers of Zanzibar supplied the East African expedition with no less than nine men's loads of the cheapest white and black beads, some of which were thrown away, as no man would accept them at a gift. Finally, the utmost economy must be exercised in beads: apparently exhaustless, a large store goes but a little way: the minor purchases of a European would average 10 strings or necklaces per diem, and thus a man's load rarely outlasts the fifth week.

Beads, called by the Arabs kharaz, and by' the Wasawahili ushanga, are yearly imported into East Africa by the ton—in quantities which excite the traveler's surprise that so little is seen of them.   For centuries there has been a regular supply of these ornaments; load after load has been absorbed; but although they are by no means the most perishable of substances, and though the people, like the Indians, carry their wealth upon their persons, not a third of the population wears any considerable quantity.   There are about 400 current varieties, of which each has its peculiar name, value, and place of preference; yet, being fabricated at a distance from the spot, they lack the perpetual change necessary to render them thoroughly attractive.   In Urori and Ubena, antiquated marts, now nearly neglected, there are varieties highly prized by the people : these might be imitated with advantage.

For trading purposes a number of different kinds must be laid in—for travelers, the coral or scarlet, the pink porcelain, and the large blue glass bead, are more useful than other colors.   Yet in places even the expensive coral bead has been refused.

Beads are sold in Zanzibar Island by the following weights :

16 Wakiyyah (ounces, each = 1 dollar in weight) = 1 Ratl (or pound? in the plural, Artál).
3 Ratl, or 48 Wakiyyah = 1 Man (Maund).
12 Amnan (Maunds) = 1 Frasilah (35 to 36 pounds).
60 Artál (pounds) = 1 Frasilah.
20 to 22 Farásilah (according to the article purchased) = 1 Kandi (Candy).

The Zanzibar lb. is the current English avoirdupois.   The Arabs use a ratl without standard, except that it should be equal to sixteen Maria Theresa dollars.   According to M. Guillain, it is four grammes (each 22.966 grs. avoir.) less than the English lb., and when reduced to seven grammes it is considered under weight.   The "man" or maund is the general measure : there are, however, three varieties.   The "man" of Zanzibar consists of three ratl, that of Maskat contains nine, and that of Oman generally 0.25 less than the Zanzibar maund.   The frasilah (in the plural farásilah) may roughly be assumed as one third of the cwt.: the word probably gave rise to the English coffee-weight called a "frail."

The measures of beads are as complicated and arbitrary as those of cloth.   The following are the terms known throughout the interior, but generally unintelligible at Zanzibar, where this merchandise is sold by weight :

4 Bitil (each a single length from index tip to wrist) = 1 Khete.
10 Khete (each a doubled length round the throat, or round the thumb, to the elbow-bone) = 1 Fundo (i. e., a " knot").
10 Fundo (in the plural, Mafundo) = 1 Ugoyye, or Ugoe.
10 Ugoyye (or 60 Fundo) = 1 Miranga, or Gana.

Of these bead measures there are local complications.   In the central regions, for instance, the khete is of half size, and the fundo consists of five, not of ten khete.

Beads are purchased for the monopolizers of Zanzibar unstrung, and before entering the country it is necessary to measure and prepare the lengths for barter.   The string, called "ut'hembwe" (in the plural " t'hembwe"), is generally made of palm-fibre, and much depends for successful selling, especially in the larger kinds of beads, upon the regularity and attractiveness of the line.   It will be remembered that beads in East Africa represent the copper and smaller silver coins of European countries; it is, however, impossible to reduce the khete, the length most used in purchases, to any average : it varies from a half-penny to threepence.   The average value of the khete in Zanzibar coin is three pice, and about 100 khete are included in the man or maund.   The traveler will find the bitil used as our farthing, the khete is the penny, the shukkah kaniki is the sixpence and shilling, the shukkah merkani and the fundo represent the half-crown and crown, while the Barsati cloth, the kitindi or coil bracelet, and the larger measures of beads, form the gold money.   The following varieties are imported in extensive outfits.   Nos. 1, 2, and 3, are the expensive kinds; Nos. 4, 5, and 6, are in local demand, cheap in the maritime, and valuable in the central regions, and the rest are the more ordinary sorts.   All those that are round and pierced are called indifferently by the Arabs madruji, or the "drilled."

1. Samsam (Ar.) sámesáme (Kis.), kimara-p'hamba (food-finishers), joho (scarlet cloth), and kifungá-mgi (town-breakers, because the women are mad for them), are the various names for the small coral bead, a scarlet enameled upon a white ground. They are known at Zanzibar as kharaz-kartasi—paper beads—because they are sent into the country ready strung, and packed in paper parcels, which ought to weigh 4

pounds each, but are generally found to vary from 8 to 10 fundo or knots. Of this bead there are 15 several sizes, and the value of the frasilah is from 13 to 16 dollars at Zanzíbar. In Unyamwezi, where the sámesáme is in greatest demand, one fundo is equivalent to 1 shukkah merkani, and 6 khete to the shukkah kaniki.

2. Next in demand to the sámesáme, throughout the country, except at Ujiji, where they lose half their value, are the pink porcelain, called gulabi (the rosy), or máguru lá nzige (locust's feet). The price in Zanzibar varies from 12 to 15 dollars per frasilah.

3. The blue porcelain, called in Venice ajerino, and in East Africa langiyo or murtutu (blue vitriol) is of three several sizes, and the best is of the lightest color. The larger variety, called langiyo mkuba, fetches, at Zanzibar, from 6 to 12 dollars per frasilah, and the p'heke, or smaller, from 7 to 9 dollars. In Usagara and Unyamwezi, where from 3 to 4 fundo are equivalent to the shukkah merkani, and 1 to 2 to the shukkah kaniki, it is used for minor purchases, where the sámesáme would be too valuable. It is little prized in other parts, and between Unyamwezi and Ujiji it falls to the low level of the white porcelain.

4. A local variety, current from Msene to the Tanganyika Lake, where, in the heavier dealings, as the purchase of slaves and ivory, a few strings are always required to cap the bargain, is called mzizima, mtunda, balghami, and jelabi, the ringel perle of Germany. It is a large flat bead of glass; the khete contains about 150, and each item acts as a copper coin. The mzizima is of two varieties; the more common is a dark blue, the other is of a whitish and opaline tint. At Zanzibar the frasilah costs from 7 to 9 dollars. In Unyamwezi 3 fundo are equivalent to 1 shukkah merkani, and 1 fundo to 1 shukkah kaniki.

5. Another local variety is the balghami mkuba, popularly called sungomaji, a bead made at Nuremberg (?). It is a porcelain, about the size of a pigeon's egg, and of two colors, white and light blue. The sungomaji, attached to a thin cord or twine, is worn singly or in numbers as an ornament round the neck, and the people complain that the polish soon wears off. At Zanzibar the price per 1000 is from 15 to 20 dollars, but it is expected to decline to 10 dollars. This bead is useful in purchasing ivory in Ugogo and Unyamwezi, and in hiring boats at Ujiji: its relative value to cloth is 19 per shukkah merkani, and 15 per shukkah kaniki.

6. The sofi, called in Italian cannettone, resembles bits of broken pipe-stems, about two thirds of an inch in length. It is of various colors, white, brick-red, and black. Each bead is termed masaro, and is used like pice in India: of these the khete contains from 55 to 60. The price varies, at Zanzibar, from 2 to 3 dollars per frasilah; in the interior, however, the value greatly increases, on account of insufficient importation. This bead, in 1858, was in great demand throughout Usagara, Unyamwezi, and the western regions, where it was as valuable as the sámesáme. Having neglected to lay in a store at Zanzibar, the East African Expedition was compelled to exchange cloth for it at Msene and Ujiji, giving 1 shukkah merkani for 30 to 35 khete, and 1 shukkah kaniki for 15 to 25. In Ujiji, however, many of the purchases were rejected because the bits had become small by wear, or had been chipped off by use.

7. The staple of commerce is a coarse porcelain bead, of various colors, known in Zanzibar by the generic name of háfizi. There are three principal kinds. The khanyera or ushanga waupa (white beads) are common throughout the country. The average value, at Zanzibar, is 6 dollars per frasilah: in Unyamwezi, 4 fundo were equivalent to the shukkah merkani, and 2 to 3 to the kaniki; but the people, glutted with this bead (as many as 20,000 strings were supplied to the East African Expedition by the Banyans of Zanzibar), preferred 1 khete of sámesáme to 3 of khanyera. The kidunduguru is a dull brick-red bead, worth at Zanzibar from 5 to 7 dollars per frasilah, but little prized in the interior, where it is derisively termed khanyera ya mk'hundu. Another red variety of háfizi is called merkani: it is finely made to resemble the sámesáme, and costs from 7 to 11 dollars per frasilah. Of this bead there are four several subdivisions. The uzanzawírá or samuli (ghee-colored) is a bright yellow porcelain, worth at Zanzibar from 7 to 9 dollars per frasilah. It is in demand throughout Chhaga and the Masai country, but is rarely seen on the central line.

8. The sukoli are orange-colored or rhubarb-tinted porcelain, which average at Zanzibar from 7 to 9 dollars. They are prized in Usagara and Ugogo, but are little worn in other places.

9. The nílí (green), or ukití wa mnazi (coco-leaves), are little beads of transparent green glass; they are of three sizes, the smallest of which is called kíkítí. The Zan-

zibar price is from 6 to 11 dollars. In Ujiji they are highly valued, and are readily taken in small quantities throughout the central line.

10. The ghubari (dust-colored), or nya kifu (?) is a small dove-colored bead, costing, in Zanzibar, from 7 to 8 dollars. It is used in Uzaramo, but its dullness of aspect prevents it being a favorite.

11. The lungenya or lak'hio is a coarse red porcelain, valued at 5 to 6 dollars in Zanzibar, and now principally exported to Uruwwa and the innermost regions of Central Africa.

12. The bubu (ububu ?), also called ukumwi and ushanga ya vipande, are black Venetians, dull dark porcelain, ranging, at Zanzibar, from 5 to 7 dollars. They are of fourteen sizes, large, medium, and small; the latter are the most valued. These beads are taken by the Wazaramo. In East Usagara and Unyamwezi they are called khuni or firewood, nor will they be received in barter except when they excite a temporary caprice.

The other beads, occasionally met with, are the sereketi, ovals of white or garnet-red, prized in Khutu; choroko or mágiyo, dull green porcelains; undriyo maupe (?), mauve-colored, round or oval; undriyo mausi (?), dark lavender; asmani, sky-colored glass; and pusange, blue Bohemian glass beads, cut into facets. The people of the coast also patronize a variety of large fancy articles, flowered, shelled, and otherwise ornamented; these, however, rarely find their way into the interior.

After piece goods and beads, the principal articles of traffic, especially on the northern lines and the western portion of the central route, are masango (in the singular sango), or brass wires, called by the Arabs hajúlah. Nos. 4 or 5 are preferred. They are purchased in Zanzibar, when cheap, for 12 dollars, and when dear for 16 dollars per frasilah. When imported up country the frasilah is divided into three or four large coils, called by the Arabs daur, and by the Africans khata, for the convenience of attachment to the banghy-pole. Arrived at Unyanyembe they are converted by artisans into the kitindi, or coil-bracelets, described in the preceding pages. Each daur forms two or three of these bulky ornaments, of which there are about 11 to the frasilah, and the weight is thus upward of three pounds. The charge for the cutting, cleaning, and twisting into shape is about 1 doti of domestics for 50 kitindis. The value of the kitindi, throughout Unyamwezi, in 1858, was 1 doti merkani; at Ujiji, where they are in demand for slaves and ivory, the price was doubled. Thus the kitindi, worth one dollar each—when cheap, nine are bought for ten dollars—in Zanzibar, are from five dollars in the lake regions. Kitindi were formerly made of copper wire; it has fallen into disuse on account of its expense—at Zanzibar from 15 to 20 dollars per frasilah. Large iron wires, called senyenge, are confined to Ugogo and the northern countries inhabited by the Wamasai. The East Africans have learned to draw fine wire, which they call uzi wa shaba (brass thread); they also import from the coast Nos. 22 to 25, and employ them for a variety of decorative purposes, which have been already alluded to. The average price of this small wire at Zanzibar is 12 dollars per frasilah. As has been mentioned, sat or zinc, called by the Africans bati (tin), is imported by the Wajiji.

The principal of the minor items are colored cloths, called by the people "cloths with names:" of these, many kinds are imported by every caravan. In some regions, Ugogo for instance, the people will not sell their goats and more valuable provisions for plain piece-goods; their gross and gaudy tastes lead them to despise sober and uniform colors. The sultans invariably demand for themselves and their wives showy goods, and complete their honga or black-mail with domestics and indigo-dyed cottons, which they divide among their followers. Often, too, a bit of scarlet broadcloth, thrown in at the end of a lengthened haggle, opens a road and renders impossibilities possible.

The colored cloths may be divided into three kinds—woolens, cottons, and silks mixed with cotton. Of the former, the principal varieties now imported are joho or broadcloth; of the second, beginning with the cheapest, are barsati, dabwani, jam-dani, bandira, shít (chintz), khuzarangi, ukaya, sohari, shali, taujiri, msutu, kikoi, and shazar or mukunguru; the mixed and most expensive varieties are the subai, dewli, sabuni, khesi, and masnafu. Traveling Arabs usually take a piece of baftah or white calico as kafan or shrouds for themselves or their companions in case of accidents. At Zanzibar the value of a piece of 24 yds. is 1 dollar 25 cents. Blankets were at first imported by the Arabs, but being unsuited to the climate and to the habits of the people, they soon became a drug in the market.

Joho (a corruption of the Arabic johh) is a coarse article, either blue or scarlet.

As a rule, even Asiatics ignore the value of broadcloth, estimating it, as they do guns and watches, by the shine of the exterior; the African looks only at the length of the pile and the depth of the tint. The Zanzibar valuation of the cheap English article is usually 50 cents (2s. 1d.) per yard; in the interior, rising rapidly through double and treble to four times that price, it becomes a present for a prince. At Ujiji and other great ivory-marts there is a demand for this article, blue as well as red; it is worn, like the shukkah merkani, round the loins by men and round the bosom by women, who, therefore, require a tobe or double length. At Unyanyembe there are generally pauper Arabs or Wasawahili artisans who can fashion the merchants' supplies into the kizbao or waistcoats affected by the African chiefs in imitation of their more civilized visitors.

Of the second division the cheapest is the barsati, called by the Africans kitambi; it is a blue cotton cloth, with a broad red stripe extending along one quarter of the depth, the other three quarters being dark blue; the red is either of European or Cutch dye. The former is preferred upon the coast for the purchase of copal. Of this Indian stuff there are three kinds, varying in size, color, and quality; the cheapest is worth at Zanzibar (where, however, like dabwani, it is usually sold by the gorah of two uzar or loin-cloths) from 5 to 7 dollars per score; the second 10 dollars 50 cents; and the best 14 to 15 dollars. The barsati in the interior represents the doti or tobe of merkani. On the coast it is a favorite article of wear with the poorer freemen, slaves, and women. Beyond the maritime regions the chiefs will often refuse a barsati, if of small dimensions and flimsy texture. Formerly, the barsati was made of silk, and cost 7 dollars per loin-cloth. Of late years the Wanyamwezi have taken into favor the barsati or kitambi banyani; it is a thin white long cloth, called in Bombay kora (Corah, or cotton piece-goods), with a narrow reddish border of madder or other dye stamped in India or at Zanzibar. The piece of 39 yards, which is divided into 20 shukkah, costs at Bombay 4.50 Co.'s rs.; at Zanzibar 2 dollars 50 cents; and the price of printing the edge is 1 dollar 75 cents.

The dabwani is a kind of small blue and white check made at Maskat; one fourth of its breadth is a red stripe, edged with white and yellow. This stuff, which from its peculiar stiffening of gum appears rather like grass-cloth than cotton, is of three kinds: the cheapest, dyed with Cutch colors, is much used in the far interior; it costs at Zanzibar 12 dolls. 50 cents per score of pieces, each two and a half yards long; the medium quality, employed in the copal trade of the coast, is stained with European dye, and superior in work; the score of pieces, each 3 yards long, costs 30 dolls.; and the best, which is almost confined to the Island of Zanzibar, ranges from 40 to 45 dolls. per kori. The dabwani is considered in the interior nearly double the value of the barsati, and it is rarely rejected unless stained or injured.

The jamdani is a sprigged or worked muslin imported from India: though much prized for turbans by the dignitaries of the maritime races, it is rarely carried far up the country. At Zanzibar the price of 10 yards is 1 doll., and the piece of 20 lengths, each sufficient for a turban, may be purchased for 15 dolls.

The bandira (flag stuff) is a red cotton bunting imported from Bombay. It is prized in the interior by women. At Zanzibar the price of this stuff greatly varies; when cheap the piece of 28 yards may be obtained for 2 dolls. 50 cents, when dear it rises to 3 dolls. 50 cents. It is sold by gorah of 7½ shukkahs.

Shít, or chintz, is of many different kinds. The common English is a red cotton, striped yellow and dark green; it fetches from 1 doll. 50 cents to 2 dolls. per piece of 28 yards, and is little prized in the interior. Those preferred, especially in Unyamwezi and Ujiji, are the French and Hamburg; the former is worth at Zanzibar from 4 dolls. 50 cents per piece of 35 yards, to 5 dolls. 50 cents per gorah of 10 shukkahs, and the latter from 5 dolls. to 5 dolls. 50 cents. The most expensive is the "ajemi," that used by the Persians as lining for their lamb's-wool caps; the price is from 50 cents to 1 doll. per yard, which renders it a scarce article even in Zanzibar Island.

The khuzarangi, a European cotton dyed a reddish nankeen, with pomegranate rind and other coloring matters, at Maskat, is almost confined to the Arabs, who make of it their normal garment, the long and sleeved shirt called el dishdashah, or in Kisawahili khanzu. It is the test of foreign respectability and decorum when appearing among the half-clad African races, and the poorest of peddlers will always carry with him one of these nightgown-like robes. The price of the ready-made dishdashah ranges from 50 cents to 2 dolls. 50 cents, and the uncut piece of 16 yards costs from 2 dolls. to 2 dolls. 50 cents.

The ukaya somewhat resembles the kaniki, but it is finer and thinner. This jaconet, manufactured in Europe and dyed in Bombay, is much used by female slaves and concubines as head-veils. The price of the piece of 20 yards, when of inferior quality, is 2 dollars 50 cents; it ranges as high as 12 dollars.

The sohari, or ridia, made at Maskat, is a blue and white check with a red border about 5 inches broad, with smaller stripes of red, blue, and yellow; the ends of the piece are checks of a larger pattern, with red introduced. There are many varieties of this cloth, which, considered as superior to the dabwani as the latter is superior to the barsati, forms an acceptable present to a chief. The cheapest kind, much used in Unyamwezi, costs 16 dollars 25 cents per kori, or score. The higher sort, of which however only 1 to 40 of the inferior is imported into the country, ranges from 22 to 30 dollars.

The shali, a corruption of the Indian shal (shawl), is a common English imitation shawl pattern of the poorest cotton. Bright yellow or red grounds, with the pear pattern and similar ornaments, are much prized by the chiefs of Unyamwezi. The price of the kori, or score, is 25 dollars.

The taujiri (from the Indian taujír burá) is a dark blue cotton stuff, with a gaudy border of madder-red or turmeric-yellow, the former color preferred by the Wahiao, the latter by the Wanyamwezi. The price per score varies from 8 to 17 dollars.

The msutu is a European cotton dyed at Surat, indigo-blue upon a madder-red ground, spotted with white. This print is much worn by Arab and Wasawahili women as a night-dress and morning wrapper; in the interior it becomes a robe of ceremony. At Zanzibar the piece of 20 lengths, each 2.25 yards long and 40 inches broad (two breadths being sewn together), costs 19 dollars. The kisutu, an inferior variety, fetches, per kori of pieces 2.50 yards long, 13 dollars.

The kikoi is a white cotton, made at Surat, coarse and thick, with a broad border of parallel stripes, red, yellow, and indigo-blue: per kori of pieces 2 yards long, and sewn in double breadths, the price is 5 dollars. A superior variety is made principally for the use of women, with a silk border, which costs from 1 to 4 dollars.

The shazar, called throughout the interior mukunguru, is a Cutch-made cotton plaid, with large or small squares, red and white, or black and blue; this cloth is an especial favorite with the Wamasai tribes. The score of pieces, each 2 yards, costs 6 dollars 25 cents. There is a dearer variety, of which each piece is 3 yards long, costing 16 dollars per kori, and therefore rarely sold.

Of the last division of "cloths with names," namely, those of silk and cotton mixed, the most popular is the subaí. It is a striped stuff, with small checks between the lines, and with a half-breadth of border, a complicated pattern of red, black, and yellow. This cloth is used as an uzar, or loin-cloth, by the middle classes of Arabs; the tambua, taraza, or fringe, is applied to the cloth with a band of gold thread at Zanzibar, by Wasawahili. The subai, made at Maskat of Cutch cotton, varies greatly in price: the cheapest, of cotton only, may be obtained for 2 dollars; the medium, generally preferred for presents to great chiefs, is about 5 dollars 50 cents; while the most expensive, inwoven with gold thread, ranges from 8 to 30 dollars.

The dewli is the Indian lungi, a Surat silk, garnished with a border of gold thread and a fringe at Zanzibar. It is a red, yellow, or green ground, striped in various ways, and much prized for uzar. The price of the cheap piece of 3.50 yards is 7 dollars, besides the fringe, which is 2 dollars more; the best, when adorned with gold, rise to 80 dollars.

The sabuni uzar, made in Maskat, is a silk-bordered cotton, a small blue and white check; the red and yellow edging which gives it its value is about one fifth of its breadth. The score of pieces, each 2.50 yards long, varies from 25 to 50 dollars; the more expensive, however, rarely find their way into the interior.

The khesi is a rare importation from Bombay, a scarlet silk, made at Tannah; the piece sold at Bombay for 10 Co.'s rs. fetches at Zanzibar 5 dolls. 50 cents to 6 dollars; this kind is preferred by the Wanyamwezi chiefs; when larger, and adorned with gold stripes, it rises to 35 Co.'s rs., or 19 dollars, and is prized by the Banyans and Hindis of Zanzibar.

The masnafu is rare like the khesi; it is a mixed silk and cotton cloth, of striped pattern, made at Maskat. The cheapest is a piece of 1.75 yards, costing 2 to 5 dollars, and highly regarded in Unyamwezi; the larger kinds, of 2.50 yards, rise from 5 to 6 dollars, and the Arabs will pay from 20 to 25 dollars for those worked with gold thread.

These notes upon the prices of importations into Central Africa rest upon the authority of the Hindoos, and principally of Ladha Damha, the collector of customs at Zanzibar. Specimens of the cloths were deposited with the Royal Geographical Society of London, and were described by the kindness of Mr. Alderman Botterill, F. R. G. S.

Remain for consideration the minor and local items of traffic.

The skull-caps are of two kinds. One is a little fez, locally called kummah. It is made in France, rarely at Bagdad, and sells at Zanzibar for 5 dolls. 50 cents to 9 dollars per dozen. The cheaper kind is preferred in Unyamwezi; it is carried up from the coast by Arab slaves and Wasawahili merchants, and is a favorite wear with the sultan and the mtongi. At Unyanyembe the price of the fez rises to 1 dollar. The "alfiyyah" is the common Surat cap, worked with silk upon a cotton ground; it is affected by the diwans and shomwis of the coasts. The "vis-gol," or 20-stitch, preferred for importation, cost 8 dollars per score; the "tris-gol," or 30-stitch, 13 dollars; and the "chalis-gol," or 40-stitch, 18 dollars.

Besides these articles, a little hardware finds its way into the country. Knives, razors, fish-hooks, and needles are useful, especially in the transit of Uzaramo. As an investment they are useless; the people who make for themselves an article which satisfies their wants, will not part with valuables to secure one a little better. They have small axes and sharp spears, consequently they will not buy dear cutlery; they have gourds, and therefore they care little for glass and china. The Birmingham trinkets and knicknacks, of which travelers take large outfits to savage and barbarous countries, would in East Africa be accepted by women and children as presents, but, unless in exceptional cases, they would not procure a pound of grain; mirrors are cheap and abundant in Zanzibar, yet they are rarely imported into the interior. The people will devise new bijouterie for themselves, but they will not borrow it from strangers. In the maritime regions, where the tribes are more civilized, they will covet such foreign contrivances as dollars, blankets, snuff-boxes, and tin cylinders, which can be converted into tobacco pouches: the Wanyamwezi would not regard them. Similarly in Somaliland, a case of Birmingham goods carried through the country returned to Aden almost full.

Coffee, sugar, and soap may generally be obtained in small quantities from the Arabs of Unyanyembe. At Zanzibar the price of common coffee is 3 dollars 75 cents, and of Mocha 5 dollars 50 cents per frasilah. Sugar is of three kinds: the buluji, or loaf-sugar, imported from America, averages 6 annas; sukkari za mawe, or sugar-candy, fetches upon the island 5 dollars 50 cents per frasilah; and the bungálá, or sukkari za mchanga (brown Bengal sugar), costs 3 dollars 50 cents; gur, or molasses, sells at Zanzibar for 1 dollar 25 cents per frasilah. Soap is brought to Zanzibar Island by the Americans, French, and India merchants.

The other articles of importation into Zanzibar, which, however, so rarely find their way into the interior, that they do not merit detailed notice, are—rice and other cereals from Bombay and Western India; shipping materials, canvas, rigging, hempen cord, planks and boards, paint, pitch, turpentine, linseed-oil, bees'-wax, and tar, from America and India; metals from Europe and India; furniture from Europe and America, China and Bombay; carpets and rugs from Turkey and Persia; mats from Madagascar; made-up clothes from Maskat and Yemen; glass-ware from Europe and America; pottery, paper, and candles from Europe and Bombay; kuzah (water-jars) from the Persian Gulf; woods and timber from Madagascar, the Mozambique, and the coast as far north as Mombasah; skins and hides from the Benadir; salt fish (shark and others) from Oman, Hazramaut, and the Benadir; brandy, rum, peppermint, eau de Cologne, syrups and pickles, tobacco, cigars, and tea, from Bombay, France, and the Mauritius; rose-water from the Gulf; attar of rose and of sandal from Bombay; dates, almonds, and raisins from Arabia and the Gulf; gums and ambergris from Madagascar, the Mozambique, and the "Sayf-Tawil" (the long low coast extending from Ras Awath, in N. lat. 5° 33', to Ras el-Khayl, N. lat. 7° 44'); aloes and dragon's-blood from Socotra; incense, gum Arabic, and myrrh from the Somali country and the Benadir; turmeric, opium, ginger, nutmegs, colombo-root, cardamoms, cinnamon, aniseed, camphor, benzoin, asafœtida, saltpetre, potash, blue vitriol, alum, soda, saffron, garlic, fenugreek, and other drugs and spices from Bombay and Western India.

The staple articles of the internal trade throughout the regions extending from the coast of the Indian Ocean to the Lakes of Central Africa are comprised in slaves and cattle, salt, iron, tobacco, mats and strainers, and tree-barks and ropes. Of these, all except salt have been noticed in detail in the preceding pages.

Salt is brought down during the season from East Arabia to Zanzibar by Arab dows, and is heaped up for sale on a strip of clear ground under the eastern face of the gurayza or fort. It is of two kinds: the fine rock salt sells at 6 annas per frasilah, and the inferior, which is dark and sandy, at about half that price. On the coast the principal ports and towns supply themselves with sea salt evaporated in the rudest way. Pits sunk near the numerous lagoons and back-waters allow the saline particles to infiltrate; the contents, then placed in a pierced earthen pot, are allowed to strain into a second beneath. They are inspissated by boiling, and are finally dried in the sun, when the mass assumes the form of sand. This coarse salt is sold after the rains, when it abounds, for its weight of holcus; when dear, the price is doubled. In the interior there are two great markets, and the regularity of communication enables the people to fare better as regards the luxury than the more civilized races of Abyssinia and Harar, where of a millionaire it is said, "He eateth salt." An inferior article is exported from Ugogo, about half way between the east coast and the Tanganyika Lake. A superior quality is extracted from the pits near the Rusugi River, in Western Uvinza, distant but a few days from Ujiji. For the prices and other conditions of sale the reader is referred to Chapters V. and VII.

The subject of exports will be treated of at some length; it is not only interesting from its intrinsic value, but it is capable of considerable development, and it also offers a ready entrance for civilization. The African will never allow the roads to be permanently closed—none but the highly refined among mankind can contemplate with satisfaction a life of utter savagery. The Arab is too wise to despise "protection," but he will not refuse to avail himself of assistance offered by foreigners when they appear as capitalists. Hitherto British interests have been neglected in this portion of the African continent, and the name of England is unknown in the interior. Upon the Island of Zanzibar, in 1857–8, there was not an English firm; no line of steamers connected it with India or the Cape, and, during the dead season, nine months have elapsed before the answer to a letter has been received from home.

The reader is warned that among the East Africans the "bay o shara"—barter or round trade—is an extensive subject, of which only the broad outlines and general indications can be traced. At present the worthlessness of time enables both buyer and seller to haggle *ad libitum*, and the superior craft of the Arab, the Banyan, the Msawahili, and the more civilized slave, has encumbered with a host of difficulties the simplest transactions. It is easy to be a merchant and to buy wholesale at Zanzibar, but a lengthened period of linguistic study and of conversancy with the habits and customs of the people must be spent by the stranger who would engage in the task of retail buying in the interior.

The principal article of export from the Zanzibar coast is copal, from the interior ivory. The minor items are hippopotamus teeth, rhinoceros horns, cattle, skins, hides, and horns, the cereals, timbers, and cowries. Concerning the slaves, who in East Africa still form a considerable item of export, details have been given in the preceding pages. The articles which might be exploited, were means of carriage supplied to the people, are wax and honey, orchella-weed, fibrous substances, and a variety of gums.

The copal of Zanzibar, which differs materially from that of the western coast of Mexico and the cowaee (Australian dammar?) of New Zealand, is the only article convertible into the fine varnishes now so extensively used throughout the civilized world.

As the attention of the expedition was particularly directed to the supplies of copal in East Africa by Dr. G. Buist, LL.D., Secretary to the Bombay branch of the R. G. Society, many inquiries and visits to the copal diggings were made. In the early part of 1857 specimens of the soils and subsoils, and of the tree itself, were forwarded to the Society.

The copal-tree is called by the Arabs shajar el sandarús, from the Hindoostani chhandarus; by the Wasawahili, msandarusi; and by the Wazaramo and other maritime races, mnángú. The tree still lingers on the island and the main land of Zanzibar. It was observed at Mombasah, Saadani, Muhonyera, and Mzegera of Uzaramo; and was heard of at Bagamoyo, Mbuamaji, and Kilwa. It is by no means, as some have supposed, a shrubby thorn; its towering bole has formed canoes 60 feet long, and a single tree has sufficed for the kelson of a brig. The average size, however, is about half that height, with from 3 to 6 feet girth near the ground; the bark is smooth, the lower branches are often within reach of a man's hand, and the tree frequently emerges from a natural ring-fence of dense vegetation. The trunk is of a yellow-whitish tinge, rendering the tree conspicuous amid the dark African jungle-growths; it is dotted with exudations of raw gum, which is found scattered in bits about the base; and it is infested by ants, especially by a long ginger-colored and semi-transparent variety, called by the people maji-m'oto, or "boiling water," from its fiery bite. The copal-wood is yellow-tinted, and the saw collects from it large flakes; when dried and polished, it darkens to a honey-brown, and being well veined, it is used for the panels of doors. The small and pliable branches, freshly cut, form favorite "bakur," the kurbaj or bastinadoing instrument of these regions; after long keeping they become brittle. The modern habitat of the tree is the alluvial sea-plain and the anciently raised beach: though extending over the crest of the latter formation, it ceases to be found at any distance beyond the landward counterslope, and it is unknown in the interior.

The gum copal is called by the Arabs and Hindoos sandarus, by the Wasawahili sandarusi, and by the Wanyamwezi—who employ it, like the people of Mexico and Yucatan, as incense in incantations and medicinings—sirokko and mámnángu. This semi-fossil is not "washed out by streams and torrents," but "crowed" or dug up by the coast-clans and the barbarians of the maritime region. In places it is found when sinking piles for huts, and at times it is picked up in spots overflowed by the high tides. The East African sea-board, from Ras Gomani in S. lat. 3° to Ras Delgado in 10° 41', with a medium depth of 30 miles, may indeed be called the "copal coast;" every part supplies more or less the gum of commerce. Even a section of this line, from the mouth of the Pangani River to Ngao (Monghou), would, if properly exploited, suffice to supply all our present wants.

The Arabs and Africans divide the gum into two different kinds. The raw copal (copal vert of the French market) is called sandarusi za miti, "tree copal," or chakází, corrupted by the Zanzibar merchant to "jackass" copal. This chakazi is either picked from the tree, or is found, as in the Island of Zanzibar, shallowly imbedded in the loose soil, where it has not remained long enough to obtain the phase of bitumenization. To the eye it is smoky or clouded inside, it feels soft, it becomes like putty when exposed to the action of alcohol,'and it viscidizes in the solution used for washing the true copal. Little valued in European technology, it is exported to Bombay, where it is converted into an inferior varnish for carriages and palanquins, and to China, where the people have discovered, it is said, for utilizing it, a process which, like the manufacture of rice paper and of Indian ink, they keep secret. The price of chakazi varies from 4 to 9 dollars per frasilah.

The true or ripe copal, properly called sandarusi, is the produce of vast extinct forests, overthrown in former ages either by some violent action of the elements, or exuded from the roots of the tree by an abnormal action which exhausted and destroyed it. The gum, buried at depths beyond atmospheric influence, has, like amber and similar gum resins, been bitumenized in all its purity, the volatile principles being fixed by moisture and by the exclusion of external air. That it is the produce of a tree is proved by the discovery of pieces of gum embedded in a touch-wood which crumbles under the fingers; the "goose-skin," which is the impress of sand or gravel, shows that it was buried in a soft state; and the bees, flies, gnats, and other insects which are sometimes found in it delicately preserved, seems to disprove a remote geologic antiquity. At the end of the rains it is usually carried ungarbled to Zanzibar. When garbled upon the coast it acquires an additional value of 1 dollar per frasilah. The Banyan embarks it on board his own boat, or pays a freight varying from 2 to 4 annas, and the ushur or government tax is 6 annas per frasilah, with half an anna for charity. About 8 annas per frasilah are deducted for "tare and tret." At Zanzibar, after being sifted and freed from heterogenous matter, it is sent by the Banyan retailer to the Indian market or sold to the foreign merchant. It is then washed in solutions of various strengths: the lye is supposed to be composed of soda and other agents for softening the water; its proportions, however, are kept a profound secret. European technologists have, it is said, vainly proposed theoretical methods for the delicate part of the operation which is to clear the goose-skin of dirt. The Americans exported the gum uncleaned, because the operation is better performed at Salem. Of late years they have begun to prepare it at Zanzibar, like the Hamburg traders. When taken from the solution, in which from 20 to 37 per cent. is lost, the gum is washed, sun-dried for some hours, and cleaned with a hard brush, which must not, however, injure the goose-skin; the dark "eyes," where the dirt has sunk deep, are also picked out with an iron tool. It is then carefully garbled, with due regard to color and size. There are many tints and peculiarities known only to those whose interests compel them to study and to observe copal, which, like cotton and Cashmere shawls, requires years of experience. As a rule, the clear and semi-transparent are the best; then follow the numerous and almost imperceptible varieties of dull white, lemon color, amber yellow, rhubarb yellow, bright red, and dull red. Some specimens of this vegetable fossil appear by their dirty and blackened hue to have been subjected to the influence of fire; others again are remarkable for a tender grass-green color. According to some authorities, the gum, when long kept, has been observed to change its tinge. The sizes are fine, medium, and large, with many subdivisions; the pieces vary from the dimensions of small pebbles to 2 or 3 ounces; they have been known to weigh 5 lbs., and, it is said, at Salem a piece of 35 lbs. is shown. Lastly, the gum is thrown broadcast into boxes and exported from the island. The Hamburg merchants keep European coopers, who put together the cases whose material is sent out to them. It is almost impossible to average the export of copal from Zanzibar. According to the late Lieutenant Colonel Hamerton, it varies from 800,000 to 1,200,000 lbs. per annum, of which Hamburg absorbs 150,000 lbs., and Bombay two lacs' worth. The refuse copal used formerly to reach India as "packing," being deemed of no value in commerce; of late years the scarcity of the supply has rendered merchants more careful. The price, also, is subject to incessant fluctuations, and during the last few years it has increased from 4 dolls. 50 cents to a maximum of 12 dollars per frasilah.

According to the Arabs, the redder the soil the better is the copal. The superficies of the copal country is generally a thin coat of white sand, covering a dark and fertilizing humus, the vestiges of decayed vegetation, which varies from a few inches to a foot and a half in depth. In the Island of Zanzibar, which produces only the chakazi or raw copal, the subsoil is a stiff blue clay, the raised sea-beach, and the ancient habitat of the coco. It becomes greasy and adhesive, clogging the hoe in its lower bed; where it is dotted with blood-colored fragments of ochreish earth, proving the presence of oxidizing and chalybeate efficients, and with a fibrous light-red matter, apparently decayed coco-roots. At a depth of from 2 to 3 feet water oozes from the greasy walls of the pit. When digging through these formations, the gum copal occurs in the vegetable soil overlying the clayey subsoil.

A visit to the little port of Saadani afforded different results. After crossing 3 miles of alluvial and maritime plain, covered with a rank vegetation of spear-grass and low thorns, with occasional mimosas and tall hyphænas, which have supplanted the coco, the traveler finds a few scattered specimens of the living tree and pits dotting the ground. The diggers, however, generally advance another mile to a distinctly formed sea-beach, marked with lateral bands of quartzose and water-rolled pebbles, and swelling gradually to 150 feet from the alluvial plain. The thin but rich vegetable covering supports a luxuriant thicket, the subsoil is red and sandy, and the color darkens as the excavation deepens. After 3 feet fibrous matter appears, and below this copal, dusty and comminuted, is blended with the red ochreish earth. The guides assert that they have never hit upon the subsoil of blue clay, but they never dig lower than a man's waist, and the pits are seldom more than 2 feet in depth. Though the soil is red, the copal of Saadani is not highly prized, being of a dull white color; it is usually designated as "chakazi."

On the line inland from Bagamoyo and Kaole the copal-tree was observed at rare intervals in the forests, and the pits extended as far as Muhonyera, about 40 miles in direct distance from the coast. The produce of this country, though not first-rate, is considered far superior to that about Saadani.

Good copal is dug in the vicinity of Mbuamaji, and the diggings are said to extend 6 marches inland. The Wadenkereko, a wild tribe, mixed with and stretching southward of the Wazaramo, at a distance of two days' journey from the sea, supply a mixed quality, more often white than red. The best gums are procured from Hunda and its adjacent districts. Frequent feuds with the citizens deter the wild people from venturing out of their jungles, and thus the Banyans of Mbuamaji find two small dows sufficient for the carriage of their stores. At that port the price of copal varies from 2 dolls. 50 cents to 3 dolls. per frasilah.

The banks of the Rufiji River, especially the northern district of Wánde, supply the finest and best of copal; it is dug by the Wawande tribe, who either carry it to Kikunya and other ports, or sell it to traveling hucksters. The price in loco is from 1 doll. 50 cents to 2 dollars per frasilah; on the coast it rises to 3 dolls. 50 cents. At all these places the tariff varies with the Bombay market, and in 1858 little was exported, owing to the enlistment of "free laborers."

In the vicinity of Kilwa, for four marches inland, copal is dug up by the Mandandu and other tribes: owing to the facility of carriage and the comparative safety of the country it is somewhat dearer than that purchased on the banks of the Rufiji. The copal of Ngao (Monghou) and the Lindi Creek is much cheaper than at Kilwa; the produce, however, is variable in quality, being mostly a dull white chakazi.

Like that of East African produce generally, the exploitation of copal is careless and desultory. The diggers are of the lowest classes, and hands are much wanted. Near the sea-board it is worked by the fringe of Moslem negroids called the Wamrima or coast-clans; each gang has its own mtu mku or akida'ao (mucaddum—headman), who, by distributing the stock, contrives to gain more and labor less than the others. In the interior it is exploited by the Washenzi or heathen, who work independently of one another. When there is no blood-feud they carry it down to the coast, otherwise they must await the visits of petty retail dealers from the ports, who enter the country with ventures of 10 or 12 dollars, and barter for it cloth, beads, and wire. The kosi—southwest or rainy monsoon—is the only period of work; the kaskazi, or dry season, is a dead time. The hardness of the ground is too much for the energies of the people: moreover, "kaskazi copal" gives trouble in washing on account of the sand adhering to its surface, and the flakes are liable to break. As a rule, the apathetic Moslem and the futile heathen will not work while a pound of grain remains in their huts. The more civilized use a little jembe or hoe, an implement about as efficient as the wooden spade with which an English child makes dirt-pies.

The people of the interior "crow" a hole about six inches in diameter with a pointed stick, and scrape out the loosened earth with the hand as far as the arm will reach. They desert the digging before it is exhausted; and although the laborers could each, it is calculated, easily collect from ten to twelve lbs. per diem, they prefer sleeping through the hours of heat, and content themselves with as many ounces. Whenever upon the coast there is a blood-feud—and these are uncommonly frequent—a drought, a famine, or a pestilence, workmen strike work, and cloth and beads are offered in vain. It is evident that the copal mine can never be regularly and efficiently worked as long as it continues in the hands of such unworthy miners. The energy of Europeans, men of capital and purpose, settled on the sea-board with gangs of foreign workmen, would soon remedy existing evils; but they would require not only the special permission, but also the protection of the local government. And although the intensity of the competition principle among the Arabs has not yet emulated the ferocious rivalry of civilization, the new settlers must expect considerable opposition from those in possession. Though the copal diggings are mostly situated beyond the jurisdiction of Zanzibar, the tract labors under all the disadvantages of a monopoly; the diwans, the heavy merchants, and the petty traders of the coast derive from it, it is supposed, profits varying from 80 to 100 per cent. Like other African produce, though almost dirt cheap, it becomes dear by passing through many hands, and the frasilah, worth from 1 to 3 dollars in the interior, acquires a value of from 8 to 9 dollars at Zanzibar.

Zanzibar is the principal mart for perhaps the finest and largest ivory in the world. It collects the produce of the lands lying between the parallels of 2° N. lat. and 10° S. lat., and the area extends from the coast to the regions lying westward of the Tanganyika Lake. It is almost the only legitimate article of traffic for which caravans now visit the interior.

An account of the ivory markets in Inner Africa will remove sundry false impressions. The Arabs are full of fabulous reports concerning regions where the article may be purchased for its circumference in beads, and greed of gain has led many of them to danger and death. Wherever tusks are used as cattle-pens or to adorn graves, the reason is that they are valueless on account of the want of conveyance.

The elephant has not wholly disappeared from the maritime regions of Zanzibar. It is found, especially during the rainy monsoon, a few miles behind Pangani Town: it exists also among the Wazegura as far as their southern limit, the Gama River. The Wadoe hunt the animal in the vicinity of Shakini, a peak within sight of Zanzibar. Though killed out of Uzaramo and K'hutu, it is found upon the banks of the Kingani and the Rufiji Rivers. The coast people now sell their tusks for 30 to 35 dollars' worth of cloth, beads, and wire per frasilah.

In Western Usagara the elephant extends from Maroro to Ugogi. The people, however, being rarely professional hunters, content themselves with keeping a lookout for the bodies of animals that have died of thirst or of wounds received elsewhere. As the chiefs are acquainted with the luxuries of the coast, their demands are fantastic. They will ask, for instance, for a large tusk—the frasilah is not used in inland sales—a copper caldron worth 15 dollars; a khesi, or fine cloth, costing 20 dollars; and a variable quantity of blue and white cottons: thus an ivory, weighing perhaps 3 frasilah, may be obtained for 50 dollars.

Ugogo and its encircling deserts are peculiarly rich in elephants. The people are eminently hunters, and, as has been remarked, they trap the animals, and in droughty seasons they find many dead in the jungles. Ivory is somewhat dearer in Ugogo than in Unyamwezi, as caravans rarely visit the coasts. It is generally bartered to return-caravans for slaves brought from the interior; of these, five or six represent the value of a large tusk.

The ivory of Unyamwezi is collected from the districts of Mgunda Mk'hali, Usukuma, Umanda, Usagozi, and other adjacent regions. When the "Land of the Moon" was first visited by the Arabs, they purchased, it is said, 10 farasilah of ivory with one frasilah of the cheap white or blue porcelains. The price is now between 30 and 35 dollars per frasilah in cloth, beads, and wire. The Africans, ignoring the frasilah, estimate the value of the tusk by its size and quality; and the Arabs ascertain its exact weight by steelyards. Moreover, they raise the weight of what they purchase to 48 lbs., and diminish that which they sell to 23.50 lbs., calling both by the same name, frasilah. When the Arab wishes to raise an outfit at Unyanyembe he can always command three gorahs of domestics (locally worth 30 dollars) per frasilah of ivory. Merchants visiting Karagwah, where the ivory is of superior quality, lay in a stock of white, pink, blue, green, and coral beads, and brass armlets, which must be made up at Unyanyembe to suit the tastes of the people. Cloth is little in demand. For one frasilah of beads and brass wire they purchase about one and a half of ivory. At K'hokoro the price of tusks has greatly risen; a large specimen can scarcely be procured under 40 doti of domestics, one frasilah of brass wire, and 100 fundo of colored beads. The tusks collected in this country are firm, white, and soft, sometimes running 6 farasilah (210 lbs.). The small quantity collected in Ubena, Urori, and the regions east of the Tanganyika Lake, resembles that of K'hokoro.

The ivory of Ujiji is collected from the provinces lying around the northern third of the lake, especially from Urundi and Uvira. These tusks have one great defect; though white and smooth when freshly taken from the animal, they put forth after a time a sepia-colored or dark-brown spot, extending like a ring over the surface, which gradually spreads and injures the texture. Such is the "jendai" or "gendai" ivory, well known at Zanzibar: it is apt to flake off outside, and is little prized on account of its lightness. At Ujiji tusks were cheap but a few years ago; now they fetch an equal weight of porcelain or glass beads, in addition to which the owners—they are generally many—demand from 4 to 8 cloths. Competition, which among the Arabs is usually somewhat unscrupulous, has driven the ivory merchant to regions far west of the Tanganyika, and geography will thrive upon the losses of commerce.

The process of elephant-hunting, the complicated division of the spoils, and the mode of transporting tusks to the coast, have already been described. A quantity of ivory, as has appeared, is wasted in bracelets, armlets, and other ornaments. This would not be the case were the imports better calculated to suit the tastes of the people. At present the cloth-stuffs are little prized, and the beads are not sufficiently varied for barbarians who, eminently fickle, require change by way of stimulant. The Arabs seek in ivory six qualities: it must be white, heavy, soft, thick—especially at the point—gently curved—when too much curved it loses from 10 to 14 per cent.; and it must be marked with dark surface-lines, like cracks, running longitudinally toward the point. It is evident, from the preceding details, that the Arab merchants gain but little beyond a livelihood in plenty and dignity by their expeditions to the interior. An investment of 1000 dollars rarely yields more than 70 farasilah (2450 lbs.). Assuming the high price of Zanzibar at an average of 50 dollars per frasilah, the stock would be worth 3500 dollars—a net profit of 1050 dollars. Against this, however, must be set off the price of porterage and rations—equal to at least five dollars per frasilah—the enormous interest upon the capital, the wastage of outfit, and the risk of loss, which, upon the whole, is excessive. Though time, toil, and sickness not being matters of money, are rarely taken into consideration by the Eastern man, they must be set down on the loss side of the account. It is therefore plain that commercial operations on such a scale can be remunerative only to a poor people, and that they can be rendered lucrative to capitalists only by an extension and a development which, depending solely upon improved conveyance, must be brought about by the energy of Europeans. For long centuries past and for centuries to come the Semite and the Hamite have been and will be contented with human labor.   The first thought which suggests itself to the sons of Japhet is a tram-road from the coast to the lake regions.

The subject of ivory as sold at Zanzibar is as complicated as that of sugar in Great Britain or of cotton in America.   A detailed treatise would here be out of place, but the following notices may serve to convey an idea of the trade.

The merchants at Zanzibar recognize in ivory, the produce of these regions, three several qualities.   The best, a white, soft, and large variety, with small "bamboo," is that from Banadir, Brava, Makdishu, and Marka.   A somewhat inferior kind, on account of its hardness, is brought from the countries of Chaga, Umasai, and Nguru. The Wamasai often spoil their tusks by cutting them, for the facility of transport ; and, like the people of Nguru and other tribes, they stain the exterior by sticking the tooth in the sooty rafters of their chimneyless huts, with the idea that, so treated, it will not crack or split in the sun.   This red color, erroneously attributed at Zanzibar to the use of ghee, is removed by the people with blood, or cow-dung mixed with water. Of these varieties the smaller tusks fetch from 40 to 50 dollars ; when they attain a length of 6 feet, the price would be £12 ; and some choice specimens 7½ feet long fetch £60.   A lot of 47 tusks was seen to fetch £1500 ; the average weight of each was 95 lbs., 80 being considered moderate, and from 70 to 75 lbs. poor.

The second quality is that imported from the regions about the Nyassa Lake, and carried to Kilwa by the Wabisa, the Wahiao, the Wangindo, the Wamakua, and other clans.   The "Bisha ivory" formerly found its way to the Mozambique, but the barbarians have now learned to prefer Zanzibar ; and the citizens welcome them, as they sell their stores more cheaply than the Wahiao, who have become adepts in coast arts.   The ivory of the Wabisa, though white and soft, is generally small, the full length of a tusk being 7 feet.   The price of the "bab kalasi"—scrivellos or small tusks, under 20 lbs., is from 24 to 25 dollars ; and the value increases at the rate of somewhat less than 1 dollar per lb.   The "bab gujrati or kashshi," the bab kashshi, is that intended for the Cutch market.   The tusk must be of middling size, little bent, very bluff at the point, as it is intended for rings and armlets ; the girth must be a short span and three fingers, the bamboo shallow, and not longer than a hand. Ivory fulfilling all these conditions will sell as high as 70 dollars per frasilah—medium size of 20 to 45 lbs., fetches 56 to 60 dollars.   The "bab wilaiti," or "foreign sort," is that purchased in European and American markets.   The largest size is preferred, which, ranging from 45 to 100 lbs., may be purchased for 52 dollars per frasilah.

The third and least valued quality is the western ivory, the gendai, and other varieties imported from Usagara, Uhehe, Urori, Unyamwezi, and its neighborhood.   The price varies, according to size, form, and weight, from 45 to 56 dollars per frasilah.

The transport of ivory to the coast, and the profits derived by the maritime settlers, Arab and Indian, have been described.   When all fees have been paid, the tusk, guarded against smuggling by the custom-house stamp, is sent to Zanzibar.   On the island scrivellos under 6 lbs. in weight are not registered.   According to the late Lieutenant Colonel Hamerton, the annual average of large tusks is not less than 20,000. The people of the country make the weight range between 17,000 and 25,000 farasilah.   The tusk is larger at Zanzibar than elsewhere.   At Mozambique, for instance, 60 lbs. would be considered a good average for a lot.   Monster tusks are spoken of. Specimens of 5 farasilah are not very rare, and the people have traditions that these wonderful armatures have extended to 227 lbs., and even to 280 lbs. each.

Among the minor articles of export from the interior, hippopotamus teeth have been enumerated.   Beyond the coast, however, they form but a slender item in the caravan load.   In the inner regions they are bought in retail ; the price ranges between 1 and 2 fundo of beads, and at times 3 may be procured for a shukkah.   On the coast they rise, when fine, to 25 dollars per frasilah.   At Zanzibar a large lot, averaging 6 to 8 lbs. in weight (12 lbs. would be about the largest), will sell for 60 dollars ; per frasilah of 5 lbs., from 40 to 45 dollars : while the smallest fetch from 5 to 6 dollars.   Of surpassing hardness, they are still used in Europe for artificial teeth.   In America porcelain bids fair to supplant them.

The gargatan (karkadan ?), or small black rhinoceros with a double horn, is as common as the elephant in the interior.   The price of the horn is regulated by its size ; a small specimen is to be bought for 1 jembe or iron hoe.   When large the price is doubled.   Upon the coast a lot fetches from 6 to 9 dollars per frasilah, which at Zanzibar increases to from 8 to 12 dollars.   The inner barbarians apply plates of the horn to helcomas and ulcerations, and they cut it into bits, which are bound with twine round the limb, like the wooden mpigii or hirizi.* Large horns are imported through Bombay to China and Central Asia, where it is said the people convert them into drinking-cups, which sweat if poison be administered in them: thus they act like the Venetian glass of our ancestors, and are as highly prized as that eccentric fruit the coco de mer. The Arabs of Maskat and Yemen cut them into sword-hilts, dagger-hafts, tool-handles, and small boxes for tobacco, and other articles. They greatly prize, and will pay 12 dollars per frasilah, for the spoils of the kobaoba, or long-horned white rhinoceros, which, however, appears no longer to exist in the latitudes westward of Zanzibar Island.

Black cattle are seldom driven down from the interior, on account of the length and risk of the journey. It is evident, however, that the trade is capable of extensive development. The price of full-grown bullocks varies, according to the distance from the coast, between 3 and 5 doti; while that of cows is about double. When imported from the main-land ports, 1 dollar per head is paid as an octroi to the government, and about the same sum for passage-money. As Banyans will not allow this traffic to be conducted by their own craft, it is confined to the Moslem population. The Island of Zanzibar is supplied with black cattle, chiefly from the Banadir and Madagascar, places beyond the range of.this description. The price of bullocks varies from 5 to 8 dollars, and of cows from 6 to 9 dollars. Goats and sheep abound throughout Eastern Africa. The former, which are preferred, cost in the maritime regions from 8 to 10 shukkah merkani; in Usagara, the most distant province which exports them to Zanzibar, they may be bought for 4 to 6 shukkah per head. The Wasawahili conduct a small trade in this live stock, and sell them upon the island for 4 to 5 dollars per head. From their large profits, however, must be deducted the risk of transport, the price of passage, and the octroi, which is 25 cents per head.

The exceptional expense of man-carriage renders the exportation of hides and horns from the far interior impossible. The former are sold with the animal, and are used for shields, bedding, saddle-bags, awnings, sandals, and similar minor purposes. Skins, as has been explained, are in some regions almost the only wear; consequently the spoils of a fine goat command, even in far Usukuma, a doti of domestics. The principal wild hides, which, however, rarely find their way to the coast, are those of the rhinoceros—much prized by the Arabs for targes—the lion and the leopard, the giraffe and the buffalo, the zebra and the quagga. Horns are allowed to crumble upon the ground. The Island of Zanzibar exports hides and skins, which are principally those of bullocks and goats brought from Brava, Marka, Makdishu, and the Somali country. The korjah or score of the former has risen from 10 to 24 dollars; and the people have learned to mix them with the spoils of wild animals, especially the buffalo. When taken from the animal the hides are pinned down with pegs passed through holes in the edges; thus they dry without shrinking, and become stiff as boards. When thoroughly sun-parched they are put in soak and are pickled in sea-water for forty-eight hours; thus softened, they are again stretched and staked, that they may remain smooth: as they are carelessly removed by the natives, the meat fat, flippers, ears, and all the parts likely to be corrupted, or to prevent close stowage, are cut off while wet. They are again thoroughly sun-dried, the grease which exudes during the operation is scraped off, and they are beaten with sticks to expel the dust. The Hamburg merchants paint their hides with an arsenical mixture, which preserves them during the long months of magazine-storing and sea-voyage. The French and American traders omit this operation, and their hides suffer severely from insects.

Details concerning the growth of cereals in the interior have occurred in the preceding pages. Grain is never exported from the lands lying beyond the maritime regions: yet the disforesting of the Island of Zanzibar and the extensive plantations of clove-trees rendering a large importation of cereals necessary to the Arabs, an active business is carried on by Arab dows from the whole of the coast between Tanga and Ngao (Monghou), and during the dear season, after the rains, considerable profits are realized. The corn measures used by the Banyans are as follows:

2 Kubabah (each from 1.25 to 1.50 lbs., in fact, our "quart") = 1 Kisaga.
3 Kubabah = 1 Pishi (in Khutu the Pishi = 2 Kubabah).
4 Kubabah = 1 Kayla (equal to 2 Man).
24 Kayla = 1 Frasilah.
60 Kayla = 1 Jizlah, in Kisawahili Mzo.
20 Farasilah = 1 Kandi (candy).

As usual in these lands, the kubabah or unit is made to be arbitrary; it is divided into two kinds, large and small. The measure is usually a gourd.

The only timber now utilized in commerce is the mukanda'a or red and white mangrove, which supplies the well-known bordi or "Zanzibar rafters." They are the produce of the fluviatile estuaries and the marine lagoons, and attain large dimensions under the influence of potent heat and copious rains. The best is the red variety, which, when thrown upon the shore, stains the sand; it grows on the soft and slimy bank, and anchors itself with ligneous shoots to the shifting soil. The white mangrove, springing from harder ground, dispenses with these supports; it is called mti wa mutu ("wild-wood"), and is quickly destroyed by worms. Indeed, all the bordi at Zanzibar begin to fail after the fifth year if exposed to the humid atmosphere; at Maskat it is said they will last nearly a century. The rafter finds its way to Aden and the woodless lands of Eastern and Western Arabia; at Jeddah they have been known to fetch 1 dollar each.

The maritime regions also supply a small quantity of the "grenadille-wood," called by the people, who confound it with real ebony (Diospyros ebenus), abnus and pingú. It is not so brittle as ebony; it is harder than lignum-vitæ (G. officinalis), spoiling the common saw, and is readily recognized by its weight. As it does not absorb water or grease, it is sent to Europe for the mouth-pieces and flanges of instruments, and for the finer parts of mills. The people use it in the interior for pipe-bowls.

The mpira or caoutchouc-tree (Ficus elastica) grows abundantly throughout the maritime regions. A few lumps of the gum were brought to Zanzibar at the request of a merchant, who offered a large sum for a few tons, in the vain hope of stimulating the exploitation of this valuable article. The specimens were not, however, cast in moulds as by the South American Indians; they were full of water, and even fouler than those brought from Madagascar. To develop the trade European supervision would be absolutely necessary during the season for tapping the trees.

A tree growing upon the coast and common in Madagascar produces, when an incision has been made in the bark, a juice inspissating to the consistency of soft soap, and much resembling the Indian "kokam." This "kanya" is eaten by Arabs and Africans, with the idea that it "moistens the body:" in cases of stiff joints, swellings of the extremities, and contractions of the sinews, it is melted over the fire and is rubbed into the skin for a fortnight or three weeks.

The produce and the value of the coco and areca palms have already been noted. Orchella-weed (Rocilla fuciformis?), a lichen most valuable in dyeing, is found, according to the late Lieut. Colonel Hamerton, growing on trees and rocks throughout the maritime regions. The important growths of the interior are the frankincense and bdellium, the coffee and nutmeg—which, however, are still in a wild state—the tamarind, and the sisam or black-wood. The largest planks are made of the mtimbati (African teak?) and the mvule; they are now exported from the coast to the island, where they have almost died out. As the art of sawing is unknown, a fine large tree is invariably sacrificed for a single board. It was the opinion of the late Lieut. Colonel Hamerton that a saw-mill at the mouth of the Pangani River would, if sanctioned by the local government, be highly remunerative.

Cowries, called by the Arabs kaure, in Kisawahili khete, and in the interior simbi, are collected from various places in the coast-region between Ras Hafun and the Mozambique. This trade is in the hands of Moslem hucksters: the Banyan, who has no objection to the valuable ivory or hippopotamus tooth, finds his religion averse to the vile spoils of the Cypræa. Cowries are purchased on the main land by a curious specimen of the "round-trade;" money is not taken, so the article is sold measure for measure of holcus grain. From Zanzibar the cowrie takes two directions. As it forms the currency of the regions north of the "Land of the Moon," and is occasionally demanded as an ornament in Unyamwezi, the return African porters, whose labor costs them nothing, often partly load themselves with the article; the Arab, on the other hand, who seldom visits the northern kingdoms, does not find compensation for porterage and rations. The second and principal use of cowries is for exportation to the West African coast, where they are used in currency—50 strings, each of 40 shells, or a total of 2000, representing the dollar. This, in former days a most lucrative trade, is now nearly ruined. Cowries were purchased at 75 cents per jizlah, which represents from 3 to 3½ sacks, of which much, however, was worthless. The sacks in which they were shipped cost in Zanzibar 1 dollar 44 cents, and fetched in West Africa 8 or 9 dollars. The shells sold at the rate of £80 (£60 was the average English price) per ton; thus the profits were estimated at 500 per cent., and a Hamburg house rose, it is said, by this traffic, from 1 to 18 ships, of which 7 were annually engaged in shipping cowries. From 75 cents the price rose to 4 dollars; it even attained a maximum of 10 dollars, the medium being 6 and 7 dollars per jizlah, and the profits necessarily declined.

Cotton is indigenous to the more fertile regions of Eastern as well as of Western Africa. The specimens hitherto imported from Port Natal and from Angola have given satisfaction, as they promise, with careful cultivation, to rival in fineness, firmness, and weight the medium-staple cotton of the New World. On the line between Zanzibar and the Tanganyika Lake the shrub grows almost wild, with the sole exception of Ugogo and its two flanks of wilderness, where the ground is too hard and the dry season too prolonged to support it. The partial existence of the same causes renders it scarce and dear in Unyamwezi. A superior quality was introduced by the traveling Arabs, but it soon degenerated. Cotton flourishes luxuriantly in the black earths fat with decayed vegetation, and on the rich red clays of the coast regions, of Usumbara, Usagara, and Ujiji, where water underlies the surface. These almost virgin soils are peculiarly fitted by atmospheric and geologic conditions for the development of the shrub, and the time may come when vast tracts, nearly half the superficies of the lands, here grass-grown, there cumbered by the primeval forest, may be taught to bear crops equaling the celebrated growths of Egypt and Algeria, Harar and Abyssinia. At present the cultivation is nowhere encouraged, and it is limited by the impossibility of exportation to the scanty domestic requirements of the people. It is grown from seed sown immediately after the rains, and the only care given to it is the hedging requisite to preserve the dwarf patches from the depredations of cattle. In some parts the shrub is said to wither after the third year, in others to be perennial.

Upon the coast the cotton grown by the Wasawahili and Wamrima is chiefly used as lamp-wicks and for similar domestic purposes; Zanzibar Island is supplied from Western India. The price of raw uncleaned cotton in the mountain regions is about 0.25 dollar per maund of 3 Arab lbs. In Zanzibar, where the msufi or bombax abounds, its fibrous substance is a favorite substitute for cotton, and costs about half the price. In Unyamwezi it fetches fancy prices; it is sold in handfuls for salt, beads, and similar articles. About 1 maund may be purchased for a shukkah, and from 1 to 2 oz. of rough homespun yarn for a fundo of beads. At Ujiji the people bring it daily to the bazar and spend their waste time in spinning yarn with the rude implements before described. This cotton, though superior in quality, as well as quantity, to that of Unyanyembe, is but little less expensive.

Tobacco grows plentifully in the more fertile regions of East Africa. Planted at the end of the rains, it gains strength by sun and dew, and is harvested in October. It is prepared for sale in different forms. Every where, however, a simple sun-drying supplies the place of cocking and sweating, and the people are not so fastidious as to reject the lower or coarser leaves and those tainted by the earth. Usumbara produces what is considered at Zanzibar a superior article: it is kneaded into little circular cakes four inches in diameter by half an inch deep: rolls of these cakes are neatly packed in plantain-leaves for exportation. The next in order of excellence is that grown in Uhiáo: it is exported in leaf or in the form called kambari, "roll-tobacco," a circle of coils each about an inch in diameter. The people of Khutu and Usagara mould the pounded and wetted material into disks like cheeses, 8 or 9 inches across by 2 or 3 in depth, and weighing about 3 lbs.; they supply the Wagogo with tobacco, taking in exchange for it salt. The leaf in Unyamwezi generally is soft and perishable, that of Usukuma being the worst: it is sold in blunt cones, so shaped by the mortars in which they are pounded. At Karagwah, according to the Arabs, the tobacco, a superior variety, tastes like musk in the water-pipe. The produce of Ujiji is better than that of Unyamwezi; it is sold in leaf, and is called by the Arabs hamúmí, after a well-known growth in Hazramaut. It is impossible to assign an average price to tobacco in East Africa; it varies from 1 khete of coral beads per 6 oz. to 2 lbs.

Tobacco is chewed by the maritime races, the Wasawahili, and especially the Zanzibar Arabs, who affect a religious scruple about smoking. They usually insert a pinch of nurah or coral-lime into their quids—as the Somal introduces ashes—to make them bite; in the interior, where calcareous formations are deficient, they procure the article from cowries brought from the coast, or from shells found in the lakes and streams. About Unyamwezi all sexes and ages enjoy the pipe. Farther eastward snuff is preferred. The liquid article in fashion among the Wajiji has already been described. The dry snuff is made of leaf toasted till crisp and pounded between two stones, mixed with a little magádí or saltpetre, sometimes scented with the heart of the plantain-tree, and stored in the tumbakira or gourd-box.

The other articles exported from the coast of Zanzibar are beeswax and honey, tortoise-shell and ambergris, ghee, tobacco, the sugar-cane, the wild arrow-root, gums, and fibrous substances; of these many have been noticed, and the remainder are of too trifling a value to deserve attention.

To conclude the subject of commerce in East Africa. It is rather to the merchant than to the missionary that we must look for the regeneration of the country by the development of her resources. The attention of the civilized world, now turned toward this hitherto neglected region, will presently cause slavery to cease; man will not risk his all in petty and passionless feuds undertaken to sell his weaker neighbor; and commerce, which induces mansuetude of manners, will create wants and interests at present unknown. As the remote is gradually drawn nigh, and the difficult becomes accessible, the intercourse of man—strongest instrument of civilization in the hand of Providence—will raise Africa to that place in the great republic of nations from which she has hitherto been unhappily excluded.

Already a line of steam navigation from the Cape of Good Hope to Aden and the Red Sea, touching at the various important posts upon the main land and the islands of East Africa, has been proposed. This will be the first step toward material improvement. The preceding pages have, it is believed, convinced the reader that the construction of a tram-road through a country abounding in timber and iron, and where only one pass of any importance presents itself, will be attended with no engineering difficulties. As the land now lies, trade stagnates, loanable capital remains idle, produce is depreciated, and new seats of enterprise are unexplored. The specific for existing evils is to be found in facilitating intercourse between the interior and the coast, and that this will in due season be effected we may no longer doubt.

APPENDIX II.

1.

"East India House, 13th September, 1856.

"Sir,—I am commanded by the Court of Directors of the East India Company to inform you that, in compliance with the request of the Royal Geographical Society, you are permitted to be absent from your duties as a regimental officer while employed with an expedition, under the patronage of her majesty's government, to be dispatched into Equatorial Africa, for the exploration of that country, for a period not exceeding two years. I am directed to add, that you are permitted to draw the pay and allowances of your rank during the period of your absence, which will be calculated from the date of your departure from Bombay.

"I am, sir, your most obedient humble servant,
"(Signature illegible).

"Lieutenant R. BURTON."

2.

"East India House, 24th October, 1856.

"Sir,—In consequence of a communication from the office of the Secretary of State for War, intimating that you are required as a witness on the trial by court-martial now pending on Colonel A. Shirley, I am desired to convey to you the commands of the Court of Directors that you instantly return to London for that purpose. In obeying this order, you are required to proceed, not through France, but by the steamer direct from Alexandria to Southampton. You will report yourself to the Secretary of State for War immediately on your arrival. The agent for the East India Company in Egypt has received instructions by this mail to supply you with the necessary funds for your passage.

"I am, sir, your most obedient humble servant,
"(Signed)   JAMES MELVILLE.

"Lieutenant BURTON."

3.
" The Military Secretary, East India House.

"Aden, 14th November.

" Sir,—I have the honor to acknowledge your official letter of the 24th of October, conveying to me the commands of the Court of Directors to return instantly to London by the steamer direct from Alexandria to Southampton.

"The steamer in question left Alexandria on November 6th, at about 10 A.M. I received and acknowledged from the British Consulate your official letter on the same day at Cairo, about noon. No steamer leaves Alexandria before the 20th inst.; it is therefore evident that I could not possibly obey the order within the limits specified.

"No mention was made about my returning to England by the next steamer, probably because the court-martial pending upon Colonel A. Shirley will before that time have come to a close. I need scarcely say, that should I, on arrival at Bombay, find an order to that effect, it shall be instantly and implicitly obeyed.

"Considering, however, that I have already stated all that I know upon the subject of the court-martial in question—that I was not subpenaed in England—that I am under directions of the Royal Geographical Society, and employed with an expedition under the patronage of the Foreign Office—that without my proceeding to Bombay, valuable government property would most probably have been lost, and the preparations for the expedition have suffered from serious delay—and lastly, that by the loss of a few weeks a whole year's exploration must be allowed to pass by—I venture respectfully to hope that I have taken the proper course, and that should I, on my arrival in India, find no express and positive order for an immediate return to Europe, I may be permitted to proceed forthwith to Africa.

" As a servant of the East India Company, in whose interests I have conscientiously and energetically exerted myself for the space of 14 years, I can not but request the Court of Directors to use their powerful influence in my behalf. Private interests can not be weighed against public duty. At the same time, I have already embarked a considerable sum in the materiel of the expedition, paid passage money, and devoted time, which might have been otherwise profitably employed, to the subject of Equatorial Africa. I remained long enough in London to enable the War Office to call for my presence as a witness, and I ascertained personally from Major General Beatson that he had not placed me upon his list. And finally, I venture to observe, that by returning to Europe now, I should be compromising the interests of the Royal Geographical Society, under which I am in fact virtually serving."

4.
" To the Secretary of the Royal Geographical Society, London.

"Sir,—I have the honor to forward, for the information of the President and members of the Expeditionary Committee, a copy of a communication to my address from the Military Secretary to the Court of Directors, together with my reply thereto. On perusal of these documents, you will perceive that my presence is urgently demanded in England to give evidence on a court-martial, and that the letter desiring me to proceed forthwith to England arrived too late in Egypt to admit of my obeying that order. Were I now to proceed directly from Bombay to England, it is evident that the expedition which I am undertaking under your direction must be deferred to a future and uncertain date. With a view to obviate this uncalled-for delay, I have the honor to request that you will use your interest to the effect that, as an officer virtually in your service, I may be permitted to carry out the views of your society; and that my evidence, which can be of no importance to either prosecutor or defendant in the court-martial in question, may be dispensed with. I start this evening from Bombay, and will report departure from that place.

"I have, etc.,   R. F. BURTON.
"Camp, Aden, 14th November, 1856."

5.
" To the Secretary of the Royal Geographical Society, London.

"Sir,—I have the honor to inform you that on the 1st of Dec., 1856, I addressed to you a letter which I hope has been duly received. On the 2d instant, in company with Lt. Speke, I left Bombay Harbor, on board the H. E. I. C's. ship of war ' Elphinstone' (Capt. Frushard, I. N., commanding), en route to East Africa. I have little to report that may be interesting to geographers; but perhaps some account of political affairs in the Red Sea may be deemed worthy to be transmitted by you to the Court of Directors or to the Foreign Office.

"As regards the expedition, copies of directions and a memorandum on instruments and observations for our guidance have come to hand. For observations, Lt. Speke and I must depend upon our own exertions, neither sergeants nor native students being procurable at the Bombay Observatory. The case of instruments and the mountain barometer have not been forwarded, but may still fail us at Zanzibar. Meanwhile I have obtained from the commanding engineer, Bombay, one six-inch sextant, one five-and-a-half ditto, two prismatic compasses, five thermometers (of which two are B. P.), a patent log, taper, protractors, stands, etc.; also, two pocket chronometers from the Observatory, duly rated; and Dr. Buist, Secretary, Bombay Geographical Society, has obliged me with a mountain barometer and various instructions about points of interest. Lt. Speke has been recommended by the local government to the government of India for duty in East Africa, and the services of Dr. Steinhaeuser, who is most desirous to join us, have been applied for from the Medical Board, Bombay. I have strong hopes that both these officers will be allowed to accompany me, and that the Royal Geographical Society will use their efforts to that effect.

"By the subjoined detailed account of preliminary expenses at Bombay, it will be seen that I have expended £70 out of £250, for which I was permitted to draw.

"Although, as I before mentioned, the survey of Eastern Intertropical Africa has for the moment been deferred, the necessity still exists. Even in the latest editions of *Horsburgh*, the mass of matter relative to Zanzibar is borrowed from the observations of Capt. Bissel, who navigated the coast in H. M's. ships ' *Leopard*' and ' *Orestes*' about A.D. 1799. Little is known of the great current which, setting periodically from and to the Red Sea and the Persian Gulf, sweeps round the Eastern Horn of Africa. The reefs are still formidable to navigators; and before these seas can be safely traversed by steamers from the Cape, as is now proposed, considerable additions must be made to Capt. Owen's survey in A.D. 1823–24. Finally, operations on the coast will form the best introduction to the geographical treasures of the interior.

"The H. E. I. Company's surveying brig ' *Tigris*' will shortly be out of dock, where she has been undergoing a thorough repair, and, if fitted up with a round-house on the quarter-deck, would answer the purpose well. She might be equipped in a couple of months, and dispatched to her ground before the southwest monsoon sets in, or be usefully employed in observing at Zanzibar instead of lying idle in Bombay Harbor. On former surveys of the Arabian and African coasts, a small tender of from thirty to forty tons has always been granted, as otherwise operations are much crippled in boisterous weather and exposed on inhospitable shores. Should no other vessel be available, one of the smallest of the new pilot schooners now unemployed at Bombay might be directed to wait upon the ' *Tigris*.' Lt. H. G. Fraser, I. N., has volunteered for duty upon the African coast, and I have the honor to transmit his letter. Nothing more would be required were some junior officer of the Indian navy stationed at Zanzibar for the purpose of registering tidal, barometric, and thermometric observations, in order that something of the meteorology of this unknown region may be accurately investigated.

"When passing through Aden I was informed that the blockade of the Somali coast had been raised, without compensation for the losses sustained on my last journey. This step appears, politically speaking, a mistake. In the case of the ' *Mary Ann*' brig, plundered near Berberah in A.D. 1825, due compensation was demanded and obtained. Even in India, an officer traveling through the states not under British rule, can, if he be plundered, require an equivalent for his property. This is indeed our chief protection—semi-barbarians and savages part with money less willingly than with life. If it be determined for social reasons at Aden that the blockade should cease and mutton become cheap, a certain percentage could be laid upon the exports of Berberah till such time as our losses, which, including those of government, amount to £1380, are made good.

"From Harar news has reached Aden that the Amir Abubakr, dying during the last year of chronic consumption, has been succeeded by a cousin, one Abd el Rahman, a bigoted Moslem, and a violent hater of the Gallas. His successes in feud and foray, however, have not prevented the wild tribes from hemming him in, and unless fortune interfere, the city must fall into their hands. The rumor prevalent at Cairo, namely, that Harar had been besieged and taken by Mr. Bell, now serving under 'Theodorus, emperor of Ethiopia' (the chief Cássái), appears premature. At Aden I met in exile Sharmarkay bin Ali Salih, formerly governor of Zayla. He has been ejected in favor of a Dankali chief by the Ottoman authorities of Yemen, a circumstance the more to be regretted, as he has ever been a firm friend to our interests.

"The present defenseless state of Berberah still invites our presence. The eastern coast of the Red Sea is almost entirely under the Porte. On the western shore, Cosseir is Egyptian, Masawwah, Sawakin, and Zayla, Turkish, and Berberah, the best port of all, unoccupied. I have frequently advocated the establishment of a British agency at this place, and venture to do so once more. This step would tend to increase trade, to obviate accidents in case of shipwreck, and materially assist in civilizing the Somal of the interior. The government of Bombay has doubtless preserved copies of my reports, plans, and estimates concerning the proposed agency, and I would request the Royal Geographical Society to inquire into a project peculiarly fitted to promote their views of exploration in the Eastern Horn of Africa. Finally, this move would checkmate any ambitious projects in the Red Sea. The Suez Canal may be said to have commenced. It appears impossible that the work should pay in a commercial sense. Politically it may, if, at least, its object be, as announced by the Count d'Escayrac de Lauture at the Société de Geographie, to 'throw open the road of India to the Mediterranean coasting trade, to democratize commerce and navigation.' The first effect of the highway would be, as that learned traveler justly remarks, to open a passage through Egypt to the speronari and feluccas of the Levant, the light-infantry of a more regular force.

"The next step should be to provide ourselves with a more efficient naval force at Aden, the head-quarters of the Red Sea squadron. I may briefly quote as a proof of the necessity for protection, the number of British protégés in the neighboring ports, and the present value of the Jeddah trade.

"Mocha now contains about twenty-five English subjects, the principal merchants in the place. At Masawwah, besides a few French and Americans, there are from sixteen to twenty British protégés, who trade with the interior, especially for mules required at the Mauritius and our other colonies. Hodaydah has from fifty to sixty, and Jeddah, besides its dozen resident merchants, annually witnesses the transit of some hundreds of British subjects, who flock to the Haj for commerce and devotion.

"The chief emporium of the Red Sea trade has for centuries past been Jeddah, the port of Meccah. The custom-house reports of 1856 were kindly furnished to me by Capt. Frushard, I. N. (now commanding the H. E. I. C's. sloop of war '*Elphinstone*'), an old and experienced officer, lately employed in blockading Berberah, and who made himself instrumental in quelling certain recent attempts upon Turkish supremacy in Western Arabia. According to these documents, thirty-five ships of English build (square-rigged) arrived at and left Jeddah between the end of September and April, from and for various places in the East, China, Batavia, Singapore, Calcutta, Bombay, the Malabar Coast, the Persian Gulf, and Eastern Africa. Nearly all carried our colors, and were protected, or supposed to be protected, by a British register: only five had on board a European captain or sailing master, the rest being commanded and officered by Arabs and Indians. Their cargoes from India and the Eastern regions are rice, sugar, piece-goods, planking, pepper, and pilgrims; from Persia, dates, tobacco, and raw silk; and from the Mozambique, ivory, gold dust, and similar costly articles. These imports in 1856 are valued at £160,000. The exports for the year, consisting of a little coffee and spice for purchase of imports, amount, per returns, to £120,000. In addition to these square-rigged ships, the number of country vessels, open boats, buggalows, and others, from the Persian Gulf and the Indian coasts, amount to 900, importing £550,000, and exporting about £400,000. I may remark, that to all these sums at least one third should be added, as speculation abounds, and books are kept by triple entry in the Holy Land.

"The next port in importance to Jeddah is Hodaydah, where vessels touch on their way northward, land piece and other goods, and call on the return passage to fill with coffee. As the head-quarters of the Yemen Pashalik, it has reduced Mocha, formerly the great coffee mart, to insignificance, and the vicinity of Aden, a free port, has drawn off much of the stream of trade from both these ancient emporia. On the African coast of the Red Sea, Sawakin, opposite Jeddah, is a mere slave mart, and Masawwah, opposite Hodaydah, still trades in pearls, gold dust, ivory, and mules.

"But if the value of the Red Sea traffic calls, in the present posture of events, for increased means of protection, the slave-trade has equal claims to our attention. At Aden energetic efforts have been made to suppress it. It is, however, still carried on by country boats from Sawakin, Tajurrah, Zayla, and the Somali coast; a single cargo sometimes consisting of 200 head gathered from the interior, and exported to Jeddah and the small ports lying north and south of it. The trade is, I believe, principally in the hands of Arab merchants at Jeddah and Hodaydah, and resident foreigners, principally Indian Moslems, who claim our protection in case of disturbances, and consequently carry on a thriving business. Our present squadron in the Red Sea consisting of only two sailing vessels, the country boats in the African ports have only to wait till they see the ship pass up or down, and then knowing the passage—a matter of a day—to be clear, to lodge the slaves at their destination. During the past year, this trade was much injured by the revolt of the Arabs against the Turks, and the constant presence of the ' Elphinstone,' whose reported object was to seize all vessels carrying slaves. The effect was principally moral. Although the instructions for the guidance of the commander enjoined him to carry out the wishes of the Home and Indian governments for the suppression of slavery, yet there being no published treaty between the imperial government and the Porte sanctioning to us the right of search in Turkish bottoms, his interference would not have been supported by the Ottoman local authorities. It may be well to state, that after a firman had been published in the Hejaz and Gemen abolishing the trade, the Turkish governments of Jeddah and Hodaydah declared that the English commander might do as he pleased, but that they declined making any written request for his assistance. For its present increased duties, for the suppression of the slave-trade, for the protection of British subjects, and for the watching over Turkish and English interests in the Red Sea, the Aden squadron is no longer sufficient. During the last two years it has numbered two sailing vessels, the ' Elphinstone,' a sloop of war, carrying twelve 32-pounders and two 12-pounders; and the ' Mahi,' a schooner armed with one pivot gun, 32-pounder, and two 12-pounders. Nor would it be benefited by even a considerable increase of sailing vessels. It is well known that, as the prevailing winds inside the sea are favorable for proceeding upward from September to April, so on the return, during those months, they are strongly adverse. A fast ship, like the ' Elphinstone,' requires 30 days on the downward voyage to do the work of four. Outside the sea, during those months, the current sets inward from the Indian Ocean, and a ship, in the event of very light winds falling, has been detained a whole week in sight of Aden. From April to September, on the contrary, the winds set down the Red Sea frequently with violence; the current inside the sea also turns toward the Indian Ocean, and outside the southwest monsoon is blowing. Finally, sailing ships draw too much water. In the last year the ' Elphinstone' kept the Arabs away from Jeddah till the meanness of the Sherif Abd el Muttalib had caused his downfall. But her great depth (about from 14 6 to 15 ft.) prevented her approaching the shore at Hodaydah near enough to have injured the insurgents, who, unaware of the fact, delayed their attack upon the town till famine and a consequent pestilence dispersed them. With little increase of present expenditure, the Red Sea might be effectually commanded. Two screw-steamers, small enough to enter every harbor, and to work steadily among the banks on either shore, and yet large enough to be made useful in conveying English political officers of rank and native princes when necessary, would amply suffice; a vessel of the class of H. M's. gun-boat ' Flying Fish,' drawing at most 9 feet water, and carrying four 32-pounders of 25 cwt. each, as broadside, and two 32-pounders of 25 cwt. each, as pivot guns, would probably be that selected. The crews would consist of fewer men than those at present required, and means would easily be devised for increasing the accommodation of officers and men, and for securing their health and comfort during cruises that might last two months in a hot and dangerous climate.

"By means of two such steamers we shall, I believe, be prepared for any contingencies which might arise in the Red Sea; and if to this squadron be added an allowance for interpreters and a slave approver in each harbor—in fact, a few of the precautions practiced by the West African squadron, the slave-trade in the Red Sea will soon have received its death-blow, and Eastern Africa its regeneration at our hands. I have, etc., etc., R. F. BURTON,

"Commanding East African Expedition.

"H. E. I. C. Sloop of War ' Elphinstone,' 15th December, 1856."

6.

No. 961 of 1857.

From H. L. ANDERSON, *Esquire, Secretary to Government, Bombay, to* Captain R. F.
BURTON, 18*th Regiment Bombay N. I.*

Dated 23d July, 1857.

"Sir,—With reference to your letter, dated the 15th of December, 1856, to the
address of the Secretary of the Royal Geographical Society of London, communicating your views on affairs in the Red Sea, and commenting on the political measures of the government of India, I am directed by the right honorable the governor
in council to state, your want of discretion, and due respect for the authorities to
whom you are subordinate, has been regarded with displeasure by government.

"I have the honor to be, sir, your most obedient servant,

"(Signed)   H. L. ANDERSON, Secretary to Government.

"Bombay Castle, 23d July, 1857."

7.

THE MASSACRE AT JUDDAH.

(Extract from the "Telegraph Courier," Overland Summary, Bombay, August 4, 1858.)

"On the 30th of June, a massacre of nearly all the Christians took place at Juddah
on the Red Sea.   Among the victims were Mr. Page, the British Consul, and the
French Consul and his lady.   Altogether the Arabs succeeded in slaughtering about
twenty-five.

"H. M. steam-ship Cyclops was there at the time, and the captain landed with a
boat's crew, and attempted to bring off some of the survivors, but he was compelled
to retreat, not without having killed a number of the Arabs.   The next day, however, he succeeded in rescuing the few remaining Christians, and conveyed them to
Suez.

"Among those who were fortunate enough to escape was the daughter of the
French Consul; and this she succeeded in doing through the fidelity of a native after
she had killed two men with her own hands, and been severely wounded in the encounter.   Telegraphic dispatches were transmitted to England and France, and the
Cyclops is waiting orders at Suez.   As it was apprehended that the news from
Juddah might excite the Arab population of Suez to the commission of similar out-
rages, H. B. M's. vice-consul at that place applied to the Pasha of Egypt for assistance, which was immediately afforded by the landing of 500 Turkish soldiers, under
the orders of the Pasha of Suez."

8.

"Unyanyembe, Central Africa, 24th June, 1858.

"Sir,—I have the honor to acknowledge the receipt of your official letter, No. 961
of 1857, conveying to me the displeasure of the government in consequence of my
having communicated certain views on political affairs in the Red Sea to the R. G. S.
of Great Britain.

"The paper in question was as is directly stated, and it was sent for transmission
to the Board of Directors, or the Foreign Office, not for publication.   I beg to express my regret that it should have contained any passages offensive to the authorities
to whom I am subordinate; and to assure the right honorable the governor in council that nothing was farther from my intentions than to displease a government to
whose kind consideration I have been, and am still, so much indebted.

"In conclusion, I have the honor to remind you that I have received no reply to
my official letter, sent from Zanzibar, urging our claims upon the Somal for the
plunder of our property.

"I have the honor to be, sir, your most obedient servant,

"RICHARD F. BURTON, Commanding East African Expedition.

"To the Secretary to Government, Bombay."

9.

No. 2845 of 1857.   "Political Department."

From H. L. ANDERSON, *Esq., Secretary to Government of Bombay, to* Capt. R. F.
BURTON, *Commanding E. A. Expedition, Zanzibar.*

Dated 13th June, 1857.

"Sir,—I am directed by the right honorable the governor in council to acknowledge the receipt of your letter dated the 26th of April last, soliciting compensation on

behalf of yourself and the other members of the late Somalee Expedition, for losses sustained by you and them.

"2. In reply, I am desired to inform you that, under the opinion copied in the margin, expressed by the late Governor General of India, the right honorable the governor or in council can not accede to the application now preferred.

Having regard to the conduct of the expedition, his lordship can not think that the officers who composed it have any just claims on the government for their personal losses.

"I have, etc.   (Signed)   H. L. ANDERSON, Secretary to Government."

END OF FIRST CORRESPONDENCE.

SECOND CORRESPONDENCE.

1.

"India Office, E. C., 8th November, 1859.

"Sir,—I am directed by the Secretary of State for India in council to forward for your information copy of a letter addressed by Captain Rigby, her majesty's consul and agent at Zanzibar, to the government of Bombay, respecting the non-payment of certain persons hired by you to accompany the expedition under your command into Equatorial Africa, and to request that you will furnish me with any observations which you may have to make upon the statements contained in that letter.

"Sir Charles Wood especially desires to be informed why you took no steps to bring the services of the men who accompanied you, and your obligations to them, to the notice of the Bombay government.

"I am, sir, your obedient servant,   (Signed)   T. COSMO MELVILLE.
"Captain R. Burton."

2.

No. 70 of 1859.   "Political Department."
From Captain C. P. RIGBY, *her Majesty's Consul and British Agent, Zanzibar, to* H. L. ANDERSON, *Esquire, Secretary to Government, Bombay.*

"Zanzibar, July 15th, 1859.

"Sir,—I have the honor to report, for the information of the right honorable the governor in council, the following circumstances connected with the late East African Expedition under the command of Captain Burton.

"2. Upon the return of Captain Burton to Zanzibar in March last, from the interior of Africa, he stated that from the funds supplied him by the Royal Geographical Society for the expenses of the expedition, he had only a sufficient sum left to defray the passage of himself and Captain Speke to England, and in consequence the persons who accompanied the expedition from here, viz. : the Kafila Bashi, the Belooch Sepoys, and the porters, received nothing whatever from him on their return.

"3. On the quitting Zanzibar for the interior of Africa, the expedition was accompanied by a party of Belooch soldiers, consisting of a jemadar and twelve armed men. I understand they were promised a monthly salary of five dollars each; they remained with the expedition for twenty months, and as they received nothing from Captain Burton beyond a few dollars each before starting, his highness the sultan has generously distributed among them the sum of (2300) two thousand three hundred dollars.

"4. The head clerk of the Custom-house here, a Banian, by name Ramjee, procured ten men, who accompanied the expedition as porters; they were promised five dollars each per mensem, and received pay for six months, viz., thirty dollars each before starting for the interior. They were absent for twenty months, during three of which the Banian Ramjee states that they did not accompany the expedition. He now claims eleven months' pay for each of these men, as they have not been paid any thing beyond the advance before starting.

"5. The head clerk also states that after the expedition left Zanzibar, he sent two men to Captain Burton with supplies, one of whom was absent with the expedition seventeen months, and received nothing whatever; the other, he states, was absent fifteen months, and received six months' pay, the pay for the remaining nine months being still due to him. Thus his claim amounts to the following sums :

```
Ten men for eleven months, at $5 per man per month ..............$550
One man for seventeen  "      "    "     "      "   ..................  85
One   "    nine      "      "    "     "      "   ..............  45
                              Total.......................$680
```

"6. These men were slaves, belonging to 'deewans,' or petty chiefs, on the opposite main land. They travel far into the interior to collect and carry down ivory to the coast, and are absent frequently for the space of two or three years. When hired out, the pay they receive is equally divided between the slave and the master. Captain Speke informs me, that when these men were hired, it was agreed that one half of their hire should be paid to the men, and the other half to Ramjee on account of their owners. When Ramjee asked Captain Burton for their pay, on his return here, he declined to give him any thing, saying that they had received thirty dollars each on starting, and that he could have bought them for a less sum.

"7. The kafila bashi, or chief Arab, who accompanied the expedition, by name Said bin Salem, was twenty-two months with Captain Burton. He states, that on the first journey to Pangany and Usumbara, he received fifty (50) dollars from Captain Burton; and that before starting on the last expedition, to discover the Great Lake, the late Lieutenant Colonel Hamerton presented him with five hundred dollars on behalf of government for the maintenance of his family during his absence. He states that he did not stipulate for any monthly pay, as Colonel Hamerton told him, that if he escorted the gentlemen to the Great Lake in the interior, and brought them in safety back to Zanzibar, he would be handsomely rewarded; and both Captain Speke and Mr. Apothecary Frost inform me that Colonel Hamerton frequently promised Said bin Salem that he should receive a thousand dollars and a gold watch if the expedition were successful.

"8. As it appeared to me that Colonel Hamerton had received no authority from government to defray any part of the expenses of this expedition, and probably made these promises thinking that if the exploration of the unknown interior were successful a great national object would be attained, and that the chief man who conducted the expedition would be liberally rewarded, and as Captain Burton had been furnished with funds to defray the expenses, I told him that I did not feel authorized to make any payment without the previous sanction of government, and Said bin Salem has therefore received nothing whatever since his return.

"9. Said bin Salem also states, that on the return of the expedition from Lake Tanganyika (70) seventy natives of the country were engaged as porters, and accompanied the expedition for three months; and that on arriving at a place called 'Kootoo,' a few days' journey from the sea-coast, Captain Burton wished them to diverge from the correct route to the coast opposite Zanzibar, to accompany him south to Keelwa; but they refused to do so, saying that none of their people ever dared to venture to Keelwa; that the chief slave-trade on the east coast is carried on. No doubt their fears were well grounded. These men received nothing in payment for their three months' journey, and, as no white man had ever penetrated into their country previously, I fear that any future traveler will meet with much inconvenience in consequence of these poor people not having been paid.

"10. As I considered that my duty connected with the late expedition was limited to affording it all the aid and support in my power, I have felt very reluctant to interfere with any thing connected with the non-payment of these men; but Said bin Salem and Ramjee having appealed to me, and Captain Speke since his departure from Zanzibar, having written me two private letters, pointing out so forcibly the claims of these men, the hardships they endured, and the fidelity and perseverance they showed, conducting them safely through unexplored countries, and stating also that the agreements with them were entered into at the British consulate, and that they considered they were serving the British government, that I deem it my duty to bring their claims to the notice of government; for I feel that if these men remain unpaid, after all they have endured in the service of British officers, our name for good faith in these countries will suffer, and that any future travelers wishing to further explore the interesting countries of the interior will find no persons willing to accompany them from Zanzibar, or the opposite main land.

"11. As there was no British agent at Zanzibar for thirteen months after the death of Colonel Hamerton, the expedition was entirely dependent on Luddah Damha, the custom-master here, for money and supplies. He advanced considerable sums of money without any security, forwarded all requisite supplies, and, Captain Speke says, afforded the expedition every assistance in the most handsome manner. Should government, therefore, be pleased to present him with a shawl, or some small mark of satisfaction, I am confident he is fully deserving of it, and it would gratify a very worthy man to find that his assistance to the expedition is acknowledged.

"I have, etc.,   (Signed)   C. P. RIGBY, Captain,
"H. M's. Consul and British Agent, Zanzibar."

3.

"Sir,—I have the honor to acknowledge the receipt of your official letter, dated the 8th of November, 1859, forwarding for my information copy of a letter, addressed by Captain Rigby, her majesty's consul and agent at Zanzibar, to the government of Bombay, respecting the non-payment of certain persons, hired by me to accompany the expedition under my command into Equatorial Africa, and apprising me that Sir C. Wood especially desires to be informed, why I took no steps to bring the services of the men who accompanied me, and my obligations to them, to the notice of the Bombay government.

"In reply to Sir Charles Wood I have the honor to state that, as the men alluded to rendered me no services, and as I felt in no way obliged to them, I would not report favorably of them.   The kafilah bashi, the jemadar, and the Baloch were servants of H. H. Sayyid Majid, in his pay and under his command; they were not hired by me, but by the late Lieut. Col. Hamerton, H. M.'s consul and H. E. I. C.'s agent at Zanzibar, and they marched under the Arab flag.   On return to Zanzibar, I reported them as undeserving of reward to Lieut. Col. Hamerton's successor, Capt. Rigby, and after return to England, when my accounts were sent in to the Royal Geographical Society, I appended a memorandum, that as those persons had deserved no reward, no reward had been applied for.

"Before proceeding to reply to Capt. Rigby's letter, paragraph by paragraph, I would briefly premise with the following remarks.

"Being ordered to report myself to Lieut. Col. Hamerton, and having been placed under his direction, I admitted his friendly interference, and allowed him to apply to H. H. the sultan for a guide and escort.   Lieut. Col. Hamerton offered to defray, from public funds, which he understood to be at his disposal, certain expenses of the expedition, and he promised, as reward to the guide and escort, sums of money, to which, had I been unfettered, I should have objected as exorbitant.   But in all cases, the promises made by the late consul were purely conditional, depending entirely upon the satisfactory conduct of those employed.   These facts are wholly omitted in Capt. Rigby's reports.

"2. Capt. Rigby appears to mean that the kafila bashi, the Baloch sepoys, and the porters received nothing whatever on my return to Zanzibar, in March last, from the interior of Africa, because the funds supplied to me by the Royal Geographical Society for the expenditure of the expedition had been exhausted.   Besides the sum of (£1000) one thousand pounds, granted by the Foreign Office, I had expended from private resources nearly (£1400) fourteen hundred pounds, and I was ready to expend more had the expenditure been called for.   But, though prepared on these occasions to reward liberally for good service, I can not see the necessity, or rather I see the unadvisability of offering a premium to notorious misconduct.   This was fully explained by me to Capt. Rigby on my return to Zanzibar.

"3. Capt. Rigby 'understands' that the party of Baloch sepoys, consisting of a jemadar and twelve armed men, were promised a monthly salary of 5 dollars each. This was not the case.   Lieut. Col. Hamerton advanced to the jemadar 25, and to each sepoy 20 dollars for an outfit; he agreed that I should provide them with daily rations, and he promised them an ample reward from the public funds in case of good behavior.   These men deserved nothing; I ignore their 'fidelity' and 'perseverance,' and I assert that if I passed safely through an unexplored country, it was in no wise by their efforts.   On hearing of Lieut. Col. Hamerton's death, they mutinied in a body.   At the Tanganyika Lake they refused to escort me during the period of navigation, a month of danger and difficulty.   When Capt. Speke proposed to explore the Nyanza Lake, they would not march without a present of a hundred dollars' worth of cloth.   On every possible occasion they clamored for 'bakhshish,' which, under pain of endangering the success of the expedition, could not always be withheld.   They were often warned by me that they were forfeiting all hopes of a future reward, and, indeed, they ended by thinking so themselves.   They returned to Zanzibar with a number of slaves, purchased by them with money procured from the expedition.   I would not present either guide or escort to the consul; but I did not think it my duty to oppose a large reward, said to be 2300 dollars, given to them by H. H. the sultan, and I reported his liberality and other acts of kindness to the Bombay government on my arrival at Aden.   This fact will, I trust, exonerate me from any charge of wishing to suppress my obligations.

"4. The Banyan Ramji, head clerk of the custom-house, did not, as is stated by Capt. Rigby, procure me (10) ten men who accompanied the expedition as porters; nor were these men, as is asserted (in par. 6), 'slaves belonging to deewans or petty chiefs on the opposite main land.' It is a notorious fact that these men were private slaves, belonging to the Banyan Ramji, who hired them to me direct, and received from me as their pay, for six months, thirty dollars each; a sum for which, as I told him, he might have bought them in the bazar. At the end of six months I was obliged to dismiss these slaves, who, as is usually the case with the slaves of Indian subjects at Zanzibar, were mutinous in the extreme. At the same time I supplied them with cloth, to enable them to rejoin their patron. On my return from the Tanganyika Lake, they requested leave to accompany me back to Zanzibar, which I permitted, with the express warning that they were not to consider themselves re-engaged. The Banyan, their proprietor, had, in fact, sent them on a trading trip into the interior under my escort, and I found them the most troublesome of the party. When Ramji applied for additional pay, after my return to Zanzibar, I told him that I had engaged them for six months; that I had dismissed them at the end of six months, as was left optional to me; and that he had already received an unusual sum for their services. This conversation appears in a distorted form and improperly represented in the concluding sentence of Capt. Rigby's 6th paragraph.

"5 and 6. With respect to the two men sent on with supplies after the expedition had left Zanzibar, they were not paid, on account of the prodigious disappearance of the goods intrusted to their charge, as I am prepared to prove from the original journals in my possession. They were dismissed with their comrades, and never afterward, to the best of my remembrance, did a day's work.

"7 and 8. The kafilah bashi received from me for the first journey to Usumbara (50) fifty dollars. Before my departure in the second expedition he was presented by Lieut. Colonel Hamerton with (500) five hundred dollars, almost double what he had expected. He was also promised, in case of good conduct, a gold watch, and an ample reward, which, however, was to be left to the discretion of his employers. I could not recommend him through Captain Rigby to the government for remuneration. His only object seemed to be that of wasting our resources and of collecting slaves in return for the heavy presents made to the native chiefs by the expedition, and the consequence of his carelessness or dishonesty was, that the expenditure on the whole march, until we had learned sufficient to supervise him, was inordinate. When the kafilah bashi at last refused to accompany Captain Speke to the Nyanza Lake, he was warned that he also was forfeiting all claim to future reward, and when I mentioned this circumstance to Captain Rigby at Zanzibar, he then agreed with me that the 500 dollars originally advanced were sufficient.

"9. With regard to the statement of Said bin Salim concerning the non-payment of the seventy-three porters, I have to remark that it was mainly owing to his own fault. The men did not refuse to accompany me because I wished to diverge from the "correct route," nor was I so unreasonable as to expect them to venture into the jaws of the slave-trade. Several caravans that had accompanied us on the down-march, as well as the porters attached to the expedition, were persuaded by the slaves of Ramji (because Zanzibar was a nearer way to their homes) not to make Kilwa. The pretext of the porters was simply that they would be obliged to march back for three days. An extra remuneration was offered to them, they refused it, and left in a body. Shortly before their departure Captain Speke proposed to pay them for their services, but being convinced that they might be prevented from desertion, I did not judge advisable by paying them to do what would be virtually dismissing them. After they had proceeded a few miles, Said bin Salim was sent to recall them, on conditions which they would have accepted; he delayed, lost time, and ended by declaring that he could not travel without his dinner. Another party was instantly sent; they also loitered on the way, and thus the porters reached the coast and dispersed. Before their departure I rewarded the kirangozi, or chief man of the caravan, who had behaved well in exhorting his followers to remain with us. I was delayed in a most unhealthy region for the arrival of some down-porters, who consented to carry our goods to the coast; and to prove to them that money was not my object, I paid the newly-engaged gang as if they had marched the whole way. Their willingness to accompany me is the best proof that I had not lost the confidence of the people. Finally, on arrival at the coast, I inquired concerning those porters who had deserted us, and was informed by the diwan and headman of the village, that they had returned to their homes in the interior, after a stay of a few days on the sea-board. This was a regretable occurrence, but such events are common on the slave-path in Eastern Africa, and the established custom of the Arabs and other merchants, whom I had consulted upon the subject before leaving the interior, is, not to encourage desertion by paying part of the hire, or by settling for porterage before arriving at the coasts. Of the seven gangs of porters engaged on this journey, only one, an unusually small proportion, left me without being fully satisfied.

"10. That Said bin Salim, and Ramji, the Banyan, should have appealed to Captain Rigby, according to the fashion of Orientals, after my departure from Zanzibar, for claims which they should have advanced when I refused to admit them, I am not astonished. But I must express my extreme surprise that Captain Speke should have written two private letters forcibly pointing out the claims of these men to Captain Rigby, without having communicated the circumstance in any way to me, the chief of the expedition. I have been in continued correspondence with that officer since my departure from Zanzibar, and until this moment I have been impressed with the conviction that Captain Speke's opinion as to the claims of the guide and escort above alluded to was identical with my own.

"11. With respect to the last paragraph of Captain Rigby's letter, proposing that a shawl or some small mark of satisfaction should be presented by government to Ladha Damha, the custom-master at Zanzibar, for his assistance to the expedition, I distinctly deny the gratuitous assertions that I was entirely dependent on him for money and supplies; that he advanced considerable sums of money without any security; that he forwarded all requisite supplies, or, as Captain Speke affirms, that he afforded the expedition every assistance in the most handsome manner. Before quitting Zanzibar for Inner Africa I settled all accounts with him, and left a small balance in his hands, and I gave, for all subsequent supplies, an order upon Messrs. Forbes, my agents in Bombay. He, like the other Hindoos at Zanzibar, utterly neglected me after the death of Lieut. Colonel Hamerton; and Captain Rigby has probably seen some of the letters of complaint which were sent by me from the interior. In fact, my principal merit in having conducted the expedition to a successful issue is in having contended against the utter neglect of the Hindoos at Zanzibar (who had promised to Lieut. Colonel Hamerton, in return for his many good offices, their interest and assistance), and against the carelessness and dishonesty, the mutinous spirit and the active opposition of the guide and escort.

"I admit that I was careful that these men should suffer for their misconduct. On the other hand I was equally determined that those who did their duty should be adequately rewarded—a fact which nowhere appears in Captain Rigby's letter. The Portuguese servants, the negro gun-carriers, the several African gangs of porters, with their leaders, and all other claimants, were fully satisfied. The bills drawn in the interior, from the Arab merchants, were duly paid at Zanzibar, and on departure I left orders that if any thing had been neglected it should be forwarded to me in Europe. I regret that Captain Rigby, without thoroughly ascertaining the merits of the case (which he evidently has not done), should not have permitted me to record any remarks which I might wish to offer, before making it a matter of appeal to the Bombay government.

"Finally, I venture to hope that Captain Rigby has forwarded the complaints of those who have appealed to him without endorsing their validity; and I trust that these observations upon the statements contained in his letter may prove that these statements were based upon no foundation of fact.

"I am, sir, your obedient servant,

"R. F. BURTON, Bombay Army."

4.

"India Office, E. C., 14th January, 1860.

"Sir,—I am directed by the Secretary of State for India in council, to inform you that, having taken into consideration the explanations afforded by you in your letter of the 11th of November, together with the information on the same subject furnished by Captain Speke, he is of opinion that it was your duty, knowing, as you did, that demands for wages, on the part of certain Belochs and others who accompanied you into Equatorial Africa, existed against you, not to have left Zanzibar without bringing these claims before the consul there, with a view to their being adjudicated on their own merits, the more especially as the men had been originally engaged through the intervention or the influence of the British authorities, whom, therefore, it was your duty to satisfy before leaving the country. Had this course been followed, the character of the British government would not have suffered, and the adjustment of the dispute would, in all probability, have been effected at a comparatively small outlay.

"Your letter, and that of Captain Speke, will be forwarded to the government of Bombay, with whom it will rest to determine whether you shall be held pecuniarily responsible for the amount which has been paid in liquidation of the claims against you.   I am, sir, your obedient servant,

                                   "(Signed)   J. Cosmo Melvill."

5.

" Sir,—I have the honor to acknowledge the receipt of your official letter of the 14th of January, 1860.

"In reply, I have the honor to observe that, not having been favored with a copy of the information on the same subject furnished to you by Captain Speke, I am not in a position to understand on what grounds the Secretary of State for India in council should have arrived at so unexpected a decision as regards the alleged non-payment of certain claims made by certain persons sent with me into the African interior.

"I have the honor to observe that I did not know that demands for wages existed against me on the part of those persons, and that I believed I had satisfactorily explained the circumstances of their dismissal without payment in my official letter of the 11th of November, 1859.

"Although impaired health and its consequences prevented me from proceeding in an official form to the adjudication of the supposed claims in the presence of the consular authority, I represented the whole question to Captain Rigby, who, had he then —at that time—deemed it his duty to interfere, might have insisted upon adjudicating the affair with me, or with Captain Speke, before we left Zanzibar.

"I have the honor to remark that the character of the British government has *not*, and can not (in my humble opinion) have suffered in any way by my withholding a purely conditional reward when forfeited by gross neglect and misconduct; and I venture to suggest that by encouraging such abuses serious obstacles will be thrown in the way of future exploration, and that the liberality of the British government will be more esteemed by the native than its character for sound sense.

"In conclusion, I venture to express my surprise, that all my labors and long services in the cause of African exploration should have won for me no other reward than the prospect of being mulcted in a pecuniary liability incurred by my late lamented friend, Lieut. Colonel Hamerton, and settled without reference to me by his successor, Captain Rigby.   I have the honor, etc., etc.,

                              "Richd. F. Burton, Captain, Bombay Army."
" The Under Secretary of State for India."

INDEX.

THE END.

A CATALOG OF SELECTED DOVER
BOOKS IN ALL FIELDS OF INTEREST

CONCERNING THE SPIRITUAL IN ART, Wassily Kandinsky. Pioneering work by father of abstract art. Thoughts on color theory, nature of art. Analysis of earlier masters. 12 illustrations. 80pp. of text. 5⅜ x 8½. 23411-8 Pa. $4.95

ANIMALS: 1,419 Copyright-Free Illustrations of Mammals, Birds, Fish, Insects, etc., Jim Harter (ed.). Clear wood engravings present, in extremely lifelike poses, over 1,000 species of animals. One of the most extensive pictorial sourcebooks of its kind. Captions. Index. 284pp. 9 x 12. 23766-4 Pa. $14.95

CELTIC ART: The Methods of Construction, George Bain. Simple geometric techniques for making Celtic interlacements, spirals, Kells-type initials, animals, humans, etc. Over 500 illustrations. 160pp. 9 x 12. (Available in U.S. only.) 22923-8 Pa. $9.95

AN ATLAS OF ANATOMY FOR ARTISTS, Fritz Schider. Most thorough reference work on art anatomy in the world. Hundreds of illustrations, including selections from works by Vesalius, Leonardo, Goya, Ingres, Michelangelo, others. 593 illustrations. 192pp. 7⅛ x 10¼. 20241-0 Pa. $9.95

CELTIC HAND STROKE-BY-STROKE (Irish Half-Uncial from "The Book of Kells"): An Arthur Baker Calligraphy Manual, Arthur Baker. Complete guide to creating each letter of the alphabet in distinctive Celtic manner. Covers hand position, strokes, pens, inks, paper, more. Illustrated. 48pp. 8¼ x 11. 24336-2 Pa. $3.95

EASY ORIGAMI, John Montroll. Charming collection of 32 projects (hat, cup, pelican, piano, swan, many more) specially designed for the novice origami hobbyist. Clearly illustrated easy-to-follow instructions insure that even beginning paper-crafters will achieve successful results. 48pp. 8¼ x 11. 27298-2 Pa. $3.50

THE COMPLETE BOOK OF BIRDHOUSE CONSTRUCTION FOR WOODWORKERS, Scott D. Campbell. Detailed instructions, illustrations, tables. Also data on bird habitat and instinct patterns. Bibliography. 3 tables. 63 illustrations in 15 figures. 48pp. 5¼ x 8½. 24407-5 Pa. $2.50

BLOOMINGDALE'S ILLUSTRATED 1886 CATALOG: Fashions, Dry Goods and Housewares, Bloomingdale Brothers. Famed merchants' extremely rare catalog depicting about 1,700 products: clothing, housewares, firearms, dry goods, jewelry, more. Invaluable for dating, identifying vintage items. Also, copyright-free graphics for artists, designers. Co-published with Henry Ford Museum & Greenfield Village. 160pp. 8¼ x 11. 25780-0 Pa. $12.95

HISTORIC COSTUME IN PICTURES, Braun & Schneider. Over 1,450 costumed figures in clearly detailed engravings–from dawn of civilization to end of 19th century. Captions. Many folk costumes. 256pp. 8⅜ x 11¾. 23150-X Pa. $12.95

STICKLEY CRAFTSMAN FURNITURE CATALOGS, Gustav Stickley and L. & J. G. Stickley. Beautiful, functional furniture in two authentic catalogs from 1910. 594 illustrations, including 277 photos, show settles, rockers, armchairs, reclining chairs, bookcases, desks, tables. 183pp. 6½ x 9¼. 23838-5 Pa. $11.95

AMERICAN LOCOMOTIVES IN HISTORIC PHOTOGRAPHS: 1858 to 1949, Ron Ziel (ed.). A rare collection of 126 meticulously detailed official photographs, called "builder portraits," of American locomotives that majestically chronicle the rise of steam locomotive power in America. Introduction. Detailed captions. xi+ 129pp. 9 x 12. 27393-8 Pa. $13.95

AMERICA'S LIGHTHOUSES: An Illustrated History, Francis Ross Holland, Jr. Delightfully written, profusely illustrated fact-filled survey of over 200 American light-houses since 1716. History, anecdotes, technological advances, more. 240pp. 8 x 10¾. 25576-X Pa. $12.95

TOWARDS A NEW ARCHITECTURE, Le Corbusier. Pioneering manifesto by founder of "International School." Technical and aesthetic theories, views of industry, economics, relation of form to function, "mass-production split" and much more. Profusely illustrated. 320pp. 6⅛ x 9¼. (Available in U.S. only.) 25023-7 Pa. $10.95

HOW THE OTHER HALF LIVES, Jacob Riis. Famous journalistic record, exposing poverty and degradation of New York slums around 1900, by major social reformer. 100 striking and influential photographs. 233pp. 10 x 7⅞. 22012-5 Pa. $11.95

FRUIT KEY AND TWIG KEY TO TREES AND SHRUBS, William M. Harlow. One of the handiest and most widely used identification aids. Fruit key covers 120 deciduous and evergreen species; twig key 160 deciduous species. Easily used. Over 300 photographs. 126pp. 5⅜ x 8½. 20511-8 Pa. $3.95

COMMON BIRD SONGS, Dr. Donald J. Borror. Songs of 60 most common U.S. birds: robins, sparrows, cardinals, bluejays, finches, more–arranged in order of increasing complexity. Up to 9 variations of songs of each species.
Cassette and manual 99911-4 $8.95

ORCHIDS AS HOUSE PLANTS, Rebecca Tyson Northen. Grow cattleyas and many other kinds of orchids–in a window, in a case, or under artificial light. 63 illustrations. 148pp. 5⅜ x 8½. 23261-1 Pa. $7.95

MONSTER MAZES, Dave Phillips. Masterful mazes at four levels of difficulty. Avoid deadly perils and evil creatures to find magical treasures. Solutions for all 32 exciting illustrated puzzles. 48pp. 8¼ x 11. 26005-4 Pa. $2.95

MOZART'S DON GIOVANNI (DOVER OPERA LIBRETTO SERIES), Wolfgang Amadeus Mozart. Introduced and translated by Ellen H. Bleiler. Standard Italian libretto, with complete English translation. Convenient and thoroughly portable–an ideal companion for reading along with a recording or the performance itself. Introduction. List of characters. Plot summary. 121pp. 5¼ x 8½. 24944-1 Pa. $3.95

TECHNICAL MANUAL AND DICTIONARY OF CLASSICAL BALLET, Gail Grant. Defines, explains, comments on steps, movements, poses and concepts. 15-page pictorial section. Basic book for student, viewer. 127pp. 5⅜ x 8½. 21843-0 Pa. $4.95

THE CLARINET AND CLARINET PLAYING, David Pino. Lively, comprehensive work features suggestions about technique, musicianship, and musical interpretation, as well as guidelines for teaching, making your own reeds, and preparing for public performance. Includes an intriguing look at clarinet history. "A godsend," *The Clarinet,* Journal of the International Clarinet Society. Appendixes. 7 illus. 320pp. 5⅜ x 8½.   40270-3 Pa. $9.95

HOLLYWOOD GLAMOR PORTRAITS, John Kobal (ed.). 145 photos from 1926-49. Harlow, Gable, Bogart, Bacall; 94 stars in all. Full background on photographers, technical aspects. 160pp. 8⅜ x 11¼.   23352-9 Pa. $12.95

THE ANNOTATED CASEY AT THE BAT: A Collection of Ballads about the Mighty Casey/Third, Revised Edition, Martin Gardner (ed.). Amusing sequels and parodies of one of America's best-loved poems: Casey's Revenge, Why Casey Whiffed, Casey's Sister at the Bat, others. 256pp. 5⅜ x 8½.   28598-7 Pa. $8.95

THE RAVEN AND OTHER FAVORITE POEMS, Edgar Allan Poe. Over 40 of the author's most memorable poems: "The Bells," "Ulalume," "Israfel," "To Helen," "The Conqueror Worm," "Eldorado," "Annabel Lee," many more. Alphabetic lists of titles and first lines. 64pp. 5³⁄₁₆ x 8¼.   26685-0 Pa. $1.00

PERSONAL MEMOIRS OF U. S. GRANT, Ulysses Simpson Grant. Intelligent, deeply moving firsthand account of Civil War campaigns, considered by many the finest military memoirs ever written. Includes letters, historic photographs, maps and more. 528pp. 6⅛ x 9¼.   28587-1 Pa. $12.95

ANCIENT EGYPTIAN MATERIALS AND INDUSTRIES, A. Lucas and J. Harris. Fascinating, comprehensive, thoroughly documented text describes this ancient civilization's vast resources and the processes that incorporated them in daily life, including the use of animal products, building materials, cosmetics, perfumes and incense, fibers, glazed ware, glass and its manufacture, materials used in the mummification process, and much more. 544pp. 6⅛ x 9¼. (Available in U.S. only.)
                                                                                           40446-3 Pa. $16.95

RUSSIAN STORIES/PYCCKNE PACCKA3bl: A Dual-Language Book, edited by Gleb Struve. Twelve tales by such masters as Chekhov, Tolstoy, Dostoevsky, Pushkin, others. Excellent word-for-word English translations on facing pages, plus teaching and study aids, Russian/English vocabulary, biographical/critical introductions, more. 416pp. 5⅜ x 8½.   26244-8 Pa. $9.95

PHILADELPHIA THEN AND NOW: 60 Sites Photographed in the Past and Present, Kenneth Finkel and Susan Oyama. Rare photographs of City Hall, Logan Square, Independence Hall, Betsy Ross House, other landmarks juxtaposed with contemporary views. Captures changing face of historic city. Introduction. Captions. 128pp. 8¼ x 11.   25790-8 Pa. $9.95

AIA ARCHITECTURAL GUIDE TO NASSAU AND SUFFOLK COUNTIES, LONG ISLAND, The American Institute of Architects, Long Island Chapter, and the Society for the Preservation of Long Island Antiquities. Comprehensive, well-researched and generously illustrated volume brings to life over three centuries of Long Island's great architectural heritage. More than 240 photographs with authoritative, extensively detailed captions. 176pp. 8¼ x 11.   26946-9 Pa. $14.95

NORTH AMERICAN INDIAN LIFE: Customs and Traditions of 23 Tribes, Elsie Clews Parsons (ed.). 27 fictionalized essays by noted anthropologists examine religion, customs, government, additional facets of life among the Winnebago, Crow, Zuni, Eskimo, other tribes. 480pp. 6⅛ x 9¼.   27377-6 Pa. $10.95

FRANK LLOYD WRIGHT'S DANA HOUSE, Donald Hoffmann. Pictorial essay of residential masterpiece with over 160 interior and exterior photos, plans, elevations, sketches and studies. 128pp. 9¼ x 10¾. 29120-0 Pa. $14.95

THE MALE AND FEMALE FIGURE IN MOTION: 60 Classic Photographic Sequences, Eadweard Muybridge. 60 true-action photographs of men and women walking, running, climbing, bending, turning, etc., reproduced from rare 19th-century masterpiece. vi + 121pp. 9 x 12. 24745-7 Pa. $12.95

1001 QUESTIONS ANSWERED ABOUT THE SEASHORE, N. J. Berrill and Jacquelyn Berrill. Queries answered about dolphins, sea snails, sponges, starfish, fishes, shore birds, many others. Covers appearance, breeding, growth, feeding, much more. 305pp. 5¼ x 8¼. 23366-9 Pa. $9.95

ATTRACTING BIRDS TO YOUR YARD, William J. Weber. Easy-to-follow guide offers advice on how to attract the greatest diversity of birds: birdhouses, feeders, water and waterers, much more. 96pp. 5³⁄₁₆ x 8¼. 28927-3 Pa. $2.50

MEDICINAL AND OTHER USES OF NORTH AMERICAN PLANTS: A Historical Survey with Special Reference to the Eastern Indian Tribes, Charlotte Erichsen-Brown. Chronological historical citations document 500 years of usage of plants, trees, shrubs native to eastern Canada, northeastern U.S. Also complete identifying information. 343 illustrations. 544pp. 6½ x 9¼. 25951-X Pa. $12.95

STORYBOOK MAZES, Dave Phillips. 23 stories and mazes on two-page spreads: Wizard of Oz, Treasure Island, Robin Hood, etc. Solutions. 64pp. 8¼ x 11. 23628-5 Pa. $2.95

AMERICAN NEGRO SONGS: 230 Folk Songs and Spirituals, Religious and Secular, John W. Work. This authoritative study traces the African influences of songs sung and played by black Americans at work, in church, and as entertainment. The author discusses the lyric significance of such songs as "Swing Low, Sweet Chariot," "John Henry," and others and offers the words and music for 230 songs. Bibliography. Index of Song Titles. 272pp. 6¹⁄₂ x 9¹⁄₄. 40271-1 Pa. $10.95

MOVIE-STAR PORTRAITS OF THE FORTIES, John Kobal (ed.). 163 glamor, studio photos of 106 stars of the 1940s: Rita Hayworth, Ava Gardner, Marlon Brando, Clark Gable, many more. 176pp. 8⅜ x 11¼. 23546-7 Pa. $14.95

BENCHLEY LOST AND FOUND, Robert Benchley. Finest humor from early 30s, about pet peeves, child psychologists, post office and others. Mostly unavailable elsewhere. 73 illustrations by Peter Arno and others. 183pp. 5⅜ x 8½. 22410-4 Pa. $6.95

YEKL and THE IMPORTED BRIDEGROOM AND OTHER STORIES OF YIDDISH NEW YORK, Abraham Cahan. Film Hester Street based on *Yekl* (1896). Novel, other stories among first about Jewish immigrants on N.Y.'s East Side. 240pp. 5⅜ x 8½. 22427-9 Pa. $7.95

SELECTED POEMS, Walt Whitman. Generous sampling from *Leaves of Grass*. Twenty-four poems include "I Hear America Singing," "Song of the Open Road," "I Sing the Body Electric," "When Lilacs Last in the Dooryard Bloom'd," "O Captain! My Captain!"–all reprinted from an authoritative edition. Lists of titles and first lines. 128pp. 5³⁄₁₆ x 8¼. 26878-0 Pa. $1.00

THE BEST TALES OF HOFFMANN, E. T. A. Hoffmann. 10 of Hoffmann's most important stories: "Nutcracker and the King of Mice," "The Golden Flowerpot," etc. 458pp. 5⅜ x 8½.   21793-0 Pa. $9.95

FROM FETISH TO GOD IN ANCIENT EGYPT, E. A. Wallis Budge. Rich detailed survey of Egyptian conception of "God" and gods, magic, cult of animals, Osiris, more. Also, superb English translations of hymns and legends. 240 illustrations. 545pp. 5⅜ x 8½.   25803-3 Pa. $13.95

FRENCH STORIES/CONTES FRANÇAIS: A Dual-Language Book, Wallace Fowlie. Ten stories by French masters, Voltaire to Camus: "Micromegas" by Voltaire; "The Atheist's Mass" by Balzac; "Minuet" by de Maupassant; "The Guest" by Camus, six more. Excellent English translations on facing pages. Also French-English vocabulary list, exercises, more. 352pp. 5⅜ x 8½.   26443-2 Pa. $9.95

CHICAGO AT THE TURN OF THE CENTURY IN PHOTOGRAPHS: 122 Historic Views from the Collections of the Chicago Historical Society, Larry A. Viskochil. Rare large-format prints offer detailed views of City Hall, State Street, the Loop, Hull House, Union Station, many other landmarks, circa 1904-1913. Introduction. Captions. Maps. 144pp. 9⅜ x 12¼.   24656-6 Pa. $12.95

OLD BROOKLYN IN EARLY PHOTOGRAPHS, 1865-1929, William Lee Younger. Luna Park, Gravesend race track, construction of Grand Army Plaza, moving of Hotel Brighton, etc. 157 previously unpublished photographs. 165pp. 8⅞ x 11¾.
                    23587-4 Pa. $13.95

THE MYTHS OF THE NORTH AMERICAN INDIANS, Lewis Spence. Rich anthology of the myths and legends of the Algonquins, Iroquois, Pawnees and Sioux, prefaced by an extensive historical and ethnological commentary. 36 illustrations. 480pp. 5⅜ x 8½.   25967-6 Pa. $10.95

AN ENCYCLOPEDIA OF BATTLES: Accounts of Over 1,560 Battles from 1479 B.C. to the Present, David Eggenberger. Essential details of every major battle in recorded history from the first battle of Megiddo in 1479 B.C. to Grenada in 1984. List of Battle Maps. New Appendix covering the years 1967-1984. Index. 99 illustrations. 544pp. 6½ x 9¼.   24913-1 Pa. $16.95

SAILING ALONE AROUND THE WORLD, Captain Joshua Slocum. First man to sail around the world, alone, in small boat. One of great feats of seamanship told in delightful manner. 67 illustrations. 294pp. 5⅜ x 8½.   20326-3 Pa. $6.95

ANARCHISM AND OTHER ESSAYS, Emma Goldman. Powerful, penetrating, prophetic essays on direct action, role of minorities, prison reform, puritan hypocrisy, violence, etc. 271pp. 5⅜ x 8½.   22484-8 Pa. $8.95

MYTHS OF THE HINDUS AND BUDDHISTS, Ananda K. Coomaraswamy and Sister Nivedita. Great stories of the epics; deeds of Krishna, Shiva, taken from puranas, Vedas, folk tales; etc. 32 illustrations. 400pp. 5⅜ x 8½.   21759-0 Pa. $12.95

THE TRAUMA OF BIRTH, Otto Rank. Rank's controversial thesis that anxiety neurosis is caused by profound psychological trauma which occurs at birth. 256pp. 5⅜ x 8½.   27974-X Pa. $7.95

A THEOLOGICO-POLITICAL TREATISE, Benedict Spinoza. Also contains unfinished Political Treatise. Great classic on religious liberty, theory of government on common consent. R. Elwes translation. Total of 421pp. 5⅜ x 8½. 20249-6 Pa. $10.95

MY BONDAGE AND MY FREEDOM, Frederick Douglass. Born a slave, Douglass became outspoken force in antislavery movement. The best of Douglass' autobiographies. Graphic description of slave life. 464pp. 5⅜ x 8½. 22457-0 Pa. $8.95

FOLLOWING THE EQUATOR: A Journey Around the World, Mark Twain. Fascinating humorous account of 1897 voyage to Hawaii, Australia, India, New Zealand, etc. Ironic, bemused reports on peoples, customs, climate, flora and fauna, politics, much more. 197 illustrations. 720pp. 5⅜ x 8½. 26113-1 Pa. $15.95

THE PEOPLE CALLED SHAKERS, Edward D. Andrews. Definitive study of Shakers: origins, beliefs, practices, dances, social organization, furniture and crafts, etc. 33 illustrations. 351pp. 5⅜ x 8½. 21081-2 Pa. $12.95

THE MYTHS OF GREECE AND ROME, H. A. Guerber. A classic of mythology, generously illustrated, long prized for its simple, graphic, accurate retelling of the principal myths of Greece and Rome, and for its commentary on their origins and significance. With 64 illustrations by Michelangelo, Raphael, Titian, Rubens, Canova, Bernini and others. 480pp. 5⅜ x 8½. 27584-1 Pa. $10.95

PSYCHOLOGY OF MUSIC, Carl E. Seashore. Classic work discusses music as a medium from psychological viewpoint. Clear treatment of physical acoustics, auditory apparatus, sound perception, development of musical skills, nature of musical feeling, host of other topics. 88 figures. 408pp. 5⅜ x 8½. 21851-1 Pa. $11.95

THE PHILOSOPHY OF HISTORY, Georg W. Hegel. Great classic of Western thought develops concept that history is not chance but rational process, the evolution of freedom. 457pp. 5⅜ x 8½. 20112-0 Pa. $9.95

THE BOOK OF TEA, Kakuzo Okakura. Minor classic of the Orient: entertaining, charming explanation, interpretation of traditional Japanese culture in terms of tea ceremony. 94pp. 5⅜ x 8½. 20070-1 Pa. $3.95

LIFE IN ANCIENT EGYPT, Adolf Erman. Fullest, most thorough, detailed older account with much not in more recent books, domestic life, religion, magic, medicine, commerce, much more. Many illustrations reproduce tomb paintings, carvings, hieroglyphs, etc. 597pp. 5⅜ x 8½. 22632-8 Pa. $12.95

SUNDIALS, Their Theory and Construction, Albert Waugh. Far and away the best, most thorough coverage of ideas, mathematics concerned, types, construction, adjusting anywhere. Simple, nontechnical treatment allows even children to build several of these dials. Over 100 illustrations. 230pp. 5⅜ x 8½. 22947-5 Pa. $8.95

THEORETICAL HYDRODYNAMICS, L. M. Milne-Thomson. Classic exposition of the mathematical theory of fluid motion, applicable to both hydrodynamics and aerodynamics. Over 600 exercises. 768pp. 6⅛ x 9¼. 68970-0 Pa. $20.95

SONGS OF EXPERIENCE: Facsimile Reproduction with 26 Plates in Full Color, William Blake. 26 full-color plates from a rare 1826 edition. Includes "TheTyger," "London," "Holy Thursday," and other poems. Printed text of poems. 48pp. 5¼ x 7. 24636-1 Pa. $4.95

OLD-TIME VIGNETTES IN FULL COLOR, Carol Belanger Grafton (ed.). Over 390 charming, often sentimental illustrations, selected from archives of Victorian graphics–pretty women posing, children playing, food, flowers, kittens and puppies, smiling cherubs, birds and butterflies, much more. All copyright-free. 48pp. 9¼ x 12¼. 27269-9 Pa. $9.95

PERSPECTIVE FOR ARTISTS, Rex Vicat Cole. Depth, perspective of sky and sea, shadows, much more, not usually covered. 391 diagrams, 81 reproductions of drawings and paintings. 279pp. 5⅜ x 8½. 22487-2 Pa. $9.95

DRAWING THE LIVING FIGURE, Joseph Sheppard. Innovative approach to artistic anatomy focuses on specifics of surface anatomy, rather than muscles and bones. Over 170 drawings of live models in front, back and side views, and in widely varying poses. Accompanying diagrams. 177 illustrations. Introduction. Index. 144pp. 8⅜ x11¼. 26723-7 Pa. $9.95

GOTHIC AND OLD ENGLISH ALPHABETS: 100 Complete Fonts, Dan X. Solo. Add power, elegance to posters, signs, other graphics with 100 stunning copyright-free alphabets: Blackstone, Dolbey, Germania, 97 more—including many lower-case, numerals, punctuation marks. 104pp. 8⅛ x 11. 24695-7 Pa. $9.95

HOW TO DO BEADWORK, Mary White. Fundamental book on craft from simple projects to five-bead chains and woven works. 106 illustrations. 142pp. 5⅜ x 8. 20697-1 Pa. $5.95

THE BOOK OF WOOD CARVING, Charles Marshall Sayers. Finest book for beginners discusses fundamentals and offers 34 designs. "Absolutely first rate . . . well thought out and well executed."–E. J. Tangerman. 118pp. 7¾ x 10⅝. 23654-4 Pa. $7.95

ILLUSTRATED CATALOG OF CIVIL WAR MILITARY GOODS: Union Army Weapons, Insignia, Uniform Accessories, and Other Equipment, Schuyler, Hartley, and Graham. Rare, profusely illustrated 1846 catalog includes Union Army uniform and dress regulations, arms and ammunition, coats, insignia, flags, swords, rifles, etc. 226 illustrations. 160pp. 9 x 12. 24939-5 Pa. $12.95

WOMEN'S FASHIONS OF THE EARLY 1900s: An Unabridged Republication of "New York Fashions, 1909," National Cloak & Suit Co. Rare catalog of mail-order fashions documents women's and children's clothing styles shortly after the turn of the century. Captions offer full descriptions, prices. Invaluable resource for fashion, costume historians. Approximately 725 illustrations. 128pp. 8⅜ x 11¼. 27276-1 Pa. $12.95

THE 1912 AND 1915 GUSTAV STICKLEY FURNITURE CATALOGS, Gustav Stickley. With over 200 detailed illustrations and descriptions, these two catalogs are essential reading and reference materials and identification guides for Stickley furniture. Captions cite materials, dimensions and prices. 112pp. 6½ x 9¼. 26676-1 Pa. $9.95

EARLY AMERICAN LOCOMOTIVES, John H. White, Jr. Finest locomotive engravings from early 19th century: historical (1804–74), main-line (after 1870), special, foreign, etc. 147 plates. 142pp. 11⅜ x 8¼. 22772-3 Pa. $12.95

THE TALL SHIPS OF TODAY IN PHOTOGRAPHS, Frank O. Braynard. Lavishly illustrated tribute to nearly 100 majestic contemporary sailing vessels: Amerigo Vespucci, Clearwater, Constitution, Eagle, Mayflower, Sea Cloud, Victory, many more. Authoritative captions provide statistics, background on each ship. 190 black-and-white photographs and illustrations. Introduction. 128pp. 8⅞ x 11¾. 27163-3 Pa. $14.95

LITTLE BOOK OF EARLY AMERICAN CRAFTS AND TRADES, Peter Stockham (ed.). 1807 children's book explains crafts and trades: baker, hatter, cooper, potter, and many others. 23 copperplate illustrations. 140pp. 4⅝ x 6.
23336-7 Pa. $4.95

VICTORIAN FASHIONS AND COSTUMES FROM HARPER'S BAZAR, 1867–1898, Stella Blum (ed.). Day costumes, evening wear, sports clothes, shoes, hats, other accessories in over 1,000 detailed engravings. 320pp. 9⅜ x 12¼.
22990-4 Pa. $16.95

GUSTAV STICKLEY, THE CRAFTSMAN, Mary Ann Smith. Superb study surveys broad scope of Stickley's achievement, especially in architecture. Design philosophy, rise and fall of the Craftsman empire, descriptions and floor plans for many Craftsman houses, more. 86 black-and-white halftones. 31 line illustrations. Introduction 208pp. 6½ x 9¼. 27210-9 Pa. $9.95

THE LONG ISLAND RAIL ROAD IN EARLY PHOTOGRAPHS, Ron Ziel. Over 220 rare photos, informative text document origin (1844) and development of rail service on Long Island. Vintage views of early trains, locomotives, stations, passengers, crews, much more. Captions. 8⅞ x 11¾. 26301-0 Pa. $14.95

VOYAGE OF THE LIBERDADE, Joshua Slocum. Great 19th-century mariner's thrilling, first-hand account of the wreck of his ship off South America, the 35-foot boat he built from the wreckage, and its remarkable voyage home. 128pp. 5⅜ x 8½.
40022-0 Pa. $5.95

TEN BOOKS ON ARCHITECTURE, Vitruvius. The most important book ever written on architecture. Early Roman aesthetics, technology, classical orders, site selection, all other aspects. Morgan translation. 331pp. 5⅜ x 8½. 20645-9 Pa. $9.95

THE HUMAN FIGURE IN MOTION, Eadweard Muybridge. More than 4,500 stopped-action photos, in action series, showing undraped men, women, children jumping, lying down, throwing, sitting, wrestling, carrying, etc. 390pp. 7⅞ x 10⅝.
20204-6 Clothbd. $29.95

TREES OF THE EASTERN AND CENTRAL UNITED STATES AND CANADA, William M. Harlow. Best one-volume guide to 140 trees. Full descriptions, woodlore, range, etc. Over 600 illustrations. Handy size. 288pp. 4½ x 6⅜.
20395-6 Pa. $6.95

SONGS OF WESTERN BIRDS, Dr. Donald J. Borror. Complete song and call repertoire of 60 western species, including flycatchers, juncoes, cactus wrens, many more–includes fully illustrated booklet. Cassette and manual 99913-0 $8.95

GROWING AND USING HERBS AND SPICES, Milo Miloradovich. Versatile handbook provides all the information needed for cultivation and use of all the herbs and spices available in North America. 4 illustrations. Index. Glossary. 236pp. 5⅜ x 8½.
25058-X Pa. $7.95

BIG BOOK OF MAZES AND LABYRINTHS, Walter Shepherd. 50 mazes and labyrinths in all–classical, solid, ripple, and more–in one great volume. Perfect inexpensive puzzler for clever youngsters. Full solutions. 112pp. 8⅛ x 11.
22951-3 Pa. $5.95

PIANO TUNING, J. Cree Fischer. Clearest, best book for beginner, amateur. Simple repairs, raising dropped notes, tuning by easy method of flattened fifths. No previous skills needed. 4 illustrations. 201pp. 5⅜ x 8½. 23267-0 Pa. $6.95

HINTS TO SINGERS, Lillian Nordica. Selecting the right teacher, developing confidence, overcoming stage fright, and many other important skills receive thoughtful discussion in this indispensible guide, written by a world-famous diva of four decades' experience. 96pp. 5³/₈ x 8¹/₂. 40094-8 Pa. $4.95

THE COMPLETE NONSENSE OF EDWARD LEAR, Edward Lear. All nonsense limericks, zany alphabets, Owl and Pussycat, songs, nonsense botany, etc., illustrated by Lear. Total of 320pp. 5⅜ x 8½. (Available in U.S. only.) 20167-8 Pa. $7.95

VICTORIAN PARLOUR POETRY: An Annotated Anthology, Michael R. Turner. 117 gems by Longfellow, Tennyson, Browning, many lesser-known poets. "The Village Blacksmith," "Curfew Must Not Ring Tonight," "Only a Baby Small," dozens more, often difficult to find elsewhere. Index of poets, titles, first lines. xxiii + 325pp. 5⅜ x 8¼. 27044-0 Pa. $12.95

DUBLINERS, James Joyce. Fifteen stories offer vivid, tightly focused observations of the lives of Dublin's poorer classes. At least one, "The Dead," is considered a masterpiece. Reprinted complete and unabridged from standard edition. 160pp. 5³⁄₁₆ x 8¼. 26870-5 Pa. $1.50

GREAT WEIRD TALES: 14 Stories by Lovecraft, Blackwood, Machen and Others, S. T. Joshi (ed.). 14 spellbinding tales, including "The Sin Eater," by Fiona McLeod, "The Eye Above the Mantel," by Frank Belknap Long, as well as renowned works by R. H. Barlow, Lord Dunsany, Arthur Machen, W. C. Morrow and eight other masters of the genre. 256pp. 5⅜ x 8½. (Available in U.S. only.) 40436-6 Pa. $8.95

THE BOOK OF THE SACRED MAGIC OF ABRAMELIN THE MAGE, translated by S. MacGregor Mathers. Medieval manuscript of ceremonial magic. Basic document in Aleister Crowley, Golden Dawn groups. 268pp. 5⅜ x 8½. 23211-5 Pa. $9.95

NEW RUSSIAN-ENGLISH AND ENGLISH-RUSSIAN DICTIONARY, M. A. O'Brien. This is a remarkably handy Russian dictionary, containing a surprising amount of information, including over 70,000 entries. 366pp. 4½ x 6⅛. 20208-9 Pa. $10.95

HISTORIC HOMES OF THE AMERICAN PRESIDENTS, Second, Revised Edition, Irvin Haas. A traveler's guide to American Presidential homes, most open to the public, depicting and describing homes occupied by every American President from George Washington to George Bush. With visiting hours, admission charges, travel routes. 175 photographs. Index. 160pp. 8¼ x 11. 26751-2 Pa. $13.95

NEW YORK IN THE FORTIES, Andreas Feininger. 162 brilliant photographs by the well-known photographer, formerly with *Life* magazine. Commuters, shoppers, Times Square at night, much else from city at its peak. Captions by John von Hartz. 181pp. 9¼ x 10¾. 23585-8 Pa. $13.95

INDIAN SIGN LANGUAGE, William Tomkins. Over 525 signs developed by Sioux and other tribes. Written instructions and diagrams. Also 290 pictographs. 111pp. 6⅛ x 9¼. 22029-X Pa. $3.95

ANATOMY: A Complete Guide for Artists, Joseph Sheppard. A master of figure drawing shows artists how to render human anatomy convincingly. Over 460 illustrations. 224pp. 8⅜ x 11¼. 27279-6 Pa. $11.95

MEDIEVAL CALLIGRAPHY: Its History and Technique, Marc Drogin. Spirited history, comprehensive instruction manual covers 13 styles (ca. 4th century through 15th). Excellent photographs; directions for duplicating medieval techniques with modern tools. 224pp. 8⅜ x 11¼. 26142-5 Pa. $12.95

DRIED FLOWERS: How to Prepare Them, Sarah Whitlock and Martha Rankin. Complete instructions on how to use silica gel, meal and borax, perlite aggregate, sand and borax, glycerine and water to create attractive permanent flower arrangements. 12 illustrations. 32pp. 5⅜ x 8½. 21802-3 Pa. $1.00

EASY-TO-MAKE BIRD FEEDERS FOR WOODWORKERS, Scott D. Campbell. Detailed, simple-to-use guide for designing, constructing, caring for and using feeders. Text, illustrations for 12 classic and contemporary designs. 96pp. 5⅜ x 8½. 25847-5 Pa. $3.95

SCOTTISH WONDER TALES FROM MYTH AND LEGEND, Donald A. Mackenzie. 16 lively tales tell of giants rumbling down mountainsides, of a magic wand that turns stone pillars into warriors, of gods and goddesses, evil hags, powerful forces and more. 240pp. 5⅜ x 8½. 29677-6 Pa. $6.95

THE HISTORY OF UNDERCLOTHES, C. Willett Cunnington and Phyllis Cunnington. Fascinating, well-documented survey covering six centuries of English undergarments, enhanced with over 100 illustrations: 12th-century laced-up bodice, footed long drawers (1795), 19th-century bustles, 19th-century corsets for men, Victorian "bust improvers," much more. 272pp. 5⅝ x 8¼. 27124-2 Pa. $9.95

ARTS AND CRAFTS FURNITURE: The Complete Brooks Catalog of 1912, Brooks Manufacturing Co. Photos and detailed descriptions of more than 150 now very collectible furniture designs from the Arts and Crafts movement depict davenports, settees, buffets, desks, tables, chairs, bedsteads, dressers and more, all built of solid, quarter-sawed oak. Invaluable for students and enthusiasts of antiques, Americana and the decorative arts. 80pp. 6½ x 9¼. 27471-3 Pa. $8.95

WILBUR AND ORVILLE: A Biography of the Wright Brothers, Fred Howard. Definitive, crisply written study tells the full story of the brothers' lives and work. A vividly written biography, unparalleled in scope and color, that also captures the spirit of an extraordinary era. 560pp. 6⅛ x 9¼. 40297-5 Pa. $17.95

THE ARTS OF THE SAILOR: Knotting, Splicing and Ropework, Hervey Garrett Smith. Indispensable shipboard reference covers tools, basic knots and useful hitches; handsewing and canvas work, more. Over 100 illustrations. Delightful reading for sea lovers. 256pp. 5⅜ x 8½. 26440-8 Pa. $8.95

FRANK LLOYD WRIGHT'S FALLINGWATER: The House and Its History, Second, Revised Edition, Donald Hoffmann. A total revision–both in text and illustrations–of the standard document on Fallingwater, the boldest, most personal architectural statement of Wright's mature years, updated with valuable new material from the recently opened Frank Lloyd Wright Archives. "Fascinating"–*The New York Times.* 116 illustrations. 128pp. 9¼ x 10¾. 27430-6 Pa. $12.95

PHOTOGRAPHIC SKETCHBOOK OF THE CIVIL WAR, Alexander Gardner. 100 photos taken on field during the Civil War. Famous shots of Manassas Harper's Ferry, Lincoln, Richmond, slave pens, etc. 244pp. 10⅝ x 8¼. 22731-6 Pa. $10.95

FIVE ACRES AND INDEPENDENCE, Maurice G. Kains. Great back-to-the-land classic explains basics of self-sufficient farming. The one book to get. 95 illustrations. 397pp. 5⅜ x 8½. 20974-1 Pa. $7.95

SONGS OF EASTERN BIRDS, Dr. Donald J. Borror. Songs and calls of 60 species most common to eastern U.S.: warblers, woodpeckers, flycatchers, thrushes, larks, many more in high-quality recording. Cassette and manual 99912-2 $9.95

A MODERN HERBAL, Margaret Grieve. Much the fullest, most exact, most useful compilation of herbal material. Gigantic alphabetical encyclopedia, from aconite to zedoary, gives botanical information, medical properties, folklore, economic uses, much else. Indispensable to serious reader. 161 illustrations. 888pp. 6½ x 9¼. 2-vol. set. (Available in U.S. only.) Vol. I: 22798-7 Pa. $10.95
Vol. II: 22799-5 Pa. $10.95

HIDDEN TREASURE MAZE BOOK, Dave Phillips. Solve 34 challenging mazes accompanied by heroic tales of adventure. Evil dragons, people-eating plants, blood-thirsty giants, many more dangerous adversaries lurk at every twist and turn. 34 mazes, stories, solutions. 48pp. 8¼ x 11. 24566-7 Pa. $2.95

LETTERS OF W. A. MOZART, Wolfgang A. Mozart. Remarkable letters show bawdy wit, humor, imagination, musical insights, contemporary musical world; includes some letters from Leopold Mozart. 276pp. 5⅜ x 8½. 22859-2 Pa. $9.95

BASIC PRINCIPLES OF CLASSICAL BALLET, Agrippina Vaganova. Great Russian theoretician, teacher explains methods for teaching classical ballet. 118 illustrations. 175pp. 5⅜ x 8½. 22036-2 Pa. $6.95

THE JUMPING FROG, Mark Twain. Revenge edition. The original story of The Celebrated Jumping Frog of Calaveras County, a hapless French translation, and Twain's hilarious "retranslation" from the French. 12 illustrations. 66pp. 5⅜ x 8½. 22686-7 Pa. $4.95

BEST REMEMBERED POEMS, Martin Gardner (ed.). The 126 poems in this superb collection of 19th- and 20th-century British and American verse range from Shelley's "To a Skylark" to the impassioned "Renascence" of Edna St. Vincent Millay and to Edward Lear's whimsical "The Owl and the Pussycat." 224pp. 5⅜ x 8½. 27165-X Pa. $5.95

COMPLETE SONNETS, William Shakespeare. Over 150 exquisite poems deal with love, friendship, the tyranny of time, beauty's evanescence, death and other themes in language of remarkable power, precision and beauty. Glossary of archaic terms. 80pp. 5$\frac{3}{16}$ x 8¼. 26686-9 Pa. $1.00

THE BATTLES THAT CHANGED HISTORY, Fletcher Pratt. Eminent historian profiles 16 crucial conflicts, ancient to modern, that changed the course of civilization. 352pp. 5⅜ x 8½. 41129-X Pa. $9.95

THE WIT AND HUMOR OF OSCAR WILDE, Alvin Redman (ed.). More than 1,000 ripostes, paradoxes, wisecracks: Work is the curse of the drinking classes; I can resist everything except temptation; etc. 258pp. 5⅜ x 8½. 20602-5 Pa. $6.95

SHAKESPEARE LEXICON AND QUOTATION DICTIONARY, Alexander Schmidt. Full definitions, locations, shades of meaning in every word in plays and poems. More than 50,000 exact quotations. 1,485pp. 6½ x 9¼. 2-vol. set.
Vol. 1: 22726-X Pa. $17.95
Vol. 2: 22727-8 Pa. $17.95

SELECTED POEMS, Emily Dickinson. Over 100 best-known, best-loved poems by one of America's foremost poets, reprinted from authoritative early editions. No comparable edition at this price. Index of first lines. 64pp. 5 3/16 x 8¼.
26466-1 Pa. $1.00

THE INSIDIOUS DR. FU-MANCHU, Sax Rohmer. The first of the popular mystery series introduces a pair of English detectives to their archnemesis, the diabolical Dr. Fu-Manchu. Flavorful atmosphere, fast-paced action, and colorful characters enliven this classic of the genre. 208pp. 5 3/16 x 8¼. 29898-1 Pa. $2.00

THE MALLEUS MALEFICARUM OF KRAMER AND SPRENGER, translated by Montague Summers. Full text of most important witchhunter's "bible," used by both Catholics and Protestants. 278pp. 6⅝ x 10. 22802-9 Pa. $12.95

SPANISH STORIES/CUENTOS ESPAÑOLES: A Dual-Language Book, Angel Flores (ed.). Unique format offers 13 great stories in Spanish by Cervantes, Borges, others. Faithful English translations on facing pages. 352pp. 5⅜ x 8½.
25399-6 Pa. $9.95

GARDEN CITY, LONG ISLAND, IN EARLY PHOTOGRAPHS, 1869–1919, Mildred H. Smith. Handsome treasury of 118 vintage pictures, accompanied by carefully researched captions, document the Garden City Hotel fire (1899), the Vanderbilt Cup Race (1908), the first airmail flight departing from the Nassau Boulevard Aerodrome (1911), and much more. 96pp. 8 7/8 x 11 3/4. 40669-5 Pa. $12.95

OLD QUEENS, N.Y., IN EARLY PHOTOGRAPHS, Vincent F. Seyfried and William Asadorian. Over 160 rare photographs of Maspeth, Jamaica, Jackson Heights, and other areas. Vintage views of DeWitt Clinton mansion, 1939 World's Fair and more. Captions. 192pp. 8⅞ x 11. 26358-4 Pa. $14.95

CAPTURED BY THE INDIANS: 15 Firsthand Accounts, 1750-1870, Frederick Drimmer. Astounding true historical accounts of grisly torture, bloody conflicts, relentless pursuits, miraculous escapes and more, by people who lived to tell the tale. 384pp. 5⅜ x 8½. 24901-8 Pa. $9.95

THE WORLD'S GREAT SPEECHES (Fourth Enlarged Edition), Lewis Copeland, Lawrence W. Lamm, and Stephen J. McKenna. Nearly 300 speeches provide public speakers with a wealth of updated quotes and inspiration–from Pericles' funeral oration and William Jennings Bryan's "Cross of Gold Speech" to Malcolm X's powerful words on the Black Revolution and Earl of Spenser's tribute to his sister, Diana, Princess of Wales. 944pp. 5⅜ x 8⅜. 40903-1 Pa. $15.95

THE BOOK OF THE SWORD, Sir Richard F. Burton. Great Victorian scholar/adventurer's eloquent, erudite history of the "queen of weapons"–from prehistory to early Roman Empire. Evolution and development of early swords, variations (sabre, broadsword, cutlass, scimitar, etc.), much more. 336pp. 6⅛ x 9¼.
25434-8 Pa. $9.95

AUTOBIOGRAPHY: The Story of My Experiments with Truth, Mohandas K. Gandhi. Boyhood, legal studies, purification, the growth of the Satyagraha (nonviolent protest) movement. Critical, inspiring work of the man responsible for the freedom of India. 480pp. 5⅜ x 8½. (Available in U.S. only.)   24593-4 Pa. $9.95

CELTIC MYTHS AND LEGENDS, T. W. Rolleston. Masterful retelling of Irish and Welsh stories and tales. Cuchulain, King Arthur, Deirdre, the Grail, many more. First paperback edition. 58 full-page illustrations. 512pp. 5⅜ x 8½.   26507-2 Pa. $9.95

THE PRINCIPLES OF PSYCHOLOGY, William James. Famous long course complete, unabridged. Stream of thought, time perception, memory, experimental methods; great work decades ahead of its time. 94 figures. 1,391pp. 5⅜ x 8½. 2-vol. set.
Vol. I: 20381-6 Pa. $14.95
Vol. II: 20382-4 Pa. $16.95

THE WORLD AS WILL AND REPRESENTATION, Arthur Schopenhauer. Definitive English translation of Schopenhauer's life work, correcting more than 1,000 errors, omissions in earlier translations. Translated by E. F. J. Payne. Total of 1,269pp. 5⅜ x 8½. 2-vol. set.
Vol. 1: 21761-2 Pa. $12.95
Vol. 2: 21762-0 Pa. $12.95

MAGIC AND MYSTERY IN TIBET, Madame Alexandra David-Neel. Experiences among lamas, magicians, sages, sorcerers, Bonpa wizards. A true psychic discovery. 32 illustrations. 321pp. 5⅜ x 8½. (Available in U.S. only.)   22682-4 Pa. $9.95

THE EGYPTIAN BOOK OF THE DEAD, E. A. Wallis Budge. Complete reproduction of Ani's papyrus, finest ever found. Full hieroglyphic text, interlinear transliteration, word-for-word translation, smooth translation. 533pp. 6½ x 9¼.
21866-X Pa. $12.95

MATHEMATICS FOR THE NONMATHEMATICIAN, Morris Kline. Detailed, college-level treatment of mathematics in cultural and historical context, with numerous exercises. Recommended Reading Lists. Tables. Numerous figures. 641pp. 5⅜ x 8½.
24823-2 Pa. $11.95

PROBABILISTIC METHODS IN THE THEORY OF STRUCTURES, Isaac Elishakoff. Well-written introduction covers the elements of the theory of probability from two or more random variables, the reliability of such multivariable structures, the theory of random function, Monte Carlo methods of treating problems incapable of exact solution, and more. Examples. 502pp. 5³/₈ x 8¹/₂.   40691-1 Pa. $16.95

THE RIME OF THE ANCIENT MARINER, Gustave Doré, S. T. Coleridge. Doré's finest work; 34 plates capture moods, subtleties of poem. Flawless full-size reproductions printed on facing pages with authoritative text of poem. "Beautiful. Simply beautiful."–*Publisher's Weekly.* 77pp. 9¼ x 12.   22305-1 Pa. $7.95

NORTH AMERICAN INDIAN DESIGNS FOR ARTISTS AND CRAFTSPEOPLE, Eva Wilson. Over 360 authentic copyright-free designs adapted from Navajo blankets, Hopi pottery, Sioux buffalo hides, more. Geometrics, symbolic figures, plant and animal motifs, etc. 128pp. 8⅜ x 11. (Not for sale in the United Kingdom.)   25341-4 Pa. $9.95

SCULPTURE: Principles and Practice, Louis Slobodkin. Step-by-step approach to clay, plaster, metals, stone; classical and modern. 253 drawings, photos. 255pp. 8⅛ x 11.
22960-2 Pa. $11.95

THE INFLUENCE OF SEA POWER UPON HISTORY, 1660–1783, A. T. Mahan. Influential classic of naval history and tactics still used as text in war colleges. First paperback edition. 4 maps. 24 battle plans. 640pp. 5⅜ x 8½. 25509-3 Pa. $14.95

THE STORY OF THE TITANIC AS TOLD BY ITS SURVIVORS, Jack Winocour (ed.). What it was really like. Panic, despair, shocking inefficiency, and a little heroism. More thrilling than any fictional account. 26 illustrations. 320pp. 5⅜ x 8½. 20610-6 Pa. $8.95

FAIRY AND FOLK TALES OF THE IRISH PEASANTRY, William Butler Yeats (ed.). Treasury of 64 tales from the twilight world of Celtic myth and legend: "The Soul Cages," "The Kildare Pooka," "King O'Toole and his Goose," many more. Introduction and Notes by W. B. Yeats. 352pp. 5⅜ x 8½. 26941-8 Pa. $8.95

BUDDHIST MAHAYANA TEXTS, E. B. Cowell and others (eds.). Superb, accurate translations of basic documents in Mahayana Buddhism, highly important in history of religions. The Buddha-karita of Asvaghosha, Larger Sukhavativyuha, more. 448pp. 5⅜ x 8½. 25552-2 Pa. $12.95

ONE TWO THREE . . . INFINITY: Facts and Speculations of Science, George Gamow. Great physicist's fascinating, readable overview of contemporary science: number theory, relativity, fourth dimension, entropy, genes, atomic structure, much more. 128 illustrations. Index. 352pp. 5⅜ x 8½. 25664-2 Pa. $9.95

EXPERIMENTATION AND MEASUREMENT, W. J. Youden. Introductory manual explains laws of measurement in simple terms and offers tips for achieving accuracy and minimizing errors. Mathematics of measurement, use of instruments, experimenting with machines. 1994 edition. Foreword. Preface. Introduction. Epilogue. Selected Readings. Glossary. Index. Tables and figures. 128pp. 5³/₈ x 8¹/₂. 40451-X Pa. $6.95

DALÍ ON MODERN ART: The Cuckolds of Antiquated Modern Art, Salvador Dalí. Influential painter skewers modern art and its practitioners. Outrageous evaluations of Picasso, Cézanne, Turner, more. 15 renderings of paintings discussed. 44 calligraphic decorations by Dalí. 96pp. 5⅜ x 8½. (Available in U.S. only.) 29220-7 Pa. $5.95

ANTIQUE PLAYING CARDS: A Pictorial History, Henry René D'Allemagne. Over 900 elaborate, decorative images from rare playing cards (14th–20th centuries): Bacchus, death, dancing dogs, hunting scenes, royal coats of arms, players cheating, much more. 96pp. 9¼ x 12¼. 29265-7 Pa. $12.95

MAKING FURNITURE MASTERPIECES: 30 Projects with Measured Drawings, Franklin H. Gottshall. Step-by-step instructions, illustrations for constructing handsome, useful pieces, among them a Sheraton desk, Chippendale chair, Spanish desk, Queen Anne table and a William and Mary dressing mirror. 224pp. 8⅛ x 11¼. 29338-6 Pa. $16.95

THE FOSSIL BOOK: A Record of Prehistoric Life, Patricia V. Rich et al. Profusely illustrated definitive guide covers everything from single-celled organisms and dinosaurs to birds and mammals and the interplay between climate and man. Over 1,500 illustrations. 760pp. 7½ x 10⅛. 29371-8 Pa. $29.95

Prices subject to change without notice.

Available at your book dealer or write for free catalog to Dept. GI, Dover Publications, Inc., 31 East 2nd St., Mineola, N.Y. 11501. Dover publishes more than 500 books each year on science, elementary and advanced mathematics, biology, music, art, literary history, social sciences and other areas.